KT-582-524

TRAVELERS
CANADA
COMPANION

The 1999–2000 Traveler's Companions

ARGENTINA • AUSTRALIA • BALI • CALIFORNIA • CANADA • CHINA • COSTA RICA • CUBA •
EASTERN CANADA • ECUADOR • FLORIDA • HAWAII • HONG KONG • INDIA • INDONESIA • JAPAN •
KENYA • MALAYSIA & SINGAPORE • MEDITERRANEAN FRANCE • MEXICO • NEPAL • NEW ENGLAND •
NEW ZEALAND • PERU • PHILIPPINES • PORTUGAL • RUSSIA • SPAIN • THAILAND • TURKEY •
VENEZUELA • VIETNAM, LAOS AND CAMBODIA • WESTERN CANADA

Traveler's CANADA Companion

First Published 1999 in the United Kingdom by
Kümmerly+Frey AG,
Alpenstrasse 58, CH 3052 Zollikofen, Switzerland
in association with
World Leisure Marketing Ltd
Unit 11, Newmarket Court, Newmarket Drive, Derby, DE24 8NW, England

ISBN: 1-8400-6070-0

© 1999 Kümmerly+Frey AG, Switzerland

Created, edited and produced by
Allan Amsel Publishing,
53, rue Beaudouin, 27700 Les Andelys, France.
E-mail: Allan.Amsel@wanadoo.fr
Editor in Chief: Allan Amsel
Editor: Anne Trager
Original design concept: Hon Bing-wah
Picture editor and designer: David Henry

Acknowledgements

The authors wish to thank the following for good company along the way, generous hospitality and expert
advice: Jo Frances and Dan Purdom, May and Sandy Gray, Barry Wood and Heidi Fengler, Jolanda of
The Hague, Manon Desforges, Jim Vetter, Jean Ouderkirk, Leo Boon, Jan Peters, Tineke Gow, Hardy and
Trix Ruf, Jean and his Old House, the Post Hotel, The Woods of Prince Rupert, Eleanor House, BC Ferries,
Eric Bélanger and Rocky Mountaineer Railtours, Alaska State Ferries, Danielle Oberle at the Calgary
Convention and Visitors Bureau, Jean François, Christine and Gilles at the Greater Montréal Convention
and Visitors Bureau, Laura Serena at Tourism Vancouver, Roger and Glenda Francœur along with
Rolf, Barry and Goldie, and Marge and Peter Kormendy along with Bertha Blondin and James Badineau.

Printed by Samhwa Printing Co. Ltd., Seoul, South Korea

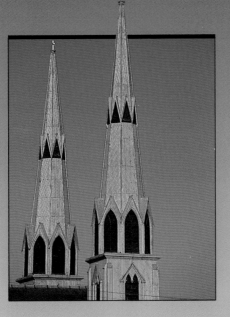

T R A V E L E R ' S
CANADA
C O M P A N I O N

by Laura Purdom and Donald Carroll

Photographed by
Robert Holmes, Nik Wheeler and David Henry

Kümmerly+Frey

Contents

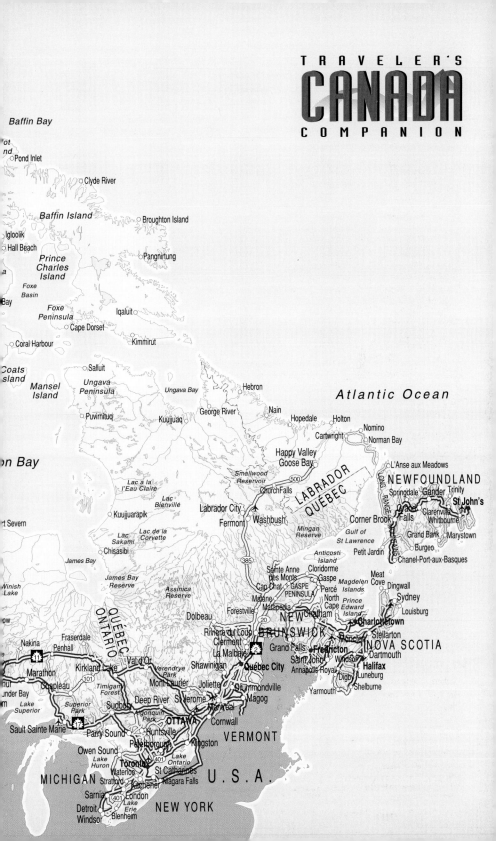

TRAVELER'S
CANADA
COMPANION

Baffin Bay

ot
nd
○Pond Inlet

○Clyde River

Baffin Island   ○Broughton Island

○Igloolik
○Hall Beach   ○Pangnirtung

Prince
Charles
Island
Foxe
Basin
Bay
Foxe
Peninsula   Iqaluit
○Cape Dorset

○Coral Harbour   ○Kimmirut

Coats
Island
Mansel   ○Salluit
Island   Ungava
Peninsula   Ungava Bay   ○Hebron
on Bay   ○Puvirnituq   ○Kuujjuaq   George River   ○Nain   ○Hopedale   ○Holton
○Cartwright   ○Nomino
○Norman Bay

Happy Valley
Goose Bay   ○L'Anse aux Meadows
Smallwood   NEWFOUNDLAND
Reservoir   500   Springdale Gander Trinity
Lac a la   ChurchFalls   LABRADOR   St John's
l'Eau Claire   QUÉBEC   Grand Clarenville
Lac   Labrador City   Falls Whitbourne
Bienville   Fermont Washbush   Corner Brook
Kuujjuarapik   Gulf of   Grand Bank
Lac de la   Mingan   St Lawrence   Marystown
Lac   Corvette   Reserve   ○Burgeo
Sakami   Anticosti   Petit Jardin Chanel-Port-aux-Basques
Chisasibi   Island
385   Cloridorme   Meat
James Bay   Sainte Anne Gaspé   Magdelen Cove Dingwall
Winish   James Bay   des Monts   Percé Islands
Lake   Reserve   Cap Chat   GASPE   North   Sydney
ow   Assinica   Matane PENINSULA Cape Prince   Louisburg
Reserve   Forestville Matapedia   Edward
Nakina   Fraserdale   Dolbeau   NEW Chatham Island
Penhall   Rivière du Loup BRUNSWICK   Stellarton
QUÉBEC   Val d'Or Clermont   Grand Falls Moncton   NOVA SCOTIA
Marathon   Kirkland Lake   La Malbaie 20   Fredericton Dartmouth
101   Verendrye   Shawinigan Québec City Saint John Windsor
Cupsleau   Timigam   Park   Mont Laurier Joliette   Annapolis Royal Halifax
under Bay   Forest   Deep River St Jerome   Drummondville Digby Luneburg
Lake   Sudbury   Agonquin   Magog   Shelburne
Superior   Superior   Park   Yarmouth
Park   17   Montreal
Sault Sainte Marie   Huntsville   Cornwall
Parry Sound   OTTAWA
Owen Sound   Peterborough   VERMONT
Kingston
Lake
Huron   Toronto
Lake
MICHIGAN   Stratford Kitchener Ontario
Waterloo St Catharines   U.S.A.
Sarnia   Niagara Falls
London 401   Lake
Detroit   Blenheim Erie   NEW YORK
Windsor

Atlantic Ocean

James Bay

Severn
Lake
Superior

TOP SPOTS

Into the Mist

"LADIES AND GENTLEMEN… THIS IS NIAGARA FALLS!" announces the captain as the *Maid of the Mist* chugs toward the roaring heart of one of the world's natural wonders. Clad in blue ponchos, we cling to the sides of the little boat and watch the spectacle in silent amazement. Niagara from this vantage point is like some terrible archangel: terrifying in its power, yet clothed in an ethereal robe of white vapor. The voyage is a total sensory experience — we not only see the falls and hear their roar, but we feel them, smell them, even taste them as the mist washes over us.

Formed as the waters of Lake Erie race downhill to join Lake Ontario, Niagara Falls plunges over a shelf of limestone cliffs at the rate of one trillion liters (almost three billion gallons) a minute. Sightseers, like pilgrims to a shrine, have been flocking to this thundering cataract since the infancy of North American tourism. And since 1846, *Maid of the Mist* boats have been carrying them to the base of the falls and back — very awed and slightly damp.

Though the *Maid of the Mist* is our favorite Niagara excursion, the last 150 years of entrepreneurial spirit have provided dozens of ways to look at the falls. At night they are lit by rainbow spotlights. You can view them from Table Rock, the point nearest the falls where there's a well-worn metal railing to cling to, and in Table Rock House, elevators take you down to tunnels which offer views from behind the falls. For an aerial view there are three towers, or if you wish to go higher still, Niagara Helicopters will fly you over the falls and river. In winter the falls are at their most dazzling when the spray freezes to form wonderful natural sculptures and Canada is linked to the United States by a bridge of ice.

Niagara, Ontario is a stone's throw from Niagara, New York, where there are still more viewing angles. After you've wandered along the promenade on the Canadian side, with its spectacular panoramic view of both the American and Horseshoe falls, cross the Rainbow Bridge by car or on foot and, for a quarter, you can leave Canada and go through a door labeled: "Exit to the USA." On the American side the falls are surrounded by gentle green parkland — the first state park to be created in the United States (1885: the same year Banff was founded in Alberta). There is an interpretive center here, and it's possible to get close to the breaking edge of the falls — quite a different view than that from the Canadian side. Those who can't get enough of meeting the falls head on can cross over to Goat Island from the American side, where you can make the hike (after donning a yellow slicker and nor'easter) down to the base of the falls along a wooden stairway… into the mist once more.

Niagara Falls — spectacular, no matter how you look at them. OPPOSITE: The American Falls gush over limestone cliffs. ABOVE: The *Maid of the Mist* chugs headlong into the thundering cataract.

Explore the Old World in the New

IT IS SOMEHOW APPROPRIATE THAT THE ONLY CITY IN NORTH AMERICA TO HAVE BEEN DESIGNATED A WORLD HERITAGE SITE BY UNESCO is also the only walled city on the continent north of Mexico. It is as if the only way to preserve and protect an Old World gem in the hurly-burly of the New World is to build a wall around it.

Perched on a cliff 110 m (360 ft) above the St. Lawrence River, Québec City is not only one of the most beautiful cities in North America, it is one of the most *French* cities anywhere — including France. As Charles Dickens wrote, "It is a place not to be forgotten, or mixed up in the mind with other places." Indeed, how could one forget a walled, cliff-top city with cobbled streets, many seventeenth- and eighteenth-century stone buildings, breathtaking views, lively bistros and outdoor cafés, magnificent churches, a city redolent of history, a city that not only speaks but breathes in French — here in North America? It would be like forgetting or confusing Gibraltar with some place else; in fact, Dickens also referred to Québec City as "the Gibraltar of America."

One of the best ways to enjoy this very European city is to park yourself on a bench or in a sidewalk café and watch city life stream by. At Terrasse Dufferin, you can stroll along the busy boardwalk and choose a bench overlooking the St. Lawrence river. (Try out the little pretzel shop about halfway down the

terrasse where you can get a giant hot pretzel topped with your choice flavors.) At the end of the terrasse climb up onto the Plains of Abraham. Towards the top, you'll find all of Québec laid at your feet — the skyline, as always, dominated by the baronial towers of Château Frontenac. In-line skaters zip by on the hilltop pathways here.

Plenty of corner-pocket parks lie hidden away throughout the city, awaiting discovery. You're likely to find yourself alone with your thoughts and a few spirited squirrels in the tiny Parc du Cavalier du Moulin behind the town house hotels that line the Jardin des Gouverneurs. If the weather is blustery, claim one of the coveted window tables at Serge Bruyère's upstairs bistro, or wander along Rues St-Louis or St-Jean and choose from dozens of cozy cafés.

Basse-ville offers yet more action to the street-scene aficionado. The picturesque Place Royale is at the heart of the summer street life; there's invariably entertainment happening here. Sunny cafés abound along Boulevard Champlain. Head north and west to Rue St-Paul where there's a clutch of truly authentic Québécois cafés. Near Rue St-Paul, at 73 rue Sault-au-Matelot, one of the newest additions

Quebec City, old and new — ABOVE LEFT: The Basilique Notre-Dame was rebuilt in 1922 according to the original 1647 plans. RIGHT: Winding narrow streets seem made for wandering. OPPOSITE TOP: Musée du Québec's modern façade. BOTTOM: Rue du Trésor, once the site of the royal treasury, now a treasure trove of souvenirs.

to the Lower City's café life is L'Échaude ℂ (418) 692-1299, a moderately priced bistro. Install yourself at one of the sidewalk tables, close your eyes and listen to the strains of Charles Aznavour on the stereo; for a moment you may think you're in Paris — a moment, perhaps to ponder Voltaire's quip when the British took over Québec: "J'aime beaucoup mieux la paix que le Canada et je crois que la France peut être heureuse sans Québec." (I love peace much more than I love Canada, and I believe that France can be happy without Québec.)

Was it sour grapes? Perhaps. Though it may be that France could live without Québec, how much richer North America is with this jewel of a city.

Jet the Lachine Rapids

"IT'S LIKE A SUBMARINE RIDE IN A CONVERTIBLE!" bellows Jack Kowalski at a crowd of men, women, and children gathered at Montréal's waterfront to shoot the Lachine Rapids with Saute Moutons (Wave Jumpers) — a fleet of hydro-powered jet-boats. (In French *moutons* refers to "sheep" as well as to the foamy "whitewater" that typifies rapids). "Two things are certain," continues Kowalski to the adventurers who've lined up to take the plunge, "you *will* get wet, and you *will* have the time of your life."

Though the St. Lawrence in summer is "like bath water," thrill seekers must nevertheless don woolen army sweaters. Then on top of a

lifejacket goes a yellow hooded rain slicker. The flat-bottomed aluminum boats are specially made for the ride. Their shallow draft allows them to take on the roughest parts of the water; but even with their 1,100-horse-power engines, the boats are at times suspended, running against the awesome currents of the Lachine.

These currents were enough to stop explorer Jacques Cartier when he arrived at the native encampment of Hochelaga in 1535, not far from the present-day Montréal, on his quest for a route to the Orient. And he named them, wistfully, *Lachine*. Later *voyageurs* (fur traders) portaged the rapids before paddling their way across the Great Lakes on their way to trading posts in the interior. It wasn't until the Victorian era that steamboats regularly traversed the rapids, shepherded by daredevil native pilots with names like Big John Canadian and Baptist Taiaiake.

Half historic sightseeing excursion and half thrill ride, Saute Moutons leap headlong through this untamed section of the mighty St. Lawrence River — right into the heart of cosmopolitan Montréal. Now in its sixteenth year, Jack Kowalski's jet-boat ride is one of Montreal's most popular attractions.

Jet-boats depart from the Quai de l'Horloge (Clock Tower Pier) in Montréal's Vieux Port every two hours for the hour-and-a-half trip to

OPPOSITE: A Québec City calèche. ABOVE LEFT: Light, shadow and color in Québec's Haute-Ville. RIGHT: Jet boaters ride the last untamed section of the St. Lawrence River in Montréal.

the rapids and back. Trips run daily from May to October, 10 AM to 6 PM. There are special package tours, such as the fireworks and dinner tour which takes place along with Montréal's annual summer fireworks festival (dates vary; contact Tourisme Montréal–Greater Montréal Convention & Tourism Bureau ((514) 844-5400 FAX (514) 844-0541 WEB SITE www.tourism-montreal.org, 1555 Peel Street, Suite 600, Montréal H3A 3L8. Tours are offered in French, German, Spanish and Italian as well as English. For information and reservations contact Saute Moutons–Lachine Rapids Tours ((514) 284-9607 FAX (514) 287-9401 E-MAIL lrt@cam.org, 105 rue de la Commune Ouest, Montréal, Québec H2Y 2C7. There's a similar ride, the Whirlpool Jet at Niagara-on-the-Lake ((905) 468-4800 FAX (905) 468-7004, George III, 61 Melville Street, Niagara-on-the-Lake, Ontario L0S1J0.

See the Wonders of Witless Bay

JUST SOUTH OF NEWFOUNDLAND'S CAPITAL CITY OF ST. JOHN'S, ALONG THE LYRICALLY NAMED IRISH LOOP, LIES THE HAMLET OF BAY BULLS, the jumping off point for boat tours to the Witless Bay Ecological Preserve, where a trio of attractions bring visitors in droves each spring.

The islands of Witless Bay are off-limits to humans, set aside since the 1920s for the sea birds of this island province. Over two million birds arrive here in early May, including 500,000 Atlantic puffins, one of the largest puffin colonies on earth. They come to nest and to feed on capelin — the sardine-sized fish that cruise the bay in sparkling schools. The capelin also attract a somewhat larger predator — humpback whales. But Newfoundlanders know that spring has truly arrived when icebergs sail like ghost yachts into the bays.

Tour boats ply the waters of Witless Bay and approach the islands, giving passengers a close-up view of the busy puffins, along with other bird populations including murres, kittiwakes, and a variety of gulls. Throughout the two-and-a-half-hour tour the sky is alive with beating wings, and from time to time the sea — of an almost surreal blue — seethes with the bobbing heads of puffins as they surface from their marathon dives into the icy water.

When icebergs are in the water, the boat gets close enough to feel the chill, and passengers can break off pieces and taste the pure, blue-hued ice. The 'bergs are "calves," sundered from their mother ice fields in the Arctic. They make their way along the northern Canadian coast and out into the Gulf Stream, where they melt in the warm water. On their long journey to the open sea the 'bergs take on fantastic forms; resembling anything from shark fins to gothic cathedrals.

The puffins arrive in early May and the icebergs are not far behind. A couple of weeks later, Newfoundland welcomes the whales. The humpbacks pass within meters of the tour boats, giving passengers up-close views of giant corrugated flippers and massive flukes (tails). Occasionally the leviathans lunge out of the water, launching their 36 tons into the air. Tour boats keep a respectful distance, but at times the animals move close enough that passengers can smell the whale's salty breath as the spray from a blow passes over the boat.

For boat tour information and reservations, contact Gatherall's Boat Tours ((709) 334-2887 TOLL-FREE (800) 419-4253 FAX (709) 334-2176, Northside Road, Bay Bulls, Newfoundland A0A 1C0 (see page 234 in NEWFOUNDLAND for additional tour-boat listings). There are six tours daily from May to October, departing from Gatherall's wharf in Bay Bulls (30 minutes south of St. John's on Route 10). Reservations are requested, but walk-aboard passengers can usually be accommodated.

Tower over Toronto

"HOW'D THEY BUILD IT? WELL, BASICALLY, THEY JUST POURED CONCRETE NONSTOP FOR 40 MONTHS," explains our youthful guide. We're looking up — way up — at the world's tallest freestanding structure: Toronto's CN Tower.

Before we know it we're preparing to be whisked up the tower's ultramodern elevator, which will take a mere 58 seconds to deliver us to the top of the 553.33-m (1,815-ft)-tall

tower — a privilege for which we've paid $12. The budget option, says our statistic-spouting guide, is to climb the 1,796 steps to the top. No thanks.

The CN Tower is a "tourist attraction" *par excellence*, but there is no denying that the view is superb. From the Space Deck, a 360-degree panorama shows us the north shore of Lake Ontario, commuter planes landing and taking off on the Toronto Islands, and the great sprawl of the city fanning north, west, and east.

As at nearby Niagara Falls, there are dozens of activities to distract visitors from the disturbingly breathtaking views. We head downstairs to the Sky Pod, where the famous glass floor is a magnet for daredevils of various stripes. Some people stand on the glass — on thin air it seems — looking down a dizzying 340 m (1,115 ft) and waving for the camera; some walk along the girders that crisscross the glass, holding hands, laughing nervously; the rest of us cling to the opposite wall and turn green — despite the fact that our guide has assured us that the glass used in this floor is three times stronger than concrete. Incidentally, the CN Tower is strong enough to withstand a direct hit from a DC-10. I feel reassured, until I start wondering what happens to the DC-10.

OPPOSITE: Gulls roost in cliffside niches at Witless Bay Ecological Preserve, Newfoundland. ABOVE: Toronto's CN Tower, Ontario.

The Sky Pod level also has the PhotoFX booth, where you can get an instant digital photo of your party looking wide-eyed at a digital representation of — you guessed it — the CN Tower. There is Horizons, "the only café in Toronto that is 1,136 ft high." You can have a continental breakfast here for $3. Upstairs is the award-winning, revolving, Restaurant 360° ((416) 362-5411, where diners pay a bit more to munch on blue-crab cakes and watch the world pass by.

At the base of the tower there are more distractions, including a visitor center, two simulation theaters, and a food court. All in all, there is plenty at Toronto's CN Tower to keep visitors of many tastes entertained for an hour or so. Even if you don't care for interactive video games, digital souvenirs and glass floors — go for the view.

Ride the Legendary Rails

UNTIL THE COMPLETION OF THE TRANS-CANADA HIGHWAY IN THE 1960S, IT WAS THE RAILWAYS THAT STITCHED CANADA TOGETHER AS A NATION. Over the years, many miles of track have closed, yet some historic and wildly scenic routes still remain, reminders of a romantic era in Canadian history.

"We're going to be highballing for the next few miles, folks, so hang on to your champagne glasses!" Thus begins a classic Canadian journey: the two-day train ride (daytime only, you overnight in Kamloops so not to miss any of the splendor) through the Rockies from Calgary to Vancouver aboard the *Rocky Mountaineer*.

After a toast to the journey ahead, you settle into plush digs — a spacious two-level coach with a glass-domed roof allowing a 360° view of the thrilling rush of scenery. Downstairs is the dining room where — a brochure informs you — you'll enjoy West Coast cuisine prepared by the onboard chef. But lunch isn't for a few hours, and just now you have some sightseeing to do.

Right out of Banff you are in the midst of jaw-dropping mountain scenery. From this point on, every mention of a photo opportunity by the train crew is like a call to battle: cameras and binoculars bristle on one or the other side of the car — training their sights on blue-streaked glaciers and mile-high mountains, aerial bridges slung over thundering rivers with names like Jaws of Death and Suicide Rapids, and silent arcades

Passengers peruse the Alberta scenery from the *Rocky Mountaineer*'s "dome car."

Station, Slipping Rock, Inspiration Point, and Deadhorse Gulch, names which give an idea of both the magnificence and misery of the route. The tiny train wraps itself around each bend, by waterfalls which churn under half-melted snow bridges — so close that you could touch them. All too soon, the ride is over. At Fraser, you can transfer to a motor coach for the rest of the 176-km (110-mile) journey to the Yukon, or return the way you came — dreaming, perhaps, of yet another legendary rail journey somewhere in Canada's vast landscape.

The *Rocky Mountaineer* runs from early May to mid-October. For information and reservations, contact your travel agent or Rocky Mountaineer Railtours ((604) 606-7245 TOLL-FREE (800) 665-7245 FAX (604) 606-7250, 1150 Station Street, First Floor, Vancouver, British Columbia V6A 2X7.

The White Pass & Yukon Railway runs four to six trips per day, from mid-May until late September. For information, contact the White Pass & Yukon Railway ((907) 983-2217 TOLL-FREE (800) 343-7373 FAX (907) 983-2734, PO Box 435, Skagway, Alaska 99840 USA.

of 1,000-year-old cedars. Over the course of the trip, wildlife sightings send passengers into yet higher ecstasies: a beaver paddling across a pond, Canada geese in V-formation, a black bear curious about the hulking giant that's passing through its berry patch, osprey fledglings in their eyrie. Across the Continental Divide and down into the Fraser Valley and onward to the Pacific shore, the *Rocky Mountaineer* is the journey of a lifetime.

Once you've crossed the Continental Divide by rail, the next adventure lies further north, where the White Pass & Yukon Railway (WP&YR crosses the 60th parallel, that latitudinal marker that for Canadians designates the transition from "north" to "true north."

White Pass. Anyone familiar with the history of the Klondike will know that this was the treacherous route to the gold fields that thousands attempted to cross on foot in the mad rush of 1898–9. One of the most famous images of that era is that of an endless stream of humanity toiling up a snow-covered incline — the trail to White Pass.

So great was the lust for gold at the turn of the century that a group of entrepreneurs conceived a plan to build a railroad over the pass. Most people said it couldn't be done, but with English capital, Canadian contractors, and American engineers, the "Stampede Rail" was completed in 1900 under extreme weather conditions.

Now the WP&YR is the last of the Canadian narrow-gage passenger service railways. All aboard! Following along a glacially fed river through the Tongass National Forest from Skagway, Alaska, to Fraser, British Columbia, you gain 900 m (3,000 ft) in elevation. Along the 32-km (20-mile) route you cross through Glacier

Walk with the Dinosaurs

WHEN YOU HEAR THE OMINOUS "BOOM... BOOM... BOOM," YOU'VE ENTERED THE ROYAL TYRRELL MUSEUM'S EXTREME THEROPOD EXHIBIT which relates the gory tale of the *velociraptor* and other meat-eating dinosaurs which once roamed Alberta's badlands. The *Jurassic Park* connection is exploited to the fullest at this world-class paleontological museum; it's just one of the many enticements attracting 350,000 visitors here each year.

Situated in Alberta's Midland Provincial Park, 140 km (90 miles) northeast of Calgary, the Royal Tyrrell Museum collects, conserves, and exhibits paleontological history through the appearance of man. That means dino bones, and lots of them. On view are 35 complete dinosaur skeletons — including the dramatic *Albertosaurus*, a fully-articulated skeleton in death pose — along with some very impressive bits and pieces (the rare "Black Beauty" *Tyrannosaurus rex* skull and a T-rex leg bone as thick as a tree trunk). Many of these specimens were found right in the extraordinary landscape of the Red Deer Valley where erosive conditions — nature's ongoing archeological dig — expose more petrified wood, fossils, and dinosaur bones with every gully-washing storm.

But, as museum staff like to point out: "It's not just bones!" Visitors with an aesthetic eye

linger at display cases sparkling with million-year-old seed ferns in endless patterns and shades. There are fragile crystallized leaves imprisoned in stone; zebra-patterned blocks of Jurassic Period limestone; and rare multicolored ammolite gemstones, unique to the province.

Kids, needless we say, have a blast here. At the museum entrance youngsters crawl over the life-size dinosaur models, hanging from giant teeth and sliding down sloping backs. Inside they find plenty of interactive computers and touchable displays. A blacklight puppet show featuring the PaleoPlayers presents the story of the "Weird Wonders": the strange marine animals of the Burgess Shale — the first multicellular animals in the fossil record. The Weird Wonders are also the subject of the museum's newest permanent exhibit, a three-dimensional Burgess Shale diorama which explores these extraordinary creatures and their underwater environment before they were buried 515 million years ago (see YOHO NATIONAL PARK, page 328, for information on hiking trips to the Burgess Shale fossil beds in British Columbia, or contact the Tyrrell Museum).

To would-be paleontologists, the Tyrrell offers not only a window through which to observe research in action, but a chance to get their hands dirty. At the museum's preparation-lab viewing area visitors can watch technicians meticulously releasing fossilized remains from massive chunks of stone. Surrounding the museum, Midland Provincial Park's trails give explorers a chance to investigate the badlands on one- and two-hour loops. They can even pitch in and excavate alongside trained technicians with the museum's Day Digs program. At nearby Dinosaur Provincial Park, the Tyrrell Museum operates an important field station where volunteers can sign up for a more intensive field experience, working for stints of a week or longer in the park's fossil rich fields.

In 1979 Dinosaur Provincial Park ((403) 378-4342 FAX (403) 378-4247 WEB SITE discoveryweb.com/aep/parks/dinosaur, PO Box 60, Patricia, Alberta T0J 2K0, was designated a UNESCO World Heritage Site in recognition of its rich fossil deposits, representing nearly 300 species of plants and animals. It is located a half-hour northeast of Brooks, Alberta.

The Royal Tyrrell Museum ((403) 823-7707 FAX (403) 823-7131 E-MAIL rtmp@dns.magtech.ab.ca WEB SITE www.tyrrellmuseum.com, PO Box 7500, Drumheller, Alberta T0J 0Y0, is open from 9 AM to 9 PM daily from the end of May through Labor Day weekend; 10 AM to 5 PM, Tuesday to Sunday in winter. An admission fee is charged.

OPPOSITE: A bridal veil cascade captures the attention of *Rocky Mountaineer* passengers. ABOVE: *Tyrannosaurus rex* towers over a tourist at Alberta's Royal Tyrrell Museum, Alberta.

Paddle the Pacific Rim

HUGGING THE FJORD-PITTED COASTLINE OF VANCOUVER ISLAND IN SOUTHWEST BRITISH COLUMBIA, PACIFIC RIM NATIONAL PARK encompasses one of the most extensive temperate rain forests in the world. Kayakers paddle here in the calm waters surrounding the Broken Islands, alighting on tiny islets framed with white sand beaches. Day hikers out of Tofino roam the rain forest under a canopy of red cedars and through a damp profusion of sword fern. Beachcombers emerge from the muted colors of the forest to the sparkling tidal pools of the coast where green sea anemones feed and fat orange starfish cling to the rocks. Here, zealous backpackers follow the challenging West Coast Trail carrying all of their supplies for the six- to nine-day trip from Port Renfrew to Bamfield. This infamous trail covers the southern third of the park weaving through 77 km (48 miles) of woods and waterfalls, scaling slippery slopes, and tracing the shoreline that has been the death of many a ship. Killer and gray whales, sea otters and black bears are commonly seen along the route.

Pacific Rim National Park is also the setting for a somewhat more genteel adventure experience. In the midst of the rain forest, a small lodge nestles in a notch carved out of the granite hillside along the emerald waters of Barkley Sound. Eagle Nook Ocean Wilderness Resort offers a taste of the rich variety of flora and fauna to be found in the Pacific Rim National Park, but here guests rough it in style, enjoying a true wilderness experience — hiking and heli-hiking, kayaking, salmon fishing, whale-, seal- and bird-watching — and returning at the end of the day to the comforts of a warm hearth, a gourmet meal, a moonlit dip in the hot tub, and a soft bed.

One constant to a trip to the park is the weather, whether you're trekking or taking it easy. Some days the sky seems to hang within yards of the water. The air is liquid. "Classic west coast weather," you'll be told by Vancouver Islanders, who seem to thrive on the misty atmosphere as much as the cedars and ferns do. But rain or shine, rough or relaxed, Pacific Rim National Park is splendid.

No roads lead to Eagle Nook Wilderness Lodge. From Port Alberni, it's an hour's boat ride to the lodge. Float plane transportation can also be arranged. For information and reservations, contact Eagle Nook Ocean Wilderness Resort ((250) 723-1000 TOLL-FREE (800) 760-2777 FAX (250) 723-9842 E-MAIL eaglenk@cedar.alberni.net, PO Box 575, Port Alberni, British Columbia V9Y 7M9.

Only experienced hikers should attempt to hike the West Coast Trail, and never alone. There is a strict quota system regulating the number of people who hike the trail. Advance reservations are strongly recommended (see PACIFIC RIM NATIONAL PARK, page 368).

Pacific Rim National Park — OPPOSITE: Starfish and sea anemone. ABOVE: Kayaking.

Cruise the Inside Passage

WITH A DEEP GROAN AND A WHISTLE, THE FERRY SHIP, MV MATANUSKA *SWINGS ROUND ITS BOW AND SAILS OUT OF PRINCE RUPERT,* on British Columbia's northern coast. We will be aboard for three days, making our way along the Inside Passage, Canada's historic inland waterway.

We're following in the wake of hundreds of thousands of prospectors who blazed this route in 1898, when gold was discovered in the Klondike region of the Yukon Territory. One hundred years later, adventurers are still booking passage on Canada's inland waterway, in search of other sorts of riches — for this is one of North America's most scenic journeys, taking voyagers through and beyond the Pacific rain forest and into the glacier-locked Coast Mountains of the north. Along the way, the scenery is astounding, and opportunities for spotting wildlife, especially marine mammals, are unparalleled.

The voyage takes us along British Columbia's northern coast and the Southeast Alaska panhandle — which shares British Columbia's rainforest flora, composed of Sitka spruce, western hemlock, and the tall cedars. As we cruise further north, the landscape changes dramatically: Alaska — we're told by the onboard Forest Service interpreter — has glaciers the size of Rhode Island. She ticks off the wildlife we have a chance of seeing during the two-day passage through this icy wilderness: brown bears (grizzlies), black bears, bald eagles, orcas (killer whales), humpback whales, Steller's sea lions, and Pacific white-sided dolphins.

The 22-m (74-ft) long MV *Matanuska* looks like a hospital in *Mayberry RFD*. Snug, clean, solid. There's a cafeteria, a cocktail lounge, and an observation lounge. The top deck has a recliner lounge and the solarium where budget travelers can camp out for the duration of the trip. We have sprung for an outside cabin — with its two portals that blink out into the Pacific day. Along the way, in addition to a stopover in Prince Rupert, we dock briefly in the Alaskan ports of Ketchikan, Wrangell, Petersburg, Juneau, and Haines. It's possible to ferry hop along the coast of British Columbia and Southeast Alaska, debarking at these picturesque towns, many of which can only be reached by boat.

The second and final evening finds many of the passengers enjoying the waning day on the ship's port side. It's the orca watch. A couple of hours pass pleasantly enough, but tension is building: Where are those whales? A

few false alarms set us to giggling: a log floats by… "Hey, look… oh, sorry." Then a resounding, "There they are!" comes from an upper deck, and we all rush to the rail. It's a large school of Pacific white-sided dolphins. Magnificent! But we still want whales. Finally, at dusk, they appear — a pod of five orcas, with their unmistakable tall black fins, curve majestically through the water. Seeing the orcas out on the open sea, it's not difficult to understand why the Pacific West Coast natives so revered these creatures, calling them sea wolves, incorporating them into their art, and endowing them with supernatural powers.

The journey ends at Skagway, Alaska, the very place where thousands of gold seekers erected a muddy tent-city 100 years ago in preparation for their trek over the White and Chilkoot passes to the Yukon.

Schedules and fare information and reservations are available from BC Ferries ((604) 669-1211 TOLL-FREE IN BRITISH COLUMBIA (800) 223-3779 FAX (250) 381-2583, 1112 Fort Street, Victoria, British Columbia V8V 4V2, for trips between Vancouver, Vancouver Island, Port Hardy, and Prince Rupert, British Columbia; and from the Alaska Marine Highway System ((907) 627-1744 or (907) 627-1745 TOLL-FREE (800) 642-0066, PO Box 25535, Juneau, Alaska 99802-5535 USA, for ports of call between Bellingham, Washington, and Skagway, Alaska. While the BC Ferries reservation system is slick and efficient, the Alaska Marine Highway is notoriously unresponsive. For better service, contact Alaska Northwest Travel Service ((206) 787-9499 FAX (206) 745-4946, 3303 148th Street SW, Suite 2, Lynnwood, Washington 98037 USA. They can make bookings for you on both systems.

Note: If you're taking the Alaska Marine Highway out of a Canadian port of call, don't forget to bring along United States dollars.

Listen to Ancient Voices

IT'S AN HOUR'S BOAT RIDE OUT OF DAWSON UP THE YUKON RIVER —A SHORT TRIP, BUT A LONG JOURNEY; taking visitors back many years as they sail into the Ancient Voices Wilderness Camp. Throughout the year, Dawson City visitors who want a change from the gold-rush hullabaloo, gladly embark on this quiet river journey where they can visit the

The Inside Passage — ABOVE: The village of Petersburg in the Alaska panhandle. BELOW: Snowcapped mountains from the deck of the ferry ship MV *Matanuska*.

descendants of the region's original inhabitants and learn about life in this valley before the gold seekers came and changed their lives forever.

This place in the woods may have originally been a Hän native hunting bivouac. Towards the turn of the century it became a logging camp, providing fuel for the riverboats that steamed up and down the Yukon at the height of the gold rush era. Now Marge and Peter Kormendy along with their family and their friends and colleagues are fulfilling a lifelong dream to reclaim and preserve their native heritage. They're part of an immensely exciting movement in the Yukon and throughout Canada of First Nations people regaining their land and their culture after a century of marginalization.

On the boat ride to the camp, Marge explains how she and Peter chose the camp's name. "We call this place Ancient Voices because it's a place of spirits. We're here because we want to keep alive our past. The voices are calling to tell us to come back to the past, because it is simple and true. The land is alive with our ancestors' voices."

Though it is a sacred place, Ancient Voices welcomes everyone. Some people come in winter to see *naoka*, the Northern Lights; some come for the summer women's retreat, knife-making workshops, wilderness survival courses, or leather- and bead-craft seminars. Others just want to be here amongst the voices — to sleep in rustic cabins, or learn the skills of building a lean-to out of spruce boughs, to bask in the *makivik*, the traditional steam-house, and to share a meal at the outdoor fire pit. While some visitors come for week-long stays, many come just for a few hours to see demonstrations of the traditional crafts being practiced: the fish wheel, moose-hide curing, storytelling, drumming and singing. After the demonstrations a picnic of traditional foods is served: *bannock*, a delicious fried biscuit, is eaten with highbush cranberry jam and dried caribou. A barbecue of moose steaks and salmon follows.

First Nations tourism is growing rapidly. These native-owned-and-run enterprises range from historical villages to tour companies to camps to lodges. What they offer in common is a chance to meet and talk to some of Canada's First Nations peoples and to learn about the culture, first hand, often in a participatory manner. These are not living history museums with costumed interpreters, but real encounters with a living culture — and one we have much to learn from.

The Yukon First Nations are among the country's most active and organized. The Yukon First Nations Tourism Association ((867) 667-7698 FAX (867) 667-7527, PO Box 4518,

Whitehorse, Yukon Y1A 2R8, can assist you with a list of contacts in the territory. For information about Ancient Voices Wilderness Camp, contact Marge Kormendy ((867) 993-5605 FAX (867) 993-6532 E-MAIL avwcamp@yukon.net, PO Box 679, Dawson, Yukon Y0B 1G0. Day visits operate through the summer; workshops and conferences are offered throughout the year; package trips and customized vacations are also available year-round.

British Columbia is also an excellent place to encounter First Nations cultures. In the Vancouver area there is the Hiwus Feasthouse ((604) 980-9311 on Grouse Mountain, with a program of Coast Salish dancing and dining. Talapus Tours ((604) 734-1716 is a First-Nations-owned sightseeing company that takes visitors around the Vancouver to aboriginal sites and concludes with traditional dancing, *bannock*, and barbecue. On Vancouver Island, there are a number of cultural centers, including the U'Mista Cultural Centre at Alert Bay, the Cowichan Native Village, in Duncan, and the Kwagiulth Museum and Cultural Centre on Quadra Island. At Cape Mudge, you can stay at the Tsa-Kwa-Luten Lodge and dine in a longhouse on traditional native cuisine. Further north in British Columbia, Prince Rupert is steeped in Tsimshian history and culture (30% of the population is aboriginal) and there is much to see and do in and near the city. From here, you can sail to the Queen Charlotte Islands, ancestral home of the Haida, or head east to the Hazelton area to visit the 'Ksan Historical Village, a restored Gitksan native village.

The Northern Ontario Native Tourism Association ((807) 623-0497 FAX (807) 623-0498 E-MAIL nonta@norlink.net, Rural Route 4, Mission Road, Thunder Bay, Ontario P7C 4Z2, is a clearinghouse for Ontario First Nations tours where participants can learn about the Oji-Cree culture. Tours can include fishing, snowshoeing and dog sledding, polar bear and beluga whale watching, and river trips on freighter canoes.

The Nunavut Tourism Association ((867) 979-6551 TOLL-FREE IN CANADA (800) 491-7910, PO Box 1450, Iqaluit, Nunavut X0A 0H0, is an excellent source of information for all things Inuit.

Finally, annual events and festivals are a good way to encounter First Nations culture. See FESTIVE FLINGS, page 52, and check with the tourism office or native tourism association of the region you are planning on visiting.

Ancient Voices Wilderness Camp, Dawson City, Yukon — ABOVE : After a barbecue of salmon and moose steaks, Nova Scotian visitors "jam" BELOW with native Canadians.

YOUR CHOICE

The Great Outdoors

Extending from the densely populated 49th parallel into the empty reaches of the north, Canada — the world's second largest country — encompasses not only a stunning breadth of wilderness, but also a mind-boggling variety of terrains. Within its embrace is an endless range of contrast: the treeless tundra of Nunavut and the sea-battered fjords of Newfoundland; the lake-dotted interior of the Canadian Shield and the pocket deserts of British Columbia; the boundless wheat fields of the western prairie lands and the picket fences and potato patches of tiny Prince Edward Island.

National parks (37 in total) have been established throughout Canada's distinct regions. While these parks serve to protect the natural habitat, most are accessible to travelers, and most offer an array of facilities

and activities. Boating, biking, skiing, dog mushing… take your pick. But a stout pair of hiking boots is all that is required to experience many of Canada's wide-open spaces.

HIKING IN THE NATIONAL PARKS

The five Rocky Mountain parks — Banff, Jasper, Kootenay, Yoho, and Waterton Lakes — straddle the provinces of Alberta and British Columbia. Banff alone has more than 1,500 km (900 miles) of marked trails. Jasper, larger than Banff, Yoho, and Kootenay combined, is the third-most visited park in Canada (after Banff and Kootenay), with some 800 lakes and mountain trails to satisfy every type of hiker. In both Banff and Jasper many trailheads are close to the townsites themselves, though for a true wilderness experience you'll want to climb to higher pastures. Yoho and Kootenay draw mountaineers and rock climbers from around the world, but also have trails for all levels of ability and interest.

Coastal British Columbia is the home of one of the world's most fabled long-distance treks, the West Coast Trail in **Pacific Rim National Park**. Originally used as a lifesaving route for shipwrecked sailors along Vancouver Island's sparsely populated coastline, this is a challenging 77-km (46-mile) trek that can take five to nine days to complete, and is only for experienced hikers.

Another long-distance hike with a fascinating history is the **Chilkoot Trail**. This grueling four- to five-day hike between Dyea, Alaska and Lake Bennett, British Columbia was the poor man's route to the Klondike gold

Springtime in the Canadian Rockies, Alberta — OPPOSITE: A glacial lake mirrors its towering neighbor. ABOVE: A ground squirrel peers out from the rocks surrounding Lake Louise.

fields in 1898. From Lake Bennet it's just a short hop to some of the best true-wilderness hiking in Canada, in the Yukon Territory's **Kluane National Park**. Canada's highest peak, Mount Logan (6,050 m or 19,844 ft) looms over vast ice fields in Kluane's back ranges, drawing alpinists from around the world. The park's front ranges are accessible to all, offering spectacular scenery and opportunities for spotting wildlife.

Some of Canada's parks are remote indeed, but well worth the effort and expense to reach. Bisected by the Arctic Circle, on Baffin Island in Nunavut, **Auyuittuq National Park Reserve** is an international draw for climbers and hikers; who follow traditional Inuit routes marked by *inukshuks*, rock cairns resembling human figures.

Most people don't think of Saskatchewan as a hiker's paradise, but **Prince Albert National Park**, where the prairie meets the forested northern region of the province, offers backpackers a 400,000-hectare (million-acre) playground. There are hiking trails for all abilities, ranging from short walks to lengthy backpacking treks. Another jewel of central Canada, **Riding Mountain National Park** has 30 hiking trails traversing Manitoba's highlands — where bison, elk, and deer roam.

Rich and varied in its landscape, Québec is the largest Canadian province. On the Gaspé Peninsula, **Parc de la Gaspésie** is laced with excellent trails leading into mountainous territory where Arctic flora grows. Further east, on the tip of the peninsula, **Parc National Forillon** has a spectacular craggy coastline from which walkers can spot whales in spring and fall.

Fundy National Park encompasses some of New Brunswick's loveliest shoreline. Here the country's most extreme tides rise and fall, and foot travelers can observe life in the tidal zone. With forested hills and gorges as well, the scenery is varied, and the park is crossed by more than 100 km (62 miles) of hiking trails, most of which are short, easy walks of no more than three hours. Long-distance backpackers link these shorter trails to walk the 50-km (30-mile) Fundy Circuit.

Some of Eastern Canada's most dramatic scenery is found in fjord-creased **Gros Morne National Park** where splendid hiking abounds, particularly at Rocky Harbour and Bonne Bay. **Terra Nova National Park** on Bonavista Bay is popular for its rugged treks such as the Outport Trail, an 18-km (11-mile) walk along the south shore of the fjord.

Eastern Canada has its long-distance trails, too. The **Rideau Trail** follows paths and side

roads for 386 km (232 miles) between Ottawa and Kingston, Ontario, and the **Bruce Trail** runs 690 km (414 miles) from Queenston, Ontario on the Niagara River to Tobermory on the Bruce Peninsula, while the **Voyageur Trail** runs along the north shores of lakes Superior and Huron.

As well as local tourist information centers, park centers are often equipped with adequate trail maps. If you are venturing into the backcountry, you'll need a topographical map, available from the **Canada Map Office (** (613) 952-7000 FAX (613) 957-8861 TOLL-FREE (800) 465-MAPS FAX (800) 661-MAPS, 130 Bentley Avenue, Nepean, Ontario K1A 0E9.

WILDLIFE

Canada's tundra, mountains, forests, and prairies support a profusion of wildlife. On Vancouver Island, **tidal pools** fascinate hikers who can gaze through clear waters at golden starfish and green sea anemone, while kayakers paddling the Broken Island Group drift through sparkling schools of sardines. Coastal British Columbia teems with **marine mammals;** from the majestic humpbacks to graceful orcas (killer whales), Steller's sea lions, and Pacific white-sided dolphins. In the northern interior of British Columbia, the

OPPOSITE: The glacially-fed Lake Annette in Jasper National Park, Alberta. ABOVE: A bald eagle perched like a totem on Queen Charlotte Island, British Columbia.

rare white **kermode bear** is sometimes spotted around Terrace. The Tsimshian natives called these white bears "ghosts," and they figure prominently in their folklore. The kermode is cousin to the **black bear**, which roams Canada's boreal forest and can sometimes be seen foraging for berries along highways.

Grizzly bears (called brown bears in Canada) are found in greater numbers in the Yukon Territory's Kluane National Park than anywhere else in Canada. **Caribou, elk, timber wolves**, and **thin horn sheep** are abundant in the Kluane Range, which also has the world's largest population of **Dall sheep**.

In April, Yukon bird watchers flock to M'Clintock Bay for the annual migration of the **trumpeter swan**, and in the Northwest Territories some 300,000 **snow geese** migrate annually to the Mackenzie Delta, and other areas of the Arctic mainland and islands. In Wood Buffalo National Park, North America's largest herd of **bison**, commonly called buffalo, roam.

Visitors to Alberta are delighted at the sight of **elk** grazing the medians and yards in Banff and Jasper townsites. Outside the towns, a drive through the parks in summer virtually guarantees sightings of **bighorn sheep**; **black bears** are also often seen.

Saskatchewan is an important migratory stop for the endangered **whooping crane**, and in late August, Last Mountain Lake, northwest of Regina, is the place to watch cranes and

pelicans. Churchill, Manitoba is the **polar bear** capital of the world and polar bears are abundant along Nunavut's Arctic coast as well as at Herschel Island in the Yukon.

Point Pelee National Park, in southern Ontario, dips into Lake Erie at Canada's southernmost reach. This peninsula attracts some **350 species of birds** each spring and fall, as well as **monarch butterflies** which gather here before their annual migration to Mexico each September.

North of Québec City, Tadoussac is an excellent place to spot beluga, fin, humpback and minke **whales** in summer months, and **snow geese** flock to Cap-Tourmente, north of Québec City, each autumn.

One of North America's highest concentrations of **bald eagles** is found in Cape Breton, Nova Scotia. July and August are the best time to see them. Nearby Bird Island is the place to see seabirds, including the **Atlantic puffin** and the endangered **piping plover**.

Newfoundland is **whale** territory, with yearly migrations of humpback, right, finback, and minke whales. Newfoundland is also well known for its seabirds: **Atlantic puffins, murres**, and **black kittiwakes** can be observed from boats at around the Witless Bay Ecological Preserve (refer to SEE THE WONDERS OF WITLESS BAY, page 18, in TOP SPOTS), and Cape St. Mary's on Newfoundland's southern Avalon Peninsula is a major nesting site for **gannets**.

Sporting Spree

Whatever your sporting passion, be it curling or croquet, watching a beer-soaked hockey match, or skiing solo down a pristine mountainside, Canada is likely to offer a time and a place for it.

CANOEING, KAYAKING, AND RAFTING

Canada is the world's most watery land with lakes and rivers that contain half of the world's supply of fresh water, and with more than 240,000 km (151,000 miles) of coastline. With so much H_2O, it's no surprise that Canada's shores and inland waterways are an irresistible draw for paddlers from all over the world.

British Columbia is well-known for its water routes. In the Okanagan region, rafts bob and weave through the whitewater rapids of **Fraser Canyon**. The 120-km (72-mile) trip on the Cariboo River to **Bowron Lakes Provincial Park** is a classic. Sea-kayaking is splendid along the Vancouver Island shoreline, especially around the **Broken Islands** and in the **Gwaii Haanas (South Moresby National Park Marine Reserve)** (part of the Queen Charlotte Islands), where most people hire a guide to help them navigate the archipelago's 180 islands.

In the Northwest Territories, the Mackenzie system presents a variety of challenging voyages, including a 300-km (180-mile) stretch of the **South Nahanni River** near Fort Simpson where the Nahanni National Park, a UNESCO World Heritage Site, has its headquarters. The Yukon river system has it all, from the gentle currents of the **Takhini** to the Class III rapids and spectacular river-level glaciers of the **Tatshenshini** and **Alsek** rivers.

Along the Québec and Ontario border, the **Jacques Cartier River** and **Rivière Rouge** in Les Laurentides offer first-class rafting. There's even a whitewater trip in the downtown heart of Montréal where Saute Moutons–Lachine Rapids Tours runs jet-boats through **Lachine Rapids** (see JET THE LACHINE RAPIDS, page 17, in TOP SPOTS).

Moving east, New Brunswick's **Fundy National Park** has facilities for river, lake and ocean canoeing and kayaking, and **Kejimkujik National Park** in Nova Scotia is a splendid place to paddle through the islets in Kejimkujik Lake or up the River Mersey beneath a canopy of red maples.

SKIING

In this land of legendary winters, where snow covers hill and vale for five months (or more!) of the year, skiing — Canadians have discovered — is a good way to stay warm. Good skiing can be had in just about every province and territory. Even in Newfoundland and the Maritimes, or in Manitoba and Saskatchewan, there are ski runs. In Ontario there are excellent ski areas near both Toronto and Ottawa. But it is in British Columbia, the Rockies, and Québec that you find ski slopes of a variety and grandeur unsurpassed anywhere in the world.

The world-famous ski resort of **Whistler/ Blackcomb** is two hours north of Vancouver along the spectacular Sea-to-Sky Highway. Whistler Mountain has a rise of 1,530 m (5,020 ft) and Blackcomb Mountain has the greatest vertical rise in North America at 1,609 m (5,280 ft). Both are well served by high-speed lift systems and between them they have 2,800 hectares (7,000 acres) of skiing, a good one and half kilometers (one mile) of it vertical, a third of it above tree-line. The area has some particularly beautiful cross-country skiing, with about 190 marked trails, and heli-skiing for intermediate or advanced skiers with Mountain Heli-Sports TOLL-FREE (888) HELISKI, or Tyax Heli-Skiing ((604) 932-7007.

OPPOSITE: A bighorn sheep finds green pasture in the Maligne Canyon parking lot, Jasper National Park, Alberta. ABOVE: Cyclists cruise the seawall in Stanley Park, Vancouver, British Columbia.

In the Canadian Rockies' Banff National Park, three world-class ski resorts are within easy reach of Banff townsite and Lake Louise: **Mount Norquay**, **Sunshine Village**, and the **Lake Louise Ski Area**. These three resorts combined offer 2,400 hectares (6,000 acres) of ski terrain with everything from groomed runs to pure powder. Over in Jasper National Park, **Marmot Basin** lays on another 400 hectares (1,000 acres) of snow.

Whistler and Banff may be Canada's most glamorous winter destinations, but Québec's **Laurentides** (Laurentians) have been attracting thousands of visitors each year since the early days of skiing in North America. And they are still going strong. There are some 20 downhill ski stations within a 50-km (32-mile) region in Les Laurentides, all within a two-hour drive from Montréal. Cross-country skiers are very well served here too, with 1,200 km (755 miles) of groomed trails. The heart of the action is at **Mont Tremblant**, a teeming town of shops, après-ski spots, and slope-side hotels. It's the largest station in Les Laurentides, with 74 ski runs, and the steepest, with vertical drops of 650 m (2,132 ft). There are dozens of other ski resorts, including a Montréaler favorite, **Le Chantecler** (see FAMILY FUN, below) on Lac Ste-Adèle with 22 ski runs, half of which are lighted so skiers can remain on the slopes until 10 PM.

Perhaps the best part of the Canada ski report is that skiing doesn't have to be an expensive undertaking. Many resorts, hotels and bed and breakfast inns offer affordable packages. In British Columbia and Alberta, some hostels offer ski packages. Hostelling International Southern Alberta ((403) 283-5551 FAX (403) 283-6503 E-MAIL SAB@ HostellingIntl.ca, Suite 203, 1414 Kensington Road NW, Calgary, Alberta T2N 3P9, will send you a brochure with the details.

SPECTATOR SPORTS

Though many North American professional spectator sports are dominated by United States leagues, on the ice rink Canada reigns supreme. There are six Canadian teams in the **National Hockey League** (NHL) whose season lasts from October to May: The Vancouver Canucks play at General Motors Place. The Edmonton Coliseum is home to the Edmonton Oilers, four times winners of the Stanley Cup, while onetime Stanley Cup winners, the Calgary Flames, play at home in the splendid Canadian Airlines Saddledome in Stampede Park. The Toronto Maple Leafs will soon leave their old digs for the new Air Canada Centre, which has some fans feeling

sentimental. For the moment ice hockey devotees still worship at the Maple Leaf Gardens. Tickets are difficult to come by despite the fact that many a long cold Toronto winter has passed since the team last captured the Stanley Cup in 1967. Though Québec's team, the Nordiques, has never been a serious contender, diehard fans watch them play at the Colisée de Québec, Parc de l'Exposition. The Montréal Canadiens play their opponents at the Molson Centre, but here again, tickets can be difficult to get. For an **NHL season schedule**, contact the National Hockey League ((514) 288-9220, 960 Sun Life Building, 1155 Metcalfe, Montréal, Québec H3B 2W2.

The Open Road

In the great tradition of ignoramuses who often say prescient things by accident, Al Capone once said, "I don't even know what street Canada is on." Everyone laughed, but old Scarface had put his chubby finger on one of Canada's most pressing needs: transportation. Nor could he have known that after his death Canada would come to live on one principal street, the **Trans-Canada Highway (TCH)**.

Completed in 1962, the TCH is only two lanes for much of its 6,978-km (4,361-mile) length from St. John's, Newfoundland, to Victoria, British Columbia. With more than 90% of all Canadians living within 80 km (50 miles) of this road, it truly is the country's main street. What's more, most of the major tourist attractions are within easy reach of the Trans-Canada Highway.

Adventurous vacationers and those with more time to spend will want to get off this well-beaten track to experience the country's more remote regions, including its incomparably beautiful national parks in the central and northern regions of the provinces. In Winnipeg, Manitoba — at about the halfway point of the TCH — cross-continental drivers can opt to veer northwest onto the **Yellowhead Highway**, the "other trans-Canada highway." Named after the blonde guide known as Tête Jaune (Yellow Head) who showed early fur traders a pass through the mountains, this road follows a First Nations trading route running 3,185 km (1,911 miles) from the prairies over the Rockies through Jasper National Park to the Pacific coast of British Columbia.

The road to Lake Louise, Alberta.

From Edmonton, Alberta, the Yellowhead Highway runs northwest to link up with "Mile 0" of the **Alaska Highway** at Dawson Creek, British Columbia. Running 1,500 km (900 miles) through often spectacular scenery, this historic route has beckoned four-wheeled adventurers since the United States government flung it hastily across the northern reaches of Canada during the early stages of World War II, when fears of a Japanese invasion via Alaska ran high. The Alaska Highway is no longer the rough-and-tumble affair that it was a decade or more ago. These days vehicles of every description, but particularly recreational vehicles, zip along the highway at a rate of one per minute. One of the most beautiful stretches of this road runs along Kluane National Park in southwest Yukon, where blue-green glacier-fed lakes and alpine scenery flank the road.

The Alaska Highway is just the tip of the iceberg when it comes to Yukon road adventures. From south of Dawson City, the **Dempster Highway** leads intrepid travelers into the wilder side of the north on an 18-hour drive that ends in Inuvik, Northwest Territories. Opened in 1979, the Dempster was Canada's first all-weather road to cross the Arctic Circle. It's a gravel surface all the way, but is well maintained. Autumn travelers are often rewarded with the sight of huge herds of caribou.

If you're not bent on making one of Canada's many epic-length road trips, plenty of scenic loops and Sunday drives remain to be enjoyed. You will find many of them described in the regional chapters.

Backpacking

Perhaps it is the length and harshness of northern winters, but when summer rolls around, Canadians just can't stay indoors. **Québec** and **Montréal**, in particular, are perfect for visitors on shoestring budgets — who can savor the city's vibrant street-life and many summer outdoor festivals without spending a *sou*. Alberta's and British Columbia's **Rocky Mountain parks** are obvious destinations, with 11 Hostelling International sites, inexpensive hikers' shuttle buses, and endless trails that are free for the taking. **Interior British Columbia** draws backpacking travelers with its miles of empty roads and spectacular waterways — perfect for long-distance biking and paddling. And the **Yukon Territory** has similar attractions as well as offering the far north's only youth hostel; at Dawson City, in the land of the midnight sun.

In short, penny-pinching travelers find much to like in Canada.

ACCOMMODATION

Canada's **hostels** are usually the least expensive places to lay your head down — especially for solo travelers — costing from $9 to $23 per night, per person. They have the added advantage of providing good company, a refreshing change from the isolation of hotels. Many of them provide cooking facilities for self-catering, offering additional savings on food cost.

Those who plan to do a fair amount of hostelling will benefit by becoming a member of Hostelling International ((613) 237-7884 FAX (613) 237-7868 E-MAIL info@hostellingintl.ca WEB SITE www.hostellingintl.ca, 400-205 Catherine Street, Ottawa, Ontario K2P 1C3. A membership not only reduces your nightly fees, but also gets you discounts at local businesses. Write to obtain their *Official Guide to Hostels in Canada and the United States of America.*

YMCA and **YWCA** residences can be found in many Canadian cities. They are often quite comfortable with extras such as inexpensive cafeterias, fitness facilities, and swimming pools. Though some residences offer dormitory accommodation for as little as $15, others can cost as much as a budget hotel.

OPPOSITE TOP: Basset hound and a Ford Edsel, Jasper National Park. BOTTOM: A truck is covered with dust after the drive up the Dempster Highway to Inuvik, Northwest Territories. ABOVE: Hanging out in sight of Old City Hall, Toronto.

YMCA Canada ((416) 967-9622 FAX (416) 967-9618, 42 Charles Street East, Sixth Floor, Toronto, Ontario M4Y 1T4, will send you the *YMCA-YWCA Residence Directory*, a complete list of all YMCA-YWCA residences in the country.

Some **university campuses** open their dormitories to travelers from May to August. Anyone can use the facilities, though preference is often given to students. Rates for single and double rooms start at $30 to $40. Most universities have an office that handles reservations, and it's a good idea to book well in advance. You'll find university accommodation contact numbers listed under WHERE TO STAY in the regional chapters.

GETTING AROUND

Have we mentioned that Canada is big? The largest part of your traveling budget will undoubtedly be transportation: gasoline is expensive in comparison to United States prices, but much cheaper than in Europe, and trains are outrageously expensive. **Greyhound Canada** TOLL-FREE (800) 661-8747 and the other bus lines ply just about every route in the country and are almost always cheaper than rail riding and driving, unless you are traveling in a group of three or more. Greyhound offers passes in seven-, 15-, 30- and 60-day limits, as well as discounts that allow a second person to ride for half price and children (under 16) to ride free with an adult (on certain routes). See TRAVELERS' TIPS, page 427.

In addition to the buses, there are a couple of other ways to reduce travel costs. With **Automobile Drive-Away** agencies, you deliver an automobile to a given destination. The demand for drive-aways is not as great in Canada as in the United States, but you might try Auto Driveaway TOLL-FREE (800) 346-2277, 310 South Michigan Avenue, Chicago, Illinois 60604-4298 USA, which has locations in Calgary **(** (403) 289-7854, 232G, 3630 Brentwood Road NW, Calgary, AB T2L 1K8; Halifax **(** (902) 832-1240 (no address available); Toronto **(** (416) 222-4700, 6120A Yonge Street, Suite 2, Toronto, Ontario M2M 3W7; Vancouver **(** (604) 985-0936, 1080A Marine Drive, Vancouver, British Columbia B7P 1S5; and Winnipeg **(** (204) 663-2966, 1579 Dugald Road, Manitoba R2J 0H3.

In Québec and Ontario Allo-Stop arranges **ride-sharing** (in Québécois, "covoiturage"); putting drivers who want company together with riders who need a lift. You can, for example, get a one-way ride between Montréal and Québec for an initial one-year membership fee of $16 and $15 for the ride. Contact **Allo-Stop** at one of the following local offices: Québec City **(** (418) 522-3430, 467 rue St-Jean, Québec, Québec G1R 1P3; **Montréal (** (514) 985-3044, 4317 rue St-Denis, Montréal, Québec H2J 2K9; **Ottawa (** (613) 562-8248, 238 Dalhousie Street, Ottawa, Ontario K1N 7E2; **Toronto (** (416) 975-9305, 398 Bloor Street West, Toronto, Ontario M5S 1X4.

Living It Up

While some vacationers come to Canada to test themselves against the great outdoors, others come to soak up the scenery at the country's luxury hotels and resorts. And, short of palm-shaded tropical beaches, Canada has just about everything the sybaritic swinger could want.

EXCEPTIONAL HOTELS

MONTRÉAL AND QUÉBEC CITY

Ask a Montréaler for a recommendation and you are likely to hear about one of Vieux Montréal's small inns, where Old World charm and excellent food are found at prices well below the large luxury hotels. The enchantingly French **Auberge du Vieux-Port** has 27 rooms on five floors of a renovated nineteenth-century warehouse. Rooms have stone or brick walls and brass beds, exposed wooden beams, tall windows, and views of the Vieux Port. Downstairs is the highly regarded French restaurant, Les Remparts. Another charmer, the nine-room **Les Passants du Sans Soucy**, is a former furrier's warehouse. Its foundations date to 1684, making it the oldest hotel in the city. There's an art gallery on the ground floor, and the inn's breakfasts include their fabulous house-baked croissants.

The same architect who designed the Banff went on to create another Canadian Pacific landmark, Québec City's **Château Frontenac**. With its distinctive copper roofs towering over Québec's romantic walled quarter, this hotel has been setting standards of excellence since 1893.

TORONTO AND NIAGARA

Our pick of Toronto's many luxury hotels is the **Toronto Marriott Eaton Centre**, mainly because of its terrific location. Staying here puts you in the vibrant core of the city's shopping district in a top-notch hotel with friendly and efficient service and lavishly comfortable rooms. Striking an entirely different decorative note is Toronto's gorgeously ornate **King Edward Hotel Meridian**. Its turn-of-the-century splendor, its columns, marble, polished wood, and beautiful ceilings make it worth a visit even if you don't stay here. It has some of the finest dining in the city and a lovely lounge offering high tea.

Niagara Falls draws thousands of tourists each year, but overnight visitors prefer the tranquil charms of nearby Niagara-on-the-Lake, where the **Prince of Wales** offers an idyllic setting, excellent cuisine and exceptional comfort.

OPPOSITE: Preparing a kayak at Eagle Nook Wilderness Lodge, Vancouver Island, British Columbia. ABOVE: *Aiguillettes de canard*, slices of cold roast duck at L'Express bistro, Montréal.

THE CANADIAN ROCKIES

No roll call of Canada's top hotels would be complete without mention of the historic **Banff Springs Hotel**, opened in 1888 by the Canadian Pacific Railway Company. Its architecture, inspired by the baronial castles of Scotland, is now a revered Rocky Mountain landmark, with 770 river- or mountain-view rooms and the European-style beauty and health spa Solace. The equally luxurious **Rimrock Resort Hotel**, near Banff's hot springs, immerses its guests in modern opulence. Smaller than its venerable neighbor, yet equally refined, the Rimrock is our pick for the best place to stay in Banff — a more restful retreat than its too popular neighbor. Nearly all rooms have views of the lovely Bow Valley.

But why stay in busy Banff when there is the laid-back Lake Louise, where our favorite Rocky Mountain retreat is nestled along the Pipestone River? The **Post Hotel**, owned by Swiss brothers André and George Schwarz, adds a European twist to mountain lodge accommodation, with its spacious and airy suites decorated in hunter green hues and Canadian pine. Some suites have cozy lofts and all have fireplaces with river-stone hearths. This Relais & Châteaux property is situated along the Pipestone River and ski lifts are just five minutes away by the hotel's complimentary shuttle service. Miles of cross-country trails start at the hotel's front door.

Further north, the **Jasper Park Lodge** is another distinctive Canadian Pacific property, noted not only for its excellent and varied accommodation, but also for its plethora of recreational offerings: year-round swimming in a heated pool, tennis, golf, horseback riding, boating, cycling, ice skating, in-line skating, sleigh rides, and more.

VANCOUVER AND ISLAND

When we're in Vancouver and in the mood for pampering, we stay at the **Wedgewood Hotel**. This intimate 97-room hotel has everything the large luxury chain hotels have, as well as what they lack: a personal touch. Owner and general manager Eleni Skalbania decorated this gorgeous property, using her own antiques and works of art to embellish the lobby and halls. Her elegant taste and characteristic warmth are evident everywhere in this charming hotel. The suites are spacious and include fireplaces and balconies that look out over leafy Robson Square.

It is virtually impossible to think of Victoria without the image of the **Empress Hotel** springing instantly to mind. This ivy-clad dowager, a Canadian Pacific property, dominates the Inner Harbour and remains a bastion of Englishness and old-style glamour. Popular with honeymooners are the secluded rooms in the attic, which have four-poster beds, as well as window seats for enjoying the beautiful views of the harbor.

EXCEPTIONAL RESTAURANTS
MONTRÉAL AND QUÉBEC CITY

One of only two restaurants in Canada to have earned the prestigious Mobil Five-Star Award, the **Beaver Club** (in the hotel La Reine Elizabeth) serves superb continental and Québec regional cuisine. **Toqué** means "loony" in French, and you would be crazy to pass up a chance to dine there; it is one of Montréal's most fashionable restaurants, where the contemporary Québec-Montréal cuisine is as good as it gets. **Nuances** (Casino de Montréal) is Canada's other Five-Star restaurant. One of the city's newer restaurants, the presentation is exquisite, the service excellent, and the food melts in your mouth. Montréalers we spoke with love it and claim that the desserts here are "built, not made."

In Québec City it was Alsatian restaurateur Serge Bruyère who set the first gourmet table, kicking off a gastronomic trend in the city that has resulted in many fine dining establishments. **À la Table de Serge Bruyère** remains one of the city's very best, having restructured its operations to include several dining choices from the informal elegance of the Café European to the hushed white-linen ambiance of La Grande Table. Elsewhere in this historic building there are covered courtyards, a cigar salon, tiny vaulted cellars warmed by ancient hearths, and our favorite Serge Bruyère spot — Chez Livernois, a bistro on the second floor where you can watch the busy street life from a window seat. The room is decorated with the original photographs taken by the Livernois brothers whose studio this was in the last century.

TORONTO

Toronto, with its rich cultural diversity, offers a profusion of excellent dining choices. **North 44°** serves exceptional international cuisine. Among the delights here are such dishes as fried oysters over jalapeño cream, roasted rack of lamb, and imaginative desserts. **Avalon** proffers such savory dishes as wood-grilled sardines and roast leg of caribou. From its 55th-floor perch, **Canoe Restaurant Bar & Grill** serves Canadian cuisine and luscious desserts along with impressive views of the city lights.

THE CANADIAN ROCKIES

The latest entry in Banff's gourmet scene is the **Dining Room at Buffalo Mountain Lodge**, where main courses center on expertly prepared caribou, rack of Alberta lamb, and sea bass. Not to be missed is the **Post Hotel** in Lake Louise Village, which offers warm hospitality in their renowned dining room. Start with one of the delightful soups, such as squash with caramelized apples, and move on to a main course of grilled salmon on a bed of mashed potatoes mixed with heavenly chunks

---

OPPOSITE: The Post Hotel in Lake Louise Village is noted for its excellent cuisine. ABOVE: High tea at the Ritz-Carlton is a Montréal tradition.

of boiled lobster. Ask for a window seat and enjoy a view of the Victoria Glacier as you dine. Breakfast is a treat here also: there's a generous cold buffet or you can tuck into eggs benedict with Pacific smoked salmon from the à la carte menu.

VANCOUVER AND ISLAND

Some say the best restaurant in Vancouver is **Diva at the Met** where the open kitchen serves "art you can eat." Others swear it's the **Chartwell** at the Four Seasons Hotel, with its inspired international cuisine. But never fear, this is one toss up you can't lose. Vancouver also has some excellent French *haute cuisine* with the upscale bistro **Le Crocodile** and the Pacific-Rim-influenced **Lumiere** leading the way in this category. Piloted by a Cordon Bleu Award-winning chef, **Floata** is the largest Chinese restaurant in Canada. Dinners are

lavish, featuring such delicacies as shark fin and bird's-nest soups.

On Vancouver Island, the internationally acclaimed **Sooke Harbour House**, west of Victoria, has wonderfully inventive Pacific Northwest cuisine; the couple who run the restaurant grow their own vegetables and herbs, and use only locally caught seafood and the meat of animals raised on nearby farms.

Family Fun

The bad news is: there is no Disneyland Canada. Or is this the good news? Whatever your opinion, this fact points to an essential, if subtle, difference between Canada and the United States when it comes to family vacations. The United States may have bigger thrill rides, glitzier cartoon characters, better-known superstars, but Canada has a small-town warmth and friendliness that we believe makes it just right for kids. It's safer, too. Canada, claims one of our American friends, reminds him of the United States of the 1950s. So, put Beaver and Wally in the car…

As long as there is snow on the ground, children seem to be impervious to the cold. So, why not take a winter vacation in Canada? If school schedules allow, visit Québec City during the first two weeks of February for the wonderful **Carnaval d'Hiver** where a potbellied snowman named Bonhomme Carnaval reigns as the mascot. Though Québec's is the most famous, many cities across Canada have terrific winter carnivals (see FESTIVE FLINGS, below).

Skiing, as you might expect, is very big in Canada. Families love British Columbia's Whistler and Blackcomb ski resorts, a short drive north of Vancouver. Both resorts have ski schools and daily supervised children's programs. In Eastern Canada, Chantecler TOLL-FREE (800) 363-2450 in Ste-Adèle, Québec, about an hour from Montréal, is a laid-back resort perfect for families. Active teenagers will appreciate this resort's new snowboarding facilities. If your tastes run to adventure, your Canadian winter break might include **dog sledding** and **snowmobiling** in the Yukon, a **canyon ice walk** in Jasper National Park, or **backcountry skiing** and **winter camping** in one of the country's national parks.

When the snow melts, Canada's vacation offerings multiply. Teenagers are thrilled by **rafting** trips in British Columbia's Fraser Valley, or Québec's Laurentides. Whether you join a tour or go it on your own, possibilities for **hiking** and **backpacking** are virtually endless and can be easily combined with **off-road biking** and **paddling** in Canada's lakes, rivers, and along its seashores. **Ranch vacations** and **farm stays** in southern Alberta, the Okanagan Valley (British Columbia), the Qu'Appelle Valley (Saskatchewan), and Quinte's Isle (Ontario) give everyone in the family a chance to share in the day-to-day operations of working ranches and farms: guests help with chores, ride horses, and round up cattle, along with a variety of leisure activities (see SPECIAL INTERESTS, below).

Children (and adults) are always delighted with animal encounters. There are zoos in most of the major cities, but one of Canada's great assets is its abundant wildlife. Each of Canada's provinces and territories has its characteristic populations (see THE GREAT OUTDOORS, above), and an entire family vacation can easily be planned around wildlife watching.

Cultural Kicks

Canada is a mosaic of cultures, an assembly of immigrant groups and native peoples, many of whom have maintained their uniqueness rather than merging into a national Canadian identity. This makes Canada in many ways a more exciting cultural destination than its southern neighbor, where ethnic origins have been obscured by the "melting pot."

Vancouver is the place to stroll in the tranquil Dr. Sun Yat-Sen Classical Garden, browse a Japanese grocery stores, or watch a Punjabi parade. You can cultivate your

OPPOSITE: A boy checks out the orthodontics at the Royal Tyrrell Museum, Alberta. ABOVE: Another toothy creature clutches its catch of halibut at the 'Ksan Historical Village, British Columbia.

cowboy image in Calgary with its world-class rodeos, country-and-western music and Wild West bars. In Manitoba, Winnipeg's historical district of St. Boniface, with the largest French-speaking community in western Canada, will have you conjugating your verbs. You can take a trip around the world in Toronto with its patchwork of lively ethnic neighborhoods — from Italian to Chinese, Portuguese, German, Jewish, Hungarian, Greek, Indian, West Indian, Vietnamese, Thai and French Canadian. Québec City needs no introduction, and Montréal is not only very French, but also very cosmopolitan, with a broad mix of ethnic communities. You'll note a strong Scottish influence in the Maritime provinces (Nova Scotia translates as "New Scotland" in Latin) — evident from the brogue you'll hear in the more remote of parts the islands, and in the Highland games staged in various communities (see FESTIVE FLINGS, page 52).

Canada's **First Nations** peoples are as culturally varied as the country's immigrant groups. In this spectrum of native bands, it is the Inuit and the Pacific Northwest Coast natives whose art first garnered international attention. The **Inuit** are known for their carvings on soapstone, ivory, antler, and whalebone, as well as for their printmaking. With the rising popularity of Inuit art, there are frequent temporary shows in galleries and museums throughout Canada. The **Pacific Northwest Coast** tribes developed a complex culture and a distinctive artistic style which can be seen today in the works of Haida, Tsimshian, West Coast (Nootka), Kwagiutl, Coast Salish, and 'Ksan artists. Animals such as the killer whale, the wolf, and the raven feature in prints, sculptures and ceremonial objects such as Chilkat blankets, totem poles, and masks. Like the Inuit, the Pacific Northwest Coast native artists are rising

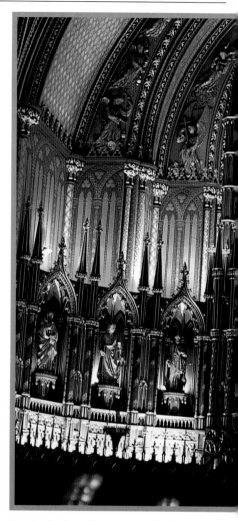

stars in the Canadian arts constellation, and every major city shows these magnificent works in a variety of venues.

European-Canadian painters began to distinguish their art from its continental influences at the beginning of the twentieth century, when the Group of Seven emerged as an artistic force, creating a uniquely Canadian school of landscape painting. Today, painters and sculptors are exhibiting their work in galleries and museums throughout Canada and the world. Canada's outstanding museums include Toronto's **Art Gallery of Ontario** and the **Royal Ontario Museum**, the **McMichael Canadian Art Collection** in Kleinburg, Ontario, the **National Gallery of Canada** in Ottawa, Montréal's **Musée des Beaux Arts**, and the **VancouverArt Gallery**.

Three large Canadian **ballet** companies perform on the international circuit: the Royal

Winnipeg Ballet, the Grands Ballets Canadiens of Montréal, and the National Ballet of Canada, based in Toronto. Widely acclaimed **modern dance** troupes include the innovative La La La Human Steps and O Vertigo. The Shaw and Stratford **theatre festivals** are well known abroad, and avant-garde theatre companies such as Carbone 14 and UBU tour the world and receive critical acclaim wherever they go.

There are **opera** companies in most major cities; the Canadian Opera Company in Toronto is one of the best. Almost every city has an orchestra, as well as smaller ensembles. Toronto, Montréal, Vancouver, and Winnipeg have **symphony orchestras** of international status.

First Nations individuals and groups are also active in the performing arts. One of the best ways to see and learn about native art and artists is to go to the **Great Northern Arts Festival** that takes place in Inuvik, Northwest Territories, each July. Native drumming and dancing, exhibitions, sales of arts and crafts, and participatory workshops are part of this growing festival.

Canadian **pop musicians** such as Bryan Adams, Céline Dion, Leonard Cohen, Roch Voisine and Daniel Lavoie are known the world over. Montréal's Festival International de Jazz is a must on the itinerary of all jazz fans. While Montréal's **Cirque du Soleil** is credited with revolutionizing the circus. Under its yellow and blue big top the troupe presents a show that is known as much for its drama, cutting edge music, and fabulous costumes as for its acrobatics.

OPPOSITE: A carving adorns the house of Haida artisan Alfie Collins in the Queen Charlotte Islands.
ABOVE: Basilique Notre-Dame, Montréal.

Shop till You Drop

The rule to remember is: look for local specialties. This means that in the **Maritime Provinces** check out the hand-knit sweaters, hunting jackets, and fishermen's gear such as oilskins. **Québec** is a good place to shop for Canadian crafts, and you will be amazed to learn how many things can be made from maple syrup. In Québec *aubaine* means "a good bargain" and Montréalers are passionate about shopping for them. There are overwhelming numbers of boutiques, shopping malls, and department stores

catering to every need or whim. In **Ontario** look for native basketwork and Mennonite quilts. In **Prairie Provinces**, especially in Alberta, you will find every sort of cowboy attire you could possibly want. In **British Columbia** look for the elaborately carved handicrafts of the West Coast natives, including Cowichan sweaters from Vancouver Island and Haida carvings from the Queen Charlotte Islands. Also keep in mind that one of the specialties of the region is salmon, which you can buy smoked and gift-packed. In the **Yukon** gold-nugget jewelry is still in style. Fossilized mastodon ivory, most often seen beautifully carved, polished, and set in earrings, is unique to the region. In the **Northwest Territories** and **Nunavut**, in addition to wonderful Inuit carvings, seek out Dene specialties: snowshoes, baskets, and drums as well as traditional clothing such as parkas, mitts and moccasins. Also in the north, Fort Liard is noted for its birch-bark baskets, and Fort Simpson for the now-rare art of moose-hair tufting.

There are two caveats to bear in mind when shopping for native Canadian arts and crafts. Although these items, when genuine, are among the loveliest things to buy in Canada, they are often swamped by cheap imitations. Be suspicious of any handcrafted article that strikes you as a bargain. To be certain that you are getting the real thing, buy from the artist or from a crafts guild or cooperative, or from a museum shop.

Short Breaks

Few visitors attempt to take Canada in as a whole. Nor is there a single entry-point at which all international flights arrive. Rather, several metropolitan areas — primarily Montréal, Toronto, Calgary, and Vancouver — serve as **transportation hubs**. Each of these cities has its unique attractions, and all of them have the distinct advantage of being within easy striking distance of the great outdoors, making them excellent choices for short vacations. All of these cities are also within an hour's drive of the United States border — over which vast numbers of Americans flock to Canada each year.

MONTRÉAL

With Montréal as your entry point into Canada, you're faced with a similarly delightful dilemma: Will you divide a week between cosmopolitan, bilingual Montréal and lovely, provincial Québec City? Or will you tackle the mountains of Les Laurentides north of the metropolis or the lush farmlands of Les Cantons de l'Est, along the United States border?

If you've never been there, you must see Québec City. A four-hour train ride whisks you into the Old World atmosphere of **Québec City**. Take a late afternoon train, splurge on first-class tickets, and enjoy dinner on the way with VIA Rail's excellent service.

One of the world's oldest mountain ranges, **Les Laurentides** is a rippling landscape of undulating hills and valleys. Just 56 km (35 miles) from Montréal, they are home to some of North America's best known ski resorts. **Les Cantons de l'Est** (formerly known as L'Estrie) is a rural area bordering Vermont, New Hampshire and Maine. Skiing here is less crowded and less commercialized than it is in Les Laurentides. In both of these regions in early spring the sugar shacks are busy with maple syrup. In summer boating, swimming, sailing, golf, in-line skating, hiking, and bicycling take over. Every fall the inns are booked solid with leaf peepers eager to take in the brilliant foliage.

TORONTO

Many visitors combine a trip to Toronto with an excursion to nearby **Niagara Falls**. This is can be accomplished as a day-trip, or you can take a more leisurely approach and include a tour of Niagara's wine country. You should plan to stay overnight in **Niagara-on-the-Lake** at one of the quaint bed-and-breakfast inns. Take in a play at the **Shaw Festival** if your schedule allows.

OPPOSITE: A souvenir shop in the Quartier Petit-Champlain, Basse-Ville, Québec City. BOTTOM: Potter Tim Alexander forms a vase in Rossport, Ontario. ABOVE: Downtown Calgary gleams from the Calgary Tower.

A less-obvious, but no less enjoyable, Toronto-based vacation would be to divide a week between Toronto's urban pleasures and the outdoor delights of the **Bruce Peninsula**, where two of Ontario's most impressive parks are found: Bruce Peninsula National Park and Fathom Five National Marine Park.

CALGARY

Calgary is the jumping off point for trips into Alberta's **badlands**, where paleontology buffs can get their fill of Tyrannosaurus-Rex bones and trilobite fossils. There's much to explore here, including Dinosaur Provincial Park, Royal Tyrrell Museum, and Midland Provincial Park. The **Rocky Mountains** are easily accessible from Calgary. Shuttles run direct from the Calgary International Airport to Banff townsite in under an hour. From here the field is wide open for all sorts of vacation pleasures, from spring and winter skiing to the art and culture at the Banff Arts Festival in June. Five days allows you enough time to do some hiking and take in a few of the area's museums. Note that if your destination is Jasper rather than Banff, you should consider flying into Edmonton International Airport.

VANCOUVER

You could easily spend five days in Vancouver city limits without fear of boredom. For those who wish to venture further afield, great side-trips abound. **Whistler**, North America's premier ski resort, is a two-hour drive away. If it's cloudy in Vancouver, take the ferry (a 40-minute trip) or charter a float plane to the laid-back **Sunshine Coast** where swimming on beaches, hiking in Canada's oldest forest, visiting charming villages, and bird watching are among the attractions. Although most British Columbia **wineries** are too far away from Vancouver to include in a day-trip, Domaine de Chaberton ℂ (250) 530-1736 is just an hour's drive east in the rural Fraser Valley. The winery offers tours and tasting, and also has a wine shop where you can pick up a bottle of their award-winning Chardonnay.

It would be a pity to visit Vancouver without a trip to British Columbia's provincial capital, **Victoria**. Thanks to the new "superferries" which sail out of Tsawwassen-Schwartz Bay, it's now possible to see Victoria on a day-trip from Vancouver (see HOW TO GET THERE, page 364, under VICTORIA). Allow time to explore the city's Inner Harbour, the Royal British Columbia Museum, Bastion Square and Chinatown. The fabulous Butchart Gardens is a half-hour drive away.

The Dr. Sun Yat-Sen Classical Garden, Vancouver.

Festive Flings

No matter what the season, Canadians love a party.

WINTER

In **Alberta**, Jasper-in-January ((403) 852-3858 means nine days of alpine skiing, canyon crawling, parades, ski workshops, and live entertainment. The Calgary Winter Festival (February) ((403) 543-5480 emphasizes the city's Olympic spirit with bobsledding and ski-jumping events.

Manitoba remembers the region's early French fur trading history in Winnipeg during the Festival du Voyageur (February) ((204) 237-7692.

Ontario has the Niagara Falls Winter Festival of Lights (January) ((716) 285-8484 with fireworks, caroling, and light shows featuring the falls. Ice boating, ice sculpting, and snowshoe races are part of the fun during Ottawa's Winterlude (February) ((613) 239-5000.

In **Québec**, La Fête des Neiges — The Winter Carnival (January/February) ((514) 872-ILES is Montréal's salute to winter, while Québec City goes wild with Carnaval d'Hiver (February) ((418) 626-3716 FAX (418) 626-7252, a two-week festival of winter sports, ice-sculpting, cross-country skiing, barrel-jumping, dog sledding, and ice canoe races.

Way up north in the **Yukon Territory** when cabin fever reaches its height, the Yukon Sourdough Rendezvous (February) ((867) 668-4711 in Whitehorse is the cure. Featured events include the crowning of the Rendezvous Queen as well as feats of strength such as the Tug-a-Truck Contest. The Yukon Quest International Sled Dog Race (February) ((867) 668-4711 is called the toughest in the world. Mushers and their dog teams travel more than 1,600 km (1,000 miles) through frozen wilderness between Whitehorse and Fairbanks (the starting point alternates from year to year between the two cities) where revelers cheer them on.

SPRING

British Columbia welcomes spring with the Okanagan Wine Festival (April to May) ((250) 861-6654 which takes place in the Okanagan Valley and features wine tasting, tours and gastronomic and sporting events.

In the **Northwest Territories** the Caribou Carnival (late March) ((867) 873-4262 in Yellowknife is a three-day event celebrating traditional northern First Nations games, music, dancing and crafts.

Halifax, **Nova Scotia**, celebrates its heritage with the Scotia Festival of Music (May to June) ((902) 429-9467.

Elmira, **Ontario**, has the Maple Syrup Festival (April) ((519) 669-2605. The renowned Shaw Festival (April) ((905) 468-2172 TOLL-FREE (800) 511-7429, in Niagara-on-the-Lake, opens its season presenting plays by George Bernard Shaw and his contemporaries. Three million blossoms herald spring at the Canadian Tulip Festival (May) ((613) 567-5757 in Ottawa, and the Stratford Shakespeare Festival (May) ((519) 273-1600 opens its much-anticipated season.

SUMMER

Edmonton, **Alberta**, swings into summer with Jazz City International (June) ((403) 432-7166, 10 days of concerts and free outdoor events. The Banff Arts Festival (June to August) ((403) 762-6300 opens its season and continues through the summer with an internationally acclaimed lineup of performances and visual arts exhibitions. Calgary hosts the "greatest outdoor show on earth," the Calgary Exhibition and Stampede (July) ((403) 261-0101, the highlight of which is the chuck wagon race and rodeo, while Edmonton's Klondike Days (July) ((403) 479-3500 relive the gold rush with a week of festivities. Edmonton wraps up the summer with its Fringe Theatre Event (August) ((403) 448-9000, one of the major festivals for alternative theater in North America.

Vancouver, **British Columbia**, hosts the World Championship Dragon Boat Festival (June) ((604) 688-2382, which features Asian cuisine and the colorful ritual of the dragon boats.

In **Manitoba**, the Winnipeg Folk Festival (July) ((204) 231-0096 features 200 gospel, bluegrass and other folk music concerts, and a crafts exhibition. The National Ukrainian Festival (July to August) ((204) 638-5645 in Dauphin presents costumed interpreters, fiddling contests, dancing and workshops. Winnipeg celebrates its rich ethnic heritage with the colorful Folklorama (August) ((204) 982-6210 where there are parades, traditional dancing, music, crafts, and wonderful opportunities to sample world cuisines.

In **New Brunswick**, the Shediac Lobster Festival (July) ((506) 532-7000 takes place in "the Lobster Capital of the World." The province has ethnic festivals galore, including the Miramichi Irish Festival (July) ((506) 887-8810, Foire Brayonne (July to August) ((506) 739-6608 in Edmundston, and the Acadian Festival (August) ((506) 727-6515 in Caraquet, the heart of French-speaking New Brunswick.

In **Newfoundland** and **Labrador**, the village of Twillingate throws the Fish, Fun and Folk Festival (July) ((709) 884-2678, and the Festival of Flight (July to August) ((709) 651-2656 takes place each year in Gander, when hot-air balloons and traditional music float on the breeze. The Royal St. John's Regatta

(August) ((709) 931-2920 is North America's oldest sporting event. The Labrador Straits Bakeapple Folk Festival (August) ((709) 931-2920 in southern Labrador pays homage to this delicious fruit. St. John's, known for its year-round folk music scene, is the venue for the Newfoundland and Labrador Folk Festival (August) ((709) 576-8508, when musicians and dancers converge for a lively weekend.

The **Nova Scotia** International Tattoo (July) ((902) 420-1114 brings Celtic music and dance to the streets of Halifax, and in Lunenberg there is the Folk Harbour Festival (August) ((902) 634-3180 with island folk music and traditional foods.

Toronto, **Ontario**, has the Metro International Caravan (June) ((416) 977-0466 when an explosion of ethnic music, dance and food sweep the city. The Changing of the Guard begins in June at Ottawa's Parliament Buildings and continues through August. Caribana (July to August) ((416) 465-4884 celebrates Toronto's vibrant West Indian community.

On **Prince Edward Island**, the Charlottetown Festival (June to September) ((902) 566-1267 opens with its annual production of the musical version of *Anne of Green Gables*. The Summerside Highland Gathering (June) ((902) 436-5377 is a weekend

Montréal — OPPOSITE: Revellers color Boulevard Réné Levesque. ABOVE: A girl wears the *fleur de lys* at the Festival of St. Baptiste.

of nonstop Celtic events. Street performers and fireworks top the festivities at Charlottetown's Festival of Lights (July) ((902) 629-1864.

The **Northwest Territories'** premier cultural event is the Great Northern Arts Festival (July) ((867) 979-3536, when visitors and northerners gather in Inuvik to participate in a variety of visual arts events including exhibitions, workshops, live performances and crafts demonstrations.

In **Québec**, the Festival International de Jazz (June and July) ((514) 523-3378 is one of Canada's best parties, attracting both internationally known and local players. Québec's **Festival d'Été International** (International Summer Festival) (July) ((418) 651-2882 steps up the fun in Québec City's lovely parks for two weeks. Just for Laughs (July) ((514) 845-3155 in Montréal showcases improvisational comedy with events all over the city.

Regina, **Saskatchewan**, presents the Mosaic Festival of Cultures (June) ((304) 757-5990, celebrating the province's ethnic heritage. Regina returns to the days of the Wild West for a week of celebration known as the Buffalo Days Exhibition (end of July) ((306) 781-9200. Citizens dress themselves and the town up in pioneer style to enjoy entertainment, livestock exhibitions, music, and parades. The Saskatoon Exhibition (July) ((306) 931-7149 is a week of agriculturally based events also featuring livestock shows, tractor pulls, music, parades, and dances; while the Shakespeare on the Saskatchewan Festival (July to August) ((306) 653-2300 brings the Bard to the bottomland.

The **Yukon** International Festival of Storytelling (June) ((867) 633-7550, Whitehorse, draws storytellers from throughout the world to the North for four days of yarn-spinning. Everyone looks forward to the Dawson City Music Festival (July) ((867) 993-5584, when Dawsonites break forth with five days of country and western and folk concerts, dances, and workshops.

AUTUMN
British Columbia bids adieu to summer with the Whistler Jazz & Blues Weekend (September) ((604) 932-2394. The Vancouver International Film Festival (autumn) ((604) 685-0260 presents 300 films from 50 countries. And the Okanagan Fall Wine Festival (October) ((250) 861-6654 throws a 10-day celebration of wine and food.

Ontario makes merry throughout the fall with the Toronto International Film Festival (September) ((416) 967-7371, the Niagara Grape and Wine Festival (September) ((905)

688-0212 in St. Catharines, Oktoberfest (October) ((519) 570-4267 in Kitchener, and the Royal Agriculture Winter Fair (November) ((416) 393-6400 in Toronto. The Canadian Aboriginal Festival (November) ((416) 870-8000, held each year at the Toronto SkyDome, is a celebration of First Nations' heritage, culture, fashions, food, theatre, films, literature and arts.

The Festival Acadien de la Region Evangeline (mid-September) ((902) 368-4410 is celebrated throughout the province of **Prince Edward Island**.

See page 431 in TRAVELERS' TIPS for a listing of national and provincial holidays.

Galloping Gourmets

It must be said that Mobil-star-spangled restaurants are few and far between in Canada (there are two; see LIVING IT UP, above). But that is not to say that you can't eat wonderfully well in every part of the country. The key is to concentrate on the regional specialties.

Thus, in the eastern half of the country, you will want to sample some of the many seafood dishes, and seal flipper pie and cod tongues, which Newfoundland has made famous. In Nova Scotia, you must try the clam chowder, Digby scallops, Lunenberg sausage, and "Solomon Gundy," a pickled-herring-and-chopped-meat concoction that is much better than it sounds. In Prince Edward Island, the Malpeque oysters and the local cheeses are the star attractions. In New Brunswick, go for the broiled Atlantic salmon and the steamed fiddleheads, which are the new shoots of an edible fern unique to the region. In all of the Maritimes you should treat yourself to the glorious desserts made with any of the berries with which the area abounds. And, in all of these eastern provinces you will find, in my opinion, the finest lobster in the world.

Québec, once the heart of New France, would be called New Normandy if it were named after its stomach; for its cuisine remains based on the French peasant cooking of its early Norman (and, to a lesser extent, Breton) settlers. Not that you can't find classic or nouvelle French cuisine in Québec — you can, famously, in both Montréal and Québec City. But you can find that in New York, Los Angeles, or Mexico City, or in dozens of other cities around the world. What makes Québec special is the way provincial Canadian

The courtyard of Serge Bruyère restaurant on Rue St-Jean, Québec City.

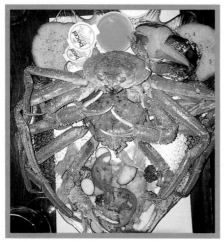

emphasis shifts to the province's game birds — you must try the Haliburton pheasant — and its dazzling variety of freshwater fish from Ontario's countless lakes and rivers. There is also, in Toronto, a wide array of first-rate ethnic restaurants: Greek, Italian, Chinese, Indian, Polish, Hungarian, Japanese, and so forth.

In the western half of the country, you will want to go for the Pacific salmon, shrimp, and king crab in British Columbia. For a change from all the wonderful seafood, you should try the lamb from Saltspring Island or the moose steaks from the Yukon. Throughout the far north, fish, such as Arctic char, and game are particular specialties. You'll find such delicacies as caribou or musk-ox jerky, and scallops and giant shrimp fresh from the frozen Arctic waters.

In Alberta, steak is the thing. Even if you are not normally a beef eater, you will be won over by Alberta's beef. Only in Argentina have I ever tasted steaks to compare with the ones you can get here. In fact, across all the Prairie Provinces the beef is exceptional — as is the freshwater fish from the thousands of lakes and rivers carved into the prairies. In Saskatchewan and Manitoba, I would urge you to order wildfowl — especially the partridge and wild duck — and even the prosaic farm birds, which are tastier here than almost anywhere else because they eat better here. In these provinces, too, you will come across a sort of Borscht Belt, where the large Ukrainian population has left its mark on the menus in the form of spicy sausages, dumplings, and a variety of cabbage dishes.

On the other hand, if you are just looking for a pit stop where you can refuel quickly, you will find coffee shops, diners, and fast-food places just about everywhere you go.

As in the United States, Canadian restaurants tend to be informal and welcoming. They also tend to serve meals at earlier hours than Europeans are used to, so if you are counting on having a late dinner you would be wise to check on kitchen closing times first.

foodstuffs have been used to create provincial French food. A few examples: *soupe aux pois*, a thick pea soup; *tourtières*, delicious minced meat pies (the meat is usually pork, but can be hare or even venison); *cretons*, pork pâté that is usually served with rye bread; *cipaille*, a pastry-layered game-and-potato pie; *andouillette aux fines herbes*, a spicy pork tripe sausage; and *trempette*, fresh baked bread saturated with maple syrup and covered in whipped cream. Maple syrup, in fact, is a theme running through (or over) almost all of Québécois cooking — in sauces, in desserts, and in cured ham — which is hardly surprising, given that the province oozes with maple syrup. What is perhaps surprising is that Montréal rivals New York as a mecca for worshippers of the great deli sandwich and the humble bagel.

Happily, the French influence — and the maple syrup — doesn't stop running when you get to Ontario, although here the culinary

DRINKING

The first time I visited Canada I asked a shopkeeper where I might find the nearest liquor store. This simple question caused utter consternation, followed by endless consultations, followed by — blank. The reason was, it turned out, that spirits may only be purchased from specially licensed liquor stores. To buy liquor by the bottle, except in parts of Québec, you have to go to one of these official stores — of which there

are maddeningly few, which are maddeningly out of the way, and maddeningly closed at night and on Sundays and holidays — and there, but only there, are you allowed to conduct your thirsty transaction. Why this should be the case I cannot say. What I can say is that it interferes with one's budgeting more than with one's drinking, because even the happiest of Happy Hours is not as economical as a couple of self-catered cocktails, and a Rémy in your room is better value than any postprandial drink in a restaurant.

Even the most convivial imbibing is complicated by local laws, which come in various shades of blue. In some places you can get a drink if you're 18, in other places you have to be 19. In some places the bars close at midnight, in other places they stay open as late as 4 AM. In most places, on Sundays you can only order a drink at a restaurant or a hotel dining room, and then only if you order a meal. In a few places you can't buy a drink — period — whatever day it is.

Equally strange, Canadians are not great whiskey drinkers, even though they make some excellent whiskies. But they are great beer drinkers, although until recently the beer they make has been at best mediocre, at worst comparable to what passes for beer south of the border. Happily, Canadian beer has improved immeasurably with the growth of microbreweries, and now good local brews are available from Toronto to Whitehorse.

Though it is true that Canadian wines don't have an international reputation, there are also some happy exceptions here. In British Columbia "ice wine" is enjoyed for dessert. It's made from grapes that are left on the vine until frozen: Quail's Gate is one of the best. Cedar Creek Wineries have an excellent Chardonnay as well as a widely respected Merlot. We enjoyed Mission Hill wines on our last visit.

Specialty of the house — OPPOSITE TOP: King crab in St. John's, Newfoundland. BOTTOM: Mussels in Québec City. ABOVE: Fiddlehead ferns in a New Brunswick market.

Special Interests

LEARNING VACATIONS

From absorbing French language and culture in a Québec café to practicing your "Eskimo roll" in a Yukon kayaking class, Canada is a veritable universe of learning opportunities.

French Canadians recommend Québec City for language learning. It offers more of an "immersion" experience — as opposed to cosmopolitan Montréal where 80% of the downtown population is fully bilingual. Berlitz TOLL-FREE (800) 257-9449, 400 Alexander Park, Princeton, New Jersey 08540 USA, tempts Francophiles with its "**Learn French** in Romantic Places" program. Two weeks of private or group instruction in Québec or Montréal might not have you conjugating like a native, but it will be fun, and you'll make progress. Francophones (and others) can polish their English at the prestigious McGill University ((514) 398-6160 FAX (514) 398-2650, 770 rue Sherbrooke ouest, Montréal, Québec H3A 1G1, which offers a nine-week **English as a Second Language** program four times a year.

Pacific Crest Outward Bound School ((604) 737-3093 TOLL-FREE (800) 547-3312 FAX (604) 737-3109, 411-1367 West Broadway, Vancouver, British Columbia V6H 4A9, offers challenging 8- to 22-day courses in **mountaineering** along British Columbia's Interior Coast Range. Ice, snow and rock climbing, off-trail hiking, backcountry navigation, first aid, and minimum impact camping are all part of the curriculum. Voyageur Outward Bound School ((612) 338-0565 TOLL-FREE (800) 328-2943 E-MAIL vobs@vobs.com, Mill Place, Suite 120, 111 Third Avenue S, Minneapolis, Minnesota 55104 USA, teaches the ins and outs of **canoeing** in Manitoba's Atikaki Provincial Wilderness Park, and **cross-country skiing** and **dog sledding** on Baffin Island, Nunavut, where would-be mushers learn to handle a team of huskies. Canoers and kayakers can perfect their Eskimo roll on Madawaska Kanu Centre's ((613) 594-KANU, 39 First Avenue, Ottawa, Ontario K1S 2G1, weekend and five-day whitewater **paddling** courses in the warm waters of the Madawaska River in southern Ontario.

Ecological study tours are the specialty of Earthwatch ((617) 926-8200 TOLL-FREE (800) 776-0188 E-MAIL info@earthwatch.org, 680 Mount Auburn Street, PO Box 9104, Watertown, Massachusetts 02471 USA, whose volunteers get a chance to contribute to ongoing studies by assisting researchers in the field. In Newfoundland it's possible to study minke, humpback and other species of **whales** for a week with Wildland Tours ((709) 722-3123 FAX (709) 722-3335 E-MAIL wildtour@nfld.com, 124 Water Street, St. John's, Newfoundland A1C 5J9. Participants also have the opportunity to see puffins and gannet colonies, caribou, and seals.

Elderhostel ((613) 530-2222 TOLL-FREE (877) 426-8056, 4 Cataraqui Street, Kingston, Ontario K7K 1Z7, offers learning vacations for the 55-and-older set. Their "Take a Closer Look at Canada" series encompasses a variety of week-long tours that explore the **culture and history** of the country from Saskatchewan's Mounties to Nova Scotia's maritime communities. Also offered are tours to the Arctic where you can learn about Inuktitut history and modern Arctic life. Elders of these First Nations communities often take part in providing the experience. Costs are very reasonable.

FARM AND RANCH VACATIONS

Everybody say, "Yeehaw!" for Canada's guest farms and ranches. These vacation spots range from working cattle ranches, where guests can try their hand at cattle drives or branding, to remote lodges in pristine backcountry, and to luxury resorts complete with room service.

Alberta Outfitters Association TOLL-FREE/FAX (800) 742-5548, PO Box 277, Caroline, Alberta T0M 0M0, represents independent ranch and farm families located throughout the southern and central province. You can contact the **British Columbia Guest Ranchers' Association** ((250) 374-6836 FAX (250) 374-

6640, c/o BCFROA, PO Box 3301, Kamloops, BC V2C 6B9, for a list of the provinces 14 guest ranches. There are a few places around Regina, Saskatchewan, that offer farm accommodation, mainly in the Qu'Appelle Valley. For details, contact the **Saskatchewan Country Vacation Association** ((306) 931-3353, Rural Route 5, PO Box 43, Saskatoon S7K 3J8, which lists farm vacations as well as bed and breakfast accommodations. Manitoba vacation farms can be found through the **Pembina Valley Travel Association** ((204) 324-8641 TOLL-FREE (800) 877-1874 E-MAIL pvdcorp@mts.net, PO Box 1180, Altona, Manitoba R0G 0B0.

OPPOSITE: Life in the tidal pools fascinates a golden retriever. ABOVE: Ice climbers scale Montmorency Falls near Québec City. RIGHT: A beluga whale at the Vancouver Aquarium.

In Ontario, **Travelinx** TOLL-FREE (800) ONTARIO WEB SITE www.travelinx.com/ bbfarm.htm (no street address) lists farm vacation operations. You can also contact the **Bruce County Office of Tourism and Agriculture** ((519) 797-1602 FAX (519) 797-2191 TOLL-FREE (800) 268-3838 E-MAIL tourism@brucecounty.on.ca, 33 Victoria Street North, PO Box 180, South Hampton, Ontario N0H 2L0, for a list of independent operators, or the **Ontario Farm and Country Accommodations** (no phone number available) E-MAIL vinceel@netrover.com, c/o Samme Putzel, Rural Route 2, Vankleek Hill, Ontario K0B 1R0. Note that these associations are not booking agents, but merely provide information; reservation booking is done directly with farms and ranches.

WINE TASTING AND TOURS

The Okanagan Similkameen Valley is British Columbia's wine country, and wine-touring opportunities abound here. Contact the **Okanagan Similkameen Tourism Association** ((250) 860-5999 FAX (250) 861-7493, 1332 Water Street, Kelowna, British Columbia V1Y 9P4. Motorists can follow the well-marked wine route through hill and valley, tasting the fruits of the season as they go (be sure to appoint a designated driver). Among the wineries to contact for details are: **Sumac Ridge Estate Winery** ((250) 494-0451 FAX (250) 494-3456, 17403 Highway 97, Summerland, British Columbia V0H 1Z0; **Kelowna's Calona Vineyards** ((250) 762-9144 or (250) 762-3332, 1125 Richter Street, Kelowna, British Columbia V1Y 2K6; **Mission Hill Winery** ((250) 768-7611 or (250) 768-5125, 1730 Mission Hill Road, Westbank, British Columbia V4T 2E4; and **Quail's Gate Estate Winery** ((250) 769-4451, 3303 Boucherie Street, Kelowna, British Columbia V1Z 2H3.

The East's wine country is the Niagara Peninsula. Contact the **Wine Council of Ontario** ((905) 684-8070, 110 Hanover Drive, Suite B205, St. Catharines, Ontario L2W 1A4, which has maps of the wine region, including locations of individual wineries and information on summer happenings in wine country. Several wineries offer wine tasting and tours; call for details at the following well-known Ontario wineries: **Château des Charmes Wines Ltd.** ((905) 262-4219 FAX (905) 262-5548, 1025 York Street, PO Box 280, St-David's, Niagara-on-the-Lake, Ontario L0S 1P0; **Hillebrand Estates Winery** ((905) 468-7123 TOLL-FREE (800) 582-8412, Highway

55, Niagara-on-the-Lake, Ontario; **Iniskillin Wines** ((905) 468-2187 FAX (905) 468-5355, SR 66, Rural Route 1, Niagara-on-the-Lake, Ontario L0S 1J0; **Konzelman Winery** ((905) 935-2866, 1096 Lakeshore Street, Niagara-on-the-Lake, Ontario L0S 150; and **Reif Winery** ((905) 468-7738, 15606 Niagara Parkway, Niagara-on-the-Lake, Ontario L0S 1J0.

Taking a Tour

Ready for adventure? Whether your idea of a thrill is dog mushing through the Arctic or riding a luxury motor coach through wine country, Canada has a tour for you. Aside from being lots of fun, a good tour takes the hassle out of trip planning, provides instant camaraderie, and puts a knowledgeable guide at your side.

ADVENTURE

Ecosummer Expeditions ((604) 214-7484 TOLL-FREE (800) 465-8884 FAX (604) 214-7485 E-MAIL trips@ecosummer.com, 5640 Hollybridge, Richmond, British Columbia V7C 4N3, has one- to two-week kayaking trips through the misty archipelago

OPPOSITE: Along Alberta's Icefields Parkway, Athabasca Falls roars through a canyon created by eons of erosion. ABOVE: Train tracks head west out of Banff, Alberta, bound for the Pacific Coast.

of the Queen Charlotte Islands and rafting trips on the Tatshenshini and Alsek rivers of the Yukon and northern British Columbia.

Nature Trek Canada (/FAX (250) 653-4265 E-MAIL naturetrek@saltspring.com WEB SITE www.saltspring.com/naturetrek, 1231 Isabella Point Road, Salt Spring Island, British Columbia V8K 1T5, specializes in hiking trips to the wild and remote Torngat Mountains in northernmost Labrador. These mountains are as high and mighty as the Rockies, but as one climber put it "there aren't any teahouses here." Guides speak German, Dutch, and English.

Butterfield & Robinson's ((416) 864-1354 TOLL-FREE (800) 678-1147 FAX (416) 864-0541, 70 Bond Street, Suite 300, Toronto, Ontario M5B 1X3, offers week-long, leisurely paced rolls through Nova Scotia's valleys and villages with stops along the way for meals of fresh lobster, mussels, and scallops. Other tours include a backcountry walks in British Columbia, Gulf Islands biking and walking trips, Nova Scotia biking, Ontario biking, and a hikes in the Rockies.

Backroads ((510) 527-1555 TOLL-FREE (800) GO-ACTIVE FAX (510) 527-1444, 801 Cedar Street, Berkeley, California 94710 USA, specializes in active adventures in an irresistible framework of luxury lodging and gourmet dining. Trips include bicycling Nova Scotia's Evangeline Trail, hiking New Brunswick's Fundy Coast, and walking tours of Banff and Yoho national parks. There are also multi-sport trips in the Rockies that can include hiking, mountain biking and rafting, heli-hiking, cross-country skiing, and snowshoeing.

Wells Gray Provincial Park, in British Columbia's Caribou Mountains, is the destination for **GAP Adventures** ((416) 922-

8899 TOLL-FREE (800) 465-5600 FAX (416) 922-0822 E-MAIL adventure@gap.ca, 266 Dupont Street, Toronto, Ontario M5R 1V7, which offers five- to nine-day hut-to-hut hiking or canoe trips. GAP also has week-long and three-day trips to Churchill, Manitoba, the "Polar Bear Capital of the World." On Vancouver Island, GAP has trips that take in killer-whale watching, grizzly bear tracking, and sea kayaking. GAP Adventures feature grassroots-style traveling, basic accommodation in simple hotels and hostels, or camping.

Each February and March hundreds of thousands of harp seals enter the Gulf of St. Lawrence to bear their young on the vast floating ice fields west of the Magdalen Islands. **Natural Habitat Adventures** ((303) 449-3711 TOLL-FREE (800) 543-8917 FAX (303) 449-3712, 2945 Center Green Court, Suite H,

Boulder, Colorado 80301 USA, takes participants by helicopter to the ice floes to walk among the mother seals and white coated pups. The tour is part of a project to protect these endangered animals. The same company takes amateur naturalists out to track gray wolves in Québec's Jacques Cartier Park. Log cabins are the accommodation and days are spent radio-tracking wolves via snowmobile, snowshoe and helicopter. Eight-day trips take place in February and March.

From May to mid-October **Equitour/FITS** ((307) 455-3363 TOLL-FREE (800) 545-0019 FAX (307) 455-2354 E-MAIL equitour@wyoming .com, 10 Stalnaker Street, Dubois, Wyoming 82513 USA, has two-day horseback riding trips along the upper St. Lawrence, with stops for swimming and trout fishing along the way; in August and September riders can

explore the wild country of the Canadian Appalachians on old woodcutters' trails. On both trips, riders stay in lodges and enjoy traditional Québécois meals and music.

In the Yukon Territory, **Walden Guiding and Outfitting** ((867) 667-7040 TOLL-FREE (877) WALDENS (9259) E-MAIL Bwalden@ hypertech.yk.ca, PO Box 4845, Whitehorse, Yukon Y1A 4N6, offers dog-mushing adventures in winter and in summer canoeing on the Big Salmon River. **Arctic Vision** ((867) 668-2411 FAX (867) 668-2642 E-MAIL arctic@yknet.yk.ca, PO Box 31210(v), Whitehorse, Yukon Y1A 5P7, specializes in tours to the Western Arctic, including day tours from Inuvik to Tuktoyaktuk where

LEFT: A canoe is waiting for you high in the Yukon's Kluane Range at St. Elias Lake. ABOVE: Coal Harbour Yacht Club, Vancouver.

you can dip your toes in the Arctic Ocean, and flights to the remote Herschel Island. **Cloudberry Adventures Yukon** (/FAX (867) 668-7711 E-MAIL cloud@cloudberry.ca, PO Box 6113, Department C, Whitehorse, Yukon Y1A 5L7, journeys to "Little Switzerland," Atlin, British Columbia, and the remote Coal River Springs Territorial Park with combined hiking, paddling and wildlife watching activities.

You can follow the trail of the old fur traders on a six-day kayaking trip on Georgian Bay with **Black Feather Wilderness Adventures** ((705) 746-1372 TOLL-FREE (800) 574-8375, Rural Route 3, Parry Sound, Ontario P2A 2X1. Black Feather also offers canoeing on the Nahanni River in the Northwest Territories combined with a four- to five-day alpine hike in the Cirque of the Unclimbables, as well as rugged 16-day kayaking and hiking trips on Ellesmere Island — the top of the world.

There are a number of excellent First Nations-owned and run tour companies. One of the longer-established of them is the **Arctic Tour Company** ((867) 977-2230 FAX (867) 977-2276 E-MAIL atc@auroranet.nt.ca, PO Box 325, Tuktoyaktuk, Northwest Territories X0E 1C0, which offers various winter and summer tours, including dog team and snowmobile excursions, wildlife viewing and bird watching, Northern Lights viewing, camping, hiking, and community tours, and native cultural and traditional tours.

GUIDED COACH AND CRUISE TOURS

Globus Tours ((303) 797-2800 TOLL-FREE (800) 851-0728 extension 7518, 5301 South Federal Circle, Littleton, Colorado 80123 USA, is a Swiss-owned company offering deluxe coach tours. Their sister company, **Cosmos** (contact Globus offers bargain-priced motor coach tours with accommodation in modest hotels. **Maupintour** ((913) 843-1211 TOLL-FREE (800) 255-4266 FAX (913) 843-8351, 1515 St. Andrews Drive, Lawrence, Kansas 66047 USA, and **Tauck Tours** ((203) 226-6911 TOLL-FREE (800) 468-2825 FAX (203) 221-6828, PO Box 5027, Westport, Connecticut 06881 USA, are two more well-established luxury coach tour operators with many Canadian destinations.

In the northwest the trend is two- to three-week combination tours that include a cruise along the Inside Passage and a motor coach ramble over the White Pass into the Yukon. **Brendan Tours** ((818) 785-9696 TOLL-FREE (800) 421-8446 FAX (818) 902-9876, 15137 Califa Street, Van Nuys, California 91411 USA, makes an interesting two-week combination cruise and motor coach tour that takes you from Vancouver to Anchorage. On the way

you spend three nights aboard the MS *Westerdam*, take a scenic ride on the White Pass & Yukon Railway, and enjoy a riverboat cruise out of Dawson City.

The city-sized ships of **Holland America**, contact Travelon Vacations ((630) 271-6004 TOLL-FREE (800) 392-2277 (no mailing address available), ply the North Atlantic and North Pacific coastlines. Their 10-day Canada–New England Northbound cruise begins in New York. After stops in the coastal cities of New England the MS *Westerdam* docks in Halifax for a day of sightseeing. Next stop is Charlottetown on Prince Edward Island where passengers can shop and explore the galleries and visit the house of *Anne of Green Gables*. Beluga whales can be spotted from the deck as the ship cruises the Saguenay Fjord, and the trip ends with a day in Québec City.

There is an abundance of cruises that chug along the gorgeous glacier-bound west coast of British Columbia, typically making their way to Anchorage, Alaska. The cruise season is generally late May through early September (see CRUISE THE INSIDE PASSAGE, page 26, in TOP SPOTS).

OPPOSITE TOP: The "Snocoach" shuttles passengers to the Athabasca Glacier, Alberta. BOTTOM: A cruise ship is docked at Canada Place, Vancouver. ABOVE: Alberta's badlands are an open book on the region's geological history.

Welcome
to Canada

IF YOU LIKE THE IDEA OF A GIGANTIC COUNTRY THAT can be enjoyed without a gigantic wallet, a New World nation that has taken care not to squander its Old World inheritance, a place where the dazzle of the landscape is matched by the kaleidoscopic mix of peoples who inhabit it, then you will like Canada — a lot.

And there is a lot of it to like. Covering almost 10 million sq km (3.9 million sq miles), it is the second largest country in the world (after Russia). Unlike Russia, however, or its next-door neighbor to the south, Canada has only 30.3 million inhabitants—slightly more than California. While the land extends northward well into the Arctic Circle, the vast majority of the population is concentrated in a narrow band along the long border with the United States.

From a strictly demographic point of view, the two most striking things about this population are that it is overwhelmingly urban — over 75% of Canadians live in cities or towns — and surprisingly heterogeneous. Unlike their American counterparts who have been historically quick to jettison their cultural baggage in the rush to become assimilated, immigrants to Canada have tended to cherish and safeguard their distinctive traditions, preserving the old in order to civilize the new. Thus it is not uncommon to see signs in Finnish by Lake Superior or to hear Ukrainian spoken on the Manitoban prairies. Likewise, members of various other nationalities and ethnic groups in Canada have created cheery enclaves without creating dreary ghettos.

It's a pity that President Kennedy appropriated the phrase "a nation of immigrants" to describe the United States, because it applies more accurately to Canada. Whereas the United States may have been founded by immigrants, and substantially populated by them for a century or more, Canada is still being shaped by immigration. At the beginning of the nineteenth century the country had a population of barely five million; since then two tidal waves of immigrants — the first before World War I and the second following World War II — have washed up on Canada's shores, helping to boost the population to its present level and helping to determine what kind of nation will enter the twenty-first century.

Unhappily, it is still uncertain whether or not this nation — whose greatest triumph has been the achievement of a multicultural, bilingual state — will unravel as the friction between the two predominant cultures, the British and the French, provokes Québec to tear itself away from Confederation. But of this more later. Happily, Canada's other great achievement, which is to have shared a continent with America without becoming totally Americanized, looks like it will continue to be a distinguishing feature of the Canadian way of life.

It won't be easy. For one thing, most Canadians live close to the United States border, the longest unguarded national boundary in the world. This means, among other things, that most Canadians are within reach of American radio and television stations. This has been a major concern of Canadian intellectuals for the better part of the twentieth century. It first surfaced as a worry in the 1920s, when Canada was absorbed into the American radio system at a time when the United States was beginning to flex its imperial muscles. Then, after the end of World War II, when America was at the zenith of its power and influence, there

came the new threat of cultural annexation by television.

So seriously was this threat viewed that no fewer than three royal commissions were set up between 1949 and 1961 to address "the problem of American culture in Canada," and specifically to seek ways of organizing "resistance to the absorption of Canada into the general cultural pattern of the United States." There was little the commissioners could do, however, apart from encouraging the Canadian Broadcasting Corporation (CBC) in its policy of featuring homegrown material. Even this rearguard action, faithfully pursued by the CBC since its creation in 1936, has never received wholehearted government

OPPOSITE: The Montréal antiques district TOP and a Toronto Greek neighborhood BOTTOM. ABOVE: In the town of Niagara Falls, motels and restaurants shout their welcome.

support. Today that support is decidedly half-hearted: during the 1990s, 11 CBC television stations had to close down because of cuts in government funding. Meanwhile, the most recent surveys show that 80% of total television viewing in the big metropolitan areas near the border is of American programs; even in Edmonton, which receives only Canadian stations, the figure is 66%.

Nor is the cross-border invasion limited to the airwaves. American films occupy most of the cinema screens, while American magazines dominate the newsagents' shelves. Even Canadian sports have not escaped American colonization. All of the top teams in the one sport about which Canadians are passionate — ice hockey — play in America's National Hockey League. Having been (quite rightly) converted to the glories of baseball, Canadians see their two baseball teams — the Toronto Blue Jays and the Montréal Expos — competing in the American major leagues. Not even their individual sporting heroes seem able to resist the Americans: within the last decade, Wayne Gretzky, "The Great One" — ice hockey's all-time superstar — abandoned Edmonton for Los Angeles, and Ben Johnson, Canada's greatest-ever sprinter, was stripped of his Olympic gold medal after failing a drug test, and then had to watch while the medal was awarded to his arch-rival, the American Carl Lewis. Perhaps the only sport in which Canadians have managed to remain somewhat aloof is American football, but that is only because they enthusiastically embraced the game, made a few minor adjustments here and there, and then renamed it Canadian football. I have watched it (with more enthusiasm, it must be said, than most Canadians) and I have to say that one needs to be a real aficionado, or perhaps a theologian, to explain how it differs from the original.

Canadian football is symbolic of Canadian society insofar as it presents the outsider with difficulties in distinguishing it from its more familiar American counterpart. This, not surprisingly, fills Canadians with an overwhelming sense of frustration. So much so, in fact, that when I told a prominent Canadian businessman over lunch (truthfully) that I had never met a Canadian I didn't like, he reacted with exasperation bordering on disgust. "That's precisely our problem," he said. "Nobody dislikes us, because nobody knows us. To the rest of the world we're just nicer, quieter Americans." Although I felt constrained to insist that this was not a bad thing to be, I could see his point: it must be maddening to be treated forever like the Canadian dollar is treated, as a slightly discounted version of the real thing.

Equally maddening, if not more so, is the fact that most Americans regard Canadians as nicer, quieter versions of themselves. No wonder, then,

that Canadians are forever worrying about their national identity being obliterated by the long shadows cast by the colossus to the south. As former prime minister Pierre Trudeau, in a celebrated quip, told Americans on a visit to Washington in 1969: "Living next to you is in some ways like sleeping with an elephant. No matter how friendly and even-tempered the beast, one is affected by every twitch and grunt."

John Bierman, the distinguished English biographer and author of *Dark Safari* who now lives in Toronto, puts it this way: "If you could perforate along the 49th parallel, tear along the dotted line and push Canada out into the Pacific or Atlantic, I'm sure they'd be a totally different people. But the identity crisis is perpetual."

To deal with this "crisis" many Canadians have chosen to reach back, sometimes way back, into their colonial past for a suitable identity. Thus there are parts of the country where stylized versions

of the British and French ways of life have been lovingly, not to say fanatically, preserved. This understandably leads outsiders to the frequent conclusion that Canadians have a neurotic preoccupation with being seen as Not-Americans. Indeed in some cases they have. But in my travels around the country I have found that for all the agonizing over their soft-focus national profile, the great majority of Canadians sensibly realize that they quite probably live in the best of all possible worlds.

After all, their country is situated in a neighborhood where there is only one neighbor — and that one is so friendly that neither of them has ever bothered to put up a fence. They have the luxury of living in cities that are not only handsome and comfortable but come equipped with the world's largest backyard, in the form of wilderness areas of awe-inspiring beauty. Their society has the civilizing patina of history while enjoying all the ben-

efits of modern technology. In short, as a member of the Commonwealth of Nations with a large Francophone population, Canada is in the privileged position of being able to boast of a British monarch but American telephones, French cooking but American plumbing.

As the country's Chinatowns attest, Canadians have managed to create cheery enclaves without creating dreary ghettos.

Canada
and Its
People

HISTORICAL BACKGROUND

Just when people first came to Canada is a matter of considerable debate among the experts—some say it could have been up to 40,000 years ago, while others insist that it was no more than 11,000 years ago — but there is no argument over who they were or where they came from. They were nomadic tribes from Asia, principally Siberia and Mongolia, who came into North America across a land bridge that crossed the Bering Strait during successive ice ages. This migration, often imagined as a mass exodus like Moses crossing the Red Sea, in fact happened gradually as bands of hunters traveled

fied landing. Arriving at the northwestern tip of Newfoundland, which they named Vinland ("land of grapevines"), they established a settlement at the site of present-day L'Anse aux Meadows. Unfortunately, the archaeological remains don't tell us how long the settlement survived or what finished it off, but it is generally assumed that a combination of the harsh winters and clashes with the region's natives drove the settlers away before they had a chance to establish a viable colony.

The next proven landing in Canada was not for another five centuries, when in 1497 the Venetian John Cabot (*né* Giovanni Caboto) arrived in Newfoundland, and then Nova Scotia, to claim

east in search of game. And the land bridge from Asia, now referred to as Beringia, was actually hundreds of miles wide, more like a small continent.

Over thousands of years, these bands and their descendants fanned out across North America, establishing different Amerindian societies and civilizations which in some cases became highly developed as early as the eighth millennium BC.

THE FIRST EUROPEANS

There is evidence, although inconclusive, to suggest that the first European to set foot in North America was a sixth-century Irish monk who, according to legend, landed briefly on the coast of Newfoundland. But Vikings sailing from Greenland around AD 1000 made the earliest veri-

these new-found lands for England and Henry VII. (For all practical — i.e., fishing — purposes the nearby sea had already been claimed by the Portuguese, Basque, and Breton fishermen who in the previous century had discovered the Grand Banks fishing grounds off the coast of Newfoundland to be among the richest in the world.) The next claimant to what was already shaping up as another stage for the worldwide Anglo-French rivalry was the Breton Jacques Cartier, who in 1534 sailed into the Gulf of St. Lawrence, landing at Prince Edward Island (which he named Île St-Jean) and the Gaspé Peninsula before sailing down the St. Lawrence as far as a native village in the shadow of an impressive hill, which he named *Mont Réal* (royal mountain). He claimed the entire area for France, referring to it by the Algonquin word for "settlement": Kannata.

NEW FRANCE

Since Cartier didn't return to France laden with the hoped-for gold and gems, French interest in Canada quickly waned, only to be revived at the start of the seventeenth century by, of all things, the demands of *haute couture*. In a word, furs. Thus in 1605 the French explorer Samuel de Champlain established the first permanent European settlement in Canada at Port Royal, Nova Scotia, on the Bay of Fundy, in hopes of trading with the natives for their beaver pelts. Three years later Champlain founded another settlement on a plateau overlooking the St. Lawrence River at the bend where the

Although the British had watched uneasily as New France expanded, their primary concerns had remained the settling and securing of their American colonies and the exploitation of the fertile fishing grounds off the Canadian coast. Canada itself was of interest only insofar as somewhere within its precincts there had to be the long-sought Northwest Passage to the Orient. Gradually, however, it began to dawn that Canada, or New France, was part of a continent that was itself a treasure trove of riches — and Britain had the key to the back door.

In 1610 the English navigator Henry Hudson sailed into the giant bay that now bears his name. Sixty years later Hudson Bay in turn gave its name

river suddenly narrows. He named the village Québec, and as the center of the fur trade it rapidly grew into the most important city in New France.

Following in the footsteps of the explorers and the fur traders, the Jesuits swiftly began the spiritual and intellectual colonization of the region. Their more contemplative lay counterparts, the Société de Notre-Dame, moved in on Cartier's "royal mountain" and founded the settlement of Montréal in 1642. Before long it had supplanted Québec as the center of the fur trade in New France.

The two decades spanning the middle of the seventeenth century were difficult ones for the French settlers, as they became inexorably drawn into the bitter tribal conflicts between the Hurons, their principal trading partners, and the warlike Iroquois. But the real threat to their colonial supremacy came, as always, from the British.

to a commercial enterprise, the Hudson's Bay Company, which was to leave an indelible mark on the history of Canada. Formed by British fur merchants to provide an alternative to Québec as an outlet for the fur trade, it was granted by Charles II right to all the lands drained by rivers flowing into Hudson Bay. Thus backed by a solicitous sovereign and a powerful navy, it was to become the largest fur trading company in North America, and today is still a force to be reckoned with in Canadian retailing.

Although British military activity in Canada was minimal during the War of the Spanish Succession (1701–1713), under the Treaty of Utrecht France was forced to relinquish all claims to

OPPOSITE: A bridal party of Kwakiutl Indians, photographed by Edward Curtis in 1914, arrives at the groom's village. ABOVE: Yukon native women and their children.

Hudson Bay and Newfoundland, and to give up Acadia, which the British promptly renamed Nova Scotia ("New Scotland"). There was a period of relative peace and tranquillity for the next 40 years, broken only in 1744 by the British seizure of the French fortress of Louisbourg on Cape Breton Island. It was handed back four years later under the Peace of Aix-la-Chapelle.

The Seven Years' War, known in America as the French and Indian War, was to be the decisive turning point in Canadian history. The war began well for the French and their native allies, as in battle after battle the British forces showed themselves to be tactically unprepared for what amounted to quasi-guerrilla warfare. But the tide

The next morning, the startled French forces, flushed out of their fortified redoubt, were slaughtered. Québec had fallen. Both Wolfe and Montcalm were killed. The battle had lasted 15 minutes.

Although it was one of the shortest battles on record, its consequences ultimately reverberated around the world. The fall of Québec effectively marked the fall of New France, and when the French handed over all of Canada under the terms of the Treaty of Paris in 1763, the British were left as undisputed masters of the entire North American continent. Some historians argue, however, that it was a Pyrrhic victory in that the British were also left overconfident and overstretched, not to mention out-of-pocket, while the many Ameri-

began to turn in 1758 with the arrival of British land and naval reinforcements. A successful siege of the fortress at Louisbourg led to its recapture, giving the British control of the entrance to the Gulf of St. Lawrence, while at the Lake Ontario end of the St. Lawrence River the British took the vital Fort Frontenac. Then, in the summer of 1759, an assault force under the command of 32-year-old General James Wolfe, the youngest general in the British army, sailed from the Atlantic down the St. Lawrence to Québec. All summer long Wolfe's artillery pounded the city, reducing it to rubble but without budging the French forces under the Marquis de Montcalm in their citadel atop the steep cliffs above the town. Then, on the night of September 12, Wolfe tried a daring maneuver. He led a force of 5,000 infantrymen in boats to a point behind the city, where they silently scaled the cliffs and assembled on the Plains of Abraham.

can colonists who fought on the British side, including one George Washington, had gained wartime experience as well as insights into British military strategy that would prove invaluable a few years later when the Americans launched their War of Independence.

BRITISH CANADA

The conquest of Canada brought another problem for Britain: what to do about the predominantly French population in the new territory over which they now ruled. In the end, they did the decent thing — and paid dearly for it. By passing the Québec Act of 1774, the British gave the French Canadians the right to continue using their own language, the secure ownership of their property, the primacy of French civil law, and the freedom to practice the Roman Catholic religion (including the Church's right to collect tithes). This did not go down at all well with the overwhelmingly Protestant population in the 13 American colonies, who were already incensed over what they considered unjust taxes imposed by Britain to help pay for the war against France. When the boundaries of the province of Québec were extended to protect the French Canadian fur traders operating in the Ohio and Mississippi River valleys, the American colonists decided that they had had enough.

The colonial rebellion became the American Revolution late in 1775 with attacks on Montréal and Québec City which, had they been successful, would almost certainly have heralded a fairly

Canada received a large transfusion of English-speaking immigrants, many of whom were well-educated and had occupied positions of responsibility and influence under the old colonial regime. Thus did the balance of power in Canada begin to shift away from the French Canadians.

In the years following the war Canada became transformed both politically and territorially. In 1791 the province of Québec was divided into Upper Canada (mainly English-speaking: now Ontario) and Lower Canada (mainly French-speaking: now Québec), each with its own Lieutenant Governor and parliament. Meanwhile, the vast and hitherto neglected lands to the west were gradually being opened up in the wake of the

swift victory for the Americans. In fact, the attack on Montréal was successful, but so brutish was the behavior of the "liberators" that most French Canadians decided they would prefer not to be thus liberated and went on to fight fiercely alongside the British, thus denying the Americans an early knockout.

By the time the war ended in 1783, Canadians had a new neighbor, the United States of America, and also a lot of new Canadians, for about 50,000 Americans who remained loyal to the British Crown had fled northwards. Most of them settled in Nova Scotia and what is now New Brunswick, although about 7,000 made their way to present-day Ontario. More still arrived at the end of the war claiming to be Loyalists, but their devotion to George III might possibly have been influenced by the offer of free land to Loyalist immigrants. In any case, as a result of the American Revolution,

pioneering explorations of Alexander Mackenzie, who in 1793 became the first white man to cross Canada all the way to the Pacific coast, and Simon Fraser and David Thompson, who were the first to map the great mountains and rivers from the Rockies to the Pacific.

The War of 1812 was the last neighborhood brawl before the United States and Canada settled down to live together more or less happily ever after. The war had a number of causes: border disputes, British interference with American shipping, fierce rivalry in the lucrative fur trade, American claims that the British were behind native raids on American border settlements, British claims that Americans were trying to export republicanism to Canada, and so forth. Whatever

OPPOSITE: Expo '86 in Vancouver. ABOVE: Similar headgear, but worlds apart — faces from the Maritimes LEFT and Inuvik RIGHT.

Canada and Its People

the justice of any of these claims, they added up to war. Although both sides suffered some telling blows — the Americans captured Toronto (or York, as it was then called) and burned it to the ground, whereupon the British retaliated by capturing Washington and burning the White House — neither side really seemed to have much appetite for the fight. The Americans wanted to get on with nation-building and the British wanted to get on with countering the Napoleonic threat at home, while the Canadians wanted to be left in peace. In 1814 they got together and declared the war over.

Not surprisingly, considering the enormous size of the two countries, the border issue was not resolved immediately. The first major step was taken in 1818 when they agreed on the 49th parallel as their mutual border from the Great Lakes to the Rockies, but it was not until 1842, after much haggling and a little skirmishing, that the Canadian border with the New England states was established. The last link, the border with the Oregon Territory west of the Rockies, was established along the 49th parallel in 1846.

As increased immigration swelled the population, French Canadians became convinced that the British were deliberately trying to dilute their power by swamping them with English-speaking newcomers. As a result, in 1837 French Canadians under the leadership of Louis-Joseph Papineau demanded autonomy for Lower Canada (Québec) so that they could establish an independent republic. When the British refused, a violent rebellion broke out which was not finally defeated until 1838. It was the first time that the call for an independent Québec had been heard. It would not be the last.

Nor were the French Canadians the only ones growing impatient with British rule around this time. In Upper Canada (Ontario) a rough and ready coalition of economic have-nots led by newspaper editor William Lyon Mackenzie rose up against the oligarchic Tory establishment and demanded that the government be remodeled along American lines. When these demands, predictably, were not met, Mackenzie too resorted to armed rebellion with even less success than Papineau, whom he soon joined in exile in the United States.

Although both insurrections had been easily put down, they succeeded in lighting an anti-colonialist fuse that would prove unquenchable.

Nevertheless, Canada at mid-century was a picture of expansion and growth. New waves of immigrants boosted the population of the Maritime Provinces, which were beginning to prosper as a result of their flourishing lumber, fishing, and shipbuilding industries. The population explosion also led to the creation of settlements further westward, in addition to providing the labor needed to build the canals, roads, and railways that made the westward expansion possible. In

less than 20 years, over 3,000 km or 2,000 miles of railroad tracks were laid. All that was needed for Canada to become a truly coast-to-coast country was for some sort of tug to be exerted from the other side of the Rockies. That tug, when it came, turned out to be a powerful yank: in 1858 gold was discovered in the Fraser River valley.

The gold rush that followed was so frenetic, and so dominated by Americans rushing northwards to stake their claims, that Britain quickly proclaimed a new Crown colony, British Columbia, to control the stampede into the territory.

British colonies now straddled the continent from the Atlantic to the Pacific.

THE DOMINION OF CANADA

With the old Anglo-French tensions still causing problems, and with the turmoil to the south caused by the American Civil War, not to mention the

ordinary growing pains brought on by rapid population growth and territorial expansion, it was widely felt that the colonies should come together and forge a stronger union among themselves. So in 1864, delegates from the various colonies convened in Charlottetown, Prince Edward Island, to begin laying the groundwork for a new confederation. Three years later, the British North America Act of 1867 created the Dominion of Canada, in which the colonies of Nova Scotia, New Brunswick, and Québec became provinces in a confederated union with self-rule under a parliamentary system of government. Manitoba joined the Confederation in 1870, British Columbia in 1871, and Prince Edward Island in 1873. The Yukon, formerly a district of the Northwest Territories, was made a separate territory in 1898 at the height of the Klondike gold rush. Alberta and Saskatchewan, also carved out of the old Northwest Territories, joined in 1905; Newfoundland,

typically, held out until 1949, when it finally became Canada's tenth province.

As important as this political union was to Canada's development, it was more symbolic than real so long as there was no corresponding physical link between the provinces. In fact, three of the provinces — Nova Scotia, Prince Edward Island, and British Columbia — only agreed to join the Confederation on condition that a transcontinental railway was built to tie the new nation together. Work on this mammoth project began in 1881 and, incredibly, was completed in only four years. In 1885, at Rogers Pass in the Selkirk Mountains, the last spike was driven: the Canadian Pacific Railway was in business.

As was to be expected, however, this mighty triumph of engineering was not achieved without casualties. The coming of the Iron Horse meant

---

The entrance to Ottawa's Confederation Building.

the virtual disappearance of the buffalo, the driving of natives from their ancestral homelands, and the deaths of hundreds of (mostly Chinese) laborers on the railroad itself. It also precipitated a bloody uprising in 1885 on the part of the Métis, who were the descendants of French trappers and Cree women, aided and abetted by several tribes of Plains natives, all of whom felt threatened by the armies of new settlers swarming over their land. Already driven out of Manitoba as far west as the southern banks of the Saskatchewan River, the Métis and their native allies, under the leadership of Louis Riel, overwhelmed the Mounted Police post at Duck Lake, attacked the town of Battleford, and captured and burned Fort Pitt. But

their successes were short-lived. Before long they were subdued by the superior firepower of the Canadian forces, and Riel was hanged. His execution became another source of resentment among French Canadians, who felt that he would not have been treated so harshly had he not been a Roman Catholic of French ancestry.

With the country now linked literally and politically from sea to sea, the final years of the nineteenth century saw Canada blossom dramatically as a nation. As thousands upon thousands of new immigrants arrived, new lands were settled and cultivated, hydroelectric projects were initiated, new manufacturing industries were started up alongside the already-thriving industries of lumbering, fishing, mining, pulp and paper. Above all, agriculture boomed as the Prairie Provinces became one of the great grain-producing areas of the world. And, for icing on the national cake, in 1896 gold was discovered in the Klondike, setting off one of the biggest gold rushes in history as 100,000 (mostly American) fortune-seekers poured into the Yukon. These were heady times.

Thus Canada entered the twentieth century in a buoyant mood. It was also blessed from 1896 to 1911 with one of its greatest prime ministers, Sir Wilfrid Laurier, a French Canadian and Roman Catholic who set himself the Herculean task of

ending the antagonism and suspicion between Canada's English and French communities. But World War I came along and deepened the rift: French Canadians violently objected to military conscription, which was introduced in 1917 after the Canadian volunteer forces fighting alongside the British in the trenches had suffered such appalling losses that there were no volunteers left to fight. The French Canadian point of view — that the war had nothing to do with them, and therefore they shouldn't be drafted to fight in it — left much residual bitterness on both sides after the war was over.

A happier legacy of the war was an economy enriched by a vastly increased manufacturing capacity, streamlined industrial development, expanded mining activity, and burgeoning exports of wheat. Along with Canada's postwar prosperity came growing independence from Britain, acknowledged by the British at the Imperial Conference of 1926 when Canada was granted the right to conduct its own international affairs without reference to London, and sealed by the Statute of Westminster in 1931, which made Canada an independent nation.

Then came the Depression, which was even worse in Canada than in the United States. Suddenly the Promised Land was a ravaged land, as drought erased the wheat fields and unemployment stalked the cities. The misery of the "Dirty Thirties," as the Canadians called the decade, lasted until September 1939 when Hitler marched into Poland. Canada, following Britain's lead, immediately declared war on Germany, whereupon the economy coughed, spluttered, then roared back to life.

Also revived, sadly, was the bitter Anglo-French debate over military conscription, which once again split the country. Again, Canada suffered battlefield losses out of all proportion to its population. On the other side of the ledger, the Canadian economy prospered out of all proportion to its prewar capacity as almost 10% of the population were engaged in war-related industries. Thanks to the war, Canada became one of the world's major industrial nations as well as an important military power, a cofounder of the United Nations, and a member of NATO.

Peace was as good to Canada as the war had been. A huge oil field was discovered near Edmonton, Alberta, in 1947. Giant uranium deposits were discovered in Ontario and Saskatchewan, and its extraordinary mineral riches made Canada the world's leading producer of nickel, zinc, lead, copper, gold, and silver. Its inexhaustible water resources made countless hydroelectric projects possible, including the world's biggest, its forests made it the world's foremost exporter of newsprint, and its oceans made it the world's foremost exporter of fish. As if that weren't enough, Canada was fortunate in having the world's best customer for raw materials right on its doorstep.

Another milestone in Canada's rise among the world's top industrial nations was the opening in 1959 of the St. Lawrence Seaway, a joint United States–Canadian project that made possible shipping from the Great Lakes to the Atlantic. Three years later the Trans-Canada Highway was completed, a concrete link spanning all 10 provinces.

In 1967 Canada celebrated its hundredth birthday by throwing itself a big party in the form of a World's Fair — Expo '67 — in Montréal. Canadians had much to celebrate: a vigorous and rapidly expanding economy; one of the highest standards of living in the world; advanced social welfare programs providing health care and other benefits for all citizens; virtually unlimited natural resources; and a history of international conduct such that Canada had managed to join the front rank of the world's nations without making any enemies. What better reasons to have a party?

QUÉBEC AND THE CANADIAN FEDERATION

Alas, there was a ghost at the birthday party. The old specter of separatism which had haunted the federation during the entire century of its existence was suddenly summoned up in a speech by visiting French President de Gaulle. Speaking to a large throng outside the Montréal City Hall, he declared, *"Vive le Québec libre!"* Considering that he was present in Canada as a guest of a nation celebrating its "unity through diversity," this was mischief-making on an epic scale.

With their clamoring having thus been endorsed by the President of France, Québec's separatists found new heart for the struggle to wrench the province away from the rest of the nation. With the ultimate goal of full independence, the Parti Québécois (PQ) was formed under the leadership of René Lévesque. The PQ won 23% of the vote in the 1970 provincial elections. That same year the separatist movement turned nasty around its fringes, as the *Front de Liberation du Québec* (FLQ) kidnapped and murdered the province's Minister of Labor, Pierre Laporte. Prime Minister Pierre Trudeau responded by invoking the War Measures Act and sending 10,000 troops into the province, an unpopular action that ultimately benefited the PQ, who came to power in 1976. They set about developing the province's economy, instituting educational reforms, and making Québec monolingual, all the while pressing for a referendum and secession from the Canadian federation. But, in 1980, when the referendum came, 60% of the province voted "non" to secession.

At the next election Lévesque's separatists were voted out of office. In 1987 the Conservative government of Brian Mulroney made a significant gesture towards the Québécois when the prime minister signed a document recognizing them as a "distinct society." The following year, in what seemed like a reciprocal gesture of appreciation, Québec gave Mulroney's Conservatives a large part of their majority in the national elections. It seemed, at last, that the flames of separatism had finally been extinguished.

Not so. As before, the desire for separation among the Québécois simply smoldered unnoticed, waiting to be reignited into the burning issue it had so often been in the past. Sure enough, it blazed back into prominence at the start of the 1990s. This time, however, nobody was able to say precisely what set it alight. The best explanation we heard came from Don Johnson, a columnist

for the Toronto *Globe and Mail*. "We are merely advised that Québeckers feel humiliated, the status quo is unacceptable and unhappiness prevails," he said with a helpless shrug. He then went on to compare it to the breakdown of a marriage — "where neither party can point to a specific cause, but there is a general feeling that a divorce would be preferable."

Whatever the cause of the latest unhappiness, and whether or not this 125-year-old marriage is headed for eventual divorce, still remains to be seen. In 1992 and again in 1995, referenda for sovereignty were held in Québec. In both cases, the electorate rejected the idea. But the 1995 vote was nearly a dead heat with 51% against. Now, at the end of the twentieth century, it is certain that if the PQ can be reelected, another "neverendum" — as Canadians have named them — will be called.

CANADA TODAY

The future of the federation is still Canada's most troublesome political issue. But it's not the only one. In 1989, the free trade agreement with the

The maple leaf or the *fleur-de-lis*? Will it be the national or the provincial flag that flies over Quebec in future?

United States (NAFTA) was pushed through parliament by Prime Minister Brian Mulroney; causing the loss of thousands of jobs, and exposing Canada's industries to American competition. The collapse of the North Atlantic cod fishery has brought hard times to Newfoundland and Nova Scotia, where unemployment now runs very high. How far the current Liberal administration will succeed in patching up the economy and easing the straining bonds of the federation remains to be seen.

One thing, however, is clear: After centuries of exploitation and marginalization, Canada's native peoples are beginning a new and happier era. Having gained political strength throughout

the late 1960s and early 1970s, the First Nations of the north launched a series of land claims against the Canadian government in the late 1970s, demanding financial compensation, funding for social programs, hunting rights and a greater role in wildlife management and environmental protection. The success of these land claims has lead to a native cultural revival and, finally, to redrawing the very map of Canada. On April 1, 1999, Canada, formerly comprised of 10 provinces and two territories — gained a new territory, when the present Northwest Territories were divided in two. The eastern half of the existing territories is now known as Nunavut, "Our Land" in the Inuit language. The western lands will remain the Northwest Territories until a name is chosen.

Both in the north and throughout the rest of the country, native Canadians (excluding the Inuit) number around 282,000 and are members of 574

separate communities, called "bands." Ethnically, many of Canada's native peoples have the same heritage as certain United States tribes: Cree, Sioux and Blackfoot, for example, are found in both countries. In Canada native people belong to 10 linguistic groups, each of which has many local dialects.

Since 1973, when the Canadian government accepted a proposal by the National Indian Brotherhood, increasing numbers of bands have begun to manage their own schools. These schools have introduced new curricula, which often include the history of native Canadians and native-language courses.

GEOGRAPHY AND CLIMATE

William Lyon Mackenzie King, Canada's longest-serving prime minister (1921–1930, 1935–1948), observed at the beginning of his third term of office in 1936: "If some countries have too much history, we have too much geography."

It's hard to argue with that. Spread over almost 10 million sq km (3.6 million sq miles), Canada stretches more than 5,500 km (3,400 miles) from Cape Spear, Newfoundland, in the east to the Alaskan border in the west, and 4,600 km (2,900 miles) from Lake Erie's Pelee Island in the south to Cape Columbia on Ellesmere Island in the north (which is only 800 km or 500 miles from the North Pole).

Within this vastness one finds stunning topographical extremes. Almost half the country, for example, is forested — one single forest zone of conifers extends for 6,000 km (3,730 miles) in a wide sweep from Newfoundland to the far north — while similarly enormous tracts of land are empty, treeless prairies. There are millions of acres of flood plains and marshy lowlands, and there are the majestic Rocky Mountains, though Canada's highest mountain, at 6,050 m (19,844 ft), Mount Logan, is not in the Rockies but in the St. Elias Mountains of southwestern Yukon.

And then there is the water. Canada is awash in lakes and rivers; they account for over seven percent of the country's total area. There are 400,000 of them in Ontario alone. Three of the 20 longest rivers in the world are to be found in Canada. In all, the country has a staggering 25% of the world's fresh water resources.

Geologically, Canada can be divided into five distinct regions, not counting the archipelago of islands inside the Arctic Circle. The Appalachian region is that hilly, wooded part of the country bounded on the west by the St. Lawrence River and on the east by the Atlantic, and includes the Maritime Provinces, Newfoundland, and the

ABOVE: A Winterlude spectator in Ottawa.
RIGHT: Formed by eons of erosion, a hoo doo towers over the sweltering Alberta badlands.

Canada and Its People

Gaspé Peninsula. It belongs to an ancient mountain system, now eroded to modest elevations, that reaches as far south as Alabama.

The St. Lawrence Lowlands comprise that swath of land from the mouth of the St. Lawrence River to the Great Lakes. This fertile flood plain is home to most of Canada's people, industry, and commerce.

The Prairies spread across the provinces of Manitoba, Saskatchewan, and Alberta, and on up into the Northwest Territories. The rich soil in the southern reaches, where the prairies join the Great Plains of the United States, yields great golden seas of wheat which gradually dry up in Alberta, giving way to huge cattle ranches.

can be found just about everywhere: squirrels and chipmunks, rabbits and hares, porcupines and skunks. Equally widespread throughout the country's forests and woodlands are deer, moose, black bears, beavers, wild geese, and ducks. The richest fishing grounds in Canada — possibly in the world — are to be found in the Gulf of St. Lawrence and the waters of the continental shelf off Newfoundland: though cod stocks have been wiped out by over-fishing, the area still teems with herring, mackerel, tuna, oysters, clams, lobsters, and scallops, along with some 800 other species of edible marine life.

In the St. Lawrence Lowlands the coniferous forests of spruce, firs, and pines that sweep from

The Western Cordillera is bounded on the east by the Rocky Mountains and on the west by the Coast Mountains. In between is the spectacular diversity of British Columbia, a province of soaring mountain peaks, alpine lakes and meadows, large boreal forests, intricate networks of rivers, deep blue lakes, hot springs and long green valleys.

The fifth region, the Canadian Shield, encompasses everything else: the immense, horseshoe-shaped land mass that surrounds Hudson Bay, and stretches from the coast of Labrador down to the St. Lawrence Lowlands, over to the Prairies, and up to the Arctic. Covering some 4.7 million sq km (1.8 million sq miles), about half the entire area of Canada, this rough-hewn, rock-strewn, lake-pitted wilderness is one of the oldest sections of the earth's crust.

The flora and fauna naturally vary from region to region. There are, however, some animals that

Labrador to the Rockies begin to be infiltrated by aspen, birch, oak, elm, beech, hemlock, and ash. In southern Québec the sugar maples appear, and in southwestern Ontario the walnut and tulip trees, the hickories and dogwoods. As for its animal life, the region is better known for its bipeds than its quadrupeds.

In the prairies, one animal in particular is conspicuous by its absence: the plains buffalo (also called bison). The few who have survived are now in the national parks, while their place has been taken by great herds of cattle. Denizens of the semiarid grasslands of the southern prairies include kangaroo rats, hares, pronghorn antelopes, and the ranchers' nemesis, coyotes.

In the mountain ranges of the Western Cordillera one can find, if one tries hard enough, brown bears, elk, mountain goats, bighorn sheep, and the bosses of the upper slopes, grizzly bears.

In the lakes and rivers there is some of the best trout and salmon fishing to be found anywhere in the world.

In the great expanse of forests across northern Canada are the largest concentrations of fur-bearing animals: mink, ermine, marten, muskrat, beaver, river otter, weasel, lynx, bobcat, wolves, and wolverines. Further north, in the tundra, are arctic foxes, lemmings, musk oxen, and caribou, as well as snow geese and trumpeter swans. Still further north, where the frigid waters are full of whales, seals, and walrus, the mighty polar bear patrols the ice packs of the Arctic.

Because words like "frigid" and "polar" and "ice" and "Arctic" — and even the subtly pre-artists, once said: "We are a nation of thermometers monitoring cold fronts. We jig to the crunch of snow." Indeed, over a third of the annual precipitation in Canada falls as snow, compared to a worldwide average of five percent. And the only national capital colder than Ottawa is Ulan Bator, the capital of Mongolia; Winnipeg is the coldest city in the world with a population of more than half a million; and residents of Montréal shovel more snow every year than residents of any other city.

But there is a bright side to all this. It's just that: brightness. Canada may be refrigerated half the time, but it is sunlit most of the time. Which means that it is beautiful all the time, brilliantly white in

judicial "north" — are all words that we readily associate with Canada, most foreigners think that Canada's climate can probably be summed up in one word: cold. This is a mistake. True, Canada occupies the northern — and therefore colder — part of the continent, but this ignores the fact that Pelee Island, Ontario is on the same latitude as Rome. True, the dominant images of western Canada are the snow-capped peaks of the Rockies, but this obscures the fact that those same Rockies form a protective wall that guarantees Vancouver milder winters than, say, Dallas. True, the eastern coast takes a beating from the Atlantic, but parts of it are also caressed by the Gulf Stream, creating swimming beaches equal to any in the Mediterranean.

Having said that, one has to admit that for much of the year Canada is a theme park called Winter. Harold Town, one of Canada's leading winter, infinitely and variously green the rest of year. What's more, its meteorological diversity mirrors its geographical diversity, so that the visitor has the luxury of choosing not only the scenery and activities that most appeal, but also the precise climate in which to enjoy both.

In the following chapters, and in the WHEN TO GO section of TRAVELERS' TIPS, page 422, we provide information about the sort of weather you can expect to find in different places at different times. For now, though, be assured that in Canada there is truly a time and place for everything.

OPPOSITE: In Kluane National Park, a forest canopy of birch trees, Yukon Territory. ABOVE: The Canadian prairies in bloom.

Ontario

ONTARIO IS BY FAR THE RICHEST, MOST POPULOUS, and most visited province in Canada. With a population of 11 million, it is home to a third of all Canadians. It has more mineral resources than any other province. It has some of the most fertile farmland in the country, along with the longest frost-free season in which to cultivate it. It has the country's industrial heartland, which produces half of all of Canada's manufactured goods. It has the country's capital, Ottawa, as well as its largest city, Toronto. And it has approximately 400,000 freshwater lakes, covering some 200,000 sq km (70,000 sq miles). It has, in a word, everything.

Originally a part of the French colony of New France, and then of the British colony of Canada,

it became a separate province in 1791 when the Constitutional Act divided the colony into the predominantly French-settled Lower Canada (Québec) and the Loyalist-dominated Upper Canada (Ontario). Its first capital was Niagara-on-the-Lake, but in 1793 Toronto was selected to be the capital and was promptly renamed York. In 1813 York came under attack from the invading Americans and was burned to the ground. (A year later the British retaliated by burning, or at least blackening, the White House.) When York was rebuilt it expanded rapidly, helped by a tide of immigration from Britain and Europe, and in 1834 was incorporated as a city, reverting to its original native name of Toronto.

When the British North America Act of 1867 created the Dominion of Canada, the former Upper Canada joined the Confederation as the new province of Ontario, a name derived from an Iroquois

word variously translated as "shining waters" and "high rocks standing near the waters" and thought to refer to Niagara Falls. Ottawa became the capital of the newly confederated Canada, with Toronto remaining the provincial capital. Since then Ontario has gone from strength to strength, becoming during the twentieth century the economic center of the nation as well as the cultural center for English-speaking Canadians.

Although Ontario is Canada's second largest province, after Québec, with an area of 1,068,587 sq km (413,000 sq miles), its industrial and commercial preeminence is due almost entirely to that chipped-arrowhead-shaped peninsula that begins at Toronto and extends southwest to the point where it pokes into Detroit. This is Canada's machine room. But that is not all. Low-lying and lapped by three of the Great Lakes (Ontario, Erie, and Huron), it is blessed with extremely rich soil, making it an agricultural center as well. Add to all this Toronto's dominance as a commercial and banking center, and you can see why the province prospers.

OTTAWA

In almost every sense, Ottawa is the ideal capital city. It is imposing: its neo-Gothic government buildings are set high on a bluff overlooking the Ottawa River. It is beautiful: its many official buildings and its many handsome residential neighborhoods share the city with numerous parks, lakes, and open spaces, all surrounded by a four-kilometer (two-and-a-half-mile)-wide greenbelt and overhung by clear, unpolluted air. It is cultured: its six national museums and stunning National Arts Centre are only the "official" end of a cultural spectrum that is splendidly varied and impressive. It is cosmopolitan. It is the most completely bilingual city in Canada, and it boasts some of the best hotels and restaurants. And it is fun: the whole reason for Ottawa's existence, the Rideau Canal that sweeps through the heart of the city, is a summer-long haven for boating and canoeing enthusiasts, while in winter it becomes the world's longest skating rink.

Thus inventorying all the attractions of this paragon among the world's capitals, it comes as a shock to recall that only 150 years ago this was a rough-and-ready, brawling backwoods village where French lumberjacks and Irish construction workers regularly and drunkenly fought with each other. In those days it was known as Bytown, after the man who built the canal, but in 1855 it changed its name to Ottawa when Queen Victoria chose it to be the capital of the short-lived United

Ottawa in bloom — OPPOSITE TOP: Spring arrives in Rockcliffe Village neighborhood. ABOVE: The Parliament building presides over the Tulip Festival BOTTOM.

Province of Canada, thus making it the natural choice as national capital when the Confederation came into being 10 years later.

It was a widely unpopular choice, and a long time passed before Canadians stopped referring scornfully to "Westminster-in-the-Wilderness." Nevertheless, the people of Ottawa immediately set about erecting buildings worthy of a national capital, and — perhaps equally important — set about changing their image. If they were tolerably successful in the former pursuit, they were too successful in the latter. For almost a century Ottawa was noted for its sobriety, propriety, dignity, and decorum — in other words, for being numbingly boring. Then in the 1960s the city

suddenly seemed to get its second wind. Wonderful new buildings went up, the city's cultural life was reinvigorated, the entertainment scene expanded, recreational facilities proliferated — it was as if the city had decided, all of a sudden, to start enjoying itself.

The result has been, as four million tourists a year will attest, a city where visitors certainly find it easy to enjoy themselves.

BACKGROUND

When Philemon Wright arrived from New England in 1800, the region was inhabited by a band of Outaouaic natives, after whom the place was named. Wright established a small settlement at the confluence of the Ottawa, Rideau, and Gatineau rivers, which he rightly considered an ideal spot from which to ship timber to Québec.

In 1826 the settlers were joined by Colonel John By and a group of Royal Engineers, accompanied by a small army of mostly Irish laborers, who had been sent by the Duke of Wellington to build a canal. After the War of 1812, Wellington had been concerned that a long stretch of the St. Lawrence was within easy reach of American guns, so he decided on the construction of an alternative waterway from the Ottawa River to Lake Ontario. The project, which was completed in 1832, resulted in a 200-km (125-mile) system of canals, rivers, locks, dams, and lakes stretching from Bytown, as the village had come to be known, to Kingston, Ontario. It was called the Rideau Canal.

By the mid-1830s Bytown had a thriving industry producing and shipping squared timber, thus confirming Philemon Wright's judgment in establishing a settlement here. But it was another aspect of Bytown's situation that led to its becoming the capital of Canada. Distressed by the bitter rivalry between the larger cities of Upper and Lower Canada over which should be chosen as the capital of the new United Province of Canada, Queen Victoria in 1855 selected Bytown because it was situated on the border between the two provinces. Having been thus honored, the people of Bytown changed its name to Ottawa and began preparing this one-industry (timber) town to handle a second industry: government.

Today, the one million inhabitants of the Ottawa-Hull area form the fourth largest metropolitan area in Canada. Inhabitants of a city once derided as "Westminster-in-the-Wilderness," Ottawans can gloat over the fact that they live near the seat of political power yet within a short drive of genuine, beautiful wilderness. It has proven a happy combination.

GENERAL INFORMATION

The **Capital Infocentre (** (613) 239-5000, at 90 Wellington Street, just across from the Parliament Buildings provides information on Ottawa and Hull. The **Ottawa and Hull Tourism Inc. Visitor Centre (** (416) 237-5158, in the National Arts Centre at 65 Elgin Street, offers visitor information as well as a free summertime reservation service.

WHAT TO SEE AND DO

The best way of sightseeing in Ottawa is on foot, as the major attractions are all within easy walking distance of one another. However, you may like to take a ride on one of the double-decker sightseeing buses that leave from Confederation Square frequently in the summer months.

Undoubtedly, Ottawa's main sight is **Parliament Hill (** (613) 996-0896, the very heart of Ottawa and a good place to start your tour. Here, high above the Ottawa River, stand some splendid sandstone structures capped with green copper roofs; a neo-Gothic extravagance of towers and pinnacles. A huge fire in 1916 destroyed most of the original buildings and they were rebuilt a few years later with the addition of the soaring 92-m (302-ft)-high **Peace Tower** at the center, a monument to Canadians who died in World War I. Take a trip up the tower (there is an elevator) for some excellent views over Ottawa. The **Parliament Buildings** (or "Centre Block") house the Senate and the House of Commons; free tours in English or French are conducted daily at half-hour intervals. When Parliament is in session you can sit in the public galleries to watch. The offices of the **East and West Blocks** are closed to the public but you can visit the

February it's the center of the winter festival known as **Winterlude** ((613) 239-5000.

Close by across the canal between George and York streets is the **Byward Market**, a down-to-earth farmers' market which has been here since 1840. Farmers have now been joined here by local artists and artisans whose works are on display in the old market building. Specialty food stores and restaurants have also sprung up here. The market is open year-round Sunday to Wednesday from 8 AM to 6 PM and Thursday to Saturday from 8 AM to 9 PM.

Looking across eastwards from the Parliament Buildings you'll see the renowned **National Gallery of Canada** ((613) 990-1985, 380 Sussex Drive,

Parliamentary Library, the one place that escaped the fire of 1916, a polygonal domed building with an impressive, paneled interior. Tours of the Parliament Buildings are offered free of charge daily year-round. It's possible to make same-day reservations at the white Infotent east of Centre Block.

From late June to late August the **Changing of the Guard** takes place daily at 10 AM on the lawns in front of the Parliament Buildings. With the military music, colorful uniforms, and magnificent backdrop it's quite a spectacle. From May to Labor Day there is a nightly free half-hour Sound and Light Show highlighting Canada's history.

To the east lies the **Rideau Canal**, which stretches 200 km (125 miles) between Ottawa and Kingston and is now used purely for recreational purposes. Lined by gardens and trees, in summer it's a lovely place to walk along or to go boating on, while in winter skaters glide over it. In early

with one of the premier collections of Canadian art in the world. It's open year-round, but closed on Monday and Tuesday during the winter; admission is free, but there may be a charge for special events.

Across Alexandra Bridge from the National Gallery and facing Parliament Hill stands the **Canadian Museum of Civilization** ((819) 776-7000 at 100 Laurier Street in Hull. This enormous building contains such exhibits as a Pacific Northwest Coast native village with six life-size longhouses, totem poles, and life-size reconstructions of an archaeological dig. The emphasis is on Canadian culture and on hands-on participation,

OPPOSITE: The "world's longest skating rink" — the Rideau Canal in winter. ABOVE and OVERLEAF: Ottawa's Parliament Buildings — "a neo-Gothic extravagance of towers and pinnacles" — have weathered many years and many seasons.

making it a good place to take children. It's open daily year-round; an admission fee is charged, free Sunday from 9 AM to noon.

The **Canadian Museum of Nature** ((613) 996-3102 at Macleod and Metcalfe streets, is housed in an historic Victorian building. As its name suggests, it is concerned with the formation of the earth and its life forms. There's a dinosaur section that rarely fails to delight children. It's open Friday to Wednesday from 10 AM to 5 PM, Thursday from 10 AM to 8 PM. An admission fee is charged; half-price on Thursday until 5 PM, free from 5 PM to 8 PM.

The **National Museum of Science and Technology** ((613) 991-3044 at 1867 Boulevard St-Laurent, with its hands-on displays, is popular

hills, and is an ideal place for fishing, boating, swimming, camping, and hiking in summer and cross-country skiing in winter.

SPORTS AND OUTDOOR ACTIVITIES

For those who enjoy the excitement of **whitewater rafting**, and those who have never tried it before but would like to, there are several companies running one- or two-day trips, such as Owl Rafting ((613) 238-7238, 39 First Street, Ottawa K1S 2G1. There are several places where you can rent **boats**, **canoes**, and **paddleboats** along the Rideau Canal, such as Dow's Lake Pavilion ((613) 232-1001, 1001 Queen Elizabeth Drive.

with both children and adults. There are some magnificent old steam engines, vintage cars, machinery, and samples of all kinds of technology, including the Apollo 7 space capsule. You can touch and test many of the exhibits. It's open daily year-round; an admission fee is charged.

Moving northwards a little, the **National Aviation Museum** ((613) 993-2010 at Rockcliffe and Aviation parkways, features a new Harrier jump jet, as well as the Virtual Glider, an exhibit of aviation art, and an extensive collection of over 100 aircraft that trace the history of aviation from the early 1900s to the present day. It's open daily, closed Monday during the winter; an admission fee is charged, free Thursday from 5 PM to 9 PM.

Gatineau Park is only a few kilometers (a couple of miles) northwest of the city center. It has 35 hectares (86 acres) of woodlands, lakes, and

In winter there's **skiing** at Mont Cascades ((819) 827-0301, 30 minutes north of Ottawa on Highway 307. The longest run is 670 m (2,200 ft). There are two day-lodges with cafeteria and restaurant-bar at the hill. (During the summer you can cool off at the water park with its six slides.) Also in winter, the Rideau Canal becomes the world's longest **skating** run, stretching from The National Arts Centre ((613) 996-5051 to Dows Lake. You can rent skates and towing sleds across from the Arts Centre; call the center for information on ice conditions.

NIGHTLIFE AND THE ARTS

It has to be said that you don't go to Ottawa for nightlife. The city after dark has changed for the better in recent years, but the best show in town is probably the nightly **sound-and-light show** on Parliament Hill.

There's a wide variety of programs at **The National Arts Centre** ((613) 996-5051, 53 Elgin Street, where there's a 2,300-seat opera auditorium, a 950-seat theater, the smaller Studio for experimental works, and the Atelier which seats only 150. You can choose from dance and variety shows, opera, and ballet. The Centre has its own National Arts Centre Orchestra and bilingual theatrical company.

You can listen to rock music at **Barrymore's** ((613) 996-5051, 323 Bank Street; or at **Molly McGuire's** ((613) 241-1972, 130 George Street. You'll find blues on Sunday afternoons and at other times upstairs at the **Rainbow Bistro** ((613) 541-5123, 76 Murray Street, where there are free

matinees between 3 PM and 7 PM on Thursday, Friday, and Saturday. **Patty's Place** ((613) 730-2434, at 1070 Bank Street, is an authentic Irish pub where you can raise a Guinness or two and listen to folk music on Thursday to Saturday nights. Good fish-and-chips and Irish stew are served as well.

WHERE TO STAY

Expensive

The renowned **Château Laurier** ((613) 241-1414 TOLL-FREE (800) 441-1414 FAX (613) 562-7030, at 1 Rideau Street, Ottawa K1N 8S7, is a beautiful castle-like building which opened in 1912 and whose guests have included the rich, the famous, and the royal. Situated at the bottom of Parliament Hill on Confederation Square, many of its 500 rooms and suites offer beautiful views. Among

its facilities are an indoor swimming pool and the elegant Zoe's lounge.

At the **Sheraton Hotel & Towers** ((613) 238-1500 FAX (613) 235-2723, 150 Albert Street, Ottawa K1P 5G2, there's every modern convenience and comfort. Built in the 1960s, this 17-floor hotel offers 236 attractive rooms. It has an indoor swimming pool, a wine bar, and its own restaurant.

Connected to the Rideau Centre, the 24-story **Westin** ((613) 560-7000 TOLL-FREE (800) 228-3000 FAX (613) 234-5396, at 11 Colonel By Drive, Ottawa K1N 9H4, overlooks the Rideau Canal. It has 475 tastefully decorated rooms, squash courts, a gym, an indoor pool, and restaurants.

The **Radisson Hotel Ottawa Centre** ((613) 238-1122 TOLL-FREE (800) 333-3333 FAX (613) 783-4229, 100 Kent Street at Queen, Ottawa K1P 5R7, is another modern highrise hotel with large and well-equipped rooms, indoor swimming pool, a piano bar, café, and the revolving restaurant with great views of the city and the river.

Mid-range

The **Capital Hill Hotel & Suites** ((613) 235-1413 FAX (613) 235-6047, at 88 Albert Street, Ottawa K1P 5E9, has recently renewed its decor and its popularity. It has 154 rooms and, considering its proximity to Parliament Hill, it is very reasonably priced. Staying close to Parliament Hill, the **Lord Elgin** ((613) 235-3333, at 100 Elgin Street, Ottawa K1P 5K8, offers very good value. Built in 1940, this stately stone building has 315 rooms and there's a Scottish style expressed in the decor and in the excellent choice of whiskies at the bar. Also close to Parliament Hill is the **Citadel Ottawa Hotel** ((613) 237-3600 FAX (613) 237-9114, at 101 Lyon Street, Ottawa K1R 5T9, which has undergone extensive renovation and offers over 400 rooms with good facilities. There's an indoor pool and two popular restaurants.

The **Hotel Roxborough** ((613) 237-9300 at 123 Metcalfe Street, Ottawa K1P 5L9, is centrally located. Its relative intimacy (there are only 150 rooms), cozy piano bar, French restaurant, and nice complimentary touches such as newspapers delivered to the room, shoeshine service and continental breakfast, make it an excellent choice. The **Cartier Place Hotel and Towers Suites** ((613) 236-5000, 180 Cooper Street, Ottawa K2P 2L5, has 130 comfortable and well-equipped apartments of differing sizes with maid service and dry cleaning included in the cost. Facilities include an indoor swimming pool and a restaurant. Under-14s stay free of charge in their parents' room. Another good choice for families, the **Place Minto Suite Hotel** ((613) 232-2200, at 433 Laurier Avenue West, Ottawa K1R 7Y4, has

Life and art — OPPOSITE: An exhibition in the National Art Gallery. ABOVE: A street entertainer in Ottawa's Byward Market.

418 suites of varying sizes with all conveniences, very well-equipped kitchens and comfortable living rooms. With its special weekend rates, children under 18 are allowed to stay free of charge. And you're literally on top of restaurants and shops.

Inexpensive

Downtown there's Swiss-style accommodation at **Gasthaus Switzerland** ((613) 237-0335, 89 Daly Avenue, Ottawa K1N 6E6, with 22 rooms, some with private bath. On Rideau Street the **Townhouse Motor Hotel** ((613) 789-5555, at No. 319, and the **Parkway Motor Hotel** ((613) 789-3781, at No. 475, are both good value.

At the high end of inexpensive the **Talisman Hotel** ((613) 722-7600 is 10 minutes west of the town center at 1376 Carling Avenue, Ottawa K1Z 7L5. It stands in Oriental-style grounds and offers attractive rooms with balconies and use of an outdoor swimming pool.

The **Ottawa International Hostel** ((613) 235-2595 TOLL-FREE (800) 461-8585 FAX (613) 569-2131, 75 Nicholas Street, Ottawa K1N 7B9, is housed in a former eighteenth-century jail building. It's within walking distance of the major sites and is open year-round. In addition to the coeducational dormitory, private rooms are available. **Carleton University Residence** ((613) 788-5609, 223 Commons Building, 1233 Colonel By, and the **University of Ottawa** ((613) 564-5400, 100 University Avenue, offer budget accommodation from May to August.

For bed and breakfast listings, contact **Ottawa Area Bed & Breakfast** ((613) 563-0161 TOLL-FREE (800) 461-7889, 488 Cooper Street, Ottawa K1R 5H9; or the **Ottawa Tourism and Convention Authority** ((613) 237-5130, 130 Albert Street, 18th Floor, Ottawa K1P 5G4.

WHERE TO EAT

Expensive

In the Westboro district of Ottawa, we would recommend the **Opus Bistro** ((613) 722-9549, at 1331 Wellington Street. This small restaurant is elegant in its simplicity and the menu features the best of contemporary cuisine. It's open Tuesday to Saturday for dinner only. **Le Jardin** ((613) 241-1424, at 127 York Street, is known for its reliably high quality. There is a French emphasis both in the menu and the decor. It is in a nineteenth-century house with a particularly beautiful upstairs dining room. It's open daily for dinner only.

In Hull the **Café Henri Burger** ((819) 777-5646, at 69 rue Laurier, which first opened in the 1920s has undergone a recent renovation and continues to enjoy a well-deserved reputation for high quality. There's French cuisine at **La Tartuffe** ((819) 771-1689, 133 rue Notre-Dame, Hull, in a relaxed,

intimate atmosphere. It's worth the short drive into the Gatineau Hills to enjoy the beautiful setting and the superb French food at **L'Orée du Bois** ((819) 827-0332, Kingsmere Road, Old Chelsea.

Moderate

The **Place Next Door** ((613) 789-7700, 320 Rideau Street, is one of Ottawa's favorite spots. It has a homey, friendly atmosphere, and delicious steaks, ribs, and seafood. There's a distinctly English feel about **Friday's Roast Beef House** ((613) 237-5353, 150 Elgin Street, where steaks and ribs again predominate in a very Victorian setting. Canadian food and Canadian wines are to be had at **Le Café** ((613) 594-5127, in The National Arts Centre on the Canal. It's a pleasant spot for any meal of the day and stays open quite late Monday to Saturday. For Indian food try the smart and popular **Haveli** ((613) 241-1700 at 87 George Street, Market Mall.

Inexpensive

The **Elephant & Castle** ((613) 234-5544, 50 Rideau Street, is a popular and central meeting place where pub-style food is served, and it's open all day every day. One of the best-value Chinese restaurants in town is **Shanghai** ((613) 233-4001, 651 Somerset Street West, near Bronson. The menu covers a wide range of dishes from Sichuan, Canton, Shanghai, and other Asian origins. For Italian, there's **The Ritz 3 Uptown** ((613) 789-9797, 89 Clarence Street, with other locations scattered around Ottawa.

There are several good eateries in the Byward Market area, including **La Folie** ((613) 562-0705, 15 Clarence Street, which serves pizzas piping hot from its wood ovens. The outdoor patio is often packed. Next door, **Memories** ((613) 232-1882, 7 Clarence Street, is an attractive bistro–café serving light lunches and sandwiches as well as weekend brunch. You can go back in time to the 1950s at **Zak's Diner** ((613) 241-2401, at 16 Byward Market, where there's lots of vinyl, chrome, and fifties music on the jukebox. **Hurley's Roadhouse** at 73 York Street ((613) 230-9347, is also a lively and popular place that does basic food such as burgers and steaks.

HOW TO GET THERE

Ottawa's **Macdonald-Cartier International Airport** is conveniently located 15 km (eight miles) south of the city, about 25 minutes from downtown. Buses as well as taxis are available for transport.

VIA Rail ((613) 244-8289 has several trains daily to and from Toronto and Montréal. **Voyageur Colonial** ((613) 238-5900, operates a bus service

TOP: Byward Market. BOTTOM: The start of the bed race during the Winterlude Festival.

SOUTHWEST OF OTTAWA

that links Ottawa with other Canadian cities. If you are traveling by car, the Trans-Canada Highway (Route 417) is the principal east-west highway into and out of Ottawa. Approaching from the south you will want to take Route 16, which crosses the border at Ogdensburg, New York, and also connects with Route 401, the main Toronto–Montréal highway.

SOUTHWEST OF OTTAWA

If you were an inhabitant of an area that had a dazzling, sophisticated city and a major world capital—say, Montréal and Ottawa—at one end, and a sprawling, wealthy metropolis — say, Toronto — at the other, you would probably feel that somehow the twentieth century had skipped over you. In the case of that area extending southwest of Ottawa, you would have every reason to feel that way. But it so happens that this is just the way the people of this part of Ontario like it, especially in Kingston and Quinte's Isle, where they have been at pains to preserve the character and quiet dignity of an earlier age.

KINGSTON

Strategically sited where Lake Ontario meets the St. Lawrence River, this was an important native trading center long before the French fur traders arrived in the first half of the seventeenth century. Although the French immediately coveted the spot as an ideal location from which to trade with the natives, constant fighting between the Iroquois and the Hurons prevented them from establishing a trading post until 1673 when a lull in the hostilities allowed Louis de Buade, Comte de Frontenac, to establish a fortified settlement here. Fort Frontenac, as it was known, survived for almost a century before falling to a force of British-American troops in advance of the Treaty of Paris that in 1763 ceded control of all of Canada to Britain. Like so many other towns and cities near the border with the eastern United States, it was resettled in the 1780s by self-exiled Loyalists, who gave it the name Kingston. Rapidly becoming a key British naval base and home to a large shipyard, Kingston survived the War of 1812 unscathed, and went on to enjoy two significant boosts to its economy: in 1832, when it became the southern terminus of the newly completed Rideau Canal, and again in 1841, when it became, briefly, the capital of both Upper and Lower Canada. Already a prospering military center, Kingston soon became an important academic center with the founding of Queen's University.

In the 150 years since then Kingston has remained remarkably unchanged in several respects. Although now a thriving city of over 60,000 people, it has remained true to the original:

even today there are few buildings more than two or three stories tall, and Kingston's main street in the latter part of the eighteenth century, Brock Street, is still an important commercial thoroughfare and still has some of the same stores it had two centuries ago. Likewise, Kingston has retained its strong military connections: the Royal Military College, the National Defence College, and the Canadian Army Staff College are all located here. But most noticeably, it has preserved — and in many instances restored — not only its graceful gray limestone public buildings from the nineteenth century but also its many fine Victorian private residences. Add to all this the parks, the attractive waterfront, and the colorful open-air markets, and you have a thoroughly delightful place to visit.

Finally, Kingston has also retained its strategic importance. Although it no longer figures in Canadian naval strategy, it occupies a crucial place

in many tourists' travel strategy because it lies, conveniently, almost exactly halfway between Montréal and Toronto. Equally conveniently, it is ideally placed for boat excursions on Lake Ontario and sightseeing trips to the Thousand Islands region.

The **Kingston Tourist Information Office** ((613) 548-4415 is at 209 Ontario Street, Kingston K7L 2Z1.

What to See and Do

The stout and forbidding **Fort Henry** ((613) 542-7388 glowers over Kingston from a high hilltop. This massive fortification was completed in 1836 to defend the naval dockyard at Point Frederick from attack. Part of the fort has reconstructed barracks, kitchens, and officers' quarters, and shows what life was like for the nineteenth-century guardsmen. The specially trained Fort Henry Guard performs military drills daily, while in July

and August there's the color and music of the spectacular Ceremonial Retreat at 7:30 PM (call for schedule). The Fort is east of the city off Route 2. It's open mid-May to late September, and in October by appointment; an admission fee is charged.

Across Navy Bay from Fort Henry on Point Frederick stands the **Royal Military College** and in its grounds a martello tower houses the **Royal Military College Museum** ((613) 541-6000 extension 6652. There are some displays on the history of the college and, somewhat bewilderingly, the small arms collection of General Porfirio Diaz, the President of Mexico from 1886 to 1912. It's open daily from the last weekend in June until Labor Day; admission is free.

The **City Hall** ((613) 546-4291 at 2162 Ontario Street was built in 1843 when Kingston was capital

---

Kingston: an oasis of Victorian serenity.

of the United Province of Canada, and this grand domed building is one of the country's finest examples of classical architecture. During the summer there are guided tours Monday to Friday. In front of the City Hall, **Confederation Park** stretches down to the water's edge and is the site of concerts and other open-air events in the summer.

Moving eastwards along the waterfront, the **Marine Museum of the Great Lakes** ((613) 542-2261, at 55 Ontario Street is devoted to the history of shipping on the lakes from the seventeenth century to the present day, including the history of shipbuilding in the area. Among the exhibits is a 3,000-ton icebreaker called the *Alexander Henry*. The museum is open daily from April to December, weekdays from January to March; an admission fee is charged.

Continuing eastwards, the **Pump House Steam Museum** ((613) 546-4696 at 23 Ontario Street, is housed within the restored Kingston Pumping Station and its exhibits include steam engines, models, and the huge steam pumps themselves — which have been restored to working order. It's open from June to Labor Day, and an admission fee is charged.

A lovely nineteenth-century house is the setting for the **Agnes Etherington Art Centre** ((613) 545-2190, at University Avenue at Queen's Crescent. The wide-ranging collection includes Canadian, African, and European art, antiques, and the house itself is furnished in period style. It's open Tuesday to Friday from 10 AM to 5 PM, weekends from 1 PM to 5 PM; admission is free.

Bellevue House ((613) 545-8666 at 35 Centre Street, is an extravagant green and white Tuscan-style villa set in attractive grounds. Built in 1840 by a wealthy merchant, its elaborate appearance quickly earned it the nicknames "Pekoe Pagoda" and "Tea Caddy Castle." In 1848 and 1849 it was home to Canada's first prime minister, John A. Macdonald, and the interior has been restored and furnished to that period with some Macdonald memorabilia displayed. The house is open to the public daily from April to October, and an admission fee is charged.

East of Kingston in the St. Lawrence River lie the **Thousand Islands**, which in fact number more than 1,000, ranging in size from quite large to a mere few meters. Some are forested and verdant, and the houses on them range from humble to palatial. This beautiful 80-km (50-mile) stretch of the St. Lawrence has long been a popular vacation spot, and there are quite a number of cruises and tours of the islands in operation. **Wolfe Island** is the largest of the Thousand Islands, if you take a free 30-minute trip on the car ferry to it you can enjoy some good views of Kingston and some of the islands.

St. Lawrence Islands National Park ((613) 923-5261, 2 Country Road 5, Mallorytown K0E 1R0,

encompasses 17 of the islands and part of the mainland at Mallorytown Landing where the park has its Visitor Centre. The center is open daily from mid-May to mid-October and has an interpretive center, a campground, and a water-taxi that runs from here to the islands, where there are some more campsites. While you're here, take a look at the wreck of the **HMS** *Radcliffe*, a gunboat that saw action in the 1812 war and is kept in a shelter close to the Interpretive Centre.

For some more of the outdoor life, **Frontenac Provincial Park** ((613) 542-2261, in nearby Sydenham, offers untouched wilderness in Canadian Shield country where you can hike, canoe or, when the weather's right, cross-country ski. Frontenac Outfitters ((613) 376-6220, in Sydenham, rent out camping gear, canoes, and kayaks for very reasonable prices.

Where to Stay and Eat

There are several choices for accommodation in the mid-range price category. Particularly good for families, the moderately priced **Seven Oakes Motor Inn** ((613) 546-3655, at 2331 Princess Street, Kingston K7M 3G1, has 40 accommodations set in acres of land with a large swimming pool; it offers excellent value. The **Prince George Hotel** ((613) 547-9037, at 200 Ontario Street, Kingston K7L 2Y9, is a beautiful early-nineteenth-century building offering rooms with views over the lake. The **Hochelaga Inn** (/FAX (613) 549-5534 TOLL-FREE (800) 267-0525 at 24 Sydenham Street South, Kingston K7L 3G9, is another attractive Victorian-era house with 23 well-equipped rooms, handsomely decorated with period pieces. Near Fort Henry the **Highland Motel Five** ((613) 546-3121, 725 Highway 15, Kingston K7L 5H6, offers 45 rooms and facilities that include tennis courts and an outdoor pool.

For inexpensive accommodation, the **Kingston International Hostel** ((613) 546-7203 TOLL-FREE (800) 461-8585 FAX (613) 546-3715, 210 Bagot Street, Kingston K7L 3G1, has good facilities and is open year-round except Christmas week. If you are looking for **bed and breakfast** accommodation in the Kingston area you can telephone Kingston Area Bed and Breakfast ((613) 542-0214.

One of Kingston's best-known restaurants is the inexpensive **Chez Piggy** ((613) 549-7673, at 68 Princess Street, set in a restored livery stable that was built in 1810. The interior is attractive and warm, and the small menu features some interesting dishes. It is open for dinner and lunch from Tuesday to Saturday, and for Sunday brunch. Also inexpensively priced, the **Kingston Brewing Company** ((613) 542-4978, at 34 Clarence Street, serves basic bar food amid the tanks in which their own very commendable beer and lager are brewed. For good (expensive) Italian food go to **Gencarelli** at 629 Princess Street ((613) 542-7976, where you can eat on the pleasant rooftop terrace in the warm weather. It's open daily for lunch and dinner.

QUINTE'S ISLE

Surrounded by the waters of Lake Ontario, Quinte's Isle is a pastoral idyll floating offshore. It, too, was settled by Loyalists, but instead of establishing the sort of commercial, industrial, cultural, and military centers that their fellow exiles created elsewhere, these Loyalists decided to take advantage of the island's position and rich soil to make it a quiet farming paradise. As a result, today it produces more vegetables and fruit than almost

any other area of comparable size in Ontario — much of which is grown by descendants of the original settlers. The island is dotted with road-side stands selling fresh produce.

It is also increasingly dotted with art galleries and craft shops, as many artists and artisans have come here to get away from the rigors and distractions of life on the other shore. The great Canadian artist D.R. Dawson, for example, settled in the town of Picton, having lived for years on a Greek island. Inevitably, too, the island has begun to undergo the experience of being "discovered," and consequently now has facilities and developments geared to the tourist trade. But it remains largely unspoiled — and thoroughly pleasant.

For visitor information concerning Quinte's Isle, contact the **Prince Edward County Chamber of Tourism and Commerce** ((613) 476-2421, at 116 Main Street, Picton K0K 2T0.

What to See and Do

Quinte's Isle is a restful place and a drive around the island along its quiet roads and through its old settlements makes a very pleasant day's outing. It is also a recreational area where the flatness of the land makes for good bicycling, while the waters offer sailing and fishing opportunities.

The small town of **Picton** is the largest in the area and the hub of the island. It's an attractive, quiet town with some interesting old buildings and a deep-water harbor. You can pick up maps and guides in the tourist office and take a look at some of the many crafts that are produced here. Each summer it's the center of a music festival called **Quinte Summer Music**, in which top Canadian performers participate (for information, contact the Prince Edward County Chamber of Tourism and Commerce, above). Also on the island, **Bloomfield** is a settlement dating from the early nineteenth century; it is a good place for crafts, pottery, and antiques. **Consecon** is a small and picturesque village with a millpond and some delightful views over the water.

East of Picton, Route 33 brings you to the **Lake on the Mountain**, a small lake 60 m (200 ft) above Lake Ontario. Its origins are unknown, but legend has it that the lake is fed from Niagara Falls. This lovely spot is well worth a stop for the spectacular views over Lake Ontario.

West of Picton you'll find **Sandbanks** and **North Beach provincial parks**, ideal for picnicking, sailing and swimming. Sandbanks is a huge sandbar that extends across a bay and has dunes that reach up to 24 m (80 ft) in height. North Beach is good for swimming, windsurfing, and sailing; there's also a place that rents out equipment and gives lessons. For information on the parks you can call Sandbanks Provincial Park headquarters ((613) 393-3319.

Where to Stay

At the high end of the medium-priced hostelries, the **Isaiah Tubbs Resort** ((613) 393-2090, at Rural Route 1, West Lake Road, Picton K0K 2T0, offers a wide variety of attractive and comfortable accommodation: rooms or suites in the restored inn, lodges, or seasonal cabins, all with excellent facilities. Standing in 12 hectares (30 acres) of land by West Lake, the resort offers its own recreational facilities in addition to those afforded by its location.

If you enjoy messing about in the water you might be particularly interested in staying at the moderately priced **Tip of the Bay Motor Hotel** ((613) 476-2156, at 35 Bridge Street, Picton K0K 2T0. It overlooks Picton Bay, has its own

Bellevue House in Kingston remains rooted in the mid-nineteenth century.

dock, and offers fishing packages. The **Merrill Inn** ((613) 476-7451, at 343 Main Street East, PO Box 2310, Picton K0K 2T0, is a charming hotel dating from the 1870s. Each of the 15 rooms is individually decorated with antiques and is also furnished with modern conveniences. Guests have the use of an attractive sitting room and a pleasant sun porch.

In the inexpensive price range, **Tara Hall Bed & Breakfast** ((613) 399-2801, 146 Main Street, Wellington K0K 3L0, is a lovely landmark house with beautiful decorative detail throughout and three guestrooms. In Bloomfield, **Mallory House** ((613) 393-3458, at Rural Route 1, PO Box 10, Bloomfield K0K 1G0, offers some of the most

Tuesday to Friday for lunch and dinner. Also in Picton, the **Wheelhouse View Café** ((613) 476-7380, on Rural Route 4, just by the Adolphustown Ferry, is a good spot for inexpensive eating.

There's fine dining in a Victorian setting at the moderately priced **Angéline's Restaurant** ((613) 393-3301, in the Bloomfield Inn, 29 Stanley Street West, Bloomfield. It's an attractive old house with a warm and welcoming interior and there's the option of dining out on the lawn in fine weather. The chef's specialties include freshwater fish and pheasant, and his Austrian origins are in evidence when his wonderful pastries are served for afternoon tea. The restaurant is open daily for lunch and dinner in July and August, and Thursday to

charming accommodation on the island. This early nineteenth-century farmhouse set in attractive grounds has three guestrooms and is comfortably and cozily decorated throughout with antique furnishings. The **Bloomfield Inn** ((613) 393-3301, at 29 Stanley Street West, Bloomfield K0K 1G0, has nine rooms and one of the best restaurants in the area, Angéline's (see below).

Where to Eat

There's an old-fashioned coziness about the **Waring House Restaurant** ((613) 476-7492, which is in an 1835 stone house located just west of Picton on Rural Route 1. It specializes in European cuisine. Its breads and pastries are home-baked, and the dining room, with its open fireplace and polished wooden floor, quite literally exudes warmth. Prices are moderate and reservations are needed for weekends and summer months. It's open

Monday the rest of the year. Reservations are essential for dinner.

HOW TO GET THERE

Most people arrive in Kingston by car. Situated on Route 401 midway between Montréal and Toronto, it is an easy morning's (or afternoon's) drive from either city—and even quicker to reach from Ottawa or Syracuse, New York. To reach Quinte's Isle from Kingston, take Highway 49 south off Route 401.

Kingston is also well-served by **Voyageur Colonial** ((613) 547-4916 buses from Montréal, Ottawa, and Toronto. **VIA Rail** ((613) 544-5600 operates daily service through Kingston from Montréal and Toronto.

Muster ceremony at Kingston's Fort Henry.

TORONTO

However hard one struggles to be open-minded, one cannot help but arrive in a new place with certain preconceived ideas about what one will find there. In the case of Toronto, we arrived thinking of Peter Ustinov's wonderful description of it as "New York run by the Swiss." But what we hadn't counted on, when chuckling at the humorous implications of the remark, was its amazing accuracy. Toronto's buildings are not just tall, they do indeed scrape the sky; its crime rate is not just low, it's the lowest of any major city in North America; its streets are not just clean, we actually

saw two city workers outside our hotel scrubbing a municipal litter bin with soap and water — in the rain!

With a metropolitan population of around four and a half million and an urban area of some 630 sq km (230 sq miles), Toronto stands (and sprawls) as a gleaming, humming rebuttal to those who argue that big cities must inevitably become breeding grounds of corruption, poverty, and violence — concrete jungles, in other words. Toronto does have a lot of concrete, of course, but it also has over 200 verdant parks. It does have a lot of shiny new skyscrapers, but it also has many lovingly preserved old buildings. It is certainly growing at a rapid pace, but its growth is carefully controlled so that adequate provision is made for housing in any development involving new office space. It is large, but it has excellent public transport, including a sparkling and efficient sub-

way system. Its schools are good, its cultural amenities are first-rate, its services are efficient, its streets are not only clean but safe, and its citizens are orderly and polite. No wonder people flock to live here.

While the spirit of the city is symbolized by the soaring CN Tower, its enterprising character is represented by the world's largest subterranean city — 12 blocks of shops, restaurants, cinemas, and cafés underground. While it was once best known for its suffocating sense of propriety — for many years it had "blue laws" restricting drinking, and was derisively as referred to as "Toronto the Good" — it is now a lively recreational, cultural, and entertainment center (it has more theaters than any city in North America except New York). But perhaps the best measure of the extent to which Toronto has managed to achieve just the right balance between the old and the new, between dynamism and tradition, is the fact that it strikes American visitors as a British city while to Europeans it seems very American. Which probably makes it the most *Canadian* city in Canada.

BACKGROUND

Ironically, considering it is now Canada's largest city, Toronto got off to a slow start. The Huron, who named the site (it means "meeting place"), saw the spot merely as the first (or last) link in a land chain connecting Lake Huron with Lake Ontario, as did the early French fur traders. In the first half of the eighteenth century the French decided that it might be worth building a fort there to protect their traders, but it was destroyed during the Seven Years' War. After the war the victorious British showed no interest in developing the site until 1793, when the Lieutenant Governor, John Graves Simcoe, decided to establish a town there. Soon thereafter it became the capital of Upper Canada in place of Niagara-on-the-Lake, which was thought to be too dangerously close to the American border. It was renamed York after George II's son, the Duke of York.

York's early days as a capital were inauspicious, to say the least. Its few dirt streets resembled linear bogs, earning the town the unflattering name of "Muddy York." Nor was its image much improved by the fact that one of its earliest industries was livestock slaughtering, which led to the sobriquet "Hogtown." Then in 1813 an American force attacked the town and burned down every building of any size. But if its first 20 years were unpromising, York's next 20 years were marked by such economic and population growth that in

OPPOSITE: Glass and concrete office buildings can't hide the world's tallest free-standing structure, Toronto's CN Tower, seen here from Front Street. ABOVE: The entrance to the Canadian National Exhibition Center.

1834 it was incorporated as a city and given back its original name, Toronto.

For better or worse, economic and political power in Toronto — indeed in the province as a whole — was held almost exclusively by an elite group of wealthy businessmen. Known as the Family Compact, this small "club" exercised such power that its influence extended far beyond the boundaries of government and commerce to have a determining impact on every aspect of life in Toronto. Because these men were Anglophilic as well as Anglophone, Toronto became English in character as well as language. Because they were puritanical as well as philistine, it became "Toronto the Good," most righteous of cities, and most boring. While its population expanded rapidly throughout the remainder of the nineteenth century — thanks largely to the arrival of Scots fleeing the Highland clearances and Irish fleeing the potato famine — its horizons didn't

expand much until after World War II, when a tidal wave of immigrants from all over the world enlarged and enlivened the city, transforming it from a dull gray zone of strictly enforced virtue into the ethnically diverse, vibrant, cosmopolitan city that today graces the north shore of Lake Ontario.

GENERAL INFORMATION

For province-wide information, visit the drop-in **Information Centre** at Toronto Eaton Centre, Level 1, 220 Yonge Street. For information on Toronto get in touch with or drop by **Tourism Toronto** ((416) 203-2500 TOLL-FREE (800) 363-1990 FAX (416) 203-6753 WEBSITE www.tourism-toronto .com, 207 Queen's Quay West, Suite 590, PO Box 126, Toronto M5J 1A7. The **Info T.O. Booth** is conveniently located at the Metro Toronto Convention Centre (near the CN Tower), 255 Front

2424. The guides are entertaining and informative, and this is a very good way to get to know the city, especially if your time is limited. You can spend the day hopping on and off the bus at various stops for the single $25 24-hour fare.

WHAT TO SEE AND DO

The Waterfront Area

The most conspicuous feature of the Toronto skyline is the **CN Tower** ((416) 868-6937, 301 Front Street West, a tall, slim concrete structure that resembles a giant needle. Ostensibly a transmitter mast, this tower stands 553.33 m (1,815 ft) high, making it the world's tallest freestanding structure. It contains a revolving restaurant, and observation platforms. A glass elevator on the outside of the building will take you to the "Sky Pod." Above this is another observation deck with curved glass windows laying the most spectacular and giddy view of the city literally at your feet (see TOWER OVER TORONTO, page 19, in TOP SPOTS). The tower is open daily and an admission fee is charged.

Close by on Front Street is the remarkable **SkyDome** ((416) 341-2770, 1 Blue Jays Way, a domed sports stadium with an ingeniously designed 86-m (282-ft)-tall retractable roof. It is home to the Canadian football team the Argonauts and the baseball Blue Jays. It seats up to 30,000 spectators, depending on the game or event, and has the world's largest scoreboard. There's a restaurant with a huge seating capacity and a 364-room hotel with 70 of the rooms overlooking the playing field. On one famous occasion the presence of these hotel windows resulted in a serious distraction from a baseball game. During a 1990 game between Toronto and Seattle, a man and a woman in one of the rooms became extremely intimate in full view of the crowd. In the words of the hotel manager, "the people, for their own particular reason, wanted to perform in front of 30,000 fans." As a result, new hotel rules forbid "activities not considered appropriate in public." Tours of the stadium are conducted between 9 AM and 6 PM, when there's no clash with events.

From the CN Tower it's a pleasant stroll through parkland down to the **Harbourfront Centre** ((416) 973-3000, an urban park providing shopping, recreation, and cultural events — many of them free — with the main activity center at 235 Queen's Quay West. To get there, walk down York Street and pass through the newly constructed Teamway which takes you through a well-lit, soundproofed tunnel and delivers you to the other side of the railway tracks that separate downtown from the harbor. The Harbourfront was once an area of dilapidated wharves, warehouses, and

Street West; the helpful staff sell tickets for attractions, transportation services, and events and make hotel reservations.

Getting Around

The Toronto Transit Commission (TTC) ((416) 393-INFO operates **streetcars**, **buses**, and **subways**. Day passes and single-ride tickets are sold at subway stations and some convenience stores. A family day pass for unlimited travel is $6.50; adult fare is $2. There are three subway lines, and the system is relatively easy to use. The Toronto Islands are reached by **ferry** ((416) 392-8193 from the docks at the foot of Bay Street; a fare is charged. Below the downtown financial district there is a 10-km (six-mile)-long network of underground walkways known as **PATH**. Color-coded signs show the way.

Narrated **sightseeing tours** of Toronto are offered by Olde Towne Toronto Tours ((416) 798-

The Skydome, home of the Blue Jays, Toronto's National League baseball team.

factories, which the federal government took over and, through extensive building and refurbishment, created an area of cinemas, restaurants, cafés, marinas, shops, and housing. Indeed, some believe that the construction work has now gone too far and that too many condominiums are spoiling the area.

At the **Queen's Quay Terminal** ((416) 203-0510, 207 Queen's Quay West, there are galleries and shops, many featuring Canadian products, crafts, souvenirs, and books. At the **York Quay Centre** there's an art gallery and theater, and nearby at **Pier 4** there are sailing schools and equipment stores. A few blocks further west is the **Harbourfront Antique Market** ((416) 260-2626, with the world's largest selection of antiques and collectibles under one roof.

Innumerable tours on land and sea depart from the waterfront area. There are one-hour Toronto Harbour cruises with **Mariposa Cruise Line** ((416) 203-0178. The harbor area is also one of the whistle-stops on the **Olde Towne Toronto Tours** (see GENERAL INFORMATION, above). You can purchase tickets at the booth marked "gift shop" on the east side of the terminal, and catch the trolley-bus or the double-decker just in front of the booth.

Moving north and westward from the waterfront, you can find out about some of Toronto's most dramatic history at **Fort York** ((416) 392-6907 on Garrison Road. The fort was first built in 1793 to defend the town, and when in 1813 the Americans captured the city the retreating British blew up fort's magazine, killing 300 Americans and 150 British. It was rebuilt in 1816 and restored in the early 1900s. It offers the visitor a good picture of the life of the British soldier in the early nineteenth century, with its furnished officers' and soldiers' quarters, and military drills performed by authentically uniformed men during the summer months. The nearest subway station is Bathurst.

Continuing west along the waterfront, at Exhibition Place you'll find the **Marine Museum of Upper Canada** ((416) 392-1765, which traces the history of shipping and trade in the area. During the summer the *Ned Hanlan*, a restored 1932 tugboat, is open to the public.

Built on three artificial islands on the lake, **Ontario Place** ((416) 314-9900, 955 Lake Shore Boulevard West, is an indoor-outdoor entertainment complex. Futuristic pod-like structures on tall steel legs house theaters where shows and films on Ontario can be seen. The **Forum** is an outdoor concert hall used for all kinds of musical entertainment; the **Canadian National Ballet** makes appearances here. The **Children's Village** is a well-designed, supervised play area. All age groups enjoy a visit to the **HMS** *Haida*, a Canadian destroyer used in World War II and the Korean War, which is moored in a marina. Ontario Place is open

daily from mid-May to September 1. An admission fee is charged.

You can take a boat trip out to the **Toronto Islands** from Ontario Place and also from the dock at the foot of Bay Street near the Westin Harbour Castle Hotel. This collection of small islands off the downtown waterfront offer recreational possibilities such as swimming, fishing, boating and cycling and are a popular retreat from the summer heat for Torontonians and visitors alike. **Hanlan's Point** has tennis courts and a pleasant beach, **Ward's Island** is good for swimming, but the most popular is **Centreville** ((416) 203-0405, on Centre Island, an eight-hectare (20-acre) theme park designed to look like an Ontario village of a hundred years ago, with a children's farm, playgrounds and rides. Admission for Centreville is free and rides cost around $2 each. All-day ride passes can also be purchased.

Downtown

Toronto's King and Bay Street area is its financial center and here you'll find the **Toronto Stock Exchange** ((416) 947-4700 at Exchange Tower, 2 First Canadian Place, where you can watch the action on the trading floor from a gallery or take a tour of the building. Admission is free. Of the bank towers the most striking is the **Royal Bank Plaza** with its two triangular towers of gold reflecting glass. It is situated at Front and Bay streets. A true cathedral of commerce, it contains an international art collection that includes a vast sculpture by Jesùs Soto composed of 8,600 aluminum tubes.

Heading north on Bay Street from the Royal Bank Plaza leads to another palace of art and commerce, the **Toronto-Dominion Centre** ((416) 982-8473, 55 King Street West. Mies van der Rohe designed this austere complex of five buildings. Inside, you'll find the **Gallery of Inuit Art** and the impressive Toronto-Dominion Bank's art collection, which focuses on Canada's northern frontier.

At 10 Front Street West is **BCE Place**. This new arcade, with its interior resembling the ribs of a capsized ship, incorporates the façade of the Canadian Chamber of Commerce Building (1845) which was disassembled, moved and reconstructed on its present site. Within the arcade are the Heritage Square Shops and a host of Mövenpick theme restaurants. Also at BCE Place, hockey fans can make their pilgrimage to the **Hockey Hall of Fame** ((416) 360-7765, 30 Yonge Street. It is open daily; an admission fee is charged.

Heading east along Front Street, you can visit the colorful **St. Lawrence Market**, between Church and Jarvis streets, a daily farmers' market housed in Toronto's first city hall building (1899). Hours are Tuesday to Thursday from 9 AM to 7 PM; Friday from 8 AM to 8 PM; Saturday from 5 AM to

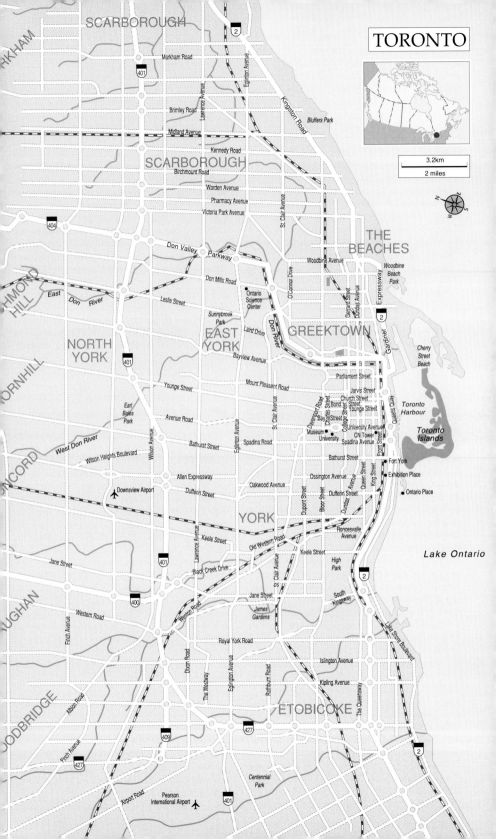

5 PM. Another fascinating market, and not to be missed, is the **Kensington Market**, between Spadina Avenue and Bathurst Street, south of College Street. It's especially lively in the early mornings when merchants and their wares and livestock create quite a scene. The market is open Monday to Saturday.

In the heart of downtown, the **New City Hall** ((416) 392-9111 at 100 Queen Street West, with its two curved towers, is a highly acclaimed piece of modern architecture. So futuristic is its design that it made an appearance in the American science-fiction television series *Star Trek*. It's open weekdays with free guided tours at 10 AM, 11 AM, and 2 PM. In front of the building stands a Henry Moore

sculpture, known locally as The Archer. Nearby on Albert and Bay streets stands the **Old City Hall**, designed by E.J. Lennox (who also designed Casa Lomam; see below). Because of years of delays and a $2.5 million budget overrun, Lennox was refused payment by the city. He promptly sued and won. In retaliation, the city forbade Lennox to take credit for the building; but Lennox got the last laugh by finishing the façade with gargoyles sculpted to resemble the leading city politicians of the day. He also carved his initials in the building; the letters are visible along the Bay Street side. The Old City Hall now functions as a courthouse.

A couple of blocks east of the city halls stands **Mackenzie House** ((416) 392-6915, 82 Bond Street, a Victorian town house which was the home of William Lyon Mackenzie, Toronto's first mayor and leader of the 1837 rebellion. Following the rebellion he lived in exile in the United States — when he was able to return to the city his friends gave him this house. Now restored and furnished in mid-nineteenth-century style, the house has displays telling the story of his life. The nearest subway stop is Dundas.

A short walk east of the city hall buildings is Toronto's main theater district where the **Elgin & Winter Garden Theatres** (TOURS (416) 314-2871 (TICKETS (416) 872-5555, 189 Yonge Street, offer

guided tours on Thursday at 5 PM and Saturday at 11 AM; a fee is charged. The larger Elgin theater has been restored to the gilt and grandeur of the Edwardian era, and upstairs the Winter Garden is a smaller theater, whimsically decorated to look like an English garden.

To the west of New City Hall, the **Art Gallery of Ontario** (AGO) ((416) 979-6648, at 317 Dundas Street West, houses one of the country's most important art collections. The **Henry Moore Sculpture Centre**, with over 300 exhibits, has the largest public collection of Moore's works in the world. The **European Collection** covers movements in art from the seventeenth century through to the early twentieth century, while three galleries are devoted to the comprehensive **Canadian Collection**. Adjoining the Art Gallery building is a beautiful Georgian brick house known as **The Grange** ((416) 979-6608. Toronto's oldest brick residence, The Grange was once the home of the prominent Boulton family, and later became the first home of the Art Gallery; it has now been restored to the elegance of an 1830s residence. The Gallery and The Grange are open daily mid-June to August, and closed on Mondays during the rest of the year. The nearest subway stops are St. Patrick and Dundas.

Queen's Park Area

Moving slightly north to the area around Queen's Park you'll find the **Royal Ontario Museum (ROM)** ((416) 586-8000, 100 Queen's Park, Canada's largest public museum and one of its most wide-ranging, as it covers art, archaeology, and the natural sciences. Among its most famous features are its Chinese art treasures, its Ming Tomb, the Dinosaur Gallery, a huge replica of a bat cave complete with special effects, and the popular hands-on Discovery Gallery. It's open daily; an admission fee is charged, free on Tuesday after 4:30 PM. Other parts of the museum are the **McLaughlin Planetarium** ((416) 586-8000; the **Sigmund Samuel Building** ((416) 586-5549, 14 Queen's Park Crescent West, which houses a large collection of Canadiana, including room settings and folk art; and the **George R. Gardiner Museum of Ceramic Art** ((416) 586-8080, at 111 Queen's Park, which includes extensive collections of Pre-Columbian pottery, Italian majolica, English Delftware, and eighteenth-century European porcelain.

West of the ROM, the **Bata Shoe Museum** ((416) 979-7799, 327 Bloor Street West, takes a street-level look at art with its exposition of footwear dating back to 4,500 years. It's a social history of shoes, from fashion statement to religious symbol. Also on display are celebrity shoes that have touched the toes of the likes of Madonna, Elvis, Elton John, and John Lennon. It's open Tuesday to Saturday from 10 AM to 5 PM, Thursday

10 AM to 8 PM, Sunday from noon to 5 PM. An admission fee is charged.

Moving south of the ROM to Queen's Park, you will find the late-nineteenth-century **Provincial Parliament Building** ((416) 325-7500, a Romanesque pink sandstone building. Free guided tours are given mid-May to Labor Day weekdays on the hour, weekends every half-hour, with frequent tours the rest of the year. You can attend parliamentary sittings when the house is in session.

Neighborhoods

Toronto's immigrant communities have been encouraged to maintain their cultural individu-

has a touch of California about it. It's largely a professional neighborhood with a beach and lakeside parkland, a three-kilometer (two-mile)-long boardwalk and a core of cafés, shops, and restaurants. The area bordered by Parliament Street, the Don River, Danforth Avenue and Gerrard Street is known as **Cabbagetown**. Originally built to provide housing for factory workers, it was a rundown slum area by the 1960s but then underwent extensive renovation to become a very pleasant residential and commercial district.

Queen Street West is Toronto's equivalent of New York's Bleaker Street, with its trendy clubs, boutiques, galleries, bistros, restaurants, and bars

ality, and the result is a rich and colorful ethnic patchwork. Around Dundas Street East is one of several Chinatown communities; another is along Dundas Street West, a third hugs University Avenue. There's a large Italian community at St. Clair Avenue West and Dufferin Street — an area rumored to have more Italians than Florence — and along Gerrard Street East you'll find Little India. Between Pape and Woodbine streets bouzouki music can be heard in the Greek district known as "the Danforth," while between Bathurst and Spadina streets south of College Street is the lively open-air **Kensington Market**, with its distinctly Portuguese accent.

Some of Toronto's other neighborhoods are characterized by lifestyle or income rather than by nationality, such as the genteel **Forest Hill** area or the wealthy **Rosedale** area. The **Beaches** area, situated along Queen Street East at Woodbine,

concentrated on the section of Queen Street West lying between University Avenue and Bathurst Street. Close to the College of Art, the street has developed a certain bohemian air and it's great fun to wander around. Moving from the hip to the seriously chic, **Bloor-Yorkville** is the smartest part of town. The area — bounded by Charles Street, Davenport Road, Yonge Street, and Avenue Road — was once a downbeat, dilapidated hippie hangout, but after renovation it is now filled with art galleries, cafés, restaurants, and upscale shops.

On and around Bloor Street, Yorkville Avenue, Hazelton Avenue and Cumberland Street, are Canada's most exclusive shops. Here you'll find such names as Chanel, Cartier, Hermès, and Louis

OPPOSITE: Restaurant 360° at the top of Toronto's CN Tower is the perfect place to watch the world go by. ABOVE: Another bird's eye view of the skyline.

Vuitton. There are shopping malls such as **Holt Renfrew Centre** ((416) 922-2333, at 50 Bloor Street West, and **Hazelton Lanes** ((416) 968-8600, at 55 Avenue Road, and attractive old houses containing art galleries, boutiques, and cafés. Avenue Road is well known for its **flower markets**, especially along the block between Davenport Road and Bernard Avenue. You will find more flowers west of Avenue Road in the Annex, a pretty, residential area.

South of Bloor Street on Markham Street, there's an altogether different kind of atmosphere around **Mirvish Village**, where entrepreneur Eddie Mirvish has his flagship store, the brash and breezy **Honest Ed's** ((416) 537-1574, 581 Bloor

wood paneling, massive ballroom, and marble-floored conservatory with stained glass dome are examples of the unfettered extravagance with which the castle was built and which eventually reduced Sir Henry to surrender his glorious dream palace to the city in payment of back taxes. Be sure to climb the stairs to the turrets for a view over the city. Casa Loma is open daily from 9:30 AM to 4 PM; an admission fee is charged. The nearest subway station is Dupont.

At **High Park** on Queen Street West you can play a game of tennis, enjoy the gardens and picnic grounds, go fishing or boating, take the children to the zoo, and on a summer's day see some Shakespeare in the open air. It is the city's largest

Street West. Walking around this huge bargain store with its lights and signs can be an overwhelming experience, but there are some good buys to be found here. With the money Ed has made he has become a well-known patron of the arts, and he was responsible for the rejuvenation of this block of pleasant Victorian buildings containing restaurants, bars, and shops selling antiques, books, and art.

Outside Downtown

The eccentrically splendid **Casa Loma** ((416) 923-1171 sits atop a hill at Davenport and Spadina roads, commanding views over the city. This 98-room, baronial-style mansion was the folly of Sir Henry Pellatt, a financier, who built it between 1905 and 1911 for $3.5 million, and with its cellars, towers, secret passageways, and stables it's rather like a set for an old Hollywood movie. Its

park and at its center is **Colborne Lodge**, a lovely Regency villa bequeathed to the city by its architect/owner John George Howard. This elegant home is open daily to the public and contains some watercolors of Toronto painted by Howard himself. He was also an engineer and his house boasts what was the first indoor flush toilet in Ontario. To get there take the subway to High Park.

For wildlife watchers and those who just enjoy a peaceful retreat, the **Tommy Thompson Park** (also known as the Leslie Street Spit) might be the place to go. Landfill from building sites created the spit that extends out into the lake, and unexpectedly the wildlife literally flocked to it. It is now a sanctuary for birds such as gulls, geese, herons, swans, and ducks, and the fox and rabbit populations are increasing. It is open to the public only on weekends and is situated south of the junction of Leslie Street and Queen Street East.

About 11 km (seven miles) north of downtown in the Don River Ravine stands the splendid **Ontario Science Centre** ((416) 696-3127, 770 Don Mills Road. Another of architect Raymond Moriyama's triumphs, the museum integrates beautifully with its environment and its series of buildings are linked by enclosed escalators and ramps which allow the visitor to enjoy stunning views. Moriyama's respect for the natural beauty of the site is rumored to have extended to penalty clauses in building contracts for each tree destroyed. This hugely popular museum presents science and technology in a way that encourages viewer participation and demonstrates its everyday relevance. Allow plenty of time to look around,

40 minutes from downtown. Over an area of 148 hectares (370 acres) there are various theme areas offering rides, shows, shops, roller coasters, water slides, and a lot of shrieking and whooping. It's open daily from June to September.

The **Toronto Zoo** ((416) 392-5900 is situated in the Rouge Valley, 35 km (22 miles) northeast of downtown on Meadowvale Road north of Highway 401. Here the natural habitats have been recreated to allow the animals greater freedom. Around the zoo an area of untouched land provides the setting for North American wildlife and can only be visited by monorail. A Zoomobile will take you around the zoo if you don't feel like walking, and in the winter there's the spe-

and remember that it gets very busy on weekends. The museum is open daily and an admission fee is charged.

Excursions from Toronto

To see what life was like in rural Ontario during the nineteenth century, take a trip to the **Black Creek Pioneer Village** ((416) 736-1733, which is 29 km (18 miles) northwest of downtown at 1000 Murray Ross Parkway. This recreated village includes a blacksmith's shop, a mill, and a general store: all run by costumed villagers who will also demonstrate their crafts and skills. Sometimes a special event such as a wedding is enacted. It's open daily from May 1 to December 31; an admission fee is charged.

Not far away is a huge theme park known as **Paramount Canada's Wonderland** ((416) 832-7000, Highway 400, exit at Rutherford Road, *Ontario*

cial option of following a cross-country skiing trail. It's open daily and with longer hours in the summer months. An admission fee is charged, and there is a fee for parking (parking is free in the winter).

We highly recommend a visit to the superb **McMichael Canadian Art Collection** ((416) 893-1121, at Islington Avenue, Kleinburg, about 40 km (25 miles) north of the city. The most important collection of the works of the Canadian painters known as the Group of Seven is housed here. These painters were a revolutionary force in Canadian art, the first to produce uniquely Canadian painting inspired by the unspoiled beauty of the northern Ontario landscape. Also represented here are Inuit and other native art. The gallery is a lovely

OPPOSITE: The Hockey Hall of Fame catalogs the feats of the men of ice. ABOVE: The Blue Jays take to the field at Toronto's Skydome.

log and stone building with a high pitched roof; and there are windows throughout giving views of the beautiful countryside that inspired the paintings within.

SPORTS AND OUTDOOR ACTIVITIES

Toronto offers great opportunities for all kinds of outdoor activities. The Ministry of Tourism and Recreation ((416) 314-0944, Queen's Park, Toronto M7A 2R2, can supply you with details, while Metro Region Conservation ((416) 661-6600, has tips on swimming areas, sledding, cross-country skiing, fishing, and boating.

Bicyclists will find plenty of trails around the parks, and there's no shortage of places renting out cycles. **Fishing** enthusiasts should bear in mind that the pollution in Lake Ontario means they have to be very careful about eating anything caught there, but each year the Great Salmon Hunt at-

tracts anglers to try their luck at landing the biggest salmon.

Toronto has over 100 natural and man-made **skating rinks**, both indoor and outdoor, so you're never far from one. For information on any city rink call ((413) 392-1111. **Cross-country skiing** is a favorite Torontonian pastime, and there are trails throughout the city, some of which go out onto the lake.

NIGHTLIFE AND THE ARTS

Toronto is a lively place after dark and offers a wide choice of entertainment. For details of what's on, you can check the listings in the *Toronto Star* on Thursday, the *Globe and Mail* on Saturday, the monthly *Toronto Life* magazine, and the free weeklies *Now* and *Eye Weekly*. Tickets for a range of plays, shows, and concerts can be bought through **Ticketmaster** ((416) 872-2222, and half-price tickets for

many of these entertainments are available on the day of the show, for cash, from the **T.O. Tix booth**, inside Eaton Centre on the Mews level; call the hotline ((413) 596-8211 for information.

Toronto has a large, lively, and varied **theater scene**. The **Royal Alexandra** ((416) 872-3333 at 260 King Street West, stages Broadway, London, and Canadian productions, and has been beautifully restored to its Victorian-era splendor. The **Elgin & Winter Garden Theatres** (TOURS (416) 314-2871 (TICKETS (416) 872-5555, at 189 Yonge Street, present musicals and theater pieces. At the **St. Lawrence Centre for the Arts** ((416) 366-7723, Front and Scott streets, classics and Canadian plays are among the works performed by Toronto repertory companies. For innovative theater there's the **Théâtre Passe Muraille** ((416) 504-7529, 16 Ryerson Avenue. At the **Tarragon Theatre** ((416) 531-1827, 30 Bridgman Avenue, excellent Canadian works are performed. You mustn't miss seeing

Toronto's legendary **Second City** ((416) 343-0011, at their new theater at 56 Blue Jays Way. This sketch comedy troupe has an illustrious list of alumni, many of whom went on to star in *Saturday Night Live* and *SCTV*. The troupe's impressive new home in the heart of the entertainment district has, in addition to the main stage, a smaller cabaret stage where other excellent comedy acts perform. There's more wacky fun at **La Cage Dinner Theatre** ((416) 364-5200, 279 Yonge Street, above the Hard Rock Café, where drag acts are performed.

The **Canadian Opera Company** ((413) 363-8231 is based at the 3,200 seat **Hummingbird Centre for the Performing Arts** ((416) 872-2262, 1 Front Street East, where it presents a program of seven operas during the period from September to June. The company also presents a series of free outdoor performances during the summer at Harbourfront. The Hummingbird Centre is also home to the highly acclaimed **National Ballet of Canada** ((416) 345-9686, with performances in November, December, February, and May. The innovative **Toronto Dance Theatre** ((416) 973-4000 is the city's leading contemporary dance company.

The **Toronto Symphony** has its home at the **Roy Thomson Hall** ((416) 593-4828, 60 Simcoe Street, and plays here from September to May when not touring. The 2,850-seat Roy Thomson Hall is also home to the **Toronto Mendelssohn Choir** ((416) 598-0422, and it attracts top names in music of all kinds. There's symphonic music in **Massey Hall** ((416) 593-4828 at 178 Victoria Street, and chamber music and recitals at the **St. Lawrence Centre for the Arts** (see above). Concerts, from gospel to opera, take place at the **Ford Centre for the Performing Arts** ((416) 872-2222, 5040 Yonge Street.

Yorkville Village was home to a large hippie population in the mid-1960s. Rich in musical history, nowadays the music of choice is jazz. **Chick 'n' Deli** ((416) 489-3363, 744 Mount Pleasant Road, has its long-running Saturday jazz set. **Albert's Parlour** ((416) 515-1449, 481 Bloor Street West, has blues and New Orleans jazz. The **Top O' the Senator** ((416) 364-7517, 249 Victoria Street, is one of the foremost jazz venues, with a reputation for presenting exciting new talent. You can also hear jazz at the **Roy Thomson Hall** and the **Massey Hall** (see above).

A major rock venue, **El Mocambo** ((416) 968-2001, 464 Spadina Avenue, is where many top bands have played over the years. Rock and country music plays at the **Birchmount Tavern** ((416) 698-4115, 462 Birchmount Road. There's World music at **Bamboo** ((416) 593-5771, 312 Queen Street West. **C'est What** ((416) 867-1573, 19 Church Street, has live music late nights, along with a menu offering Niagara wines and flame-cooked meats.

Morning breaks at Union Station on Toronto's Front Street.

Dance clubs here, as everywhere else, change with frequency, and you need to check the listings for details. Among those that attract the crowds are **The Government (** (416) 869-9261 or (416) 869-0045, 132 Queens Quay East, with its gigantic dance floor and hot Thursday disco; **Joker (** (416) 598-1313, 318 Richmond Street W, another big space with three floors of new rock, electronica and lasers; and across the street, **Whiskey Saigon (** (416) 593-4646, at 217 Richmond Street, which serves up more of the same, but has a younger crowd. **The Living Room Lounge (** (416) 979-3168, 330 Adelaide Street West, is a tad more sophisticated, attracting an affluent crowd of hipsters for acid jazz, R&B, and hip-hop. You can perfect your salsa with Latin dance lessons Tuesday at the upscale **Berlin (** (416) 489-7777, 2335 Yonge Street.

WHERE TO STAY

Accommodation in Toronto can become quite scarce at the peak of the summer season, so if you plan to come around this time of year reservations are recommended well in advance. **Tourism Toronto/Accommodations Toronto (** (416) 203-2500 TOLL-FREE (800) 363-1990 FAX (416) 203-6753 E-MAIL mtcvainf@pathcom.com, can help you find the right accommodation and in addition provides a free booking service. Discounts are usually offered over weekends, and senior citizens will usually find themselves entitled to a discount of up to 15%.

Expensive

Close to the downtown theater district the **King Edward Hotel Meridian (** (416) 863-9700 TOLL-FREE (800) 543-4300 FAX (416) 863-0642, 37 King Street East, Toronto M5C 1E9, is a truly grand hotel. The rooms are beautiful, spacious, and well-equipped, and it has 24-hour room service.

For modern luxury in the heart of the city, the **Marriott Toronto Eaton Centre (** (416) 597-9200 FAX (416) 597-9211, 525 Bay Street, Toronto M5G 2L2, can't be beat. Rooms and suites have fascinating views over the busy commercial and cultural area of Eaton Centre and are very comfortable and soothingly decorated in dusty rose and gray. The suites have larger bedrooms than most other Toronto hotels. The indoor rooftop swimming pool offers a fabulous view of the city.

Dominating the Harbourfront skyline are two more top-of-the-line hotels: The **Radisson Plaza Admiral Harbourfront (** (416) 203-3333 FAX (416) 203-3100, 249 Queen's Quay West, Toronto M5J 2N5 is conveniently located close to Harbourfront entertainment and cultural activities. Rooms have harbor views and there's also a lounge with lovely views over the marina. The twin-towered **Westin Harbour Castle (** (416) 869-1600 TOLL-FREE (800) 228-3000 FAX (416) 869-0573,

1 Harbour Square, Toronto M5J 1A6, has nearly 1,000 comfortable and well-equipped rooms with views of either the lake or the skyline. It has some good restaurants including the Lighthouse, one of Toronto's two revolving restaurants, and a free shuttle service will take you downtown.

Next to the CN Tower, **Crown Plaza Toronto Centre (** (416) 597-1400 TOLL-FREE (800) 422-7969 FAX (416) 597-8128, 225 Front Street West, Toronto M5V 2X3, is ideally suited for business people. All 560 rooms and suites are spacious and have computer ports and work desks. In the same neighborhood, opposite Union Station stands the **Royal York (** (416) 368-2511 TOLL-FREE (800) 441-1414 FAX (416) 368-2884, 100 Front Street West, M5J 1E3, one of Toronto's best known hotels, which was the tallest structure in the British Empire when it was built in 1929. Among the hotel's illustrious guests have been the Beatles, the Rolling Stones, and Queen Elizabeth. It has 1,200 rooms, which tend to be on the small side, but it has excellent facilities, over a dozen restaurants, and shops. High tea is served in the **Royal Tea Room**, Monday to Friday from noon to 5 PM, Saturday and Sunday from 2 PM to 5 PM.

Moving midtown near Queen's Park, the **Sutton Place Hotel (** (416) 924-9221 TOLL-FREE (800) 268-3790 FAX (416) 924-1778 E-MAIL sales@tor .suttonplace.com, at 955 Bay Street, Toronto M5S 2A2, maintains extremely high standards. Its rooms are furnished in elegant French style and have the usual array of facilities.

In Yorkville, the **Four Seasons Hotel Toronto (** (416) 964-0411 TOLL-FREE (800) 332-3442 FAX (416) 964-2301 at 21 Avenue Road, Toronto M5R 2G1, is part of this superb chain and manages even to surpass the expected high standards. The hotel has 210 attractive and very comfortable rooms, many of which offer excellent views of the city, and there is a swimming pool, restaurants, and attentive service.

Mid-range

Conveniently located in downtown, the **Delta Chelsea Inn (** (416) 595-1975 TOLL-FREE (800) 268-9070 FAX (416) 585-4366, 33 Gerrard Street West, Toronto M5G 1Z4, is a very busy hotel with 1,600 modern rooms, some with kitchen facilities. It has three restaurants, two lounges, a supervised children's program, and a family pool area. If you're planning a cultural binge, the **Hotel Victoria (** (416) 363-1666 TOLL-FREE (800) 363-8228 FAX (416) 363-7327, at 56 Yonge Street, Toronto M5E 1G5, might be of particular interest as it's very close to both the O'Keefe and St. Lawrence Centres. There are 48 small, modern rooms with private bath, a dining room, bar, and an elegant reception area. It offers very good value.

The centrally situated **Comfort Hotel-Downtown (** (416) 924-1222 TOLL-FREE (800) 221-2222

FAX (416) 927-1369, 15 Charles Street East, Toronto M4Y 1S1, is a delightful place with friendly service and 100 spacious rooms. It has a restaurant, a piano bar, and a patio for warm summer days.

Fitness and sports fanatics will love the **Inn on the Park** ((416) 444-2561 TOLL-FREE IN CANADA (800) 268-6282 FAX (416) 446-3308, located northeast of downtown near the Ontario Science Centre at 1100 Eglinton Avenue East, Toronto M3C 1H8. It is beautifully positioned above a ravine and is set in 200 hectares (500 acres) of land. The rooms are not terribly special, but it has swimming pools, tennis courts, squash and racquetball courts, aerobics classes, and there's horseback

The **Strathcona Hotel** ((416) 363-3321 TOLL-FREE (800) 268-8304 FAX (416) 363-4679 at 60 York Street, Toronto M5J 1S8, is an older hotel, opposite the Royal York and offering excellent value. There are 200 rooms with private bath and television.

At the lower end of the mid-range, **Bond Place** ((416) 362-6061 TOLL-FREE (800) 268-9390 FAX (416) 360-6406, 65 Dundas Street East, Toronto M5B 2G8, is convenient to the Eaton Centre and has 285 smallish but well-appointed rooms with air conditioning and television.

Inexpensive
Hostelling International–Toronto ((416) 971-4440 TOLL-FREE (800) 668-4487 FAX (416) 971-4088, 76

riding in the grounds. There are supervised activities for children throughout the day.

About 16 km (10 miles) outside the city, **The Guild Inn** ((416) 261-3331, 201 Guildwood Parkway, Scarborough M1E 1P6, offers a beautiful and unusual setting. In 1932 this manorial building housed the art and craft workshops of the Guild of All Arts; its popularity brought about the need for guestrooms and attracted many famous visitors. Spread over the 36-hectare (90-acre) grounds are important architectural fragments salvaged from old Toronto buildings that were pulled down to make way for new developments. Included in the collection are the marble façade from the Imperial Bank of Canada, several columns, and a sign from Toronto's old firehall. The hotel has a good dining room, a verandah where you can take cocktails, an outdoor swimming pool, and a tennis court. Prices range from moderate to expensive.

Church Street, Toronto M5B 1Y7, is centrally located and open year-round. There are 88 beds, a kitchen, laundry facilities, family rooms, and city tours are offered. Reservations are advisable during the summer months. The nearest subway stations are King and Queen.

For lists of **bed and breakfast** accommodation you can contact Toronto Bed & Breakfast ((416) 690-1407 FAX (416) 690-5089, 21 Kingswood Road, Toronto M4E 3N4; Metropolitan Bed & Breakfast ((416) 964-2566 FAX (416) 960-9529, at 615 Mount Pleasant Road, Suite 269, Toronto M4S 3C5; or Bed and Breakfast Homes of Toronto (416) 363-6362, PO Box 46093, College Park Postal Station, Toronto M5B 2L8. You can also write the Federation of Ontario Bed and Breakfast Accommodation

Vestige of another era: When it was built in 1929, the Royal York Hotel was the tallest structure in the British Empire.

(FOBBA), PO Box 437, 253 College Street, Toronto M5T 1R5, which publishes the booklet *Ontario Bed and Breakfast*, or you can pick up the booklet at any provincial travel information center.

WHERE TO EAT

Dining in Toronto is a delightful experience because of the many ethnic groups that make up the population. In addition to the spots we've listed, you can cruise the various ethnic neighborhoods and invariably find good, moderately priced restaurants (see NEIGHBORHOODS, above).

Expensive
At the award-winning **Auberge du Pommier** ((416) 222-2220, 4150 Yonge Street, classic French dishes are simply and beautifully presented in a romantic, French-country-house setting. It's open Monday to Friday for lunch and for dinner daily. **Canoe Restaurant Bar & Grill** ((416) 364-0054, 66 Wellington Street West, has a Canadian-themed menu along with top-notch desserts and a top-floor view of the city. The smooth service and simple elegance of **Avalon** ((416) 979-9918, 270 Adelaide Street West, make it a Toronto favorite. Try the wood-grilled sardines, *foie gras* with caramelized quince and brioche, or the grilled yellowfin with potato gnocchi and roasted-tomato sauce. Lunch is served Wednesday to Friday and dinner Monday to Saturday.

Continental food with a French and nouvelle accent is served in candlelit elegance at **Scaramouche** ((416) 961-8011, 1 Benvenuto Place. The food is of the highest quality and the desserts are legendary. The restaurant offers a wonderful view of the city, and the atmosphere is formal; dinner is served Monday to Saturday. The quite chic **Centro Grill and Wine Bar** ((416) 483-2211, 2472 Yonge Street, offers fine Italian dining with a Californian flare. It's open for dinner Monday to Saturday. Eclectic North American cooking is to be had at **North 44°** ((416) 487-4897, 2537 Yonge Street, in attractive surroundings of burnished metal and stone. An exceptional wine list rounds out the inventive menu. A fixture on the Toronto restaurant scene for nearly 40 years, **Carman's** ((416) 924-8697, 26 Alexander Street, prepares steaks, seafood, veal, back ribs, lobster, and rack of lamb to perfection. Fireplaces and soft lighting lend an intimate atmosphere.

Tom Jones Steakhouse ((416) 366-6583, 17 Leader Lane, is an old inn decorated in warm Old English style where the steaks are simply and beautifully prepared and accompanied with steamed and sautéed vegetables. The menu also features seafood specialties and the emphasis is on traditional fare. It's open throughout the day Monday to Friday and for dinner only Saturday and Sunday. A piano bar upstairs serves cocktails.

The **Rosewater Supper Club** ((416) 214-5888, 19 Toronto Street, offers a reduced *prix-fixe* menu before 7 PM. Specialties here include scallops, roast rack of lamb, and Atlantic salmon. The large airy dining room is splendidly decorated and a blue teardrop lamp glows on each table.

Moderate
At **Toronto Life Café** ((416) 214-1852, 57 Front Street East, the food — from haute cuisine to Irish pub grub — focuses on rich, updated homestyle flavors. Music, from Gregorian chant to folk, puts everyone in the proper mood for the chef's latest. **Arlequin** ((416) 928-9521, 134 Avenue Road, serves French bistro food from *croques monsieurs* (like a grilled cheese sandwich) to *steak frites* (steak and french fries) as well as North African dishes such as chicken tagine, and at **Bistro 990** ((416) 921-9990, 990 Bay Street, there's more excellent French cuisine, simply prepared, and a good selection of wines. The place has the look of a grand wine cellar with arches and unusual pictures lining the walls; lunch is served Monday to Friday and dinner Monday to Saturday. There's a casual atmosphere at **Marketta** ((416) 924-4447, 138 Avenue Road, where the Mediterranean influenced fare includes spicy paella brimming with roasted chicken, homemade sausage, and scallops; lunch and dinner are served daily.

Bangkok Garden ((416) 977-6748, 18 Elm Street, is a very good and popular Thai restaurant, where the waiters are extremely helpful and the setting is somewhat exotic. The **Mata Hari Grill** ((416) 463-3663, at 39 Baldwin Street, near the Art Gallery of Ontario, serves authentic Malaysian cuisine such as seafood curries and rice noodles. It's open for lunch Tuesday to Friday, dinner Tuesday to Sunday.

Katsura (Westin Prince Hotel) ((416) 444-2511, 900 York Mills Road, is an excellent Japanese restaurant which serves traditional Japanese food, teppanyaki, and sushi, and **Edo** ((416) 481-1370, 359 Eglinton Avenue West, serving both sushi and other traditional Japanese fare such as tempura and teriyaki.

There's a wide variety of northern Indian dishes at **Cuisine of India** ((416) 229-0377, 5222 Yonge Street, including tandooris and excellent homemade breads. **Arani** ((416) 506-1037, 402 Spadina Avenue, serves the spicier southern Indian cuisine, with a Malaysian influence; lunch (buffet and à la carte) and dinner are served daily.

The **Fish House** ((416) 595-5051, 144 Front Street West, with its seafaring decor, has specials created from the daily catch as well as an oyster bar. It's open for lunch and dinner daily.

Inexpensive
On Queen Street West, **Tiger Lily's** ((416) 977-5499, at No. 257, is a noodle shop with dim sum fusion

brunch on Saturday and Sunday. This tiny and unpretentious storefront café is located on the edge of the theatre district.

In Mirvish Village, Ed Mirvish's restaurant **Ed's Warehouse** ((416) 593-6676, 270 King Street West, serves straightforward food such as roast beef and steak in kitschy and fun surroundings. It is the only one of Ed's eateries to insist (surprisingly) on jacket and tie. Other Ed Mirvish restaurants in the street include **Ed's Chinese**, **Ed's Italian** and **Ed's Seafood**, and all are good value.

For traditional deli fare consult "Canada's Cornbeef King," **Shopsy's** ((416) 365-5333, 33 Yonge Street. Opened in 1922 as an ice cream shop by the Shopsowitz family, this Toronto institution has a

The handsome **Indian Rice Factory** ((416) 961-3472, at 414 Dupont Street, offers a small but excellent menu which includes a selection of vegetarian dishes. The **Kensington Kitchen** ((416) 961-3404, at 124 Harbord Street, serves Middle Eastern food with particularly good appetizers and pastries, and there's Moroccan cuisine served in exotic surroundings at the **Sultan's Tent** ((416) 961-0601, in Yorkville at 1280 Bay Street, with live music and belly dancing.

HOW TO GET THERE

Toronto's Lester B. Pearson International Airport, 27 km (17 miles) from downtown, handles both

voluminous menu including all the classics plus sandwiches such as the Royal Canadian Mounted Beef with sautéed peppers, Bermuda onions, and mushrooms with melted mozzarella and cheddar cheese. Breakfast is served all day. It's open daily with take-out also available.

Sai Woo ((416) 977-4988, at 130 Dundas Street West, is one of the city's oldest and best-known Chinese restaurants, serving good Cantonese food in busy, basic surroundings. Dim sum is served at lunchtime on weekdays, and twice a year they hold banquets where as many as 15 courses may be served. For authentic Japanese dining, try the **Masa Dining Lounge** ((416) 977-9519, 205 Richmond Street West, an attractive restaurant where you'll find sushi and vegetarian dishes on the menu, or **Sasaya** ((416) 487-3508, at 257 Eglinton Avenue West, which has sushi and tempura bars in addition to an extensive traditional menu.

foreign and domestic flights. The drive takes about 20 to 45 minutes, longer in rush hour. Pacific Western ((416) 564-6333 operates buses to three subway stops each hour from 8 AM to 11:30 PM. The service to and from selected downtown hotels operates every 20 minutes.

VIA Rail ((416) 366-8411 operates intercity trains from Toronto Union Station (which is also the hub of the GO Train network). VIA trains from Toronto run to Montréal, Ottawa, Niagara Falls, Windsor, Sarnia, and Vancouver, and points in between. VIA Rail and **Amtrak** TOLL-FREE (800) 872-7245 jointly operate trains from Union Station to New York and to Chicago.

The **Greyhound** terminal ((416) 367-8747 TOLL-FREE (800) 231-2222 is at 610 Bay Street, north of

One of Toronto's trendy downtown bars, Masquerade, in BCE Place.

Dundas Street, near Eaton Centre. Several other companies offer a variety of bus routes, arriving and departing from the Bay Street terminal.

If you are driving from Detroit/Windsor in the west or Montréal in the east you will want Route 401. From Niagara Falls you will take the Queen Elizabeth Way, which turns into the Gardiner Expressway as it enters Toronto.

THE GOLDEN HORSESHOE

"The Golden Horseshoe," the sliver of land that arcs around from Oshawa, east of Toronto, to Niagara Falls, is so called because in addition to being horseshoe-shaped it is one of the wealthiest regions in the country. A large proportion of Canada's manufacturing industry is concentrated here, especially in and around the steelmaking city of Hamilton.

If Hamilton is Canada's Pittsburgh, the Niagara peninsula is its Napa Valley: almost 80% of Canada's wine grapes are grown here, and at last count there were 15 wineries in the area. There is also history among the vines, for it was here that Laura Secord snuck away from the American-held village of Queenston and set out on her 30-km (19-mile) hike through the bush to warn the British of American plans for a surprise attack. Her home still stands in Queenston, as does a monument to General Isaac Brock, who died leading the first counterattack against the Americans in the War of 1812.

But however much blood and wine may have flowed here, it's still the water that brings the tourists: Niagara Falls and Niagara-on-the-Lake, two of the most beautiful spots on earth.

St. Catharines

St. Catharines is in the heart of Ontario's wine-producing and fruit-growing region, and nowhere is this more evident than in the outdoor **Farmer's Market** near City Hall, where you see the abundance of the local produce. It's a popular rest place for visitors to the many festivals that the area has to offer.

The 42-km (26-mile) **Welland Canal** connects Lake Ontario to the much higher Lake Erie through a series of eight locks. From nearby Port Weller it cuts through to Port Colborne on Lake Erie, allowing oceangoing ships to navigate the Great Lakes. The original canal was built in St. Catharines and at **Port Dalhousie** you can see sections of the first three canals built in 1829, 1845, and 1887, where some of the locks, warehouses and other nineteenth-century structures still stand. The present Welland Canal was completed in 1933, and there's a smart new **Welland Canal Viewing Complex** at Lock 3 where you can watch the oceangoing giants pass through the locks.

For lodging, there's the **Ramada Parkway Inn** ((905) 688-2324 FAX (905) 684-6432, 327 Ontario Street, St. Catharines L2R 5L3. Conveniently situated in downtown, it has 125 comfortable rooms and its facilities include an indoor pool and a bowling alley. Prices are within the mid-range category. The **Holiday Inn** ((905) 934-8000 TOLL-FREE (800) HOLIDAY FAX (905) 934-9117, at 2 North Service Road, St. Catharines L2N 4G9, has 140 rooms with television, private bath and facilities which include indoor and outdoor swimming pools. Both of these hotels are in the mid-range category.

Lists of **bed and breakfast** accommodation are available through Bed and Breakfast Accommodations — St. Catharines and Niagara Region ((905) 937-2422 FAX (905) 935-0059 E-MAIL bbassoc @chardonnay.niagara.com, 28 Cartier Drive, St. Catharines L2M 2E7.

For a delightful meal, try the **Wellington Court** ((905) 682-5518, 11 Wellington Street, located downtown in a flowered-bedecked Edwardian town house. Fish and pasta are featured items along with thoughtfully prepared meat dishes often accompanied by fruit chutneys.

HAMILTON

Hamilton, population 650,000, sits in the western corner of Lake Ontario on a landlocked harbor spanned at the lakeside by a sandbar, cut through to allow ships into the port. Across this sandbar sweeps the Burlington Skyway, a section of the Queen Elizabeth Way that links Toronto with Niagara Falls. It is Canada's steel-producing capital and its heavy industry has brought Hamilton more than its fair share of pollution. It's not all a landscape of satanic mills, however. There are some renovated old buildings and some impressive new ones, the result of new development schemes and urban renewal projects. One such development, Hamilton Place, is a large new arts center that has helped put Hamilton on the cultural map.

For information about Hamilton contact the **Greater Hamilton Visitor and Convention Services** ((905) 546-4222 TOLL-FREE (800) 263-8590 FAX (905) 546-4107, 1 James Street, Third Floor, Hamilton L8P 4R5.

Like Toronto's Yorkville, **Hess Village** at Hess and George streets is a very pleasant area of renovated clapboard buildings that now house shops, restaurants, and cafés. It is a nice place for a stroll. There is plenty of activity on nearby York Boulevard where the local produce is displayed in the huge and bustling indoor **Farmer's Market** on Tuesdays, Thursdays, Fridays, and Saturdays. A striking modern building houses the **Art Gallery** ((905) 527-6610 FAX (905) 577-6940, at 123 King Street West. The gallery has a large

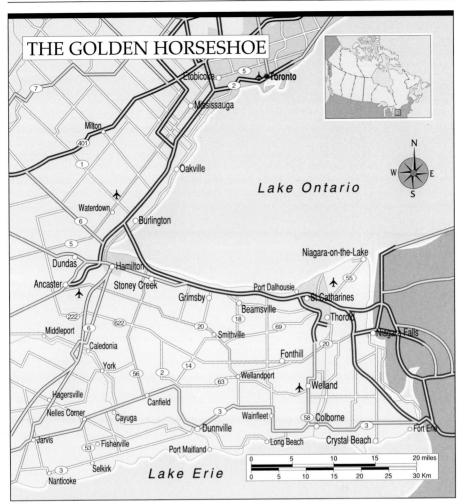

THE GOLDEN HORSESHOE

Lake Ontario

Lake Erie

collection of twentieth-century Canadian and American art. It is open Tuesday to Sunday, closed on Mondays and holidays, and an admission fee is charged.

Just outside the town at Dundern Park on a hill stands **Dundern Castle** ((905) 546-2872, on York Boulevard, an impressive 35-room white stone mansion with a dignified columned portico overlooking the bay. It was built in the 1830s by Sir Allan Napier MacNab, prime minister of the United Provinces of Canada from 1854 to 1856. It has been furnished in the style of the 1850s and restored to its former splendor. Throughout the year there are special exhibitions here, and there's a military museum in the grounds of the castle. It's open daily June to September, closed Mondays the rest of the year. An admission fee is charged.

A little further out of town at Routes 2 and 6, the **Royal Botanical Gardens** ((905) 527-1158 FAX (905) 577-0375, cover 20,243 hectares (50,000

acres) of land along the lakeside. The greater part of this area is given over to natural parkland threaded with trails, but among the most stunning sights are the Rock Garden, the Rose Garden, and the gorgeous Lilac Garden in the Arboretum. It's open daily from dawn to dusk, and an admission fee is charged.

About 32 km (20 miles) northwest of Hamilton off Highway 8 is the **African Lion Safari** ((519) 623-2620. You can take a safari tram through the various reserves where the animals roam free. Alternatively you can drive your own car through the park, bearing in mind that the baboons in the Monkey Jungle enclosure will climb all over it and remove anything they can. Convertibles are not allowed, for obvious reasons. There are many side attractions, including a scenic railway, a cruise, and a playground. It's open daily early April through October; an admission fee is charged.

For lodging, there is the **Sheraton Hamilton** ((905) 529-5515 FAX (905) 529-8266, centrally located downtown at 116 King Street West, Hamilton L8P 4V3, has 300 modern rooms which are nicely furnished and well-equipped. Guests have use of an indoor pool with an attractive poolside area. The hotel has two restaurants. There's a sense of grandeur about the **Royal Connaught Howard Johnson Plaza Hotel** ((905) 546-8111 TOLL-FREE (800) 446-4656 FAX (905) 546-8118, 112 King Street East, Hamilton L8N 1A8, which first opened its doors in 1904. The entrance hall is lavishly decorated with chandeliers and columns, and the hotel's rooms all have luxuriously large bathrooms. There are two restaurants and an indoor swimming pool. Both of these hotels are in the mid-range category.

A comprehensive guide to **bed and breakfast** establishments, including those in Hamilton, is published by the Federation of Ontario Bed and Breakfast Accommodation ((416) 964-2566, PO Box 437, 253 College Street, Toronto M5T 1R5.

Shakespeare's Steak House ((905) 528-0689, at 181 Main Street East, is decorated, as you'd expect, in Olde English style; it serves quite decent steaks at prices ranging from inexpensive to moderate. It's open Monday to Friday for lunch and dinner, and for dinner only on Saturdays.

NIAGARA-ON-THE-LAKE

Situated where the Niagara River meets Lake Ontario, delightful Niagara-on-the-Lake is one of North America's best-preserved nineteenth-century towns. Settled by Loyalists in the late eighteenth century, Niagara-on-the-Lake, then known

as Newark, became the first capital of Upper Canada in 1792. In 1813 it was completely destroyed by the Americans, was quickly rebuilt, and seems to have changed very little since. Its attractive situation and pretty tree-shaded streets lined with clapboard and brick houses make it a delightful stopping point during a trip to Niagara Falls.

For information about Niagara-on-the-Lake contact the **Niagara-on-the-Lake Chamber of Commerce** ((905) 468-4263, 153 King Street, PO Box 1043, Niagara-on-the-Lake L0S 1J0.

What to See and Do
Queen Street is the town's focal point, and the only part of it that gets busy. It is one chain wide (22 yards, or around 20 meters) and its lovely old buildings house bakeries, tea shops, restaurants, and shops selling all manner of goods such as crafts, jams, and confectionery. The splendid old **Niagara Apothecary Shop** ((905) 468-3845 dates from 1866 and maintains its original walnut counters, beautifully labeled drawers, and old jars. Its medications are no longer dispensed, as the place is only a museum now, and looking at such remedies as "Dragon's Blood" or "Pink Pills for Pale People" you can't help but feel that it's probably just as well.

The town's main attraction is the annual **Shaw Festival** ((905) 468-2172 TOLL-FREE (800) 511-7429 FAX (905) 468-3804 E-MAIL bxoffice@shawfest.com, PO Box 774, Niagara-on-the-Lake L0S 1J0, which draws theater-goers from far and wide and presents top-name actors in a season of plays by George Bernard Shaw and his contemporaries.

There are three theaters in the town, the main one being the **Festival Theatre**, a modern brick and glass structure with an attractive interior, at Queen's Parade and Wellington Street. The festival is held from April to October with performances daily except on Mondays. Ticket prices range from $15 for lunchtime one-acts to $65 for the best weekend seats.

South on Niagara Parkway on River Road is the **Fort George Historic Site** ((905) 468-4257. Built between 1797 and 1799, the Fort was a major British post in the War of 1812. It was destroyed by the Americans in 1813, rebuilt in 1815, and later abandoned. It was restored in the 1930s, so that you can now visit the officers' quarters, the soldiers' barracks, the forge, and the powder magazine, and watch a display by the Fort George Fife and Drum Corps. The fort is open daily from April to November; an admission fee is charged. To find out some more of Niagara's history you could visit the **Niagara Historical Society Museum** ((905) 468-3912 at 43 Castlereagh Street at Davy, one of the oldest and largest museums of its kind in Canada. It's open daily March to December, weekends only in January and February; an admission fee is charged.

Near Niagara-on-the-Lake are several wineries which offer tasting tours, such as the Hillebrand Estates Winery, an attractive place which would not look out of place in the French countryside (see WINE TASTING AND TOURS under SPECIAL INTERESTS, page 61, in YOUR CHOICE).

Where to Stay

Niagara-on-the-Lake is a small town and its hostelries can fill up in the summer, so if you plan your visit at this time of year try to book well in advance.

One of the foremost hotels is the **Prince of Wales** ((905) 468-3246 TOLL-FREE (800) 263-2452 FAX (905) 468-1310 or (905) 468-5521, PO Box 46, 6 Picton Street, Niagara-on-the-Lake L0S 1J0, a beautiful old inn with 100 rooms — including a royal suite which was once actually graced by royalty — all decorated with antique furniture and with large bathrooms. It combines Old World charm with a full range of facilities, including an indoor pool, tennis court, restaurants, and bars. Prices are mid-range to expensive. The **Pillar & Post Inn** ((905) 468-2123 TOLL-FREE (800) 361-6788 FAX (905) 468-3551, PO Box 1011, 48 John Street, Niagara-on-the-Lake L0S 1J0, is another lovely hotel, with 130 rooms furnished in early colonial style, combining old-fashioned elegance with modern amenities. It has very pleasant indoor and outdoor pools. It, too, is priced in the moderate to expensive range. In contrast, the **Gate House Hotel** ((905) 468-3263 FAX (905) 468-7400, PO Box 1364, 142 Queen Street, Niagara-on-the-Lake L0S 1J0, has 10 rooms decorated in chic, modern Milanese

style. Prices are mid-range to expensive. One of the town's best hotels, the **Oban Inn** ((905) 468-2165, PO Box 94, 160 Front Street, Niagara-on-the-Lake L0S 1J0, is a delightful early eighteenth-century building overlooking the lake. It has beautiful gardens, 23 comfortable rooms with antique furniture, a piano bar, a good restaurant, and its very own ghost, so they say. Prices are moderate to expensive.

The **White Oaks Inn & Racquet Club** ((905) 688-2550 TOLL-FREE (800) 263-5766 FAX (905) 688-2220, just outside the town at 253 Taylor Road, Rural Route 4, Niagara-on-the-Lake L0S 1J0, has 90 smart and well-equipped rooms with lots of nice touches, but the real attraction lies in

amenities such as its tennis courts (four outdoor and eight indoor), squash and racquetball courts, child-care facilities, cafés, and a restaurant. To make yourself feel really good, you can also treat yourself to a session on the sun bed or to a massage.

For details of **bed and breakfast** accommodation you can write to or ring the Niagara-on-the-Lake Bed and Breakfast Association ((905) 468-0123 E-MAIL admin@bba.notl.on.ca, or the Federation of Ontario Bed and Breakfast Accommodation ((416) 964-2566, PO Box 437, 253 College Street, Toronto M5T 1R5.

Where to Eat

There are quite a few good restaurants in the town and it's generally a much better place for dining than Niagara Falls. The **Oban Inn** ((905) 468-2165, 160 Front Street, has a reputation for fine dining in tasteful surroundings and is possibly the best restaurant in the area. Traditional English dishes feature on the menu, prices are moderate, and lunch and dinner are served in the cozy pub or the formal dining room. There's fine European cuisine in an elegant setting at the **Prince of Wales Hotel** ((905) 468-3246, 6 Picton Street. Royals, the

Niagara-on-the-Lake — OPPOSITE: A sailboat plies Lake Ontario. ABOVE: The Inniskillen Winery.

elegant main dining room, is open daily for lunch and dinner, and prices are moderate; the more casual Queen's Royal Lounge serves inexpensive soups and sandwiches and is a pleasant place for cocktails or afternoon tea. For a more raucous dining experience, **The Buttery** ((905) 468-2564, at 19 Queen Street holds weekend Henry VIII banquets where costumed wenches serve old English food and minstrels supply entertainment. It's open daily and prices are moderate.

The Angel ((905) 468-3411, at 224 Regent Street, The Old Market Square, serves English pub food and 26 varieties of beers. The dining room serves continental food and prices are inexpensive to moderate. It's open daily from lunchtime through the evening. Classic Italian food is served in chic, modern surroundings at **Restaurant Giardino** ((905) 468-3263, in the Gate House Hotel, 142 Queen Street. Prices are inexpensive to moderate. **Fans Court** ((905) 468-4511, at 135 Queen Street, is a pleasant spot where you can taste some very good inexpensively priced Cantonese and Sichuan food.

NIAGARA FALLS

Midway between Lake Erie and Lake Ontario, the Niagara River hurtles over a 61-m (200-ft) cliff at a rate of 130 million liters or 34 million gallons each minute, thus creating one of the greatest wonders of the world. Divided by a small island, the Canadian Horseshoe Falls are 793 m (2,600 ft) wide and the American Falls much less wide at 305 m (1,000 ft). At times over 75% of the water is diverted by canals to power stations on both the American and Canadian sides, resulting in a variation of the water volume depending on time of day and year. It is said that the erosion caused by the plunging water will eventually flatten the Falls, but it is estimated that this will take about 25,000 years to happen.

Since the seventeenth century, people have traveled huge distances to see the falls, and today an average of 12 million people come every year to wonder at the spectacle. No one quite knows why it has become a tradition for honeymooning couples to come here, but one legend has it that the idea caught on after Napoleon's brother brought his new bride here in 1804, riding all the way from New Orleans in a coach. Anyway, it's everything it's cracked up to be — and more. One can only echo Rupert Brooke's feelings on seeing the falls: "I was so impressed by Niagara. I had hoped not to be, but I horribly was." So is everyone, it seems.

General Information

For information the falls and surrounding area, contact the **Niagara Falls Canada Visitor and Convention Bureau** ((905) 356-6061, 5433 Victoria Avenue, Niagara Falls L2G 3L1, or the **Niagara Parks Commission** ((905) 356-2241 or (905) 354-6266, 7400 Porage Road South, Niagara Falls L2E 6T2. There are drop-in information centers in summer at Table Rock, Maid of the Mist Plaza, Rapids View Parking Lot, and Niagara-on-the-Lake.

What to See and Do

There are dozens of ways to enjoy the Falls, but however you look at them, they are hopelessly spectacular. Best of all are the boat trips on the *Maid of the Mist* ((905) 358-0311, which afford a tremendously exciting, if damp, experience. Kitted out in blue hooded raincoats, you are taken to the base of the American Falls, as close as you can get to its deafening might. The boarding dock is at the Maid of the Mist Plaza elevator at the foot of Clifton Hill. Trips run from April 4 to October 24 leaving approximately every 15 minutes starting at 10 AM with closing time depending on the season; a fare is charged (see INTO THE MIST, page 13, in TOP SPOTS). The **Niagara River Boat Company** ((416) 468-4219/5154 runs tours, dances, and dinners aboard an old-fashioned cruise ship called the *Senator* during May to October. For an aerial view, there are three towers, the best being the **Skylon** at 5200 Robinson Street ((905) 356-2651, open daily. Exterior elevators carry you to the top where there's a revolving dining room, and an indoor and outdoor viewing deck.

The downtown area of **Clifton Hill**, called "the street of fun at the falls," is where visitors escape the stress of dealing with too much Nature. Attractions such as The House of Frankenstein, The Haunted House, and Ripley's Believe It Or Not are strung out along the strip along with souvenir shops, bars, and fast food joints.

The area's newest attraction is the sparkling **Casino Niagara** TOLL-FREE (888) WIN-FALL, 5705 Falls Avenue. It has an 8,900-sq-m (96,000-sq-ft) gaming area bursting with 3,000 slot machines and over 100 gaming tables. Several restaurants and seven bars are found on the premises, so you won't have to go far to drown your sorrows. The casino is open 24 hours a day, seven days a week, year-round.

The **North Niagara Parkway** stretches between the falls to Niagara-on-the-Lake, a distance of 26 km (16 miles) following the river on its way to Lake Ontario. With its parks, gardens and historic buildings and sites, it makes a delightful drive or walk. Along the way you'll find the **Great Gorge Adventure** ((905) 354-5711 which operates daily from mid-May to Labor Day, and from Labor Day to mid-October when the weather permits. An

Neon signs wink at strollers along Clifton Hill in downtown Niagara Falls. In the background: the Falls.

elevator takes you to the bottom of the gorge for a close view of the rapids in violent action. A fare is charged. A little further along, **Niagara Spanish Aero Car** ((905) 356-2241 FAX (905) 354-6041 offers cable trips over the Whirlpool Rapids for some dramatic views of the swirling water below. The fare is charged for the ride. At **Niagara Glen**, trails lead to the river's edge and the forest offers a lovely and peaceful retreat for the weary traveler. Nearby the **Niagara Parks Commission School of Horticulture** has acres of beautiful gardens filled with shrubs and flowers maintained by students of the school. It's open daily in the summer months from dawn until dusk. A little further north is **Queenston Heights**, the place where in 1812 the British finally defeated the American attempt to take Queenston. It's now a peaceful park and a good spot for a picnic.

Where to Stay

The Falls can easily be seen as part of a day trip from Toronto. If you do plan to spend the night, you should consider staying at nearby Niagara-on-the-Lake (see NIAGARA-ON-THE-LAKE, page 122). There are, however, accommodation signs screaming at you everywhere around Niagara Falls. It's quite difficult to categorize accommodation in terms of price as there's such a great fluctuation according to the time of year, added to which prices seem to change according to daily demand. It really is worth bargaining for a drop in price. For help in finding accommodation you can ring the Niagara Falls, Canada Visitor & Convention Bureau (see GENERAL INFORMATION, above).

MID-RANGE TO EXPENSIVE

The **Skyline Foxhead** ((905) 374-4444 TOLL-FREE (800) 263-7135 FAX (905) 371-0157, 5875 Falls Avenue, Niagara Falls L2E 6W7, has 395 well-equipped rooms, some with balconies and views of the falls. It is connected to Casino Niagara as well as the Hard Rock Café via a bizarre multi-story lobby built to resemble a London square with a miniature Niagara Falls running through it. There are very good facilities, with a rooftop swimming pool, and a good restaurant. Next door, the **Skyline Brock** ((905) 374-4444 TOLL-FREE (800) 263-7135 FAX (905) 358-0443, 5685 Falls Avenue, Niagara Falls L2E 6W7, is a less expensive alternative to the Foxhead and possibly the most popular place to stay in town. It has been in business since 1929 and there's some elegance about it. About three-quarters of the 210 rooms look towards the falls and there's a restaurant with great views on the tenth floor. Prices vary between mid-range and the low end of the expensive range. Less expensive rooms come with an unfortunate view of the parking lot. From just outside the two Skyline hotels a pleasant garden walk leads down to the falls.

The **Old Stone Inn** ((905) 357-1234 TOLL-FREE (800) 263-6208 FAX (905) 357-9299, at 5425 Robinson Street, Niagara Falls L2G 7L6, has 114 spacious, modern rooms, although the building itself is built to look like an old-fashioned inn. The emphasis is on couples at the **Honeymoon City Motel** ((905) 357-4330 TOLL-FREE (800) 668-8840 FAX (905) 357-0423, 4943 Clifton Hill, Niagara Falls L2G 3N5, where there are 80 units, some of which are honeymoon suites with special decoration. All rooms have private bath and television, and a few have balconies.

INEXPENSIVE

The **Best Western Fallsview Your Host Motor Hotel** ((905) 356-0551 TOLL-FREE (800) 263-2580, 5551 Murray Street, Niagara Falls L2G 2J4, is quite centrally located with 233 modern rooms, some of which are suites catering for the honeymoon market with round beds and large baths. Ameni-

ties include an indoor swimming pool and a restaurant and bar.

The **Ameri-Cana** ((905) 356-8444 TOLL-FREE (800) 263-3508 FAX (905) 356-8576 at 8444 Lundy's Lane, Niagara Falls L2H 1H4, offers motel accommodation set in large grounds with tennis courts and indoor and outdoor swimming pools. It has 90 well-equipped rooms, some of which are honeymoon suites. With self-catering facilities, it's an appealing option for families.

For information on **bed and breakfast** accommodation, contact the Federation of Ontario Bed and Breakfast Accommodation ((416) 964-2566, PO Box 437, 253 College Street, Toronto M5T 1R5.

Where to Eat

The moderately priced **Skylon Tower** ((905) 356-2651 TOLL-FREE (800) 927-2251, 5200 Robinson Street, has another revolving restaurant — the Summit Suite, which is open for breakfast, lunch, and dinner. There's a happy country atmosphere and international cuisine at **The Old Stone Inn** ((416) 357-1234, 5425 Robinson Street, and you'll find good Italian food among columns and friezes at **Casa d'Oro Dining Lounge** ((905) 356-5646, 5875 Victoria Avenue.

The Niagara Parkway Commission owns the **Victoria Park Cafeteria and Dining Room** ((416) 356-2217, situated near the falls, where you can dine inexpensively inside or on an outdoor terrace. The Commission also runs **Queenston Heights** ((905) 262-4274, on Niagara Parkway North, again offering indoor or outdoor dining, beautifully located with some great views. **Betty's Restaurant** ((905) 295-4436, 8921 Sodom Road, is a very low-budget eatery where generously

Visitors enjoy the walkway above the American Falls in Niagara Falls, USA.

portioned scallops, chicken, and burgers are served all through the day.

How to Get There

The major road linking all the towns and cities of the Golden Horseshoe, from Toronto to Niagara Falls, is the Queen Elizabeth Way. The principal American highway leading to the vicinity of the falls, from both the southwest and the southeast, is Interstate-90. There is an hourly bus service between Toronto and Niagara Falls, and a bus twice daily between the falls and the Prince of Wales Hotel in Niagara-on-the-Lake. The station, however, is quite a hike from the tourist area. There is also a regular shuttle from nearby Buffalo International Airport to Niagara.

VIA Rail TOLL-FREE (888) 842-7733 has five trains a day from Toronto to Niagara Falls, while **Amtrak** TOLL-FREE (800) 872-7245 has frequent service from various American cities.

SOUTHERN ONTARIO

Southern Ontario, the "land between the lakes," consists of miles and miles of gently rolling farmland laced with rivers and streams and sprinkled with charming towns and villages. Thanks to its rich alluvial soil and temperate climate, the area produces an abundance of fruit and vegetables. This means that the larger towns are genuine market towns, where you can find a mouth-watering selection of local produce. Almost anywhere you go you can find a welcoming array of inns and taverns on the English model.

Speaking of the English model, fruit and vegetables are not the only things cultivated here; so is Englishness itself. The region is a cultural as well as an agricultural seedbed, where the English way of life that was first planted in the eighteenth century has blossomed in the form of communities called London, Windsor, Cambridge, Essex, Waterloo, Woodstock, Blenheim, and Stratford — where the summer-long Shakespeare Festival provides a unique celebration of the Bard's work.

BACKGROUND

The Hurons were the first to appreciate the agricultural potential of this fertile region, but their efforts at farming the land were constantly interrupted by the belligerent, rampaging Iroquois. It wasn't until after the Anglo-French treaty in 1763 that settlers moved into the area, and not until after the American Revolution, when the Loyalists began arriving, that it acquired its distinctly British character. The first farming-based settlement was at Windsor; others followed at London and Stratford. At about the same time Germans settled in the area, as did many Mennonites from Pennsylvania whose resolute pacifism during the American Revolution had made them unpopular with their American neighbors.

Today the German and Mennonite presence is still very marked, but the peninsula as a whole remains what it was two centuries ago: still very pretty to look at, still very British in outlook.

For information about southern Ontario communities, contact **Ontario Travel** ((416) 314-0944 TOLL-FREE (800) ONTARIO, Queen's Park, Toronto M7A 2E5.

STRATFORD

Set in farmlands, this attractive town with a population of 26,000 has many things in common with the famous English town of the same name, and these similarities are far from accidental. Back in 1830 proprietor William Sargint called his inn the Shakespeare Inn, which prompted the community to change its name to Stratford and its river's name to Avon. The most important link, however, was forged in 1953, with the inauguration of the world-famous Shakespeare Festival that is held here each summer and attracts a large international audience.

The **Shakespeare Festival** was the dream of local journalist Tom Patterson, a dream that was realized with the help of Sir Tyrone Guthrie in 1953 when the first festival productions were staged inside a tent. The idea took off, an award-winning theater was built, and the festival has grown in size, popularity and reputation; it now attracts an audience of around 500,000. The season usually extends from June to October, and while the plays performed are predominantly Shakespearean, other classic and contemporary works also feature. International stars appear in the highly rated productions. There are three theaters in the town — the Festival Theatre at 55 Queen Street, the Avon Theatre at 99 Downie Street, and the Tom Patterson Theatre on Lakeside Drive. For information on the festival write to or call the Stratford Festival ((519) 273-1600 TOLL-FREE (800) 567-1600 FAX (519) 271-2734 E-MAIL stratford-festival.com.ca, PO Box 520, Stratford N5A 6V2. Tickets go on sale in early February, and the season runs from early May to mid-November, with shows daily except Monday.

The center of the festival is the **Festival Theatre**, which was built in the late 1950s, innovatively designed along the lines of the Elizabethan stage and reminiscent of the tent in which the plays were originally performed. The nearby **Queen's Park** provides a beautiful setting, with lawns stretching down to the riverside. Around here the river is dammed to form Victoria Lake, which with its swans and ducks furthers the resemblance to

The Shakespeare Garden in Queen's Park, Stratford, features a bust of the bard RIGHT as well as green lawns and swan ponds OVERLEAF.

England's Stratford. There are many pleasant walks and spots for picnicking. Footpaths lead you beyond the dam through an old-fashioned gate into the delightful **Shakespeare Garden**, an English-style garden complete with a bust of the bard.

In an old building near Confederation Park is **The Gallery (** (519) 271-5271, at 54 Romeo Street North, where there are often temporary exhibitions of international modern painting and sculpture, plus lectures and films. There are three galleries, so there's always a choice of exhibitions. It's open daily in the summer and closed on Mondays during the rest of the year. An admission fee is charged.

Where to Stay and Eat

One of the oldest hotels in Stratford is the **Queen's Inn at Stratford (** (519) 271-1400 TOLL-FREE (800) 461-6450 FAX (519) 271-7373, at 161 Ontario Street, Stratford N5A 3H3, which is conveniently central and handy for all three theaters. It has 30 attractive, air-conditioned rooms all with private bath, and there are two restaurants. The prices vary from mid-range to expensive. The moderately priced **Albert Place–Twenty Three (** (519) 273-5800 FAX (519) 273-5008, 23 Albert Street, Stratford N5A 3K2, has 35 spacious, modern rooms with television and air-conditioning, and some mini-suites are available.

A little closer to town is the **Noretta Motel (** (519) 271-6110 FAX (519) 273-1625 at 691 Ontario Street, Stratford N5A 3J6, which has 15 air-conditioned units.

For **bed and breakfast** accommodations, contact the Federation of Ontario Bed and Breakfast Accommodation **(** (416) 964-2566, PO Box 437, 253 College Street, Toronto M5T 1R5.

For dinner, the place to go has to be the **Church Restaurant and Belfry (** (519) 273-3424, at Brunswick and Waterloo streets, but if you're planning to dine here during the festival then reservations really do need to be made at the same time you book your theater tickets, i.e. up to six months in advance. Fine French food is served in this nineteenth-century converted church, which retains its altar, stained glass, and original woodwork. The Belfry grill room and bar is upstairs for a less expensive menu, snacks, and drinks. Prices range from moderate to expensive.

Rundles ((519) 271-6442, at 9 Coburg Street, is another excellent restaurant, which is beautifully located by Victoria Lake. Its interior is modern and adorned with contemporary paintings and sculptures, the food is mouth-watering and imaginative, and the three-course *table d'hôte* is recommended. They also prepare delicious packed lunches for festival-goers. The restaurant's opening hours adapt to the theater program, but usually it is open for lunch and dinner Wednesday to

Saturday, for lunch only on Sunday, and is closed during the winter. Prices, again, vary from moderate to expensive.

Local produce features largely on the menu at **The Old Prune (** (519) 271-5052, located in an older building at 151 Albert Street. The food is light, fresh, and delicious; for dinner there is an expensive *prix-fixe* menu, but there is quite a wide choice.

LONDON

Situated at the fork of the River Thames (pronounced as it is spelled), London is the area's industrial center, and the province's fourth largest metropolitan area. However, this is not immediately obvious thanks to the town's attractive old houses, tree-lined streets and squares, and exceptional amount of greenery — a result of an extensive tree-planting scheme that started a hundred years ago and is still in progress.

Information and maps for London and the region are available through the **Southwestern Ontario Travel Association (** (519) 652-1391 TOLL-FREE (800) 661-6804 FAX (519) 652-0533, 4023 Meadowbrook Drive, Suite 112, London N6L 1E7.

What to See and Do

Overlooking the river is the **London Regional Art Museum (** (519) 672-4580, 421 Ridout Street North, a striking modern building designed by Raymond Moriyama. This unusual structure is a series of interlocking barrel vaults that form large and airy galleries with domed skylights providing natural lighting. The gallery holds changing exhibitions of national and international work, and has its own large collection of Canadian art. It is open Tuesday to Sunday from noon to 5 PM; admission is free.

Children have a wonderful time at the **London Regional Children's Museum (** (519) 434-5726 FAX (519) 434-1443, at 21 Wharncliffe Road South, where they are encouraged to explore, participate, and play. They can dress up in costumes or uniforms and "be" a firefighter, a doctor, or a builder in the gallery called "The Street Where You Live." They can see what life was like in the past, explore the Computer Hall, or look into outer space. The museum is open Monday to Saturday and Sunday afternoons, year-round, and an admission fee is charged.

For a glimpse of what life was like before the settlers arrived in southwestern Ontario, visit the **London Museum of Archaeology (** (519) 473-1360, at 1600 Attawandaron Road, where there are displays on the area's prehistory as well as a reconstructed Attawandaron Village. It is open daily May to November from 10 AM to 5 PM; an admission fee is charged. About 32 km (20 miles) southwest of the city is the **Ska-Nah-Doht Village**, a recreation of a prehistoric Iroquois village with exhibits and audiovisual presentations that show all aspects of everyday life. It's in the Longwoods Road Conservation area off Route 2 and is open daily.

Life in a pioneer community is recreated at the **Fanshawe Pioneer Village** in Fanshawe Park ((519) 451-2800, 14 km (nine miles) northeast of the city. This reconstructed village consists of 24 buildings, where you can watch demonstrations of pioneer crafts and take a ride in a wagon. It's open daily from early May to Labor Day. The park itself covers 600 hectares (1,500 acres) of land, with a large lake and a pool where you can swim, fish, canoe, windsurf, and sail. It's open all year except for winter weekends.

Where to Stay and Eat

The best accommodation is probably the **Idlewyld Inn** ((519) 433-2891, at 36 Grand Avenue, London N6C 1K8, a splendid 1878 mansion with tall windows, ornate woodwork, and a grand central staircase. It has 25 guestrooms, each uniquely decorated and with a happy combination of antique furnishings and modern facilities. The **Delta London Armouries Hotel** ((519) 679-6111 TOLL-FREE (800) 668-9999 FAX (519) 679-3957, 325 Dundas Street, London N6B 1T9, provides quite luxurious accommodation in an unusual setting. A thick-walled and turreted armory forms the main floor of the building, above which rises a glass tower. Rooms are attractively furnished, all have private bath and television, and guests can enjoy the indoor swimming pool.

For lists of **bed and breakfast** accommodations contact the London and Area Bed & Breakfast

Association ((519) 673-6797, 2 Normandy Gardens, London N6H 4A9.

For first-rate seafood go to **Anthony's** ((519) 679-0960, 434 Richmond Street, where the atmosphere is warm and friendly, the food is beautifully presented, and the desserts are homemade. It's open for lunch from Monday to Friday, for dinner Monday to Thursday, and prices range from moderate to inexpensive.

For continental cuisine there's the **Wonderland Riverview Dining Room** ((519) 471-4662, 284 Wonderland Road South, which is a popular spot with an outdoor terrace and a dance floor that overlooks the river. It's open all day every day and prices again range from moderate to inexpensive. Similarly priced is **Miestro's** ((519) 439-8983, at 352 Dundas Street, where the menu features dishes from all around the world.

HOW TO GET THERE

Route 401 between Toronto and Windsor is the concrete spine of the peninsula. Driving along it, Kitchener is about an hour from Toronto, London is about an hour and a half from Kitchener, and Windsor is about two hours from London. To continue on to Stratford, follow Highway 8 west from Kitchener onto Highway 7/8 west. If you are coming from the United States, Detroit and Windsor are connected by both a bridge and a tunnel. **Amtrak** TOLL-FREE (800) 872-7245 and **VIA Rail** ((519) 256-5511 operate several trains daily along the Toronto-Kitchener-Stratford-London-Chicago route. **Canadian Airlines International** flies into both Windsor and London.

NORTHERN ONTARIO

Northern Ontario is generally considered to be everything north and west of Lake Nipissing, which lies between the Québec border and the northern tip of Georgian Bay. In other words, it is almost all of Ontario in terms of size — but very little of it in terms of interest to visitors. Thickly forested and thinly populated, this vast wilderness has no towns of any size except near rich mineral deposits and along the shores of Lake Huron and Lake Superior.

On the other hand, its many lakes and rivers and its forests teeming with wildlife make it ideal for the sportsman who really wants to get away from it all.

SUDBURY

The town of Sudbury sits in the vast Sudbury Basin, a mineral-rich geological formation 37 km (59 miles) long and 27 km (17 miles) wide which

A demonstration in the Fanshawe Pioneer Village, northeast of London.

is the world's largest single source of nickel. Sudbury is one of Canada's major mining towns with the biggest nickel mining plant in the world, and the resulting pollution has contributed to the bleakness that afflicts parts of the landscape. However, this is compensated for by the surrounding Canadian Shield countryside, wild and wonderful with its forests, rocks, and lakes, offering the outdoor enthusiast all kinds of possibilities.

Of Sudbury's population of around 165,000, about a quarter are Francophone. Laurentian University, which is situated on the shores of Lake Ramsey, is bilingual, and French culture thrives here.

For visitor information, get in touch with the **Sudbury and District Chamber of Commerce** ((705) 673-7133 or the **Community Information Service and Convention and Visitors Service** ((705) 674-3141.

What to See and Do
The major attraction here is probably **Science North** ((705) 522-3700, an impressive science center which stands at the edge of Lake Ramsey. This dramatic building was designed by architect Raymond Moriyama and consists of two snowflake-shaped buildings set over a cavern in the rock. The smaller hexagonal structure is the reception area; it is linked to the larger "snowflake," containing the exhibition halls, by a tunnel through the rock. In the darkness of the cavern you can see a 3-D film of the Northern Ontario landscape before ascending to exhibition areas where a hands-on experience of science awaits you. You can test to find your ideal body weight, measure your fitness, visit a weather station, or find out what the local pollution levels are and how they test for them at the Atmosphere Laboratory. Computers encourage involvement in the center's wide range of displays, that cover subjects such as insects, animals, communications, and outer space. The center offers dining facilities, a bar, and a bookstore. Science North is situated one and a half kilometers (one mile) south of the Trans-Canada Highway on Ramsey Lake Road and is open daily year-round. The museum charges an admission fee.

To the west of the town stands Sudbury's famous landmark, the nine-meter (30-ft)-tall **Big Nickel**, which stands among four other huge replicas of coins, and below lies the **Big Nickel Mine** ((705) 673-5659, a hard-rock mine run by Science North and open to the public. You go down in a cage to the tunnels where the mining process is demonstrated. Tours are operated from May to November; an admission fee is charged.

From the Big Nickel you can take **The Path of Discovery**, a two-and-a-half hour bus tour of the Sudbury Basin, also organized by Science North, which gives the visitor a glimpse of the massive

mining, refining, and smelting operations here and includes a visit to the **Inco Refinery**. Tours operate three times daily from late June to Labor Day. Contact Science North ((705) 522-3700 for details.

Lovers of the Great Outdoors will enjoy an excursion to the **Killarney Provincial Park** ((705) 287-2900, which lies about 80 km (50 miles) southwest of Sudbury. It covers 363 sq km (140 sq miles) of rugged Canadian Shield wilderness at its most beautiful, against a backdrop of the snow-capped **La Cloche Mountains**. Apart from some campgrounds, there are few facilities here, and you make your way on foot, by canoe, or on ski. For fishing and whitewater canoeing the place to go is **French River**, which is south of Sudbury and runs between Lake Nipissing and Georgian Bay. Also to the north and all around Sudbury the countryside offers endless opportunities for outdoor recreation, and there are plenty of lodges, camps, and organized trips to ease the way.

Where to Stay
Most guest accommodation in Sudbury is to be found in motels located on the outskirts of town. In the city center there is the reliable **Ramada Inn Sudbury** ((705) 675-1123 FAX (705) 675-7727, at 85 St. Ann Road, Sudbury P3E 4S4, with 145 rooms, an indoor swimming pool, and near the beach there is **Howard Johnson** ((705) 675-1273 FAX (705) 671-1766, at 390 Elgin Street, Sudbury P3B 1B1, offering similarly good facilities. Prices at both these hotels fall within the mid-range.

SAULT STE. MARIE

Known as "the Sault" (pronounced "the Soo"), Sault Ste. Marie is separated from its twin town in the United States by the rapids of the St. Mary's River, which links Lake Superior and Lake Huron. Long before the explorers came, the rapids were a meeting place for natives who came there to catch whitefish. Established by Jesuit missionaries in 1668, Sault Ste. Marie has grown into an industrial town with a population of over 80,000. It has a large steelworks, pulp and lumber mills, and is also a very important shipping center. A series of locks on the St. Mary's River enable huge ships to pass between Lakes Huron and Superior, bypassing the rapids and making the canal the busiest section of the St. Lawrence Seaway with 90 million metric tons (100 million tons) of cargo passing through annually.

The Soo is also linked to its Michigan twin by road and railway bridges, and it's therefore a popular stopping place for travelers. To the north lies the unspoiled and untamed Algoma wilderness; the excursion train that runs from the town to the Agawa Canyon is a famous attraction.

For visitor information, contact the **Sault Ste. Marie Chamber of Commerce** ((705) 949-7152 FAX (705) 759-8166.

At the bottom of Huron Street you can see the **Soo Locks** that connect the lakes. You can watch the continuous stream of ships passing through from a viewing platform or down by the locks, around which you'll find pleasant walking trails. There are four American locks and one Canadian — which dates from 1895 and is the oldest of the system. This Canadian lock, now operated by Parks Canada, is used only by pleasure craft, and has some lovely spots for picnicking. **Boat trips** about the MV *Chief Shingwauk* ((705) 253-9850 run from Roberta Bondar Dock, next door to the

trips are available: The nine-hour journey into beautiful **Agawa Canyon** takes in some spectacular scenery. Starting from Sault Ste. Marie, the train plunges deep into the unspoiled wilderness, through forests, over rivers and gorges, along trestle bridges, on mountain ledges and around lakes. The trip allows two hours for exploring, fishing, climbing, and camera clicking. A full breakfast and lunch menu are available. The fare is $52. In winter, the **Snow Train** makes the same journey, when a lovely white mantel covers the landscape. The fare is $53. Finally there is the 480-km (300-mile) excursion to the French-Canadian town of **Hearst**. An overnight stay in modern accommodations is included in the fare of $130.

Holiday Inn, and operate from mid-May to mid-October. The trip takes you through all five locks and lasts about two hours. A fare is charged.

The **Ermatinger Old Stone House** ((705) 759-1443 at 831 Queen Street East, is a lovely Georgian building dating from 1814 and is the oldest surviving dwelling in Northern Ontario. Built by wealthy fur trader Charles Oakes Ermatinger for his wife — who was an Objiwa princess — it served as a way station for many explorers. One floor has been restored and furnished in the style of the early nineteenth century, and the other floor houses a museum. It's open weekdays in April, May, October, and November, and daily from June to September. Admission is by donation.

The main attractions here are excursions north of the city aboard the Algoma Central Railway ((705) 946-7300 TOLL-FREE (800) 242-9287, 129 Bay Street, PO Box 130, Sault Ste. Marie P6A 6Y2. Three

To appreciate more of the area's natural beauty, take the Trans-Canada Highway (Route 17) north to Wawa, a journey of 230 km (143 miles) known as the **Lake Superior Drive**. The route takes you by **Batchawana Bay** on the shore of Lake Superior with miles of sandy beaches. You'll find plenty of accommodation of all kinds here. Continuing along the Trans-Canada Highway beyond the lovely **Alona Bay**, the road takes you through **Lake Superior Provincial Park**, a majestic wilderness of cliffs and forests. Here, rising from the lake, is **Agawa Rock**, on which a series of native pictographs are painted telling stories that were the inspiration of Longfellow's epic poem, *Hiawatha*.

For a spectacular view of the lake and St. Mary's River, go 26 km (16 miles) west of the

Sudbury's famous Big Nickel which stands above the entrance to the Big Nickel Mine.

town along Route 550 to the ridge known as **Gros Cap**, where there's a marked trail along the edge.

Sports and Outdoor Activities
Lake Superior Provincial Park is a beautiful setting for **boating** and **canoeing**, and also offers **fishing**. At Batchawana Bay the rivers offer good inland fishing and there are more opportunities during the two-hour stop on the Agawa Canyon trip. For **swimming** Batchawana Bay has some lovely beaches although the waters are cool, and in the Kinsmen-Crystal Creek Conservation Area, also known as Hiawatha Park, a short drive northwest of town, there's a swimming pond and waterfalls.

Within city limits, **Hiawatha Highlands** has many kilometers of cross-country ski trails. Cross-country as well as downhill skiing are found at the **Searchmont Resort** ((705) 781-2340 TOLL-FREE (800) 663-2546, about 30-minutes from the city on Highway 556. There are also hundreds of kilometers of groomed **snowmobile** trails in the region.

Where to Stay
Close to the Algoma Central train station there's the moderately priced **Holiday Inn** ((705) 949-0611 FAX (705) 945-6972, at 208 St. Mary's River Drive, Sault Ste. Marie P6A 5V4, with an indoor pool, restaurant, and 195 rooms. Ideally situated for shopping, the **Ramada Inn** ((705) 942-2500 FAX (705) 942-2570, 229 Great Northern Road, Sault Ste. Marie P6B 4Z2, has an excellent range of facilities and additional features such as an indoor miniature golf course, also moderately priced.

The Hostelling International-affiliated **Algonquin Hotel** ((705) 253-2311, 864 Queen Street East, Sault Ste. Marie P6A 2B4, is located close to the harbor front, the museum, and the art gallery. There are private rooms, and linens and towels are included in the rock-bottom price. There is a restaurant serving lunch and dinner, a bar, as well as on-site parking. It's located about two kilometers (under one and a half miles) from the train and bus station.

THUNDER BAY

The port of Thunder Bay stands on the shores of Lake Superior, virtually at the exact center of Canada. Situated at the western end of the St. Lawrence Seaway, it is the terminus for freighters and is a pivotal point in the transportation of grain, forest products, and other materials. Thirteen huge grain elevators dominate the skyline, but in recent years reduced grain shipments have meant a reduction in traffic through the **Lakehead**. However, the city's economy remains typically Canadian, being largely dependent on grain, forest products, and mineral resources.

Jobs in shipping attracted many immigrants to Thunder Bay, which today has a population of around 130,000. There is a rich ethnic mix — including a large Finnish community and some 10,000 First Nations people. With the forest and mountains to the north, the wilderness is never far away and it's not uncommon to see moose and bear wandering about the town. In fact someone swears she once saw a moose running around a high school track.

In the days before the St. Lawrence Seaway, Fort William, as it was then known, was an important fur-trading center. Natives and trappers came here to the mouth of the Kaministikwia with their furs for their meeting — known as the Great Rendezvous — with the buyers who brought their European goods up the St. Lawrence. In 1801 the British built Fort William here, where it served as the headquarters of the North West Trading Company, and each summer more than 2,000 voyageurs

met there for the Great Rendezvous, a time of discussion and celebration — and no insignificant amount of drinking — that lasted six weeks. Fort William remained a fur trading post until the late nineteenth century. In 1970 Fort William merged with the community of Port Arthur to form the city of Thunder Bay.

Visitor information can be obtained from **Tourism Thunder Bay** ((807) 625-2149 TOLL-FREE (800) 667-8386, 500 East Donald Street, Thunder Bay P7E 5V3.

What to See and Do
The best way to get an idea of Thunder Bay's economic role and its geography is to take a **Harbour Cruise**. Outside downtown, **Old Fort William** ((807) 577-8461 has been reconstructed along with 50 village buildings. At the fort you can see trappers, voyageurs, natives and traders going about their business. To get to the Old Fort

William you go 16 km (10 miles) along Broadway Avenue or take a boat from Port Arthur marina. It's open daily from mid-May to early October; an admission fee is charged.

The **Thunder Bay Art Gallery** at Confederation Campus focuses particularly on contemporary First Nations art, and has examples of the work of Norval Morrisseau, a well-known native artist who was born in Thunder Bay. There are changing exhibitions that include crafts, sculpture, and photography.

At the eastern end of the city, the wooded **Centennial Park** covers a 57-hectare (140-acre) area and has a logging camp, museum, and nature trails. It is open daily throughout the year, while the logging camp is open mid-June to Labor Day.

Kakabeka Falls, a few miles west of Thunder Bay.

Further out and to the east of the city is the scenic **Sibley Provincial Park** with trails, cliffs, woods, and shoreline. At one end you'll see the **Sleeping Giant** rock formation stretching out into the lake, attached to which is a legend involving a silver mine, a treacherous native, and a Great Spirit. There are several **amethyst mines** 56 to 72 km (35 to 45 miles) to the east of the town on Route 11/17, which are open to the public. You can either gather your own amethysts from the mines or choose them from displays.

Sports and Outdoor Activities
There's good canoeing territory between the Lakehead and Rainy River, and at Centennial

Park you'll find canoes and boats for rent. Between Thunder Bay and Kenora there are many **fishing** lodges, details of which can be obtained from the Tourist Office. Sibley Provincial Park is a good spot for swimming, and there are beaches at Kakabeka Falls, situated 25 km (16 miles) to the west of the town.

The long winters and short summers here have given rise to the local saying that here there's "six months of good **skiing**, six months of poor skiing." Certainly, there is plenty of it. In the immediate vicinity there are three downhill areas with excellent facilities and snowmaking equipment. There are also five cross-country trails close to the city, with plenty of après-ski and package deals to be had. The Big Thunder Ski Jump is the world's largest with 90-m (295-ft) and 70-m (230-ft) jumps. It's southwest of the city and is where the national ski-jumping team trains.

Where to Stay
Near the airport the **Airlane Hotel** ((807) 473-1600 FAX (807) 475-4852, 698 West Arthur Street, Thunder Bay P7E 5R8, is one of the best hotels in the area. It has 155 rooms, good service, and a host of amenities such as an indoor pool, a good restaurant, and a complimentary shuttle service to the airport. The **Landmark Inn** ((807) 767-1681 FAX (807) 767-1439, 1010 Dawson Road, Thunder Bay P7B 5J4, has similarly high standards and amenities. It offers 106 air-conditioned rooms with private bath and television.

HOW TO GET THERE

The **Algoma Central Railway** TOLL-FREE (800) 242-9287 operates trains service four times a week between Sault Ste. Marie and Hearst, Ontario, but only between May 16 and October 13. There is a daily **VIA Rail** TOLL-FREE (888) 842-7733 train eastbound from Winnipeg that stops at Thunder Bay and Sudbury on its way to Ottawa and Montréal, and one westbound daily along the same route. There is also daily train service between Sudbury and Toronto.

Greyhound TOLL-FREE (800) 661-8747 has frequent buses from major Canadian cities to Sudbury, Sault Ste. Marie, and Thunder Bay, as well as daily buses to Sault Ste. Marie from Detroit and Chicago.

If you are coming by car, the Trans-Canada Highway (Route 17) links Sudbury, Sault Ste. Marie, and Thunder Bay with each other as well as with eastern and western Canada. Approaching from the south, Sudbury can be reached by Route 69 from Toronto; Sault Ste. Marie can be reached by Interstate-75 from Detroit; and Thunder Bay can be reached by Interstate-35 from Minneapolis/St. Paul and Duluth, which becomes Route 61 when it crosses the border.

ABOVE: The windmill at Thunder Bay's Friendship Gardens. OPPOSITE TOP: Once an important fur trading post, Old Fort William has been reconstructed along with 50 village buildings where you can see trappers, voyageurs, natives, and traders going about their business. BOTTOM: Boat builder John DeForge plies his trade on Manitoulin Island.

Québec

QUÉBEC, THE LARGEST OF CANADA'S PROVINCES, is very large indeed: it covers over one and a half million square kilometers (almost 600,000 sq miles), or one-sixth of Canada. Or to put it another way, it is twice the size of Texas and three times the size of France. But it is as "La Belle Province," a bastion of French culture in an Anglo-dominated continent, that Québec is best known. And rightly so, because for almost four centuries the people of Québec have stubbornly resisted every effort by others to interfere with their way of life — first by the natives who wanted to drive them out, then by the British who wanted to stamp them out, and latterly by their fellow Canadians who have tried to buy them out. All to no avail. The Québécois

are determined not to surrender any part of the heritage left them by their ancestors. This determination is succinctly captured in the province's defiant motto, which is displayed on all Québec license plates: *Je me souviens* ("I remember").

They have much to remember from their unique history. Although Jacques Cartier landed at Gaspé in 1534 and claimed the region for France, it was not until 1608 that the French-speaking history of the province began when Samuel de Champlain arrived at a place on the St. Lawrence River that the natives called *Kébec*, which means "narrowing of the waters." De Champlain established a small fur trading post here, and then three years later he established another trading post on the river at a spot now occupied by Montréal. Permanent settlements followed at Trois Rivières in 1634 and Ville-Marie (now Montréal) in 1642. Although constantly raided by the hostile Iroquois, the settlements grew steadily and more were founded along the shores of the St. Lawrence. By 1700 there were 25,000 French colonists living along the St. Lawrence, while the French colony of New France stretched from Hudson Bay to the Gulf of Mexico, and from the St. Lawrence almost to the Rockies.

French dominion over Québec continued more or less undisturbed for the next half-century, but

the outbreak of the Seven Years' War in 1756 changed all that. Or, to be precise, it was the 15-minute battle on the Plains of Abraham, where the British forces under General James Wolfe routed the French under the Marquis de Montcalm, that broke forever France's political hold on Québec. Under the Treaty of Paris in 1763 France ceded all its Canadian possessions to England. In 1774 Parliament passed the Québec Act, recognizing the right of French Canadians to keep their language, religion, property, and legal system. Incensed by these and other concessions to the French Canadians, especially regarding special advantages in the fur trade, the American colonists sent an army under General Richard Montgomery to attack Montréal and Québec City. Montréal fell, but Québec City held out, and the following year Montréal was recaptured by the British.

In 1791 Parliament passed the Constitutional Act dividing Québec into mainly English-speaking Upper Canada (present-day Ontario) and mainly French-speaking Lower Canada (present-day Québec). The arrangement worked reasonably well for the next four decades, despite growing resentment among the people of Lower Canada at being swamped by English-speaking immigrants, and at being governed by a British lieutenant-governor with his handpicked legislative council. This led to a violent but unsuccessful rebellion by French Canadians in 1837. While the insurrection itself may have been put down, the desire for more control over their own affairs would linger on. And on.

In 1867 the newly created provinces of Québec and Ontario joined Nova Scotia and New Brunswick in the confederated Dominion of Canada. Québec City was made the provincial capital. During the rest of the century, Québec's economy remained largely dependent on trade and agriculture. Québec City consolidated its position as the center of government as well as chief custodian of French Canadian heritage and culture, while Montréal emerged as a great port and the province's financial and industrial center. By 1911 Montréal's population had reached half a million — and it doubled in the next two decades.

Unfortunately, the suspicions and enmities that had long bedeviled Québec's relations with the other provinces surfaced again, with renewed virulence, in 1917 when Canada was forced to introduce conscription to replace the horrific numbers of servicemen lost in the fighting in Europe. To the French Canadians, conscription was a sinister ploy to use them as cannon fodder in Britain's war with Germany. To the rest of Canada, the revolt of the Québécois against conscription was little short of treasonable.

The old wounds, thus reopened, never really healed. And when the Union Nationale

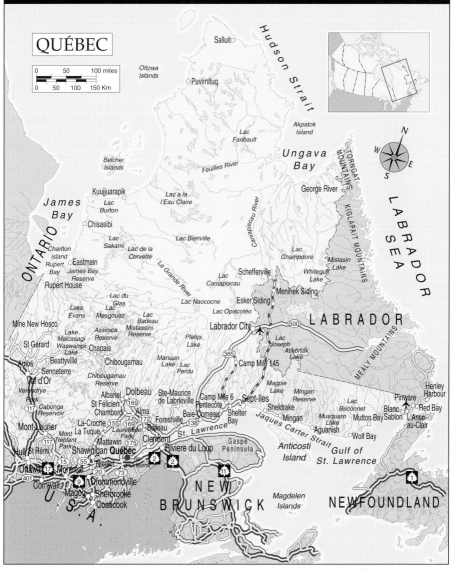

QUÉBEC

0   50   100 miles
0   50   100   150 Km

Inset map of Canada showing Québec location

Hudson Strait

Salluit

Ottowa Islands

Puvirnituq

Akpatok Island

Lac Faribault

Belcher Islands

Ungava Bay

Feuilles River

Kuujjuarapik

Lac Burton

Lac a la l'Eau Claire

George River

James Bay

Chisasibi

Lac Sakami

Lac de la Corvette

Lac Bienville

Caniapiscau River

Lac Champdoré

Mistasin

LABRADOR SEA

TORNGAT MOUNTAINS

KIGLAPAIT MOUNTAINS

ONTARIO

Charlton island

Rupert Bay

Eastmain

James Bay Reserve

La Grande River

Schefferville

Whitegull Lake

Lac Caniapiscau

Menihek Siding

Rupert House

Lac du Glas

Lac Naococne

Esker Siding

Lake Evans

Lac Mesgouez

Lac Badeau

Lac Opiscotéo

LABRADOR

Mine New Hosco

Lake Maicasagi

Assinica Reserve

Mistassini Reserve

Pletipi Lake

Labrador City

500

St Gérard

Waswanipi Lake

Chapais

Lac Joseph

MEALY MOUNTAINS

Amos

Beattyville

Chibougamau

Manuan Lake

Lac Perdu

Atikonak Lake

385

Senneterre

Chibougamau Reserve

Camp Mile 145

Val d'Or

Verendrye Park

Albanel

Dolbeau

Ste-Maurice de Labrieville

Camp Mile 6

Sept-Iles

Magpie Lake

Mingan Reserve

Lac Briconnet

Pinware

Henley Harbour

117

Cabonga Reservoir

St Félicien

169

Chambord

Alma

172

Pentecôte

Sheldrake

Mingan

Musquaro Lake

Blanc Sablon

Red Bay

Mont-Laurier

La-Croche

155

169

Beileau

Foresthville

138

Baie-Comeau

Shelter Bay

Jacques Carter Strait

Aguanish

Mutton Bay

L'Anse-au-Clair

Mont Treblant Park

La Tuque

Laurentide Park

Clermont

St. Lawrence

Wolf Bay

117

Mattawin

175

Riviere du Loup

Gaspé Peninsula

Anticosti Island

Gulf of St. Lawrence

Hull St Rémi

Shawinigan

Québec

d'Orleans

Ottawa

17

Montreal

Nicolet

20

73

NEW

401

15

55

73

Cornwall

9

Drummondville

Magog

Sherbrooke

BRUNSWICK

Magdelen Islands

NEWFOUNDLAND

U.S.A.

Coaticook

4

---

party of Maurice Duplessis took control of the provincial government in the 1930s the estrangement looked set to become permanent — all the more so when the fight over conscription flared up again during World War II. Indeed, by 1960, when the Union Nationale finally lost power to the Liberals, Québec was not only far apart from the rest of Canada, but far behind as well. Industrial expansion had been sacrificed in an attempt to preserve Québec's traditional agrarian economy, science and economics had been woefully neglected in the province's Church-run schools, and most progressive ideas for revitalizing the province had been successfully suppressed.

In 1960, however, the Liberals under Jean Lesage gained power and set in motion the "Quiet Revolution," an ambitious program of economic and social reform, which nudged Québec towards a modern society and a dynamic economy. At the same time, alas, it exposed the lack of French Canadians who had been properly trained for managerial responsibilities, which meant that most of the bosses were Anglos — a situation guaranteed to sow further discord. And it did. In the late 1960s the separatist Parti Québécois rose to prominence under René Lévesque, taking 23%

A sylvan scene in the Laurentians, north of Québec City.

of the vote in the 1970 provincial elections and then, astonishingly, taking power in the 1976 elections. But Lévesque's radicalism, tinged with Anglophobia, frightened Anglo-run businesses out of the province, which in turn frightened the people, who somehow thought they could lose their bosses without losing their jobs. In a 1980 referendum the voters of Québec overwhelmingly rejected the idea of declaring independence, and in 1985 the Parti Québécois was turned out of office in favor of the Liberals. But now the pendulum seems to have swung back towards the separatists. Only time will tell.

Whichever path the people of Québec decide to take — continued provincial status with

perhaps enhanced autonomy, or independent nationhood — one thing is certain: in either version Québec will be a formidable economic power. Its natural resources alone guarantee that. With 16% of the world's freshwater resources, it is able to generate (and sell) vast amounts of hydroelectric power. With its gigantic forests, it has a thriving lumber industry and is the top producer of paper in North America. With more than its share of the ancient rocks of the Canadian Shield, it is rich in such minerals as iron, copper, gold, silver, lead, zinc, and nickel; it is one of the world's foremost producers of aluminum. With the fertile flood plain of the St. Lawrence, its farmland supports a thriving agriculture industry. With all of these blessings, and with a population of only 7.4 million, it is no wonder that Québec is able to export 40% of its total production.

What to say of those seven million Québécois? To begin with, they are not as homogeneous as they may appear at first glance. At least 10% are of British ancestry, most of who live in Montréal, and another 10% are immigrants from Europe, Asia, Latin America, and the Caribbean. While French may be the official language of Québec, with English as the widely understood second language, there are 35 other languages one can hear spoken in the province; such is the ethnic diversity of its immigrant population. Nor are the French-speakers the fanatical malcontents they are often portrayed to be. On the contrary, they are warm, garrulous, hospitable, informal, and affectionate, with a *joie de vivre* that underlines their primarily Norman and Breton ancestry.

If it is their destiny to carry the torch of French civilization in the Americas, not only do they do it proudly, but with a big smile.

QUÉBEC CITY

The first European to visit the spot the natives called *Kébec* was Jacques Cartier in 1535. Optimistically, he named the cliff Cap Diamants ("Diamond Cape") in honor of the great mineral wealth he hoped (and failed) to find there. When Samuel de Champlain arrived in 1608 he took a much more realistic view of the site's potential importance. Recognizing its strategic location, he established a trading post at the foot of the cliff, and then in 1620 built a fort at the summit. It was captured by the British under Admiral David Kirke in 1629, but was regained by the French three years later. For the next 130 years it found itself repeatedly under siege by either the British or the Iroquois, finally falling on the morning of September 13, 1759, when General Wolfe's troops surprised the French forces (under the Marquis de Montcalm) on the Plains of Abraham.

In 1763, with the signing of the Treaty of Paris, the city that had been the heart and soul of New France became the capital of a new British colony. After the American attack on the city in 1775 was repulsed, the British strengthened the fortifications and built the Citadel, but, happily, they were never needed.

GENERAL INFORMATION

The office of the **Greater Québec Area Tourist Information Centre** ℭ (418) 649-2608 is in Haute-Ville on Avenue Wilfrid-Laurier. The provincial government operates the massive **Maison du tourisme** ℭ (418) 873-2015 TOLL-FREE (800) 363-7777 FRENCH-ONLY WEB SITE www.destinationQuébec .ca/. It's located on Place d'Armes, at 12 rue Ste-Anne, across from the Château Frontenac. **Internet access** is available at the Cyber-Bar L'Étrange, 275 rue St-Jean, Haute-Ville.

WHAT TO SEE AND DO

When speaking of Québec City one should probably refer to it as Québec Cities, because there is Haute-Ville (Upper Town), which includes the romantic and historic Vieille-Ville (Old City) with its walled fortifications, lovely residential areas, and the Plains of Abraham, as well as some extramural concessions to the twentieth century in the form of modern office buildings and shopping malls; and there is Basse-Ville (Lower Town) wrapped around the foot of the cliff and extending into the valley of the Rivière St-Charles, where the industrial suburbs begin. Although the city

30-minute tour with an English-speaking driver costs around $50. They operate all summer, rain or shine.

Situated in the heart of Haute-Ville, the **Place d'Armes** is a good place to begin a walking tour, and makes a useful orientation point. The square, and indeed the city, is dominated by the imposing **Château Frontenac**, an enormous red brick structure with a profusion of towers, turrets, and parapets that give it the air of a medieval castle. Built on the site of Château St. Louis, the residence of the governors of New France, it takes its name from a former governor, the Comte de Frontenac. Guided tours depart from the lobby hourly, year-round, between 10 AM and 6 PM; a fee is charged.

has an official population of about 700,000, it never has that few people in it, as its attractions make it one of the most visited cities on the entire continent (see EXPLORE THE OLD WORLD IN THE NEW, page 14, in TOP SPOTS).

The city has stairways and a funicular to bring you up (or down) the escarpment between Haute-Ville and Basse-Ville. With the attractive old stone buildings, narrow winding streets, pleasant squares and parks, there's a lot to see within a small area, which is comforting news for the visitor as the narrow and sometimes pedestrianized streets make walking by far the best means of getting about.

For a very relaxed (but expensive) sightseeing tour you can take a ride in one of the **horse-drawn calèches** that you'll find waiting at Place d'Armes (see below), or on Rue d'Auteuil by the city walls, near the tourist information office. A

Next to Château Frontenac is the **Jardin des Gouverneurs**, once the garden of the Château St. Louis. At the center of this little park stands a monument which pays tribute to both General Wolfe and the Marquis de Montcalm, and in the summer there's often some kind of entertainment to be found here. Running along the south side of the park the **Avenue Ste-Geneviève** is lined with European-style inns, behind which is hidden the lovely little **Parc du Cavalier du Moulin** with its vestiges of the seventeenth-century French fortifications.

Just off the Place d'Armes is the awning-covered **Rue du Trésor**, so named because the royal treasury once stood here. During the summer

Québec City — The airy spires of Haute-Ville OPPOSITE contrast with weighty Château Frontenac overlooking Basse-Ville and the St. Lawrence River ABOVE.

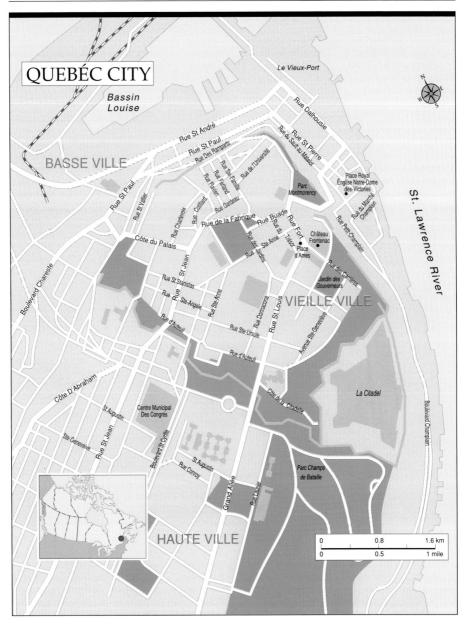

months the tiny alley is jammed with artists of varying talent displaying their works and sketching visitors' portraits. Just off this little street is the entrance to Les Promenades de Vieux-Québec, an indoor retail area with shops, the pleasant Café Buade and a **sound-and-light show entitled "The Québec Experience"** ((418) 694-4000, (call for schedule).

At the end of the Rue du Trésor turn left onto the Rue de Buade, and at the corner of Côte de la Fabrique you'll find the **Basilique-Cathédrale Notre-Dame** ((418) 692-2433. This somber, gray stone cathedral has an ornate interior and some interesting paintings. The basilica was destroyed during the British invasion in 1759, rebuilt only to be destroyed by fire in 1922, following which it was rebuilt using the original 1647 plans. One of its unique features is the fabulous golden umbrella-like *baldaquin* (altar canopy). To the right of the nave is the tomb of François Xavier de Laval, Canada's first bishop. The map over Laval's sepulcher shows the outlines of the original diocese of Québec, which stretched from Newfoundland to Louisiana! Guided tours are offered free of charge, daily from May to early October, and include a visit to the crypt where the bones of Samuel de Champlain may or may not be interred. A **sound-and-light show**, "Act of Faith" ("Don't miss it!" cries the cathedral's publicity material) plays daily at 3:30 PM, 5 PM, 6:30 PM, and 8 PM. An admission fee is charged.

To the left of the basilica stands the **Seminary**, the entrance to which is at 9 rue de l'Université. It was founded in 1663 by Québec's first bishop, François Xavier de Laval, and developed into the Université Laval. It has a beautiful and tranquil inner courtyard and its main chapel is notable for its relics and the beautifully crafted tomb of Laval. In order to visit other parts of the seminary you

des Ursulines contains some interesting relics and the Marquis de Montcalm is buried here (at least in part: his skull is in the museum). The convent, museum, and chapel are open Tuesday to Saturday and Sunday afternoons, and an admission fee is charged. Just along the Rue des Jardins is the **Holy Trinity Anglican Cathedral**, a fine building in the English Baroque style. Built in 1804, it was the first Anglican cathedral built outside the United Kingdom.

If by now you feel the need to blow away the cobwebs, behind Château Frontenac you'll find the **Terrasse Dufferin**, a wide boardwalk stretching south overlooking the St. Lawrence and offering good views of Basse-Ville and the opposite

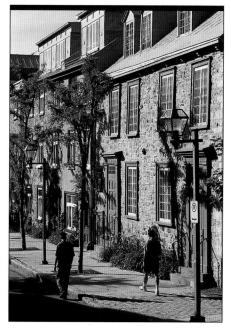

have to take a guided tour, for which a small fee is charged. Tours run daily from mid-May to mid-August.

Nearby in Rue Charlevoix is the **Hôtel-Dieu**, a large hospital founded by the Augustine nuns in 1639. It houses the **Musée des Augustines** ((418) 692-2492, 32 rue Charlevoix, where some religious paintings and relics of the hospital's past can be seen. The museum is closed on Mondays, and admission is free.

Moving back south and still on a religious note, at 12 rue Donnacona stands the **Couvent des Ursulines**. Founded in 1693, it is the oldest girls' school in North America. The **Musée des Ursulines** ((418) 694-0694 lies within the convent walls. Here displays show you how the Ursulines lived under French rule, and there are paintings, furniture, and some exquisite examples of their embroidery on show. The recently restored **Chapelle**

shore. It leads to the **Promenade des Gouverneurs**, a stairway and boardwalk clinging to the edge of the cliff and taking you by La Citadelle and on to the Plains of Abraham.

From Terrasse Dufferin either the funicular (reopened in 1998 after a two-year renovation) or the Côte de la Montagne leading to the Escalier Casse-Cou (Breakneck Stairway) will bring you down to **Rue Petit-Champlain**, the oldest and narrowest street in the city. It's a bustling, arty area where an abundance of craft shops and cafés tempt you to indulge yourself or just stroll and browse.

At 60 rue du Marché-Champlain, stands the **Maison Chevalier** ((418) 643-2158. This former inn was built in 1752 for shipowner Jean-Baptiste

LEFT: Rue du Trésor, a miniature Montmartre.
RIGHT: Cobblestones and copper roofs — a typical old Québec street scene.

Chevalier. Handsomely restored, it now houses a museum with changing exhibits on Québec's history and culture. Texts are in French but English-language guidebooks are available. It's open daily June to October from 10 AM to 5 PM. Admission is free.

North and slightly to the east is **Place Royale**, a small eighteenth-century square. The square was once the hub of the city's thriving commercial center until business moved away in the nineteenth century. Now the whole area has been carefully restored and in the square some of the beautiful steep-roofed buildings now house museums, art galleries, restaurants, and shops, making it once again the lively center of Basse-Ville.

On the south side of Place Royale stands **Église Notre-Dame-des-Victoires**. This little church was built in 1688, and was extensively restored after the bombardment of 1759. It has some interesting features such as the fort-shaped altar, and a wooden model of a boat that hangs from the ceiling. These furnishings were brought here by the early settlers as offerings to ensure safe voyages. There's a **Welcome Center** ((418) 643-6631 in Place Royale, at 215 rue du Marché-Finlay.

Just north of Place Royale in the Vieux-Port area stands the excellent **Musée de la Civilisation** ((418) 643-2158, 85 rue Dalhousie, an interesting modern building designed to integrate with the surrounding architecture. It has some lively multimedia exhibitions on humankind, society, and culture, and has a particularly good exhibition on Québec's history and society. It's open daily from June 24 to September 4, and is closed Monday the

rest of the year; an admission fee is charged. Next to the Musée de la Civilisation there's the **Explore Sound-and-Light Show** ((418) 692-2063 — "Québec and the Age of Exploration" — telling the story of local hero, Samuel de Champlain. It's located at 63 rue Dalhousie (at St-Antoine). An admission fee is charged.

If you wander by the water's edge, south of Place Jacques-Cartier you'll find **Le Vieux-Port**, a redevelopment of the old port area where there are parks, restaurants and cafés — and in the summer months cruises, exhibitions, and free open-air entertainment of all kinds and for all ages. The days when it functioned as one of the world's great ports are recalled in **Centre d'interprétation du**

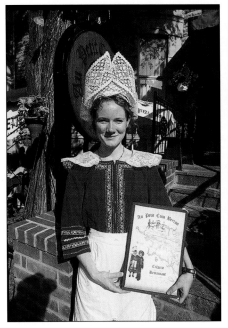

Vieux-Port ((418) 648-3300 at 100 rue St-André (at Rioux) where Parks Canada offers a range of films, exhibits, and demonstrations on shipbuilding and the lumber trade. It's open May to November daily, December to April by appointment; an admission fee is charged. At the northwestern tip of the port is the **Marché du Vieux-Port**, where farmers sell their fresh produce daily from May to October.

Continuing west from the Vieux-Port is the **antique shop district** along Rue St-Paul; another reclaimed urban area whose cafés and galleries have made it one of the city's most fashionable spots.

The Fortifications
Returning to Haute-Ville, **Les Fortifications de Québec** ((418) 648-7016, 100 rue St-Louis, warrant a tour to themselves. Built mainly by the British to protect the city from American attack, they were never needed but instead have added to the unique

character of the city. The city wall encircles the old town and has four *portes*, or gates. Standing at the south end is **La Citadelle** ((418) 694-2815, the large star-shaped fortress that looms high over the banks of the St. Lawrence. It was constructed (1820–1832) at great expense and is now occupied by the Royal 22e Régiment. Guided tours of the fortress and its museum are given and you can watch the Changing of the Guard and Beating of the Retreat ceremonies during the summer. To reach the entrance, go up Côte de la Citadelle from St-Louis Gate. It's open daily from April to October. An admission fee is charged.

Near the Porte St-Louis the **Poudrière de l'Esplanade** (Powder Magazine) at 100 rue St-Louis

of the St. Lawrence. The park encompasses the Plains of Abraham, on which the bloody battle of 1759 was fought. Two early nineteenth-century Martello towers remind us of this with their displays on the battles fought here.

At the south end of the park is the **Musée du Québec** (GENERAL ENQUIRIES (418) 643-2150 (TICKETS (418) 643-3377 (GUIDED TOURS (418) 643-4103, which occupies two buildings, a neoclassical structure and a former jailhouse, linked by a tall glass-roofed atrium. The museum houses North America's largest collection of Québécois art, in eight galleries containing works from the colonial era to the present. The jailhouse is a new addition (one cellblock has been left intact as an

now holds an interpretation center explaining the development of the fortifications. Guided tours start from here, and it's the place to start a walk of the ramparts. Moving north along the wall, just inside Porte St-Jean is the **Parc de l'Artillerie National Historique** ((418) 648-4205, 2 rue d'Auteuil, a complex of buildings dating from the early eighteenth century, which have served a variety of purposes over the years, mainly military. There's an interpretation center, and the exhibitions on offer are mostly on military themes. The park is open daily from March to October, and Monday to Friday the rest of the year; an admission fee is charged.

Outside the Walls

West of the fortress is the **Parc des Champs-de-Bataille (National Battlefields Park)** ((418) 648-4071, large and pleasant, sprinkled with gardens and monuments and offering impressive views

exhibit). This building's four galleries host temporary shows, and the tower contains a David Moore sculpture called *Le Plongeur*. In the atrium you'll find the reception area, a cafeteria and gift shop. The Parc des Champs-de-Bataille interpretation center is located here. Both the museum and park open daily from mid-May to mid-September and closed on Monday during the rest of the year. An admission fee is charged.

From here head back in the direction of the Old City towards the **Grande-Allée**, the wide avenue that is alive with cafés, bars, and restaurants, and at the north side near the corner of Avenue Dufferin you'll come to the **Hôtel du Parlement (National**

OPPOSITE: Why the sign? Imagine Québec under more than a meter of snow. RIGHT: Restaurants such as Au Petit Coin Breton RIGHT and Aux Anciens Canadiens ABOVE offer warm welcome and ancestral Québec cuisine.

Assembly)((418) 643-7239, a stately Renaissance-style building built between 1877 and 1886, and home of the provincial government. There are free guided tours of some of the most splendid rooms, daily from mid-June to 2 September and Monday to Friday the rest of the year.

Further north, about two miles from the Porte St-Jean on the banks of Rivière St-Charles, lies the **Cartier-Brébeuf National Historic Park**. ((418) 648-4038 at 175 rue de l'Espinay. Here an interpretive center focuses on the exploration and development of the colony and also the harshness of the conditions in which Cartier and his crew lived. There's a replica of the *Grande Hermine* on which Cartier sailed to North America.

Excursions from Québec City

A short distance east of Québec City lies **Île d'Orléans**, a rural oasis and a popular Québécois vacation spot. The island's winter population of approximately 6,000 doubles during summer, but it's still a tranquil escape from the city with — at last count — one traffic light and no movie theaters. The largest hotel has 14 rooms and there are a couple of dozen bed and breakfasts. Before the bridge was built in 1935, ferries and the winter ice bridge were the island's only connection to the mainland.

Just beyond the bridge to Île d'Orléans is **Parc de la Chute-Montmorency**, with its impressive falls — 30 m (98 ft) higher than Niagara (but

In early July, the town is busy with the annual **Québec Festival d'Été International** (International Summer Festival) ((418) 692-4540. It's a cultural celebration with concerts, theater, folk music, jazz, and dancing. Book your accommodation in advance. For festival information write to the festival office, PO Box 24, Station B, Québec City G1K 7A1. The **Carnaval d'Hiver** ((418) 626-3716 FAX (418) 626-7252 is an altogether more rambunctious affair. This 15-day celebration is held the first two weeks in February, and it's when Québec really lets its hair down. It starts when the two-meter (seven-foot) snowman is erected and activities center around the wonderful ice and snow sculptures. There are concerts, dances, parades, skiing, ice-skating, and an awful lot of *caribou*, the local mixture of alcohol and wine, is consumed. Book accommodation well in advance as this is a big event and the city is glazed with revelers.

much narrower). A cable car will take you to the top, where you can cross over the falls on a suspension bridge. Pack a picnic or have a delightful gourmet lunch at **Manoir Montmorency** ((418) 663-3330. Québécois cuisine is featured and there are fine views of the St. Lawrence River, Île d'Orléans and the falls. The park is about a 10-minute drive from downtown Québec.

A bit farther along lies the **Basilique Ste-Anne-de-Beaupré**. From here you can easily reach **Station Mont-Ste-Anne**, renowned for its world-class skiing and year-round outdoor activities, and the **Cap Tourmente National Wildlife Area**, visited by hundreds of thousands of snow geese in

OPPOSITE: Seen here from the Breakneck Stairway, Rue Petit-Champlain is the oldest street in the city. ABOVE: A footbridge traverses the falls at Parc de la Chute Montmorency, northeast of the city.

migration season. North of Québec City you can take in the Huron village of **Wendake**, or push on just a bit farther to **Jacques Cartier Park** or to the **Réserve Faunique des Laurentides**, another wildlife reserve.

SPORTS AND OUTDOOR ACTIVITIES

Battlefields Park, just outside the city walls, is a good place for **jogging** and **bicycling**. There are 1.3 km (.8 miles) of **in-line skating** paths within the Plains of Abraham ((418) 648-4071 with equipment rental available.

The **ice-skating** season runs roughly from December until March. You can join the throng in

service that runs between major hotels in Vieux-Québec, the nearby suburb of Ste-Foy, and the ski stations.

If you want to go **fishing** the Québec authorities insist you have a permit. Most sports shops can provide you with one. Contact the Ministry of Wildlife and Environment ((418) 643-3127, place de la Capitale, 150 boulevard René-Lévesque est, for their pamphlet on fishing regulations, or pick up the pamphlet at a tourist information office. Armed with the rules and your permit you can then go north to the lakes of the Réserve Faunique-des-Laurentides ((418) 686-1717, about 50 km (30 miles) north of the city via Route 73.

the Parc de l'Esplanade or skate along the stretch of the Rivière St-Charles between the Dorchester and Lavigueur bridges. North of the city in St-Gabriel-de-Valcartier, at the Village des Sports ((418) 844-3725 at 1860 boulevard Valcartier, you can skate through the woods or go **tobogganing**; there's also nighttime skating here. If you're a **skiing** enthusiast, the Plains of Abraham ((418) 648-4071 has cross-country skiing trails as do many of the nearby parks. Call *Regroupement des stations de ski de fond* ((418) 653-5875, for further information.

Station Mont Ste-Anne ((418) 827-4561 is northeast of the Québec City along Route 360, with 50 downhill trails, 10 lifts and over 200 km (125 miles) of cross-country trails. There are another three alpine ski resorts around the Québec City, accessible by car or by the Winter Shuttle ((418) 525-4953 or (413) 525-5191 which is a taxi

NIGHTLIFE AND THE ARTS

There's plenty to do in Québec City at night, mostly in or just outside the Old City. For events listings in English, check the *Québec Chronicle-Telegraph* which comes out each Wednesday. The French-language daily *Le Soleil* lists events in their "Où Aller à Québec" section ("Where to Go in Québec"). *Voir* is a free, French-language weekly with arts events and reviews; it appears every Thursday. Finally, *Québec Scope* is a free, bilingual monthly listing events of all kinds.

You can purchase tickets for most shows at **Billtech**. Outlets are located at: the Grand Théâtre de Québec ((418) 643-8131, 269 boulevard René-Lévesque est; Colisée ((418) 691-7211; Théâtre Périscope ((418) 529-2183, 2 Crémazie est; Palais Montcalm ((418) 670-9011; Salle Albert-Rousseau ((418) 659-6710, 2410 chemin Ste-Foy; La Baie department store ((418) 627-5959, 2740 boulevard Laurier, second level; and at Provigo supermarkets. Hours vary, and in some cases tickets must be bought at the venue.

Theater productions are all in French. At the **Grand Théâtre de Québec** ((418) 643-8131, 269 boulevard René-Lévesque est, classic and new plays are performed by le Théâtre du Trident. The open-air **Agora du Vieux-Port** ((418) 692-4672, at 84 rue Dalhousie, stages shows and plays — but, for obvious reasons, only in the summer. If you like theater in a casual café atmosphere go to **Théâtre Petit-Champlain** ((418) 692-4744, at 78 rue Petit-Champlain.

L'Orchestre Symphonique de Québec ((418) 643-8131 plays at the Grande Théâtre de Québec (see above).

Nightclubbing centers around the bars of Rue St-Jean. There are several good places for live rock music within the walls. Start the evening early at **Le Bistro Disco-Plus**, No. 1063, which has happy hours from 4 PM to 7 PM. **Bar L'Arlequin**, No. 1070, is a rock club hosting intriguing local names such as Strange Bubbles and Porno Como; pitchers of beer are very reasonably priced. Less obvious to visitors is the section of Rue St-Jean that radiates west, away from the Old City where you can find scores of hip bars and casual restaurants. **Le Sacrilège** at No. 477 is a boisterous bar with a terrace that's open until 3 AM; **Restaurant Carthage** at No. 395 has belly dancing on Friday and Saturday nights, and good moderately priced Middle Eastern food.

The **Grande-Allée** and **Vieux-Port** areas are also lively nightspots where the bars and clubs tend to attract a slightly older crowd. Québec's jazz mecca is the **Café Bar L'Emprise** ((418) 692-2480 in the Hôtel Clarendon at 57 rue Ste-Anne.

WHERE TO STAY

During the Carnaval d'Hiver in February hotels get booked up, so if you're planning your visit then it's essential to book far in advance.

Expensive

Le Château Frontenac ((418) 692-3861 TOLL-FREE (800) 441-1414 FAX (418) 692-1751, 1 rue des Carrières, Québec G1R 4P5, may no longer be the ultra-luxury hotel that it was in its heyday, but there's still an air of romance about staying in the most famous — and obvious — landmark in Québec City. Situated on Terrasse Dufferin and right by the Place d'Armes, its location could not be better. There's a huge ballroom, an indoor pool, a piano bar, a café, shops, and a very good restaurant called Le Champlain, and an air of decaying splendor. There are 600 rooms, which vary widely in size and location, but most of them have splendid views of the St. Lawrence and the Old City.

At Place d'Youville, just outside Porte St-Jean, **Hôtel du Capitole** ((418) 694-4040 FAX (418) 694-1191, 972 rue St-Jean, Québec G1R 1R5, is a dramatically post-modern 1992 renovation of the beautiful beaux-arts-style theater building. The 40 rooms look out on the three-story atrium-lobby with its cascades of flowers and potted palms. Rooms and miniature suites are equipped with eiderdown quilts, whirlpools, and compact disc players. The complex includes the gorgeously restored Théâtre Capitole and an Italian restaurant. Rates range from mid-range to expensive.

Outside the walls, the contemporary **Radisson Hôtel des Gouverneurs** ((418) 647-1717 TOLL-FREE (888) 910-1111 or (800) 333-3333, at 690 bou-

levard René-Lévesque est, Québec G1R 5A8, is a highrise hotel which faces the Parliament buildings and has 377 large rooms, an outdoor pool, and a restaurant. The poured-concrete interior is less than inspirational, and the hotel could do with some interior renovation, but the rooms are very spacious and the location is convenient, putting you within a short walk of the old city. Nearby, at the **Québec Hilton** ((418) 647-2411 TOLL-FREE (800) 447-2411 FAX (418) 647-2986, at 1100 boulevard René-Lévesque est, Québec G1R 4X3, you'll find service that cannot be bettered. The rooms are spacious, the decor is modern, and the facilities are typically Hiltonesque. It has a bar and restaurant, and a heated outdoor pool in summer. Near the Parliament buildings, the location is good, and to make life even easier it's connected underground to the large shopping complex, Place Québec. For a superb view of the Old City, make sure you get a room on one of the upper floors.

Overlooking the Parc des Champs-de-Bataille, the **Hôtel Loews Le Concorde** ((418) 647-2222 TOLL-FREE IN CANADA (800) 463-5256 TOLL-FREE IN THE UNITED STATES AND MEXICO (800) 23LOEWS,

OPPOSITE: Playbills announce the latest offerings at Palais Montcalm. ABOVE: Toning up in Lower Town.

1225 place Montcalm, Québec G1R 4W6, is just a short and pleasant walk from the heart of the city, and ideally placed for the cafés and nightlife of Grande-Allée. Among the luxury facilities there's an outdoor pool, VIP floors, café terrace, dance club, and, perched on top of this soaring concrete tower, a revolving restaurant.

Mid-range

In the Upper Town, the **Hôtel Clarendon** ((418) 692-2480 TOLL-FREE (800) 463-5250 FAX (418) 692-4652, at 57 rue Ste-Anne, is in itself a landmark. It's the city's oldest hotel with a wonderful art deco interior and loads of character. It has 150 pleasantly decorated rooms, and it boasts an excellent jazz bar, a cocktail lounge, and an atmospheric French restaurant. Standing next to City Hall, its location is ideal for sightseeing. Prices vary from mid-range to expensive. Further along at 115 rue Ste-Anne, the **Fleur-de-Lys** ((418) 694-0106 TOLL-FREE IN CANADA AND EASTERN UNITED STATES (800) 567-2106 FAX (418) 692-1959 is a bit of a surprise as it's a modern hotel in the heart of the Old City. Service is very good here, and there are 30 well-equipped and smartly decorated rooms, some with kitchenettes.

    Hôtel Le Château de Pierre ((418) 694-0429 FAX (418) 694-0153, at 17 avenue Ste-Geneviève, Québec G1R 4A8, is a charming Victorian mansion, elegantly decorated throughout. Its 15 rooms have a genteel look but modern conveniences. The **Hôtel Manoir Ste-Geneviève** ((418) 694-1666, at 13 avenue Ste-Geneviève, overlooks the Jardin des Gouverneurs. This early nineteenth-century building is filled with old English country furniture, creating a cozy and comfortable atmosphere. It offers nine accommodations, all air-conditioned and with television; some have kitchenettes.

    Outside the city walls, **Château Laurier** ((418) 522-8108 TOLL-FREE (800) 463-4453 FAX (418) 524-8768, at 695 Grande-Allée est, Québec G1R 2K4, offers 55 simple, well-equipped rooms, and the restaurants and nightlife of the Grande-Allée are literally (and noisily) on the doorstep.

Inexpensive

Many small family-run hotels and guesthouses can be found in the Rue St-Louis, including the **Auberge St-Louis** ((418) 692-2424 FAX (418) 692-3797, at 48 rue St-Louis, Québec G1R 3Z3, which offers 27 very pleasant rooms and very good value. The nineteenth-century building is in the heart of the walled city, and rates include breakfast. At **Hôtel Le Clos St-Louis** ((418) 694-1311 TOLL-FREE (800) 461-1311 FAX (418) 694-9411, 71 rue St-Louis, Québec G1R 3Z2, rooms are clean and neat. A good choice of similar accommodation can be found along the peaceful Rue Ste-Ursule: **Hôtel La Maison Demers** ((418) 692-2487 TOLL-FREE (800) 692-2487 TOLL-FREE IN FRANCE (0 800) 90 31 87, 68 rue

Ste-Ursule, Québec G1R 4E6, offers eight cozy rooms, and at No. 40 the **Hôtel Maison Ste-Ursule** ((418) 694-9794, Québec G1R 4E6, offers 15 rooms, the majority of which have private bathrooms.

    For details of **bed and breakfast** lodging in private homes around Québec City and the region, contact Bonjour Québec ((418) 524-0524 or (418) 527-1465 FAX (418) 648-8995, 540 rue Champlain, Québec G1K 4J3.

    Québec has plenty of options for backpacking travelers. The **Auberge de Jeunesse** ((418) 694-0755 or (514) 252-3117 TOLL-FREE IN QUÉBEC (800) 461-8585 FAX (418) 694-2278 or (514) 251-3119, 19 rue Ste-Ursule (at Rue Dauphine), Québec G1R 4E6, is housed in a former Ursuline girls'

residence. The tidy dorm-style rooms sleep eight and there is a poolroom and a picnic area. There is also the **Auberge de la Paix** ((418) 694-0735, 31 rue Couillard, Québec G1R 3T4.

    The university offers **campus accommodation** from May 1 to August 22. For details write to: Le Service des résidences de l'Université Laval, Pavillon Alphonse-Marie-Parent, Local 1634, Cité Universitaire, Ste-Foy; or call ((418) 656-5632.

WHERE TO EAT

Expensive

À la Table de Serge Bruyère ((418) 694-0618, at 1200 rue St-Jean, is the city's most famous restaurant and arguably its best. Here you can enjoy classic French and Alsatian cuisine in the elegant interior of a nineteenth-century building. There are actually dozens of dining rooms in the complex, but the formal **La Grande Table** is the pinnacle (and the most expensive). The food is both imaginative and immaculately presented. There's only one sitting per night, hardly surprising as the eight-course meal takes place at luxurious, leisurely pace.

Situated in one of the city's a seventeenth century buildings, **Aux Anciens Canadiens** ((418) 692-1627, 34 rue St-Louis, serves a mix of ancestral Québec and nouvelle cuisine. You'll find pea soup, *creton*, *tourtière*, pig's knuckles, and ragout side by side on the menu with sweet-and-sour duckling with maple syrup. The building is filled with period antiques, which gives it the look of an early settler's house.

Moderate to Inexpensive

Serge Bruyère (see above) also houses **Chez Livernois**, a bistro on the upper floor of the building with three arched windows and interesting views of the street. The decor is based on the lives of the former occupants, brothers who ran a photographic studio here. Down below is the **Café European**, where you can get a healthy breakfast with freshly squeezed fruit juices.

Café Suisse ((418) 694-1320 is at 32 rue Ste-Anne, and no prizes for guessing the cuisine here. The extensive menu offers some particularly good fondues and raclettes, and with its sidewalk terrace and exceptionally late opening hours, it's an ideal place to spend an evening. Moving east in

French haute cuisine can be found at **Le St-Amour** ((418) 694-0667, 48 rue Ste-Ursule, an attractive restaurant with a warm and informal atmosphere. Rabbit is always a good choice here, and the chocolate desserts are famous. The **Restaurant au Parmesan** ((418) 692-0341, at 38 rue St-Louis, offers fine Italian dining to the accompaniment, nightly, of an accordionist. There's free parking with valet service here.

Seafood Italian-style is the specialty at **Gambrinus** ((418) 692-5144, 15 rue du Fort (opposite the Château Frontenac). This cozy restaurant also serves meat dishes, but the pastas with seafood sauce are splendid. Probably the best seafood dishes are to be found at **Le Marie-Clarisse** ((418) 692-0857, situated in the Lower Town at 12 rue du Petit-Champlain (near the funicular). The fish is cooked to perfection and with great flair, but committed carnivores are also well catered to.

culinary terms, the **Fleur de Lotus** ((418) 692-4286, at 38 Côte de la Fabrique (opposite the Hôtel de Ville), offers delicious Vietnamese, Thai, and Cambodian food, and you can bring along your own bottle of wine.

Moving into the inexpensive category there is **Chez Temporel** ((418) 694-1813, 25 rue Couillard, a very French café in look and menu, which is an ideal place for breakfast or a snack. At **Au Relais de la Place d'Armes** ((418) 694-9063, 16 rue Ste-Anne, you can sit outside on the square and enjoy some good, hearty food. For reliably good Italian fare try **Pizzeria d'Youville** ((418) 694-0299, at 1014 rue St-Jean, and **La Petite Italie** ((418) 694-0044, at 49A rue St-Louis.

OPPOSITE: Chef Marie-Chantal Le Page presents excellent Québécois cuisine at Manoir Montmorency. ABOVE: Dining at the landmark Château Frontenac runs from casual to chic.

At **Le Casse-Crêpe** ((418) 692-0438, 1136 rue St-Jean, you can watch your dinner being made. Main course crêpes come with two to five ingredients of your choice. **Le Figaro**, 32 rue St-Louis, has *moules frites à volonté* (all-you-can-eat steamed mussels and french fries) on Monday and Tuesday evenings. On the daily lunch menu are ribs, omelets, and lasagna.

Pub VII Alexandre, 1087 rue St-Jean, has dozens of imported and beers to nurse along with steak and fries. **Brûlerie Tatum Café** ((418) 692-3900, 1084 rue St-Jean, is a slick new *maison de torréfaction* with a chrome-and-coffee-colored interior. The house specialty is *café au sirop d'érable*, maple syrup coffee, which comes piping hot in a tall glass, topped with whipped cream.

With its consignment shops, used-book stores, coffee shops and galleries, the St-Jean-Baptiste neighborhood, Rue St-Jean (outside the walls), is also a good place to seek out inexpensive eats. At No. 860 the vegetarian restaurant, **Le Commensal** is open seven days a week; **La Playa** at No. 788 serves excellent west-coast cuisine with some innovative options such as half-portions and meals to share. They're famous citywide for their pastas, which come with a choice of 24 different sauces. At No. 565, **Kookening Café** is open from 11 AM to midnight, specializing in tortilla pizzas. You can get a cheap and filling breakfast at **Café Bobon** at No. 475 place d'Youville.

HOW TO GET THERE

Although Québec City is served by many major airlines, most airborne visitors to the city come via Montréal or Toronto. The **airport shuttle**, Le Québécois ((418) 872-5525, stops at various hotels in Haute-Ville and Vieille-Ville; it takes about 45 minutes to get to the city center from the airport.

If you are driving from the Maritime provinces you will want to take the Trans-Canada Highway. From Montréal either the Trans-Canada Highway (Route 20) or Route 40 will take you to Québec City. From the Atlantic coast of the United States (except Maine) the best route is up Interstate-91, which goes through Vermont and becomes Route 55 when it crosses the border. This soon joins Route 10 which in turn becomes Route 51 before joining the Trans-Canada Highway at Drummondville, 155 km (96 miles) southwest of Québec City. Those coming from New York will enter Canada via Interstate-87.

VIA Rail ((418) 692-3940 has five daily trains to Québec City from Montréal, three daily from Toronto. Trains from the west arrive at the Gare du Palais in Basse-Ville. Coming from the Atlantic provinces, trains arrive at Lévis; across the St. Lawrence from which there is a regular ferry to Québec.

MONTRÉAL

Montréal has a lot in common with Manhattan: it is an island, it was once occupied by Native Americans, it is a major port, it is the most cosmopolitan and "European" city in the nation, it has hosted a memorable World's Fair, it has the largest Jewish population in the country, it is noted for its excellent restaurants and exciting nightlife, it is home to more than 130 different ethnic groups, and it has a National League baseball team which is the annual source of much hope and much suffering among its devoted fans.

But this train of thought will take you only so far, after which point the landscape becomes notable — and illuminating — for the differences between the two places. *Unlike* Manhattan, Montréal is a large island (51 km or 32 miles long, and at its widest, 16 km or 10 miles across). It is a thousand miles from the ocean, has a extensive and safe métro (or subway) system, and the overwhelming majority of its three and a half million citizens speak French as a first language. Indeed, it is the second largest French-speaking city in the world. And there is also a certain *je ne sais quoi* — let's call it *joie de vivre* — that clearly distinguishes Montréal from Manhattan, or from almost any other urban center you can think of.

LEFT: Designed by Buckminster Fuller, Montréal's Biosphere explains the ecosystems of the St. Lawrence River and the Great Lakes. ABOVE: View from the tower of Notre-Dame-de-Bonsecours.

Built around a mound of volcanic rock (Mont-Royal, known locally simply as "the mountain"), Montréal stands as a living monument to happy coexistence, for here one finds happily coexisting two principal languages, two cultures, two traditions, two school systems (one French, one English), and even two eras: that of New France, which celebrates the past by preserving its landmarks, and that of the new Québec, which began celebrating the present and future with Expo '67, the World's Fair that brought more than 50 million visitors to the city, and continued with the 1976 summer Olympics, and has now produced a city that is gleamingly, efficiently modern without having sacrificed any of its Gallic zest for life.

When the city fell to the British in 1760 it had a population of 5,000, all of whom lived in present-day Vieux-Montréal. As a result of the British conquest, and the subsequent cession of Canada to Britain in 1763, there was a large exodus of French nobility and military officers back to France. At the same time there was a large influx of immigrants from Scotland, who quickly became prominent in the burgeoning fur trade. The occupation of Montréal by the Americans under General Montgomery, which lasted for seven months during the winter and spring of 1775–1776, made very little impact on the city, although the American Revolution itself did affect Montréal by prompting thousands of Loyalists to flee the new republic and resettle there.

BACKGROUND

Whereas Montréal's name apparently dates from 1535, when Jacques Cartier is said to have described the island's volcanic rock peak as "un mont réal" ("a royal mountain"), the city's foundation dates from 1611, when Samuel de Champlain established a fortified trading post on the island. Some 31 years later, in 1642, Paul de Chomeday, Sieur de Maisonneuve, arrived with 53 Frenchmen and founded a permanent settlement named Ville-Marie on the site of what is now known as Vieux-Montréal. For the remainder of the century the settlers were under constant attack by the Iroquois, but during the eighteenth century the threat faded and the bustling town of Montréal — it ceased to be called Ville-Marie during this period — prospered thanks to its ever-expanding fur trade.

In 1783 a new enterprise was set up — the North West Trading Company — by a partnership of Montréal's leading fur traders. This consolidated Montréal's preeminence in the fur trade and made possible the large-scale export of furs to Europe. The importance of the fur trade gradually diminished after 1821, when the North West Trading Company was merged with its more powerful rival, the Hudson's Bay Company, but the economic boom continued with other industries beginning to flourish. It was also the early part of the nineteenth century that saw the arrival of a large wave of European Jewish immigrants, who brought with them skills crucial to Montréal's development as a major business and financial center. Thus, by the time the city was incorporated in 1832 it was already a significant force in

The 1705 Château de Ramezay, now a museum.

Canadian life; by the time of Confederation in 1867 it was the most important city in Canada.

Its importance and growth continued into the twentieth century, although in the period between the two World Wars it acquired a rather unsavory reputation as "Sin City." Illegal gambling, prostitution, and gangsterism all thrived under the protection of corrupt authorities. This slide into decadence came to an abrupt end, however, in 1954 with the election of Jean Drapeau as mayor. Corruption among city officials was weeded out, hoodlums were prosecuted, and brothels and gambling houses were closed down. At the same time there was extensive redevelopment and renovation of derelict areas, a modern subway

system was installed, and the ambitious Place Ville-Marie, a downtown underground shopping complex, was built. With the exception of a short spell in the early 1960s, Drapeau continued in office until the mid-1980s; a remarkable span of 30 years during which he literally changed the face of the city with spectacular shopping complexes, the métro, the stunning array of buildings and structures associated with Expo '67, the magnificent cultural and performing arts center, Place des Arts, and many other less-obvious examples of his determination to beautify and modernize the city.

GENERAL INFORMATION

For informational materials in advance of your trip contact **Tourisme Montréal–Greater Montréal Convention & Tourism Bureau** ((514) 844-5400

FAX (514) 844-0541 WEB SITE www.tourism-montreal.org, 1555 Peel Street, Suite 600, Montréal H3A 3L8. The **Infotouriste Centre** ((514) 873-2015 WEB SITE www.tourism-montréal.org, 1001 rue du Square-Dorchester, at the corner of Rue Peel and Rue Ste-Catherine, also has a range of services, such as hotel booking, bus tours, car rentals, and currency exchange. There is also an information kiosk at Place Jacques-Cartier, 174 rue Notre-Dame est, in Vieux-Montréal. There is **Internet access** at Cybermonde, 15 rue de la Commune, Vieux-Montréal.

Museum buffs can reap savings by purchasing a **Montréal Museum Pass** ((514) 845-6873, which allows entry to 19 museums and comes as one-day and three-day versions.

Getting Around

Many of Montréal's sites of interest can be reached on foot from downtown and Vieux Montréal hotels. For purposes of orientation, remember that the city is laid out on the American plan, a grid that in Montréal's case is divided into east and west, with St-Laurent being the center. East and west numbering is taken from St-Laurent, and north and south numbers begin at the Vieux-Port.

The city also has an excellent public transportation system, STCUM (*Société de transport de la communauté urbaine de Montréal*) which operates the bus and métro (subway) systems on the island. They have a 24-hour recorded information service in both French and English ((514) 288-6287. STCUM offers the **Carte touristique (Tourist Pass)**, which costs $5 for a one-day pass and $12 for a weekly pass. Individual ride tickets cost $1.85 — do the arithmetic. You can also save by buying your tickets in a *lisière* of six for $8. When purchasing tickets (though not passes), seniors and students with ID get a reduced price. The last métro is around 1 AM, after which a night bus runs between the popular nightspots.

WHAT TO SEE AND DO

Vieux-Montréal

Vieux-Montréal, or the Old Town, is bounded by Rue Berri, Rue St-Antoine, Rue McGill, and the waterfront; and until the nineteenth century all of Montréal was contained within this area. By the 1960s, no longer the city's center, the Old Town had fallen into disuse and disrepair, so the

on top of a high column erected in 1809 to honor his victory at Trafalgar. This might be a good time to pick up some information from the Tourist Information Bureau at the Notre-Dame end of the square, and browse through it while soaking up the atmosphere and some refreshment at one of the square's cafés. Running along the south side of the square is the **Rue St-Paul**, a lively main street that is filled with fashionable shops, art galleries and restaurants.

Moving up the incline from Place Jacques-Cartier you'll find, just across from the square on Rue Notre-Dame, the **Hôtel de Ville** (City Hall) — a dignified Second-Empire-style building — and just west of it is the domed **Old Courthouse**

government stepped in and declared it an historic area — whereupon a program of restoration and renovation of its attractive older buildings began. It is now alive and well, bustling with restaurants, bars, shops, galleries, outdoor cafés, and street entertainment. The best way to see the historic Old Town is to wander around on foot along its narrow streets and beautiful squares. Vieux-Montréal is served by three métro stations: Place d'Armes, Victoria Square and Champs-de-Mars.

The delightful **Place Jacques-Cartier** is a large cobbled square lined with old houses, restaurants, cafés, and craft shops. **Galerie le Chariot (** (514) 875-4994, is located here at No. 446; it is Canada's foremost showcases for Inuit art. In the summer, tourists and Montréalers alike are drawn here by the outdoor cafés, the colorful craft and flower markets, and the street performers. At the north end of the square a **statue of Lord Nelson** stands

building. The broad field that the city hall looks out onto is the **Champs-de-Mars**, which was a parking lot until just recently. Facing the Hôtel de Ville on the corner of Notre-Dame and St-Claude is the elegant **Château de Ramezay (** (514) 861-3708, 280 rue Notre-Dame est, which dates from 1705. Originally the home of the French governors, it was subsequently used for a variety of purposes, its most recent incarnation being that of a museum where you can see period furnishings, costumes, artifacts, and displays on the history of the city, including the story of the area's original native inhabitants. It is open daily from June to September, and from Tuesday to Sunday the rest of the year. An admission fee is charged.

OPPOSITE: Ornate façades LEFT of Montréal's Vieux Port contrast with downtown's soaring lines RIGHT. ABOVE: Cathédrale-Basilique Marie-Reine-du-Monde, a scaled-down version of St. Peter's in Rome.

One block east of here, running between Rues Notre-Dame and St-Paul, is **Rue Bonsecours**, a beautiful little street that is well worth a visit. The **Maison Pierre-du-Calvet** stands here, an attractive French Colonial house that dates from 1725 and has been furnished with antiques. At the bottom of the road is the lovely **Chapelle Notre-Dame-de-Bonsecours**, known as the Sailors' Chapel, which stood at the waterside until the land was reclaimed. The original church was built here in 1657 by Marguerite Bourgeoys, the founder of an order of teaching nuns. It was rebuilt in 1678 and again in 1772. It has a quaint and interesting interior where model ships, votive offerings from sailors, hang from the ceiling, and the life of the

the square, tucked away behind old stone walls, is Montréal's oldest building, the **Séminaire St-Sulpice**, which dates from 1685. You can't explore this fine old building because it is still used by Sulpician monks, and not open to the public.

Next to the seminary is the vast **Basilique Notre-Dame**, a twin-towered neo-Gothic structure, built over a period of 46 years and completed in 1869. The huge and richly decorated interior contains some very fine carving. There is a splendidly ornate main altar, made of red and white pine, and the pulpit was hand-carved from the trunk of a single walnut tree. The stained glass windows, made in Limoges, France, tell of the religious history of Montréal. Notice the slope of

founder is depicted in its small museum in a curious series of tableaux made with dolls. Climb up the church tower for some good views of the old city and the harbor. Next door is the newly renovated **Marché Bonsecours** ((514) 872-4560, 350 rue St-Paul, with its boutiques, restaurants, exhibitions and summer farmer's market. It's open daily 9 AM to 5 PM.

A few blocks west of Place Jacques-Cartier along Rue Notre-Dame is the **Place d'Armes**, which in 1644 was the site of a battle between settlers and the Iroquois. A statue of the Sieur de Maisonneuve in the center of the square commemorates the French victory. To the north side of the square you'll see the **Banque de Montréal**, a dignified Classical building with its stately columned portico. It houses a small and quite interesting banking museum that you can visit between 10 AM and 4 PM on weekdays. At the south end of

the floor; architect James O'Donnell chose to rake the sanctuary, following the natural slope of the land downward toward the St. Lawrence. The sanctuary is occasionally used for concerts (Pavarotti once performed here). The lovely **Chapel of the Sacred Heart** was rebuilt after being all but destroyed by a deranged arsonist in 1978; many of the remaining 1888 elements were incorporated within the modern design. Its bronze sculpture depicting the stages of human life is one of the largest in the world. The church ((514) 849-1070 is open daily and offers guided tours (except Sunday morning).

The nearby **Pointe-à-Callière (Montréal Museum of Archaeology and History)** ((514) 872-9150, 350 place Royale (corner of Commune), is the pride of the city. An archeological dig in Vieux-Port found remains of Chomeday's 1652 original settlement along with Amerindian remains. Rather than removing the artifacts, this museum was built on top of the site. The multimedia presentation "Montréal, a Crossroads of Cultures and Trade" on the founding of Montréal kicks off the tour. It's open July to August, Tuesday to Friday from 10 AM to 6 PM, and Saturday and Sunday from 11 AM to 6 PM; September to June, Tuesday to Friday from 10 AM to 5 PM, and Saturday to Sunday from 11 AM to 5 PM. An admission fee is charged.

A block and a half west of the Point-à-Callière is the **Centre d'Histoire de Montréal (** (514) 872-3207 housed in the old fire station at 335 place d'Youville, where the history of the city is described in a series of audiovisual displays. The museum is open Tuesday to Sunday from September to

Dame Ouest between Guy and Atwater is the main antiques area.

Downtown (Centre-Ville)

The downtown district of Montréal, bordered by Atwater, St-Denis, St-Antoine, and Sherbrooke, has quite a different character. In the 1960s steel and glass skyscrapers, highrise hotels, and complexes began to appear here. This sweeping modernization was also happening below ground with the development of Montréal's **Cité Souterraine (Underground City)**, a huge 29-km (18-miles) network of passages among shopping and business centers, cinemas, and restaurants; with access to hotels, railway stations, and many other

early May, open every day in summer. An admission fee is charged. Just around the corner, the **Musée Marc-Aurèle Fortin (** (514) 845-6108 at 118 rue St-Pierre, houses the works of Québécois landscape painter Fortin (1887–1970), and also temporary exhibitions of the work of other local artists. The museum is closed Mondays.

Just across from the Centre d'Histoire stands the **Écuries d'Youville**, a group of early nineteenth-century warehouse and factory buildings enclosed by old stone walls. The buildings have been renovated and function as offices and shops, and there are some pleasant restaurants here. The attractive courtyard provides a peaceful haven for tired sightseers.

There are plenty of tacky souvenir shops in Vieux Montréal, but it also has its share of **boutiques**, **antique**, and **craft shops**, especially around Rues St-Paul, St-Amble, and St-Jacques. Notre-

facilities. Whether or not you like the idea of shopping malls, going about your business without having to be outdoors can be quite an appealing prospect in the winter rain and snow. Underground walkways link such complexes as **Place Bonaventure**, **Place du Canada**, and **Place Ville-Marie**, while others are a métro ride away.

The center of this system, and the first complex to have been built, is the **Place Ville-Marie** (often referred to as the PVM). Aboveground the square is dominated by the 45-story **Royal Bank Tower**, a remarkable cruciform structure designed by architect I.M. Pei and now one of Montréal's most famous landmarks.

It could be said that **Dominion Square** is the heart of Montréal, and with calèches and tour

LEFT: The new Pointe-à-Callière museum of archaeology and history is the pride of the city. ABOVE: Montréal's waterfront.

buses waiting here, it's a good place to start your explorations. But before taking off, look around the square. On one side stands the **Sun Life Building**, a great gray wedding cake of a place which was Montréal's first skyscraper, and once Canada's largest building. Facing it stands the **Bank of Commerce**, a slick, glass skyscraper, and the **Marriott Château Champlain** hotel, another vast modern structure sometimes referred to as "the cheese-grater" because of its semicircular windows. At the southern end of the square along the Boulevard René-Lévesque (formerly known as Boulevard Dorchester) **Cathédrale-Basilique Marie-Reine-du-Monde**, a scaled-down copy of St. Peter's in Rome, stands valiantly in the midst of the modern giants.

Eastwards along Boulevard René-Lévesque past the PVM, turn left (motorists: only after 6 PM) onto Rue de l'Université and two blocks along at Rue Ste-Catherine you'll find **Cathédrale Christ Church**; a fine Gothic-style church dating from the 1850s. In summer there are free organ concerts here each Wednesday. **Rue Ste-Catherine** is Montréal's main shopping street. At Rue Ste-Catherine Ouest you'll find just about everything at the major department stores such as La Baie, Eaton, Simon (chic clothing), and Ogilvy's. However, the most exclusive fashion-only store, Holt Renfrew, is found along the "Gold Square Mile" of Rue Sherbrooke Ouest, at the corner of Rue de la Montagne. At 2025 rue Peel, the **Canadian Guild of Crafts** ((514) 849-6091 has a particularly good selection of Canadian arts and crafts, with knowledgeable staff to offer advice. Further west along Ste-Catherine on and around **Rues Crescent** and

Bishop is Montréal's center of chic, where restored Victorian mansions house exclusive and trendy boutiques, cafés, and restaurants.

For a cultural interlude, go eastwards along Rue Ste-Catherine to the **Place des Arts** ((514) 842-2112, an arts complex for theater, opera, ballet, music, and visual arts. It's the venue for the annual Festival International de Jazz (see NIGHTLIFE AND THE ARTS, page 168). The **Musée d'Art Contemporain** ((514) 847-6226, is part of the complex. It's Canada's only museum dedicated to contemporary art. The museum is open Tuesday to Sunday; an admission fee is charged, free on Wednesday evening. If you haven't had enough of shopping malls by this time, there's an underground

link from Place des Arts to the nearby **Complexe Desjardins**, an enclosed mall that extends above and below ground level. For a completely different kind of shopping, south of here near Place d'Armes métro and centered on Rue de la Gauchetière is Montréal's **Chinatown**.

On the north side of Rue Sherbrooke, where it intersects with Rue de l'Université, stands the famous **McGill University**, where you might like to wander around the pleasant green campus lying at the foot of Mont-Royal. Facing the campus on the south side of Sherbrooke is **Musée McCord de l'Histoire Canadienne** ((514) 398-7100, 690 rue Sherbrooke ouest, which traces the history of Montréal and Canada as a whole with collections of art, costume, artifacts, and a massive photographic collection, including the story and artifacts of the region's First Nations peoples. It's open Tuesday to Sunday, and an admission fee is charged.

Continuing westwards, Canada's first museum, the **Musée des Beaux-Arts** (Fine Arts Museum) ((514) 285-1600 at 1379–1380 rue Sherbrooke ouest, houses an art collection that spans all ages and all parts of the world, so whatever your taste you'll find something to please you here. As you might expect, it has a large collection of Canadian art; European art movements are also well represented. Inuit sculptures, African masks, and pre-Columbian figures are among the permanent exhibits and the museum also hosts major international exhibitions. The museum is open Tuesday to Sunday, and admission to the permanent collection is free, with a fee charged for special exhibitions.

which is home to many writers, artists, and musicians. At the western end of the square runs **Rue Prince Arthur**, a lively pedestrian-only street that offers shops, ethnic food, and street entertainment.

For some more ethnic flavors, turn off Prince Arthur at **Boulevard St-Laurent**, an immigrant neighborhood that is rapidly becoming a fashionable culinary focal point. It's a busy area of shops, bars, cafés, delis, and restaurants. St-Laurent, also known as "The Main," was once the ostensible dividing line between the French- and English-speaking communities, and although this is no longer strictly true, there are still hints of this cultural split. It remains the east-west dividing line for street numbers.

Le Centre Canadien d'Architecture ((514) 939-7000, at 1920 rue Baile, is one of the world's most important architectural museums. Exhibition halls are open to the public with scale models and hands-on demonstrations. It's open Wednesday to Sunday; an admission fee is charged.

Outside Downtown

Centered around the **Rue St-Denis** is Montréal's **Quartier Latin**. St-Denis has an academic chic about it with its cafés, restaurants, nightclubs, bars, art galleries, and trendy boutiques where local designers sell their one-of-a-kind conceptions: it's an area that's big on atmosphere, and a haunt of students from the local **Université du Québec**. Proceeding northwards, one block beyond the intersection with Sherbrooke you'll find **Square St-Louis** on the left, an attractive square of beautiful Victorian houses looking onto a small park,

During your visit to the Latin Quarter, you might like to combine a trip to the **Parc Lafontaine** ((514) 872-2644, Rue Sherbrooke and Avenue Parc-Lafontaine (nearest métro: Sherbrooke). It's an ideal place to do a spot of rowing, stroll around the French- and English-style gardens or have a picnic while enjoying the free open-air entertainment that is often presented here. The park is open year-round.

Further along Sherbrooke, on the eastern edge of the city, is **Parc Maisonneuve**, where you'll find the **Parc Olympique**, originally built for the 1976 Summer Olympics (although not completed until 1987). This huge and vastly expensive complex is bold and striking in its design; the centerpiece

OPPOSITE: An antique merchant LEFT buys and sells religious articles, while a "video sex" store RIGHT offers goods of a more secular nature. ABOVE: The Biodôme.

is the gigantic **Stade Olympique (Olympic Stadium)** ((514) 252-8687, which can seat 80,000 spectators who come to see the Montréal Expos baseball games, rock concerts, and trade shows. The striking tilted tower overlooking the stadium was designed for winching the retractable roof. The original roof, however, proved too expensive to maintain; it has recently been replaced by a stationary one. From the tower, which leans at a 45-degree angle, runs a funicular on which you can ride to an observation deck for a view over the metropolis. Daily guided tours of the Olympic complex, including its six swimming pools, leave from the tourist hall ((514) 252-8687 in the base of the tower. Tours at 12:40 PM and 3:40 PM are in English and the ones at 11 AM and 2 PM are in French; a fee is charged. The pools are open for public swimming also. During summer the tower is open Monday from noon to 9 PM, Tuesday to Thursday from 10 AM to 9 PM, and Friday and Saturday from 10 AM to 11 PM; from early September to mid-January it opens Tuesday to Sunday from noon to 6 PM (closed mid-January to mid-February). An admission fee is charged. To get there you can take the métro to Via or Pie-IX.

Next to the Stade Olympique is the **Biodôme de Montréal** ((514) 868-3000, at 4777 avenue Pierre-de-Coubertin. Built as the Olympic vélodrome for the 1976 Olympics, it is now an environmental museum and one of the city's most popular attractions. Replicas of four distinct ecosystems have been constructed inside the building: polar tundra, tropical forest, boreal forest, and the St. Lawrence River. Each of the rooms features flora and fauna and appropriate temperatures, as well as changing seasons. It is open daily 9 AM to 8 PM (to 6 PM in winter); an admission fee is charged. Inclusive admission fees for the Biodôme, Olympic Tower and/or the Jardin Botanique and Insectarium are available.

A free shuttle bus links the Parc Olympique to the **Jardin Botanique** (Botanical Garden) ((514) 872-1400, where about 26,000 species of plants from all around the world are displayed in a series of gardens and greenhouses, over an area of 72 hectares (180 acres). The summer is undoubtedly the time to see the gardens at their spectacular best, but in winter the visitor can escape into the exotic atmospheres of the greenhouses. The **Chinese Garden** was a joint project of Montréal and Shanghai, and is the largest of its kind outside Asia. You can wander amongst its pavilions, courtyards, carp ponds, and myriad indigenous Chinese plants. The truly celestial **Japanese Garden** is a must. There is a cultural pavilion and art gallery, a tearoom where the ancient tea ceremony is performed, and a Zen garden. Also within the grounds is the **Insectarium** ((514) 872-0663, with more than 4,000 mounted insects including scarab beetles, locusts, butterflies, maggots, tarantulas,

and live creepy crawlers including cockroaches, praying mantises, and scorpions. It's open daily in summer from 9 AM to 7 PM and the rest of the year from 9 AM to 5 PM; an admission fee is charged. A small train will take you on a guided tour of the gardens for a small fee. The garden is open daily from 9 AM to 8 PM (to 5 PM in winter). An admission fee is charged.

In the St. Lawrence River, facing Vieux-Montréal is **Île Ste-Hélène**, which was enlarged using landfill during the 1960s. Ste-Hélène and the completely man-made neighboring **Île Notre-Dame** were the setting for the World's Fair, Expo '67. The former French pavilion now houses one of the world's biggest gambling palace — the Casino de Montréal (see NIGHTLIFE AND THE ARTS, below). The giant geodesic dome designed by Buckminster Fuller was once the American Pavilion and now houses **La Biosphère** ((514) 283-5000, 160 tour-de-l'Île (Île Ste-Hélène). Not to be confused with

the Biodôme at the Parc Olympique, this is an environmental exhibit area devoted to promoting awareness of the St. Lawrence/Great Lakes ecosystem. There are multimedia shows and hands-on displays, and good views of the river from the observation deck. It's open June to September daily from 10 AM to 8 PM, October to May Tuesday to Sunday from 9 AM to 6 PM. An admission fee is charged. For lighter entertainment there's **La Ronde (** (514) 872-4537 TOLL-FREE (800) 797-4537, Île Ste-Hélène's enormous amusement park, featuring Le Cobra, a stand-up roller coaster with a 360 degree loop, and all the shows, rides, and thrills needed to keep the shrieks and the laughter going. It's open mid-May to late June daily from 11 AM to midnight; and from late June to Labor Day, Sunday to Thursday 11 AM to 11 PM and Friday and Saturday 11 AM to midnight. An admission fee is charged. Île Ste-Hélène can be reached by métro from Île Ste-Hélène Station, or by car via either La Concorde or Jacques Cartier bridges. A shuttle bus takes would-be millionaires from the island métro station to the casino.

Easily accessible by métro (Lionel Giroulx station), **Marché Atwater**, at 138 avenue Atwater, is a charming year-round farmer's market housed in a brick art deco building that also has cafés and delis and arts and crafts. On a sunny summer's day it's one of the most photogenic spots in the city, with crusty farmers chatting up the customers over meticulously arranged vegetables. You can get some Eastern Canadian food specialties here, such as maple syrup *(sirop d'érable)* and fiddlehead ferns. It's open daily from 7 AM to 6 PM.

One of Montréal's most stunning features is, of course, the mountain that dominates the cityscape, **Mont-Royal**. The **Parc du Mont-Royal** is the city's finest park and, was skillfully planned by

Inside Montréal's Biodôme visitors walk through the tropical forest exhibition.

the architect of New York's Central Park, Frederick Law Olmstead. In the summer it's a popular place for walking, jogging, picnicking, riding, sitting, sunbathing, or just taking in the views of the city below. In winter, skates, sleighs, skis, and snowshoes are brought here. How you get to the park depends on your mood: you can go there by calèche, drive most of the way there by car, or walk from Rue Peel, Avenue du Parc, or Rue Drummond.

You might like to make a pilgrimage to the **Oratoire St-Joseph** (St. Joseph's Oratory) ℂ (514) 733-8211, 3800 chemin Queen-Mary, on the northwest slope of Mont-Royal. In 1904 a monk called Brother André, who was said to have great healing powers, raised a chapel to St. Joseph here, from where he worked tirelessly to treat the sick. A large domed basilica was built here in the late 1930s, although the interior was not completed until the 1960s; the original chapel still stands. Inside the basilica is a museum dedicated to Brother André: abandoned crutches and wheelchairs bear witness to his powers. If you are looking for a miracle yourself, you can light a candle or touch Brother André's tomb; hardcore pilgrims climb the stairs to the church on their knees saying a prayer at every step. St-Joseph's is open daily and can be reached by taking the métro to Côte des Neiges or Snowdon stations.

SPORTS AND OUTDOOR ACTIVITIES

General information on summer and winter sports activities in Montréal is available from the Sports and Leisure Department of the City of Montréal ℂ (514) 872-6211.

The Parc Mont-Royal is a popular spot for **jogging**. There are over 20 **cycling** paths running through Montréal covering 240 km (149 miles); popular rides include the Lachine Canal, Vieux-Port, Angrignon Park, and Rue Notre-Dame, between the Parc Rivière-des-Prairies and Rue Berri. Maps are available widely. Bicycles can be rented at the Vieux-Port from Vélo Aventure ℂ (514) 847-0666 on the Promenade du Vieux-Port, which also rents in-line skates. The métro allows cyclers to bring their bikes on board during non-rush-hour periods; use the last two doors of the tail car.

Jet-boating over the Lachine Rapids is an exhilarating experience. Excursions leave six times a day May to September. Contact Saute Moutons–Lachine Rapids Tours ℂ (514) 284-9607 FAX (514) 287-9401 E-MAIL lrt@cam.org, 105 rue de la Commune Ouest, Montréal, Québec H2Y 2C7 (see JET THE LACHINE RAPIDS, page 17, in TOP SPOTS).

There are more than 200 **skating** rinks in Montréal, most of which are outdoors, and the biggest of which is the one-and-a-half-kilometer (one-mile)-long Olympic Basin on Île Notre-Dame. Winter also brings **cross-country skiing**, **tobogganing** and **snowshoeing** to the snow-covered city parks.

Two hours north of the city, **Les Laurentides** (the Laurentians) were so named in 1845 by a French historian because they parallel the St. Lawrence River. These rolling hills are a mecca for outdoor activities, from paddling to sailing to trout fishing to mountain biking. But the region's greatest fame is as a ski destination. There are a wealth of slopes, including **Mont Tremblant** ℂ (819) 681-2000 TOLL-FREE (800) 461-8711, 3005 chemin Principal; and **Le Chantecler** ℂ (514) 229-3555 or (514) 393-8884, chemin Chantecler, Route 15, in Ste-Adèle.

NIGHTLIFE AND THE ARTS

Montréal has long had a well-deserved reputation for scintillating nightlife, with a choice of entertainment that ranges from the highbrow to the downright tacky, and there are masses of bars and clubs to choose from. *Voir* (in French) and its English counterpart, *Hour*, are hefty free publications with all the listings of all the local events (available in shops and cafés all over town). Voyage Astral ℂ (514) 866-1001, at the Infotouriste office, 1001 Square-Dorchester, sells **tickets** to all of these sporting, as well as many cultural, events. Bars close at 3 AM.

The world-famous **Orchestre Symphonique de Montréal** ℂ (514) 842-9915 plays at Salle Wilfrid-Pelletier at the Place des Arts when they're not on tour or playing at one of the city's parks or at the Basilique Notre-Dame. The **Orchestre Métropolitain du Grand Montréal** ℂ (514) 598-0870, an orchestra of younger musicians, also play at Place des Arts. Classical music can also be heard at **Pollack Concert Hall** ℂ (514) 398-4547 at McGill University. Opera fans will be interested to know that the **Opéra de Montréal** ℂ (514) 985-2258 stages four or five major operas each year at the Place des Arts. Operas are presented with bilingual scripts projected on screens above the stage.

Balletomanes can see the excellent **Grands Ballets Canadiens** ℂ (514) 849-8681, at the Salle Wilfrid-Pelletier when they're not touring, the popular **Les Ballets Jazz de Montréal** ℂ (514) 982-6771, and several other thriving contemporary dance troupes.

There are around a dozen theaters in the city with more than 65 theater companies; most productions are in French—the **Centaur Theatre** ℂ (514) 288-3161, 453 rue St-François-Xavier in Vieux-Montréal, is the foremost English-language theater company. **Théâtre du Nouveau-Monde** ℂ (514) 866-8667, 84 rue Ste-Catherine ouest, is the place for French classics, while **Théâtre du Rideau Vert** ℂ (514) 844-1793, 4664 rue St-Denis, specializes in contemporary French works. Each July the 12-day **Just For Laughs Festival** ℂ (514) 845-3155 is held in concert halls and outdoor venues around Rue St-Denis and all over the city.

The big-name pop and rock concerts take place at **Centre Molson** ((514) 932-2582, 1260 rue de la Gauchetière. The **Spectrum de Montréal** ((514) 861-5851, 318 rue Ste-Catherine ouest, is another biggy that hosts all kinds of shows, while the smaller **Club Soda** ((514) 270-7848, 5240 avenue du Parc, is a well-established venue for a variety of rock bands, including international acts.

For jazz on a summer's day there's the 11-day **Festival International de Jazz** which takes place both in and out of doors from the end of June to the beginning of July at Place des Arts. Bell Info-Jazz ((514) 871-1881 TOLL-FREE (888) 515-0515 has information; or to purchase tickets call ((514) 790-1245 TOLL-FREE (800) 678-5440 TOLL-FREE IN

and attracts McGill students; St-Laurent is the dividing line between east and west, and traditionally between English (east) and French (west) — and it's trendy right now. It's a great place for a late-night espresso and people-watching at sidewalk cafés. Or you can hip hop your way from one discotheque to another: **Wax Lounge** ((514) 282-0919, No. 3481 has guest DJs spinning house music. **DiSalvio** ((514) 845-4337, No. 3519 blasts its young clientele with house music, too, but throws in some R&B and some classic rock and roll. **Angels** ((514) 282-9944, No. 3604, has two floors to choose from with music ranging from hip hop to house, R&B, alternative, Britpop, '60s, and electronica; and **Allegra** ((514) 288-4883,

CANADA (800) 361-4595. Montréal does like its jazz and one of the favorite spots is **L'Air du Temps** ((514) 842-2003 in the Vieux-Montréal at 191 rue St-Paul ouest, which is a small and friendly place. Downtown you could go to **Biddles** ((514) 842-8656 at 2060 Aylmer, and nibble a spare rib or a chicken leg while you enjoy the sounds.

There is the vast **Casino de Montréal** ((514) 392-2746, 1 avenue du Casino, on Île Notre-Dame in the St. Lawrence River. In addition to almost 3,000 slot machines and more than 100 gaming tables, there are five restaurants, including the Mobil-Five-Star awarded Nuances, and a bilingual cabaret theater. You can take the métro to the Île Ste-Hélène station and transfer to bus 167. The casino is open 24 hours a day.

Clubs and bars center around several areas: St-Denis is more or less French, near the University of Québec; Rue Crescent is more or less English,

No. 3523A, has live Latin music on Thursdays, and on other nights world beat, R&B, funk, and an occasional swing band. Children of the 1970s will delight in **Le Limelight** ((514) 866-5463, 1254 Rue Stanley. This place was a flower-power-era disco and has recently been revived just as it was in those feverish days. Don't forget your bell-bottoms.

WHERE TO STAY

Expensive

The **Westin Mont-Royal** ((514) 284-1110 TOLL-FREE (800) 228-3000 FAX (514) 845-3025 is prestigiously located at 1050 rue Sherbrooke ouest, Montréal H3A 2R6, and is one of the very best hotels Montréal has to offer. The service is impeccable, the elegant rooms are equipped with just

The Casino de Montréal is a vast gambling palace, one of the world's largest.

about everything you could want, and if it isn't there then it can probably be arranged. Its rival is the nearby **Ritz-Carlton Montréal** ((514) 842-4212 TOLL-FREE (800) 363-0366 FAX (514) 842-4907, at 1228 rue Sherbrooke ouest, Montréal H3G 1H6. Established in 1912, this was the first Ritz in North America and has catered for the whims of many of the rich and famous over the years. The rooms are elegant and spacious, the service is everything you could wish it to be, and afternoon tea in the garden is a tradition.

Close to Dominion Square, the **Marriott Château Champlain** ((514) 878-9000 TOLL-FREE (800) 200-5909 or (800) 228-9290 FAX (514) 878-6777, 1 place du Canada, Montréal H3B 4C9, is a tall and unmistakable building with crescent-shaped windows. Rooms are airy and fitted out with French-style furniture. Views of Dominion Square and the downtown are inspirational. It is connected to Place Bonaventure, shopping, and restaurants via the city's underground network of walkways. Directly on top of place Bonaventure is the **Montréal Bonaventure Hilton** ((514) 878-2332 TOLL-FREE (800) 267-2575 FAX (514) 878-3881, 1 place Bonaventure, PO Box 779, Montréal H5A 1E4, with a shopping mall, restaurants, and métro below. There is a rooftop swimming pool in use year-round, a hectare (two and a half acres) of gardens, and the usual Hilton high standards.

La Reine Elizabeth ((514) 861-3511 TOLL-FREE (800) 441-1414 FAX (514) 954-2256, at 900 boulevard René-Lévesque, Montréal H3B 4A5, with more than 1,000 rooms and suites, is the city's largest hotel and you can rely on the service being excellent. It houses several restaurants including the famous Beaver Club.

The 37-floor **Sheraton Le Centre** ((514) 878-2000 TOLL-FREE (800) 325-3535 FAX (514) 878-3958, at 1201 boulevard René-Lévesque, Montréal H3B 2L7, is conveniently situated for the smart shops and restaurants of the Rue Crescent area. The hotel has several bars of its own, a nightclub, restaurant, and a smart, modern interior. The top five floors contain the most luxurious suites and rooms and have extra-special service.

Mid-range

One of Montréal's most charming downtown hotels is the **Château Versailles** ((514) 933-3611 TOLL-FREE IN CANADA (800) 361-7199 TOLL-FREE IN THE USA (800) 361-3664 FAX (514) 933-6867, at 1659 rue Sherbrooke ouest, Montréal H3H 1E3, which now fills four lovely old stone houses and offers 70 comfortable, well-equipped rooms with bathrooms and warm, friendly service. Across the street at No. 1808, is the 100-room Tour Versailles, a converted apartment hotel that has been added as an annex to the original town houses. Slightly further west in a residential area of downtown near the Forum sports and concert arena, **Manoir**

le Moyne ((514) 931-8861 TOLL-FREE (800) 361-7191 FAX (514) 931-7726, at 2100 boulevard de Maisonneuve ouest, Montréal H3H 1K6, is an all-suites hotel. With its 24-hour restaurant, and self-contained apartments, it creates the home-away-from-home environment that is popular with families or those who plan long stays. Taking advantage of weekly rates can bring a stay here into the inexpensive category.

Ideally placed for the restaurants and nightlife of the Latin Quarter, the **Crown Plaza Metro Centre** ((514) 842-8581 TOLL-FREE (800) 561-4644 FAX (514) 842-8910, at 505 rue Sherbrooke est, Montréal H2L 1K2, has good facilities including an indoor pool.

Centrally situated, the **Hôtel l'Appartement-In-Montréal** ((514) 284-3634 TOLL-FREE (800) 363-3010 FAX (514) 287-1431, at 455 rue Sherbrooke ouest, Montréal H3A 1B7, has 125 apartments of varying sizes, and guests have use of an indoor swimming pool, rooftop terrace, and laundry facilities. People certainly don't stay at the **Hôtel de l'Institut** ((514) 282-5120 TOLL-FREE (800) 361-5111 for the look of the place, but they do stay there for the service, convenient location, and good value. Students of the Institute of Tourism and Hotel Management train here, and they are determined to please. The rooms are comfortable, the hotel looks across to square St-Louis, and it's on top of Sherbrooke métro station at 3535 rue St-Denis, Montréal H2X 3P1. Close to Rue St-Denis and to Old Town is the **Hôtel Lord Berri** ((514) 845-9236 TOLL-FREE (888) 363-0363 FAX (514) 849-9855, at 1199 rue Berri, Montréal H2L 4C6, where the rooms have comforts such as in-room movies, some floors are set aside for nonsmokers, and there's a bright and busy sidewalk café.

Two delightful bed-and-breakfast inns in Vieux-Montréal, under the same ownership, are the most romantic places to stay in the city. **Auberge du Vieux-Port** ((514) 876-0081 FAX (514) 876-8923 TOLL-FREE (888) 660-7678, 97 rue de la Commune est, is an 1882 building with a cellar restaurant. Hardwood floors, massive beams, and the original windows typify its cozy rooms, many of which have whirlpool baths. Light meals and cocktails are served on the rooftop terrace, which has good views of the Vieux-Port. **Les Passants du Sans Soucy** ((514) 842-2634 FAX (514) 842-2812, 171 rue St-Paul ouest, Montréal H2Y 1Z5, near Pointe-à-Callière, is smaller and somewhat less expensive. There are nine guestrooms upstairs with stone walls, wood floors, wrought-iron beds, and lace curtains. Both of these hotels include a full breakfast in the room rate.

Inexpensive

Just off Sherbrooke, **Manoir Ambrose** ((514) 288-6922 TOLL-FREE (800) 665-1528 extension 115, at 3422 rue Stanley, Montréal H3A 1R8, offers an assortment of 22 accommodations in an attractive old building near the heart of downtown. Near Rue St-Denis the **Hôtel Bon Accueil** ((514) 527-9655 at 1601 rue St-Hubert, Montréal H2L 3Z1, has 20 rooms all with bathroom and television and offers very good value, as does **Hôtel Le Breton** ((514) 524-7273, at 1609 rue St-Hubert, Montréal H2L 3Z1, which has 13 rooms, seven of which have bathrooms and all of which have television. Just south of Rue Sherbrooke Est is the clean and cozy **Hôtel Castel St-Denis** ((514) 842-9719, at 2099 rue St-Denis, Montréal H2X 3K8, which has 14 rooms.

There is plenty of **bed and breakfast** accommodation in Montréal, ranging from basic to luxurious, and several agencies to help you find some-

thing to suit your needs, including: Bed and Breakfast Downtown Network ((514) 289-9749 TOLL-FREE (800) 267-5180, 3485 avenue Laval, Montréal H2X 3C8; or Relais Montréal Hospitalité ((514) 287-9653 TOLL-FREE (800) 363-9635, 3977 avenue Laval, Montréal H2W 2H9.

For backpackers there is the **Auberge de Montréal** ((514) 843-3317 TOLL-FREE (800) 461-8585 FAX (514) 934-3251 at 1030 rue Mackay, Montréal H3G 2H1. Also in downtown, **McGill University** ((514) 398-6367 FAX (514) 398-6770, Bishop Mountain Pavillion, 3935 rue de l'Université, Montréal H3A 2B4, **Collège Français** ((514) 495-2581, 185 avenue Fairmount ouest, Montréal H2T 2M6 (métro: Laurier) and the **Université de Montréal** ((514) 343-6531 FAX (514) 343-2353, 2350, boulevard Édouard-Montpetit, Montréal H3T 1J4 (métro: Édouard-Montpetit) all offer accommodation at low prices from mid-May to mid-August.

WHERE TO EAT

It's easy to see why eating out is favorite pastime of Montréalers. With some 4,000 restaurants representing the national cuisines from more than 80 different ethnic groups, you could eat out every night of the year at a different restaurant without fear of monotony. In addition to ethnic, there are also an abundance of Québécois regional restaurants and bistros. A large number of restaurants in the Latin Quarter allow you to bring your own wine, which will save on the final tab, so check this out in advance.

Expensive

The **Beaver Club** ((514) 861-3511 was a club formed by the early fur traders which by the 1800s had evolved into a gentlemen's club. It survives as a restaurant in the hotel La Reine Elizabeth at 900 boulevard René-Lévesque ouest, where its origins are very much in evidence in its formal atmosphere and the pelts and mementos that are hung about the walls. The cuisine is both continental and Québécois regional, and the service is superb. More excellent French food is served at **Les Chênets** ((514) 844-1842, 2075 rue Bishop, one of Montréal's priciest restaurants, where warm, glowing colors set the scene. **Le Café de Paris** ((514) 844-4212 at the Ritz-Carlton, 1228 rue Sherbrooke ouest, is classical in its cuisine and its elegant decor, and strains of piano music accompany your superb meal. Its venerable wine cellar provides an excellent list of wines ranging in price from moderate to very, very expensive. We recommend you pop in on a chilly morning for their Japanese breakfast — grilled salmon, spinach leaves with sesame dressing, miso soup, steamed rice, and dried toasted seaweed.

Toqué ((514) 499-2084, 3842 rue St-Denis, is one of Montréal's top tables. The contemporary Québec-Montréal cuisine emphasizes intense flavors and the freshest market ingredients. At the splendid **Nuances** ((514) 392-2708, 1 avenue du Casino, in the Casino de Montréal on Île Notre-Dame, chef Jean-Pierre Curtat reigns over one of Montréal's most admired kitchens. The cuisine is authentically French with a nod to contemporary trends, so that Asian or Mediterranean flavors complement classic French fish or poultry dishes.

The interior of **Le Lutétia** ((514) 288-5656, at 1430 rue de la Montagne, in the Hôtel de la Montagne, is an explosion of ornate decorative styles; baroque in the broadest sense and an ideal place for romantic *dîner à deux*. The excellent menu offers fine French and Italian cuisine, and the wine list is of a similarly high standard.

The sunny waterfront terrace of Café Helios is a favorite lunchtime gathering spot.

Ardent carnivores will think they have died and gone to heaven in **Moishe's** ((514) 845-3509 at 3961 boulevard St-Laurent, a steak house of the highest order. The meat is expertly prepared and aged in the restaurant's own cold rooms, and steaks are grilled over wood. The old Jewish neighborhood around Rue St-Laurent is now *très branché* (very trendy: literally "plugged in") and here you'll find a host of excellent restaurants—and the who's who of Montréal dining in them. Your taste buds can travel the world over on Rue St-Laurent. **Globe** ((514) 284-3823, at No. 3455, has a *fin-de-siècle* decor rather like a Hollywood notion of a luxury cruise liner's dining room. The menu is cosmopolitan, but with special emphasis on Mediterranean

flavors. **Mediterraneo** ((514) 844-0027, at No. 3500, could be the best place on this gastronomic street. A glowing jet-set atmosphere and a menu that accents the flavors of southern France guarantee a memorable evening. **Soto** ((514) 842-1150, at No. 3527, offers divine sushi of all varieties as well as sashimi, yakitori, and teriyaki. The setting is as elegantly styled as the food.

In Vieux-Montréal, perfectly prepared fresh seafood is served in **Chez Delmo** ((514) 849-4601, at 211-215 rue Notre-Dame ouest, in comfortable, old-fashioned surroundings. There are oyster bars at the front of the restaurant, popular for informal lunchtime dining. At **La Marée** ((514) 861-9794, 404 place Jacques-Cartier, you can dine in the beautiful surroundings and intimate atmosphere of an eighteenth-century house. The seafood is also cooked to perfection and served with delicious sauces.

Moderate

Trendy Rue St-Laurent also offers some less loftily priced restaurants. Though **Pizzadelic** ((514) 522-2286, 1250 rue St-Laurent, is franchising its heart out, they haven't forgotten how to make an excellent pizza. Toppings range from the classic to the bizarre, and pastas, salads, and other Italian specialties are also on offer. **L'Express** ((514)

845-5333 at 3927 rue St-Denis, is another Montréal place to see and be seen. It is a crowded bistro and the food and the wine list are excellent. Try the *aiguillettes de canard*, slices of cold roast duck complemented by stir-fried vegetables with Thai peanut sauce, and save room for their famous *tarte au chocolate*. The kitchen is open until 3 AM making it a good late-night spot.

For good Greek food, **Milos** ((514) 272-3522, at 5357 avenue du Parc, is an excellent choice. You select the ingredients of your meal from the fresh seafood, meat, and vegetables that are displayed. One of the best Indian restaurants around is **Le Taj** ((514) 845-9015, 2077 rue Stanley, where the menu is northern Indian and includes tandoori dishes.

Katsura ((514) 849-1172, 2170 rue de la Montagne, provides elegant and tranquil Japanese surroundings and a menu that includes all the sushi dishes. You can book a private tatami room for dining in the traditional Japanese manner, and there's also the option of the restaurant's sushi bar.

To sample Québécois food you should go to the **Auberge le St-Gabriel** ((514) 878-3561, 426 rue St-Gabriel, an old and interesting building in Vieux-Montréal which is said to be North America's oldest restaurant.

Inexpensive

For good-value Asian fare, we like **Chao Thai** ((514) 868-0657, 1029 rue Clarke (at the corner of Rue de la Gauchetière). From its second floor location there is a view over the windswept Sun Yat-Sen Park and the blinking lights of Chinatown. It's a friendly place, bustling with families tending their steaming hot pots — partitioned bowls with two types of soup in which you cook greens and noodles. There's also a short list of specials including squid, chicken, and vegetarian dishes. Service is quick, and spicy dishes are not at all wimpy.

For hamburgers, **Restaurant La Paryse** ((514) 842-2040, at 302 rue Ontario est, is the best place in town, where they make them with good ground beef and lashings of everything to satisfy the largest appetites.

There's hearty Polish food and ridiculously low prices in the **Restaurant Mazurka** ((514) 844-3539, 64 rue Prince Arthur est, and so it's not surprising that the place is always busy. **Laurier Barbeque** ((514) 273-3671, 381 avenue Laurier ouest, is something of an institution where traditional Québécois food is served and French-Canadian families gather; try their barbecued chicken, and save room for their legendary desserts.

Montréal has some excellent delicatessens where smoked meat — brisket of beef that is marinated for two weeks then steamed and served with rye bread and pickle — is the classic fare.

Remember rue St-Laurent? It's is also home to the humble **Hoffner's** ((514) 845-9809, at No. 3671, where you can have sausage on a bun. **Ben's** ((514) 844-1000 at 990 boulevard de Maisonneuve ouest, **Schwartz's** ((514) 842-4813 at 3895 boulevard St-Laurent, and **Reuben's Restaurant Delicatessen** ((514) 861-1255, 888 rue Ste-Catherine ouest, all have their devoted customers.

Montréalers claim their city produces the best bagels in the world, and the best of the best are found at **St-Viateur Bagels** ((514) 276-8044, 263 rue St-Viateur ouest. Try one with smoked salmon and cream cheese. At **Squeeze Juice Bar** ((514) 866-9941 extension 303, in the YWCA building, on Boulevard René-Lévesque at the corner of rue Crescent, the owner doesn't just mix a great juice drink, he's also an artisan who created the decor from scratch. Sit at the sinuously curved bar with its octopus lamps and rococo glass bowls full of exotic plastic fruits and sip one of his dozens of fresh fruit juice concoctions.

EXCURSIONS FROM MONTRÉAL

From Montréal, Autoroute 10 runs east to Sherbrooke. This road takes you through the scenic terrain and tidy villages of **Les Cantons de l'Est (Eastern Townships)**. Its a snowbelt region and a growing ski destination, yet on the whole much quieter and more bucolic than the pulsing Laurentian ski stations to the north. The four main resorts have a total of 143 trails, verticals up to 540 m (1,770 ft), and 900 km (560 miles) of cross-country trails. As befits the birthplace of the inventor of the snowmobile, Joseph-Armand Bombardier, there are 2,000 km (1,200 miles) of trails for snowmobiling. Resorts include: **Mont Sutton** ((514) 538-2339, PO Box 280, Sutton J0E 2K0; **Station Touristique de Mont Orford** ((819) 843-6548 TOLL-FREE (800) 361-6548, PO Box 248, Magog-Orford J1X 3W8; **Station touristique Owl's Head** ((514) 292-3342 TOLL-FREE (800) 363-3342, 40 chemin du Mont Owl's Head, PO Box 35, Mansonville J0E 1X0.

Accommodation is plentiful and varied in the region. For information on visiting the Eastern Townships, contact **Tourism Estrie** ((819) 820-2020 TOLL-FREE (800) 355-5755 FAX (819) 566-4445 E-MAIL ate@multi-medias.ca, 25 rue Bocage, Sherbrooke J1L 2J4, or visit the **Maison régionale du tourisme des Cantons-de-l'Est** ((514) 375-8774 FAX (514) 375-3530, Eastern Townships Autoroute (10), Exit 68.

HOW TO GET THERE

All flights to Montréal are handled by **Aéroport de Dorval** ((514) 633-3105, 25 km (15 miles) west of the city. (Aéroport Mirabel is now used primarily for cargo.) The ride into the city takes about 25 minutes. **Autobus Connaisseur** ((514) 934-1222

has a regular shuttle service. The shuttle runs on the half hour and drops off at La Reine Elizabeth, Le Centre Sheraton, Le Château Champlain and the Voyageur terminal. When flying out of Montréal you will have to pay a departure tax of $10.

Montréal is also connected to many of the country's major cities by **VIA Rail's** ((514) 989-2626, intercity and transcontinental trains which arrive at and depart from Gare Centrale (Central Station), 935 rue de la Gauchetière ouest, under Le Reine Elizabeth at the corner of Boulevard René-Lévesque and Rue Mansfield. The station is connected underground to the Bonaventure, McGill, and Peel métro stations (and the Windsor railway

station for the local commuter trains). If you are coming by train from the United States, **Amtrak** TOLL-FREE IN THE UNITED STATES (800) 835-8725 has two East Coast trains to Montréal: the *Vermonter*, which leaves from Penn Station in New York City daily just before noon and stops in St-Albans where a bus takes you to Montréal for arrival just before midnight; and the *Adirondack*, which goes every morning from Penn Station, getting into Montréal by early evening.

Greyhound TOLL-FREE (800) 661-8747 has a regular bus service to Montréal from cities all over North America and **Voyageur Colonial** ((514) 842-2281 covers eastern Canada. The depot is at 505 boulevard de Maisonneuve est (connected to the Berri-UQAM métro station).

OPPOSITE: The gleaming dome of the Marché Bonsecours on Rue St-Paul. ABOVE: A water lily blossoms in Montréal's Jardin Botanique.

Motorists will want to take the Trans-Canada Highway (Route 20) from the Maritimes, and either the Trans-Canada Highway or Route 40 from Québec City. From Toronto you will take Route 401. From the United States there are three principal routes: Interstate-87 through New York State, which becomes Route 15 at the Canadian border; Interstate-89 from Boston through New Hampshire and Vermont, becoming Route 133 at the border; and Interstate-91 from New Haven, Connecticut through western Massachusetts and Vermont, which becomes Route 55 at the border before joining Route 10 into Montréal.

GASPÉ PENINSULA

Not far from Montréal, yet a world away, is the Gaspé Peninsula. Jutting out into the Gulf of St. Lawrence like a clenched fist, the peninsula is an ancient landmass bounded on the north by the vast estuary of the St. Lawrence River and on the south by the Baie des Chaleurs ("Bay of Warmth"). Rising out of the heavily forested interior are the Chic Chocs Mountains, a continuation of the Appalachian chain, with peaks of over 1,220 m (4,000 ft) above sea level, the highest in the province. Some of the world's best moose and deer hunting, as well as salmon fishing, are to be found in the uplands and river valleys of these mountains. The wild, boulder-strewn north coast, from Matane around to Percé, has some of the most dramatic scenery in Canada, punctuated at frequent intervals by tiny fishing villages. The gentler, warmer, less precipitous coastline of the south shore, though still dotted with little fishing villages, has most of the peninsula's farms and small industries.

But what is so striking about the Gaspé, apart from its stunning scenery, is its overwhelming sense of isolation. Not only is it geographically somewhat isolated from the rest of the country, but the little villages themselves are isolated from each other, even when they are only a few kilometers apart. And the villagers all seem isolated from the twentieth century, preferring to go about their business — usually as fishermen, but sometimes as merchants and craftsmen — in exactly the way that generations of their forefathers did. It is this simplicity, this stubborn respect for tradition, that makes the Gaspé an enchanting as well as scenic place to visit.

BACKGROUND

The first European visitors to the Gaspé were the Vikings in the eleventh century, followed four centuries later by the Basque fishermen who had discovered the rich fishing grounds of the Gulf of

The twentieth century arrives, modestly, in the Gaspé

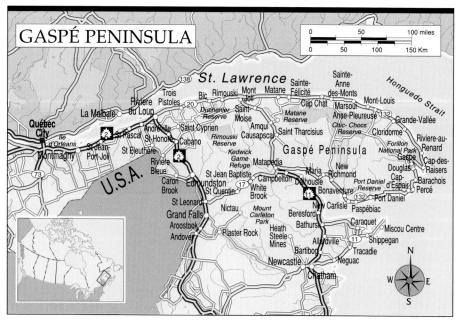

St. Lawrence. Then in 1534 Jacques Cartier — who else? — landed at the present site of the city of Gaspé, where, in the presence of a small band of bewildered Mi'kmaq natives, he erected a tall wooden cross on a hill overlooking the bay and claimed the area for France. He named it Gaspéche, from the native word Gaspeg, meaning "land's end." It wasn't until the early seventeenth century that French fishermen began arriving and establishing little coastal villages which, despite the harsh and primitive conditions, survived thanks to the rich harvest from the sea. Acadians deported by the British from Nova Scotia settled more villages in the mid-eighteenth century. At about the same time, English settlers began establishing farming communities along the south coast, which were then augmented by the arrival of Loyalists in the aftermath of the American Revolution.

Since then, it's as if time stood still. A few waves, or ripples, of immigrants arrived from Scotland and Ireland, but nothing much changed. The pattern of village life was set: cling to the coast, and the sea will provide. And the formula worked. The sea has provided not only fish in abundance, but in the eighteenth and nineteenth centuries it provided bonus extras in the form of shipwrecks along the Gaspé's rocky northern coastline. In fact, the survivors of shipwrecks founded entire villages with the stores and equipment they salvaged from their wrecked vessels. In cases where there were no survivors, the residents of existing villages would bury the dead sailors and then help themselves to the sunken cargo.

There are no longer any shipwrecks or roaming tribes of natives, or primitive outdoor plumbing, but in many essential respects the Gaspé today remains untouched — and therefore unspoiled — by the modern world.

GENERAL INFORMATION

Apart from the wealth of information you can get from the provincial tourist information offices, there is more specific information available from the **Gaspé Tourist Association** ((418) 775-2223 TOLL-FREE (800) 463-0323 FAX (418) 775-2234, which has offices at 357 route de la Mer, Ste-Flavie G0J 2L0.

WHAT TO SEE AND DO

As you make your way eastwards across the north coast of the Gaspé you really shouldn't pass through **Grand Métis** without stopping to see the magnificent **Jardins de Métis** ((418) 775-2221, 200 Route 132. When Elsie Reford inherited her uncle's estate near Grand Métis in 1919 she used her remarkable horticultural talents to create this series of beautifully landscaped settings for a vast variety of shrubs, perennials, and annuals, and her achievement is all the more remarkable because many of the species are found nowhere else this far north. Her home, the elegant Victorian Villa Reford, still stands in the park and is now a museum with a restaurant and shop. You can visit the park every day between June 1 and October 14; an admission fee is charged.

Continuing eastwards on Route 132 you'll come to **Matane**, a fishing town well known for its salmon and shrimp, so it stands to reason that it's a good place to stop for a bite or to buy your fish and bite on it elsewhere. Starting in June Atlantic salmon swim up the Matane River to their spawning grounds. The dam here has a specially constructed passage through which the salmon swim and there's an observatory by the dam where you can listen to taped information as you watch them struggle by. South of Matane a little way and just off Route 195, the **Réserve Faunique de Matane** is a good place to pitch your tent and do some canoeing, boating, or fishing, or just to take a hike.

Back along Route 132, **Cap-Chat** offers keen fishermen lots of opportunities. The lakes are brimming with trout, the river teems with salmon, and some of the locals will take you cod fishing at an hourly rate.

The next village is **Ste-Anne-des-Monts**, and from it Route 299 will take you south into the **Parc de la Gaspésie**, a magnificent wilderness of some 200 hectares (500 acres) which encompasses lakes, forests, and the wildlife reserve in the Chic Chocs Mountains. Moose, caribou, deer, and a few black bears roam. Mont Jacques-Cartier is the tallest peak, and if you can take the cold, the wet, and the hike, the views are breathtaking. The park is laced with hiking trails and roads, there's some good fishing and during winter it's popular for cross-country skiing. About 40 km (25 miles) from Ste-Anne-des-Monts along Route 299 is the **Gîte du Mont-Albert** ((418) 763-2288, a lodge from

which all trails begin, and where you'll find accommodation, campsites, a restaurant, an information point, and a nature center.

You can return to the coastal road at **Mont-St-Pierre**, a little village sheltering in a beautiful bay. It's one of the top Canadian spots for **hang-gliding** and if you fancy trying it yourself, a hang-gliding school operates there between June and August. There's also a two-week hang-gliding festival, **La Fête du Vol Libre**, held here each summer. For information, contact: Corporation Vol Libre ((418) 797-2222 FAX (418) 797-2558, CP 82, Mont St-Pierre, Gaspésie.

The northeastern tip of the peninsula that juts out into the gulf forms the **Parc National Forillon**

((418) 368-5505, 238 sq km (92 sq miles) of spectacular coastline and forest where wildlife abounds. The northern side is characterized by dramatically sheer limestone cliffs, pebble beaches, and impressive headlands from which seals and whales can be sighted between May and October. There is a rich and remarkable variety of flora, and among the many forms of wildlife you may find moose, lynx, and black bears. The park offers a wealth of activities for you to choose from: there are guided tours, nature walks, hiking trails, boat trips to seal colonies, an island bird sanctuary and trips for whale watching, scuba diving, or fishing — plus beaches to relax on when you've done all those things. In winter there are trails for cross-country skiing and snowshoeing.

At Fox River Route 197 takes you south along the western side of the park to Gaspé, but you should follow Route 132 if you want to see the magnificent northern coastline at this point. Route 132 brings you along the coast to the old village of **Cap-des-Rosiers**, the site of many shipwrecks, and you can visit Canada's tallest **lighthouse** which dates from 1858, or learn more about the park at the interpretive center. Some privately owned boats offer deep-sea fishing trips and

LEFT: The lighthouse at La Martre. RIGHT: A house in the fishing village of Percé.

cruises with the sanction of the park authorities. From here the Route 132 brings you to the south side of the **Parc National Forillon**, where the coastline along the Baie de Gaspé is softer and there are sandy beaches.

The port of **Gaspé** is the industrial and administrative center of the peninsula. It doesn't have a great deal to offer the tourist other than its historical significance, for it was here in 1534 that Jacques Cartier first landed on North American soil and claimed it in the name of the King of France, an event commemorated with a **monument** that depicts scenes of Cartier's journey in bas-relief. Near the monument and overlooking the bay stands the **Musée de la Gaspésie (** (418)

nearly 91 m (300 ft) high and is pierced by a natural hole at its eastern end, from which the name Percé ("pierced") originates. Beside it stands a pillar of stone; all that is left of a second arch that collapsed in the nineteenth century. At low tide you can walk out to the rock and wonder at it from close quarters, but if the tide is in you can take a path that leads to a nearby cave.

Mont Ste-Anne affords some wonderful views of the area, including the Rock, and despite a height of 320 m (1,050 ft) it is not a difficult walk if you follow the trail near the church. Another trail, the Route des Failles, takes you to **La Grande Crevasse**, a dramatic split in the rock to the west of Mont Ste-Anne.

368-2536, 80 boulevard Gaspé, where you can spend a pleasant hour learning about the peninsula's history. The museum is open daily from June 24 to September 2, but closed Monday and Saturday the rest of the year. An admission fee is charged.

Those interested in fishing should take note that three Atlantic salmon rivers run into the sea at Gaspé; these can be fished through prior arrangement with the government office that strictly controls the waters. Other than this, there's nothing to keep you here.

The fishing village of **Percé** is a small and pleasant place set against a mountainous backdrop, but it is renowned for the strangeness and splendor of its geological landscape. Cliffs rise steeply from the sea, but nothing quite prepares you for the sight of the famous **Percé Rock**. This majestic reddish-gold limestone rock is 427 m (1,400 ft) long,

Boat trips run from the wharf to the **Île Bonaventure**, an island that is now a bird sanctuary, home to various species of seabirds and an enormous colony of over 50,000 gannets. You can either be content to circle the island or you can disembark and catch another ferry back. Go armed with binoculars and walking shoes; a hat may also be a good idea.

Attracting tourists as it does, the town is busy by Gaspésian standards, and there are souvenir and craft shops, cafés, and some excellent restaurants.

Continuing southeast along Route 132, the south coast of the Gaspé assumes a very different character to that of the north. The coastline is low, the beaches are sandy, and some of the land is farmed. During the American Revolution many Loyalists fled to this area and many of the towns bear English names as a result.

A little north of the town of Port-Daniel, **Port-Daniel Park** is a good spot for trout and salmon fishing, while further west the little town of **Bonaventure** sits in a pleasant bay. Its **Musée Historique Acadien** ((418) 534-4000, at 95 avenue Port-Royal, features period furniture and old domestic appliances. At the attractive town of Carleton, it's worth a walk or bus ride to the top of **Mont St-Joseph** for a panoramic view of the south coast of the Gaspé and the shore of New Brunswick across the Baie des Chaleurs.

At the **Parc de Miguasha** ((418) 794-2475, 231 route Miguasha ouest, the museum is devoted to the study of fossils, and specimens from the area are supplied to other museums around the

and tucked-away villages, so allow yourself time to enjoy it.

WHERE TO STAY

At Matane, the elegant **Riotel Matane** ((418) 566-2651 TOLL-FREE (800) 463-7468 FAX (418) 562-7365, at 250 avenue du Phare est, Matane G4W 3N4, has good facilities including a swimming pool, snowmobiling, and a good restaurant. There are 96 rooms, many of which offer pleasant sea views, with prices from the lower end of mid-range up. The **Quality Inn Inter-Rives** ((418) 562-6433 TOLL-FREE (800) 463-2466 FAX (418) 562-9214, 1550 avenue du Phare ouest, Matane G4W 3M6, has a

world. You can take a look at the cliffs where the fossils are found and also see the laboratory processes used to separate them from the rock. It's open daily from June to late September, and admission is free. Further along Route 132 is Restigouche, where the final naval battle between the French and English was fought in 1760 — this is commemorated in the **Battle of Restigouche Historic Park** at Pointe-à-la-Croix. An interpretive center (open mid-June to early September) includes among its exhibits parts of the *Machault*, the French warship sunk during the battle.

Matapédia is an attractive little village at the confluence of the Matapédia and Restigouche rivers, both of which are full of salmon. From here Route 132 goes north to Ste-Flavie on the northern shore, a distance of roughly 160 km (100 miles). This is a very scenic route which takes you through the Matapédia valley with its pine-covered hills

swimming pool, a babysitting service, and snowmobiling facilities, and some of its rooms come with fireplaces. Rates are slightly higher than those at the Riotel. **Motel la Vigie** ((418) 562-3664 TOLL-FREE (800) 856-2288 FAX (418) 566-2930, further along at 1600 avenue du Phare ouest, Matane G4W 3M6, is an inexpensive 32-roomed motel near the dock, and the **Hôtel-Motel Belle Plage** ((418) 562-2323 TOLL-FREE (800) 244-2323 FAX (418) 562-2562, at 1310 rue Matane-sur-Mer, Matane G4W 3M6, is reasonably good value, with rates running from inexpensive to mid-range. For information on **campsites** at the Matane Wildlife Preserve call (418) 562-3700.

On the beach at Cap-Chat the seasonal **Cabines Goemons sur Mer** ((418) 786-5715, 195 rue Notre-Dame est, Cap-Chat G0J 1G0, provides inexpen-

OPPOSITE and ABOVE: Bird watchers and watched birds flock to Île Bonaventure.

sive self-catering accommodation. At Ste-Anne-des-Monts, both the **Motel à la Brunante** ((418) 763-3366 TOLL-FREE (800) 463-0828 FAX (418) 763-7380, at 94 boulevard Ste-Anne ouest, Ste-Anne-des-Monts G0E 2G0, and the smaller, slightly more expensive, **Monaco des Monts** ((418) 763-3321 TOLL-FREE (800) 463-7468 FAX (418) 763-7846, 90 boulevard Ste-Anne ouest, Ste-Anne-des-Monts G0E 2G0, offer comfortable accommodation and reasonably good dining facilities at prices which are inexpensive to moderate. The **Motel Beaurivage** ((418) 763-2291 FAX (418) 786-5388, at 100 avenue Première ouest, Ste-Anne-des-Monts G0C 2G0, offers inexpensive accommodation and has a very good restaurant.

some well-equipped **campsites**, and on the south coast of the Forillon peninsula there's a Hostelling International facility, **Auberge de Cap-aux-Os** ((418) 892-5153 TOLL-FREE (800) 461-8585 FAX (418) 892-5292, 2095 boulevard Grande-Grève, Cap-aux-Os, Gaspé G0E 1J0. The 56-bed auberge is open year-round and offers a cafeteria in summer and kitchen in winter. The seasonal **Hôtel le Pharillon** ((418) 892-5200 FAX (418) 892-5832, at 1293 boulevard Cap-des-Rosiers, in Cap-des-Rosiers G0E 1E0, has 38 inexpensive rooms with television and kitchenettes, and there's a restaurant.

At Gaspé you'll find one of the best hotels on the peninsula: the **Quality Inn des Commandants** ((418) 368-3355 TOLL-FREE (800) 462-3355 FAX (418)

In the Parc de la Gaspésie, the **Gîte du Mont Albert** ((418) 763-2288, PO Box 1150, Parc de la Gaspésie G0E 2G0, offers accommodation either in the lodge itself or the chalets around it. The rooms are basic, but none the less pleasant for that. With the peaceful setting, fresh mountain air, views of Mont Albert, and a crackling fire in the grate, who's complaining? Prices here range from inexpensive to moderate and reservations are essential. Camping is also available here.

At Mont-St-Pierre, the **Motel au Délice** ((418) 797-2850 TOLL-FREE (888) 797-2955 FAX (418) 797-5032, 100 rue Prudent-Cloutier, Mont-St-Pierre G0E 1V0, has 17 comfortable rooms, as well as a restaurant, and is probably the best accommodation on offer, while the **Motel Mont-St-Pierre** ((418) 797-2202, 60 rue Prudent-Cloutier, Mont-St-Pierre G0E 1V0, also has a restaurant; both are inexpensive. In Parc National Forillon there are

368-1702, 178 rue de la Reine, Gaspé G0C 1R0. All rooms are air-conditioned with television and the prices are mid-range. At Percé, the best choice has to be the **Hôtel La Normandie** ((418) 782-2112 TOLL-FREE (800) 463-0820 FAX (418) 782-2337, at 221 Route 132 ouest, Percé G0C 2L0. In this attractive wooden building, well-situated for views of the sea and Percé Rock, there are 45 pleasant rooms all with private bath and television, a sitting area, a restaurant, and guests have the use of a gym. Prices range from inexpensive to mid-range, depending on the view. The similarly priced **Motel les Trois-Sœurs** ((418) 782-2183 TOLL-FREE IN CANADA (800) 463-9700, at 77-B Route 132, Percé G0C 2L0, is also very comfortable, has a restaurant, and the service is good. At 222 Route des Failles, Percé G0C 2L0, the **Auberge du Gargantua** ((418) 782-2852 FAX (418) 782-5229 has 11 inexpensive to lower mid-range accommodations with great views of the Rock and probably the best restaurant in the Gaspé (breakfast and dinner only), and there's an old-fashioned charm about the **Maison Avenue House** ((418) 782-2954, at 38 avenue de l'Église, Percé G0C 2L0, where five simple and clean rooms are offered at very inexpensive rates.

Moving to the south shore of the peninsula, at Bonaventure there are a couple of quite good motels: The **Motel Grand-Pré** ((418) 534-2053 TOLL-FREE IN QUÉBEC (800) 463-2053 FAX (418) 534-4530, at 118 avenue Grand-Pré, Bonaventure G0C 1E0, offers a wide variety of accommodation in its 38 rooms, with prices ranging from inexpensive to expensive. Some rooms have kitchenettes, some have whirlpools, and there's a swimming pool and playground. The **Motel de la Plage** ((418) 534-2934, at 136 avenue Port-Royal, Bonaventure G0C 1E0, has 10 inexpensively priced rooms, all with bath, television, and telephone. At Carleton the two best places to stay are the moderately priced **Motel Carleton** (/FAX (418) 364-3288 TOLL-FREE IN QUÉBEC AND NEW BRUNSWICK (800) 510-3288, at 1746 boulevard Perron, Carleton G0C 1J0, which offers 33 inexpensive accommodations and a restaurant, and the **Manoir Belle Plage** ((418) 364-3388 TOLL-FREE IN QUÉBEC (800) 463-0780 FAX (418) 364-7289, at 474 boulevard Perron, Carleton G0C 1J0, also with a restaurant and with prices varying from inexpensive to mid-range.

WHERE TO EAT

It is hardly surprising that the menus of Gaspésian cafés and restaurants are swimming with seafood that is well-prepared and inexpensively priced. Cod tongues in batter are a Gaspésian specialty and have a surprisingly subtle flavor. As the Gaspé is such an outdoor place, there's always the option of buying your smoked fish from one of the many excellent fisheries and having a picnic somewhere along the way.

At the center of **Jardins de Métis** ((418) 775-2221, the Villa Reford has a busy restaurant where you can taste some traditional Canadian fare. In Matane there's a good and moderately priced restaurant at the **Hôtel-Motel Belle Plage** ((418) 562-2323, where you can sit watching the river flow.

At Ste-Anne-des-Monts it's again a case of looking to the hotels, with the best restaurant being at the **Hôtel Beaurivage** ((418) 763-2291, and another reasonably good one in **Monaco des Monts** ((418) 763-3321. Before leaving the town, you might want to gather the makings of a picnic for your trip to the Parc de la Gaspésie, in which case you can buy some smoked fish down by the dock.

In the Parc de la Gaspésie itself there's a real treat in store at the restaurant in the **Gîte du Mont-Albert** ((418) 763-2288, situated on Route 299. The

highly acclaimed restaurant specializes in classic French cuisine and also regional dishes. Students from the Québec Institute of Tourism and Hotel Management serve here as part of their training and are eager to please. Prices are moderate and reservations are essential.

Gastronomic delights await you in Percé's **Auberge du Gargantua** ((418) 782-2852. Beautifully situated with a fine view of the Percé Rock, the restaurant specializes in French cuisine, seafood, Gaspésian dishes, and a sinful array of desserts. Prices here fall within the moderate category but are the most expensive in the area. Still, a meal here is a real must. The restaurant at the **Hôtel La Normandie** ((418) 782-2112 offers very good

dining in attractive surroundings and with good views of that Rock. At the wharfside, **La Maison du Pêcheur** ((418) 782-5331, place du Quai, is also very good, moderately priced, and serves excellent lobster. Its location makes it an interesting spot at lunchtime and its large windows afford views of you-know-what.

At Carleton, the good and moderately priced restaurant at the **Motel Baie Bleue** ((418) 364-3355, 482 boulevard Perron, Route 132, is probably the best spot to dine.

HOW TO GET THERE

VIA Rail TOLL-FREE (888) 842-7733 serves Gaspé, Percé, via Halifax, (Nova Scotia), Moncton (New Brunswick), and Matapédia, but to get the most out of being there, you'll need a car. From Montréal or Québec City, the Trans-Canada Highway (Route 20) goes to Rivière-du-Loup, from where the coastal highway, Route 132, does a complete loop of the peninsula. From New Brunswick, Routes 11 and 17 converge on Campbellton at the Québec border, where you cross over and pick up Route 132.

OPPOSITE: The famous Percé Rock stands sentry at the water's edge. ABOVE: A fisherman at Rivière-du-Renard, north of the port of Gaspé.

New
Brunswick

NEW BRUNSWICK, THE "GATEWAY TO ATLANTIC CANADA," can lay claim to two of the wonders of the natural world: the tides in the Bay of Fundy and the leaves on its trees. Twice a day 100 billion tons of water swirls up the funnel-shaped Bay of Fundy, creating tides of up to 15 m (50 ft), the highest in the world. Once a year the trees of New Brunswick put on such a spectacular show of color — as their leaves in the autumn turn to gold, red, orange, and purple — that the Department of Tourism operates a toll-free hotline which people from all over North America can call to get daily updates on the colors the leaves are turning.

There are a lot of leaves to turn, because more than 80% of New Brunswick's 74,437 sq km (28,354 sq miles) is covered in forest. Bordered in the west by Maine, in the north by Québec, and joined to Nova Scotia in the southeast by the Isthmus of Chignecto, New Brunswick still has approximately 2,250 km (1,400 miles) of coastline. Along these shores are to be found dozens of first-rate beaches in addition to hundreds of charming little fishing villages.

Like the other Maritimes, New Brunswick was inhabited by the Mi'kmaq for at least 2,000 years before it was "discovered" by Jacques Cartier in 1534. Seventy years later Samuel de Champlain established a settlement on Saint Croix Island, but the French settlement of the province didn't begin in earnest until the early eighteenth century. In 1751, with British pressure mounting, the French built Fort Beauséjour to protect the settlers. It failed. Four years later, in 1755, it fell to the British under Colonel Moncton, and shortly thereafter the order for the deportation of the French-speaking Acadians was proclaimed.

In 1783 the first ships bearing Loyalists from the former American colonies arrived at Parrtown (now Saint John). By the following year the Loyalist population had grown to 14,000, and in response to their demands the new province of New Brunswick was formally established and named after the German duchy then still ruled by the British Crown. In 1785 Saint John became Canada's first incorporated city, while Fredericton was named the provincial capital. Around this time, some of the Acadians who had been deported 30 years before began to return, and today one-third of the province's 724,000 people are French-speaking. In fact, in 1969 New Brunswick was the first province to become officially bilingual.

FREDERICTON

As the home of the provincial legislature and the University of New Brunswick, Fredericton is the political and intellectual center of the province. Thus, with a population of only about 44,000, it is not surprising that a majority of its inhabitants work either for the government or the university, nor that Frederictonians seem to spend most of their free time planning or attending gala dinners, charity balls, and garden parties. This "City of the Stately Elms," with its tree-lined avenues and elegant houses, is definitely and observably the heartland of New Brunswick high society.

It is also, thanks to lavish benefactions from the city's most famous native son, Lord Beaverbrook, an important cultural center, with an excellent art gallery, theater, and library. In addition, the city in recent years has become a center for all kinds of crafts, making it an ideal place to look for hooked rugs, batiks, pottery, enamelware, jewelry,

stained glass, and pewter ware. Fredericton, in other words, has managed the difficult feat of providing the perfect setting for both gentility and creativity.

BACKGROUND

Although as early as 1692 the French built a fort here where the Nashwaak River joins the St. John River, it was several decades before there was a French settlement of any size. Called Pointe-Ste-Anne, it lasted only until 1759, when British troops drove the settlers out and renamed it Fredericton after the second son of George II. With the arrival of the Loyalists in 1783 it came into its own as a British town, the first major inland settlement. The following year New Brunswick was declared a province with Thomas Carleton as its first governor, and in 1785 Carleton decided that the provincial capital should be Fredericton rather than the larger Saint John because it was less vulnerable to attack from the sea. It quickly grew into an attractive and prosperous city — and remains one to this day.

Fredericton — OPPOSITE: Autumn foliage frames St. Andrew's Church. ABOVE: The St. John River.

GENERAL INFORMATION

Before you set out for New Brunswick, you may want to call the **Fredericton Convention and Vistors Bureau** ((506) 460-2941 for informational materials. In Fredericton, you should stop by **City Hall** ((506) 460-2129, downtown at 397 Queen Street. In addition to the usual mound of maps and brochures, you can also get a parking pass here which will allow you to park for free in city lots and at meters around town. If you are entering Fredericton from the west, look for the **information center** just off the Trans-Canada Highway, at Exit 289.

Lord Beaverbrook designed the original building himself and gave it, along with his personal art collection, to the people of New Brunswick. First opened in 1959, it has expanded considerably in recent years and is particularly renowned for its wide range of masterpieces by British artists, although its most striking work is the huge *Santiago El Grande* by Dali that hangs by the entrance.

Another of Lord Beaverbrook's gifts to the city where he grew up is the **Playhouse**, 686 Queen Street, built in 1964 and now the home of Theatre New Brunswick ((506) 458-8344. Also on Queen Street, between Carleton and Regent, is **Officers' Square** ((506) 453-2324, an old parade ground that is now the site of lunchtime theater on weekdays

WHAT TO SEE AND DO

Most of the places you will want to visit in Fredericton are centrally located on Queen Street. **Christ Church Cathedral**, a fine Gothic edifice modeled on the parish church of Saint Mary in Snettisham, Norfolk, was consecrated in 1853 and had the distinction of being the first new cathedral foundation on British soil since the Norman Conquest of 1066. The silver-domed **Legislative Assembly** ((506) 453-2527, built in the 1880s, has one of the rare copies of the original Doomsday Book. In the rotunda, there is a set of Audubon prints to admire. Opposite the Legislative Assembly, at 703 Queen Street, is the **Beaverbrook Art Gallery** ((506) 458-8545, which houses one of the most impressive art collections in North America.

during July and August as well as free weekly band concerts. Between Queen Street and the river is **The Green**, a large and beautiful landscaped park.

If you are a sports enthusiast, you should know about the **Mactaquac Provincial Park** ((506) 363-4747, just 24 km (15 miles) west of Fredericton on Route 105, off the Trans-Canada Highway. This 570-hectare (1,400-acre) "superpark," the largest park in New Brunswick, stretches along the north shore of the headpond of the Mactaquac Dam and offers sailing, boating, waterskiing, fishing, and lovely beaches for swimming. It also has an 18-hole golf course, supervised playgrounds, guided nature trails, and 300 campsites. A per-vehicle entrance fee is charged in summer, free in the off-season. Further along the St. John River, 37 km (23 miles) west of Fredericton, is **King's Landing Historical Settlement** ((506) 363-5090, Exit 259, Trans-Canada Highway, near Prince William, a

Pumpkins for sale outside Fredericton.

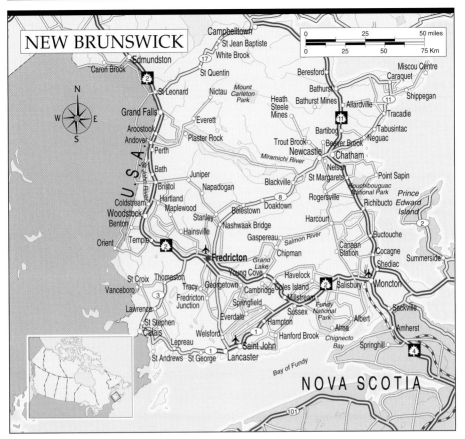

NEW BRUNSWICK

reconstruction of a typical nineteenth-century Loyalist village. Beautifully situated on the banks of the river, the village has over 50 buildings, including a working sawmill and grist mill, and 100 "villagers" who go about their daily routines exactly as they would have done in the last century, all the while explaining to visitors what they are doing. Typical food and drink of the period is served in the King's Head Inn. The settlement is open June to mid-October. An admission fee is charged.

WHERE TO STAY

The good news is that even the best hotels in Fredericton — and there are some very good ones — are moderately priced. The venerable **Keddy's Lord Beaverbrook Hotel (** (506) 455-3371 TOLL-FREE (800) 561-7666 FAX (506) 455-1441 is the best in town. Conveniently located across from The Playhouse, at 659 Queen Street, Fredericton E3B 5A6, it has all the luxuries one would expect, including an indoor heated pool, and many of its rooms overlook the river. It also has one of the city's best restaurants. Similarly priced and equipped is the **Auberge Wandlyn Inn (** (506) 452-

8937 TOLL-FREE IN CANADA (800) 561-0000 TOLL-FREE IN THE UNITED STATES (800) 561-0006 FAX (506) 452-7658, at 58 Prospect Street West, Fredericton E3B 2T8. Also in this category are the **Fredericton Inn Limited (** (506) 455-1430 TOLL-FREE (800) 561-8777 FAX (506) 458-5448 at 1315 Regent Street, Fredericton E3C 1A1, and the **Howard Johnson Hotel and Restaurant (** (506) 460-5500 TOLL-FREE (800) 596-4656 FAX (506) 472-0170, located on the Trans-Canada Highway, Fredericton E3B 5E3, with the edge going to Howard Johnson.

Dropping down in price, there are three particularly good hotel bargains in Fredericton: **Keddy's Inn (** (506) 454-4461 TOLL-FREE (800) 561-7666 FAX (506) 452-6915 at 368 Forest Hill Road, Fredericton E3B 5G2, in a delightful location with a heated indoor swimming pool; the **Town and Country Motel (** (506) 454-4223 FAX (506) 454-6264 E-MAIL delmas@nbnet.nb.ca, at 967 Woodstock Road, Fredericton E3B 7R7, overlooking the river just west of the city; and the **Carriage House Inn (** (506) 452-9924 TOLL-FREE (800) 267-6068 FAX (506) 458-0799 at 230 University Avenue, Fredericton E3B 4H7, a Victorian mansion built in 1875 for the city's mayor, adjacent to The Green, with excellent facilities for its seven guestrooms.

There's no restaurant, but a full breakfast is served. In Mactaquac Park, near King's Landing, there is the **Chickadee Lodge** ((506) 363-2759 (May to November) ((506) 363-2288 (November to April) FAX (506) 363-2929, a superb bed and breakfast overlooking the headpond with kayaks and canoes available for guests' use. For additional bed and breakfast listings, contact the New Brunswick Bed and Breakfast Association ((506) 385-2398 FAX (506) 385-1999 E-MAIL bba@nbnet.nb.ca, C/o Jim MacIsaac, in Lakeville Corner E0E 1M0.

WHERE TO EAT

If you are staying at the Lord Beaverbrook Hotel (see WHERE TO STAY, above), you could spend weeks without exhausting its dining possibilities. To begin with, there is the hotel's elegant **Terrace Room** with a seasonal deck overlooking the river; in the basement there is the popular **Maverick Room**, which has excellent steaks and a lively bar that stays open until midnight; the **River Room** stays open even later, and has live entertainment every evening; while on the roof the **Top Deck** serves meals under large umbrellas throughout the summer.

For Chinese cooking Sichuan and Cantonese style, **Mei's** ((506) 454-2177, 73 Carlton Street, is very good. There are two restaurants next to each other on Queen Street that both deserve a visit. For Greek food, **Dimitri's** ((506) 452-8882, 596 Queen Street, is the place to go, and **Café du Monde** ((506) 457-5534, 610 Queen Street, serves classic French cuisine at reasonable prices.

HOW TO GET THERE

Fredericton is served by **Air Canada** ((506) 458-8561 (from more distant cities). The airport is located 10 minutes southeast of downtown on Route 102. Taxi cabs run from the airport to downtown.

If you are coming by car, the Trans-Canada Highway passes through Fredericton, entering New Brunswick from Nova Scotia across the Isthmus of Chignecto and from Québec near Edmundston, whence it follows the St. John River Valley into Fredericton. Coming from Maine, Interstate 95 enters New Brunswick near Woodstock, where it links up with the Trans-Canada Highway on its way down the St. John River Valley.

SAINT JOHN

Known as "Loyalist City" to its inhabitants, Saint John is never known as St. John. It is Canada's oldest incorporated city, having been incorporated by its Loyalist settlers in 1785, and New Brunswick's largest, with a population of 125,000. Situated in the estuary of the St. John River, it has

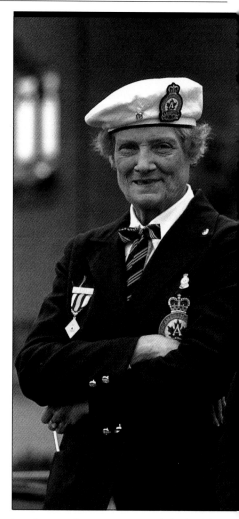

long been an important port and shipbuilding center, although today most of its income comes from its oil refineries and its big pulp and paper mill.

More often than not the city is shrouded in fog, hence its nickname, but the sea mists can have a welcome cooling effect on summer days when the rest of the province is sweltering. While Saint John has never been famous for its beauty, the city has been transformed in recent years by an ambitious development and restoration project that has done wonders for the waterfront and has skillfully blended the past with the present elsewhere in the city. Now, when the fog lifts, it can be quite a pleasant city to look at.

BACKGROUND

On Saint John the Baptist's Day in 1604, Samuel de Champlain landed at the mouth of the river,

and in 1631 Charles de la Tour founded a fort and a trading post there. For the next century and a half the history of Saint John mirrored the history of the region, with the Acadian population being dispossessed by the British in 1755 and the city itself being formally ceded to England in 1763. But its real birthday was May 18, 1783 — the day that ships carrying more than 3,000 Loyalists arrived. What had been an obscure trading post instantly became a thriving Loyalist town, growing into a flourishing Loyalist city that so prospered from its trade and shipbuilding that it became known in the nineteenth century as the "Liverpool of America."

The growth and prosperity that the city had enjoyed almost uninterrupted since the arrival of the Loyalists came to an abrupt end in the latter part of the century. As wooden sailing ships became obsolete, Saint John's shipyards sank into bankruptcy. Then, as if to demonstrate the cru-

elty of the fates, a devastating fire in 1877 swept through the city's wooden buildings, wiping out over half of the city. It was a long time before Saint John recovered. But recover it did, so that the Saint John of today once again resembles the proud, bustling Saint John of yesterday.

GENERAL INFORMATION

Motorists arriving from the west should look for the **Visitor Information Centre** ((506) 658-2940 in the triangular building just off Route 1. It's open mid-May to mid-October. There's a secondary information center ((506) 658-2937 inside the restaurant overlooking the Reversing Falls on Route 100. Downtown, you can drop by the **City Centre Tourist Information Centre**

The happy, proud countenances of Legionnaires in Fredericton.

((506) 658-2855 inside Market Square, a downtown shopping center near the waterfront. It is open daily from mid-June to mid-September from 9 AM to 8 PM, the rest of the year daily from 9:30 AM to 6 PM.

WHAT TO SEE AND DO

There are sights and sights to see in Saint John, and then there is The Sight: the famous phenomenon of the **Reversing Falls** that occurs twice daily, when the mighty tides in the Bay of Fundy confront the St. John River and drive it back upstream. At the point where the river empties into the bay the level of the river is over four meters

Most of the sights in the city itself are within easy walking distance of King Square, and most have a distinctly Loyalist flavor. **King Square** itself advertises the city's past and present orientation: Flowerbeds are laid out in the form of a Union Jack. Nearby, at the corner of Union Street and Germain Street, is **Loyalist House** ((506) 652-3590, a Georgian mansion built in 1816 and one of the very few existing buildings to have survived the terrible fire of 1877. It is open daily from June to September; an admission fee is charged. East of King Square, the old **Loyalist Burial Grounds** has tombstones dating all the way back to 1784, the year after the Loyalists arrived. Across the street, on the harborfront, is **Barbour's General Store**

(14 ft) above that of the bay at low tide, but at high tide the river is more than four meters (14 ft) below the oncoming sea water — which has now risen by 8.5 m (28 ft)! — so the river is forced to reverse its course. Because the river narrows dramatically and curls around a sharp bend just before it reaches the bay, whirlpools and plunging rapids are created: reversing falls. There is an observation point at Reversing Falls Bridge, which is ideal for witnessing this trick of nature. The **Interpretive Centre** ((506) 658-2937, Route 100, Reversing Falls Bridge (West Side), explains it all.

Also west of downtown is the historic **Carleton Martello Tower**, a stone fortification built during the War of 1812 and which today provides a commanding view of the city and the estuary. Ask for directions at the Reversing Falls Interpretive Centre.

((506) 658-2939, a red clapboard building dating from 1867, stocked with merchandise of the time and staffed by people in period costume. It also includes a vintage barbershop. The **New Brunswick Museum** ((506) 643-2300, at Market Square, is Canada's oldest museum, having been founded in 1842. It features national and international art treasures, historic artifacts, and a natural science gallery. The museum is open daily, year-round. An admission fee is charged.

Saint John is also the home of Canada's oldest market, the **Old City Market** ((506) 658-2820, which has been held in the same building since 1876 and where many of the same families have operated stalls for generations. In addition to the fish, fruit, and vegetables on sale there is a wide variety of crafts and antiques. But if you're interested in either crafts or antiques, the place to go is **Prince William Street**, which is packed with shops and galleries. For more contemporary shopping, the **Market Square** complex, opened in 1983, offers several levels of shops to go along with its hotel and convention center.

WHERE TO STAY

The best hotel in Saint John is the **Saint John Hilton** ((506) 693-8484 TOLL-FREE (800) 561-8282 FAX (506) 657-6610, 1 Market Square, Saint John E2L 4Z6. Along with all the luxury comes the splendid location in Market Square, with direct access to more than 60 shops, boutiques, and restaurants in the complex as well as to the convention center, and beautiful views over the harbor.

Country Inn & Suites by Carlson ((506) 635-0400 TOLL-FREE (800) 456-4000 FAX (506) 635-3818, 1011 Fairville Boulevard, Saint John E2M 5T9, but there are compensations, such as videocassette players in all the rooms and free video movies, complimentary continental breakfasts, and microwave ovens in the two-room suites.

In the western part of Saint John, just north of and parallel to Route 100 (Fairville Boulevard), is Manawagonish Road. Along this road you will find motels and guesthouses of every type and description, all inexpensive. Four of the best are: the **Island View Motel** ((506) 672-1381 TOLL-FREE (888) 674-6717 FAX (506) 674-1089, 1726 Manawagonish Road, Saint John E2M 3Y5, which

Larger and more moderately priced than the Hilton is **The Delta Brunswick Hotel** ((506) 648-1981 TOLL-FREE (800) 268-1133 FAX (506) 658-0914 at 39 King Street, Saint John E2L 4W3. Luxurious and comfortable, it is also centrally located.

For my money, the best bargain in Saint John is **Keddy's Fort Howe Hotel** ((506) 657-7320 TOLL-FREE (800) 561-7666 FAX (506) 693-1146, at Main and Portland streets, Saint John E2K 4H8. It has all the amenities of a luxury hotel — air conditioning, cable color television, indoor heated pool, on-site parking — and yet is very moderately priced. Its top-floor restaurant overlooking the city and harbor is one of the best. Not quite so central, but again offering good value, is the **Colonial Inn** ((506) 652-3000 TOLL-FREE (800) 561-4667 FAX (506) 658-1664, 175 City Road, Saint John E3L 3T5. Apart from the usual amenities, it has a 24-hour restaurant. There is no restaurant at the

has a heated pool and kitchenettes; the **Fundy Ayre Motel** (/FAX (506) 672-1125 at 1711 Manawagonish Road, Saint John E2M 3Y2, which also has housekeeping units and apartments; the **Seacoast Motel** ((506) 635-8700 FAX (506) 634-0617 E-MAIL renton@mi.net at 1441 Manawagonish Road, Saint John E2M 3X8, overlooking the bay; and the **Hillside Motel** ((506) 672-1273, 1131 Manawagonish Road, Saint John E2M 3X5, which is the least expensive of the lot and has 16 units overlooking the bay, all with cable television.

WHERE TO EAT

Easily the three best places to eat in Saint John are the **Turn of the Tide** ((506) 693-8484 in the Hilton,

OPPOSITE: The famous Reversing Falls at Saint John. ABOVE: Saint John's Old City Market, the oldest market in Canada.

the **Top of the Town** ((506) 657-7320 at Keddy's
Fort Howe Hotel, and the restaurant in the **Delta
Brunswick** ((506) 648-1981. You will pay handsomely to eat at these places, but you will eat
handsomely as well.

For less sumptuous dining your best bet is to
go to Market Square, where you will find an array of restaurants and cafés to appeal to every
appetite and every budget. As difficult as it is to
single out any one of them, we would mention
Grannan's ((506) 634-1555, a seafood restaurant
and oyster bar which has delicious dishes at quite
moderate prices. If you have trouble choosing
between all the restaurants, or if you are just in
a hurry, there is the **Food Hall** at Market Square,
which is full of fast-food places selling pizzas,
burgers, sandwiches, fried chicken, ribs, and so
on. A short walk from Market Square is the popular **Incredible Edibles** ((506) 633-7554 at 42 Princess Street, which specializes in pastas and local
desserts.

HOW TO GET THERE

Like Fredericton, Saint John is served by **Air
Canada** ((506) 632-1500.

If you are traveling to Saint John by car, the
principal north-south highway into the city is
Route 1, which links with the Trans-Canada Highway about 70 km (43 miles) to the north at Sussex
and in the south crosses the border into Maine at
St. Stephen and becomes US Highway 1. From
Fredericton the main road is Route 7, but the
meandering Route 102, which follows the St. John
River, is much more picturesque.

If you are coming by train, you will take the
VIA Rail ((506) 857-9830 network to Moncton and
then change for one of the two daily (except
Wednesday) buses to Saint John.

Bay Ferries ((504) 649-7777 TOLL-FREE (888) 249-
7245, PO Box 3427, Postal Station B, Saint John
E2M 4X9, operates a year-round ferry service
across the Bay of Fundy between Digby, Nova
Scotia, and Saint John. The journey takes three
hours. During peak season, the ferry sails three
times daily. In Digby, contact Bay Ferries ((902)
245-2116, PO Box 418, Digby B0V 1A0.

Farm boys cycling on the road north from
Saint John.

Prince Edward Island

A GLANCE AT SOME OF THE SOBRIQUETS GIVEN to Prince Edward Island tells you a great deal about the province. Variously and affectionately known as Canada's "million-acre farm," "Spud Island," and "the Garden of the Gulf," it is indeed small (over half a million hectares or 1.4 million acres actually, spread over an island 224 km (140 miles) long and 6 to 64 km (4 to 40 miles) wide), it is mostly rolling farmland, it is famous for its potatoes, and it is lovely and unspoiled.

Separated from the mainland by the Northumberland Strait, the island was inhabited by Mi'kmaq when Jacques Cartier in 1534 came upon "the fairest land 'tis possible to see," named it Île St-Jean, and claimed it for France. French settlers didn't begin to arrive in any numbers, however, until the early eighteenth century, to be reinforced in 1755 by Acadians expelled from Nova Scotia by the British, and again in 1758 by French colonists fleeing Nova Scotia after the fall of the for-

tress at Louisbourg. But it didn't remain a safe haven for long. Later that same year, 1758, a British expeditionary force under Lord Rollo captured the island and deported most of the French-speaking population. Five years later Île St-Jean was renamed the "Island of St. John" and was annexed to Nova Scotia. In 1764, Charlottetown, named in honor of Queen Charlotte, the wife of George III, was designated as the capital, and in 1769 the island became a colony in its own right.

In the years following the American Revolution both the colony's population and its Anglophile orientation received a boost from the arrival of Loyalists fleeing the new republic to the south; and in 1799 it was renamed one final time, in honor of Prince Edward, later to be Duke of Kent and father of the future Queen Victoria. In 1851 the colony was granted self-governing status, and in 1864 it hosted the historic conference that led to the confederation of Canada in 1867.

Prince Edward Island joined the Confederation in 1873.

Although the island's population is only 137,000, it is nonetheless Canada's most densely populated province — because it's easily the smallest province. It is even more densely populated in the summer, when it attracts over a million visitors who come to enjoy its idyllic scenery and long sandy beaches. Indeed, after agriculture, tourism is now the island's most important industry.

CHARLOTTETOWN

This lovely little city of tree-shaded streets and squares, stately Victorian clapboard houses, and monumental churches is not only the provincial capital but also the center of the island's commerce and tourism. It is situated on an arm of Hillsborough Bay, off the Northumberland Strait, 55 km

(34 miles) from the ferry landing at Wood Islands. Known as the "cradle of Confederation," it was here that the discussions were held in 1864 which led to the birth of the Dominion of Canada.

BACKGROUND

Charlottetown lies just across the harbor from the spot where 300 French colonists founded the first European settlement on Prince Edward Island in 1720, naming it Port-la-Joye. After the British captured it in 1758 they built Fort Amherst on the site, and six years later founded Charlottetown. Over the next century, despite the influx of Loyalists following the American Revolution and successive waves of immigrants from Ireland and the Scottish Highlands, the town's population grew at a slow but steady pace — much like the pace of life in Charlottetown today. Then in 1864 it became the birthplace of Canada, when delegates from Britain's North American colonies convened in Province House and signed the articles that led to the Canadian Confederation.

With much of its colonial architecture still handsomely preserved, Charlottetown is a delightful and attractive place to start any visit to the island.

The **Charlottetown Visitor Information Centre** ((902) 368-4444 is on Water Street next to Confederation Mall.

WHAT TO SEE AND DO

Charlottetown

The heart and soul of Charlottetown is to be found in the **Confederation Centre of the Arts** ((902) 566-4648, 145 Richmond Street. Built in 1964 to commemorate the 100th anniversary of the historic conference where the first steps were taken towards a united, confederated Canada, it covers two city blocks and contains a memorial hall, a theater, an art gallery, a museum, a library, and a restaurant. It is the principal venue of the annual, summer-long Charlottetown Festival, which always includes a popular musical based on the classic children's book, *Anne of Green Gables*. It's open daily, year-round. Opposite the Centre on Richmond Street is **Province House** ((902) 566-7626, a three-story, neo-Georgian sandstone edifice built between 1843 and 1847, which is where the delegates met in 1864 to begin the process that created Canada. The room on the second floor where their meetings were held is now called the **Confederation Chamber** and is set out exactly as it was in 1864. The building also houses the provincial Legislative Assembly. This National Historic Site is open year-round, daily throughout the summer, weekdays the rest of the year. Admission is free.

A typical corner of Canada's "million-acre farm."

South of Province House on Richmond Street is **St. Dunstan's Basilica**, one of Canada's largest churches, easily recognizable by its twin Gothic spires. Inside you will find some exceptionally fine Italian carvings. On Church Street is **St. Paul's Anglican Cathedral**, which dates from 1747, making it the oldest Protestant church in the province. Several murals by the portraitist Robert Harris distinguish its interior.

Captain Garry's Cruises ((902) 962-2494, Route 4, northeast of Wood Islands Murray River, offers **seal-** and **bird-watching cruises** to the largest seal colony on Prince Edward Island. See seal pups and bull seals up to 450 kg (1,000 lbs), as well as Bird Island, where thousands of cormorants, great

blue herons, and terns, bald eagle. Chowder and mussels are served aboard the vessel.

Shoppers will find Prince Edward Island a treasure trove of traditional **crafts** such as stitchery, quilting, pottery, glasswork, leather, woodwork, and weaving. For information contact the Prince Edward Island Crafts Council ((902) 892-5152, 156 Richmond Street, Charlottetown C1A 1H9.

The North Shore

If you take Route 2 north of Charlottetown you will come to Route 6 just beyond Dunstaffnage; Route 6 will then take you to **Dalvay** at the eastern entrance to a protected area with spectacular coast, **Prince Edward Island National Park** ((902) 672-6359, 2 Palmers Lane, Charlottetown C1A 5V6, the province's premier tourist attraction. The park stretches for 40 km (25 miles) along the north shore and is hugely popular thanks to having some of the finest white sand beaches in North America and beautiful clear water warmed by the Gulf Stream. **Dalvay Beach** is usually the least crowded of the park's beaches, while **Cavendish Beach** at the other end of the park is one of the busiest in all of Canada. All of these beaches

are accessible from Route 6, which after **Brackley Beach** becomes part of the scenic Blue Heron Drive that loops around the central part of the island. The drive is named for the beautiful blue herons that make their home in **New London Bay**, just beyond Cavendish at the western end of the park. There are park information centers in Cavendish (Routes 6 and 13) and Brackley (Routes 6 and 15). The park is open year-round, and an entrance fee is charged from June to September.

Off Route 6 in Cavendish is **Green Gables House** ((902) 672-6350, the old green and white farmhouse that belonged to the grandfather of Lucy Maud Montgomery, who used it as Anne's home in her novel, *Anne of Green Gables*. Now carefully restored, it is visited by thousands of people every year. It's open from May to October; an admission fee is charged.

WHERE TO STAY

Charlottetown

The biggest and best hotel is the new 10-story **Prince Edward Hotel** ((902) 566-2222 TOLL-FREE (800) 441-1414 FAX (902) 566-2282 overlooking the waterfront at 18 Queen Street, Charlottetown C1A 8B9. A Canadian Pacific hotel, it has a swimming pool, two restaurants and a lounge. The other really top-flight hotel is **The Charlottetown** ((902) 894-7371 TOLL-FREE (800) 565-RODD FAX (902) 368-2178, at the corner of Kent and Pownal streets, PO Box 159, Charlottetown C1A 7K4. Operated by Rodd Hotels & Resorts, it's marginally less expensive than the Prince Edward and about half the size, but offers the same basic range of amenities in the heart of downtown.

Of the mid-range hotels, my pick would be the **Dundee Arms Inn and Motel** ((902) 892-2496 FAX (902) 368-8532, 200 Pownal Street, Charlottetown C1A 3W8, a restored turn-of-the-century mansion furnished with antiques and situated in a tree-lined residential area. Its restaurant, the Griffon Dining Room, is probably the best on the island. There's also a pub with a terrace. Rooms in the motel wing are less expensive than those in the inn. The **Elmwood Heritage Inn** ((902) 368-3310 FAX (902) 628-8457 E-MAIL elmwood@pei .sympatico.ca, is situated on elm-lined North River Road, PO Box 3128, Charlottetown C1A 7N8. It's a lovely setting, and the large Victorian house is furnished with antiques and distinguished by its friendly, personal service. Full breakfast is included in the price of the room and rates range from moderate to expensive.

Of the less expensive accommodation, the two best-equipped places are conveniently clustered together on the Trans-Canada Highway just a couple of kilometers (a little over a mile) west of the city. The fanciest of these is the **Queen's Arms Inn** (/FAX (902) 368-1110 TOLL-FREE (800) 539-1241,

Oyster beds in Malpeque Bay.

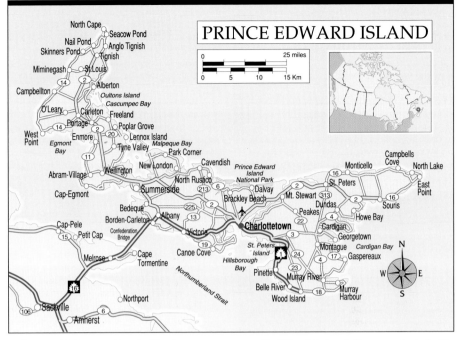

PRINCE EDWARD ISLAND

20 Lower Malpeque Road, Charlottetown C1A 7J9. Its 40 rooms and 20 housekeeping units are all air-conditioned and have cable television, and there is a restaurant and a swimming pool. Smaller and cheaper still, the **Royalty Maples Cottages and Motel** ((902) 368-1030 TOLL-FREE (800) 831-STAY, Rural Route 7, Charlottetown C1A 7J9, has 16 housekeeping units, 10 of them cottages, set in spacious grounds near a shopping mall and golf course. It's located two kilometers (one and a quarter miles) west of Charlottetown, left off the Trans-Canada Highway on Route 2. Happily for the bargain-hunter, there is an abundance of **tourist homes** and **bed and breakfast** accommodations in Charlottetown, as well as in the rest of the island. A full list of these is available from the Visitor Services office in Charlottetown, or contact Bed & Breakfast/Country Inns of Prince Edward Island ((902) 892-4353 E-MAIL santer@ pei.sympatico.ca, PO Box 2551, Charlottetown C1A 8C2.

The North Shore

At the eastern end of the national park near Dalvay Beach is the magnificent old **Dalvay-by-the-Sea Inn** ((902) 672-2048, PO Box 8, Little York C0A 1P0. Built in 1895 as the summer residence of Alexander Macdonald, a Standard Oil tycoon, it is set in lovely grounds only 180 m (590 ft) from the beach, with an excellent restaurant, a two-hole fairway, a bowling green, a lake with canoes, tennis courts, playgrounds, and nature trails. Its 26 rooms are expensive, but what do you expect for a little bit of

paradise? Breakfast and dinner are included in the rate. This is a seasonal hotel, open June 9 to September 30. Further west, on Route 25 overlooking Covehead Bay, is the moderately priced **Stanhope by the Sea** ((902) 672-2047 TOLL-FREE (888) 999-5155 FAX (902) 672-2951, Little York C0A 1P0, which has been a country inn since 1817. There are 35 rooms in the original inn, 24 in the new inn, 17 motel units, and one expensive apartment; all recently renovated. The inn is near the beach and is open from June 1 to October 15. Prices are mid-range.

At Brackley Beach the class act is **Shaw's Hotel & Cottages** ((902) 672-2022 FAX (902) 672-3000, on Route 15, Brackley Beach C1E 1Z3. Run by the Shaw family since 1860, it has 22 rooms in the hotel proper and 12 cottages (including eight luxury chalets) on the well-manicured grounds, which are only about 600 m (just over 650 yards) from the beach. The cottages are open year-round, while the inn is open May 29 to October 3. Meals are provided in the (expensive) rates.

Around Rustico Bay there are three delightful places to stay, all very reasonably priced. In South Rustico there is the **Barachois Inn** ((902) 963-2194, PO Box 1022, Charlottetown C1A 7M4. It is a Victorian house on Route 243, built in 1870, recently refurbished, with five tastefully decorated rooms and two suites. Rates, with full breakfast included, are in the upper mid-range.

As you would expect, given the presence of Green Gables House as a mecca for tourists, not to mention the enormous popularity of Cavendish Beach, the entire area around Cavendish is crammed with places to stay. Within walking distance are the **Sundance Cottages** ((902) 963-2149 or (902) 566-1256 (in winter) TOLL-FREE (800) 565-2149, Hunter River, Rural Route 2, Cavendish C0A 1N0, which also offers 11 deluxe cottages with the same amenities. Prices are in the expensive range. It's open early May to late October. In the heart of Cavendish, the **Kindred Spirits Country Inn and Cottages** (/FAX (902) 963-2434, Route 6, Memory Lane, Cavendish C0A 1N0, is a charming, antique-filled inn on a beautiful estate right next to Green Gables House and Golf Course. There are 10 large rooms at the inn and 12 cottages, plus a large swimming pool. It's open

mid-May to mid-October; rates range from the top end of inexpensive to expensive. Also next to Green Gables Golf Course is the **Lakeview Lodge and Cottages** ((902) 963-2436 or (902) 8925424 (in winter) TOLL-FREE (800) 565-7550, Cavendish C0A 1N0 (in winter: 20 Loridale Drive, Charlottetown C1E 1P1) which has two rooms in the lodge, 20 cottages, and six motel units. There's a pool and two and a half hectares (six acres) of landscaped grounds. It's open June 1 to September 25; prices, range from inexpensive to mid-range. On Route 13 in the center of Cavendish is the **Shining Waters Country Inn and Cottages** (/FAX (902) 963-2251, Cavendish C0A 1N0, another moderately priced and delightful inn. It has 10 rooms in the main lodge and 20 cottages, with a splendid array of recreational facilities.

Nor should one forget that all along this coast there are excellent budget accommodations in farmhouses and tourist homes.

WHERE TO EAT

Charlottetown
The best place to eat in Charlottetown, perhaps in the whole province, is the colonial-style **Griffon Dining Room** ((902) 892-2496 in the Dundee

Arms Inn. It is expensive, of course, but not quite as expensive as the **Selkirk** ((902) 566-2222 in the Prince Edward Hotel. In any case, both are excellent, as is the **Confederation Room** ((902) 894-7371 in The Charlottetown, which is somewhat easier on the wallet. **Samuel's** ((902) 894-8572 at the Quality Inn on the Hill has delicious seafood at reasonable prices.

Charlottetown has a good selection of moderately priced eateries serving above-average food. One such is the **Lobsterman-on-the-Wharf** ((902) 368-2888 on the Prince Street Wharf overlooking the harbor, where the clams and mussels are exceptionally delicious. The **Queen Street Café** ((902) 566-5520, at 52 Queen Street, offers some very tasty bargains on its menu in addition to its attractive decor. Another popular place is the **Town & Country Restaurant** ((902) 892-2282, at 219 Queen Street, which has good steaks and salads.

Charlottetown also has some worthwhile ethnic restaurants. My favorite is **Cedar's Eatery** ((902) 892-7377, at 81 University Avenue, a welcoming sort of place that specializes in Lebanese dishes and mountainous servings.

The North Shore
If you have taken my advice on where to stay along the north shore, then you will be well placed to eat well. The dining room at **Dalvay-by-the-Sea** ((902) 672-2048 is excellent, with an Anglo-French accent to its seafood. The seafood dishes are similarly scrumptious, if not as elaborate, at **Stanhope by the Sea** ((902) 672-2047. When you get to Brackley Beach, you are in for a treat at the dining room of **Shaw's Hotel & Cottages** ((902) 672-2022, especially if you arrive in time for their Sunday buffet. A bit further down the road, on Route 6 in Oyster Bed Bridge, you can enjoy a delightful meal in delightful surroundings at **Café St. Jean** ((902) 963-3133, at delightfully reasonable prices. It operates from early June to late September.

In North Rustico the whole world, or so it seems, heads for **Fisherman's Wharf** ((902) 963-2669 on the harbor, where it is claimed that 10 tons of live lobsters are kept for the hundreds (yes, hundreds) of customers who can be accommodated at one sitting. It's open seasonally. For somewhat quieter dining in North Rustico, we recommend the **Idle Oars Restaurant** ((902) 963-2534 on Route 6, which has first-rate steaks in addition to its seafood, and has views which look out over rolling farmland. It's open May to late October.

In Cavendish there are many — too many — diners, snack bars, and fast-food places, but little of decent quality. One happy exception is **The Galley** ((902) 963-2354 on Route 13, which also has steaks as well as seafood and lobster dinners.

But for fun with your food we would go to **Fiddles & Vittles (** (902) 963-3003, next to the Bay Vista Motor Inn on Route 6. The fiddles in the background are mostly western and unobtrusive, the vittles in the foreground are mostly seafood and delicious, while the service in the middle is unfailingly friendly.

HOW TO GET THERE

If you are flying, **Air Canada (** (902) 892-1007 has daily flights to Charlottetown from several cities across Canada.

The new 13-km (nine-mile)-long **Confederation Bridge** links Prince Edward Island to the mainland, cutting crossing time to a mere 12 minutes. You pay your toll on the return trip — as the tourism brochures say — "if you decide to leave" the province. There's a free shuttle service for pedestrians and bicyclers.

There is also a ferry that crosses from Caribou, Nova Scotia, to Wood Islands, Prince Edward Island, sailing 10 times daily (approximately every hour and a half) beginning at 5:30 AM. It operates May to December and takes about 75 minutes to make the crossing. For information and schedules call **Northumberland Ferries (** (902) 566-3838 TOLL-FREE (888) 249-7245 FAX (902) 566-1550, 94 Water Street, PO Box 634, Charlottetown C1A 7L3.

OPPOSITE: The House that Anne Built — Green Gables House, near Cavendish, is a perennial tourist attraction. ABOVE: A small Prince Edwardian takes it easy.

Nova
Scotia

APPROPRIATELY FORMED AS IF TO HONOR ITS MOST celebrated culinary delight, the lobster-shaped province of Nova Scotia is Canada's anchor in the Atlantic. Its 52,842 sq km (20,402 sq miles) is divided into two parts: a long peninsula connected to the adjoining province of New Brunswick by the narrow Isthmus of Chignecto, and Cape Breton Island, which is linked to the peninsula by a one-and-a-half-kilometer (one-mile)-long causeway. With Prince Edward Island and New Brunswick, it is one of the three Maritime Provinces.

Like Newfoundland, Nova Scotia is thought to have been visited by the Vikings around AD 1000, but dates its "discovery" to 1497, when John Cabot arrived at the northern tip of Cape Breton Island

ment at Halifax, as a counterweight to France's military stronghold to the north.

In 1755, as Britain and France squared up to fight another war, the British governor of Nova Scotia ordered the deportation of all French settlers, or Acadians, who refused to take an oath of allegiance to the British Crown. Over the next few years 15,000 Acadians were forcibly removed from their homes and shipped off to the American colonies, where they found themselves equally unwelcome. Most of them eventually settled in the bayou country of Louisiana, where they survive to this day as Cajuns.

After the end of the Seven Years' War in 1763 all of Nova Scotia, including Cape Breton Island,

and claimed the territory for England. The first settlement, however, was French: Samuel de Champlain founded Port Royal, now Annapolis Royal, on the peninsula's northwest coast in 1605. Sixteen years later, England's Scottish King James I granted the region to another Scot, Sir William Alexander, so that he might establish a "New Scotland" there. Which he did, though using the Latin form of the name in the original charter.

For the next century Nova Scotia was caught up in the Anglo-French struggle for possession of eastern North America. Finally, in 1737 it was agreed that the British would have sovereignty over the peninsula while the French would control Cape Breton Island. Then in the early 1740s the French completed building a great fortress in a commanding position at Louisbourg on the east coast of the island, prompting Britain to send a large group of settlers to establish a fortified settle-

came under British rule. The Anglicization of the region received a further boost after the American Revolution, when 30,000 Loyalists fled the new republic and resettled in Nova Scotia, mostly along the Atlantic coast. In 1867 it became one of Canada's four founding provinces.

Today, with a population of around 950,000, Nova Scotia is by far the most populous of the Maritime Provinces. Fishing, naturally, has always been at the heart of the province's economy, and today still accounts for the largest share of its revenues. There is also a thriving timber industry to go alongside the agricultural output of the orchards and dairy farms of the Annapolis Valley.

OPPOSITE: Lunenberg, once a haven for pirates, is now home to a less swashbuckling breed of seafarers. ABOVE: Long after the flames died, the story of a terrible forest fire still lives in Cape Breton Highlands National Park.

But probably its fastest growing industry is tourism. Thanks to its great natural beauty, which includes the spectacular Cape Breton Highlands National Park, and its excellent recreational facilities, Nova Scotia is the Maritime Province that is the most popular with both American and European tourists.

HALIFAX

Originally founded for purely strategic reasons, Halifax remains militarily important as the home of Canada's largest naval base. But as a bustling provincial capital with a metropolitan population of around 345,000, which makes it the largest

city in the Maritime Provinces, Halifax is more important today as the commercial center of the Maritimes.

Situated on a small peninsula on the western shore of a deep inlet of the Atlantic, Halifax has a superb natural harbor — and indeed the busiest port on Canada's east coast. The historical as well as the contemporary center of the city is that part which lies between the harbor installations and the hilltop Citadel that dominates the peninsula. As the oldest British town on the Canadian mainland, and home of Canada's first Protestant church, Halifax wears its age gracefully. At the same time, as a modern financial center and government seat, the city has a liveliness and sophistication seldom found in cities of comparable size. In short, Halifax is in the enviable

A fisherman with his catch in picturesque Peggy's Cove, west of Halifax.

position of being able to boast both small-town virtues and big-city amenities.

BACKGROUND

Although the Mi'kmaq had long inhabited the area, the town of Halifax came into being almost overnight when, in 1749, Colonel Edward Cornwallis led a flotilla of 20 ships, carrying 3,000 settlers, into the harbor and immediately began work on constructing a town. Built in response to the perceived threat posed by the new French fortress at Louisbourg, it was named after the Earl of Halifax, who was then the president of England's Board of Trade and Plantations.

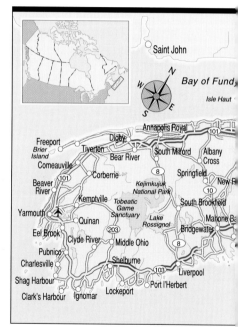

Ironically, having been established in the first place solely because of its strategic location in case of war, Halifax went on to prosper greatly from wars fought in other lands. First, the British victory in the Seven Years' War removed any potential threat from Louisbourg. Then during the American War of Independence the harbor became an important naval base for British warships, which pumped a lot of money into the local economy; and after the British were defeated the resulting influx of fleeing loyalists, many of whom were educated and well-to-do, further invigorated the local economy as well as having a profound and beneficial impact on the local culture. Then came the War of 1812, which brought the warships back from Britain, and with them more money to swell the municipal coffers. Even the American Civil War led to increased military activity in Halifax, and thus increased military spending, and the resulting increased employment.

Twentieth century wars, too, were profitable for the town. During World War I, thanks to its 16 sq km (10 sq miles) of deep-water anchorage in the harbor's Bedford Basin, it was used as a distribution center for the supply ships heading for Europe. During World War II it was the port from which the great convoys—some 17,000 ships in all — sailed across the North Atlantic.

Only once, in 1917, has Halifax suffered a war wound of its own—but it was a horrible wound, and left a permanent scar on the collective memory of its citizens. In December 1917 a French munitions ship, the *Mont Blanc*, loaded with ex-

WHAT TO SEE AND DO

Thanks to a city ordinance banning the construction of buildings that interfere with various "view planes" across the city, Halifax has been uniquely successful in preserving the "human scale" as it has grown. The center of Halifax since its founding has been the **Grand Parade**, a square running along the west side of Barrington Street, Halifax's main shopping thoroughfare. At the north end of the square is **City Hall**, with its enormous wooden flagpole, and at the south end is the timber-framed **St. Paul's** (1750), the oldest Protestant church in Canada. Going up George Street from the Grand

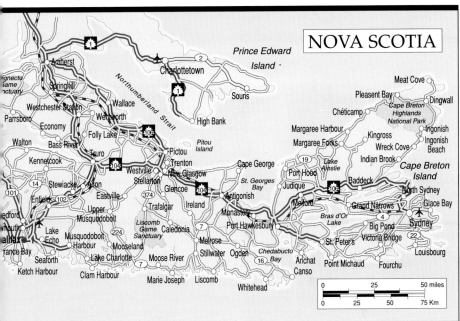

plosives headed for Europe, collided with a Belgian relief ship in the harbor and blew up. The explosion leveled the entire north end of town, killing over 2,000 people and injuring 9,000, of whom 200 were blinded by the blast. It is not the sort of thing a community recovers from quickly or easily.

But recover it did, and during the past half-century has shown that it can flourish in peacetime just as well as in wartime.

GENERAL INFORMATION

Tourism Nova Scotia operates two year-round Visitor Information Centres. One is in the Red Store at the Historic Properties ((902) 424-4248, on the downtown harbor boardwalk. The second is at the International Visitors Centre ((902) 490-5946, corner of Barrington and Sackville streets.

Parade towards The Citadel, you come upon the **Old Town Clock**, erected in 1803, the symbol of Halifax. Further up is **The Citadel** itself, a many-angled, star-shaped fortress. Originally built by Cornwallis on his arrival in 1749, it was rebuilt and expanded after the American Revolution and then again after the War of 1812. Finally, in 1828, the Duke of Wellington ordered that a permanent fortress of masonry be built.

On the other side of the hill from the downtown area, at 1747 Summer Street, is the **Nova Scotia Museum of Natural History** ((902) 424-7353. It has exhibits covering every aspect of the province's history — geographical, natural, social, and industrial. It's open daily from mid-May to October, closed Mondays the rest of the year; an admission fee is charged. The **Public Gardens** just south of the museum were first opened in 1867 and remain to this day seven hectares (17 acres) of classic Victoriana: a bandstand, fountains, statues, duck pond, and formally planted Oriental trees. Even more attractive for would-be strollers and picnickers is **Point Pleasant Park** at the southern tip of the Halifax peninsula. This heavily wooded 79-hectare (186-acre) park has a restaurant in addition to its many walking trails and picnic spots.

Down on the **harborfront** north of Duke Street you will find the **Historic Properties**, a group of old wharves and buildings dating from as early as 1800, now restored and refurbished, in an all-pedestrian area which includes shops, galleries, restaurants, and street entertainers. The buildings include the **Privateers' Warehouse**, the oldest structure in the area, where nineteenth-century

634-1963, is moored at the wharf of the Maritime Museum and goes on two-hour cruises of the harbor at 9:30 AM and 1 PM during July and August.

NIGHTLIFE AND THE ARTS

Halifax is lively at night, especially along **Grafton Street** and **Spring Garden Road**, which on Friday and Saturday nights is the scene of one long party. There is a multilevel partying at **Privateers' Warehouse** ((902) 422-1289 in the Historic Properties: below the Upper Deck restaurant (see WHERE TO EAT, below) is the **Middle Deck**, a lounge where rock and jazz bands play, and below that the **Lower Deck**, where maritime folk music fills the air. The

pirates stashed their loot, and the **Old Red Store** building, which now houses the tourist office. A few blocks south of the Historic Properties is the **Maritime Museum of the Atlantic** ((902) 424-7490, at 1675 Lower Water Street. Its newest exhibit, *Titanic: The Unsinkable Ship and Halifax*, traces the link between the disaster and the city — the closest major port to the disaster site, telling the story of the rescue and search ships chartered from this city. The exhibit displays salvaged artifacts, including what is reputed to be John Jacob Astor's lifejacket. Ship models, naval instruments, weapons, and many other items illustrating Halifax's maritime history make up the rest of the museum's collection. It is open daily year-round, and an admission fee is charged from June 1 to October 15.

Fittingly, the best tours of Halifax are waterborne. A replica of Canada's most famous boat, the unbeaten racing schooner *Bluenose II* ((902)

Palace ((902) 429-5959, at 1721 Brunswick Street, is open nightly and offers varied musical fare.

Concerts of all kinds are performed regularly at the **Metro Centre** ((902) 451-1202, 5248 Duke Street, near The Citadel, while the intimate **Neptune Theatre** ((902) 429-7300 at 1593 Argyle Street, stages drama and comedy.

EXCURSIONS FROM HALIFAX

Dating back to 1811, **Peggy's Cove**, 43 km (27 miles) west of Halifax on Route 333, is built around a narrow ocean inlet and is dominated by a lighthouse perched on massive granite boulders. Here brightly colored clapboard houses cling to the granite cliffs surrounding the lovely little harbor where the fishing boats are moored and where the fishermen's shacks stand on stilts in the water. Unfortunately — such is the fame of Peggy's Cove — it is packed with tourists during summer. The best time to go is early morning before the hoards descend, and if you're driving the best place to park is in the public lot at the top of the village.

WHERE TO STAY

Expensive

The most luxurious address in Halifax is the **Sheraton Halifax (** (902) 421-1700 TOLL-FREE (800) 325-3535 FAX (902) 422-5805, in the Historic Properties at 1919 Upper Water Street, Halifax B3J 3J5. Although large and modern and equipped with all the luxuries, it has been so well designed and decorated that it manages to blend in beautifully with the historic buildings around it. Not far away, in the Scotia Square complex, is the **Hotel Halifax (** (902) 425-6700 TOLL-FREE (800) 441-1414 FAX (902) 425-6214, 1990 Barrington Street, Halifax B3J 1P2. As it is attached to the Scotia Square shopping mall, this Canadian Pacific hotel offers not only the amenities you would expect of a luxury hotel, but also the convenience of having every conceivable type of shop within easy walking distance. Connected by underground walkway to the World Trade and Convention Centre is the **Prince George Hotel (** (902) 425-1986 TOLL-FREE (800) 565-1567 FAX (902) 429-6048, at 1725 Market Street, Halifax B3J 3N9. Opened in 1986, this elegantly appointed hotel has not only a handy location next to the convention center but also boasts an award-winning restaurant.

Mid-range

Halifax is blessed with a large number of superb mid-range hotels. The **Citadel Halifax (** (902) 422-1391 TOLL-FREE IN CANADA (800) 565-7162 FAX (902) 429-6672, is marginally the best of these. Located at 1960 Brunswick Street, Halifax B3J 2G7, the Citadel Inn has 270 luxurious rooms, some of which are on no-smoking floors and some of which overlook the harbor. Another top-class hotel in this category is the **Delta Barrington (** (902) 429-7410 TOLL-FREE (800) 268-1133, at 1875 Barrington Street, Halifax B3J 3L6. Near the Historic Properties, it's another classic example of how to build a modern hotel without upsetting the neighbors. For elegance and charm it would be hard to beat the **Halliburton House Inn (** (902) 420-0658 FAX (902) 423-2324, 5184 Morris Street, Halifax B3J 1B3. This registered Heritage property with 30 rooms was built in 1820, and it has been completely renovated and modernized without sacrificing any of its original charm. It also has one of the best restaurants in Halifax.

The **Westin Nova Scotian (** (902) 421-1000 TOLL-FREE (800) 228-3000 FAX (902) 422-9465, 1881 Hollis Street, Halifax B3H 2P6, is a rather elderly hotel next to the railway station, but it has been tastefully refurbished and now enjoys the addition of a number of luxury rooms as well as a swimming pool and a tennis court. It also runs a free shuttle service to downtown. The **Lord Nelson (** (902) 423-6331 TOLL-FREE (800) 565-2020 FAX (902) 423-7128 is another venerable hotel, located opposite the Public Gardens at 1515 South Park Street (corner Spring Garden Road), Halifax B3J 2T3. Finally, there is the **Waverley Inn (** (902) 423-9346 FAX (902) 425-0167 at 1266 Barrington Street, Halifax B3J 1Y5. This friendly 30-room inn has been here since 1876, and boasts Oscar Wilde among its former guests. Now fully modernized, it is an attractive bargain.

Inexpensive

Although it is some way from downtown, the **Chebucto Inn (** (902) 453-4330 TOLL-FREE (800) 268-4330 FAX (902) 454-7043 is probably the best of the inexpensive hotels. It has 30 air-conditioned rooms, with all the standard facilities, in an attractive two-story building at 6151 Lady Hammond Road, Halifax B3K 2R9. Another good value is the **Travelers Motel (** (902) 835-3394 TOLL-FREE (800) 565-3394 FAX (902) 835-6887 on the Halifax city limits at 773 Bedford Highway, Bedford B4A 1A4. It has 25 motel units, an outdoor pool, and a restaurant.

Across the harbor from Halifax in Dartmouth are two places that represent excellent value. The first is **Keddy's Dartmouth Inn (** (902) 469-0331 FAX (902) 466-6324 TOLL-FREE (800) 561-7666, at

Halifax — OPPOSITE: The restored Historic Properties. ABOVE: The Victorian bandstand, focal point of the Public Gardens.

9 Braemar Drive, Dartmouth B2Y 3H6, which has 116 air-conditioned rooms, a licensed lounge and dining room. Also in Dartmouth at 101 Yorkshire Avenue Extension, is the **Country Inn & Suites** ((902) 465-4000 TOLL-FREE (800) 456-4000 FAX (902) 465-6006, which has an innovative array of complimentary services in addition to its creature comforts.

For **bed and breakfast** accommodation, call the Nova Scotia Bed and Breakfast Association ((902) 423-4480 TOLL-FREE (800) 948-4267 E-MAIL tians@ns.sympatico.ca, 1800 Argyle Street, Suite 402, Halifax B3J 3N8.

WHERE TO EAT

As with any smallish city, the best restaurants generally are in the best hotels. In Halifax, we would recommend the superb restaurant in the **Halliburton House Inn** ((902) 420-0658.

The **Upper Deck restaurant** (see above) on the third floor of Privateers' Warehouse in the Historic Properties has excellent food as well as courteous service to go with its maritime decor. Of course, it's not difficult to find wonderful seafood in Halifax, but if you want to find it in an unusual and lovely setting, go to the **Five Fishermen** ((902) 422-4421 at 1740 Argyle Street across from the Grand Parade. The restaurant is upstairs in a converted schoolhouse and is lit by genuine Tiffany lamps.

Ryan Duffy's Steak and Seafood ((902) 421-1116, in the Spring Garden Place shopping center at 5640 Spring Garden Road, is as moderate (or as expensive) as you want it to be. If you order a steak, for example, the meat is cut and trimmed to your specifications at your table before it is cooked, and the price is strictly according to the weight of the cut you have chosen.

For a tasty, inexpensive, bite, **Lawrence of Oregano** ((902) 425-8077, at 1726 Argyle Street, is a very cheerful and popular Italian restaurant serving excellent pizzas and spaghetti dishes.

HOW TO GET THERE

Air Canada ((902) 429-7111 has daily flights to Halifax from New York, Boston, Toronto, and Montréal, while **Canadian Airlines International** TOLL-FREE IN CANADA (800) 565-1800 TOLL-FREE IN THE UNITED STATES (800) 426-7000 flies in daily from many Canadian cities.

If you are driving, highways from all over the United States and Canada join the Trans-Canada Highway, which crosses from New Brunswick into Nova Scotia at Amherst. Similarly, **Greyhound** TOLL-FREE (800) 661-8747 buses from the United States and Voyageur buses from Montréal link up with the SMT bus lines in New Brunswick which in turn connects with the Acadian Lines in Nova

Scotia at Amherst. Halifax is the eastern terminus of the **VIA Rail** TOLL-FREE (888) 842-7733 network with one train daily (except Tuesday) from Montréal via Moncton, New Brunswick.

There are no ferries into Halifax, but there are ferries from Newfoundland to North Sydney, discussed in the preceding chapter, and there is a daily ferry from Wood Islands, Prince Edward Island, to Caribou, Nova Scotia, from May to December, operated by **Northumberland Ferries** ((902) 566-3838 TOLL-FREE (888) 249-7245 FAX (902) 566-1550, 94 Water Street, PO Box 634, Charlottetown, Prince Edward Island C1A 7L3. There are also ferries to Yarmouth from Bar Harbor, Maine and Portland, Maine.

OUTSIDE HALIFAX

Nova Scotia may divide into two parts geographically — the peninsula and Cape Breton Island — but ethnically it is a jigsaw puzzle. While Halifax is very English both in its history and its character, the rest of the province shows the cultural influences of the English, the Irish, the French, the Germans, and the Scots — whose descendants today make up over a third of the population. As you travel around Nova Scotia these influences will become apparent.

Tourism Nova Scotia in Halifax (see GENERAL INFORMATION, page 207, under HALIFAX) is your best source of information about the province. The free Check-In reservation service ((902) 425-5781 TOLL-FREE (800) 565-0000 provides up-to-date accommodation information and makes reservations. In addition there are drop-in tourist information centers throughout the province.

THE SOUTH SHORE

On Route 3 southwest of Halifax, the charming seaside village of **Chester** is situated on a penin-

OPPOSITE TOP: A barn and farmhouse in their wooded context. BOTTOM: The shingled exterior of a barn. ABOVE: Preparing salmon for smoking.

sula at the head of scenic, island-strewn Mahone Bay. Settled by New Englanders in 1760 (who originally gave it the name Shoreham), it is still the summer home of quite a few American families — as well as a favored retirement home of wealthy Canadians. Although visitors are welcome to use its tennis courts and its 18-hole golf course on a promontory overlooking the bay, most people come for the sailing and yachting. Indeed, the high point of the summer season is Chester Race Week in the middle of August, the largest sailing regatta in the Maritimes.

There are **visitor information centers** in Lunenburg ((902) 634-8100, at the top of Blockhouse Road; in Shelburne ((902) 875-4547 in a waterfront

sidered Nova Scotia's premier fishing port. Like its neighbor, it was a favorite haven for pirates until well into the nineteenth century. Settled in 1753 by Protestants from the German town of Lunenburg, it has a long and colorful seafaring heritage, but is probably best known as the town that in 1921 built the *Bluenose*, the famous racing schooner that never lost an international race and which is depicted on the back of the Canadian dime. (In 1963 Lunenburg also built its replica, *Bluenose II*, which can usually be seen in the harbor at Halifax.) Situated on a picturesque peninsula with a front and back harbor, Lunenburg has lately become an important tourist stopover, with shops, galleries, and all sorts of recreational

building at the corner of King and Dock streets; and in Yarmouth ((902) 742-6639 up the hill from the ferry terminal, at 228 Main Street.

The little town of **Mahone Bay**, 21 km (13 miles) southwest of Chester on Route 3, is today best known as a crafts and antiques center, with its trademark three churches standing side-by-side at the head of the harbor. But there was a time, in the century after its founding by Captain Ephraim Cook in 1754, when it was known primarily as a haunt of pirates and smugglers. In fact, the name Mahone is thought to be derived from the Old French *mahonne*, a type of raiding boat used by pirates. One of the most delightful aspects of the town is that many of its shops, studios, galleries, and restaurants are housed in historic early nineteenth-century buildings.

Just down the coast from Mahone Bay is **Lunenburg**, a UNESCO World Heritage Site, long con-

facilities, including the nine-hole **Bluenose Golf Course** overlooking Front Harbour. It is also home to the interesting **Fisheries Museum of the Atlantic** ((902) 634-4794, with three floors of exhibits and an aquarium. It's open daily from June to mid-October. An admission fee is charged.

Further down Route 103 is **Shelburne**, "The Loyalist Town," settled in 1783 when 3,000 Loyalists fleeing New York City, many of them rich, arrived in 30 ships and instantly created a prosperous town where there had been nothing but wilderness. That is to say, nothing but wilderness and one of the best natural harbors in the world. Within a few years the population had quintupled, making it the largest community in British North America. However, the population shrank again almost as quickly as it had expanded, whereupon the settlers who stayed began turning Shelburne into a fishing and shipbuilding center — in fact, it went on to become the birthplace of many of the world's great yachts. There are still quite a few houses in Shelburne that date from the Loyalist period, but two in particular deserve mention. **Ross-Thomson House** was built in 1784; originally a general store today it is a Loyalist museum that includes shelves still stocked with goods that were in demand in the 1780s, while **David Nairn House**, built in 1787, is now the home of the Shelburne County Museum.

Although **Yarmouth**, with a population of 7,800, is Nova Scotia's largest seaport west of Halifax, and has a great shipping tradition going back to its settlement in 1761, it is principally of interest today as the "Gateway to Nova Scotia;"

Hill Road, Chester B0J 1J0, perched atop a hill with unobstructed views of Mahone Bay. There are nine rooms, ranging in price from the low end of the expensive category upwards. Three of the rooms are in the main lodge and the others are scattered about the property in cottages. Four rooms have wood fireplaces, three have Jacuzzis, and two have kitchenettes. The (expensive) dining room is very good and you should be sure to make reservations for a table on the front porch with its lovely vistas. Chester also has the inexpensive and informal **Mecklenburgh Inn** ((902) 275-4638 E-MAIL frnthrbr@auracom.com, at 78 Queen Street, Chester B0J 1J0. Located in a residential neighborhood, the inn has large porches on its two floors,

the terminus for ferries from Portland and Bar Harbor in Maine.

Yarmouth is also notable for its well-preserved **Victorian architecture** and for its famous **Runic Stone** on Main Street, which bears inscriptions suggesting that the Vikings reached here 1,000 years ago. The **Yarmouth County Museum** ((902) 742-5539, 22 Collins Street, is an excellent regional museum, with displays of seafaring artifacts, Victorian furniture, costumes, and examples of early decorative arts. It's open June to mid-October, Monday to Saturday from 9 AM to 5 PM and Sunday from 2 PM to 5 PM; mid-October to May, Tuesday to Sunday from 2 PM to 5 PM. An admission fee is charged.

Where to Stay

In Chester you can enjoy stylish luxury at **Haddon Hall** ((902) 275-3577 FAX (902) 275-5159, 67 Haddon

which fill up with guests rocking and watching small town life. The Victorian-style rooms have shared bath. Robes are provided.

Nearby in Hubbards there are two delightful places on Shore Club Road. One is the **Anchorage House & Cabins** ((902) 857-9402, Rural Route 2, Hubbards B0J 1T0, which has seven housekeeping cottages, two cabins, and five rooms in the main lodge. It has fishing charters and small-boat rentals from its own private wharf. Very reasonably priced. At 167 Shore Club Road, Hubbards B0J 1T0, is the rather more expensive **Dauphinee Inn** ((902) 857-1790, which has only six rooms but has a licensed dining room and lounge, a gift shop, and boat docking facilities.

OPPOSITE: The church in Grand Pré National Historic Site that memorializes the deported Acadians. ABOVE: Annapolis Royal's Historic Gardens.

In Mahone Bay there are two charming bed and breakfasts. The **Sou'Wester Inn** ℂ (902) 624-9296, at 788 Main Street, Mahone Bay B0J 2E0, has four rooms, some with private bath. It's decorated throughout with antique furniture, and a verandah overlooks the bay. The inn's inexpensive price includes full breakfast and evening tea. **Longacres Bed & Breakfast** ℂ (902) 624-6336 is in a house that dates from 1800 at 122 Clearland Road, Mahone Bay B0J 2E0. It has three rooms with two and a half private baths, a walking trail, beach bikes, a pond. The price, which is in the mid-range category, includes full breakfast.

The two most elegant hostelries in **Lunenburg** are both restored Victorian mansions full

Shelburne B0T 1W0, a splendidly refurbished 1785 house on the waterfront with an excellent licensed restaurant. It has three rooms with private baths; breakfast is included in the inexpensive price. More inexpensive still is the **Loyalist Inn** ℂ (902) 875-2343 downtown at 160 Water Street, Shelburne B0T 1W0, which has 18 air-conditioned rooms with bath and cable television. Another bargain is the **Ox Bow Motel** ℂ (902) 875-3000, PO Box 459, Rural Route 2, Shelburne B0T 1W0, on the shores of Lake George about five kilometers (three miles) east of Shelburne. It has 47 units, including 13 housekeeping, a heated pool, licensed dining room and lounge, and a coffee shop.

of antiques and period pieces. The **Boscawen Inn and MacLachlan House** ℂ (902) 634-3325 FAX (902) 634-9293, 150 Cumberland Street, PO Box 1343, Lunenburg B0J 2C0, is slightly more expensive than **Bluenose Lodge** ℂ (902) 634-8851, 10 Falkland Avenue, Lunenburg B0J 2C0, and somewhat larger, with 20 rooms. Like the Boscawen Inn it has a licensed dining room serving three meals daily. An excellent bargain is the **Homeport Motel** ℂ (902) 634-8234, at 167 Victoria Road, Lunenburg B0J 2C0, which has nine air-conditioned units as well as six new housekeeping units, cable television, whirlpool tub, queen-size beds, etc., at very competitive rates. There is also a campground right next to the tourist information center on Blockhouse Hill Road.

In Shelburne you should try to get into **The Cooper's Inn** ℂ (902) 875-4656, 36 Dock Street,

The poshest hotel in Yarmouth is easily the **Rodd Grand Hotel** ℂ (902) 742-2446 TOLL-FREE IN THE MARITIMES (800) 565-0207 TOLL-FREE IN QUÉBEC AND ONTARIO (800) 565-0241, TOLL-FREE IN THE UNITED STATES (800) 565-9077 FAX (902) 742-4645, at 417 Main Street, Yarmouth B5A 4B2. Its 138 comfortable rooms occupy seven floors overlooking Yarmouth harbor, with all the usual trimmings at mid-range prices. Its lower-priced sister hotel, the **Rodd Colony Harbour Inn** ℂ (902) 742-9194 (toll-free numbers the same as the Rodd Grand), is across from the ferry terminal, at 6 Forest Street, Yarmouth B5A 3K7. The hotel's Colony Restaurant is deservedly celebrated, while its bar, Hawthorne's Lounge, is a most convivial watering hole. Four kilometers (two and a half miles) from Yarmouth on Route 1 at Dayton is the **Voyageur Motel** ℂ (902) 742-7157 TOLL-FREE IN THE MARITIMES (800) 565-5026,

PO Box 1020, Rural Route 1, Yarmouth B5A 4A5. Overlooking Doctors Lake, it has 29 motel units and four housekeeping units. All of its rooms, even the deluxe ones, are priced in the middle range.

Where to Eat

In Chester, if you are staying at **Haddon Hall** ℂ (902) 275-3577, eat there. Otherwise go down Route 3 to **The Galley** ℂ (902) 275-4700, 115 Marina Road, which has an enchanting view over the marina at Marriott Cove as well as lovely, and inexpensive, seafood and homemade desserts. In Mahone Bay, **The Innlet Café** ℂ (902) 624-6363, Edgewater Street, is a smartly decorated dining room in the wing of

Hotel ℂ (902) 742-2446. After those you ought to check out **Captain Kelley's Kitchen** ℂ (902) 742-9191 at 577 Main Street, which serves very good food at popular prices. Also, out on Route 1 across from the Voyageur Motel, there is **Harris's Quick 'n' Tasty** ℂ (902) 742-3467, which is much better than it sounds, and also boasts of "cholesterol-free frying."

ANNAPOLIS VALLEY

To go up Route 1 from Yarmouth to Windsor, through the beautiful Annapolis Valley region, is to go up the **Evangeline Trail**, named after the eponymous heroine of Longfellow's famous poem

a 200-year-old house. It specializes in coffees and desserts, but what comes before is quite edible.

In Lunenburg, the best dining is at the **Boscawen Inn and MacLachlan House** ℂ (902) 634-3325 and the **Bluenose Lodge** ℂ (902) 634-8851 (see WHERE TO STAY, above). Also good is **Capt'n Angus Seafood Restaurant** ℂ (902) 634-3030 on the second floor of the Fisheries Museum of the Atlantic, which offers several traditional Lunenburg dishes.

In Shelburne, apart from **The Cooper's Inn** ℂ ((902) 875-4656 and the **Loyalist Inn** ℂ (902) 875-2343, in one of which you might be staying anyway (see WHERE TO STAY, above), there is **McGowan's** ℂ (902) 875-3602, a licensed dining room and lounge at 1 Dock Street on the upper level, above Bruce's Wharf.

In Yarmouth, once again, the best places to eat are in the best places to stay: **Rodd Colony Harbour Inn** ℂ (902) 742-9194 and the **Rodd Grand**

about the tragedy of the Acadians who were expelled from here in 1755. This was the heartland of Acadia.

There is a **Tourist Information Centre** ℂ (902) 245-5714, in Digby on the harbor at 110 Montague Row. In Annapolis Royal, the **Annapolis District Tourist Bureau** ℂ (902) 532-5454, is at the Annapolis Tidal Power Project on Route 1.

The first town of any size that you come across is **Digby**, home of the (justly) celebrated Digby scallops. In fact, the town itself celebrates its best-known product with the Digby Scallop Days in August. Almost as well known are the locally cured smoked herring, called Digby Chicks. Digby's site, on an inlet of the Bay of Fundy, is not only beautiful but handy: it is the terminus for the ferry from Saint John, New Brunswick.

Lobster pots piled up on Cape Breton Island.

Founded in 1605 by Samuel de Champlain, **Annapolis Royal** was originally called Port-Royal, and for over a century was at the center of the battles that raged between the French and English for control of the area. Finally, in 1710, the English triumphed and renamed the town Annapolis Royal in honor of Queen Anne. Although it then became the capital of Nova Scotia until the founding of Halifax, it remained an English island in a sea of French-speaking Acadians until 1755, when the Acadians were expelled from the province. The centerpiece of the town is the **Fort Anne National Historic Site** ((902) 532-2397, with its well-preserved earthwork fortifications, a museum, and a gunpowder magazine dating from 1708 (open

daily, mid-May to mid-October; an admission fee is charged). Also well worth a visit are the **Annapolis Royal Historic Gardens** ((902) 532-7018 near the fort on Upper George Street, where you can see the history of the area in its gardens (open daily, mid-May to mid-October; an admission fee is charged). At Port **Royal National Historic Site** ((902) 532-2898, 10 km (six miles) west of Annapolis Royal, you will find a restoration of the original French fur-trading post that stood here from 1605 to 1613 (open daily, mid-May to mid-October; an admission fee is charged).

Wolfeville (population 3,500) is a trim little Victorian village with a thoroughly New England feel to it. The reason for this ambiance is clear: The region was largely populated in the wake of the American Revolution by transplanted New

Rural scenes on Cape Breton Island.

Englanders. These new inhabitants forced out the Acadian settlers who had been working the land here since the late 1600s.

Grand Pré, the "great meadow" of diked land along the shore a few kilometers (a couple of miles) east of Wolfeville, was the most important Acadian settlement before the Deportation, and was the setting for Longfellow's *Evangeline*. The **Grand Pré National Historic Site** ((902) 542-3631 features a bronze statue of Evangeline, as well as an Acadian well, a blacksmith's shop, and a stone church that stands as a memorial to the Acadians and houses an exhibit on the Deportation (open daily, mid-May to mid-October; an admission fee is charged).

The Evangeline Trail ends at **Windsor**, at the eastern end of the Annapolis Valley, which also happens to be located exactly midway between the equator and the North Pole. Settled by the Acadians at the end of the seventeenth century, not long after the founding of Grand Pré, it disappeared as an Acadian town in 1755 and became a Loyalist stronghold shortly thereafter. Today it is best known as the home of Judge Thomas Chandler Haliburton, the "Canadian Mark Twain" who created the memorable character of Sam Slick, many of whose coinages are now everyday expressions. **Haliburton House** ((902) 798-2915, 414 Clifton Avenue, which he built in 1833, is now a museum.

Where to Stay

If you know anything about Digby, you know it is the home of the **Pines Resort Hotel** ((902) 245-2511 TOLL-FREE (800) 667-4637 FAX (902) 245-6133 on Shore Road, PO Box 70, Digby B0V 1A0, where the rooms in the main lodge and cottages are expensive — and well worth it. The Pines, which is one of three grand resort hotels operated by the provincial government, has an 18-hole golf course, floodlit tennis courts, a heated and glass-enclosed swimming pool, croquet lawns, hiking trails, you name it.

In Annapolis Royal there is no shortage of delightful places to stay. For creature comforts, you can't do better than the **Auberge Wandlyn Royal Anne Motel** ((902) 532-2323 FAX (902) 532-7277, PO Box 628, Route 1, Annapolis Royal B0S 1A0, with its modern rooms, and restaurant. It is just west of town. For charm and taste (and convenient location) we would recommend three places. The **Bread and Roses Country Inn** ((902) 532-5727, at 82 Victoria Street, Annapolis Royal B0S 1A0, is a brick mansion built in 1882, in which the nine rooms all have en suite bathrooms and antique furnishings. The **Garrison House Inn** ((902) 532-5750, at 350 St. George Street, Annapolis Royal B0S 1A0, is directly across from Fort Anne and was built in 1854. The **Queen Anne Inn** ((902) 532-7850, at 494 Upper St. George Street, Annapolis

Royal B0S 1A0, is a registered Heritage Property with 10 rooms, all with private bath, and cable television in the sitting room.

In **Wolfeville**, the **Blomidon Inn** ((902) 542-2291 TOLL-FREE (800) 565-2291 FAX (902) 542-7461, at 127 Main Street, PO Box 839, Wolfeville B0P 1X0, has 25 elegantly furnished rooms, as well as recreational facilities and a first-class dining room. Also moderately priced. If you're looking for a bargain, you need look no further than the **Evangeline Motel** ((902) 542-2703 TOLL-FREE (888) 542-2703, Grand Pré B0P 1M0, at the intersection of Route 101 and the road into the park. Its 21 rooms are comfortable, there is a pool and restaurant, and it costs what you would pay in tax alone at some other places.

In Windsor, the pick of the accommodations is easily the **Hampshire Court Motel and Cottages** ((902) 798-3133, 1081 King Street, Windsor B0N 2T0. In beautiful surroundings, with air con-

ditioning, tennis courts, cable television, and a lovely picnic area, it is surprisingly inexpensive.

Where to Eat

In Digby the **Pines Resort Hotel** ((902) 245-2511 (see WHERE TO STAY, above) is tops. In Annapolis Royal, the **Secret Garden** ((902) 532-2200, at 471 St. George Street, serves delicious light fare in a Victorian house overlooking beautiful gardens. At 218 St. George Street is **Newman's** ((902) 532-5502, which is more for gourmands than gourmets, but its basic and well-prepared dishes are very reasonably priced.

In Wolfeville, the best place to eat is **Chez La Vigne** ((902) 542-5077, at 117 Front Street, where you will find classic French cuisine in a romantic setting. More homespun is the **Colonial Inn Restaurant** ((902) 542-7525, on Main Street across from the post office in the center of town. Everything here is homemade, including the pastries, and

served in a colonial setting. For elegant food in an elegant atmosphere, you can't beat the **Blomidon Inn** ((902) 542-2291 (see WHERE TO STAY, above).

CAPE BRETON ISLAND

Connected to the mainland by the one-and-a-half-kilometer (mile)-long Canso Causeway, Cape Breton Island consists of 10,300 sq km (3,980 sq miles) of some of the most beautiful scenery in North America. Once across the causeway, most visitors continue on up the Trans-Canada Highway as far as Baddeck, where they join the **Cabot Trail**, a 294-km (184-mile) loop that rivals California's famous Highway 1 for unbelievably spectacular views.

The forested mountains and steep, verdant valleys of Cape Breton Highlands National Park provide a paradise for hikers and campers. OVERLEAF: The rugged beauty of Cape Breton Island's coastline.

There are nine tourist information centers on the island. The main branch and a wise first stop is the **Tourist Information Centre** ((902) 625-4201 in Port Hastings on the right after crossing the causeway. There is also a **Cape Breton Highlands National Park information office** ((902) 285-2691 at Ingonish Beach, another at Chéticamp, and the **Louisbourg Visitor Centre** ((902) 733-2280.

After leaving the Trans-Canada Highway, heading clockwise, you follow the Cabot Trail over Hunter's Mountain into the Middle River Valley before joining the Margaree River in a lush valley renowned for its salmon pools. The highway then cuts across gentle farmland until it reaches Margaree Harbour on the coast, where it crosses the estuary of the Margaree River and heads up the coast, affording excellent views of the Northumberland Strait and the Gulf of St. Lawrence. About half an hour's drive up the coast from Margaree Harbour is **Chéticamp**, an Acadian, French-speaking fishing village known for the hooked rugs and mats handmade by the local women. In addition to the large number of craft shops, the **Musée Acadien** has a splendid collection of hooked rugs as well as a café and a shop where all kinds of locally made items are for sale.

About five kilometers (three miles) east of Chéticamp is the entrance to **Cape Breton Highlands National Park**, 958 sq km (370 sq miles) of steep mountains, stony shores, deep forests, green valleys, sandy beaches, and stunning ocean views — not to mention all kinds of wildlife — in a wilderness area furnished with many campgrounds and picnic sites. The most important resort area along the Cabot Trail is in the **Ingonish** region at the eastern entrance to the park, 105 km (65 miles) from Chéticamp. Here you will find the park's administrative headquarters and a great variety of recreational facilities: a golf course, tennis courts, supervised swimming, campsites, picnic areas, hiking trails, boating, sailing, and, in winter, skiing. Ingonish Beach, south of Ingonish, is also the home of the Keltic Lodge, one of the finest resort hotels in eastern Canada (see WHERE TO STAY, below). From there you climb the 366 m (1,200 ft) of Cape Smokey, a mist-capped promontory whence the trail plunges back to the coast and continues along the "North Shore," an area originally settled by Highland Scottish pioneers, down to South Gut St. Ann's, below St. Ann's Harbour, where it rejoins the Trans-Canada Highway for the final 18 km (11 miles) back to Baddeck, completing the loop.

If you take the Trans-Canada Highway (Route 105) in the other direction — east — it will take you to North Sydney, where it is met by the ferry to Newfoundland. Before entering North Sydney, if you turn right onto Route 125 it will take you across the Sydney River to the outskirts of Sydney, the "Steel City," Nova Scotia's third

largest (and certainly drabbest) urban area. From there you take Route 22 south for 37 km (23 miles) to reach the **Fortress of Louisbourg National Historic Site**, the largest in Canada. The fortress itself, guarding the entrance to the St. Lawrence and therefore the approach to Québec, took the French a quarter of a century to build (1719–1744) and really wasn't completely finished when it was attacked in 1745 by an army of 4,000 New Englanders who captured it after a 49-day siege. It was handed back to France in 1748 under the Treaty of Aix-la-Chapelle, but was retaken by the British in 1758. Two years later Prime Minister William Pitt ordered the fortifications blown up. Since 1961 the fortress and the town have been the site of the largest historical reconstruction project ever undertaken in Canada. Over 40 buildings have been meticulously reconstructed, while the streets and shops are full of people in period dress and the inns and taverns serve authentic eighteenth-century food and drink. It is remarkable in the way it captures the feel of a French colonial outpost of the time.

We would add just one word of caution. As the weather at Louisbourg is often foggy and cold, bring along a sweater and a raincoat just in case.

Where to Stay

On the Canso Causeway at the junction of Routes 19, 104, and 105 are two very comfortable and moderately priced motels. **Keddy's Motel Inn** ((902) 625-0460 FAX (902) 625-1275, PO Box 50, Port Hastings B0E 2T0, is the larger and slightly more expensive of the two. **Travelodge Cape Breton Island** ((902) 625-1300 FAX (902) 625-1966, 353 Port Hastings, Port Hawkesbury B0E 2T0, has the better restaurant.

In Chéticamp, the cream of the crop is **Laurie's Motel** ((902) 224-2400 TOLL-FREE (800) 959-4253, on Main Street, Chéticamp B0E 1H0. It has 55 rooms, some with private balcony, and a good restaurant. Rates are in the high mid-range. A good deal cheaper but still in the mid-range category is the **Park View Motel** ((902) 224-3232, PO Box 117, Chéticamp B0E 1H0, on Route 19 north of town, with a view of the Gulf of St. Lawrence, along with a licensed dining room and friendly lounge.

In Ingonish, the **Glenhorm Beach Resort** ((902) 286-2049, PO Box 39, Ingonish B0C 1K0, offers astonishingly good value for its inexpensive to mid-range prices. It has 54 motel units and 11 housekeeping cottages on nine hectares (22 acres) with ocean frontage and a swimming pool. Near the eastern entrance to the park at Ingonish Beach is the spectacular, and spectacularly expensive, **Keltic Lodge** ((902) 285-2880 TOLL-FREE (800) 565-0444, PO Box 70, Ingonish Beach B0C 1L0, another resort complex operated by the provincial government. Set on a peninsula jutting out into the Atlantic, it features a baronial main lodge with 32 rooms, the White Birch Inn with 40 rooms, and nine cottages. It has an 18-hole golf course and absolutely everything else that the dedicated vacationer might want.

In Baddeck, the moderate-to-expensive **Inverary Inn** ((902) 295-3500 TOLL-FREE (800) 565-5600 FAX (902) 295-3527, PO Box 190, Route 205 and Shore Road, Baddeck B0E 1B0, offers a wide variety of motel rooms and cottages — 160 in all — in addition to a private beach on Bras d'Or Lake, spacious grounds, indoor and outdoor swimming pools, tennis courts, and a wonderful restaurant.

ferries arrive at Yarmouth, Nova Scotia. The ferry from Bar Harbor, which takes about three hours, is operated by **Bay Ferries Limited** ((902) 566-3838 TOLL-FREE (888) 249-7245 FAX (902) 566-1550. Tickets must be picked up one hour before sailing. Bay Ferries also operates daily service year-round between Saint John, New Brunswick and Digby, Nova Scotia, with three trips daily during peak months. Reservations are recommended. From Portland to Yarmouth there is daily service from early May through October (reservations required) provided by **Prince of Fundy Cruises** ((207) 775-5616 TOLL-FREE (888) 341-7540 or (800)-482-0955, 468 Commercial Street, Portland, Maine 04101-4637 USA.

Where to Eat

About three kilometers (two miles) off the Cabot Trail, the **Normaway Inn** ((902) 248-2987, Egypt Road in Margaree Valley has a wonderful dining room in the main lodge. In Chéticamp, **Laurie's Motel** ((902) 224-2400 (see WHERE TO STAY, above) has a very fine restaurant, although it closes a bit early. You probably don't have to be told that the place to eat in Ingonish is the **Keltic Lodge** ((902) 285-2880 (see WHERE TO STAY, above) which probably has the best food on the island — and the dearest. In Baddeck, the restaurant in the **Inverary Inn** ((902) 295-3500 (see WHERE TO STAY, above) is worth a visit even if you're not staying there.

HOW TO GET THERE

For those going to Nova Scotia from Maine there are ferries from Bar Harbor and Portland; both

In addition, **Marine Atlantic** TOLL-FREE (800) 341-7981 FAX (902) 564-7480, 355 Purves Street, North Sydney, NS B2A 3V2; or PO Box 520, Port aux Basques, NF A0M 1C0, operates a daily ferry service year-round between Port-aux-Basques, Newfoundland and North Sydney, Nova Scotia, with additional service mid-June to September. There is also service between North Sydney and Argentia, Newfoundland on Monday, Wednesday and Friday from mid-June to mid-September. Reservations are recommended and tickets must be picked up one hour before sailing. From May 1 to December 20, **Northumberland Ferries** ((902) 566-3838 TOLL-FREE (800) 565-0201, link Caribou, Nova Scotia to Wood Islands, Prince Edward Island.

Fishing boats moored in Peggy's Cove.

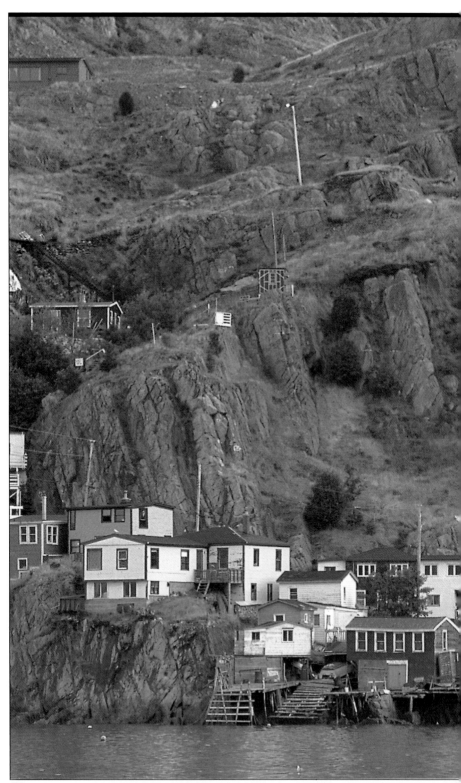

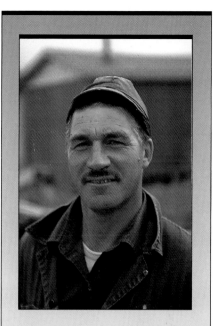

New-
foundland

IT IS ALMOST IMPOSSIBLE TO READ OR HEAR ANYTHING about Newfoundland without coming across the word "rugged" to describe both the place and the people who live there. It is an apt word. The island is indeed rugged (although Labrador, on the mainland, is officially a part of the province, whenever people speak of Newfoundland they mean the island) — very rugged, as you would expect of a land that only 10,000 years ago was still covered by glaciers, and today is regularly lashed by Atlantic winds and rain. And the people, or "Newfies" as they are known throughout Canada, are every bit as rugged as the landscape they inhabit.

They are also ruggedly independent. Although a confederated Canada was formed in 1867, and spanned the continent by 1905, the Newfies stubbornly refused to join the Confederation until 1949. They still refer to their compatriots from the mainland as "Canadians," while inquiring of visitors if they come "from Canada." They have their own distinctive accents and dialects, with their own colorful (if not always comprehensible) vocabulary. They even have their own time zone — "Newfoundland Time" — which is a half-hour ahead of Atlantic Standard Time. They are happy to point out that the provincial capital, St. John's, is closer to Europe than it is to Winnipeg in the middle of Canada.

Given this fiercely independent streak, it is not surprising that they have become the butt of countless "Newfie jokes" among other Canadians, rather like the Irish jokes the English enjoy telling. The Newfies themselves take all this in their good-humored stride, and in turn seem to have made the island itself the butt of their own little jokes: just look at the map. There you will find places with names like Stinking Cove, Useless Bay, Sitdown Pond, Come By Chance, Blow Me Down, Tickle Cove, Witless Bay, Joe Batt's Arm, Jerry's Nose, Nick's Nose Cove, Cuckold Cove, Dildo Pond, Happy Adventure, Heart's Desire, Heart's Content, and Little Heart's Ease.

The island of Newfoundland, known to Newfies as "The Rock," is the eighteenth largest in the world, and was already inhabited by Inuit and natives when the Vikings first arrived a thousand years ago and established a settlement near L'Anse aux Meadows at its northern tip. The next Europeans to arrive came with John Cabot, who arrived in the harbor of what is now St. John's in June 1497. He reported back to Henry VII that he had discovered a *"new founde lande"* surrounded by rich fishing grounds. Thirty years later a Captain John Rut arrived and wrote back to the new king, Henry VIII, urging that a permanent settlement be established here. This was done the following year, but it was not until 1583 that Queen Elizabeth I sent Sir Humphrey Gilbert to officially claim the island for England. Thus did Newfound-

land become the first British colony in the New World.

Anchored as it was in the then-rich Grand Banks fishing grounds, the island became the scene of repeated military confrontations between the British claimants and others, usually the French. Under the Treaty of Utrecht in 1713, Newfoundland was formally recognized as belonging to Britain, but there was to be another half-century of hostilities before the British finally secured undisputed control of the island, when they decisively defeated the French at St. John's in 1762.

There followed a period of increased immigration from Britain, swelling the colony's population to 40,000 by 1800. In 1832 it was granted self-gov-

ernment in domestic affairs, and in 1855 achieved full dominion status in the British Commonwealth. Especially hard hit by the Depression, Newfoundland in 1934 suffered the dual humiliation of bankruptcy and reversion to being a mere colony. Finally, in 1949, but only by the narrowest of margins, Newfies voted to end their long holdout and join the rest of Canada as the nation's tenth province.

With its population of 560,000 concentrated almost exclusively along its 9,660 km (6,000 miles) of deeply indented coastline, Newfoundland's economy was for 500 years based on fishing. There was a time when the island's fishermen brought in an annual haul of over 500,000 tons of fish, mostly cod. (In fact, when Newfies say "fish" they

Cape Spear, North America's most easterly point — OPPOSITE: The new lighthouse shines its beacon out into the Atlantic. ABOVE: The road to the cape meanders through a subalpine forest.

always mean cod; other types of fish are given their individual names.) But overfishing has destroyed what was the greatest fishing ground in history, Grand Banks. With the death of the cod-fishing industry, Newfoundland is struggling to set a new economic course based on tourism, mining, and hydroelectric activity.

ST. JOHN'S

First settled in 1528, St. John's can legitimately claim to be the oldest city in North America. Its past has not only been long but colorful, sometimes violently so. Given its strategic location as the nearest point to Europe in the New World, as well as being

BACKGROUND

Although it has been settled only since 1528 (and then sparsely), the 178,000 citizens of St. John's date their city from June 24, 1497, the saint's day of St. John the Baptist, when John Cabot sailed into the lovely little harbor and named the place after the saint.

If the next three centuries were tumultuous, with the British and French (and occasionally the Dutch) fighting for control of the city, the nineteenth century was one of rapid growth interrupted by devastating fires: St. John's burned down no fewer than five times in the nineteenth

alongside what were some of the richest fishing grounds in the world, and blessed with a wonderfully sheltered natural harbor, St. John's was a prize to be coveted. It was repeatedly fought over, for two and a half centuries, until British supremacy was finally and lastingly established in 1762, at the end of the Seven Years' War. But just because there was peace afterwards doesn't mean that St. John's was suddenly peaceful. Far from it. It became a favorite haven for pirates who preyed on ships on their way to and from Europe. As a result, by the end of the eighteenth century there were 80 taverns in the town and over 750,000 liters (200,000 gallons) of rum was being imported annually.

It is markedly quieter today, but still colorful, with its brightly painted clapboard houses lining narrow winding streets, that climb up from a harbor where fishing boats from many nations lie at anchor.

century. Each time the townspeople, undaunted, rebuilt it — in wood. As it has escaped the flames in the last hundred years, the oldest buildings in St. John's date back to the Victorian period.

One of these buildings, Cabot Tower on Signal Hill, is of particular historical interest. Built in 1897 to mark the fourth centenary of Cabot's landing as well as Queen Victoria's diamond jubilee, it was here on December 12, 1901 that Guglielmo Marconi received the first transatlantic radio message from his station in Cornwall.

Now the colorful wooden houses that crowd the waterfront are beginning to be overshadowed by modern buildings and high-rises, but it can truthfully be said that after five centuries the oldest city in North America has lost little of its character. Perhaps the sailors who went to war over it, and the pirates who took refuge in it, would have trouble recognizing it today, but they would still find something awfully familiar about it.

GENERAL INFORMATION

For information in advance of your trip, you can contact **the City of St. John's Tourism Division** ((709) 576-8455 FAX (709) 576-8246, PO Box 908, St. John's, A1C 5M2. In summer, visitor information is available at the **Tourist Information Rail Car** ((709) 576-8514 on Harbour Drive, along the waterfront. Outside of summer, you can get information at **City Hall** ((709) 576-8106 E-MAIL cityedev@nfld.com, on New Gower Street. There is a seasonal information booth at the

name because it was originally used by the various sailing companies to hoist their flags in order to signal to the dock workers and merchants that one of their ships was approaching. At **Cabot Tower**, you can see the birthplace of modern telecommunications, for this is the site where Guglielmo Marconi received the first wireless transatlantic broadcast. Outside you can see cannon of the Queen's Battery dating from 1796 as well as ruined fortifications from the War of 1812.

Just over the hill on the north side is the picturesque fishing village of **Quidi Vidi** (pronounced "kiddy viddy"), an absolutely charming port community set on a small inlet with something of the flavor of the typical Newfoundland

St. John's airport—in the baggage claim area. Off season, you'll find a supply of brochures and maps free for the taking. **Internet access** is available at the excellent bookstore-coffeeshop Wordplay ((709) 726-9193, downtown at 221 Duckworth Street.

WHAT TO SEE AND DO

Possibly much to the chagrin of the tourism association which has given St. John's the sobriquet "City of Legends," St. John's is more widely know as "Fog City." Nowhere is this aspect of the city seen from greater advantage than on **Signal Hill** ((709) 772-5367, with its sunlight and fog, mist-shrouded ponds, crying seagulls and, on a good day, a magnificent view of the Narrows—the inlet that leads into St. John's Harbour. Signal Hill which rises steeply at the mouth of the harbor, got its

fishing village, or "outport." If you won't have the chance to go further afield on the island, this is a good way to get the flavor of this type of hamlet. Among the little wharves and boats are some wonderful seafood restaurants. Nearby a boardwalk circling Quidi Vidi Lake makes for a pleasant walk.

Back in town, take a stroll along **Water Street**, one of the oldest streets in North America, which runs parallel to the harbor through the middle of town. At the corner of Duckworth and Prescott streets is the **Newfoundland Museum** ((709) 729-2329, which has exhibits on the early native peoples of Newfoundland and on the history of St. John's, with particular emphasis on daily life in the nineteenth century. Summer hours are Friday to

Although St. John's is the oldest city in North America, almost all of its oldest buildings were built in the twentieth century.

Wednesday from 9 AM to 5 PM and Thursday from 10 AM to 9 PM. In winter it opens Tuesday, Wednesday, and Friday from 9 AM to 5 PM, Thursday from 9 AM to 9 PM, and Saturday and Sunday from 10 AM to 6 PM. Admission is free.

The **Roman Catholic Basilica Cathedral of St. John the Baptist** (1855) on Military Road is well worth a visit. It's the one with the Gothic façade and twin granite-and-bluestone towers that dominate the city's skyline. Further along Military Road is the distinctly more modest **St. Thomas' Church**, which dates from 1836 and is one of the few buildings to be spared in the terrible fires that swept the city in the nineteenth century. In fact it is the oldest church still standing anywhere in the province.

Next door to the church is **Commissariat House** ((709) 729-6730, a clapboard structure with tall chimneys which dates from 1821. It, too, escaped the fires and was used by the military commissariat until 1871, when it became the rectory for the church. Beautifully restored and furnished with period pieces, it is open daily 10 AM to 5:30 PM from mid-June to mid-October; admission is free.

At the corner of Allendale Road and Prince Philip Drive, near the university, is the **Arts and Culture Centre**, which includes two galleries featuring contemporary Canadian art, two theaters, three libraries, and a fine restaurant, Act III. In the summer there is a festival of the arts with free outdoor concerts.

Duckworth Street and the **Murray Premises** shopping center down on Water Street are the places to go for boutiques and luxury goods. Duckworth Street is also good for antique shops. For arts and crafts the area around the War Memorial at the eastern end of Water Street is the best hunting ground. For new and used books, there is **Wordplay** ((709) 726-9193 E-MAIL wordplay.com, 221 Duckworth Street. Among the selection are books on Newfoundland travel and history. Upstairs the James Baird Gallery is an exhibition space for contemporary art.

NIGHTLIFE AND THE ARTS

St. John's has an excellent folk music scene, which you should certainly check out. There are many places, but you might start with the **Blarney Stone** ((709) 754-1798, on George Street, features Newfoundland and Irish folk music; arrive early to get a seat. **Trapper John** ((709) 579-9630, 2 George Street, is also know for outstanding provincial folk music. For blues there's **Fat Cat** ((709) 722-6409, at 5 George Street.

In keeping with its rum-soaked past, St. John's probably has more drinking spots per capita than any other city in Canada. Most of them seem to be

Here at Cabot Tower on Signal Hill, Guglielmo Marconi received the first transatlantic radio message in 1901.

clustered on and around George Street downtown, where you can find pubs, clubs, and discos to suit almost any state. We also like the **Ship Inn** ((709) 753-3870, at 265 Duckworth Street, down the stairs, off the alley, which has live music and is popular with the sailors.

WHERE TO STAY

Expensive

The new **Hotel Newfoundland** ((709) 726-4980 TOLL-FREE (800) 441-1414 FAX (709) 726-2025, Cavendish Square, PO Box 5637, St. John's, A1C 5W8, is easily the grandest hotel in Newfoundland, with 280 elegantly furnished rooms and 20 suites, a for-

affording glorious views over the harbor and city, plus an indoor swimming pool.

Also in this category is Old Reliable: the **Holiday Inn St. John's** ((709) 722-0506 FAX (709) 722-9756, 180 Portugal Cover Road at the intersection of Cove Road and MacDonald Drive, two and a half kilometers (a mile and a half) from downtown, near the Arts and Culture Centre. It has all the amenities one associates with Holiday Inns, including here an outdoor pool, an above-average restaurant, and 24-hour room service.

Inexpensive

About six kilometers (under four miles) from downtown on the Trans-Canada Highway is the

mal dining room, a restaurant and a lounge, an indoor swimming pool, squash courts, and a disco. Very reasonable for what it has to offer — and it has discount weekend packages. The 11-story **Delta St. John's Hotel** ((709) 739-6404 TOLL-FREE (800) 268-1133 FAX (709) 570-1622, 120 New Gower Street, St. John's A1C 6K4, is another newish hotel. Overlooking the harbor, with 276 rooms and nine suites, it has nonsmoking floors as well as the swimming and health facilities you would expect, and a highly rated restaurant.

Mid-Range

Though bland from the exterior, the **Battery Hotel and Suites** ((709) 576-0040 TOLL-FREE (800) 563-8181 FAX (709) 576-6943 E-MAIL battery@voyager .newcomm.net, 100 Signal Hill Road, St. John's A1A 1B3, is nevertheless a comfortable choice, offering good value, with 125 rooms and 20 suites

First City Motel ((709) 722-5400 FAX (709) 722-1030, 479 Kenmount Road, St. John's A1B 3P9, which happens to be just about the first city motel you encounter when driving into St. John's. It is very comfortable and quiet. The **Airport Plaza Hotel** ((709) 753-3500 TOLL-FREE (800) 563-2489 FAX (709) 753-3711, 106 Airport Road, PO Box 21142, St. John's A1A 5B2, is right next to the airport, within walking distance of the terminal, about five kilometers (three miles) from downtown. Its rooms and suites are nicely furnished, and its restaurant and lounge are both superior to what one expects to find nestling up against an airport, even a small one.

If you want a real bargain in civilized surroundings, head for the **Prescott Inn** ((709) 753-7733 FAX (709) 753-6036 E-MAIL arier@public.compusult .nf.ca, at 19 Military Road, St. John's A1C 2C3, which has 12 large rooms with balconies, and

10 suites overlooking the harbor, each splendidly and differently decorated with local arts and crafts, and each with color television and private bath. Five of the suites are equipped with kitchens. A delicious full breakfast is included in the price of the room. There's no more helpful or friendlier host than Jan Peterson, who offers, in addition to excellent accommodation, itinerary-planning services, and is pleased to set you up with your own self-drive itinerary.

There are scores of other **bed and breakfast** accommodations sprinkled throughout the city, indeed throughout the province. Get a copy of the *Newfoundland and Labrador Accommodations Guide*, available free from the Newfoundland Department of Development and Tourism (see TOURIST INFORMATION, page 421, in TRAVELERS' TIPS).

cuisine gives variety to the menu. This is a formal place and jackets are required for men.

Moderate

Classic Café ((709) 579-4444, 364 Duckworth Street, offers a casual ambiance and warm service, in a cozily rustic room. Seafood is expertly prepared and reasonably priced. I recommend the king crab. It's open 24 hours a day and big breakfasts are served at all hours. At 108 Duckworth Street, the **Casa Grande (** (709) 753-6108 serves award-winning Mexican and Canadian food in cozy surroundings. If you are willing to stray a bit further afield, we would suggest you stray out along Route 60 about 11 km (seven miles) to the

WHERE TO EAT

Expensive

With one exception, the best restaurants in St. John's are in luxury hotels. That exception is the **Stone House Restaurant (** (709) 753-2380 at 8 Kenna's Hill, near Quidi Vidi Lake. Set in a restored early nineteenth-century stone cottage, it used to be a top Canadian restaurant, although locals call it merely "adequate." Innovative dishes featuring local game and seafood are complemented by an extensive wine list. Of the restaurants in the best hotels, we prefer the elegant **Cabot Room (** (709) 726-4980 in the Hotel Newfoundland (see WHERE TO STAY, above). A mix of traditional Canadian fare — such as caribou medallions — and continental

Woodstock Colonial Inn ((709) 722-6933, where you will find some delicious food served (generously) in a delightful colonial setting.

Inexpensive

For fish and chips, **Ches's** is something of an institution in St. John's. Its three restaurants are at 655 Topsail Road (** (709) 368-9473, 9 Freshwater Road (** (709) 722-4083, and 29-33 Commonwealth Avenue (** (709) 364-6837. For something a bit more sophisticated wander over to **Nautical Nellie's (** (709) 738-1120, 201 Water Street. This restaurant looks as though it might serve typical pub grub, but there's nothing mediocre about the menu. Try the curried scallop pasta with peach chutney. This place is an excellent value.

OPPOSITE: A St. John's softball team gets ready to take the field. ABOVE: Quidi Vidi village is set on a small inlet on the north side of St. John's.

HOW TO GET THERE

St. John's International Airport is eight kilometers (five miles) from the city, and the drive to downtown takes 10 to 15 minutes. **Air Canada (** (709) 726-7880 operates regular service to Newfoundland and Labrador airports, with connections available from all major centers in Canada and the United States. **Air Labrador** TOLL-FREE (800) 563-3042 provides regular services within the province and offers daily scheduled services from St. John's to points throughout the province. There are also regularly scheduled services from St. John's to the island of St-Pierre.

ELSEWHERE ON THE ISLAND

It is known that bands of First Nations peoples roamed the island up to 4,000 years before the Vikings landed, including some who left behind stone tools that are among the most delicate ever discovered. Whether it was due to the arrival of the Vikings or to some other phenomenon, the island's original inhabitants disappeared around AD 1000 and were replaced by the Beothucks. These were the natives that Cabot and the later settlers encountered. As they tended to cover their bodies in red powdered ochre, they became known as the "Red Paint People" — possibly the origin of the term "Red Indian". In any case, the arrival of the white man spelled doom for the red man. Over the next centuries the Beothucks were systematically exterminated by the settlers. The last known surviving Beothuck died in 1829.

Except around its edges, the island that the Beothucks and their predecessors occupied for millennia is still pretty much the way it was throughout its prehistory. Perhaps the only real difference, apart from the obvious inroads made by the modern world, is that the forests are being nibbled away — not devoured, just nibbled — by the timber, paper and pulp manufacturing industries which have now surpassed fishing in the economy of the western part of Newfoundland. Otherwise the land, or most of it anyway, retains the same wild beauty that the natives enjoyed long before Europeans ever set foot on it.

THE AVALON PENINSULA

With its coastal fog-bound cliffs and inland bogs, the Avalon has some of Newfoundland's most dramatic scenery. Most of the peninsula is accessible on day trips from St. John's, making the Avalon a good choice for travelers with limited time.

Cape Spear National Historic Park is only 11 km (seven miles) southeast of St. John's. Here

at North America's most easterly point you will get a stunning view of the ocean (which in springtime includes the sight of whales heaving its way up and down the coast). There is also a square, white clapboard **lighthouse (** (709) 772-5367 dating from 1835, which makes it the oldest lighthouse in Newfoundland. The park is open daily, and from mid-June to mid-September there are guided tours of the lighthouse for which an admission fee is charged.

About 35 km (21 miles) south of the capital there is world-class birding at **Witless Bay Ecological Preserve**, a cluster of islands located a few kilometers off shore. Each spring the largest Atlantic puffin colony in North America descends on the islands for nesting. Murres, kittiwakes, and gulls also inhabit the tiny islands. Tour boats take visitors out of Bay Bulls (named for the bull walruses that used to frequent its harbor) to observe the birds, as well as the humpback whales and

icebergs which also migrate here. **Whale** and **bird-watching boat tours** are offered by Gatherall's Boat Tours ((709) 334-2887 TOLL-FREE (800) 419-4253 FAX (709) 334-2176, Northside Road, Bay Bulls, Newfoundland A0A 1C0 (refer to SEE THE WONDERS OF WITLESS BAY, page 18, in TOP SPOTS); and O'Brien's Boat Tours ((709) 753-4850 or (709) 334-2355 FAX (709) 753-3140 E-MAIL obriens@netfx-inc.com; or Captain Murphy's Bird Island & Whale Tours ((709) 334-2002 TOLL-FREE (888) 738-3467 FAX (709) 368-4040, PO Box 149, Puffin Cove, Witless Bay A0A 4K0.

Listen for the Irish burr in the speech of the local residents. The original settlers of the bay were Irish conscripts who jumped ship here.

About 40 km (24 miles) south of Witless Bay is Ferryland, a seaside town where a major **archeological dig** ((709) 432-3200, Route 10, is going on. A 370-year-old cobblestone street has been unearthed here. The street section was part of the Colony of Avalon, which was established in the 1620s by Lord Baltimore. The site includes an archeology laboratory and exhibit center.

Moving into the southwest corner of the Avalon, the drive down Route 100 south of Placentia is dotted with lovely coves and cliffy viewpoints. At the end of the line is **Cape St. Mary's Ecological Reserve** ((709) 729-2431. You're way off the beaten track if you've made it this far (100 km or 60 miles) from the Trans-Canada Highway. But this remote corner of the island is worth the effort it takes to get here. Some 5,400 pairs of gannets nest here, along with 10,000 pairs of murres, 10,0000 kittiwakes, and 100 razorbills. The nesting birds are approached from the top of a 100-m (300-ft)-high cliff, so that visitors can get quite close without disturbing them. The reserve is open daily from May to October. There is a visitor

The old lighthouse at Cape Spear with its signature red and white striped dome.

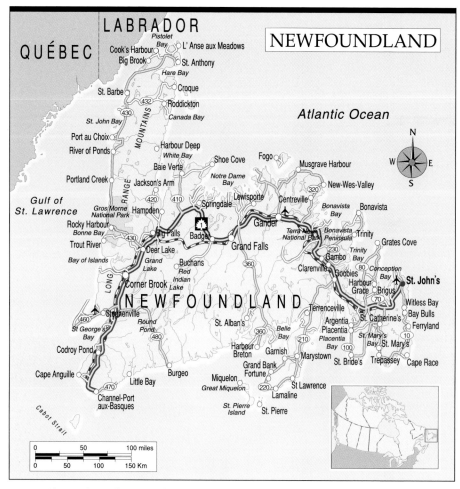

LABRADOR

QUÉBEC

NEWFOUNDLAND

Pistolet Bay
Cook's Harbour
Big Brook
St. Anthony
L' Anse aux Meadows
Hare Bay
Croque
St. Barbe
Roddickton
St. John Bay
Canada Bay
Port au Choix
River of Ponds
Harbour Deep
White Bay
Baie Verte
Portland Creek
Jackson's Arm
Shoe Cove
Fogo
Musgrave Harbour
Notre Dame Bay
New-Wes-Valley

Atlantic Ocean

Gulf of
St. Lawrence
Gros Morne National Park
Hampden
Lewisporte
Springdale
Centreville
Bonavista Bay
Bonavista
Rocky Harbour
Bonne Bay
Big Falls
Badger
Gander
Terra Nova National Park
Bonavista Peninsula
Trinity
Grates Cove
Trout River
Deer Lake
Grand Falls
Trinity Bay
Bay of Islands
Grand Lake
Buchans
Red Indian Lake
Gambo
Clarenville
Goobies
Conception Bay
St. John's
Corner Brook
Harbour Grace
Brigus
Witless Bay
Stephenville
Terrenceville
St. Catherine's
Bay Bulls
St. Alban's
Argentia
Placentia
Ferryland
St. George's Bay
Round Pond
Belle Bay
Placentia Bay
St. Mary's Bay
St. Mary's
Codroy Pond
Harbour Breton
Garnish
Marystown
St. Bride's
Trepassey
Cape Race
Cape Anguille
Burgeo
Little Bay
Miquelon
Great Miquelon
Grand Bank
Fortune
St Lawrence
Lamaline
Channel-Port aux-Basques
St. Pierre Island
St. Pierre
Cabot Strait

NEWFOUNDLAND

0   50   100 miles
0   50   100   150 Km

center with a good introduction to the cape's bird life. A small admission fee is charged for the interpretive exhibit.

If are you heading west from Witless Bay you can circle back toward St. John's along Conception Bay, stopping in the beautiful little village of **Brigus** (19 km or 12 miles off of Route 1 and Route 80). There's a public garden, winding lanes, and a teahouse to enjoy in this village. Aside from its lovely atmosphere, Brigus is best known as the birthplace of Captain Bob Bartlett, who accompanied Admiral Peary on polar expeditions during the first decade of the twentieth century. His house, **Hawthorne Cottage** ((709) 753-9262, dates from 1830 and is a National Historic Site.

Nearby is **Cupids**, the oldest English colony in Canada, founded in 1610 by John Guy. You can visit the Cupids Archaeological Site ((709) 528-3477 during the summer months, where archaeologists have unearthed remnants of the original colony. Further north, **Harbour Grace** was the

former headquarters of the seventeenth-century pirate, Peter Easton. Starting in 1919, this town was the takeoff point for many attempts at transAtlantic flight. Amelia Earhart departed from Harbour Grace in 1932 to become the first woman to fly solo across the Atlantic.

Where to Stay and Eat

In Ferryland there is the **Downs Inn** ((709) 432-2808 or (709) 432-2659, Route 10, Ferryland A0A 2H0, a handsome building overlooking the harbor. Formerly a convent, the furnishing is uninspired — tending to reflect its history as an institution — but the price is inexpensive, and if you can get one of the front rooms you can watch for whales from your windows. There is a tearoom for light lunches and desserts. The innkeepers offer customized touring packages.

RIGHT: Clouds gather over Conception Bay, just north of St. John's. OVERLEAF: The village of Brigus, Bonavista Peninsula.

At the southwest corner of the peninsula, **Bird Island Resort** ((709) 337-2450 FAX (709) 337-2903, Route 100, St. Bride's A0B 2Z0, is an inexpensive modern motel offering basic amenities, including some rooms with kitchenettes.

Fish and chips is offered just about anywhere you eat in Newfoundland. When you're on the road look for a branch of the Irving's chain; they're always open and it's one of the few places where you'll find codfish broiled, not fried. Try their Jigg's Dinner (meat, potatoes, cabbage, and carrots all cooked together) on Sunday. Though cod fishing is officially banned, "by-catch" (cod that happens to be collected during other fishing operations) has thus far insured a steady supply to the island.

BONAVISTA PENINSULA

The Avalon Peninsula may be home to Newfoundland's capital, St. John's, and most of its population, but the rest of the island has most of the land — land which includes two great national parks, a mountain range, mighty forests, and countless lakes and rivers.

Cape Bonavista, at the northern tip of the peninsula, is said to have been Cabot's first North American landfall. He gave it its name in 1497 — accurately, one should add, because there is a beautiful view from the cape. The fishing village of **Bonavista**, five kilometers (three miles) away, has an outer harbor as well as a sheltered inner harbor for smaller fishing boats. It was a favorite port of European fishing fleets in the sixteenth century before the British settled it, and is now a favorite spot for whale-watchers in the early summer.

The picturesque little village of **Trinity** on Bonavista Bay (not be confused with the village of the same name on Trinity Bay) was discovered by the Portuguese navigator Jozo Vas Corte Real in 1500. Its settlement was so rapid that the first Admiralty Court in North America was convened here in 1615. Thanks to a program of renovation and restoration, the character of the village has been beautifully preserved.

From Trinity, you can explore **abandoned fishing villages**, such as Kerleys Harbour, a short drive south of the village. The last inhabitants left the Kerleys Harbour in the 1950s but the remnants of their lives still remain. From the churchyard in New Bonaventure it's a 20-minute walk past ponds and stands of trees to the site. At the site, there is a picnic table at the head of the harbor, a magnificent spot for a pause.

Where to Stay and Eat
Trinity boasts the best place to stay on the island: **Campbell House** ((709) 464-3377 (summer) or (709) 753-8945 (winter) MAILING ADDRESS 24 Circular Road, St. John's A1C 2Z1. Proprietor Tineke

Gow personally oversaw the restoration of the historic building, which was an 1840s home. Careful attention was paid to maintaining the authenticity of the property. Rooms are spacious and comfortable with luxurious touches such as down comforters and views of the lovely harbor. Loyal guests return here year after year for Tineke's excellent hospitality and hearty breakfasts. A cottage nearby is also part of the property. You must reserve well in advance for July and August.

On the Trans-Canada Highway (Route 1) at Clarenville, just before you turn off to head out onto the Bonavista Peninsula, there is a **Clarenville Inn** ((709) 466-7911 FAX (709) 466-3854, Routes 1 and 1A, Clarenville A0E 1J0. With 64 rooms at mid-range prices, it's a convenient and comfortable pit stop. If you are keen on whale-watching, or other types of oceangoing expeditions, the **Village Inn** ((709) 464-3269 FAX (709) 464-3700, PO Box 10, Trinity A0C 2S0, organizes trips and charters with their resident marine biologist. It is small (12 rooms) and inexpensive, but very comfortable, with a licensed dining room and private bar.

Also in Trinity, the **Old Trinity Cookery** ((709) 464-3615 serves traditional Newfoundland fare; and the **Dock Marina Restaurant** specializes in thick steaks. If you're visiting outside of the peak season, the dependable **Cooper's Meat Market, Restaurant and Convenience Store** ((709) 464-3832 in the nearby hamlet of Port Rexton is open year-round. It's a friendly, family-run place where fried cod is always a good choice.

teems with wildlife: black bear, moose, beaver, otter. There is even a nine-hole seaside golf course, from which in early summer you can see any number of icebergs floating in the coastal waters. There are 80 km (50 miles) of nature trails in the park, and both canoes and bicycles can be rented at the park's new **Marine Interpretation Centre** ((709) 533-2801 at the Saltons Day-Use Area, about five kilometers (three miles) north of the Newman Sound Campground. It's open daily from 9 AM to 9 PM from June to mid-October.

Where to Stay and Eat

The **Terra Nova Park Lodge & Golf Course** ((709) 543-2525 FAX (709) 543-2201, Route 1, Port

TERRA NOVA NATIONAL PARK

The older and smaller of Newfoundland's two national parks, the 396 sq km (153 sq miles) of **Terra Nova National Park** is divided north to south by the Trans-Canada Highway. To the east are the beaches, tidal flats, and rocky coast along Bonavista Bay, as well as the park's two developed campgrounds at **Newman Sound** and **Malady Head**. The one at Newman Sound has 400 campsites, a general store, laundry, cabins, showers, fireplaces — the works; the one at Malady Head is smaller (165 campsites) and a little more Spartan. There are also more primitive campsites spread around the park.

To the west of the highway are the woods, lakes, ponds, streams, and bogs so typical of the island's interior. And on both sides of the highway — indeed sometimes on the highway itself — the area

Blandford A0C 2G0, is a modern resort with 79 rooms and suites. You'll find it south of the park's southern entrance. Though somewhat characterless, it is clean and comfortable and well-located as a base from which to explore the park. The golf course is probably one of the more scenic in Atlantic Canada. The lodge's dining room is open for all meals, with standard island fare such as fried cod dinners and surf-and-turf. Both lodge and restaurant are moderately priced.

The seasonally operated **Clode Sound Motel** ((709) 664-3146 FAX (709) 664-4471, PO Box 10, Charlottetown A0C 1L0, has 19 housekeeping units, a

Ready for winter in Trinity, Bonavista Peninsula — OPPOSITE: Newfoundlanders still store their winter vegetables in root cellars such as this one. Wood is stacked RIGHT for a long cold spell. ABOVE: Afternoon sunbeams play on an antique cupboard at the circa 1840s Campbell House inn.

heated pool, and a tennis court, and is only 10 minutes from the nine-hole golf course at Twin Rivers.

GANDER

About the only thing Gander has going for it is its **airport**, which in the pre-jet era was the western takeoff and landing point for transatlantic flights. It was chosen for this role not only because of its proximity to Europe, but also because it is far enough inland not to be affected by the fog that often shrouds the coast. It played a critical part in World War II as a refueling stop for the thousands of military aircraft headed for Europe, but its importance has declined since the advent of the jet engine.

Gander's only other point of interest, unless you are excited by shopping centers, lies west of the town, where the **Gander River** flows under the Trans-Canada Highway. Apart from being beautiful to look at, either from the bank or a canoe, it is one of the island's best salmon rivers. Bring your angling gear.

Where to Stay and Eat

The four best hotels in Gander are all mid-range in price. Marginally more expensive than the others, the **Irving West Hotel** ℂ (709) 256-3981 TOLL-FREE (800) 663-5711 FAX (709) 651-3297, 1 Caldwell Street, Gander A1V 1T6, has a heated outdoor swimming pool and a children's activity room. The **Albatross Motel** ℂ (709) 256-3956 TOLL-FREE (800) 563-4900 FAX (709) 651-2692, is on the Trans-Canada Highway — PO Box 450, Gander A1V 1W8 — and has 100 nicely furnished rooms. **Sinbad's Motel**

ℂ (709) 651-2678 TOLL-FREE (800) 563-8330 FAX (709) 651-3123, is on Bennett Drive, across from the Gander Mall, PO Box 450, Gander A1V 1W6. Many of its rooms are efficiency units. At the **Hotel Gander** ℂ (709) 256-3931 TOLL-FREE IN CANADA (800) 563-2988 FAX (709) 651-2641 E-MAIL hotelgan@ newcomm.net, is right at 100 Trans-Canada Highway, Gander A1V 1P5, you can enjoy an indoor pool, fitness facilities, and a restaurant.

GROS MORNE NATIONAL PARK

Gros Morne ("Big Knoll") is probably the most spectacular national park in all of eastern Canada. Within its 1,815 sq km (700 sq miles) are moun-

tains, gorges, lakes, and fjords of stunning beauty. The flat-topped **Long Range Mountains**, which rise to a barren plateau some 600 m (2,000 ft) tall, are cut by deep lakes and fjords bordered by towering rock cliffs. The entire park is glorious, and crisscrossed by hiking trails, but there are two areas of special beauty. One is **Western Brook Pond**, 29 km (19 miles) north of Rocky Harbour, which is reached by hiking about four kilometers (two and a half miles) through the forest from the highway. When you get there, the "pond" turns out to be a lake 16 km (10 miles) long that resembles a fjord because of the soaring, near vertical cliffs rising alongside it. It is truly breathtaking. There are three boat tours of the lake daily during the summer.

The other must-see scenic spot is **Bonne Bay**, which you can appreciate without getting out of the car. Bonne Bay is a deep fjord on the Gulf of St. Lawrence, with two arms thrusting deep into the park. The drive along the South Arm must be one of the most gorgeous drives in the world, and only slightly less so is the drive up along the East Arm to Rocky Harbour.

Where to Stay and Eat

Just south of Rocky Harbour on Route 430, there is a **Visitor Reception Centre** ((709) 458-2066, where you can get details of all the campgrounds in the park. The handiest private campground is the **Juniper Campground** ((709) 458-2917, on Pond Road off Route 230 close to Rocky Harbour — PO Box 114, Rocky Harbour A0K 4N0. It has 72 campsites, 25 of them full-service. For inexpensive accommodation in Rocky Harbour, we

L'ANSE AUX MEADOWS NATIONAL HISTORIC PARK

At the northern tip of Newfoundland's Northern Peninsula is the site of the only authenticated Viking settlement in North America, preserved as **L'Anse aux Meadows National Historic Park** ((709) 623-2608, Route 436. It had long been known that Norsemen sailing from Iceland had landed somewhere along North America's Atlantic coast, and had named the spot Vinland after the wild grapes they found there, but it was not until 1960 that the Norwegian explorer Helge Instad came upon a cluster of overgrown mounds near

would recommend **Gros Morne Cabins** ((709) 458-2020 or ((709) 458-2369 FAX (709) 458-2882, PO Box 151, Rocky Harbour A0K 4N0, where there are 22 log, ocean-view cabins equipped with kitchenette and gas barbecue. The complex includes a convenience store, a laundromat, and a recreation area.

The **Victorian Manor** ((709) 453-2485, Main Street, PO Box 165, Woody Point A0K 1P0, has three rooms, three efficiency units, and a guesthouse. The property is located a short walk from the harbor. The inexpensive-to-moderate rates include a continental breakfast.

In Trout River you'll find a restaurant that is a cut above the usual island offerings. The **Seaside Restaurant** ((709) 451-3461, on Main Street, serves excellent pan-fried cod and a number of other seafood dishes. There is a splendid view of the harbor from the dining room.

L'Anse aux Meadows. For the next seven years he excavated the site, and established beyond doubt that here were the remains of a 1,000-year-old Norse settlement.

In 1978 L'Anse aux Meadows was named the first UNESCO World Heritage Site. Today three of the original six sod houses have been reconstructed, and artifacts from the site are on display in the Visitor Reception Centre, together with an exhibit on the Norse way of life. The site is open daily from 9 AM to 8 PM from mid-June to mid-September, but is closed the rest of the year. An admission fee is charged.

OPPOSITE: Kerley's Harbour, a fishing village abandoned in the 1950s, bears witness to the island's changing economy. ABOVE: Fishing boats at rest along the Viking Trail.

Where to Stay

The nearest good motel to the historic site is the inexpensive **Loon Motel** ((709) 454-3541, on Pistolet Bay at the junction of Routes 430 and 437, PO Box 552, Pistolet Bay, St. Anthony A0K 4S0. It has 11 rooms, a restaurant and bar, and even a helicopter landing space; it is also only 20 minutes' drive from the local airport. St. Anthony, 27 km (17 miles) away from L'Anse aux Meadows, has the **Vinland Motel** ((709) 454-8843 TOLL-FREE (800) 563-7578 FAX (709) 454-8468, PO Box 400, St. Anthony A0K 4S0, which is in the lower reaches of the mid-range category. In addition to its 40 motel rooms it has two cottages.

CORNER BROOK

A population of a little over 30,000 makes Corner Brook Newfoundland's second largest town. With an economy based almost exclusively on the town's giant pulp and paper mill and the herring fishing industry, it cannot be said to have overpowering appeal for the visitor, unless one needs to buy the sort of goods and services generally unavailable in smaller places.

However, Corner Brook does have the advantage of being near some appealing places indeed. To begin with, it is an ideal starting point for a drive along either the northern or southern shore of the scenic Humber Arm of the **Bay of Islands**.

Lichen covers some seaside rocks in the abandoned fishing village of Kerleys Harbour.

A drive out along the southern shore will take you to **Bottle Cove**, where there is a lovely public beach as well as campsites and hiking trails up into the mountains. Also, there is fabulous salmon fishing in the **Humber River** near Corner Brook: catches of salmon weighing over 13 kg (30 lb) have been recorded here. Finally, there is excellent hunting nearby, and only eight kilometers (five miles) away is the **Marble Mountain Ski Resort**, the only proper ski resort in Newfoundland.

Where to Stay and Eat

The three best hotels in Corner Brook are all mid-range in price, and all three belong to hotel chains. The **Best Western Mamateek Inn** ((709) 639-8901 TOLL-FREE (800) 563-8600 FAX (709) 639-7567, is on the Trans-Canada Highway at Maple Valley Road, PO Box 787, Corner Brook A2H 6G7. Nearby at 41 Maple Valley Road is the least expensive of the four, the **Comfort Inn** ((709) 639-1980 TOLL-FREE (800) 228-5150 FAX (709) 639-1549, PO Box 1142, Corner Brook A2H 6T2. The best of the three, in my opinion, is the Tudor-style **Glynmill Inn** ((709) 634-5181 TOLL-FREE (800) 563-4400 FAX (709) 634-5106, at 1 Cobb Lane, PO Box 550, Corner Brook A2H 6E6. Overlooking Glynmill Pond, it has 80 handsome rooms and suites, and a splendid steak house, as well as a more intimate restaurant downstairs.

PORT AUX BASQUES

Named for the Basque fishermen who were fishing the waters of the Cabot Strait as early as 1500, and probably earlier, Port aux Basques is still an important fishing port as well as being the island's main ferry port. If you arrive in Newfoundland by ferry, and you are intending to do some hunting and fishing, you will be happy to discover that you needn't go further than 200 km (125 miles) beyond Port aux Basques to find the best hunting and fishing on the island.

As you take the Trans-Canada Highway north towards Corner Brook, you go through the wooded valley of the **Grand Codroy River**, perhaps the best salmon river in Newfoundland. Moreover, this whole region, all the way to Corner Brook, is noted for its abundance of game, especially moose and caribou.

Where to Stay and Eat

The best hotel in this area is the **Hotel Port aux Basques** ((709) 695-2171 FAX (709) 695-2250, PO Box 400, Port aux Basques A0M 1C0. It is on the Trans-Canada Highway just two kilometers (a bit over a mile) from the ferry terminal and has 50 rooms and a good restaurant. Another inexpensive hostelry, **St. Christopher's Hotel** ((709) 695-7034 TOLL-FREE (800) 563-4779 FAX (709) 695-

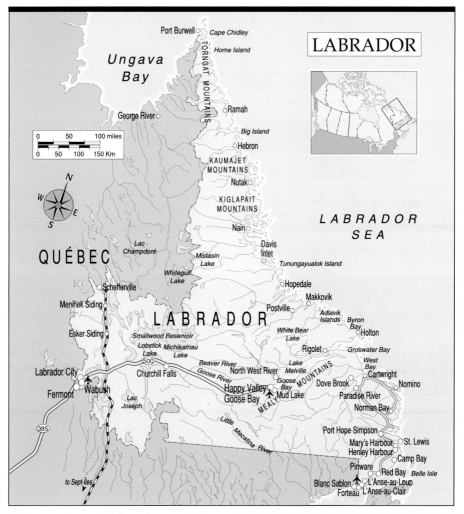

9841 E-MAIL clomond@nlnet.nf.ca, on Caribou Road, PO Box 2049, Port aux Basques A0M 1C0, has a nice restaurant and a lounge with a large-screen television showing sports and movies via satellite.

HOW TO GET THERE

There is an international airport at Gander, as well as airports at Stephenville, Deer Lake, and St. Anthony. To find out about services contact **Air Atlantic (** (709) 722-0222 TOLL-FREE IN NEW-FOUNDLAND (800) 565-1800 TOLL-FREE IN THE UNITED STATES (800) 426-7000. For information about the ferry from North Sydney, Nova Scotia, to Port aux Basques, contact Marine Atlantic Reservations Bureau TOLL-FREE (800) 341-7981 FAX (902) 564-7480, 355 Purves Street, North Sydney, NS B2A 3V2; or P.O. Box 520, Port aux Basques, NF A0M 1C0.

LABRADOR

At the top of the Gulf of St. Lawrence there is a strip of water 16 km (10 miles) wide that separates Newfoundland island from Labrador, the mainland part of the province. Covering 293,347 sq km (113,261 sq miles), Labrador is almost three times the size of the island, yet has only 35,000 inhabitants. Until fairly recently it was virtually uninhabited except for the Air Force base at Goose Bay and the dozens of tiny villages huddled in coves and inlets along the eastern seaboard.

Though Labrador remains one of the world's last great wilderness areas, it is beginning to be opened up due to its fabulous natural resources. At Labrador City and Wabush near the Québec border large mining complexes produce almost half of Canada's iron ore, while a giant hydro-electric plant at Churchill Falls supplies power to the eastern United States. At the same time,

Labrador's other great natural resources, its fish and wildlife, are beginning to attract anglers and hunters in ever-increasing numbers.

BACKGROUND

You could say that Labrador looks its age: it forms the eastern edge of the Canadian Shield, one of the oldest unchanged geological formations on the planet. As a result, it apparently looks very much the same as it did before animal life appeared on earth. The first humans are thought to have arrived in Labrador almost 9,000 years ago. In any case, it is known that the Inuit and other natives were here for thousands of years before the arrival of the first Europeans; Basque whalers who established a settlement at Red Bay, just across the strait from the northern tip of Newfoundland, in the sixteenth century. New arrivals since then have been few and far between, but this will undoubtedly change as more people begin to realize the extent of the unspoiled beauty that awaits them here.

Tourist information is available from **Destination Labrador** ((709) 944-7788 FAX (709) 944-7787, 118 Humphrey Road, Bruno Plaza, Labrador City A2V 2J8.

WHAT TO SEE AND DO

Labrador's 293,347 sq km (113,261 sq miles) contain some of the most spectacular scenery in North America. Don't think in terms of specific sights you ought to see or specific things you ought to do at a particular time or place. Labrador is just *there*, in all its vastness and prehistoric splendor, to be enjoyed by anyone who likes to hunt or fish or hike or ski or camp or simply breathe fresh, unpolluted air.

For details of organized hunting and fishing excursions by airplane into the interior, contact Destination Labrador (see above).

WHERE TO STAY

As you might expect, Labrador is not exactly chock-a-block with hotels. As you might not expect, what accommodations there are tend to be, in my opinion, overpriced — although none of those we know about is yet in the expensive category where prices (or amenities) are concerned.

Happy Valley–Goose Bay has three comfortable hotels. The largest and plushest is the **Labrador Inn** ((709) 896-3351 TOLL-FREE (800) 563-2763, 380 Hamilton Road, PO Box 58, Station C, Happy Valley–Goose Bay A0P 1C0. It also has a superb restaurant. The **Aurora Hotel** ((709) 896-3398 TOLL-FREE (800) 563-3066 FAX (709) 896-9608, 382 Hamilton River Road, PO Box 1320, Station A, Happy Valley–Goose Bay A0P 1F0, is similarly comfort-

able, and cleverly offers a fax and photocopying service to guests. The smallest and in many ways the most charming of the three is the **Royal Inn** ((709) 896-2456 FAX (709) 896-5501, at 3 Royal Avenue, PO Box 69, Station B, Happy Valley–Goose Bay A0P 1E0, with nine rooms and nine housekeeping units.

In L'Anse-au-Clair, **Northern Light Inn** ((709) 931-2332 E-MAIL nli@porthole.entnet.lb.ca, on Route 510, PO Box 92, L'Anse-au-Clair A0K 3K0, is similarly priced and offers most of the same facilities as Happy Valley-Goose Bay hostelries, plus housekeeping units and all kinds of recreational opportunities and facilities nearby.

HOW TO GET THERE

A summer car-and-passenger ferry operates between Lewisporte, Newfoundland and Happy Valley-Goose Bay, Labrador, with a stop at Cartwright, Labrador. For information on these services call the **Newfoundland and Labrador Department of Tourism, Culture, and Recreation** ((709) 729-2830 TOLL-FREE (800) 563-6353, PO Box 8700, St. John's A1B 4K2. During the summer months **Marine Atlantic** TOLL-FREE (800) 341-7981 FAX (902) 564-7480, 355 Purves Street, North Sydney, NS B2A 3V2; or P.O. Box 520, Port aux Basques, NF A0M 1C0, operates a ferry service to Goose Bay from Lewisporte, near Gander, via Cartwright, Labrador. A coastal boat also operates during the summer between St. Anthony, Newfoundland and ports north to Nain, Labrador. From May to November there is a daily ferry between St. Barbe, on Newfoundland's Northern Peninsula, and Blanc-Sablon, Québec, just across the border from L'Anse-au-Clair.

Motorists can reach Labrador City and Wabush via Toure 389, a partially paved highway from Baie-Comeau, Québec. The total distance is 581 km (366 miles) and travel time is eight and a half hours. The Trans-Labrador Highway, Route 500, is a gravel road between Labrador City and Happy Valley-Goose Bay.

Rail service between Sept-Îles, Québec, and Labrador is provided by the **Québec, North Shore & Labrador Railways** (QN&L) ((418) 968-7805 (in Québec) or (709) 944-8205 (in Labrador), and **Québecair** ((514) 376-1682 flies to Blanc-Sablon from Montréal, Québec City, and Sept-Îles.

Black water — Sunlight glints off a northern stream.

Manitoba

OFTEN REFERRED TO AS CANADA'S "KEYSTONE PROVINCE" because of its central position, Manitoba is bordered by the states of North Dakota and Minnesota to the south, by the province of Saskatchewan to the west, Ontario to the east, and Nunavut and Hudson Bay to the north. It stretches over a vast 650,088 sq km (251,000 sq miles), approximately one-sixth of which is covered with rivers and lakes. It has a population of just over one million, more than half of whom live in the capital city of Winnipeg, the province's only major city.

Of all three Prairie Provinces, Manitoba has the smallest portion of prairie land, with the wheat-growing belt intruding only into its southwest corner. Beyond the prairies lie the Great Lakes of Winnipeg, Manitoba, and Winnipegosis; beyond them a vast, rugged, rocky wilderness of forests, bogs, and more lakes stretch northwards to the sub-Arctic coastline of Hudson Bay. With the Northern Lights and polar bears of Hudson Bay, around 100,000 lakes, the desert-like landscape of Spruce Woods Provincial Park, and numerous parks offering escape routes into the wilderness, there is a lot more to Manitoba than wheat fields.

Agriculture, however, has always played an important role in the province's growth and economy. Wheat is the major crop, with other grains and cattle-raising also important sources of revenue. Food processing and manufacturing are the province's main industries, and the rich mineral deposits of the Canadian Shield form the basis of several others. The tourist industry is developing and outdoor enthusiasts are attracted to the province by the wonderful opportunities that the lakes and forested wilderness have to offer. The climate, however, is a limiting factor for adventurers: it varies between hot summers, when the temperature often soars above 30°C (90°F), particularly in the southwest, and bitterly cold winters, when it's often well below freezing.

In 1612 an Englishman named Thomas Button sailed into Hudson Bay and spent the winter at the mouth of the Nelson River. He came in search of the fabled Northwest Passage to the Orient, but the disappointment at coming up against the mass of mid-Canada was diminished by the discovery that it was a hunter's paradise, teeming with furry animals and cut by rivers that brimmed with fish. In 1668 the ketch *Nonsuch* sailed from England to Hudson Bay and returned laden with furs. As a result, the Hudson's Bay Company was formed and was granted the vast territory, then known as Rupertsland, by Charles II, and trading posts were established around the province.

French trappers were the first white settlers in the prairie and they were the fathers of the Métis race, a half-French, half-Cree people who held with the Catholic faith but led the native way of life. The fur trade continued to flourish and eventually the French posts were surrendered to the British.

Because of the success of trade and transportation in the area, the province began to open up, but this success brought with it a threat to the Métis way of life.

In 1870 the Hudson's Bay Company sold its lands to the Dominion of Canada, which immediately commissioned surveys of the area in preparation for land allotment to new settlers. This prompted the Métis people to rise up in defense of their land rights, and, under the leadership of the young Louis Riel, they set up their own provisional government. As a result of their action and negotiations, a small area around the Red River Valley was declared the province of Manitoba with land allocated to the Métis, and in 1870 Manitoba was incorporated into the Dominion of Canada.

The coming of the Canadian Pacific Railway in the 1880s heralded a period of great change, bringing with it immigrants from Ontario, Iceland, Eastern and Western Europe, and the Ukraine. By 1912 the ever-growing province had been extended to its present-day boundaries, farming was flourishing, and good communications increased the province's supply lines, thus strengthening the economy.

WINNIPEG

Halfway across Manitoba, at the very center of Canada, the city of Winnipeg rises out of the vast flat prairie land rather like a mirage, so far away is it from any other city. It lies at the junction of the Assiniboine and Red rivers, 2,093 km (1,300 miles) west of Toronto, and 572 km (355 miles) east of Regina, connected by rail and the Trans-Canada Highway. It is Manitoba's only major city. Around 675,000 people live in it, over half the entire population of the province. It is also Western Canada's oldest city, and its nucleus is, and always has been, the junction of Main Street and Portage Avenue, streets that stretch out for miles across the prairie, following the direction of the city's two rivers.

Winnipeg is a very likable city, quite cosmopolitan in character and very cultured. It has pleasant parks, lovely riverside walks, wealthy suburbs with old mansion houses, and at the northeastern end of the city an old area of warehouses and depots reminds visitors of its early importance as a distribution center. The buildings along the wide, flat downtown streets testify to a policy of urban development that has respect for the city's stately older buildings, while remaining unafraid of change and innovation.

The famous corner of Portage Avenue and Main Street has benefited from such innovation, with an underground mall and walkways now offering shelter from what is billed as the windiest and coldest spot in Canada. The summer temperatures in the city can hit upwards of 30°C (the high 80s Fahrenheit), but the winter sees temperatures of minus 20°C (minus 4°F) with snow and blizzards that chill to the bone. Winnipeggers seem to take pride in their ability to withstand the bitterness of these long winters, and they will boldly go forth in search of an evening's entertainment. The combination of this harsh weather and Winnipeg's isolation from other urban centers may be the reason why it has created such a gloriously rich cultural scene for itself. It boasts the world-famous Royal Winnipeg Ballet, a widely acclaimed symphony orchestra, the Manitoba Opera, the excellent Manitoba Theatre Centre, and one of the country's finest museums, the Manitoba Museum of Man & Nature.

Another enriching factor in Winnipeg's cultural life is the diverse ethnic mix of its population. It started out with a mixture of natives, British, French, and Métis, but the coming of the Canadian Pacific Railway added more to the melting pot. Chinese came as laborers working on the construction of the railway, then came other Western and Eastern Europeans, Ukrainians, Mennonites, and Icelanders. The various nationalities tended to settle in ethnic-based communities around the city, and though this arrangement has to a large extent broken down, certain districts still retain a strong cultural identity. The downtown area has a sizable Chinatown, while the St. Boniface district to the south of the river has a large French-speaking community, and the southern part of town generally tends to be British in origin. Each August the city celebrates its ethnicity with the Folklorama festival that takes place in 40 pavilions throughout the town, each representing a different culture. You buy a "passport" which gains you admission to the various pavilions and also allows you to travel on the special buses that shuttle you between pavilions.

Maybe it is again the city's isolation and self-sufficiency that underlies its strong character. Even the cityscape, with its cast-iron buildings, huge stockyards, warehouses, and mansion-like houses, has solidity and a sense of security about it. Winnipeggers are themselves a resilient bunch, proud of their city, whose feelings of intense loyalty bind them to it wherever they wander.

BACKGROUND

This was once a region where the Cree and Assiniboine roamed, but change began when the first white man set foot in the area in 1738. He was the French explorer and fur trapper Pierre Gaultier de la Verendrye, and he established a fort near the confluence of the Red and Assiniboine rivers. The fur trade flourished in the area, albeit with a good deal of friction between rival factions, and in 1812 the Hudson's Bay Company gave land in the Red River valley to Lord Selkirk, allowing him to establish a Scottish settlement, thus creating a supply center for the traders.

These Scottish Highlanders came here in search of a more prosperous life, and they began to farm the area, slowly at first, as regular flooding and pestilence made for a difficult start. To the Métis people who lived by hunting buffalo, the settlement and farming of the area was a threat to their survival, and in 1816 they attacked the settlement, killing 20 of the Scots in what has become known as the Seven Oaks Massacre. The colony faltered, but continued to grow slowly. A commercial center developed around the junction of the two rivers that served as trading trails, with river and road transportation linking it to the United States.

In 1870 the province of Manitoba was created, and by 1873 the city of Winnipeg was incorporated. The Canadian Pacific Railway arrived in 1886, sparking the rapid expansion of the city and bringing large numbers of immigrants to the city. The agricultural industry flourished, and Winnipeg's position as a distribution center and financial capital was strengthened. Today it has a thriving manufacturing industry, and it remains a major financial and distribution center with a large Commodity Exchange. The junction of Portage Avenue and Main Street, shadowing the two old trade routes, remains at the center of the city's financial district, a reminder of its past.

GENERAL INFORMATION

At The Forks waterfront complex (next to the Johnston Terminal), you can visit the huge **Manitoba Travel Idea Centre** ((204) 945-3777, extension SJ9, where exhibits and travel counselors will help you sort through your options; another walk-in visitor center is located at the Legislative Building at Broadway and Osborne Street. Information on camping in Manitoba can be obtained from **Manitoba Natural Resources** ((204) 945-6784 TOLL-FREE (800) 214-6497. For information specifically on Winnipeg, there is **Tourism Winnipeg** ((204) 943-1970 TOLL-FREE (800) 665-0204, 279 Portage Avenue, Winnipeg R3B 2B4, with a second location at the Winnipeg International Airport ((204) 774-0031, main Level, North End, and a third at the Legislative Building, at Broadway and Osborne Street.

WHAT TO SEE AND DO

The **Exchange District** lies at the very heart of Winnipeg, a 20-block area stretching from Portage Avenue and Main Street to the Centennial Centre, and incorporating the famous Canadian cold spot at the corner of Portage Avenue and Main Street. Today the large buildings that stand here

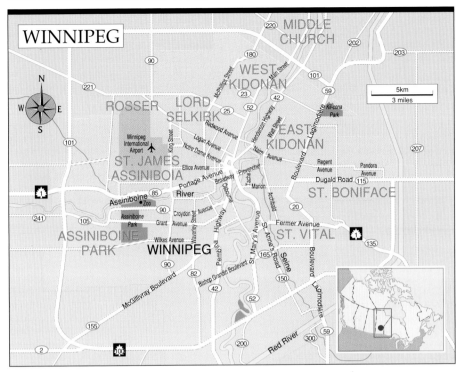

WINNIPEG

are all linked together by an underground shopping mall. This area has always been the commercial hub of the province and many of its beautiful old buildings still stand. The **Winnipeg Commodity Exchange** ((204) 925-5015, after which the district is named, is still located here. Originally the world's largest grain exchange, it has expanded into other commodities and now occupies the fifth floor of a tower block at 360 Main Street. Visitors can watch the action on the trading floor from a gallery and join a guided tour. Trading takes place between 9:30 AM and 1:20 PM. One particularly attractive building in the area is the ornate **Electric Railways Chambers Building**, which is a reminder of the importance of the railway in Winnipeg's development.

This is not purely a business district, however, as many of the restored buildings now house restaurants and boutiques. The **Market Square** at King Street and Bannatyne Avenue is a popular gathering place where there are shops, market stalls selling arts and crafts, trendy restaurants, and street entertainment during the summer months. The Exchange District is also a lively nighttime spot when the theaters, clubs, and restaurants open up.

On the edge of the Exchange District at Main Street stands the **Centennial Centre**, a complex comprising several buildings, including the **Centennial Concert Hall** ((204) 956-2171 (information) or (204) 986-6069 (tours), the **Planetarium**

((204) 943-3142, and the **Manitoba Museum of Man and Nature** ((204) 956-2830 or (204) 943-3139 (24-hour recorded information), 190 Rupert Avenue. As its name suggests, this splendid museum is devoted to the development of the province in geological, natural, historical, and cultural terms. There are realistic dioramas of Manitoba's various natural regions — combining sight, sound, and smell — and there's a gallery devoted to the prairie lands with reconstructions of pioneer dwellings and displays describing the native way of life. The highlight of a visit here is the *Nonsuch*, a full-scale replica of the ketch that left London in 1668 for Hudson Bay and returned laden with furs. It was this success that brought the famous Hudson's Bay Company into existence. The museum is open daily year-round, and an admission fee is charged.

Close by stands the **Ukrainian Cultural and Educational Centre** ((204) 942-0218 FAX (204) 943-2857, 184 Alexander Avenue East. Housed within this old building is an art gallery and a museum that contains archival material and presents changing exhibitions on the history and rich culture of the Ukrainian people, the second largest group of immigrants to settle in the province. Exhibits include samples of embroidery, ceramics, carving, costumes, and the delicately painted Easter eggs called *pysankys*. It's open Tuesday to Saturday and Sunday afternoons; an admission fee is charged.

Moving south along Main Street and opposite the railway station there's a tiny park in which you can see **Upper Fort Garry Gate**, all that remains of the early nineteenth-century Hudson's Bay Fort. To the east along Broadway, another Winnipeg landmark carries on the name — the **Fort Garry**, a château-like hotel built by the Grand Trunk Railway in 1913.

Behind the station, on four hectares (10 acres) of land is the **Forks National Historic Site** ((204) 943-6757, where you can learn about the region's history through interpretive displays, or wander along riverside pathways. Next to the historic site and sharing the riverside promenade with it is **The Forks** ((204) 943-7752, a sprawling complex

of renovated railway buildings and parkland. There's a lively public market in a former stable, a playground, Johnston terminal with shops and restaurants, and the **Manitoba Children's Museum** ((204) 956-5437, a state-of-the-art hands-on space that appeals equally to adults. Five different sections cover aspects of history, science, nature and technology. Kids can climb aboard a vintage steam-engine, try out a fully functioning television studio, and more. It's open daily; an admission fee is charged.

The magnificent **Legislative Building** ((204) 945-5813 stands at the junction of Broadway and Osborne Street, an excellent example of neoclassical architecture, built in 1919 and designed by English architect Frank Worthington Simon. It is an H-shaped structure made of Tyndall limestone, a substance rich in fossil deposits that gives it a special texture. Atop its dome stands the gold-

plated figure of the **Golden Boy**. This figure of a boy holds the torch of progress in one hand and carries a sheaf of wheat in the other to symbolize its importance in the development of Winnipeg. It is the work of French sculptor Charles Gardet, and has become itself a symbol of the city. The building is set in lovely grounds dotted with statuary honoring the city's various ethnic groups with depictions of some of their distinguished countrymen. One statue of particular note is that of Louis Riel. The interior of the building is also quite spectacular and free guided tours that allow visitors a look at the Legislative Chamber are conducted between July and Labor Day, weekdays from 9 AM to 6 PM; Labor Day to June by appointment.

South of Broadway, you can take a look at what high-tech meant to the late Victorians at the **Dalnavert Museum** ((204) 943-2835, 61 Carlton Street, a house that was built for the son of John A. Macdonald, Canada's first prime minister. It is a red-brick building that was built with indoor plumbing, electric lighting, and was fitted with all kinds of household gadgetry. It is closed on Fridays and Mondays. Call for opening hours; the admission fee includes a guided tour.

Winnipeg has a superb **Winnipeg Art Gallery** ((204) 786-6641 housed in an unmissable wedge-shaped building at 300 Memorial Boulevard. It has a varied collection of international art, but is most famous for its wonderful collection of Inuit works, which are exhibited in continually changing displays. The gallery hosts some major temporary exhibitions, and is a center for other cultural events. It is open Tuesday and Thursday to Sunday from 11 AM to 5 PM, Wednesday from 11 AM to 9 PM (though times may vary with seasons). An admission fee is charged, free on Wednesday.

Across the Red River lies the **St. Boniface** district, the oldest French-speaking community in Canada and the largest in the west. French traders lived in the area from 1738 when Pierre Gaultier de la Verendrye arrived here. In 1819, following the building of a church here, a French community began to develop that included French Canadians and Métis. The **St. Boniface Basilica** ((204) 233-7304, 190 avenue de la Cathédrale, that stands today is a modern structure built among the ruins of an earlier cathedral that burned down in 1968. In the old cemetery lies the body of Louis Riel, who was executed following the defeat of the Northwest Rebellion.

Next to the basilica stands an oak structure that was built in 1846 as a convent for the Grey Nuns who arrived here from Montréal. It now contains the **St. Boniface Museum** ((204) 237-4500, 494 avenue Taché, which has a large collection of artifacts belonging to the Métis and to other early settlers in the district and includes some memorabilia of Louis Riel. The museum is open daily. Also in the area is the **Church of the Precious**

Blood, an interesting modern structure that is shaped like a teepee.

At the southern edge of the city you can visit **Riel House** ((204) 257-1783, which stands close to the river at 330 River Road in St. Vital. It was the home of the Riel family although Louis Riel never lived there. It has been restored to the year 1885, when Riel was executed, and tours and exhibits offer glimpses into Métis life of the period. It's open daily, mid-May to Labor Day, and an admission fee is charged. Moving eastwards, a striking glass pyramid houses the **Royal Canadian Mint** ((204) 257-3359, at 520 Boulevard Lagimodière. The mint produces coins for Canada and various foreign nations. Guided tours — offered in English and

The **Fort Whyte Centre for Environmental Education** ((204) 989-8355, 1961 McCreary Road, stands on 80 hectares (200 acres) of land in Winnipeg's southwest corner. Here the natural habitat of the province's lakes and rivers has been recreated in and around several former cement quarries. Self-guided nature trails and an interpretive center tell all about it. It's open weekdays from 9 AM to 5 PM, weekends from 10 AM to 5 PM; an admission fee is charged.

Excursions from Winnipeg

Lower Fort Garry ((204) 785-6050, about 32 km (20 miles) north of Winnipeg along Highway 9, was built by the Hudson's Bay Company in the

French — show you the processes and high-tech equipment involved in making money. It's open year-round, and an admission fee is charged. Tours run weekdays from May to August, and by appointment from September to April

Assiniboine Park ((204) 986-3130, at 2355 Corydon Avenue, over in the west end of the city is a large, pleasant park with recreation areas, a miniature railway, flowerbeds, an English garden where a statue of Queen Victoria stands, and an attractive old pavilion where you can sometimes catch a game of cricket. It also contains a **zoo** ((204) 986-6921 with a population of around 1,300 — including many native species — and a conservatory where there are tropical plants, birds, and monkeys. The park is on the southern bank of the Assiniboine River about 11 km (seven miles) from downtown. There is an admission fee for the zoo, which is open daily, year-round.

1830s and is the only remaining stone fort of that era in North America. It has been carefully restored and visitors can see the various living quarters, the fur loft, and the governor's residence as they were when the fort functioned as an important trading post. Before you begin your tour of the buildings, it's a good idea to watch the film shown in the reception area, which fills you in on the background. Inside the compound, costumed "workers" will demonstrate crafts in the various workshops. In the grounds you'll see a restored York boat, a vessel that was designed for transporting furs. Buses run to the fort from the downtown bus station. The fort is

OPPOSITE: Walking out the past in Lower Fort Garry. ABOVE: Part of the façade of the Legislative Building, LEFT, and the towers of the Ukrainian church at the Ukrainian Cultural and Educational Centre.

open daily from mid-May to Labor Day; an admission fee is charged.

The **Mennonite Heritage Village** ((204) 326-9661 lies 61 km (38 miles) southeast of Winnipeg, about two and a half kilometers (one and a half miles) outside the village of Steinbach, a living museum where you can see a working mill and watch the Mennonites demonstrate their crafts, just as they would have in the nineteenth century. The Mennonite sect is one that is totally committed to pacifism and has been frequently persecuted because of its beliefs. The Mennonites who settled in Manitoba came from Russia in the 1870s and 1880s, and this heritage village presents a colorful picture of their way of life. There is a restaurant here that serves traditional Mennonite food. The village is open daily from May to September. To get there from Winnipeg, take Highway 1 to Highway 12 North, and watch for signs just north of Steinbach. It's open daily from May to September, weekdays only from October to April. An admission fee is charged.

If you like scenic train rides you should find out if the *Prairie Dog Central* is back in operation. At the time of research the train was not operating, but it may resume service in 1999; check with Tourism Winnipeg (see GENERAL INFORMATION, above). A trip aboard this early twentieth-century steam train takes you on a two-hour trip to **Grosse Isle**, 58 km (36 miles) northwest of Winnipeg. It's worth the trip not only to see the countryside rolling by, but also for the delightful experience of traveling in grand old-fashioned style.

SPORTS AND OUTDOOR ACTIVITIES

There are **hiking** trails and **cycling** paths in the city parks, details of which are available from information centers. There are several **skating** rinks throughout Winnipeg, and when the snow comes there's **snowmobiling** at Birds Hill Provincial Park, about 32 km (20 miles) northeast of the city.

There's excellent **fishing** in the province, as you would expect with so many lakes, but you need to venture outside Winnipeg. The tourist information centers can help you with information on where to go and how to get there. Likewise they can help you with details of the excellent **canoe** routes that the province is famous for.

NIGHTLIFE AND THE ARTS

Winnipeg has a lively nightlife. To find out what's going on check the entertainment listings that appear in the daily *Winnipeg Free Press* and the *Winnipeg Sun*. The **Centennial Centre** ((204) 956-1360, 555 Main Street, is the hub of Winnipeg's cultural scene. The area comprises the Centennial Concert Hall, the Manitoba Theatre Centre, the Warehouse Theatre, and the excellent Manitoba Museum of Man and Nature.

The theatre season in Winnipeg is really under way between September and early May, and during those months the **Manitoba Theatre Centre** (BOX OFFICE (204) 942-6537, 174 Market Avenue, stages a variety of comedy and serious drama, while nearby the smaller **Warehouse Theatre** ((204) 956-1340, stages experimental productions. There are several other companies scattered around town, including the innovative **Gas Station Theatre** ((204) 284-9477 FAX (204) 284-9478, 445 River Avenue, in Osborne Village.

The most cherished and famous of Winnipeg's cultural institutions is the **Royal Winnipeg Ballet**, which performs a program of classical and modern works at the **Centennial Concert Hall** ((204) 956-2792, Room 101-555 Main Street, and also gives a free open-air performance in Assiniboine Park in the summer. The acclaimed

Winnipeg Symphony Orchestra and the **Manitoba Opera** also perform at the Centennial Concert Hall.

A mixture of jazz, folk, and classical music can often be heard at the **Winnipeg Art Gallery (** (204) 786-6641, 300 Memorial Boulevard. You'll find rock and other live music playing at various bars and clubs in the town, often in hotel lounges. The **Palamino Club (** (204) 772-0454, 1133 Portage Avenue, is a country-and-western hangout. Winnipeg has quite a lively nightclub scene and one that is rapidly changing, like the city itself. The Exchange District is a nighttime hot spot where many of these clubs can be found.

Winnipeg has two **casinos**, both of which were under renovation at the time of research: Club Regent TOLL-FREE (800) 493-4652, at 1425 Regent Avenue, is installing a gigantic walk-through saltwater aquarium; and McPhillips Station TOLL-FREE (888) 493-4652, 484 McPhillips Street, will have

the Manitoba Millenium Theatre where multimedia and "multisensory" presentations will explore the province's history and culture. In addition to their new, John Waters-esque attractions and the usual mass of gaming tables, both casinos feature Vegas-style entertainment, restaurants and lounges.

WHERE TO STAY

Expensive
The **Crown Plaza Winnipeg Downtown (** (204) 942-0551 TOLL-FREE (800) 2CROWNE FAX (204) 943-8702, 350 St. Mary Avenue, Winnipeg R3C 3J2, is part of a complex that connects with the Convention Centre. There are 390 pleasant rooms including several suites, indoor and outdoor pools, and a good range of services. There's a choice of

Feathers for sale in the Old Market Square.

restaurants within the hotel, and several more inside the complex. Also top notch, the **Radisson Winnipeg Downtown** ((204) 956-0410 TOLL-FREE (800) 333-3333 FAX (204) 947-1129, 288 Portage Avenue, Winnipeg R3C 0B8, is a downtown highrise hotel with 270 rooms above its multistory parking facility. The rooms are smart and have good views; the service is first-rate. There are two attractive restaurants, one formal and one casual, and a comprehensive range of amenities that include an indoor swimming pool, a cinema, and a supervised children's activity center. Under renovation at the time of writing, the Radisson will sport a new lobby and entrance by the spring of 1999.

Mid-range

The Lombard ((204) 957-1350 TOLL-FREE (800) 441-1414 FAX (204) 956-1791, at 2 Lombard Place, Winnipeg R3B 0Y3, is in the very center of town and is one of the city's top-rated hotels. There are 340 luxurious rooms, excellent service, and guests have the use of an indoor swimming pool. There is a choice of restaurants, a café, and in-house entertainment. The hotel is conveniently linked to a large shopping complex. The **Sheraton Winnipeg** ((204) 942-5300 TOLL-FREE (800) 463-6400 FAX (204) 943-7975 is another top downtown hotel located close to the Convention Centre at 161 Donald Street, Winnipeg R3C 1M3. Rooms here are large, well-equipped, and have balconies with some excellent views from the top floors. The hotel has an indoor pool, a sun deck, and a pleasant restaurant, with nightly entertainment in the lounge. Both hotels have prices that vary between mid-range and expensive.

For some old-style grandeur, you must go to **Hotel Fort Garry** ((204) 942-8251 TOLL-FREE (800) 665-8088 FAX (204) 956-2351, 222 Broadway, Winnipeg R3C 0R3. This castle-like hotel was built by the Grand Trunk Railway in 1913 and subsequently underwent extensive renovation. The refurbishment has been done with great care, so the original splendor has been preserved throughout the hotel. There are 240 elegant rooms and suites, and two beautiful dining rooms. Breakfast is included in the price of accommodation.

For accommodation with lots of character and excellent service, book in at the **Ramada Marlborough Hotel** ((204) 942-6411 TOLL-FREE (800) 667-7666 FAX (204) 942-2017, 331 Smith Street, Winnipeg R3B 2G9, which is in the town's financial district. It is a Victorian Gothic building with a grand interior of vaulted ceilings, stained glass, and polished wood. The rooms and suites are stylish with modern conveniences, and the hotel has a delightful restaurant as well as a coffee shop.

Inexpensive

The **Gordon Downtowner Motor Hotel** ((204) 943-5581 FAX (204) 947-3041, 330 Kennedy Street, Winnipeg R3B 2M6, has comfortable, convenient accommodation, bars, and a restaurant, and is excellent value. The **Charter House Hotel** ((204) 942-0101 TOLL-FREE (800) 782-0175 FAX (204) 956-0665, 330 York Avenue, Winnipeg R3C 0N9, is a good downtown choice. It has 90 rooms, some of which have balconies, a dining room, and an outdoor swimming pool. The **St. Regis** ((204) 942-0171 TOLL-FREE (800) 663-7344 FAX (204) 943-3077, 285 Smith Street, Winnipeg R3C 1K9, has basic but pleasant rooms, and a nice atmosphere.

The **Ivey House International Hostel** ((204) 772-3022, 210 Maryland Street, Winnipeg R3G 1L6, is located in a turn-of-the century residence within walking distance of the city's cultural attractions. It's open year-round. During the summer break the **University of Manitoba** has accommodation for visitors. For details contact the Conference Coordinator ((204) 474-9942, 26 MacLean Crescent, Pembina Hall R3T 2N1.

For a list of bed and breakfast accommodation in the area contact an Information Centre or Bed and Breakfast of Manitoba ((204) 661-0300, 434 Roberta Avenue, Winnipeg R2K 0K6. If a rural retreat appeals, get in touch with the **Manitoba Country Vacations Association** ((204) 776-2176, c/o Ernest Fraser, Fairfax R0K 0V0. The Information Centres also have information on campgrounds in the region.

WHERE TO EAT

Winnipeg's diverse ethnic mix makes for some exciting dining, and there are a surprisingly large number of restaurants for a city of its size. Many of the restaurants, like the shops, are closed on Sundays.

Moderate to Expensive

Restaurant Dubrovnik ((204) 944-0594 FAX (204) 957-7750, 390 Assiniboine Avenue, is one

Winnipeg's skyline.

of the city's best restaurants. It is in a large Victorian house on the riverbank, with a charming interior that has retained many of the original features. Some beautiful examples of Yugoslavian crafts adorn the walls. The food is continental but with Yugoslavian specialties on the menu, and it is quite delicious. Proof of its excellence lies in its popularity, so be sure to make a reservation. Prices vary between expensive and moderate.

Another popular dining spot is the **Royal Crown Revolving Restaurant** ((204) 947-1990, at Fort Garry Place, 83 Garry Street. The menu here is continental on the whole, and the interior is quite plush. There are two restaurants that revolve in different directions, the Tiara Dining Room being the more exclusive of the two. Although the food is quite good, people come here mainly for the panoramic views of the city. In addition to daily à la carte dining, there's a Sunday brunch and a Sunday evening buffet. The **Velvet Glove** ((204) 985-6255 in The Lombard, 2 Lombard Place, is a top-rated restaurant that specializes in continental food prepared to gourmet standards. The setting is one of formal elegance amid warm tones of wood and brass, and the dining booths add an element of intimacy. Prices vary widely, but unless you choose some particularly expensive dishes your bill is likely to land in the moderate range.

Victor's ((204) 947-2751, in the Ramada Marlborough, 331 Smith Street, bears out the Gothic exterior of this lovely hotel with arches, stained glass, and Victorian furnishings creating a delightful atmosphere. The menu concentrates on steaks, seafood, and continental dishes. Over in the French district of St. Boniface, **Le Beaujolais** ((204) 237-6306, 131 Provencher Boulevard, serves traditional French and nouvelle dishes, all expertly prepared, and elegantly served in attractive surroundings.

For good northern Italian cooking in a cultivated setting, go to **Amici** ((204) 943-4997, 326 Broadway. There's delicious Swiss fare at the **Old Swiss Inn** ((204) 942-7725, 207 Edmonton Street, where you'll find more than fondue on the menu, and warm, friendly surroundings. **Hy's Steak Loft** ((204) 942-1000, 216 Kennedy Street, serves good quality steaks and seafood in old-fashioned surroundings, and **Rae and Jerry's** ((204) 783-6155, in the west end of the city, at 1405 Portage Avenue, is another popular steak house that includes chicken and fish dishes on its menu. Prices here vary between inexpensive and moderate. For steaks served in a rather different way, go to the **Ichiban Japanese Steak House and Sushi Bar** ((204) 925-7400, 189 Carlton Street, where meats and vegetables are stir-fried with tremendous flair in front of diners. There's also a wide choice of other traditional dishes. The decor here is easy on the eye, and an artificial brook adds the soothing sound of running water. The Ichiban is a good

choice for a Sunday when your options are limited in Winnipeg.

Inexpensive

One of Winnipeg's ever-popular restaurants is the **Bistro Dansk** ((204) 775-5662, 63 Sherbrooke Street. It is a cheerful, friendly place with good Danish food and pleasant, helpful staff.

The north end of town has a plethora of delis and cafés that make for some interesting and enjoyable dining. **Alycia's** ((204) 582-8789, 559 Cathedral Avenue, serves homemade Ukrainian food in cozy surroundings decorated with traditional arts and crafts. Both **Oscar's** ((204) 947-0314, 175 Hargrave Street, and **Simon's** ((204) 589-8269, 1322 Main Street, are well-established Jewish delicatessens which are open into the small hours. For a taste of Indonesia, try **Betsy's Place** at 1134 Main Street North.

In Osborne Village you can go English at the **Tea Cozy** ((204) 475-1027, 99 Osborne Street. Here you can eat breakfast, or have a spot of lunch, or take tea with crumpets, cakes, or biscuits. For a completely different cultural experience, **Carlos and Murphy's** ((204) 284-3510, 129 Osborne Street, has a bar and a restaurant serving good Mexican food in a congenial atmosphere.

Winnipeg's **Chinatown** lies to the north of the Exchange District, stretching between James and Logan avenues and covering an eight-block area. As is the norm, you'll find good-value Chinese restaurants here and a variety of Chinese cuisines.

How to Get There

Winnipeg International Airport is approximately 10 km (six miles) northwest of downtown, about a 20-minute drive away, but allow longer during rush hours. An airport shuttle runs between the airport and some of the big hotels.

The **VIA Rail** ((204) 949 1830 TOLL-FREE (888) 842-7733 station is downtown at 101-123 Main Street. Trains run to Vancouver via Kamloops, Jasper, Edmonton, and Saskatoon. From the east the line runs into Winnipeg from Toronto. VIA Rail runs the *Hudson Bay* train to Churchill via Dauphin, The Pas, and Thompson.

The bus station is downtown at 487 Portage Place. **Greyhound** ((204) 982-8747 buses operate to and from this terminal. **Grey Goose Lines** ((204) 784-4512, 301 Burnell Street, links Winnipeg with other towns in Manitoba.

Winnipeg is quite isolated, so if you're driving the chances are that wherever you're coming from (unless it's the airport), you'll have quite a long drive ahead. The Trans-Canada Highway (Highway 1) runs through the city, linking it with Toronto, 2,093 km (1,300 miles) east, and Calgary, 1,359 km (844 miles) to the west. Minneapolis in Minnesota is 734 km (456 miles) from

Winnipeg via Interstate-94 and Interstate-29 in the United States, becoming Highway 75 in Manitoba.

ELSEWHERE IN MANITOBA

WHITESHELL PROVINCIAL PARK

There are wonderful opportunities for all kinds of outdoor pursuits in this large wilderness park that lies close to the Ontario border, 144 km (89 miles) east of Winnipeg. It is Canadian Shield country, an area rich in lakes, rivers, forest, and wildlife — ideal for hiking, canoeing, horseback riding, fishing, and all kinds of water sports. Areas of the park have been developed for tourism, and at **Falcon Lake** a recreational development offers a golf course, tennis courts, a ski resort, shops, and accommodations. If you prefer to get away from all that, there are quieter areas in the northern reaches of the park.

LAKE WINNIPEG

This vast lake lies to the north of Winnipeg and is lined with sandy beaches, making it an excellent place for relaxation and water sports. The fishing town of **Gimli** stands at the southwestern shores of the lake, 90 km (56 miles) north of Winnipeg. Back in the 1870s Icelanders came to the area in search of a new home free of the tyranny of the volcanoes that so disrupted their lives in their native land. They found that this area could offer them a good living through fishing and farming, and for a time the region was an independent country known as New Iceland. The community of Gimli retains a strong Icelandic identity and culture, and in August it celebrates the **Icelandic Festival**, a celebration of sports, music, parades, art, and traditional food. There is a museum on the waterfront that has displays on the history of the settlement.

Hecla Provincial Park ((204) 378-2945, PO Box 70, Riverton ROC 2R0, encompasses a collection of islands in Lake Winnipeg. These islands are wildlife preserves and a bird-watcher's delight, while hikers, fishermen, canoeists, and winter sports enthusiasts also find much to enjoy here. Hecla Island is accessible by car, and at its northern end the **Gull Harbour Resort** (204) 475-2354 TOLL-FREE (800) 475-5992 manages to offer recreation facilities, attractive accommodation, and good Icelandic hospitality without marring the natural beauty of the island. The hotel is open year-round.

RIDING MOUNTAIN NATIONAL PARK

Riding Mountain National Park is an outdoor playground that lies 248 km (154 miles) northwest of Winnipeg, on the highlands of a prairie escarp-

ment. It has been partially developed in **Wasagaming** on the shores of Clear Lake, where there's a variety of accommodation and extensive recreational facilities, but the area remains largely unspoiled, with bison, elk, deer, and beaver inhabiting the parkland. In the winter there are cross-country skiing trails through the park and downhill skiing at Mount Agassiz. The **Visitor Centre** ((204) 848-PARK TOLL-FREE (800) 707-8480, in Wasagaming, will provide guides and maps. Close to Wasagaming the **Elkhorn Resort & Conference Centre** ((204) 848-2802 FAX (204) 848-2109, PO Box 40, Onanole R0J 1N0, has chalets and suites, a nine-hole golf course, and organized horseback riding treks. Prices vary from mid-range to expensive.

CHURCHILL

The small town of Churchill lies on the southwestern shore of Hudson Bay at the estuary of the Churchill River, and is one of the few places in the north accessible from the south — though not by road. It is one of the world's largest grain-handling ports, with huge grain elevators looming overhead, but it is increasingly becoming a popular tourist destination because of its substantial natural attractions. Although weather conditions are very difficult here, with snow during most of the year creating a sparse, subarctic vegetation, the wildlife draws the visitors. It is a great place for **polar bear watching**, especially during October and early November when migration is at its height and the bears are regularly seen wandering around the town. **Tundra Buggy Tours** ((204) 675-2121 TOLL-FREE (800) 544-5049 operates specially built buggies that take visitors out on bear-spotting safaris. Half-day tours are offered July to September, full-day tours in October and early November.

Getting there, as you might expect, is half the fun. **Canadian Airlines International** runs flights between Winnipeg and Churchill; there's also the option of a two-night **VIA Rail** ((204) 949-1830 journey from Winnipeg. VIA's Winnipeg address is 103-123 Main Street, Winnipeg R3C 2P8.

OPPOSITE: Waterfowl and moose share the unspoiled beauty of Riding Mountain National Park.

Saskatch-
ewan

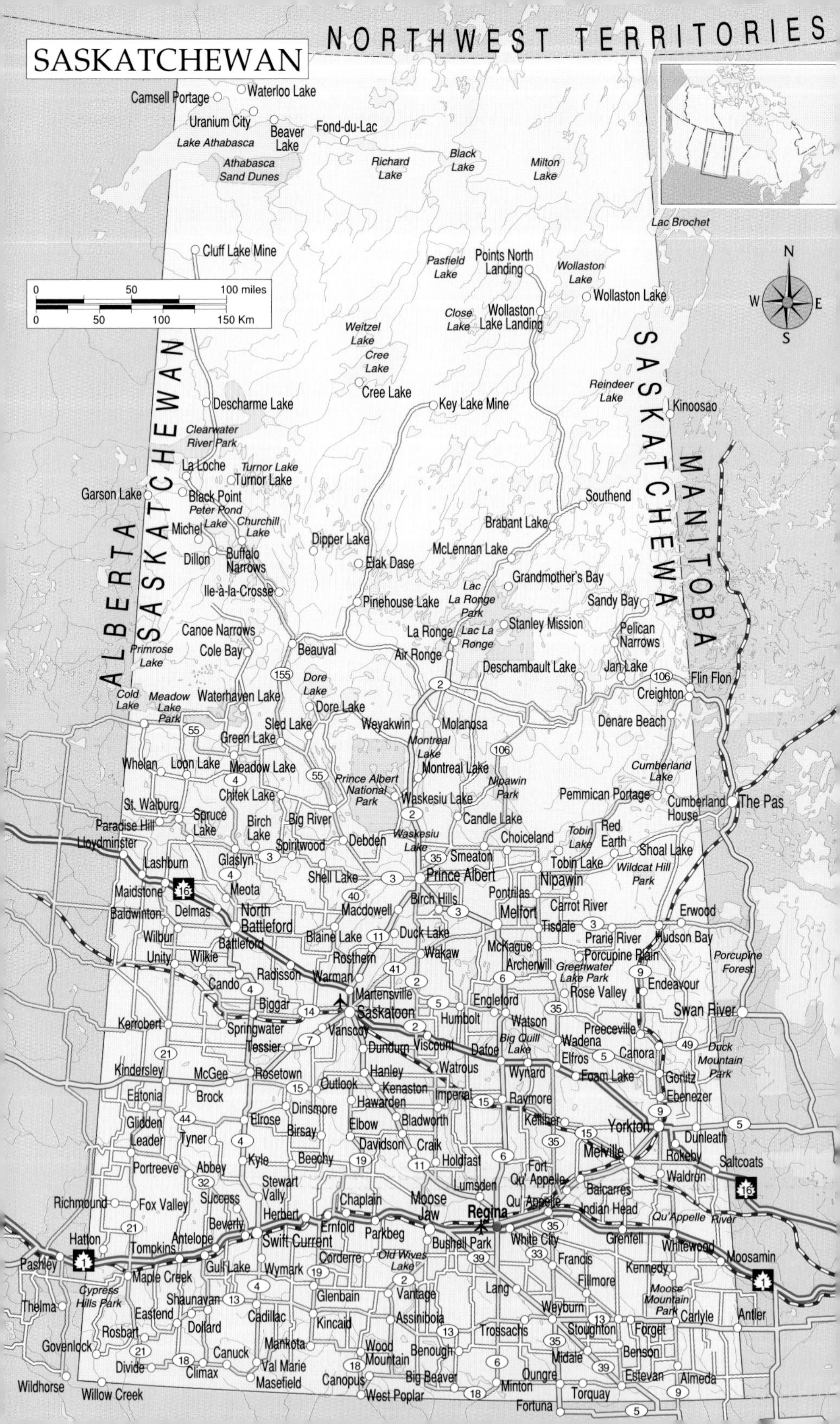

SASKATCHEWAN

Camsell Portage
Waterloo Lake
Uranium City
Lake Athabasca
Beaver Lake
Fond-du-Lac
Athabasca Sand Dunes
Richard Lake
Black Lake
Milton Lake

Lac Brochet

Cluff Lake Mine

Pasfield Lake
Points North Landing
Wollaston Lake
Wollaston Lake

Weitzel Lake
Close Lake
Wollaston Lake Landing
Cree Lake

0   50   100 miles
0   50   100   150 Km

Descharme Lake
Cree Lake
Key Lake Mine

Reindeer Lake
Kinoosao

Clearwater River Park
La Loche
Turnor Lake
Turnor Lake
Garson Lake
Black Point
Peter Pond
Churchill Lake
Michel
Lake
Dillon
Buffalo Narrows
Ile-à-la-Crosse
Dipper Lake
Elak Dase
Pinehouse Lake
Southend
Brabant Lake
McLennan Lake
Grandmother's Bay
Lac La Ronge Park
Sandy Bay
Stanley Mission
Pelican Narrows
Jan Lake

Canoe Narrows
Cole Bay
Beauval
Air Ronge
La Ronge
Lac La Ronge
Deschambault Lake
Flin Flon
Creighton

Primrose Lake
155
Dore Lake
Cold Lake
Meadow Lake Park
Waterhaven Lake
Dore Lake
Weyakwin
Molanosa
Denare Beach

55
Sled Lake
Green Lake
Montreal Lake
Cumberland Lake

Whelan
Loon Lake
Meadow Lake
55
106
Pemmican Portage
Cumberland House
The Pas

St. Walburg
4
Chitek Lake
Prince Albert National Park
Nipawin Park
Waskesiu Lake

Paradise Hill
Spruce Lake
Birch Lake
Big River
Spiritwood
Debden
Waskesiu Lake
Candle Lake
Choiceland
Tobin Lake
Red Earth
Shoal Lake

Lloydminster
Lashburn
Glaslyn
3
Shell Lake
3
Smeaton
Prince Albert
35
Tobin Lake
Nipawin
Wildcat Hill Park

Maidstone
16
Meota
40
Birch Hills
Pontrilas
Melfort
Tisdale
Carrot River
Erwood

Baldwinton
Delmas
North Battleford
Macdowell
Duck Lake
Wakaw
McKague
Archerwill
Prairie River
Hudson Bay
Porcupine Forest

Wilbur
Battleford
Blaine Lake
11
Rosthern
41
Warman
McAdam
Greenwater Lake Park
Rose Valley
Endeavour
Swan River

Unity
Wilkie
Radisson
Martensville
Saskatoon
Engleford
Watson
35
Preeceville

Kerrobert
Cando
4
Biggar
14
Vanscoy
Humbolt
Wadena
Canora
49
Duck Mountain Park

21
McGee
Springwater
7
Dundurn
Viscount
Dafoe
Big Quill Lake
Elfros
Foam Lake
Goritz
Ebenezer

Kindersley
Brock
Rosetown
15
Outlook
Hanley
Watrous
Wynard
Raymore
Kelliher
9

Eatonia
Glidden
Elrose
Dinsmore
Birsay
Elbow
Bladworth
15
Kuroki
15
Yorkton
Dunleath
5

Leader
44
Tyner
Kyle
Beechy
Davidson
Craik
Holdfast
Melville
Rokeby
Saltcoats

Portreeve
Abbey
32
Stewart Valley
Chaplain
11
Lumsden
Fort Qu'Appelle
Balcarres
Waldron
16

Richmound
Fox Valley
Success
Herbert
Moose Jaw
Regina
Indian Head
Qu'Appelle River

Hatton
21
Antelope
Beverly
Ernfold
Parkbeg
Bushell Park
White City
Grenfell
Whitewood
Moosomin

Pashley
Tompkins
Swift Current
Corderre
Old Wives Lake
39
Francis
33
Kennedy
Moose Mountain Park
1

Thelma
Maple Creek
Gull Lake
Wymark
19
Glenbain
Vantage
Assiniboia
Weyburn
13
Forget
Carlyle

Cypress Hills Park
Eastend
4
Shaunavon
13
Cadillac
Kincaid
Trossachs
Stoughton
Midale
Antler

Govenlock
Rosbart
21
Dollard
Mankota
Wood Mountain
Benough
Oungre
Benson
Almeda

Wildhorse
Willow Creek
Divide
18
Climax
Val Marie
Masefield
Canopus
Big Beaver
West Poplar
18
Minton
Torquay
Estevan
9

ALBERTA
SASKATCHEWAN
MANITOBA

SITUATED BETWEEN MANITOBA IN THE EAST AND ALBERTA IN THE WEST, Saskatchewan contains the largest area of Canada's three Prairie Provinces. It is the country's most important wheat producer, and has become a byword for the endless, treeless plain that in the minds of many typifies the word "prairie." This is unfortunate and somewhat unfair, as Saskatchewan does have quite a varied landscape, both within the prairie and beyond it. Besides that vast, flat, and treeless wheat-growing belt, there are some 100,000 jewel-blue lakes for fishing and recreation, 200,000 hectares (five million acres) of parkland, the lunar-like landscape of the badlands, as well as green valleys and acres of boreal forest.

In the south of the province the badlands, a mixture of semiarid grasslands and desert-like areas, occupy a large semicircular portion of the prairie. This section is surrounded by a wheat-growing belt in which the provincial capital of Regina lies, and beyond that strip is the outer section of the prairie, known as the parkland, an area of gently rolling hills and trees, through which the North and South Saskatchewan rivers flow. Beyond the prairie, Prince Albert National Park stands at the edge of the remote North Country, a wilderness of forests and marshlands, crisscrossed with a latticework of lakes and rivers, much of which is Canadian Shield country. Here the roads peter out, and it is very sparsely populated. These wide-open spaces, ideal for fishing and canoeing, attract adventurers and urban refugees.

When in 1858 John Palliser led an expedition through the southwest of the province, he deemed the land unsuitable for agriculture, but subsequent irrigation proved his assessment wrong, turning Saskatchewan into North America's largest wheat-growing region. More than 50% of Canada's crop is produced here, while the grasslands of the south have made good cattle-raising country. The mineral wealth of the province has also proved profitable; oil is now an important part of the economy. The favorable summer weather and hundreds of parks attract outdoors lovers, making the tourist industry a newer strand in an economy that is rapidly growing.

Saskatchewan has a population of about a million in an area of 651,900 sq km (251,700 sq miles), leaving a lot of empty space, and the citizens of its two major cities revel in the opportunities that their parklands provide. The relaxed character of the people masks a fighting spirit and a willingness to work together for the common good that has brought them through some very difficult times. They are also unafraid of change: In 1944 Saskatchewan elected the first Socialist government in North America and embarked upon a series of innovative social programs. The people are proud of their pioneering past, which they commemorate in many museums — Saskatchewan has the most museums per capita of all the provinces.

There are frequent reminders of the remarkable contribution made by the North West Mounted Police in the development of the area, and also of the bitter Northwest Rebellion that once shook the province and still seems to send out shock waves.

Saskatchewan has quite a colorful history. The first white man to explore the territory was Henry Kelsey in 1690, acting on behalf of the Hudson's Bay Company. Trading posts were then established in the region, and throughout the nineteenth century the fur trade flourished here. As a result the Métis people came into being, children of French fathers and native mothers who lived the native way of life but followed Roman Catholicism.

In 1870 the Canadian government, seeing the agricultural potential, bought the land from the Hudson's Bay Company and began to negotiate treaties in preparation for the settlement of the area. The government advertised free land to settlers, and ranchers began to move their herds into the southwest. In 1873 the North West Mounted Police was formed to enforce law and order in the Northwest Territories. But it was the coming of the Canadian Pacific Railway in 1882 that began to reel in settlers from the United States, Britain, and Europe.

The arrival of the settlers and the surveying of the land in preparation for further immigration caused great consternation among the Métis, who stood to lose rights to the lands they already inhabited. As their pleas to the government went

A vehicle decorated for Regina's Buffalo Days.

unheeded, they turned to the leadership of a young man named Louis Riel. They set up their own provincial government in an attempt to establish their rights, but the English Métis did not lend their support to this faction, and conflict arose between Riel's people and some of the settlers. This resulted in Riel having one of them killed following an attempt on his life. The Métis were eventually granted some land for settlement and Riel was forced into exile, but when the Métis and the natives again found themselves about to be dispossessed, Riel returned to lead them in the Northwest Rebellion of 1885, dubbing himself "Prophet, Infallible Pontiff and Priest King."

starving cattle. Now, half a century later, the region thrives; like the other Prairie Provinces, the 1990s have ushered in a period of great economic growth in Saskatchewan.

REGINA

Saskatchewan's capital is one of Canada's sunniest cities, and as befits its name Regina rises regally from the center of the flat prairie wheat fields. With the Canadian Pacific Railway and the Trans-Canada Highway running through the city, it is the financial, industrial, and agricultural center of Saskatchewan, with a population of around 200,000. It has a healthy cultural life with a good

This was a bitter conflict that ended with a hopeless but noble stand by the rebels at Batoche, against government troops using Gatling guns. Riel surrendered, was brought to trial in Regina, and was hanged for treason there.

Subsequently the Métis received the land rights they had sought, but the death of Riel had other political repercussions. For many it came to represent the French-English conflict, and to this day it remains an emotive subject. Saskatchewan does much to keep the memory alive, and each year in Regina the trial of Riel is reenacted.

In 1905 Saskatchewan was incorporated, with Regina as its capital, and immigration to the province steadily continued along with prosperity and growth. The Depression of the 1930s hit Saskatchewan particularly hard, and to add to the misery 10 years of drought brought crop failure, creating a depressing brown landscape dotted with

number of theatre and dance companies, as well as Canada's oldest symphony orchestra and one of her top concert halls. Regina is home to Canada's only training academy for the Royal Canadian Mounted Police, which adds a splash of red color and some ceremonial pomp to the city. The museum that traces the development of the force and other museums throughout the city afford visitors a fascinating window on the province's past.

Once a miserable, muddy, and unpromising site along the banks of the Wascana, Regina has been transformed into a dignified and serene city of parklands and well-considered public facilities, offering travelers welcome respite from the vast plains that surround it. The core of the city and the buildings that house some of its major attractions lie in Wascana Centre, a pleasant parkland of trees and gardens surrounding a man-made lake.

BACKGROUND

When the Canadian Pacific Railway was planning its route across the plains, the government, realizing that the erstwhile capital of the Northwest Territories would be nowhere near the railway, entered into discussions with the Canadian Pacific Railway to decide on a site for a new settlement that would lie along the line. The place they settled upon was far from being an obvious choice. It lay along the banks of an almost dried-up creek, with only a few stagnant pools remaining — an area that varied from being too muddy to too dusty. The banks had been used by the Cree for slaughtering buffalo and drying the skins, and because of the large numbers of buffalo skeletons there they had given it the inauspicious name Oskana — meaning "Pile of Bones." However, settlement was soon under way, and in 1882 the first train chuffed into the station. Princess Louise, wife of Canada's governor-general, bestowed upon it the more dignified name of Regina, in honor of her mother, Queen Victoria.

The North West Mounted Police set up headquarters here, and in 1885 Regina became the focus of attention when, following the Northwest Rebellion, it was the scene of the trial of the Métis leader, Louis Riel. Opinion was divided over Riel, as many believed his cause to be a just one that highlighted the French-British conflict in Canada, but Riel was found guilty of treason and hanged in November of that year.

When the province of Saskatchewan was incorporated in 1905, Regina was its capital city and immigrants began to flood in. Gradually the problems of the location were solved: the creek was dammed to create an artificial lake, the surrounding parkland was landscaped, the dignified Legislative Building was planned, and present-day Regina began to take shape.

GENERAL INFORMATION

For information on Regina and vicinity contact **Tourism Regina** ((306) 789-5099 TOLL-FREE (800) 661-5099 extension 277 FAX (306) 789-3171, which is located on the Trans-Canada Highway at the eastern edge of the city at Highway 1 East, PO Box 3355, Regina S4P 3H1. It's open year-round, seven days a week in summer and weekdays only in winter.

WHAT TO SEE AND DO

Along the banks of Wascana Creek lie several parks, but Regina's pride is the **Wascana Centre**, a 930-hectare (2,300-acre) park that forms the heart of the city. Once a muddy area with an uncertain water supply, settlers dammed the creek here to create Wascana Lake and a water reserve. It is now one of the largest urban parks in North America — a beautiful green space where trees have been planted and flowerbeds cultivated. Around the lake a pleasant marina has been built where you can take a ferry over to Willow Island, a lovely spot for a picnic. With canoeing, sailing, boating, windsurfing, and many picnic areas, it is a place of recreation, but the art gallery and science center located here also make it a place of culture and education.

On the western side of the park stands the stately domed **Legislative Building** ((306) 787-5357, built between 1908 and 1912 in the style of the English Renaissance Revival, lavishly deco-

rated within, and set in pleasant gardens. It is open to the public and tours can be arranged that take visitors around the huge library, the Legislative Chamber, and the art galleries on the lower levels. Admission is free.

Over on the north bank of Wascana Lake at the corner of College Avenue and Albert Street stands the **Royal Saskatchewan Museum** ((306) 787-2815, a low building built in Tyndall stone and decorated with a frieze. If you intend visiting the Saskatchewan that lies beyond the cities, this is an excellent introduction to the flora and fauna you will encounter. There are dioramas of various regions, complete with wildlife and sound effects that add to the realism, and with displays

OPPOSITE: Regina's skyline as seen from the Wascana Centre. ABOVE: The iron-and-wood stitchery that since 1885 has sewn Canada together.

on wildlife biology. The Earth Sciences Gallery traces the province's geological history and features some hands-on displays, while another gallery deals with Native American history.

Close by stands the **Mackenzie Art Gallery** ((306) 522-4242, at Albert Street and 23rd Avenue. This began as a private collection bequeathed to the University of Regina, and it now includes both contemporary and older works from a variety of countries, but with an emphasis on Canadian art. It is open daily, with evening hours on Wednesday and Thursday, and admission is free. In August a theatre company reenacts the trial of Louis Riel here from court transcripts, which never fails to stir up controversy.

many other species. There's a naturalist on hand to answer questions and to arrange guided tours. As well as the information center, there's a gift shop and a small art gallery. It's open daily, year-round.

Close to the Legislative Building stands **Government House** ((306) 787-5717, Dewdney Avenue at Connaught Street. This served as the residence of the Lieutenant-Governors between 1891 and 1945. The rooms have been beautifully restored and contain period furnishings. Hours are Tuesday to Sunday from 1 PM to 4 PM. Admission is free.

North of the Wascana Centre, the famous Royal Canadian Mounted Police, or Mounties, have their

Also on the north shore of the lake the old city power station has been converted to house the **Saskatchewan Science Centre** ((306) 522-4629 TOLL-FREE (800) 667-6300, on the corner of Winnipeg Street and Wascana Drive, where hands-on exhibits help to explain some of the laws of physics. It is open daily year-round. An admission fee is charged.

Also within the Wascana Centre on Lakeshore Drive you'll find the **Saskatchewan Centre of the Arts** ((306) 565-4500, which contains two theaters, the larger of which serves as an excellent concert hall where you can hear the Regina Symphony Orchestra play, Canada's oldest continuously operating symphony orchestra. The Centre presents operas, theatrical productions, dance, and other musical presentations. Nearby on the lake shore is the **Waterfowl Park** (306) 522-3661, where you can see Canada geese, swans, pelicans, and

training academy and also the **RCMP Centennial Museum** ((306) 780-5838, off of Dewdney Avenue West. The museum traces the colorful history of the Mounties and the vital role they played in Canada's development — a role that far exceeds that normally fulfilled by a police force. Archival material, uniforms, weaponry, artifacts, and a wealth of memorabilia recall the famous and grueling march that the newly formed force made through the west to establish law and order. Various other events in the force's history are also recalled. There are some curiosities on display here, such as Chief Sitting Bull's tobacco pouch, while some exhibits add a lighter touch, such as the Hollywood representations of those who "always get their man." It's open daily; admission is free.

For lovers of military drills, the **Sergeant Major's Parade** takes place weekdays at 1 PM, and from July to mid-August the colorful **Sunset**

Retreat Ceremony draws the crowds on Tuesday evenings when the flag is lowered.

Excursions from Regina

Seventy-one kilometers (44 miles) west of Regina along the Trans-Canada Highway lies **Moose Jaw**, Saskatchewan's third largest city. A prosperous railroad and industrial center, Moose Jaw was renowned in the Roaring Twenties as a haven for American bootleggers. Various schemes to attract tourists based on the city's gangster-ridden past have proved unpopular with residents, especially those who experienced this unhappy period.

The city's principal attraction is the huge **Western Development Museum (** (306) 693-5989,

decent accommodation on offer. If you visit in late May or early June, you can catch the **Yorkton Short Film and Video Festival**. The **Western Development Museum (** (306) 783-8361, is on the west side of town along Highway 16. The museum depicts "The Story of People," daily life in Saskatchewan during the eighteenth and nineteenth centuries, with displays of tools and machinery both old and new. The interiors of early homes are recreated, reflecting the style of the various ethnic groups, such as the Plains natives, the English, French, Ukrainians, and Swedes. It's open daily May to mid-September; an admission fee is charged.

The **Qu'Appelle Valley** cuts through the prairie from Lake Diefenbaker to the northwest of

50 Diefenbaker Drive at the junction of the Trans-Canada Highway and Highway 2. There are four Western Development museums in Saskatchewan, each dealing with a different area of provincial history. This branch covers the history of transportation, with displays on aviation, the railway, plus land and water transportation. Exhibits include vintage cars and aircraft, an old Canadian Pacific Railway train, a reconstructed railway station, wagons, and old snowmobiles. It's open daily during summer, closed on Mondays during winter; an admission fee is charged.

If you're keen on visiting another of the four of the Western Development museums, then you need to travel to Yorkton, which 187 km (116 miles) northeast of Regina along Highway 10 (for the two others, see WHAT TO SEE AND DO, page 274, under SASKATOON). Yorkton is a major distribution center with a population of around 16,000, and some

Regina up to the Manitoba border to the east, a route that stretches across roughly two-thirds of the province. This long, green valley of trees and lakes was a favorite place for fur traders and natives as it offered welcome respite from the prairie and was a valuable source of wood. Today it is as green as ever and is lined with parks, villages, and resorts. Route 10 from Regina will bring you to **Fort Qu'Appelle**, some 70 km (43 miles) away, which is a good place to buy local crafts. In this stretch of the valley there are a series of lakes that are excellent for fishing and swimming. The string of lakes here is popular with boaters and water-skiers. These are also ideal fishing lakes, but make sure to get a license first and familiarize yourself with the regulations.

OPPOSITE: Pinning down enthusiasm for Buffalo Days. ABOVE: The Legislative Building in Regina.

WHERE TO STAY

Expensive to Mid-range

The **Regina Inn** ((306) 525-6767 TOLL-FREE (800) 667-8162 FAX (306) 525-3630, 1975 Broad Street, Regina S4P 1Y2, is a top-rank modern hotel and convention center in the heart of downtown. It has 235 rooms and suites, most of which have balconies, and good facilities. There is a fitness center with a massage therapist on call, two attractive dining spots, and a dinner theater. There are similarly high standards at the **Sands Hotel and Resort** ((306) 569-1666 TOLL-FREE (800) 667-6500 FAX (306) 525-3550, 1818 Victoria Avenue, Regina S4P 0R1. It has particularly attractive public areas and 250 rooms and suites, all very well-equipped. There's a lovely indoor swimming pool, a restaurant and a pub. Prices at both hotels vary between expensive (for a suite with a Jacuzzi) and inexpensive (for a standard room on the weekend).

For first-class accommodation in older surroundings, book into the **Hotel Saskatchewan Radisson Plaza** ((306) 522-7691 TOLL-FREE (800) 333-3333, 2125 Victoria Avenue, Regina S4P 0S3, a grand building that dates from 1927. The public areas have an old-fashioned grandeur, and the generously proportioned rooms are furnished in modern style and with many creature comforts. There are 215 rooms and suites, including the "Royal Suite," which has indeed housed royalty. There is a cocktail lounge, and a restaurant. Prices here are in the expensive category.

Situated downtown, the **Chelton Suites Hotel** ((306) 569-4600 TOLL-FREE (800) 667-9922 FAX (306) 569-3531, at 1907 11th Avenue, Regina S4P 0J2, has 56 large rooms and suites, attractively decorated and equipped with refrigerator, microwave, and wet bar. A restaurant, a friendly atmosphere, and prices that vary from inexpensive to mid-range make this good value.

Inexpensive

The **Plains Motor Hotel** ((306) 757-8661 TOLL-FREE (800) 665-1000 FAX (306) 525-8522, downtown at 1965 Albert Street, Regina S4P 2T5, has 60 rooms with bathrooms and television. There's a pub and a dining room. Slightly to the north of the center, the **Inntowner Motor Inn** ((306) 525-3737 TOLL-FREE (800) 667-7785 FAX (306) 525-5548, 1009 Albert Street, Regina S4R 2P9, has 43 good size rooms with television, some with queen-size beds, and the hotel has a dining room and a coffee shop.

South of downtown the **Landmark Inn** ((306) 586-5363 TOLL-FREE (800) 667-9811 FAX (306) 585-2303, 4150 Albert Street South, Regina S4S 3R8, is virtually a resort hotel incorporating a large recreational complex including an indoor swimming pool with a water slide. There are 186 rooms, all well-equipped, a restaurant, and a pub.

Close to Wascana Park, the **Turgeon International Hostel (HI, IYHF)** ((306) 791-8165 TOLL-FREE (800) 467-8357 FAX (306) 721-2667, 2310 McIntyre Street, Regina S4P 2S2, is a restored heritage house with lots of character, offering dormitory-style rooms, good self-catering facilities, a laundromat, and a lovely old sitting room. It operates February 1 to December 23, and doors are open from 7 AM to 10 AM and from 5 PM to midnight.

WHERE TO EAT

The **Diplomat** ((306) 359-3366, 2032 Broad Street, is one of Regina's most elegant restaurants. Seafood and steaks, prepared expertly, are complemented by an excellent wine list.

A multitude of choices is available for moderately priced to inexpensive dining. Good Cajun cuisine is served at **Orleans Café and Oyster**

Bar ((306) 352-2000, in the Chelton Inn, 1907 11th Avenue, which is a favorite with locals who appreciate the fine service and the room's casual elegance. **Bartleby's** ((306) 565-0040, at 1920 Broad Street, is a popular dining spot and bar, with a menu that has a United Nations feel, but it's the decor that they really come here for. Heaps of Victorian curiosities adorn the place and just about every corner has some piece of memorabilia or hardware poking out of it. For English-style pub grub go to the **Elephant & Castle** ((306) 757-4405, in the Cornwall Centre at 11th Avenue and Scarth Street.

There's spicy Caribbean fare at **Brown Sugar** ((306) 359-7355, including jerk, curry dishes, and salads featuring tropical fruits and vegetables. It's located downtown at 1941 Scarth Street. **Heliotrope** ((306) 569-3373, at 2204 McIntyre Street (14th Avenue), serves vegetarian food with global influences. And, **Orleans** ((306) 525-3636, down-town at 1822 Broad Street, serves authentic Cajun cuisine in a lively Mardi-Gras style atmosphere.

HOW TO GET THERE

The **Regina Airport** is seven kilometers (just over four miles) southwest of the city center. It's about a 10- to 20-minute ride to downtown.

Greyhound TOLL-FREE (800) 661-8747 buses run from Regina to Saskatoon where connections can be made with **VIA Rail** TOLL-FREE (888) 842-7733. Buses also run to Calgary and Vancouver, Winnipeg, Toronto, and Montréal. The bus station is close to downtown at 2041 Hamilton Street ((306) 787-3340.

The two main highways into Regina are the Trans-Canada Highway (Highway 1) that runs

Royal Canadian Mounted Police at their training academy in Regina.

east and west of the city, and Highway 6 that runs from the United States Montana border to the south through the town, continuing northwards beyond Melfort. Just north of the city, Highway 11 from Saskatoon links with Highway 6, just north of Regina, which runs into the city center.

SOUTHERN SASKATCHEWAN

In the southwest corner of Saskatchewan, and stretching into southern Alberta, **Cypress Hills Interprovincial Park** ((306) 662-4411 comes as something of a surprise. It is an area of forests, hills, valleys, lakes, and streams that rise out of the prairie plains to heights of almost 1,500 m

Creek along Highway 271. The fort has been restored both inside and out, so that visitors can see for themselves the tough living conditions that the men endured. The interpretive center here shows films and has displays on the fort and the history of the police force. Among the more difficult tasks assigned to them was that of trying to persuade Chief Sitting Bull and his 5,000 braves to return to the United States after they had fled here following their defeat of Custer at Little Big Horn.

A bus from the fort will take visitors to **Farwell's Trading Post**, where costumed guides take you through the buildings and help recreate the lawless days of the whisky traders. It's open daily mid-May to mid-October; admission is free.

(5,000 ft). There are pine forests (which were mistaken by the French explorers for cypresses, hence the name), rare flowers, birds, and other wildlife. An area of the park is set aside for a resort with campsites, cabins, hiking trails, riding stables, tennis courts, golf courses, and a beach. Located on Route 21, it is open daily and a per-vehicle admission fee is charged.

This is also an area of historical significance. In 1873 it was the scene of a massacre when some Montana wolf hunters who mistakenly believed the Assiniboines were responsible for stealing their horses killed Assiniboine. The illegal trading of whisky in the area had played its part in the affair, and the massacre spurred the creation of the North West Mounted Police. In 1878 they set up headquarters at Fort Walsh, now the center of the **Fort Walsh National Historic Site** ((306) 662-3590. It is located 55 km (34 miles) southwest of Maple

SASKATOON

Saskatoon sits in the center of the prairie parkland, an area of trees and farmland that lies to the north of the wheat-growing belt and south of the forested northern wilderness. It is a small, pleasant city of around 220,000 people that lies along both banks of the South Saskatchewan River, which runs northeast to southwest through the city. Several bridges cross the river, and its banks are lined with parks offering peaceful retreats and recreation. There is a mixture of old and new buildings, generally low-rise, and there are wide downtown streets that die out around the edges of the town.

Saskatoon was founded as a temperance colony in 1882 by a group of Methodists from Ontario. They christened it after the purple berries that grew plentifully in the area. Temperance seems to have been unpopular, for at the turn of the century there were only 113 inhabitants, and even the coming of the railroad in 1890 didn't tempt new settlers here. However, in the early 1900s the agricultural potential of the area began to attract settlers from Europe and the Ukraine, and in 1906 the city was incorporated. A year later Saskatoon University was founded.

The city can offer its visitors some decent accommodation, several interesting eateries, and a warm, friendly welcome, making it a good stopover if you are on your way to the wild North Country. The Saskatoon University campus, the city's largest employer, dominates the east bank of the river. Although the university has been at

22nd Street cuts across the city dividing it into north and south, while Idylwyld Drive forms the east-west dividing line. Several galleries and shops downtown sell **arts**, **crafts**, and **antiques**, and some other outlets can be found on the east side of the river, particularly along Victoria and Broadway Avenues.

The river banks are lined with pleasant parks, trees, and recreation areas. One of the most distinguished landmarks on the west bank is the **Delta Bessborough Hotel**, a 1930s railway hotel built in the grand château style favored by the railway companies of that time. Near the Bessborough Hotel lies **Kiwanis Park**, a picnicking spot, where you can rent a canoe if you fancy some paddling.

the forefront of medical technology development, the city has still not shaken off the aura of a frontier town.

GENERAL INFORMATION

The local branch of **Tourism Saskatchewan** ((306) 242-1206 TOLL-FREE (800) 567-2444 FAX (306) 242-1955 offers information on the province and is situated in the Old Canadian Pacific Railway station, at 305 Idylwyld Drive North S7L 0Z1.

WHAT TO SEE AND DO

The downtown core lies along the west bank of the South Saskatchewan River and is a fairly small area, so most of the main attractions, with a few exceptions, are within walking distance of one another. The streets conform to a grid system, and

A little further north along the river bank, the **Ukrainian Museum of Canada** ((306) 244-3800, 910 Spadina Crescent East, preserves examples of the culture of these peasant immigrants who settled in the region during the late nineteenth and early twentieth centuries. There are displays of costumes, arts and crafts, artifacts, textiles, and photographs documenting the history of their immigration. The gift shop here sells Ukrainian cookery books, arts, and crafts. The museum is open daily from mid-May to September and closed on Mondays during the rest of the year. An admission fee is charged.

Continuing northwards along the riverbank, the **Mendel Art Gallery and Civic Conservatory** ((306) 975-7610 is housed in a modern building at

OPPOSITE: The campus of Saskatoon University. ABOVE: Bison roam at the Forestry Farm Park and Zoo in Saskatoon.

950 Spadina Crescent East. The gallery has a permanent collection of contemporary and older works from Europe and Canada, and also hosts visiting exhibitions. The building contains a small but pleasant conservatory and an interesting gift shop. It's open daily, and admission is free.

Looking across the river from the gallery you'll see the attractive gray-stone buildings of the **University of Saskatchewan** ((306) 244-4343. Tours of the campus start from Place Riel Campus Centre; places of interest here include the Biology Museum ((306) 966-4399 (open weekdays), and the Museum of Antiquities ((306) 966-7818 (open weekdays). The university's Diefenbaker Canada Centre ((306) 966-8384 (open daily) is a museum, art gallery, and research center in Canadian studies commemorating Canada's 13th prime minister. Also on the campus stands the Little Stone School House ((306) 966-8384 (open daily in summer, weekdays the rest of the year), Saskatoon's first schoolhouse and oldest public building, dating from 1887. Admission is free for all of these museums.

One of Saskatoon's two major tourist attractions is the **Western Development Museum** ((306) 931-1910 at 2610 Lorne Avenue South. It is one of four such museums in Saskatchewan (the others are in Yorkton, Moose Jaw — see WHAT TO SEE AND DO, page 267, under REGINA; and North Battleford — see below), each of which is devoted to a different aspect of the province's history. The subject dealt with by this museum is "Boomtown 1910," and the museum brings that period of Saskatchewan's history very much to life in an impressive indoor reconstruction of an entire street of that year, complete in every detail. Care has been taken to represent the period not only in visual terms but also in smells and sounds, creating a vivid impression of life at that time. As you stroll along the wooden sidewalks, past the horse-drawn buggies and automobiles, you can peruse the remedies on display at the pharmacy, look in the windows of the stores, and even see a silent movie at the picture house. The street also has a fully equipped Chinese laundry, a bank, a railway station, and a school. Other areas of the museum have collections of old cars, aircraft, and farming equipment. There's also a display on the mail order services that were an important part of life for many families until quite recently. The No. 1 bus will take you from Second Avenue downtown to the museum. The museum is open daily, year-round; an admission fee is charged.

Saskatoon's other big attraction is **Wanuskewin Heritage Park** ((306) 931-6767, RR 4, located five km (three miles) north of Saskatoon on Highway 1. This museum complex is built around the ongoing archeological excavation of 19 ancient Indian sites. You can walk the trails and observe archeological digs in progress, including living

areas, teepee rings, bison jumps, and other remnants of the Northern Plains peoples who once inhabited the area. At the amphitheater, there are performances presented by native dancers and storytellers, while at the outdoor activity area visitors can learn how to build a teepee, bake bannock, or tan a moose hide. The main exhibition halls feature artifacts, interactive computer displays, multimedia shows exploring the archeology and culture of the Plains peoples, and contemporary art. The park complex is open from Victoria Day to Labor Day daily from 9 AM to 9 PM; fall and winter Wednesday to Sunday from 9 AM to 5 PM. An admission fee is charged.

Eight kilometers (five miles) northeast of downtown along Attridge Drive lies the **Saskatoon Zoo** ((306) 975-3382. This pleasant verdant area houses around 300 animals and birds, mainly those indigenous to North America. There are recreation areas as well (including cross-country skiing in winter) along with picnic and barbecue facilities, making it a nice spot for a family outing. It is open daily throughout the year, and an admission fee is charged, with a additional vehicle fee in the summer months.

Excursions from Saskatoon

The **Batoche National Historic Site** ((306) 423-6227, lies 88 km (55 miles) northeast of Saskatoon along the banks of the South Saskatchewan River, and is a must for anyone interested in the history of the Northwest Rebellion. Batoche was the site of a major Métis settlement in the nineteenth century and was the headquarters for Louis Riel's Provisional Government, which was set up to fight for the lands of the Métis people. At the park you can tour four battlefield areas and view a film at the visitor center. The Interpretive Centre has displays on the Métis culture and the rebellion, and altogether the park pays a moving tribute to Métis people and their plight. The park is open from mid-May until mid-October; an admission fee is charged. To get there, take Highway 11 from Saskatoon, turn onto Highway 312 at Rosthern, then north onto Highway 225, which brings you to the park.

There are more history lessons in store, quite fun ones too, at the **Battlefords**, the two communities of Battleford and North Battleford, divided from one another by the North Saskatchewan River and lying 140 km (87 miles) northwest of Saskatoon. Battleford sits on the south side of the river and was once the capital of the Northwest Territories, but it lost this status when the Canadian Pacific Railway laid their line further south. It was the site of a North West Mounted Police fort built in 1876, and at **Fort Battleford National Historic Site** ((306) 937-2621, Central Avenue, you can see the restored fort which has been fitted with authentic artifacts and furnishings. Within the palisades there are five buildings, including the Officers' Quarters, the Commanding Officer's Residence, and the Barracks. The Interpretive Centre provides some good displays on the 1885 rebellion. It's open daily, and an admission fee is charged.

Across the bridge, North Battleford was created because the Canadian National Railway ran its line along the north shore of the river, and it contains another **Western Development Museum** ((306) 445-8033 located at the junction of Highways 16 and 40. This one takes the "Heritage Farm and Village" as its theme, and there are extensive displays on agricultural equipment and techniques, as well as a reconstruction of a small village of 1925 vintage. The village includes pioneer homes, a Ukrainian Orthodox church, and a railway station. It is open from the beginning of May until mid-September. To get to the Battlefords from Saskatoon, the most direct route is along the Yellowhead Highway (Highway 16) to North Battleford. An admission fee is charged.

Protecting a slice of northern coniferous forest and wildlife at the center of Saskatchewan, **Prince Albert National Park** ((306) 663-4522 TOLL-FREE RESERVATIONS (888) 333-7267 FAX 306-663-5424, PO Box 100, Waskesiu Lake, SK S0J 2Y0, lies 200 km (124 miles) north of Saskatoon and 90 km (54 miles) north of Prince Albert, is a preserve of lakes, streams, hills, and forest — where coyotes, black bears, elk, moose, beavers, and many others roam free. As well as canoeing it offers its visitors hiking trails ranging from easy walks to backpacking hikes that last for days, and cross-country skiing in winter.

Just inside the eastern entrance of the park lies **Waskesiu Lake**, and along its shores the Waskesiu townsite. With accommodation of all descriptions, cafés, and shops, it makes an excellent base from which to explore the park. Waskesiu has a beach, a golf course, tennis courts, stables, and boat rentals, and you can take a leisurely cruise along the lake aboard a paddle-wheel. The **Nature Centre** ((306) 663-4509, gives interesting and entertaining presentations on the park, telling the story of Grey Owl, the self-styled naturalist who lived in the park during the 1930s and spoke out for the cause of conservation. There's an interactive exhibit on the boreal forest and its inhabitants, and the center offers guided walks. It's open daily from June to September.

WHERE TO STAY

Expensive to Mid-range

The **Sheraton Cavalier** ((306) 652-6770 TOLL-FREE (800) 325-3535 FAX (306) 244-1739, 612 Spadina Crescent East, Saskatoon S7K 3G9, is a modern downtown hotel that has just about all the facilities you could wish for, including special executive facilities. There are 250 rooms, with lots of

comforts and enough recreational features to keep all the family happy. There are two indoor water slides, a sun deck, an attractive dining room, a café, and a nightclub.

Close to the airport, the **Saskatoon Inn** ((306) 242-1440 TOLL-FREE (800) 667-8789 FAX (306) 244-2779, 2002 Airport Drive, Saskatoon S7L 6M4, has 250 sumptuously decorated rooms with sitting areas. The hotel has a lovely courtyard filled with tropical plants, a pleasant indoor pool and whirlpool, a smart restaurant, and a more casual dining spot. There's nightly entertainment and dancing in the hotel lounge.

The **Delta Bessborough** ((306) 244-5521 TOLL-FREE (800) 268-1133 FAX (306) 653-2458, 601 Spadina

Crescent East, Saskatoon S7K 3G8, is Saskatoon's most distinguished hotel, built in the grand château style of railway hostelries and set in attractive gardens overlooking the river. The hotel retains its 1930s splendor while incorporating modern conveniences. There are 225 rooms, all slightly different but quite spacious with old-style furnishings. There is an indoor swimming pool, a Japanese steak house, a bistro, a pleasant lounge, and a coffee shop. The hotel also has special business facilities. Also on the riverbank is the **Radisson Hotel Saskatoon** ((306) 665-3322 TOLL-FREE (800) 333-3333 FAX (306) 665-5531, 405 20th Street East, Saskatoon S7K 6X6, a newish 18-story building with an ornate lobby and 290 well-decorated rooms. There are luxury suites available, and

There is superb fishing to be found in the many lakes of central Saskatchewan.

the hotel offers guests an excellent range of recreational facilities, including two indoor water slides. There are also several dining spots to choose from.

At Prince Albert National Park there is lodge and convention center in Waskesiu townsite at the **All Season Waskesiu Lake Lodge** ((306) 663-6161 FAX (306) 663-6144, 175 Lakeshore Crescent, Saskatoon S7J 3T4. Despite the name, it's open May to mid-October.

Inexpensive

The **King George Hotel** ((306) 244-6133 TOLL-FREE (800) 667-1234 FAX (306) 652-4672, 157 Second Avenue North, Saskatoon S7K 2A9, is conveniently located downtown opposite The Bay department store. The building dates from 1905, but all rooms are equipped with modern facilities. There's a restaurant and a bistro. The **Senator Hotel** ((306) 244-6141 FAX (306) 244-1559 is of a similar vintage and is also in the downtown area at 243 21st Street East, Saskatoon S7K 0B7. The hotel retains a rather grand style throughout, and its 45 rooms are all slightly different but with the same modern amenities. The dining room has lots of character and there is an English-style pub. Also centrally located, the **Park Town Hotel** ((306) 244-5564 TOLL-FREE (800) 667-3999 FAX (306) 665-8697, 924 Spadina Crescent East, Saskatoon S7K 3H5, has newly renovated and attractive rooms all with televisions and telephones, and offers guests the use of an indoor pool.

There's no hostel in Saskatoon, but the **Patricia Hotel** ((306) 242-8861, 345 Second Avenue North, Saskatoon S7K 2B8, is just as inexpensive as one. It's located a couple of blocks from the bus depot, on the corner of 25th Avenue.

For details of **farm vacations** and **bed and breakfast** accommodations, contact the Saskatchewan Country Vacation Association ((306) 664-3278 FAX (306) 664-6822, 1308 Fifth Avenue North, Saskatoon S7K 2S2.

WHERE TO EAT

This is prairie land and consequently there are some excellent steak houses in town. **Cousin Nik's** ((306) 374-2020, 1110 Grosvenor Avenue, specializes in moderately priced surf and turf, but adds a Greek touch, both in the food and the decor. The attractive outdoor courtyard makes a particularly appealing dining spot. The splendid Delta Bessborough Hotel, 601 Spadina Crescent East, houses the two reliable restaurants: the **Samurai Japanese Steak House** ((306) 244-5521, and the **Garden Bistro**. You'll find elegant continental dining at the Ramada Inn's **R.J. Wiloughby** ((306) 665-7576, 90 22nd Street East.

St. Tropez Bistro ((306) 652-1250, 238 Second Avenue South, is a pretty and popular spot for inexpensive snacking. **Fuddruckers** ((306) 955-

7777, 2910 Eighth Street East, also inexpensive, serves good homemade hamburgers.

HOW TO GET THERE

Saskatoon International Airport is about a 10- to 20-minute drive west of downtown.

The **VIA Rail** TOLL-FREE (888) 842-7733 terminal, is at the western edge of the city on Chappell Drive. It's a five-minute walk to the bus that takes you downtown.

The **Greyhound** bus station ((306) 933-8000 is downtown at 50 23rd Street East, and it handles services between Saskatoon and Regina, Winnipeg, Calgary, Edmonton, and Jasper.

If you're **driving** to Saskatoon from Regina, you'll arrive on Highway 11, and if you're coming from Manitoba in the east or Alberta in the west, you'll probably need to take the Yellowhead Highway (Highway 16) which becomes Idylwyld Drive within the city limits. If you're driving from Prince Albert National Park or Lac La Ronge Provincial Park further to the north, you need to take Highway 2 and then pick up Highway 11 south of Prince Albert, which will bring you to the northern edge of Saskatoon.

NORTHERN SASKATCHEWAN

About 150 km (95 miles) north of Prince Albert National Park lies **Lac La Ronge Provincial Park** ((306) 425-4245 TOLL-FREE (800) 772-4064, with 340,500 hectares (841,035 acres) of lakes and forests. Over 100 lakes, including the huge Lake la Ronge, plus waterfalls and rapids, make this an ideal place for canoeing and fishing. It is open year-round. Accommodation can be found in the town of La Ronge on the southwestern edge of the lake, as well as agencies offer canoeing and camping package trips.

Northeast of Prince Albert National Park lies **Meadow Lake Provincial Park** ((306) 236-7680, a horizontal strip of parkland that surrounds a string of lakes. Like Prince Albert, it is an area of forests, lakes, and rivers that marks the transition between the northern Saskatchewan wilderness and the prairie parkland area. Visitors come here to enjoy its beautiful lakeside beaches and its wildlife, and to canoe, fish, and hike. There are tennis courts, stables, and in the winter cross-country skiing trails. The park is open year-round, and there are campsites in the park and cabins for rent.

OPPOSITE: Images of life on the prairies.

Alberta

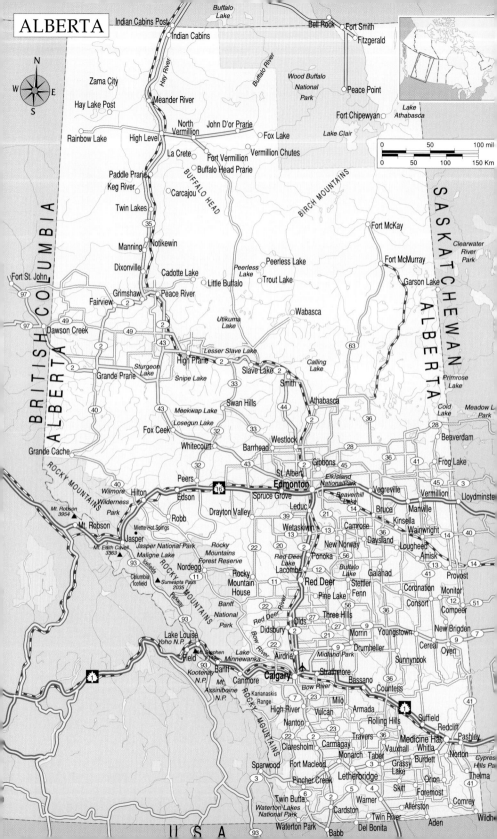

REACHING FROM THE NORTHWEST TERRITORIES to Montana, Alberta is bordered by the Canadian Rockies to the west and Saskatchewan to the east. It shares Canada's vast prairie land with Saskatchewan and Manitoba, and, covering 650,000 sq km (250,000 sq miles), it is the largest of the three Prairie Provinces. It has a population of 2.8 million, half of whom live in Calgary and Edmonton, leaving vast areas of the province uninhabited by humans.

Alberta has the cowboys, cattle, and wide-open spaces that epitomize prairie land, but it is also famous for the magnificent Rocky Mountain landscape of snowy peaks, sweeping slopes, and brilliant lakes that characterize the Banff, Jasper, and Waterton Lakes national parks to the southwest. The prairie lands of the southeast offer three different landscapes: in the southeastern corner there is an area of arid cattle-raising grassland and badlands surrounded by a larger wheat-growing belt that in turn gives way to an even larger area of parklands, trees, and mixed farming. It is in this last region that the province's major cities, Calgary and Edmonton, are located. The north of the province is a sparsely inhabited region of forests and lakes.

The exploitation of the province's oil and natural gas resources sparked a period of rapid growth and prosperity in the 1970s that brought the cities of Edmonton and Calgary to the fore. Fluctuations in oil and grain prices brought hard times in the 1980s, but these days Alberta is booming again with the fastest-growing economy in Canada. The province remains a producer of beef and grain as well as a major producer of oil and gas, with forestry. The endless outdoor opportunities that the province offers and the stunning scenery of the national parks contribute to a flourishing tourist industry.

The first European to explore the area was Anthony Henday, who acted on behalf of the Hudson's Bay Company. Among those who eased the way for the settlement of the area was Father Albert Lacombe, who founded a mission, schools, and churches, and established good relations with the Prairie natives. In 1869 the Hudson's Bay Company sold the land to the government and so Alberta became part of Canada's Northwest Territories. Whisky peddlers and fur traders descended on the area, and there followed a period of lawlessness and bloodshed, which continued until the arrival in 1874 of the North West Mounted Police.

The traders introduced guns to the native tribes, and the ease with which the buffalo could be slaughtered spelled the end of the massive herds that once roamed the prairie and had been the mainstay of the native way of life. With the herds gone, the natives were willing to negotiate treaties, and cultivation of the prairie by the whites

began in the 1880s along with immigration from Europe, Russia, and the United States. The province of Alberta was created in 1905 and the subsequent world wars and various political upheavals brought more immigrants to the province in search of a new life.

Although the discovery of oil brought Alberta prosperity and wealthy, modern cities, the province has steadfastly retained the spirit of its early ranching days. The picture-book image of the cowboy riding among herds on the plains is not an uncommon sight in the south of the province, while the days of the Wild West are celebrated each year with great gusto in the famous Calgary Stampede and Edmonton's Klondike Days festival.

EDMONTON

Alberta's capital city stands on the outer rim of the prairie, right at the center of the province, and is set around the deep valley of the North Saskatchewan River. Shiny modern high-rises testify to the prosperity of this oil town, a wealth that Edmonton seems to have handled wisely. The town is well planned: Streets conform to a grid system, underground and sheltered walkways protect citizens from the winter cold, and the river banks have been turned into parklands that provide winter and summer recreation.

With a population of 890,000, Edmonton is the largest city in Alberta and the northernmost major city in North America. It is Canada's oil capital, with some 2,000 wells within 40 km (25 miles) of

The West Edmonton Mall is not just for shopping.

the city, producing approximately 10% of Canada's oil. It deals with all the technological and scientific aspects of the oil industry, having refineries and petrochemical plants, but it leaves the administrative side of the industry to Calgary.

BACKGROUND

In the late eighteenth century two fur trading posts were established in the area, one belonging to the Hudson's Bay Company and the other to its rival the North West Trading Company. When the two companies merged in 1821 the fort that had been established in 1795 by the Hudson's Bay Company, known as Edmonton House, became the

This period of Edmonton's history is affectionately remembered every year in the town's annual Klondike Days celebrations.

When the province of Alberta was created in 1905, Edmonton, then with a population of 8,000, was elected its capital, much to the disappointment of the rival town of Calgary. It continued to grow rapidly, with a further surge of immigration during the construction of the Alaska Highway. The biggest boom of all started with the discovery of oil in 1947 at Leduc, to the south of Edmonton. The discovery of further oil fields followed and by 1965 the population had quadrupled. The 1960s and 1970s brought a period of great prosperity and frantic urban development,

trading and administrative center of the northwest and the jewel in the company's crown. The fort traded with the Blackfoot confederacy of warrior tribes who together with the Cree then inhabited the land.

In 1870 the Hudson's Bay Company sold the land to the Canadian government and the area opened to settlers. Here as elsewhere in Alberta there followed a wild and lawless period during which the town of 600 inhabitants was incorporated. Law and order finally arrived with the North West Mounted Police in 1875. In 1891 the railroad reached Edmonton, increasing its importance as a transportation center and triggering an influx of settlers. The discovery of gold in the Klondike in 1898 brought Edmonton its first boom period as prospectors flooded to the town to prepare for the long trek, increasing the population to around 4,000 and bringing prosperity to the merchants.

which in the 1980s declined with the drop in oil prices. The economic mood of the 1990s, however, has been decidedly upbeat. Edmonton remains Canada's oil center, but is not wholly dependent on this one commodity. It is also the handling and supply center for the rich agricultural area that surrounds it. Its situation also makes it the main distribution center for the mineral-rich northern Alberta, and for northern Canada as a whole.

GENERAL INFORMATION

There are visitor centers at all of the major points of entry into the province. For information on Edmonton visit one of the **Edmonton Tourism Information Centre**'s three locations: Gateway Park ((403) 496-8400 TOLL-FREE (800) 463-4667 E-MAIL edeinfo@ede.org WEB SITE www.info edmonton.com/, 2404 Calgary Trail Northbound

SW; downtown at the Shaw Conference Centre, 9797 Jasper Avenue NW; and in the Spruce Grove & District Chamber of Commerce Building, Highway 16A West, one kilometer (half a mile) west of Spruce Grove. In advance of your trip you can write to **Edmonton Tourism**, Department VG98, 9797 Jasper Avenue NW, Edmonton T5J 1N9.

Getting Around

Like most Canadian cities, Edmonton's **street plan** is laid out on a numbered grid, making it easy to find your way around. Numbered avenues run east to west. Numbered streets run north to south. Odd numbered buildings are on the east side of the street and on the south side of the avenue. Edmonton's **Light Rail Transit (LRT) System** ((403) 496-4611 runs north from the city center to Commonwealth Stadium, the Coliseum and Northlands Park, across downtown from Churchill Station to Grandin Station at 111th Street and then south to the university.

WHAT TO SEE AND DO

Should you find yourself with time on your hands, there are a handful of sites in downtown where you can while away a few hours. In the heart of the downtown area is the **Edmonton Art Gallery** ((403) 422-6223, 2 Sir Winston Churchill Square. The gallery holds temporary exhibitions of works from its own collection of contemporary and historical art, or visiting exhibitions, usually of quite a high standard. It's open daily; an admission fee is charged, free Thursday from 4 PM to 8 PM.

Southwest of the downtown core, the **Alberta Legislature**, home of the provincial government, is a dignified building of yellow sandstone, fronted with a columned portico and capped with a stately dome. Built between 1907 and 1912, it occupies the site of the original Fort Edmonton, overlooking the river and surrounded by landscaped grounds with fountains, pools, formal gardens, and lawns. Below ground, the Government Centre Pedway links the Legislature building to other government buildings and has an exhibition area where there are displays on various aspects of Alberta. The Legislature Building is at 109th Street and 97th Avenue, and there are free **tours** ((403) 427-7362 daily throughout the year.

Over on the south side of the river close to Macdonald Bridge is the unmistakable **Muttart Conservatory** ((403) 496-8755, 9626 96A Street, a group of four striking glass pyramids. Three of the structures simulate different climatic zones — tropical, arid, and temperate — and contain plants indigenous to each climate. The fourth pyramid houses changing displays. The conservatory is open daily, and an admission fee is charged.

West of downtown the **Provincial Museum of Alberta** ((403) 453-9100, 12845 102nd Avenue,

is pleasantly situated in parkland that overlooks the riverbank. This modern building contains four galleries, each devoted to a different aspect of Alberta's natural and cultural heritage. The Habitat gallery has displays that recreate the various aspects of Alberta countryside such as the mountains, the forests of the north, and the grasslands, complete with animal and plant life. The Natural History gallery deals with the geology of the area, its fossils, and the days of the dinosaurs, while the History gallery looks at the white settlement of the province. The Aboriginal Peoples Gallery has a fine collection of native artifacts. It's open daily from May 16 to September 1, Tuesday to Sunday the rest of the year. An admission fee is charged.

For a particularly enjoyable history lesson visit one of Edmonton's top attractions, the **Fort Edmonton Park** ((403) 496-8787 on the south bank of the river just west of Whitemud Freeway and close to Quesnel Bridge. This is an ambitious project that aims to recount the history of the white settlement of Edmonton in the most vivid terms. It has a detailed reconstruction of the palisaded Fort Edmonton, the 1846 Hudson's Bay Company trading post complete with "inhabitants" who are happy to chat to you about their life in the employ of the company. Outside the fort there is a recreation of village life in Edmonton during 1885 before the coming of the railroad, an Edmonton street in 1905 when the town was an expanding capital city, and a 1920 street scene showing Edmonton as a prosperous business city. Meticulous attention is given to detail, and there are shops that carry stock appropriate for the period, as well as schools, churches, and offices. To complete the experience you can ride in a restored streetcar, a steam train, a stagecoach, or a horse wagon. Special events are held here throughout the year. It's open daily, and an admission fee is charged.

OPPOSITE: The little steam train chugs its way across Fort Edmonton Park. ABOVE: Edmonton's skyline at night.

Local history will tell you that to the south of the river lies an area that was once the town of Strathcona, which joined with Edmonton in 1912. In the **Old Strathcona Historic Area** ((403) 433-5866, between 101st and 106th streets and Saskatchewan Drive and 80th Avenue, many of the buildings predate the union and have been restored. Pick up a walking tour brochure from a Tourism Information Centre and enjoy a stroll along these Victorian streets.

Coming back to modern times with a jolt, the **West Edmonton Mall** ((403) 444-5300, at 170th Street and 87th Avenue, is to date the world's largest mall, which covers a staggering 500,000 square meters (five and a half million square feet). Despite recent reports of shady dealings and mismanagement by its owners the mall is still thrivingly devoted to shopping and recreation. It holds about 800 stores, including six major department stores, over 100 places to eat, 20 cinemas, a vast water park, a large amusement park with roller coaster, a mini-golf course, and a casino. There are caged animals and performing dolphins for your entertainment, and much more besides. Like it or hate it, it's there and worth a visit for the experience alone. The mall is open weekdays from 10 AM to 9 PM, Saturday from 10 AM to 6 PM and Sunday from noon to 5 PM. An admission fee is charged.

The **Space and Science Centre** ((403) 452-9100, 11211 142nd Street, northwest of the city center in Coronation Park, is a suitably spaceship-like building containing Canada's largest planetarium, displays on astronomy and science. It's open daily from mid-June to early September from 10 AM to 10 PM; and early September to mid-June from Tuesday to Sunday from 10 AM to 10 PM. An admission fee is charged.

Each year, Edmonton really lets its hair down around mid-July when it celebrates **Klondike Days** ((403) 479-3500. Not to be outdone by Calgary's Stampede celebration, Edmonton introduced this 10-day knees-up in honor of the 1898 gold rush that brought prospectors here on their way to Dawson City. There are parades, silly competitions, music, dancing, parties, and breakfasting in the open air. Northlands Park becomes Klondike Village, and everyone from the bank manager to the shopkeeper joins in by dressing up in period costume.

Excursions from Edmonton

If you hear the call of the wild it could be coming from **Elk Island National Park** ((403) 922-3293, Site 4, Rural Route 1, Fort Saskatchewan T8L 2N7, an unspoiled wilderness of forests and lakes which is a wildlife reserve, only 48 km (29 miles) east of Edmonton on Route 16 (the Yellowhead Highway). Elk, wood bison, moose, and deer roam here, and hundreds of species of birds can be seen. The park has hiking trails varying in length from

2.5 to 18 km (1.5 to 11 miles), cross-country skiing trails over rolling terrain, and a lake for canoeing and swimming. Camping is permitted throughout the year. The Astontin Interpretive Centre tells you all about the park, which is open year-round. An admission fee is charged.

Further east along Highway 16 and about 50 km (31 miles) east of Edmonton lies the **Ukrainian Cultural Heritage Village** ((403) 662-3640, a reconstruction of an early settlement of these immigrants who arrived in Alberta in droves during the 1890s and contributed greatly to the cultural development of the province. A reception area has exhibitions on the lives of these pioneers and on the story behind their immigration. It's open daily between May 15 and October 14; an admission fee is charged.

SPORTS AND OUTDOOR ACTIVITIES

The North Saskatchewan River snakes its way east-west through the city with a long green belt of parkland running along both banks. This is Canada's largest stretch of city parkland, one long recreation area strewn with cycling paths and trails. The River Valley Parks and Outdoor Centre ((403) 496-7275 that stretches for nearly 30 kilometers (19 miles) along both banks of the North Saskatchewan River has all kinds of facilities, including networks of **jogging**, **running**, and **cycling** trails. In the winter there are **cross-country skiing** trails here and also at Elk Island Park. In the summer Elk Island is also a pleasant spot for **swimming**.

NIGHTLIFE AND THE ARTS

You'll find Edmonton to be particularly well-endowed with theaters and theatrical companies. To check what's on in Edmonton, pick up a copy of one of the free monthlies, *The Edmonton Bullet* or *Something Entertaining*.

The **Citadel Theatre** ((403) 425-1820, 99th Street and 101A Avenue, is a major Canadian performing arts center. This impressive glass-and-brick complex houses five theaters where a variety of first-rate stage and musical productions are performed, and there is also a pleasant indoor garden where you can while away some time. The **Northern Alberta Jubilee Auditorium** ((403) 427-9622, 87th Avenue and 114th Street, is another venue for theater, ballet, and concerts, and is home to the **Edmonton Symphony Orchestra** ((403) 429-1414, the **Edmonton Opera** ((403) 424-4040, and the **Alberta Ballet Company** ((403) 428-6839. There are also many other theater venues scattered throughout Edmonton, including a couple of dinner theaters. Edmonton holds the **Fringe Theatre Festival** ((403) 448-9000 for 10 days in late August when alternative theater productions crop up all over the city, both indoors and outdoors.

For jazz, there's the **Yardbird Suite** ((403) 432-0428, 10203 86th Avenue, and there are occasional jazz concerts at the **Northern Alberta Jubilee Auditorium** (above). The city has dozens of bars and eateries that double as nightclubs and feature a wide range of music. You can hear rhythm and blues at the **Sidetrack Café** ((403) 421-1326, 10333 112th Street, where you can also enjoy some excellent food.

Café Select ((403) 423-0419, 10018 106th Street, is the after-theatre spot for a quiet drink. The city's biggest patio at **Earl's** ((403) 448-5822, 11830 Jasper Avenue, is jammed every Friday night before the club scene gets underway. Don't forget, though, that this is cowboy country: Down a cold one at **Cowboys Country Saloon** ((403) 481-8739, 10102 180th Street, then move along to the dance floor at **Cook County Saloon** ((403) 432-2665, 8010 103rd Street, voted Canada's nightclub of the year for five years running.

Edmonton's casino is the **Baccarat** ((403) 413-3178, downtown at 10128 104th Avenue. It's open every day from 10 AM to 3 AM for the slot machines and from noon to 2 AM for live action gambling.

WHERE TO STAY

Mid-range

The superb **Sheraton Grande Edmonton** ((403) 428-7111 TOLL-FREE (800) 263-9030 FAX (403) 441-3098, 10235 101st Street, Edmonton T5J 3E9, has some of the best accommodation in town and is conveniently connected to a major shopping mall. The hotel has two good restaurants, a beautiful lounge set amid an indoor garden, a pub, and an indoor swimming pool. The rooms are elegantly

A ride in one of Fort Edmonton Park's horse-drawn wagons.

furnished and have well-equipped bathrooms. The **Westin Hotel** ((403) 426-3636 TOLL-FREE (800) 228-3000 FAX (403) 428-1454, at 10135 100th Street, Edmonton T5J 0N7, is another first-rate hotel. Its rooms and suites are beautifully decorated and luxuriously furnished. It houses the excellent Carvery Restaurant, and has an indoor pool.

If you feel like being really frivolous, take one of the themed rooms at the **Galaxyland Hotel & Resort** ((403) 444-3000 TOLL-FREE (800) 661-6454, 17700 87th Avenue, Edmonton T5T 4V4, over in northwest Edmonton in the larger-than-life West Edmonton Mall (formerly called Fantasyland). There is a Polynesian room, a Roman room, a Hollywood room, an Arabian room, and the in-

3982 FAX (403) 426-6260, 10049 103rd Street, Edmonton T5J 2W7, has 86 apartments comfortably furnished with compact but well equipped kitchens. The hotel has an exercise room, a sun deck, and most things you need for self-catering. For an added touch there's complimentary coffee, fruit juice, and morning paper. Weekly and monthly rates are available.

For accommodation in one of Edmonton's few older establishments, try **La Bohème** ((403) 474-5693, 6427 112th Avenue, Edmonton, T5W 0N9. Known primarily as a very good French restaurant, it now offers a few charming suites, which, like the service, are continental in style and quite charming. Breakfast is included in the price.

triguingly named Truck room, to name but a few, all with whirlpools, and some with steam baths. Prices vary between mid-range and expensive.

Mid-range to Inexpensive

Downtown, the **Edmonton House Suite Hotel** ((403) 420-4000 TOLL-FREE (800) 661-6562 FAX (403) 420-4008, at 10205 100th Avenue, Edmonton T5J 4B5, has 300 attractive suites with balconies and kitchens; and a very good range of facilities and services that include an indoor pool, an exercise room, and a bar. They also offer a free shuttle to the Edmonton Mall. The neighboring **Econo Lodge** ((403) 428-6442 TOLL-FREE IN CANADA (800) 613-7043 FAX (403) 428-6467, at 10209 100th Avenue, Edmonton, T5J 0A1, is very good value with 73 nicely furnished rooms. There's a pub as well as a restaurant. Also downtown, the **Alberta Place Suite Hotel** ((403) 423-1565 TOLL-FREE (800) 661-

Assistance with **bed and breakfast** accommodation is available through Alberta's Gem B&B Reservation Agency (/FAX (403) 434-6098, 11216 48th Avenue, Edmonton T6H 0C7.

The **Edmonton International Hostel (HI)** ((403) 429-0140 FAX (403) 421-0131 E-MAIL eihostel @HostellingIntl.ca, is located at 10422 91st Street, Edmonton T5H 1S6, and has 50 beds and offers mountain bike rentals.

WHERE TO EAT

Edmonton's cultural mix makes for a healthy restaurant scene with a wide choice of cuisines, but as a prairie town it has its own specialty: some of the best beef in Canada. You will find concentrations of restaurants in the Old Strathcona district between 101st and 106th streets, the downtown area, and the Boardwalk Market at 103rd Street.

La Bohème ((403) 474-5693, at 6427 112th Avenue, is housed within an older building close to downtown and is decidedly French in both cuisine and ambiance. You'll find some of the best French fare in town here, and there is a wine cellar to match. It is open throughout the week; reservations are recommended. The menu is also French at **La Ronde** ((403) 428-6611, the revolving restaurant at the top of the Crown Plaza Château Lacombe, 10111 Bellamy Hill. Unlike many of its counterparts, it is not only a feast for the eyes: the food and the service are also of a high standard.

One of the best steak houses in town, **Hy's Steak Loft** ((403) 424-4444, 10013 101st Street, is a good place to sample some of the province's first-rate

107th Avenue, and on the south side ((403) 434-4448, at 7909 104th Street.

The stylish **Russian Tea Room** ((403) 426-0000, 10312 Jasper Avenue, does indeed serve Russian tea along with wonderful cakes and pastries; it also has a restaurant menu where you'll find traditional Russian dishes.

HOW TO GET THERE

Edmonton International Airport is located 28 km (17 miles) south of the city along Highway 2, and the drive into downtown takes about 30 minutes. The **Sky Shuttle** ((403) 465-8515 runs between some of the big downtown hotels and the airport.

beef. The **Unheardof** ((403) 432-0480, at 9602 82nd Avenue, offers *prix-fixe* menus featuring excellent international cuisine prepared with fresh ingredients; desserts are to die for. **The King and I** ((403) 433-2222, 8208 107th Street, in Old Strathcona, serves the best Thai cuisine in town.

The family-run **Smokey Joe's Hickory Smokehouse** ((403) 413-3379, at 156th Street and 87th Avenue, serves hickory-smoked ribs, poultry, and sausages in large helpings and in a warm, friendly atmosphere. There are light meals at the much-loved **Vi's** ((403) 454-4300, 13408 Stony Plain Road, where desserts, including homemade pies, are a specialty. The cozy and affordable **Crêperie** ((403) 420-6656, at 10220 103rd Street, is Edmonton's most romantic restaurant, where the French cuisine is country style.

Doan's has authentic Vietnamese cuisine at two locations: downtown ((403) 424-3034, at 10023

Edmonton lies at the center of the what remains of Canada's trans-national rail network, with three weekly **VIA Rail** ((403) 422-6032 TOLL-FREE (888) 842-7733 trains scheduled, which also connect with Jasper. The new station is at 12360 121st Street.

The **Greyhound** bus terminal ((403) 413-8747 is at 10324 103rd Street, and operates services that extend north to Hay River in the Northwest Territories and to Whitehorse in the Yukon Territory, west to Prince Rupert, and south to Drumheller and Calgary. **Red Arrow** ((403) 424-3339 TOLL-FREE IN ALBERTA (800) 232-1958, 10014 104th Street, serves Calgary, Red Deer, Rocky Mountain House and Fort McMurray. **Motorists** will find the Trans-

Children splash OPPOSITE while adults ABOVE shop at the West Edmonton Mall, the world's largest shopping complex. OVERLEAF: Telephone poles march single-file across the prairies of eastern Alberta.

Canada Yellowhead Highway (Highway 16) — which runs from Winnipeg through Edmonton to British Columbia — easy to join. Highway 2 runs the 514 km (320 miles) from the United States Montana border via Calgary to Edmonton, and continues northwards.

CALGARY

Calgary sprawls over prairie land that seems to stretch ever eastwards, but it lies in the foothills of the Canadian Rockies and so to the west of the city you can see the magnificent snow-tipped mountains some 80 km (50 miles) away. Originally a small settlement at the confluence of the Bow and Elbow rivers, Calgary now spreads over the largest land area of any Canadian city, and has become a high-powered city of mirrored high-rises, malls, and other modernities. The climate here is generally dry and sunny with hot summers, and winters that can get bitterly cold but are tempered by the warming Chinook winds from the mountains. These winds can raise temperatures quite dramatically within hours and also have the delightful effect of creating some of the most dramatic sunsets that you'll see anywhere on the prairie.

The character of the city also has its contrasts: On the one hand it is undeniably an oil boom town, with glittering skyscrapers and busy traffic, but it also retains the identity of the cow town it once was, and this is the image that the residents are eager to nurture. The people behave in a way you don't quite expect from the inhabitants of an oil-rich city of glass and steel: they are almost aggressively friendly, and they love to lay on the welcome for visitors. And of course it's almost impossible to think of Calgary without the word "Stampede" springing to mind. This annual festival—held in early July—seems to get the whole of Canada reaching for cowboy hats and boots. Visitors and cowboys pour in from all over the world to join in the yeehawing and the explosion of rodeos, chuck-wagon races, dancing, parades, and general merrymaking.

BACKGROUND

In 1875 the newly formed North West Mounted Police were sent here to restore peace to an area where whisky traders and fur trappers had been cooking up trouble and fanning wars between the natives. They set up a fort at the point where the Bow and Elbow rivers meet; the commander of police named it after Calgary Bay in his native Scotland. Settlers clustered around the post almost immediately, and in 1877 a treaty was signed, without bloodshed, in which the native tribes who roamed the area relinquished the land to the government in return for certain provisions and rights.

The Canadian Pacific Railway came to Calgary in 1883, and this together with the offer of free land to settlers brought about rapid population growth. The excellent grazing lands of the prairie brought the ranchers and their huge herds from the United States, so the town continued to expand, becoming an important meat-packing center and the hub of the farming and ranching region. By 1891 the population was around 4,000; in 1893 the city was granted a charter.

In 1914 the discovery of oil in the Turner Valley just southwest of Calgary brought prosperity to the area, but it was the big strike in Leduc in 1947 and subsequent discoveries in the Edmonton area that triggered the meteoric rise in Calgary's fortunes. The city has become the administrative center for Canada's petroleum industry and now over 500 oil and gas companies have their headquarters here. In the late 1960s there began a 20-year period of frantic development with sky-

scrapers breaking out like a rash, dramatically changing the face of the city and turning it into a perpetual building site while the population exploded to around 640,000. Though things quieted down in the 1980s, the city's hosting of the Olympic Games in 1988 brought the area to the world's attention. The 1990s have brought yet another surge of development and Calgary is now second only to Toronto as a Canadian financial center. The city is growing at an astonishing rate, and the visitor information center is as much a welcome wagon as it is a tourist service.

GENERAL INFORMATION

For information on Calgary and the surrounding area, call or drop by the **Calgary Convention and Visitors Bureau** ((403) 263-8510 TOLL-FREE (800) 661-1678 E-MAIL tourismcalgary.com WEB SITE www.visitor.calgary.ab.ca/, whose main office

is at 237 Eighth Avenue SE, Suite 200, Calgary T2G 0K8. There is also a year-round visitor center at the Tower Centre, junction of Ninth Avenue and Centre Street and two others at the Calgary International Airport on the arrivals and departures levels, open 10 AM to 10 PM daily.

Getting Around

Calgary is divided into northwest, southwest, southeast, and northeast sections, and this is important to note as you'll find NE, SE, SW, or NW forming part of the addresses here. The east and west dividing line is Centre Street, and the Bow River separates north from south. Streets follow a grid system, and virtually all of them in the downtown section are one-way. Getting around the city is easy if you use the network of enclosed walkways called "Plus 15s" (because they are a

A polar bear in Calgary Zoo.

minimum of 15 ft or 4.5 m above the ground). Although this all makes for a somewhat characterless shopping scene, it provides welcome protection from the bitter cold of the winters. Just about everything in Calgary—excluding the Stampede grounds — is accessible on foot, but should you want to save some shoe leather, there is a public transportation system consisting of the **C-Train** — which runs along Seventh Avenue SW — and a bus network.

WHAT TO SEE AND DO

Begin your tour of the downtown section with a trip up **Calgary Tower** ((403) 266-7171 at Ninth

One of the most noteworthy sections here is the excellent collection of native art, including Inuit crafts. The Alberta Children's Museum is a recent addition to the complex. The museum is open daily Saturday to Thursday from 9 AM to 5 PM, Friday from 9:30 AM to 9 PM, closed Monday in winter. An admission fee is charged.

If you feel like a respite from the concrete jungle, take yourself up to the fourth level of the nearby Toronto Dominion Square at 317 7th Avenue SW, where you'll find the **Devonian Gardens** ((403) 268-3888, a one-hectare (2.5-acre) indoor oasis with fountains, pools, waterfalls, a stage for lunchtime entertainment, and, we were told, some 20,000 local and Californian tropical plants. This

Avenue and Centre Street South. A high-speed lift will whisk you to the observation deck close to the top of this 190-m (625-ft) landmark, from where you can see seemingly endless prairie land stretching to the east and the magnificent Canadian Rockies to the west. The tower contains the almost statutory revolving restaurant, and there's a café for light lunches. The Olympic flame atop the tower is lit on occasion. The observation deck is open daily year-round 7:30 AM to midnight, with slightly shorter hours between September and May; an admission fee is charged.

Over the road from the tower is the excellent **Glenbow Museum** ((403) 777-5506, 130 Ninth Avenue SE, which has an art gallery on one floor with permanent and temporary exhibitions, a floor devoted to the history of western Canada, and another to an extensive military and weaponry collection that spans medieval to modern times.

entirely organic indoor botanical garden gives visitors a clue about how Calgarians make it through those long days of 30-below winter weather. In addition to the foliage, there are fish ponds where muscular carp-koi-goi and turtles swim, as well as waterfalls and garden sculptures. There are a few snack bars here and it makes a very agreeable meeting place. It is accessible daily from 9 AM to 9 PM, except for times when it is rented out for a private function.

To understand a little more about what made Calgary rich, visit the **Energeum** ((403) 297-4293 at the main floor of the Energy Resources Building, 640 Fifth Avenue SW. The formation, exploitation, and uses of Alberta's energy resources are described through fascinating displays that involve models, computer games, hands-on presentations, and even hands-in (you can feel the oil with gloved hands). It's open Monday to

Friday all year from 10:30 AM to 4:30 PM and on Sundays between June and August. Admission is free.

Turning from the ground to the heavens, slightly to the west is the **Alberta Science Centre and Centennial Planetarium** ((403) 221-3700 at 701 11th Street SW, where there are star shows and hands-on displays that help you understand the laws of physics. There's also a small observatory where you can stargaze through telescopes. It's open Tuesday to Sunday, 10 AM to 5 PM, and an admission fee is charged. Walking distance away and to the north of downtown, **Prince's Island Park** in the Bow River offers a very pleasant and shady retreat. It makes a good

1,200 animals — in environments that simulate their natural habitats. Glass panels allow visitors to observe the seals, polar bears, penguins, and others in the water. A large **Botanical Gardens** filled with thousands of tropical plants also provides an ideal setting for exotic birds and butterflies. Attached to the zoo is the **Prehistoric Park**, where a group of life-size replica dinosaurs are set in a prehistoric landscape. The zoo is open daily throughout the year, and an admission fee is charged. There's yet more wildlife to be seen at the **Inglewood Bird Sanctuary** ((403) 269-6688, about two and a half kilometers (one and a half miles) from the zoo and southeast of the city center at Ninth Avenue and Sanctuary Road SE. In

picnic spot, with cycling and jogging trails, and is accessible by footbridge from both banks of the river.

Fort Calgary Historic Park ((403) 269-7747, 750 Ninth Avenue SE, lies at the east end of the city center at the confluence of the rivers. This was once the site of Fort Calgary, established by the North West Mounted Police in 1875. It was the birthplace of the city. Set in 16 hectares (40 acres) are the 1875 fort reconstruction, and a number of historical buildings. The Interpretive Centre offers a vivid picture of life in the days of the early settlers and traces the history of the city. It's open every day from 9 AM to 5 PM, May 1 to October 13; an admission fee is charged.

From Fort Calgary, cross the bridge to St. George's Island to see the excellent **Calgary Zoo** ((403) 232-9300. Here some 300 species of creatures great and small are represented by over

this forested reserve on the west bank of the Bow River there have been sightings of over 250 species of birds. A new Visitor Centre here offers information and natural history courses. It's open year-round; admission is free.

Stampede Park ((403) 261-0101, southeast of downtown at 14th Avenue and Olympic Way SE, is where the big events take place during the Calgary Stampede (see THE CALGARY STAMPEDE, below). It's worth a trip even when the Stampede isn't in progress just to see the stunning **Canadian Airlines Saddledome** ((403) 777-2177, a sports arena with a roof in the shape of a gigantic saddle. The Saddledome ((403) 777-2177 is the home of the Calgary Flames, the city's National Hockey League

Costumed interpreters talk shop OPPOSITE at Heritage Park's turn-of-the-century village. ABOVE: Calgary's Old City Hall, an architectural survivor amongst the modern skyscrapers.

team. While you're in the park you might like to visit the **Grain Academy** ((403) 263-4594 on the upper floor of the Round-Up Centre, a museum where models and a miniature railway show how grain is transported from the prairies to the Vancouver docks. It's open Monday to Saturday; admission is free.

For a full reconstruction of life in pioneer times and other periods of Calgary's history, you must go to **Heritage Park** ((403) 259-1900, 16 km (10 miles) southwest of town at the Glenmore Reservoir. This is the largest "living-history" village in Canada. Many original buildings have been brought here from various parts of Alberta, and an early-1900s village has been reconstructed with

a working bakery, a mill, a newspaper office, stocked-up stores, and housing. You can enjoy the antique midway rides, take a trip on a restored steam train or go out onto the reservoir aboard the old sternwheeler the **SS** *Moyie*. There are also plenty of places to snack or dine here. It's open daily year-round; an admission fee is charged. An old-fashioned pancake breakfast (9 AM to 10 am) is included in the price of admission.

Continuing south along the Macleod Trail, then left along Bow Bottom Trail SE, you'll come to **Fish Creek Provincial Park** ((403) 297-5293 which spreads out along eight kilometers (five miles) at the edge of the city boundary. This parkland, through which Fish Creek runs, is a wildlife sanctuary but is also where people come simply to escape from city life. There is a magnificent colony of great blue heron here as well as archeological sites, a lake for swimming — and in winter there's cross-country skiing and ice skating. The park is open daily and admission is free.

The impressive facilities which Calgary built for the 1988 Winter Olympics are still in use, and the **Olympic Park** ((403) 286-2632, which was the main site for free-style skiing, ski jump, luge and bobsleigh events, stands to the west of town, a 10-minute drive along Highway 1 (the Trans-Canada

Highway) from the center. You can explore the site for yourself or join a guided tour (highly recommended). A ski lift takes you to the top of the course from where you can gaze down the 90-m (295-ft) ski jump tower and see the courses from the perspective of the Olympic athletes who tackled them. The **Olympic Hall of Fame and Museum** has three floors stacked with Olympic memorabilia, photographs, and films and a virtual trip down all 14 twists and turns of the bobsleigh track. You can also take the Bobsleigh Bullet — a summer luge ride on the ice. Olympic park is open year-round. Admission fees are charged for the tour, museum, and Bobsleigh Bullet.

The Calgary Stampede

Billed as "The Greatest Outdoor Show on Earth," the Calgary Stampede is a 10-day celebration of Calgary's Wild West days. It takes place every July and has been going since 1912. Everyone gets into the spirit of it, donning Stetsons, jeans, and boots. There is a big parade with dancing in the streets, while hearty breakfasts are served up around town. Calgary's nightlife percolates, too, with all sorts of special events. The **Radisson** and **Westin** feature nonstop dancing in the hotel ballrooms. Southeast of the town at Stampede Park there are bands, more dancing, food, livestock shows, and the real business of the Stampede: the rodeo and the chuck-wagon races. For the professional cowboys who take part in the rodeo and make their living from the sport, this is serious business with big prize money awaiting only the first-prize winner in each of seven main events. Visitors need to reserve their tickets and accommodation well in advance. For details of the event contact the Calgary Exhibition and Stampede ((403) 261-0101 TOLL-FREE (800) 661-1260, PO Box 1060, Station M, Calgary T2P 2K8.

Excursions from Calgary

The foothill region of **Kananaskis Country** lies between Calgary and the Rocky Mountains. This area is protected by several provincial parks, created to take some of the pressure off Banff. Along the Trans-Canada Highway 106 km (66 miles) west of Calgary and 20 minutes east of Banff townsite, the community of **Canmore** is nestled at the base of the Three Sisters Mountain Range. The

The small town of **Fort Macleod** is approximately a two-hour drive south of Calgary, and is one of Alberta's earliest settlements. It is the site of the first North West Mounted Police post, and is named after their first commander, Lieutenant Colonel James Macleod. This force (now the Royal Canadian Mounted Police) was formed in 1873 to enforce law and order in the west, where at that time the whiskey traders were wreaking havoc, and their first action was to set forth on a grueling march from Manitoba through the northwest which brought them here in 1874. The **Fort Macleod Museum** ((403) 553-4703 is built in the fashion of a police post, with log buildings surrounded by a wooden palisade. The log build-

town center has plenty of shops, and eateries and is a good base for outdoor activities in the Kananaskis region which encompasses three provincial parks, including the **Peter Lougheed Provincial Park** ((403) 591-6344, Alberta's largest. With 500 sq km (190 sq miles) of valleys and lakes and hiking trails. Canmore was the sight of the 1988 Olympic cross-country skiing and biathlon events, and the **Canmore Nordic Centre** ((403) 678-2400 still draws skiers in winter and mountain bikers in summer.

The resort of Kananaskis Village and the adjacent **Nakiska Ski Area** ((403) 591-7777, and **Kananaskis Country Golf Course** ((403) 591-7272 are reached via Highway 40, south of the Trans-Canada Highway. The Canmore Nordic Centre and Nakiska Ski Area were 1988 Winter Olympic sites. Kananaskis Village is the departure point for many hiking and cross-country skiing trails.

ings contain displays on the way of life of the Mounties, of the province's pioneers, and of the natives. The **town center** is itself worth a visit as it contains many old buildings and has been declared a Provincial Historical Area. Drop by the visitor booth ((403) 553-2500 for information on self-guided tours.

The luridly named **Head-Smashed-In Buffalo Jump** lies 18 km (11 miles) northwest of Fort Macleod along Highway 2 and Secondary Highway 785. For over 5,000 years natives stampeded herds of buffalo to their deaths over the edge of this steep cliff. These hunts were an important part of the native culture, involving hundreds of men,

OPPOSITE: In the badlands a Richardson's ground squirrel packs in the peanuts. Calgary's Olympic Park LEFT and ABOVE — the main site for the 1988 Winter Olympics — is now enjoyed year-round by skiers, bobsledders and mountain bikers.

precise planning, and religious rituals. The hunt would provide the natives with food, hides, and bone. Archaeological digs at this UNESCO World Heritage Site have uncovered bones, village sites, and First Nations artifacts. The Head-Smashed-In Buffalo Jump **Interpretive Centre ℂ** (403) 553-2731 is a seven-level complex built into the cliff; it describes the culture of the Plains native people, in particular the Blackfoot, and the business of the hunt itself through films, displays, and guided walks of the site. It's open daily throughout the year; an admission fee is charged.

Approximately 55 km (33 miles) south of Fort Macleod, the lower peaks of **Waterton Lakes National Park** ascend abruptly from grasslands

of the extreme southwestern corner of Alberta — giving rise to the park's sobriquet "the place where the mountains meet the prairie." Waterton Lakes is situated along the Montana-Alberta border where it joins with the United States' Glacier National Park — with which it shares the designation of a "Biosphere Reserve" that is a UNESCO World Heritage Site because of the region's unique geological history.

Accommodation and visitor services are located in the townsite of **Waterton Park**, and the Parks Canada Visitor Centre ℂ (403) 859-2445 or (403) 859-2224 is just north of the townsite, on Highway 5.

Though only 525 sq km (189 sq miles) in area, Waterton Lakes contains scenery as wondrous as any of the bigger Canadian Rockies parks, as well as abundant recreational activities. Backpackers and hikers can enjoy the park's 225 km (135 miles) of trails. There are motorboating and boat tours on Upper Waterton Lake, as well as canoeing at the townsite marina and at Cameron Lake. Upper Waterton Lake has an almost constant wind, averaging 32.5 kph (19.5 mph) making windsurfing a top draw. Scuba divers can explore the wreck of a sunken paddle steamer in Emerald Bay. Picnicking, tennis, bicycling, and swimming round out the summer activities. Winter access is restricted

by road closures, but skiing, snowshoeing, and waterfall ice climbing take place.

A one-and-a-half-hour drive northeast of Calgary will bring you to the strange, lunar-like landscape of the **badlands**, characterized by gullies and deeply carved canyons. This area was once a subtropical marshland where dinosaurs roamed, and there have been many discoveries of fossils and skeletons in the area.

Located in this strange landscape is the small city of **Drumheller**, the starting point of the **Dinosaur Trail**, a 48-km (30-mile) circular driving route taking you to various places of interest in the area and offering some good views of the badlands. The Infocentre ℂ (403) 823-6300 is at 703 Second Avenue West, where you can pick up a copy of the *Visitors Guide to the Drumheller Valley* which lists 30 separate stop-offs.

Though mostly commercial and an attempt to capitalize on the dinosaur theme that is well-enough spun out by the Royal Tyrrell Museum and the provincial parks (see below), the Dinosaur Trail is a fun jaunt through the badlands history and geography. You can take an all-terrain vehicle ride through **Horsethief Canyon**, cross the Red Deer River on the 1913-vintage **Bleriot Ferry** that works on a pulley system, cross the **Rosedale Swinging Suspension Bridge**, visit the tumbleweed town of Rosedeer, and drop in to the **Last Chance Saloon** where wagon wheels and elk horns decorate the façade and bullet holes riddle the interior.

On Highway 10, shortly after the hamlet of Cambria (don't blink), turn left into the **Hoodoos Provincial Recreation Area**. These bizarre rock formations were created by 10,000 years of wind and rain erosion; protective caps of hard sandstone prevent the pillars from eroding as quickly as the surrounding rock. Cross-sections of the regions geological history, the hoodoo's shale base was once the floor of an ancient sea, now some 73 million years old; the sandstone above this was deposit by swamps and streams in the dinosaur era 70 million years ago.

About six kilometers (four miles) northwest of Drumheller, the **Royal Tyrrell Museum** TOLL-FREE (888) 440-4240 FAX (403) 823-7131 E-MAIL rtmp@dns.magtech.ab.ca WEB SITE www.tyrrellmuseum.com, PO Box 7500, Drumheller, Alberta T0J 0Y0, contains the largest exhibition of dinosaurs in the world. This excellent paleontological museum presents theories about evolution up until the appearance of man with over 35 complete dinosaur skeletons, hands-on displays, and a variety of special programs. You can watch museum technicians at work behind a glass window, chipping away a millimeter at a time at huge stone-encrusted skeletons. The curators are clearly aware of the esthetic as well as the scientific interest of the fossils, and offer displays emphasizing the myriad patterns and colors of petrified organisms, such as delicate million-year-old seed ferns, swirling ammonites, a rainbow-hued ammolite, a gemstone that is unique to Alberta. The star exhibit at the Tyrrell is the Burgess Shale blacklight presentation where you can see the oldest known multicellular marine animals — "weird wonders" — at 12 to 20 times their actual size.

There are multilingual audio-guides available for taking a self-guided tour of the museum. It's open in summer daily from 9 AM to 9 PM, and in winter Tuesday to Sunday from 10 AM to 5 PM. An admission fee is charged.

The museum is situated in **Midland Provincial Park** and a trail system gives you the chance to walk through the grounds where exposed fossils are often found. But remember that Alberta has strict laws to preserve the province's heritage. All fossils are the property of the people of Alberta; collecting is permitted only outside of the provincial parks.

The museum's Day Digs program gives you the chance to go out and **dig for dinosaurs** with trained technicians, and do the actual work of excavating.

Those who have caught the dinosaur bug may want to extend their journey to the **Dinosaur Provincial Park**, environs and excursions Dinosaur Provincial Park ((403) 378-4342 FAX (403) 378-4247 WEB SITE discoveryweb.com/aep/parks/dinosaur, PO Box 60, Patricia T0J 2K0, 140 km (87 miles) southeast of Drumheller, an area of the Red Deer Valley badlands that is also a UNESCO World Heritage Site. It is one of the most extensive dinosaur graveyards in the world, and throughout the park skeletons are on view exactly in the position that they were discovered. So extensive are the remains that they say you're never more than two feet from a fossil here. In the park you can visit the **Royal Tyrrell Museum Field Station** ((403) 378-4342 where you can see the paleontologists working on finds. It's open daily from mid-May to mid-October, weekends only in winter. An admission fee is charged.

There's an interpretive display here, and it is also the starting point for a bus tour of the park and guided walks. Interpretive programs run daily mid-May to early September. Admission is free; there is a fee for the bus tour To reach the park from Drumheller, take Route 56 to Brooks then Highway 873 and follow the signs.

Those who wish to continue to walk with the dinosaurs can journey even further back into prehistory with trips to the Burgess Shale fossil beds in Yoho National Park (see YOHO NATIONAL PARK, page 328).

Cochrane, 25 km (16 miles) west of Calgary, is a favorite spot for trail rides and canoe trips on the Bow River. It's western style buildings house some interesting local arts and crafts. The **Western Heritage Centre** ((403) 932-3514, near the junction of Highways 22 and 1A, is a new hands-on interpretive center with exhibits that tell the story of ranching, farming, and rodeos in the province. You can learn about the first Alberta ranchers and the families who still perform those same chores today. It's open daily year-round and an admission fee is charged.

SPORTS AND OUTDOOR ACTIVITIES

There are **cycling**, **hiking**, and **jogging** trails in the pleasant Prince's Island Park, which is accessible by footbridge from downtown, and also at

Fish Creek Provincial Park at Calgary's southern border. The Olympic Park has a brand new **mountain bike** course with lots of challenging trails; bikers and their steeds ride the ski lift to the top of the mountain and zigzag their way down. For **horseback riding**, the Happy Trails Riding Stable ((403) 251-3344 in Fish Creek Park, gives lessons and also operates guided or unguided trail rides.

The Bow and Elbow rivers are popular for **canoeing**, particularly at Bowness Park ((403) 288-5133 at 48th and 90th Street NW. There's world-class fly **fishing** and trout fishing in the section of the Bow River between Carseland and east Calgary, and lists of the many places that offer fishing trips are available from information centers.

In winter there's **skating** on the lagoon at Bowness Park, 48th Avenue and 90th Street NW, also at Fish Creek Provincial Park, and year round in the covered speed-skating track at the Olympic Speed Skating Oval ((403) 220-7954 at the University of Calgary, which is open for public use. In all, there are 17 skating rinks in Calgary; contact Calgary Parks and Recreation ((403) 268-3888

OPPOSITE: One of the Royal Tyrrell Museum's Jurassic monsters. This scale model shows a T-Rex, one of the dinosaurs that once walked the badlands. ABOVE: Home on the range — a latter-day monster haunts the streets of Calgary.

for information. The **downhill ski slopes** at the Olympic Park are open to the public, and there's **cross-country skiing** at Fish Creek Provincial Park.

NIGHTLIFE AND THE ARTS

For **entertainment listings** you should check the local daily and weekly newspapers, especially the Friday *Herald*, and the *Sun*. Several large hotels have nightclubs, and offer quite a variety of entertainment.

Calgary's cultural life centers around the **Centre for the Performing Arts (** (403) 294-7455 at 205 Eighth Avenue SE. This excellent arts complex comprises the Jack Singer Concert Hall, which is

home to the Calgary Philharmonic Orchestra. The Alberta Ballet Company performs at the **Jubilee Auditorium (** (403) 297-8000, 14th Avenue and 14th Street NW. The **Pumphouse Theatre (** (403) 263-0079, 2140 Ninth Avenue SW, features a variety of theatrical performances during its September to June season. Concerts and dramatic works both classical and contemporary are presented at the **University of Calgary Theatre (** (403) 220-4900, 2500 University Drive NW.

Calgary has hundreds of bars and clubs, many of which have live music. Jazz and blues can be enjoyed at **Kaos Jazz and Blues Bistro (** (403) 228-9997, 718 17th Avenue SW, or at **McQueen's (** (403) 269-8889, 317 10th Avenue SW. Local and touring alternative bands can be seen at **Republik (** (403) 244-1844, at 219 17th Avenue SW, or at **The Night Gallery (** (403) 266-5116, 1209B First Street SW, which is primarily known for its theme nights, often with live bands. For country & western there's the **Ranchman's Restaurant (** (403) 253-1100, 9615 Macleod Trail South, where there's also beer swilling and dancing; or **Dusty's Saloon (** (403) 263-5343, 1088 Olympic Way SE, where there are free two-step lessons on Tuesday and Wednesday nights. There's a stretch of 11th Avenue known as **Electric Avenue** that consists of a stretch of bars, clubs and pubs, or there's

the less noisy and older neighborhood of **Kensington** centered around Kensington Road and 10th Street NW — a good area for restaurants, pubs, bars, and nightlife.

Calgary has several casinos, including Alberta's largest, the **Stampede Casino (** (403) 261-0422, at Stampede Park. It's open Monday to Saturday from noon to 1 AM.

WHERE TO STAY

Expensive

Downtown, the **Palliser Hotel (** (403) 262-1234 TOLL-FREE (800) 441-1414 FAX (403) 260-1260, at 133 Ninth Avenue SW, Calgary T2P 2M3, was built by the Canadian Pacific Railway in 1914. With its pillars, stately staircases, and crystal chandeliers, it remains an oasis of old-fashioned splendor in this city of steel high-rises. It has just about every comfort provided for. There are exercise facilities, a splendid dining room, a café, and a lovely bar. For a more modern kind of elegance there's the centrally located **Calgary Marriott (** (403) 266-7331 TOLL-FREE (800) 333-3333 FAX (403) 262-8442, at 110 Ninth Avenue SE, Calgary T2G 5A6, which is within the Convention Centre complex. It is luxurious without being brash, and the service echoes this quality with its understated excellence. Rooms and suites have all kinds of special features, and there's an indoor pool and garden, two dining rooms, and a bar with live entertainment.

Also downtown, the **Westin Hotel (** (403) 266-1611 TOLL-FREE (800) 228-3000 FAX (403) 233-7471, 320 Fourth Avenue SW, Calgary T2P 2S6, offers modern luxury with 525 attractive bedrooms and suites, and lots of complimentary touches. The lobby is large and sumptuously decorated, there is a beautiful indoor swimming pool, and the hotel has several dining spots including the city's famous Owl's Nest restaurant. The **Delta Bow Valley Inn (** (403) 266-1980 TOLL-FREE (800) 665-8571 FAX (403) 266-0007, 209 Fourth Avenue SE, Calgary T2G 0C6, is another large, top-rated, downtown hotel that has exercise facilities, a children's center, indoor swimming pool, and a restaurant. The **International Hotel of Calgary (** (403) 265-9600 TOLL-FREE IN WESTERN CANADA (800) 661-8627 TOLL-FREE IN EASTERN CANADA AND THE UNITED STATES (800) 223-0888 FAX (403) 265-6949, 220 Fourth Avenue SW, Calgary T2P 0H5, is a modern highrise that exudes luxury. It has 250 attractive suites. All have balconies and are extremely comfortable. It also has a health spa, a gym, a restaurant, and a piano bar.

Located in a leafy residential area, northwest of the city center, **A Good Knight Bed & Breakfast (** (403) 270-7628 TOLL-FREE (800) 261-4954, 1728 Seventh Avenue NW, Calgary T2N 0Z4, is one of the new breed of luxury bed and breakfast accommodations. A happy combination of homespun style and soothing comforts make this a good choice for anyone looking for a relaxing, friendly stay. Throughout the house, decor is quaint in the extreme — all part of your eager hosts' efforts to make you feel at home. Their teddy bear collection is astounding. While two of the three individually decorated rooms are smallish, a third is quite spacious; a cathedral ceiling, a king-size bed and a jet bath complete the picture. An ample breakfast is served downstairs in the dining room each morning, and special dietary needs are gladly catered for. Rates range from moderate to expensive.

Mid-range

The **Sandman Hotel (** (403) 237-8626 TOLL-FREE (800) 726-3626 FAX (403) 290-1238, 888 Seventh Avenue SW, Calgary T2P 3J3, is centrally situated and offers an excellent range of facilities. It has 300 attractively furnished rooms, some with good views, with all kinds of comforts and conveniences. There is a fitness center, a glass-roofed swimming pool, and a Denny's Restaurant, which is open 24-hours. The **Prince Royal Inn All Suite Hotel (** (403) 263-0520 TOLL-FREE (800) 661-1592 FAX (403) 298-4888, downtown at 618 Fifth Avenue SW, Calgary T2P 0M7, has 300 one- or two-bedroom suites with kitchens, making it good value for families. The hotel has laundry facilities, a health club, and a dining room.

In northwest Calgary there is a motel strip along Banff Trail, near the point where Crowchild Trail crosses the Trans-Canada Highway. Along this strip, the **Quality Inn-Motel Village (** (403) 289-1973 TOLL-FREE (800) 661-4667 FAX (403) 282-1241, 2359 Banff Trail NW, Calgary T2M 4L2, has one of the best ranges of facilities. The 100 suites and rooms have telephones and televisions, and there is a poolside dining room as well as a cocktail lounge.

Inexpensive

Downtown is the **Lord Nelson Inn (** (403) 269-8262 TOLL-FREE (800) 661-6017 FAX (403) 269-4868, 1020 Eighth Avenue SW, Calgary T2P 1J2, with 55 rooms and suites that have private bathrooms, refrigerators, televisions, and telephones. There are also some bridal and executive suites. The hotel has a warm and attractive lobby, a dining room, and a pub.

There is a cluster of motels along Macleod Trail near Stampede Park. Among them is the **Elbow River Inn & Casino (** (403) 269-6771 TOLL-FREE (800) 661-1463 FAX (403) 237-5181, 1919 Macleod Trail SE, Calgary T2G 4S1. It sits on the banks of the Elbow River and is connected by an underpass walkway to Stampede Park. All of its 75 rooms have bathrooms, some have kitchenettes. There is a dining room with pleasant riverfront views, and a full breakfast is included in the rates,

which vary from mid-range to inexpensive. The **Flamingo Motor Hotel (** (403) 252-4401 FAX (403) 252-2780, 7505 Macleod Trail South, Calgary T2H 0L8, is set in pleasant grounds and has 50 good-sized rooms and suites with bathrooms, some with kitchenettes. Rates here range between inexpensive and mid-range. The **Stampeder Inn (** (403) 243-5531 TOLL-FREE (800) 361-3422 FAX (403) 243-6962, at 3828 Macleod Trail SW, Calgary T2G 2R2, has nicely appointed rooms and suites, meeting facilities, an indoor pool, shops, a pub, a cocktail bar, and a dining room that lays on an generous buffet.

For **bed and breakfast, farm** and **ranch** or **backcountry lodge accommodation**, contact the Bed

& Breakfast Agency of Alberta **(** (403) 277-8486 TOLL-FREE (800) 425-8160, 410 19th Avenue Northeast, Calgary T2E 1P3. In Drumheller, there's the Drumheller Valley Bed and Breakfast Association **(** (403) 823-5379 FAX (403) 823-9712 E-MAIL gkashuba@telusplanet.net, 71 McDougall Lane, Drumheller T0J 0Y1. Specifically for guest ranch accommodation in the area there's the **Homeplace Guest Ranch & Trail Rides (**/FAX (403) 931-3245, Rural Route 1, Priddis T0L 1W0. Rooms come with private bathrooms, family meals are provided, riding lessons and trips are organized, and horse pack trips up into the Rockies with tee-pee accommodation are also available. The ranch is just outside the city's south perimeter.

OPPOSITE: Calgary's nighttime skyline rides the Saddledome, home of the city's National Hockey League team, the Flames. ABOVE: Public art in downtown Calgary.

The **University of Calgary** has some good accommodation during the summer months, and also a few rooms available during term-time. For details contact the university at ((403) 220-3210, 2500 University Drive NW, Calgary T2N 1N4.

The **Calgary International Hostel (HI)** ((403) 269-8239 FAX (403) 266-6227 E-MAIL chostel@ HostellingIntl.ca, has six- to eight-bed dormitory rooms and is located at 520 Seventh Avenue SE, Calgary T2G 0J6.

WHERE TO EAT

La Chaumière ((403) 228-5690, at 139 17th Avenue SW, offers traditional French cuisine prepared

to gourmet standards and excellent service in a charming, intimate setting. The **Owl's Nest** ((403) 266-1611 in the Westin Hotel, 320 Fourth Avenue SW, is one of Calgary's best-known and finest dining spots. It is a splendidly decorated place serving continental cuisine, with the region's excellent beef featuring largely on the menu.

The **Green Street Restaurant** ((403) 266-1551, 815 Seventh Avenue SW, is a popular downtown spot, with a glass wall affording good views of the nearby park. The surrounding greenery, a restful color scheme, and the spaciousness make for a relaxing atmosphere. There are Cajun, French, and Italian dishes, steaks and seafood — in short, a bit of everything — on offer. Prices here range between moderate and inexpensive.

Informal and inexpensive places abound. **4th Street Rose** ((403) 228-5377, at 2116 Fourth Street SW, is a trendy place where you can get very good

pizzas, salads, and pasta. There are several other eateries around this section of Fourth Street. Along 17th Avenue SW you'll find another such cluster of restaurants. The **Unicorn Restaurant and Pub** ((403) 233-2666, at 304 Eighth Avenue SW, is a busy, snug place that serves traditional pub grub and lots of beer on tap. Over in the Kensington neighborhood the **Take Ten Café** ((403) 270-7010, 304 10th Street, has German food and lots of home baking on the menu.

Calgary's **Chinatown**, the second largest in Canada, begins at the downtown end of the Centre Street Bridge and extends across the river. There are plenty of Asian restaurants to choose from, some of which serve dim sum. In the back of the Hang Fung supermarket, 119 Third Avenue SE, is the **Hang Fung Foods** ((403) 269-4646, one of the best places in the city to get salt and pepper squid. It's a bit difficult to find (go through the supermarket) but worth the effort for some truly authentic Chinese food.

HOW TO GET THERE

The **Calgary International Airport** is about eight kilometers (five miles) northeast of downtown, a 30-minute drive. Canadian Airlines International runs a frequent Airbus service between Calgary and Edmonton. To get you to the town, there's the **Airporter Bus** ((403) 531-3909 which runs every 30 minutes from Level 1.

With the closure of its more scenic southern rail route through Calgary, VIA Rail no longer serves Calgary. **Rocky Mountain Railtours** TOLL-FREE (800) 665-7245 operates a scenic two-day rail tour from Calgary to Vancouver, with a one-night hotel stay in Kamloops included in the price of the fare (see RIDE THE LEGENDARY RAILS, page 20, in TOP SPOTS).

Greyhound ((403) 265-9111 operates bus services to Calgary from all directions. **Red Arrow** ((403) 531-0350 TOLL-FREE IN ALBERTA (800) 232-1958, serves Edmonton, Red Deer, and Rocky Mountain House. The station is at Eighth Avenue SW and 16th Street. It's a 30-minute walk from the city center, but during the day there's a free shuttle that will connect you with the C-Train.

The Trans-Canada Highway (Highway 1) runs through Calgary, linking it with British Columbia to the west and Saskatchewan to the east. West of Calgary the Trans-Canada Highway runs through Banff National Park and through Glacier National Park in British Columbia. Highway 2 runs north from the United States–Montana border to Calgary, continuing on to Edmonton and beyond.

ABOVE: Calgary's Chinatown is the second-largest in Canada. OPPOSITE: A Plains Indian in full regalia.

The Canadian Rockies

STRADDLING THE BORDER OF ALBERTA AND BRITISH COLUMBIA, the Rocky Mountain parks encompass some of the most breathtakingly beautiful scenery on earth. The area encompassing Kootenay, Banff, Jasper, and Yoho national parks, together with Mount Robson Provincial Park and Mount Assiniboine, is recognized as a UNESCO World Heritage Site, one of the largest protected areas in the world. In this vast nature preserve, white mountain peaks and glaciers tower over aquamarine lakes, rivers and waterfalls rush through forested valleys, and wild animals run free. North American mountaineering had its birthplace in these mountains, and adventurers from all over the world continue to pour in each year.

All of the parks present a wealth of opportunities for outdoor enthusiasts, with trails to be walked, mountains to be climbed, lakes and rivers to be fished and navigated, and in the winter a thick coat of snow turns it all into a skiers' paradise. Here in the mountains the temperature varies quite a lot, and the higher you are, the colder it is, making warm clothing an essential part of vacation luggage, even in July.

Wildlife abounds in this protected area and visitors need not go off the beaten track for glimpses of elk, deer, bighorn sheep, and an abundance of clever squirrels. Moose, black bears and grizzlies, and mountain goats are often spotted by hikers. Throughout your visit you will be constantly reminded not to feed the animals, both for their good and for your own, and to keep your distance. These animals are wild, despite their apparent ease around people. To drive the message home, the park authorities have imposed heavy fines on those caught feeding animals.

Besides being rich in wildlife and spectacular scenery, the Rocky Mountains are an open book on the earth's geological history. The sedimentary rock that makes up the mountain chain was laid down over eons beginning 600 million years ago when a vast sea covered the region. Eventually these sediments built up a 20-km (12-mile) thick

layer of rock. One hundred and forty million years ago, continental drift caused the mountains to begin to rise of out of the sea. At the same time that the mountains were lifting up the force of water and weather were wearing them down, reshaping the landscape until it began to take on the grand aspect that we see today.

BANFF NATIONAL PARK

Banff National Park is the most famous of the mountain parks, and the most popular. Situated about 113 km (70 miles) west of Calgary along the Trans-Canada Highway, Banff has two townsites that attract thousands of visitors from around the world: Banff and the smaller Lake Louise, both of which have splendid and superbly located castle-like hotels built by the Canadian Pacific Railway. The town of Banff is the park's main center for entertainment, accommodation, and restaurants, and is also the starting point for tours and trails into the park.

Banff was the first national park to be established in Canada. The region was explored in 1841 by the governor of the Hudson's Bay Company, but it was in the 1880s with the coming of the Canadian Pacific Railway that word of the area's great beauty began to spread. During the laying of the tracks three workers discovered some hot sulfur springs, and as soon as word of them got out, visitors began to arrive. In 1885 the government created the Rocky Mountain Park around the springs to preserve the area, and in 1888 the Canadian Pacific Railway opened the magnificent Banff Springs Hotel, a summer resort that was the last word in luxury. A beautiful golf course was laid, trips and expeditions were organized for its guests, and every whim was catered for. People came from far and wide, the town developed, the boundaries of the park were expanded and its name was changed to Banff National Park. Today it covers an area of 6,640 sq km (2,600 sq miles).

GENERAL INFORMATION

Travel Alberta ((403) 427-4321 TOLL-FREE (800) 661-8888 WEB SITE www.discoveralberta.com/html/Canada/Alberta/, PO Box 2500, Edmonton, Alberta T5J 2Z4, **Tourism British Columbia** ((604) 685-0032 TOLL-FREE (800) 663-6000 WEB SITE www.tbc.gov.bc.ca/tourism/, Parliament Buildings, Victoria, British Columbia V8V 1X4, and **Parks Canada** ((403) 292-4401 TOLL-FREE (800) 651-7959 FAX (403) 292-6004 WEB SITE parkscanada.pch.gc.ca/, 220 Fourth Street SE, Room 552, Calgary T2G 4X3, are all good sources of informa-

Visitors to Banff and Jasper need not get off the beaten track for glimpses of bighorn sheep ABOVE and elk OPPOSITE BOTTOM. A snow-covered Banff church TOP rests below Mount Rundle.

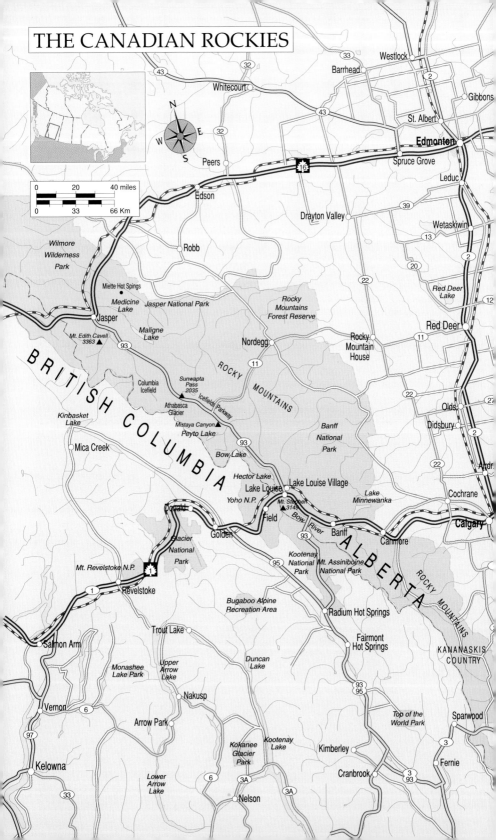

tion on the parks. The park information centers carry maps, pamphlets, and brochures, which include details of the various trips and trails throughout the area. They also give valuable advice on how to protect yourself against attack from animals, on weather conditions, and on survival skills.

For information specifically on Banff and region, contact or visit the **Park Information Centre** ((403) 762-1550 at 224 Banff Avenue, PO Box 900, Banff T0L 0C0, **Banff-Lake Louise Tourism Bureau** ((403) 762-8421 at the same address, or the **Lake Louise Visitor Centre** ((403) 522-3833, Village Road, beside Samson Mall, PO Box 213, Lake Louise T0L 1E0. If you're planning on an overnight hiking trip, you must sign in at either the Banff or Lake Louise information center. **Internet access** is available in Banff at Internet Services ((403) 762-5149, 210 Bear Street, but rates are steep.

WHAT TO SEE AND DO

Banff

Sixteen kilometers (10 miles) beyond the park gates, the town of Banff lies in the Bow River valley, nestling close to the base of Cascade Mountain and shadowed by snowy peaks on all sides. It is the hub of the Banff National Park and Canada's favorite year-round resort. You'll find everything you need here. It is the starting point for scores of trips, some on horseback, some in the bicycle saddle, some on coaches, and others tailored for a variety of outdoor pursuits. There are all kinds of walking trails to places that cars cannot reach, and the most timorous to the most intrepid of hikers will all find something to suit them. But unless you are prepared to hike long distances you will require transport to take you at least part of the way to many of the top attractions.

The town is small, however, and during the peak season of July and August it gets jam-packed, parking becomes a problem, and it can get quite claustrophobic — especially along Banff Avenue, the town's busy main street lined with shops and restaurants.

A Victorian wooden building houses the **Banff Park Museum** ((403) 762-1558, 93 Banff Avenue, where you can see old-fashioned displays of stuffed animals and birds from the park: the only place where you can study some of them up close. There is also a reference library where you can read up on the area. It's open daily year-round; an admission fee is charged. A little further along the road, the **Natural History Museum** ((403) 762-4747, 112 Banff Avenue, deals with the geological formation of the Rockies and the early life forms that inhabited them. There are audiovisual displays, exhibits on dinosaurs, and a model of Sasquatch, the Rockies' version of the abominable snowman. It's open daily; admission is free.

At the southern end of the town near the Bow River, a fortified log building houses the **Luxton Museum** ((403) 762-2388, 1 Birch Avenue, where there are displays on the various native tribes of Alberta, featuring photographs, clothing, and crafts. It's open year-round, daily in summer, Wednesday to Sunday afternoon in winter; an admission fee is charged. The **Whyte Museum of the Canadian Rockies** ((403) 762-2291, at 111 Bear Street, has a gallery devoted to paintings and sculptures of the mountains as well as exhibits chronicling the human history of the region. It also houses archival material, and some historical log cabins. Tea is served on weekend afternoons by the fireside. The museum is open daily from mid-May to

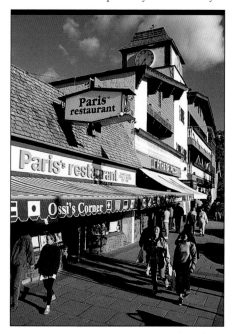

mid-October, and is closed on Mondays and on Thursday mornings during the rest of the year. An admission fee is charged.

West of downtown along Cave Avenue you can see the original hot sulfur spring that first brought tourism to the area. Railway workers discovered the Cave and Basin Hot Springs in 1883 and the spa building that surrounds them has been rebuilt in the original 1914 style. Here at the **Cave and Basin Centennial Centre** ((403) 762-1566 you can visit the interpretive display that details the history of the area. It is open daily throughout the year; an admission fee is charged. At the **Upper Hot Springs Pool** ((403) 762-1515, south of town at the top of Mountain Avenue, you can enjoy a dip in the outdoor hot-spring pool (average

Banff Avenue — a corridor of commercialism, but the mountains are never out of view for long.

temperature: 40°C or 108°F), and soak up the glorious mountain views. It's open daily year-round; an admission fee is charged.

About three kilometers (two miles) south of town and next to the Upper Hot Springs is the **Sulphur Mountain Gondola Lift(** (403) 762-2523. Completely remodeled in 1998, the gondola is a gleaming, Swiss-made state-of-the-art aerial tramway to the top of Sulphur Mountain (2,285 m or 7,500 ft). Once at the top you can feast your eyes on the wonderful views from an observation deck with its 360-degree view of the Bow Valley, or follow one of several hiking trails and see bighorn sheep grazing. You can also enjoy a repast at the moderately priced Panorama Room with set dinners

see the strange column-like rock formations known as **hoodoos**.

For a different angle on the landscape take a trip to **Lake Minnewanka** 11 km (seven miles) west of the town where Lake Minnewanka Tours **(** (403) 762-3473 will take you on a 90-minute cruise across the waters. Boats sail daily at 10:30 AM, 12:30 PM, 3 PM, and 5 PM, with an evening cruise in July and August at 7 PM; a fare is charged. You can contact the same outfit for guided fishing trips. Nearby, **Two-Jack Lake** is a popular spot for rowing and canoeing.

Northwest of Banff, 28 km (17 miles) along Highway 1A, there's a lovely one-and-a-half-hour hiking trail leading from **Johnston Canyon** that

featuring salmon and prime rib; or have a light meal or a snack at the Summit Restaurant. The gondola is open daily year-round; a fare is charged.

Following the discovery of the springs, the Canadian Pacific Railway built the **Banff Springs Hotel** (see WHERE TO STAY, below), a magnificently located tourist resort close to the springs. So great was its success that in 1910 the hotel was rebuilt to accommodate the growing number of visitors, and a majestic Scottish baronial-style structure emerged from the pine-covered slopes. If you're not staying at Banff Springs during your visit, you should at least make sure to have a meal there, or take the historical tour, so you can take a look around it and admire the beautiful setting.

The other mountains around the town also have hiking trails, and one of the more gentle climbs close to downtown is up **Tunnel Mountain** along Tunnel Mountain Drive, where you can

takes you by waterfalls and pools. You can extend the hike by a couple of miles into a lovely meadow where there are some deep-colored underground springs known as the **Ink Pots**.

Lake Louise

In 1882, the explorer Tom Wilson became the first European to lay eyes on Lake Louise, proclaiming: "As God is my judge, I never, in all my explorations of these five chains of mountains throughout western Canada, saw such a matchless scene." The lapis-blue Lake Louise, mirroring the 3,464-m (1,154-ft) tall Victoria Glacier, has been enchanting visitors ever since.

The first question most people ask on arriving at Lake Louise is: "Where's the lake?" That's because the *village* of Lake Louise is located some distance below the actual *lake* of Lake Louise. Most of the amenities are located in the village along with restaurants and lodging. Up at the lake, the Canadian Pacific hotel, Château Lake Louise is piled high along the shore and a few other hotels are strung out along the road to the lake.

The **Samson Mall** is the center of village commercial life with several retail shops and restaurants. Right next door is the **Lake Louise Information Centre (** (403) 522-3833, Village Road and Lake Louise Drive, just off the Trans-Canada Highway. Parks Canada staffs the center year-round and the Banff/Lake Louise Tourism Bureau operates there during summer months. There is an excellent and entertaining interpretive display on mountain formation — a good overview of the fascinating geological history of the Rockies.

Of course, you can't miss seeing Château Lake Louise. Though its exterior is an eyesore, the interior is tastefully lavish. The lobby has a lovely lounge with an arched window looking out on the Victoria Glacier, a wonderful place to stop for refreshment.

Back in the village there are a couple of side trips worth considering. On the other side of the Trans-Canada Highway, four and a half kilometers (almost three miles) from the village, the **Lake Louise Summer Sightseeing Lift (** (403) 522-2095 takes you up Mount Whitehorn (2,040 m or 6,700 ft). There's a teahouse, picnic areas and all sorts of hiking trails to explore at the top. The lift runs daily from June 1 to September 15. And 15 km

There are several options for laid-back **hikes** around the village, the most obvious being a the valley-bottom stroll along the Riverside Loop (seven kilometers or four and a half miles) which takes you along the Bow River and past the old train station. If you want to stretch your lungs a bit, take the four-and-a-half-kilometer (three-mile)-long footpath to Lake Louise from the village.

Up at the lake the favorite pastime is gazing at the scenery. As you stroll around the shore on the paved footpaths, look for golden-mantled ground squirrels amongst the rocky banks and Clark's nutcrackers, large gray and black birds with a long black beak. The lake is the starting point for some challenging hikes that lead to the base of the glacier or to a number of other, smaller but equally beautiful glacier-fed lakes. The visitor center has complete and current information on all of the hikes and activities in the area.

(eight miles) south of Lake Louise lies **Moraine Lake**, another beautiful and improbably colored lake that is surrounded by the Wenkchemna Peaks, named for the Stoney native word for the number "ten." Until 1989, these mountains were featured on the Canadian twenty-dollar bill. You will find picnicking and boating facilities here in season.

SPORTS AND OUTDOOR ACTIVITIES

Both Banff and Lake Louise have a wealth of **hiking** trails of all lengths. Some are little more than short walks, while others are wilderness expeditions that take several days to complete. Parks

All quiet at the boat house — OPPOSITE: Inside Maligne Lake Boathouse, guidesman Barry Wood organizes his gear. ABOVE: Lake Louise canoes wait patiently for the spring melt.

Canada ((403) 292-4401 TOLL-FREE (800) 651-7959 FAX (403) 292-6004 WEB SITE parkscanada.pch .gc.ca/ produces brochures detailing the trails, and copies of these can be picked up from the information centers. If you're planning an overnight hike into the backcountry you will need to buy a permit from either an information center or a park warden. There are also numerous **cycling** trails, which must be strictly adhered to. A few companies operate cycling tours, and renting bikes is easy in both towns. Several companies offer **heli-hiking**, which involves a helicopter trip out to remote spots high on the mountaintops or onto glaciers for some extra-special hiking. If you intend to do a spot of **fishing**, and there certainly

During the winter there's excellent **skiing** throughout the parks. Banff's nearest slopes are at Mount Norquay ((403) 762-4421 SNOW PHONE (403) 762-4421 extension 6, only five kilometers (three miles) away from town, and the well-equipped Sunshine Village Resort ((403) 762-6500 SNOW PHONE (403) 760-6543, about 16 km (10 miles) west of the town, where there are ski lifts and more than 60 runs. Sunshine Village comprises a 1960s-era hotel and several restaurants. In summer there are hiking trails that lead through alpine meadows. At Lake Louise there's the Lake Louise Ski Area ((403) 522-3555 SNOW PHONE (403) 762-4766 offering runs of up to eight kilometers (five miles), some of the longest runs in the Rockies.

are some ideal opportunities in both parks, you must get a national parks fishing license, which can be bought either from an information center or an outfitter. Several places run fishing trips and rent out tackle.

Rivers throughout both parks offer opportunities for **whitewater rafting**, and information centers can supply you with lists of the companies who operate guided trips. If you're interested in **boating** or **canoeing**, there are many beautiful lakes to choose from, most of which have places that rent out a variety of vessels. **Motorboats** are permitted only on Minnewanka Lake.

Horseback riders have a choice of many treks of varying lengths and designed for all abilities. There are several stables in both parks, including one at the Banff Springs Hotel. The information centers have details of where the stables are and what they have to offer.

NIGHTLIFE AND THE ARTS

Banff's cultural life revolves around the **Banff Centre** ((403) 762-6300 TOLL-FREE (800) 413-8368, which is near downtown at St. Julien Road. You'll almost always find there's a concert, a play, or a film presented here, and between June and August it is the venue for the world-famous **Banff Arts Festival**, when a program of theater, music, and dance is presented. For information on current and upcoming events, phone or visit the box office in the lobby of the Eric Harvie Theatre ((403) 762-6301 TOLL-FREE (800) 413-8368, St. Julien Road.

There are several busy bars in Banff, mostly around Banff Avenue, and some in the hotels. Several have live musical entertainment. **Barbary Coast** ((403) 762-4616, 119 Banff Avenue, has blues, funk, and jazz bands in its upstairs lounge. Celtic and maritime bands are featured at the **St. James's Gate Olde Irish Pub** ((403) 762-9355, 205 Wolf Street. For country and western as well as live rock bands, there's **Wild Bill's** ((403) 762-0333, upstairs at 201 Banff Avenue, which also has line-dancing lessons every Wednesday night.

WHERE TO STAY

Reservations are strongly advised for the summer season in both Banff and Lake Louise. **Banff/ Lake Louise Central Reservations** ((403) 762-5561 TOLL-FREE (800) 661-1676 can help you sort out the dizzying options.

you can bask in the myriad mineral pools or simply lounge by the fireside. A frighteningly thorough list of "therapies" is available here, from "fresh cell RNA/DNA" to "alphahydroxy AHA peels" — all designed to make you beautifully relaxed. Despite its many offerings, this massive hotel may not be to everyone's tastes. Its very fame works against it: Tour groups may receive preferential treatment, and overbooking can be a problem in peak seasons. Rates start in the expensive category and mount skyward.

Though the Banff Springs is more famous, many say the **Rimrock Resort** ((403) 762-3356 FAX (403) 762-4132 TOLL-FREE (800) 661-1587, 100 Mountain Avenue, Banff, Alberta T0L 0C0,

Banff
EXPENSIVE

The most renowned accommodation in the Rockies is at the **Banff Springs Hotel** ((403) 762-2211 TOLL-FREE (800) 441-1414 FAX (403) 762-5755, on Spray Avenue, PO Box 960, Banff, Alberta T0L 0C0, a splendid château overlooking the Spray Valley and surrounded by towering peaks. It was here in 1882 that the Canadian Pacific Railway built its first resort hotel, to encourage tourism in the area. It was so popular that it soon had to be replaced by this larger structure, which was completed in 1928 — with no expense spared. It remains a resort with riding stables, skiing and fishing packages available, almost every kind of sports facility, including one of the most spectacular golf courses anywhere. There are 841 beautiful rooms and suites, 14 restaurants, a library, shops, and services. At the new European-style spa **Solace**

on the road to the Sulphur Mountain Gondola, is the place to go if you want to do Banff in style. This 345-room hotel is magnificently situated, and amenities are superlative. Equally luxurious, but with a rustic Rocky-mountain atmosphere, the **Buffalo Mountain Lodge** ((403) 762-2400 FAX (403) 762-4495 TOLL-FREE (800) 661-1367, on Tunnel Mountain Road, PO Box 1326, Banff, Alberta T0L 0C0, has 100 rooms and suites with fireplace, whirlpool, and kitchenette. Recent renovations have made this old standby quite popular.

A number of Banff hotels offer good value at the low end of the expensive price range: The **Banff Park Lodge** ((403) 762-4433 TOLL-FREE (800) 661-9266 FAX (403) 762-3553, 222 Lynx Street,

OPPOSITE: The view from Château Lake Louise.
ABOVE: The elegant Banff Springs Hotel.

PO Box 2200, Banff, Alberta T0L 0C0, is just a couple of blocks away from the town's main street, and elegantly decorated throughout, with 210 rooms with balconies. There is an indoor swimming pool, restaurants, and a lounge. **Inns of Banff** ((403) 762-4581 TOLL-FREE (800) 661-1272 FAX (403) 762-2434, 600 Banff Avenue, PO Box 1077, Banff, Alberta T0L 0C0, is an attractive resort, where the rooms have balconies and lots of luxurious touches. It has an indoor and a large outdoor swimming pool, a squash court, a good dining room and lounge, and a Japanese restaurant. The hotel offers special winter ski packages with a ski rental and repair shop on site. The newly renovated **Douglas Fir Resort and Chalets** ((403) 762-5591 FAX (403) 762-8774, PO Box 1228, Banff, Alberta T0L 0C0, is a particularly good choice for families with its tangle of indoor water slides. Accommodation is in rustic chalets with kitchenette, fireplace and patio looking out onto wooded grounds where elk graze. There's a small grocery store on the premises.

MID-RANGE TO INEXPENSIVE

At the high end of the mid-range price category, there are two hotels at which share the excellent facilities at the Inns of Banff resort: **Rundle Manor Apartments/Hotel** ((403) 762-5544 TOLL-FREE (800) 661-1272 FAX (403) 762-0703, 348 Marten Street, PO Box 1077, Banff, Alberta T0L 0C0, is an attractive stone building which has 24 large units with kitchenettes, including some one- and two-bedroom suites. The **Swiss Village** ((403) 762-4581 TOLL-FREE (800) 661-1272 FAX (403) 762-2434, 600 Banff Avenue, Banff, Alberta T0L 0C0, has 50 units and offers ski packages.

Whatever the season, our favorite place to stay in Banff is **Eleanor's House** (403) 760-2457 FAX (403) 762-3852 E-MAIL info@bbeleanor.com, 125 Kootenay Avenue, PO Box 1553, Banff, Alberta T0L 0C0. Here guests have the best of both worlds: a friendly host with boundless energy (that's Eleanor) and the comfort and privacy of an inn (rooms are located in an addition to a private home). You can enjoy the company of other guests at breakfast or at evening cocktails in front of the cozy fireplace. Rooms are tastefully and comfortably furnished with en-suite bath, and the house is conveniently located in a quiet residential area within a few paces of downtown. Rates are in the high end of the mid-range. Winter ski-week packages are inexpensive — an excellent deal.

In all there are some 25 bed and breakfast places in Banff. For a list, contact the **Bed and Breakfast Bureau** ((403) 762-2110, 121 Cave Avenue, Banff, Alberta T0L 0C0.

The **Banff International Hostel** (403) 762-4122, PO Box 1358, Tunnel Mountain Road, Banff, Alberta T0L 0C0, three kilometers (two miles) out-side downtown on Tunnel Mountain Road, is an attractive building with good facilities and accommodation for 154 people.

Lake Louise

In Lake Louise Village, the **Post Hotel** ((403) 522-3989 TOLL-FREE (800) 661-1586 FAX (403) 522-3966, PO Box 69, Lake Louise, Alberta T0L 1E0, is a lovely alpine-style building with 100 rooms and suites, some of which have lofts and large river-stone fireplaces, while others have self-catering facilities. Suites have generous bathrooms with Jacuzzi and plush bathrobes to snuggle into afterwards. Balconies look out over neatly trimmed lawns with stands of spruce and the sparkling Pipestone River. The hotel has an indoor swimming pool, the best dining room in the region, and a cozy tavern. In winter, the Post is the perfect ski lodge; in summer, it's just plain paradise. Rates are solidly in the expensive category.

Above the village, overlooking the beautiful ultramarine-blue waters of the lake, **Château Lake Louise** ((403) 522-3511 TOLL-FREE (800) 441-1414 FAX (403) 522-3834, Lake Louise, Alberta T0L 1E0, is another historic Canadian Pacific hotel. This pile of a hotel adds nothing to the scenic beauty of the lake, but inside there are 510 attractive rooms and suites with spectacular views. The hotel boasts a good restaurant, evening entertainment, riding stables, indoor pools — and there's canoeing on the lake. Room rates are in the expensive range. Canadian Pacific recently announced an expansion of the hotel with 80 new guestrooms to be added. This will be the last expansion of this already immense property as the government of Alberta has (thankfully) banned further construction around Lake Louise. Renovations are slated to be completed in 2002.

The **Lake Louise Inn** ((403) 522-3791 TOLL-FREE (800) 661-9237 FAX (403) 522-2018, 210 Village Road, PO Box 209, Lake Louise, Alberta T0L 1E0, has 220 rooms and suites, including some with fireplaces and kitchenettes, all with beautiful views of the surrounding woods. It has tennis courts, and an indoor swimming pool. The inn runs a free shuttle to Ski Lake Louise. Prices here vary between mid-range and expensive.

Despite its reputation as an exclusive destination, Lake Louise does have a good budget option. Conveniently located in the village center, the **Canadian Alpine Centre & International Hostel** (HI) ((403) 522-2200, PO Box 115, Village Road, Lake Louise, Alberta T0L 1E0, is jointly run by Hostelling International and the Alpine Club of Canada. There are two-, four-, and six-person rooms, private showers and bathrooms, laundry facilities, a central kitchen for self-catering, and a café.

Skiers at Lake Louise.

WHERE TO EAT

Banff

Many of Banff's best tables are found in its hotels. You could eat your way through the restaurants at Banff Springs Hotel for two weeks without exhausting the options. The top table here is the elegant **Rob Roy Dining Room** ((403) 762-6860, specializing in tableside flambées. But you'd miss something special indeed if you limited yourself to Banff Springs' 11 restaurants, because the best restaurant in Banff is the **Dining Room at the Buffalo Mountain Lodge** ((403) 762-2400 FAX (403) 762-4495 TOLL-FREE (800) 661-1367 on Tunnel

Mountain Road. Here, under a high ceiling built of rough-hewn timbers, diners enjoy unique Canadian cuisine featuring game and fresh flavors. Also at the lodge is the less formal **Cilantro Café** ((403) 760-3008, where California and Southwestern cuisine is served in a quaint log cabin setting or on a pleasant patio.

At least two other hotel restaurants merit mentioning. **The Pines** (Rundlestone Lodge) ((403) 760-6690 serves inventive Canadian cuisine, and like Buffalo Mountain, wild game is a specialty. Under the same ownership is **Ticino's** (High Country Inn) ((403) 762-3848, 415 Banff Avenue, where Swiss-Italian cooking is featured. The antipasto of air-dried beef, coppa ham, and mountain cheeses is a great way to begin your repast. Raclette (melted cheese with boiled potatoes, cured meats and pickles) and pasta dumplings are specialties of the house. You must save room for a *gelato* made from Ticino's specially brewed coffee.

Grizzly House ((403) 762-4055, 207 Banff Avenue, is known for its exotic fondues, some of which feature alligator and rattlesnake. For a more classical approach, there is excellent French cuisine at **Le Beaujolais** ((403) 762-2712, at the corner of Buffalo Street and Banff Avenue. Choose from à la carte dining, the three-course *table d'hôte*

dinner, or the six-course "chef's surprise." The sophisticated menu is complemented by an award-winning wine list.

Banff has a multitude of informal dining spots. Steak features on the menu along with burgers at **Melissa's** ((403) 762-5511, at 218 Lynx Street. For good Italian fare try **Giorgio's Trattoria** ((403) 762-5114, at 219 Banff Avenue, where there's a warm, intimate atmosphere, or if pizzas and subs will do, you could go to **Aardvark's** ((403) 762-5500, 304a Caribou Street. For English-style food try the **Rose and Crown** ((403) 762-2121, 202 Banff Avenue (upstairs), and for pan-European dining try the **Paris' Restaurant** ((403) 762-3554, 108 Banff Avenue, with its reputation for

generous servings of steak and seafood. Whole Atlantic lobster and schnitzel are house specialties. **Bruno's Café & Grill** ((403) 762-8115, 304 Caribou Street, is a great spot for a casual lunch or dinner; "wraps" (burritos) and paninis are popular choices — but not as popular as the cookies. There's a takeout counter for those in a rush.

The best place for coffee and morning pastries is **Evelyn's Coffee Bar** ((403) 762-0352. Located on Banff Avenue near corner of Caribou Street. This cozy hole-in-the-wall is renowned for its delicious homemade baked goods, which you can enjoy along with French roast coffee or iced cappuccino.

ABOVE: The wintery landscape LEFT at Lake Louise, and the Weeping Wall RIGHT along the Icefields Parkway. OPPOSITE: Moraine Lake, a few kilometers east of Lake Louise.

Lake Louise

Canada's highest village has some very high-caliber dining establishments. Most notable, and not to be missed, is the **Post Hotel** ((403) 522-3989, in Lake Louise Village. Many people consider this the best table in the Rockies. Built in 1942 for alpine enthusiasts, the Post offers European cuisine with a California influence. The dining room is cozy with its low exposed-beam ceiling and wood-burning fireplace. Reserve early to get a window table and a view of the Victoria Glacier. Among the four restaurants at Château Lake Louise is the elegant **Edelweiss Dining Room** ((403) 522-3511 where diners can also revel in glacier views and enjoy Canadian and continental cuisine.

The Samson Mall has a number of inexpensive places to eat, including **Bee Line** ((403) 522-2077, with chicken and takeout pizza by the slice; the small eat-in or takeout café/bakery **Laggans Deli** ((403) 522-2017; and the **Village Grill and Bar** ((403) 522-3879, for a family sit-down dinner. At the end of Sentinel Street is the **Lake Louise Station Restaurant** ((403) 522-2600, situated in a hundred-year-old log station surrounded by vintage rail cars and gardens. The food is good, if not too imaginative, with Alberta beef and pasta dishes dominating.

HOW TO GET THERE

The nearest major airport to Banff is **Calgary International**. At the airport you can rent a car from one of several car rental companies if you wish to drive the 120 km (75 miles) to Banff. There is scheduled Airporter motor coach service between Calgary International, Banff, and Lake Louise with **Brewster** ((403) 762-6767 or **Laidlaw Canadian Rockies** ((403) 762-9102 TOLL-FREE (800) 661-4946.

You can join the private train tour to Vancouver, the **Rocky Mountaineer Railtours** ((604) 606-7245 TOLL-FREE (800) 665-7245, at Banff. The depot is at the end of Lynx Street.

In Banff, **Greyhound** ((403) 762-6767 TOLL-FREE (800) 661-8747 operates frequent service to Calgary, Edmonton, and Vancouver. The bus station is on Gopher Street near the train depot. The Trans-Canada Highway (Highway 1) runs through Banff National Park, linking it with Calgary in the east and with Vancouver in the west.

THE ICEFIELDS PARKWAY

Linking Banff with Jasper, the Icefields Parkway is one of the most beautiful drives anywhere, offering those who travel it a spectacular overview of the two national parks. It follows the continental divide along a route lined with glaciers, lakes, valleys, and mountains, where wildlife roams — sometimes into the middle of the road, so you must beware. You should set aside at least a day for

traveling the Parkway to allow time for stopping and enjoying the views.

Start at the Lake Louise Visitor Centre (see GENERAL INFORMATION, page 307, under BANFF NATIONAL PARK) where you can get a map and up-to-the-minute information on road conditions (also available by calling ((403) 762-2266). The Parkway runs north from the Trans-Canada Highway. Some 16 km (10 miles) along the Parkway north of Lake Louise you'll see the bright waters of **Hector Lake** fringed by dark green forest. Eighteen kilometers (11 miles) further along the road, the glacial waters of **Bow Lake** reflect the surrounding peaks, and a few miles beyond a trail leads to **Peyto Lake** where the waters change from green to blue as the year advances — a phenomenon caused by the presence of glacial silt. Other sights along the way include the **Mistaya Canyon** and the **Weeping Wall**, where melting snow streams down the cliff face at the bottom of Cirrus

Mountain. It is most spectacular in June when the snow melt is at its highest; in winter climbers come from all over to scale the ice.

At the **Sunwapta Pass**, 122 km (76 miles) north of Lake Louise and 108 km (67 miles) south of Jasper town, you enter Jasper National Park. This is the edge of the huge **Columbia Icefield**, an area of glaciers and snow that covers 325 sq km (129 sq miles) of the Canadian Rockies. The **Icefield Interpretive Centre (** (403) 762-6735 has a museum detailing the geological and human history of the area, with a scale model of the **Athabasca Glacier**, the toe of which stops just short of the Parkway — so close in fact that you can wander up to its edge. Between May and late September, **Brewster Snocoaches** will take you right out onto the glacier for a closer look. The six-wheel-drive Snocoaches are built especially for traveling on the Athabasca Glacier and surrounding gravel fields. Up on the ice you can walk around and even take

a sip of pure glacial water. Tours operate from the interpretive center; a fee is charged. Guided ice walk tours of the glacier will safely shepherd you over the surface, away from the deep and treacherous crevasses that thread through the ice. There is a **Parks Canada Information Desk (** (403) 852-6288 within the Icefields Centre.

Continuing towards Jasper, there are two spectacular waterfalls to be seen. The first is the **Sunwapta Falls**, 175 km (108 miles) north of Lake Louise and 55 km (34 miles) south of Jasper, which is reached via a short access road off the Parkway, and further along the Parkway there's access to the **Athabasca Falls**, where the river rushes over a ledge and down into a narrow gorge.

The spectacular Icefields Parkway links Banff with Jasper following the Continental Divide along a route lined with glaciers, lakes, and mountains. OVERLEAF: The Pipestone River tumbles down the mountainside to Lake Louise Village.

Where to Stay and Eat

Forty kilometers (25 miles) north of Lake Louise, **Num-Ti-Jah Lodge** ((403) 522-2167 FAX (403) 522-2425 E-MAIL reserve@num-ti-jah.com, PO Box 39, Lake Louise, Alberta T0L 1E0, nestles in a lovely spot on the banks of Bow Lake below the Crowfoot Glacier. An old hunting lodge (circa 1898), its common areas are decked with animal pelts and unusual furnishings — check out the moose-antler chairs in the library. There are 25 comfortable guestrooms and a large restaurant and lounge. It's a wonderfully isolated spot with marvelous cross-country skiing and snowshoeing in winter and horseback riding, fishing, and hiking in summer. The lodge is closed in

early nineteenth century the Athabasca River and Pass were part of the overland fur trading route, and at one time a trading post existed not far away from the present town of Jasper. Apart from these traders and some gold prospectors on their way to the Cariboo (the Canadian Wild West in British Columbia), the area was not visited until the national park was created in preparation for the transcontinental railway that was to cross the Rockies at Yellowhead Pass. The railway brought with it visitors, and the opening of the Icefields Parkway in 1940 made Jasper Park even more accessible. Although Jasper is today a major tourist attraction, it remains quieter and wilder than its older neighbor.

November; rates are in the expensive to mid-range category.

JASPER NATIONAL PARK

Jasper sits in a broad valley at the point where the Icefields Parkway crosses the Yellowhead Highway. It is smaller than Banff, less spectacular in its setting, but quieter and considerably less congested during the summer season. The main street is Connaught Drive, and along it stands the Canadian National Railway station which links the town with Edmonton to the east and Vancouver to the west. The town is the starting point for many excellent hiking trails, riding treks, rafting tours, and various other excursions into the beautiful wilderness beyond that teems with wildlife.

Jasper National Park, the largest of the mountain parks, was developed later than Banff. In the

GENERAL INFORMATION

The **Visitor Information Centre** ((403) 852-6176 is at 500 Connaught Drive; information is also available from the **Superintendent, Jasper National Park**, PO Box 10, Jasper, Alberta T0E 1E0, or **Jasper Tourism and Commerce** ((403) 852-3858 at the same address. As in Banff, it is necessary to sign in at the information center if you're planning an overnight hike in the park. There is **Internet access** at the Soft Rock Jasper Internet Café ((403) 852-5850, in the Connaught Mall, 622 Connaught Drive.

WHAT TO SEE AND DO

Before you head out of town to enjoy the scenery, you might want to drop by the **Jasper-Yellowhead Museum and Archives** ((403) 852-3013 on Pyramid Lake Road. Historical exhibits show what life in the area was like when the first European explorers and settlers arrived a century ago. It's open daily from mid-May to early September; donations are accepted.

Once you have an historical overview, you can take in a visual overview by taking a ride on the **Jasper Tramway(** (403) 852-3093, seven kilometers (four miles) south of Jasper. The tramway whizzes you up Whistlers Mountain for panoramic views of the ice field and of Mount Robson — the highest mountain in the Canadian Rockies. At the top terminal you'll find a restaurant, a café, an interpretive center, and hiking trails that lead up to the top of the mountain. Once at the top you

has a bike trail. Closer to town still is **Lac Beauvert**, where the famous **Jasper Park Lodge** (see WHERE TO STAY, below) spreads out along the shore, offering some of the area's best accommodation and catering for all kinds of activities.

To the east of the town lies **Maligne Canyon**, which is reached by the Yellowhead Highway and then Maligne Road, about 10 km (six miles) outside Jasper. The water has worn away the limestone to create this deep, and in parts very narrow, slash across the landscape, which can be explored by means of paths and bridges. Begin your hike along the canyon at the trailhead to the right of the tea house for maximum drama. Six bridges span the canyon at heights of up to 50 m

may discover for yourself the reason for the name of the mountain when you hear the whistling noises made by the little animals there, known as hoary marmots. The tramway operates from March 28 to October 31; a fare is charged.

There are several lakes within easy reach of the town that make lovely spots for outdoor sports and general relaxation. Just seven kilometers (four miles) northwest of town at Pyramid Lake Road, **Patricia** and **Pyramid lakes** are set amidst cottonwood forest and make fine places to picnic, boat, ride horses, hike, or canoe. The former was the sight of the bizarre *Project Habbakuk*, a wartime scheme to create the ultimate weapon: an unsinkable boat made of ice. (Needless to say, the project failed.) Three kilometers (two miles) east of town at Lodge Road, **Lake Edith** and **Lake Annette** both have picnic areas, beaches and hiking trails, and Lake Annette

(150 ft). In winter there are guided ice walks through the canyon (see SPORTS AND OUTDOOR ACTIVITIES, below) when you can explore fantastically shaped and colored ice formations.

Fourteen kilometers (nine miles) further along Maligne Road lies the mysterious **Medicine Lake**, where the water level changes throughout the year, causing it virtually to disappear during the autumn, although water is seen to enter continually. The reason behind this phenomenon is that the water constantly seeps away through holes in the bedrock, but during summer the water level is maintained because melting snow increases the amount of water entering the lake.

The crowning glory of this trip — some might say of the entire tour of the parks — is **Maligne**

Along the Icefields Parkway in Jasper National Park — OPPOSITE: The Athabasca Glacier and Num-ti-Jah Lodge ABOVE.

Lake, which lies a further 21 km (13 miles) along Maligne Road. This delightful lake stretches a length of 22 km (14 miles) and the amount of still and motion film that has been shot here would probably cover that distance several times over. Snowcapped mountains rise up from the deep blue glacial waters, and at its center lies the magical **Spirit Island**; a tiny spit of land — not really an island at all — crowned with trees. A Maligne Tours boat trip will take you along the lake and to Spirit Island between mid-May and mid-October; a hefty fare is charged.

At the Maligne Lake Boat House you can rent rowboats, canoes or kayaks, as well as rod and tackle. Professionally guided fishing trips and fly-fishing lessons can also be arranged. You can make reservations for all of your Maligne Lake activities in Jasper at **Maligne Tours** (403) 852-3370, 626 Connaught Drive.

For a relaxing treat after a hard day's hiking or skiing, visit the **Miette Hot Springs (** (403) 866-3939 which lie 60 km (37 miles) northeast of the town off Highway 16 on Miette Road. The springs are the hottest in these mountains, and their soothing properties can be enjoyed in out-door pools against a stunning alpine backdrop. The pools are open to the public from mid-May until mid-October; an admission fee is charged. The road to the springs runs through big horn sheep country.

To the south of the town **Mount Edith Cavell** looms magnificently. For a closer look, take a 30-km (18-mile) trip south of Jasper along Highway 93 and turn onto Highway 93A, a winding access road (open only from June to October) that will bring you to the foot of the mountain. It was named in honor of the heroic British nurse shot by the Germans in 1915 for helping Allied soldiers, and such a majestic sight makes a fitting memorial. A trail will take you to **Angel Glacier**, a wing-shaped tongue of ice that clings to the northeastern slopes of the mountain. There's another path that will take you into the alpine Cavell Meadows, and further back along the access road a trail leads to **Cavell Lake**.

If you'd like to see the area with a knowledge-able guide by your side, contact **Thompson Tours (** (403) 852-7269 MOBILE (403) 852-0146 E-MAIL tomtour@telusplanet.net, which offers personalized tours for individuals and small groups at reasonable rates. The owner–guides have years of experience in the Rockies with some of the best historical-cultural commentary and wilderness-sports guiding in the Jasper area. Tours are offered in English, German, and French.

Excursions from Jasper

Contiguous with the Jasper Park boundary, **Mount Robson Provincial Park** makes a nice hour-long trip from Jasper townsite. Following Highway 16, the terrain and scenery are similar to Jasper's; though more lush, as this area receives more rainfall.

The highest mountain in the Canadian Rockies, Mount Robson towers 4,324 m (12,972 ft) high. After five unsuccessful attempts, Robson was finally scaled in 1913. Certain routes on this forbidding mountain are still considered to be among the worlds' most difficult. Viewing conditions are rarely perfect, as Mount Robson is notorious for bad weather and clouds often obscure the top.

There are good views of the mountain (weather permitting) from the parking lot of the **Mount Robson Visitor Information Centre (** (250) 566-9174, which is open mid-May to early October;

there is also a small restaurant here. The park has five hiking trails, ranging from eight-kilometer (five-mile) day hikes to 70-km (44-mile) tramps; a permit is required.

SPORTS AND OUTDOOR ACTIVITIES

You can get a complete list of **day hikes**, the *Day Hiker's Guide to Jasper National Park*, from the Visitor Centre. **Horseback riding** and a dozen other outdoor activities are available at Jasper Park Lodge (** (403) 852-3301 which also has an excellent 18-hole **golf** course.

With so many lakes, Jasper is a boater's paradise. There are several outfitters offering **river rafting**, while **canoeing** is mostly reserved for

---

OPPOSITE: The blue ice of Maligne Falls remains locked in winter's embrace. ABOVE: Fog shrouds Spirit Island on Maligne Lake.

experienced paddlers, as the mountain waterways are swift and dangerous. Route information is available at the park information center. **Motorboating** is allowed only on Pyramid Lake.

There's excellent **skiing** at Marmot Basin ((403) 852-3816 SNOW PHONE (403) 488-5909, 19 km (12 miles) south of Jasper on Highway 93-93A. Here there are slopes to suit beginners and experts, and cross-country trails sweep through the stunning scenery surrounding Maligne Lake. For information on **ski packages** in the area you can call Ski Jasper ((403) 852-5247 TOLL-FREE (800) 473-8135. Also in winter, the popular **Canyon Crawl** offered by Maligne Tours ((403) 852-3370, 626 Connaught Drive, takes the hardy adventur-

ers on ice-climbing and walking trips along the multicolored ice falls at Maligne Canyon. Ice-gripping "super soles" and boots are provided on this three-hour tour.

NIGHTLIFE

Jasper is a much quieter place than Banff, and most people like it that way. What drinking and dancing goes on there tends to take place in the hotel lounges, sometimes to the accompaniment of live music. The **De'd Dog Bar & Grill** ((403) 852-3341, 404 Connaught Drive, in the Astoria Hotel, has a good selection of local ales and rare scotch, and there's a big-screen television and pool and darts. **The Whistlestop Pub** ((403) 852-3361, at the Whistlers Inn, Connaught Drive and Miette Avenue, is a similar setup. There's a nightclub at the **Athabasca Hotel** ((403) 852-3386, 510 Patricia

Street, hosting top-40 bands and dancing until 2 AM. For a quiet drink in an elegant setting, there's the Jasper Park Lodge's **Emerald Lounge** (with fireplace) and **Palisade Lounge**, overlooking beautiful Lac Beauvert.

WHERE TO STAY

In splendid solitude, the **Jasper Park Lodge** ((403) 852-3301 FAX (403) 852-5107, PO Box 40, Jasper, Alberta T0E 1E0, unrolls along the milky green Athabasca River to the east of the townsite. This Canadian Pacific hotel on Lac Beauvert has riding stables, luxurious log cabin lodges, and a famous golf course. A famous resort hotel, it has entertained many celebrities since it opened in 1922, and between the main lodge, cabins, and outbuildings it has 440 accommodations — some with fireplaces, all with beautiful views, lots of character, sitting rooms, and creature comforts. It also offers fishing, boating, and skiing packages. Prices vary according to the type of accommodation and the setting, but generally fall high in the expensive bracket. Many of the activities offered here can be enjoyed by non-guests as well.

Charlton's Château Jasper ((403) 852-5644 TOLL-FREE IN CANADA (800) 661-9323 FAX (403) 852-4860, 96 Geikie Street, PO Box 1418, Jasper, Alberta T0E 1E0, tries hard to live up to its expensive bracket prices, but is frankly overpriced. Rooms and suites are very large, but the hotel suffers from ambient noise, and some of the highest-priced rooms look out over a dreary jumble of air-conditioning vents. The dining room has a good reputation, however, and there is an attractive indoor pool.

Lobstick Lodge ((403) 852-4431 TOLL-FREE IN WESTERN CANADA (800) 661-9317 FAX (403) 852-4142, close to the center on the corner of Geikie and Juniper Street, PO Box 1200, Jasper, Alberta T0E 1E0, has 140 comfortable motel units and lots of home-away-from-home comforts, making it an ideal choice for families. There is an indoor pool, outdoor hot tub, a restaurant and lounge. Prices straddle the mid-range and expensive brackets. Located just opposite the VIA Rail station, **Whistlers Inn** ((403) 852-3361 TOLL-FREE (800) 282-9919 FAX (403) 852-4993, 105 Miette Avenue, PO Box 250, Jasper, Alberta T0E 1E0, is a busy hotel with 40 nicely furnished rooms and suites, all with bathrooms, televisions, and telephones. It has an outdoor rooftop hot tub, a cocktail lounge, and two restaurants, and prices vary from the low to the high end of the mid-range category.

Also mid-range in price, the **Athabasca Hotel** ((403) 852-3386 TOLL-FREE (800) 563-9859 FAX (403)

ABOVE: Rocky Mountain flora — a tiny conifer welcomes spring. RIGHT: Eons of erosion by the rushing water of Maligne Falls dug this deep canyon.

852-4955, 510 Patricia Street, PO Box 1420, Jasper, Alberta T0E 1E0, has simply furnished rooms, about two-thirds of which have private bathrooms. There's a popular pub, an attractive dining room, and a cocktail lounge.

Mid-range to inexpensive accommodation is available on the outskirts of the townsite: A kilometer (about half a mile) south of the town, nestled along the Athabasca and Miette rivers, **Tekarra Lodge (** (403) 852-3058 TOLL-FREE (800) 661-6562 FAX (403) 852-4636, off Highway 93A, PO Box 669, Jasper, Alberta T0E 1E0, offers cozy and peaceful self-catering cabins with fireplaces at inexpensive to mid-range prices. It's open May to October. At **Patricia Lake Bungalows (** (403) 852-3560, PO Box 657, Jasper, Alberta T0E 1E0, 35 tidy, rustic cottages and clumps of aspen and fir dot the banks of an ultramarine lake. There's a new playground, and cabins come equipped with kitchenettes, making this a good place for families. **Pyramid Lake Resort (** (403) 852-4900, PO Box 388, Jasper, Alberta T0E 1E0, has a restaurant that serves seafood and barbecue. Some accommodations have fireplaces. Rates here are in the mid-range, but more expensive than at Patricia Lake.

The mainstay of the Jasper lodging scene is **home accommodation**, a tradition since the park's early days. You'll see signs posted throughout the residential area of Jasper. These accommodations range from basic to very comfortable, from full apartments with kitchen to rooms with private or shared bath. Many are self-contained; some provide breakfast. Rates range from very inexpensive to the low end of the mid-range category, depending on facilities. The association prints an annual brochure that provides contact information for the individual homes. Write to Jasper Home Accommodation Association, PO Box 758, Jasper, Alberta T0E 1E0.

The hostels nearest to the townsite, both open year-round, are the **Maligne Canyon Hostel-HI (** (403) 852-3584 FAX (403) 852-5560, PO Box 387, Jasper, Alberta T0E 1E0, on Maligne Lake Road, 11 km (six and a half miles) east of town; and the **Jasper International Hostel-HI (** (403) 852-3215 FAX (403) 852-5560 E-MAIL jihostel@telusplanet.net, PO Box 387, Jasper, Alberta T0E 1E0, on Whistler's Mountain Road, seven kilometers (four miles) southwest of the townsite. The Jasper International offers downhill skiing packages.

WHERE TO EAT

Fiddle River ((403) 852-3032, 620 Connaught Drive, is one of the newest entry in the Jasper dining arena and is quickly gaining an excellent reputation for its delightful Pacific Rim cuisine featuring innovative dishes such as their pan-seared, peanut-crusted shrimp in strawberry purée. **Something Else Greek Taverna (** (403) 852-3850,

621 Patricia Street, is well-loved and well-patronized for its mouth-watering traditional dishes and suitably Greek decor.

For sushi and other Japanese dishes go to **Tokyo Tom's (** (403) 852-3780, 410 Connaught Drive. The **Soft Rock Jasper Internet Café (** (403) 852-5850, Connaught Mall, 622 Connaught Drive, spins the town's best selection of CDs — from Bob Marley to native chants. Breakfast is served all day with bagels, omelets, waffles, pancakes, and more for a very reasonable price. You'd never know the modern **Mountain Foods & Café (**/FAX (403) 852-4050, 606 Connaught Drive, is housed in a former dance hall. "Jaspers best bartender" and a pack of friendly locals are two among many reasons to

pay a call. Quesadillas, bagel sandwiches, and creatively conceived omelets are all made from fresh ingredients. It's directly across from the train station.

Outside the townsite, the **Jasper Park Lodge (** (403) 852-3301 on Lac Beauvert has nine restaurants. The flagship is the Four-Diamond-Award-winning Edith Cavell Dining Room, featuring freshly baked breads and herbs grown in the lodge greenhouse. The cafeteria-style **Maligne Canyon Teahouse (** (403) 852-5565, at Maligne Canyon, has a generous salad bar and hot meals which can be enjoyed on chilly days by the hearth or in summer on the terrace; avoid peak hours as this is a favorite pit stop for coach tour groups. The **Maligne Lake Restaurant**, at Maligne Lake, is another good spot run along similar lines. There's a pleasant terrace and the cafeteria serves hot meals, big sandwiches, and homemade breads and pastries.

How to Get There

Jasper is 292 km (184 miles) north of Banff along the Icefields Parkway, making Calgary International Airport 412 km (259 miles) away from Jasper. Edmonton International Airport is 350 km (215 miles) away from Jasper along the Yellowhead Highway. If you're aiming for Jasper during the winter you may want to drive via Calgary and Edmonton rather than taking the Icefields Parkway from Banff—winter conditions on this mountain road are sometimes hazardous.

The **VIA Rail** station TOLL-FREE (888) 842-7733 is in the town center along Connaught Drive, and

trains run west to Kamloops and Vancouver, eastwards to Edmonton, Winnipeg and beyond, and northward to Prince George and Prince Rupert. The **Greyhound** station ((403) 852-3332 shares the train station in the town center, and regular services operate to Vancouver via Kamloops, to Edmonton, and to Banff.

The Yellowhead Highway runs through Jasper from Edmonton in the east and to Prince George in the west, also linking with Vancouver via Kamloops.

YOHO NATIONAL PARK

Making up British Columbia's share of the Rocky Mountain national parks, Yoho and Kootenay lie alongside Banff, accessible off the Trans-Canada Highway for day trips. Both have much to offer outdoor enthusiasts and easily merit extended stays.

Yoho National Park is a land of towering rock walls and thundering waterfalls, and has 28 peaks over 3,000 m (9,000 ft) high. Once you visit, you'll understand why the Cree natives called this place "Yoho," an expression of wonder and astonishment. In addition to its scenic attractions, the park is noted for its fossil beds where the remains of more than 120 species of marine animals from 515 million years ago is the subject of ongoing investigation.

Field, British Columbia, is the administrative and supply center for the park, a compact little village with a history as a railway and mining town. Here you'll find the Field Visitor Centre ((250) 343-6783, which has all the information

you'll need for your visit, including up-to-date news on trail and weather conditions.

There are some 400 **hiking trails** in Yoho that lead to glaciated peaks, rolling alpine meadows, deep forests and thundering waterfalls. If you're making a drive-through tour, look for roadside signs pointing the way to the **Spiral Tunnels** viewpoint where you can watch passing trains corkscrew down a 2.2% grade. **Takakkaw Falls** ("magnificent" in Cree) are the highest in Canada at 254 m (84 ft). There is a parking lot, and several popular hiking trails begin here.

With so much natural history and beauty packed into such a small space (1,310 sq km or

Water, water everywhere — OPPOSITE: The Pipestone River at Lake Louise Village. ABOVE LEFT: The glacially-fed Lake Annette in Jasper National Park. RIGHT: Ice clings to the surface of the Pipestone.

507 sq miles), Yoho is sometimes overburdened with admirers. Park authorities have thus established limited access to certain areas: There is a quota on the number of people who may use the bus service up to **Lake O'Hara**. In addition, no bicycles are permitted; however, there is no limit on the number of people who may hike in. Reservations for the bus service to the lake must be made up to 90 days in advance by calling ((250) 343-6433.

Walcott's Quarry and its **Trilobite Beds** can be visited by guided hikes only. Yoho-Burgess Shale Foundation ((250) 343-6006 TOLL-FREE (800) 343-3006 E-MAIL burgshal@rockies.net, PO Box 148, Field, British Columbia V0A 1G0, offers earth science hikes to both sites. The Walcott's Quarry hike departs from the Yoho Brothers' Trading Post each Friday, Saturday, Sunday, and Monday morning at 8 AM. Guided hikes to the **Mount Stephen Fossil Beds** depart every Saturday and Sunday at 10 AM, also from the Trading Post. This hike is shorter than the Walcott's Quarry hike is, but more difficult. The local mountaineering club cut the trail; it climbs up at a very steep grade and trilobites are everywhere — you have to be careful to avoid stepping on them and crushing them. You must be in good physical condition to undertake either hike. Reservations are required.

For accommodation in Yoho, there is the **Cathedral Mountain Lodge & Chalets** ((250) 343-6442 FAX (403) 762-0514, Yoho Valley Road, Yoho National Park, PO Box 40, Field, British Columbia V0A 1G0. Located four kilometers (two and a half miles) east of Field, along the road to Takakkaw Falls, the lodge offers log cabins with fireplaces situated in quiet wooded grounds along the Kicking Horse River. There is a licensed restaurant and a grocery store. The lodge is open mid-May to mid-October and can be contacted during the off season period at the above fax number. Rates range from moderate to expensive.

From Takakkaw Falls, you can hike up to the **Twin Falls Chalet** (/FAX (403) 228-7079, PO Box 23009, Connaught Post Office, Calgary, Alberta T2S 3B1, where there is more cabin accommodation. Day hikers are welcome here for lunch, which is served between noon and 4 PM. It's open from July to Labor Day, and reservations are required. Rates, which include all meals, are in the mid-range category. A number of other **backcountry lodgings** are dotted throughout Yoho. For information, write to the Superintendent, Yoho National park, PO Box 99, Field, British Columbia V0A 1G0. Anyone who is planning an overnight trip into the backcountry must buy a wilderness pass. They're available from any Parks Canada center.

The **Whiskey Jack Hostel (HI)** ((403) 762-4122 FAX (403) 762-3441, at Yoho National Park, PO Box

1358, Banff, Alberta T0L 0C0, has an ideal setting about a kilometer from Takakkaw Falls; it's open mid-June to mid-September.

When you're in Field, be sure to stop in at the **Yoho Brothers Trading Post** ((250) 343-6030, where you can pick up souvenirs and have one of their great sandwiches of barbecued wild game or salmon.

Continuing west from Field brings you to the town of Golden in Glacier National Park (see GLACIER AND MOUNT REVELSTOKE NATIONAL PARKS, page 378), 78 km (48 miles) from Lake Louise.

KOOTENAY NATIONAL PARK

Lying southwest of Banff and Yoho national parks, Kootenay is accessible via Highway 93 off the Trans-Canada Highway south of Castle Junction. Highway 93, the Banff-Windermere Highway was the first major road to cross the Rockies and runs right through the park to its southern edge; it's a magnificent drive. As you travel through Kootenay look out for such marvels as **Marble Canyon** (take the 20 minute interpretive walk) and the ochre-tinted **Paint Pots**.

At the southern edge of the park, **Radium Hot Springs** ((250) 347-9485 features a hot pool (40°C or 104°F) and swimming pool (27°C or 80.6°F); towel and suit rentals are available. The **Visitor Information Centre** ((250) 247-9595 is located at the hot springs and has the usual raft of maps, brochures, and backcountry permits.

Kootenay and Yoho excursion specialists, **Kootenay Country Expeditions** ((403) 762-5627 TOLL-FREE (888) 899-7999, are located at the corner of Wolf and Bear streets in Banff townsite. They offer all sorts of ways to enjoy the British Columbia Rockies including glacier air tours, whitewater rafting, golf packages, horseback riding, four-wheel-drive tours, nature tours, jet-boating, and parasailing. They will also arrange accommodation in all price ranges from luxury resorts to backcountry cabins. Tours depart from Banff and Canmore.

The town of Radium Hot Springs is 129 km (80 miles) from Banff, and **Panorama Resort** ((250) 342-6941 TOLL-FREE (800) 663-2929 FAX (250) 342-3395, Toby Creek Road, Panorama V0A 1T0, is a further 20-minute drive. **The Springs at Radium Golf Resort** ((250) 347-9311 TOLL-FREE (800) 667-6444 FAX (250) 347-6299, 8100 Golf Course Road, Highway 93/95, PO Box 310, Radium Hot Springs V0A 1M0, is a year-round destination packed with activities. Its 119 rooms are mid-range in price and there is a restaurant and lounge as well as an indoor swimming pool.

Pebbles sparkle like flakes of gold in Banff's Bow River.

British
Columbia

BRITISH COLUMBIA IS THE COUNTRY'S THIRD LARGEST and most westerly province, and perhaps its most beautiful. It stretches from the Rockies to the Pacific and from the 49th to the 60th parallel. It is thus bordered by the United States' states of Washington, Idaho, and Montana at its southern edge, the Yukon and Northwest Territories to the north, Alaska at its northwest corner, and Alberta to the east beyond the Rockies. The rugged, snowcapped Coast Mountains rise above the deeply indented Pacific coastline, and beyond them the landscape is rippled by mountain ranges running northwest to southeast that give way to valleys and wide, rolling prairies carpeted with ancient forests and dotted with lakes.

British Columbia's climate is as varied as its landscape. The coast, warmed by the Pacific current and shadowed by the high Coast Mountains, has mild, wet winters and cool summers. The more exposed interior is generally drier, with more extreme temperatures, while northeastern winters are the coldest of all and have the heaviest snowfall.

The province covers an enormous area — 947,800 sq km (366,255 sq miles) — big enough to hold a handful of European countries. There are less than four million inhabitants in the entire province, the majority of whom live in the southwestern corner, and almost half the entire population can be found in Greater Vancouver. This leaves an awful lot of space. There are literally hundreds of parks covering millions of acres of wilderness, making ideal habitats for all kinds of wildlife and a heaven for outdoor enthusiasts. With

so many people huddled in its bottom corner, and with the great barrier created by the Rockies, it is not surprising that British Columbia seems separated from the rest of the country. It has often been observed that its lifestyle and easygoing attitudes owe more to California than to Canada.

The First Nations tribes who once populated the West Coast enjoyed prosperity and had a highly developed culture, expressed in art forms that are still much in evidence. Stunning examples of woodcarving are carefully preserved, most strikingly in the form of totem poles. Many First Nations communities still exist in British Columbia and, like the bands of the far north, they are in the midst of an exciting cultural renaissance, resulting in the revival of their languages and traditional arts and crafts.

Europeans were slow to arrive here because of the enormous physical barriers presented by the terrain. It was 1774 when tentative Spanish exploration began, and 1778 when Captain James Cook landed on Vancouver Island, where he traded with natives for furs which he later sold to the Chinese at a large profit. News of this began to speed things up, and the inevitable skirmishes ended with the Spanish conceding control to the British. So in 1792 Captain George Vancouver was dispatched by the British to map the coast. In the meantime intrepid fur traders were exploring overland routes to the Pacific and establishing trading posts.

The Hudson's Bay Company established its headquarters on Vancouver Island. In 1849 the English colonized the island in the name of the Crown, and Victoria was declared its capital. The discovery of gold along the banks of the Fraser River brought a rush of prospectors, and to secure its hold on their territories the British Government made the mainland (then known as New Caledonia) a British colony and renamed it British Columbia in 1858. In the 1860s the construction of the Cariboo Highway opened up the area. Lumber mills and canneries began to spring up, and in 1866 the colonies of Vancouver Island and British Columbia joined together. When the United States acquired Alaska, a further attack of nerves prompted British Columbia to consider joining the Canadian confederation as a security measure against American invasion, but it was with caution and only upon the promise that a transcontinental railway would reach its coast that in 1871 British Columbia finally joined.

This promise was fulfilled by 1885, and industries based on the province's natural resources were able to develop. A further boost came with the opening of the Panama Canal, which made transportation easier and therefore cheaper. Today

ABOVE: Vancouver's Marine Building with its art deco façade. OPPOSITE: A fjord parts the mountains in the Queen Charlotte Islands.

the economy still rests largely on natural resources such as fishing, forestry, mining, energy, agriculture (particularly in the lower Fraser Valley and the irrigated Okanagan), and the tourism attracted by the area's extraordinary natural beauty. The logging industry is currently at the center of a battle between conservationists, First Nations activists and the British Columbia government, with the province's image of caring environmentalism being severely challenged by the rapid destruction of the rain forests and the pollution resulting from logging activities.

VANCOUVER

Magnificent in its setting, sophisticated and cosmopolitan in character, Vancouver must rate as one of the world's most livable and beautiful cities. The air is fresh, the atmosphere is vibrant and youthful, and being only a little over 100 years old, this youngster is suitably seated in the lap of nature. To the north it is shadowed by the Coast Mountains, to the west are the peaks of Vancouver Island, and wilderness surrounds the city. Water is all around: Burrard Inlet separates the city core from the residential North Shore area, while the Strait of Georgia lies to the west and the Fraser River to the south. Water of another kind also figures largely in the life of Vancouverites. The rain is a popular topic of conversation — which is hardly surprising, as the city averages 145 cm (57 inches) of it a year. However, protected by the bulk of Vancouver Island and warmed by the Japan Current, Vancouver has a gentle climate and, unlike so much of Canada, has very little snowfall. May to September are the warmest months with the least rainfall, although even in July and August there may be days when the mountains will be shrouded in mist. On the bonus side, the rain keeps the air fresh and the city green.

Vancouver is the third largest city in Canada as well as being British Columbia's business center, but with a metropolitan population of only 1.8 million, and being so close to nature, it can afford a small-town lifestyle. Here, where there is a noticeable tendency to stroll instead of rush, the residents positively rejoice in the delights of their parklike city. It is said that Vancouverites are considered by Eastern Canadians to be a little too hedonistic. With the endless recreational opportunities offered them by the sea and mountains, who can blame them? There are over 14 km (nine miles) of beaches within the city limits, a rain forest within walking distance of the business core, and ski slopes only 20 minutes away.

The sea plays a major role in the city's economy, for Vancouver has the largest port on the North American Pacific coast. It's from here that grain, timber, and minerals are exported, and especially valuable trade links with Japan have been forged.

Timber, fishing, and tourism are Vancouver's major industries, but increasingly the economy is becoming more dependent on international finance. With the high rate of foreign investment here and the latest wave of immigration from Hong Kong, in some quarters the city has been dubbed "Hongkouver."

BACKGROUND

When the Spanish explorer José María Narváez sailed up the Georgia Strait in 1791, the shores on which Vancouver now stands were densely carpeted with trees and inhabited by Salish natives who fished the waters. The following year Captain George Vancouver quite literally put the area on the map when he explored and charted Burrard Inlet on behalf of the British Navy. The next white man to explore the area was Simon Fraser who in 1808 reached the Pacific by means of an overland

route. This brought him to the mouth of the river now named after him, and in his wake fur trading posts were set up.

The site then seems largely to have been ignored until the 1860s when sawmills started to appear around Burrard Inlet. Alcohol was not allowed on company land, and so when a Yorkshireman named Jack Deighton turned up with a keg of whiskey, he answered the prayers of the thirsty workers. He persuaded the men to help him build a saloon, and that was when things began to happen. The year was 1867, and the rough-and-ready community that quickly sprang up around the bar was named Gastown after its loquacious saloonkeeper, who by then had become known as "Gassy Jack." The town kept on growing and in 1869 the provincial government officially renamed it Granville.

The next major development came in 1884 when William Van Horne, builder of the Cana-

dian Pacific Railway (CPR), decided to make Granville the site of the West Coast terminus. He also suggested that the town be renamed; and in 1886 it became incorporated as the city of Vancouver. Within months the city was destroyed by fire but with speed and determination it was rebuilt by the time the first CPR passenger train chugged into town in 1887.

It was at this time that unpleasantness and disgrace shadowed Vancouver's history. Many Chinese had arrived to work on constructing the railroad, and a series of clashes between them and the white community spurred Vancouver authorities to deport them to Victoria. The incensed provincial government intervened to right this injustice and the Chinese community continued

The Vancouver skyline at dusk seen from Stanley Park. On the left-hand side of the photograph is the city's most recognizable landmark, Canada Place with its white sails.

to live in the area that developed into the city's Chinatown. The racism did not end there, however, and to the city's further shame until the late 1940s the Chinese were denied many of the rights granted to other citizens.

The twentieth century saw Vancouver's rapid growth: The port grew in importance as trade with the Far East developed, the fishing and timber industries thrived, the opening of the Panama Canal in 1914 facilitated export of grain to Europe, thus increasing the port's importance, and the demands created by World War II served to boost the mining and timber industries. After that, urban development hurtled onwards, making Vancouver the envy of many older cities.

Where once a wilderness of 1,000-year-old trees greeted the eyes of the first explorers, shiny high-rise buildings glitter against the splendid background of the Coast Mountains. The city gently tends the little history it has: old buildings have been restored and First Nations art has been carefully preserved.

GENERAL INFORMATION

For information on Vancouver, contact or drop by the excellent **Visitor Information Centre** ((604) 683-2000 WEB SITE www.tourism-vancouver.org/, Plaza Level, 200 Burrard Street, Vancouver V6C 3L6. The main **North Vancouver Visitor Information Centre** ((604) 987-4488 is at 131 East

Gastown shops offer a wide variety of Canadian crafts such as this pottery proudly displayed by a neighborhood shopkeeper.

Second Street. There is an information kiosk at Lonsdale Quay by the SeaBus Terminal, another at the airport, and several more dotted within and around the city. **Internet access** is available at the Electric Zoo ((604) 801-5788, located at 679 Denman Street at Georgia. It's open 24 hours a day.

Many of Vancouver's points of interest can be reached by public transportation. The Visitor Information Centre (above) provides schedules and maps. **BC Transit** ((604) 521-0400 bus stops are clearly marked and often list the route numbers serving the stop. The **SkyTrain** is an automated light rail that follows an elevated 29-km (17-mile) route with 20 stations, running from downtown east to the suburb of Surrey. The **Aquabus** ((604) 689-5858 runs to Granville Island from the Hornby Street dock, and the **SeaBus** ((250) 521-0400 takes passengers and their bicycles (but not cars) to the North Shore via a scenic 12-minute harbor crossing. It sails are every 15 minutes, departing from the SkyTrain Waterfront station downtown, and from the south foot of Lonsdale Avenue at Lonsdale Quay on the North Shore.

WHAT TO SEE AND DO

Downtown

One of the city's most distinctive landmarks is **Canada Place** ((604) 775-8687, which boldly projects into the harbor north of Burrard Street. With its unmistakable roof of white Teflon-coated "sails" that whiten in the sunlight, it has inevitably been referred to as "Vancouver's answer to the Sydney Opera House," and like the Opera House it quickly became an emblem of the city it graces. Originally built as the Canada Pavilion for 1986 World's Fair, the complex now comprises the World Trade Centre, the Vancouver Trade and Convention Centre, a luxury hotel, restaurants, shops, and a major cruise ship terminal. An outdoor promenade runs around the structure and offers excellent views of the harbor and mountains of the north shore.

Also of architectural note is the nearby **Canadian Pacific Railway Station** on Cordova Street. This splendidly restored structure was built in the 1880s as the Canadian Pacific Railway terminus, and now the SkyTrain elevated rail line to the eastern suburbs and the SeaBus ferry operate from here.

To fully appreciate the city's glorious setting you should take a trip up the nearby 40-story-tall **Harbour Centre** at 555 West Hastings Street. The views from the top will take your breath away, if you have any left to take after the journey up the outside of the building in the glass "Skylift" elevator. The circular observation deck is equipped with telescopes and information plaques, and an excellent special-effects film about the city is

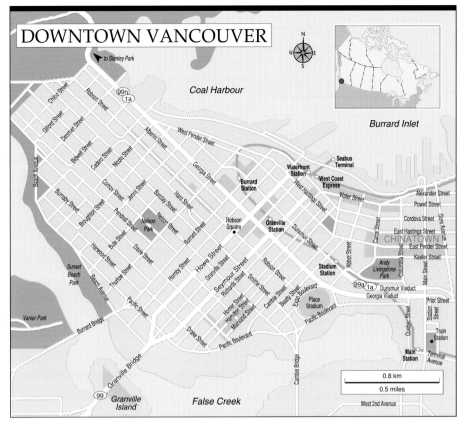

DOWNTOWN VANCOUVER

to Stanley Park

Coal Harbour

Burrard Inlet

CHINATOWN

Vanier Park

Granville
Island

False Creek

0.8 km
0.5 miles

shown. It is open May to September daily from 8:30 AM to 10:30 PM and October to April from 10 AM to 8 PM; an admission fee is charged.

Three blocks south of the Harbour Centre and then a couple east along Georgia Street lies **Robson Square**, which covers the area between Howe and Hornby streets. This complex, built in 1979, contains government buildings, a seven-story law court building with a vast sloping glass roof, restaurants, terraces, waterfalls, and, during the colder months, an ice-skating rink in the open-air plaza. The old courthouse building still stands across from the modern complex, and this dignified neo-classical building has been converted to house the **Vancouver Art Gallery (VAG)** ((604) 662-4700, 750 Hornby Street. The building was designed in 1907 by British Columbia's foremost architect of the time, Francis Rattenbury, and it seems fitting that the interior of the building was redesigned by Arthur Erickson, the internationally renowned Vancouver architect who was responsible for the square's modern complex. The gallery holds temporary exhibitions of international and Canadian art and its permanent collection includes Canadian, European, and North American paintings. One of its main attractions is the large collection of works by the famous British Columbia artist

Emily Carr, whose paintings capture the mystery of the rain forests and echo the native art of Canada's Pacific coast. During June to September the VAG is open Monday to Wednesday and Friday from 10 AM to 6 PM, Thursday from 10 AM to 9 PM (pay what you can 5 PM to 9 PM), Saturday from 10 AM to 5 PM, and Sunday from noon to 5 PM. From October to May the hours are reduced to Monday, Wednesday, Friday, and Saturday from 10 AM to 5 PM. An admission fee is charged.

You can soak up a bit of European atmosphere when you stroll along the section of Robson Street that runs between Howe and Broughton streets. Once a mainly German neighborhood, this stretch is known locally as **Robsonstrasse**, and here you can sample all varieties of European food in the restaurants, cafés, and delicatessens that line the street, or take a look at the high fashion shops.

Gastown

A few blocks east of the Harbour Centre between Richards and Columbia streets lies the neighborhood of Gastown, the birthplace of Vancouver and the oldest part of the city. In 1867 it was here that the Englishman John "Gassy Jack" Deighton built his saloon with the willing help of thirsty mill workers. The shantytown that sprung up around it grew to eventually become Vancouver, and although the 1886 fire destroyed the town, it was quickly rebuilt using more robust materials. By the 1960s these buildings had degenerated into slums, and so it came about that during the 1970s Gastown underwent the familiar rags-to-riches story of gentrification. The nineteenth-century buildings were restored, modern but matching additions were built, streets were cobbled, imitation nineteenth-century streetlights popped up, and the area filled with bistros, restaurants, galleries, and shops. This recipe proved successful yet again and Gastown is now a major tourist draw both by day and by night. The center of Gastown is Maple Tree Square, where the original Globe

Chinatown

Just south of Gastown between Carrall Street and Gore Avenue, centered along Pender and Main streets, is **Chinatown**, home to Canada's third largest Chinese community. The neighborhood developed in the 1880s and some of the original buildings still stand. It's a bustling area filled with the noises and smells of Hong Kong, and it brims with restaurants, bakeries, herbalists, and shops selling all kinds of Chinese goods from ginseng, green tea and exotic fresh produce to embroidered linens and silk robes.

Behind the Chinese Cultural Centre on East Pender Street is the delightful **Dr. Sun Yat-Sen Classical Garden** ((604) 689-7133 or (604) 662-

Saloon once lay and where a statue of Gassy Jack and his barrel of whiskey now stands in memory. At the corner of Cambie and Water streets there's an unusual object, which a plaque proudly proclaims to be the first **steam-powered clock** in the world. It pipes out its very own version of the Westminster chimes on the quarter-hour and truly lets off steam on the hour.

Gastown has the city's largest selection of cheap souvenirs, but also offers good shopping for quality Canadian crafts. **Frances Hill's** ((604) 685-1828, 151 Water Street, is one of the best outlets carrying Canadian-made crafts, clothing and gifts. Water Street is also the place for Northwest Coast and Inuit arts and crafts, including Cowichan sweaters, moccasins and carved silver jewelry, which can be purchased at the government-licensed **Inuit Gallery of Vancouver** at No. 345 and **Images for a Canadian Heritage** at No. 164.

3207, at 578 Carrall Street, which offers a peaceful sanctuary from the city. The only one of its kind outside China, it was designed in Ming Dynasty style by a team from the city of Suzhou, in honor of the revolutionary Sun Yat-Sen, who visited Vancouver while planning the overthrow of China's last dynasty. Everything in the garden was manufactured in China and brought over for the 1986 World's Fair, the 100th anniversary of the founding of Vancouver. (That same year was an important anniversary for the city of Suzhou — its 2,500th.) The garden is an exquisite composition of sculptural limestone rocks, plants, trees, bridges and water, and it's a good idea to join the guided tour which explains the principles behind the design. It's open daily year-round; an admission fee is charged. A small section of the garden is accessible free of charge.

While you're in the area, keep your eyes peeled so not to miss the **Sam Kee Building**, reputedly the world's narrowest building, which stands at the corner of Pender and Carrall streets, one block wide and a mere 1.3 m (six feet) deep.

Stanley Park

The city's pride and joy, Stanley Park is regarded by Vancouverites with great reverence. This 400-hectare (1,000-acre) urban park covers the whole of the western tip of the downtown peninsula that juts out into Burrard Inlet, and consists of some 280 hectares (700 acres) of lush rain forest. The rest is given over to gardens, sandy beaches, and public facilities.

town on foot or via No. 19 city bus along West Pender Street. There is a free shuttle bus around the park from mid-May to mid-September. Information is available from the Park Board ((604) 257-8400.

At **Brockton Point** there are great views across Burrard Inlet of the north shore mountains, and nearby is a display of totem poles. At **Prospect Point**, the Lion's Gate Bridge forms the only land link between the downtown area and the north shore, and from here you get a good view of the ships passing through First Narrows to and from the port. At the southwest tip of the park peninsula, **Ferguson Point** looks over to Third Beach and the peaks of Vancouver Island.

Back in 1886 Ottawa granted this land to Vancouver, and in 1889 Canada's governor-general Lord Stanley dedicated it "to the use and enjoyment of people of all colors, creeds and customs for all time." It is laced with hiking trails and dotted with picnic sites. There are tennis courts, a biking, in-line skating and running track, a walking path, miniature golf courses, cricket pitches, restaurants and snack bars, and an open-air theater. At the Georgia Street entrance is the marshy lake known as the Lost Lagoon, a bird sanctuary where you'll see Canada geese, Trumpeter swans, great blue heron, and other wildfowl. The 10-km (six-mile) scenic **seawall** that encircles the park is popular with cyclists and strollers, and for the less energetic there's a **scenic drive** which starts from the Georgia Street entrance to the park, taking you around the peninsula in an counterclockwise direction. Stanley Park is within easy reach of down-

Also in the park is the **Vancouver Aquarium** ((604) 268-9900. This award-winning exhibition of marine life is the largest of its kind in North America: over 8,000 aquatic specimens are on display here. Star performances are given by the acrobatic orcas (killer whales), who can be watched through glass, with strong support from the playful beluga whales, Pacific white-sided dolphins, and sea otters. While you're here you can take a turn in the Amazonian jungle, recreated under cover with sloths, turtles, and bird life indigenous to that area. It's open July to September 4, daily from 9:30 AM to 8 PM; the rest of the year, daily from 10 AM to 5:30 PM. An admission fee is charged.

OPPOSITE: Vancouver's Chinatown not only has the largest Chinese Community in Canada, but many of its buildings were erected by the original settlers. ABOVE: The Dr. Sun-Yat Sen Garden is an oasis of calm.

Outside Downtown

Over on the south side of False Creek is **Granville Island**, which is in fact a small peninsula connected to the downtown core by Granville Bridge. Once the center of Vancouver's shipbuilding industry, by the 1960s the area had degenerated into a grim spot full of dingy factories and warehouses. Renovation began in the 1970s and it is now a lively neighborhood of businesses, craft studios, industry, theaters, galleries, restaurants, markets, and shops. A huge warehouse underneath Granville Bridge has been converted to house the popular **Public Market**, where stalls sell seafood, produce, and foods of many countries. It's open daily in summer and Tuesday to

structed period interiors. It's open daily in summer from 10 AM to 5 PM; winter, Tuesday to Sunday from 10 AM to 5 PM. A general admission is charged with an extra charge for special exhibitions. Situated on the second floor of the museum is the **H.R. Macmillan Planetarium**, which has up to four astronomy shows daily, and laser shows set to rock music at night. It is open July to early September daily, from 11 AM to 4 PM; admission fee varies. Next to the museum is the **Gordon Southam Observatory**, where you gaze at the heavens with the aid of a Zeiss telescope. Hours are daily 7 PM to 11 PM; ring for opening times as they are subject to weather conditions. Admission is free.

Sunday in winter. On the west of the island you'll find the **Maritime Market** which sells just about everything needed for pleasure boating. The island is a fun place to have lunch and enjoy some views. There is also a collection of shops known as the **Kid's Only Market** with children's clothing and toys and lots of arts and crafts studios. To get there from the center peninsula you can take the passenger ferry that runs from Sunset Beach near the Aquatic Centre or take a bus from downtown.

Close by and to the west of Burrard Bridge in Vanier Park stands the **Vancouver Museum** ((604) 736-4431, 1100 Chestnut Street. The museum has a gallery devoted to West Coast native culture, where some stunning examples of native art and artifacts are displayed. In a gallery that charts the area's history, exhibits include a replica of a Hudson's Bay Company trading post and recon-

Also in Vanier Park, the **Pacific Space Centre** ((604) 738-7827, which underwent major renovation in 1997, has dozens of hands-on space-themed exhibits from laser shows to space artifacts. Computer games take you around the solar system, give you the chance to dock a space shuttle, touch a real moon rock, and then "morph" yourself into an alien. It's open daily in July and August; an admission fee is charged. Nearby, the **Vancouver Maritime Museum** ((604) 257-8300, 1905 Ogden Avenue, north end of Cypress Street, looks at voyagers of an earlier era. Here exhibits trace the history of shipping in the region and the development of the port of Vancouver. The centerpiece is the *St. Roch*, a fully restored Royal Canadian Mounted Police ship that during World War II became the first vessel to navigate the Northwest Passage in both directions. Guided tours are given. It's open May to August, daily from 10 AM to 5 PM;

September to April, Tuesday to Sunday from 10 AM to 5 PM; an admission fee is charged. Outside you can see some of the museum's restored boats in **Heritage Harbour**.

Moving west, the **University of British Columbia** is magnificently sited on the headland of Point Grey, which is tipped with forest and overlooks the Georgia Strait and English Bay. Its **Museum of Anthropology (MOA)** ((604) 822-3825, at 6393 NW Marine Drive, is a concrete and glass building worthy of its dramatic setting. Designed by Vancouver architect Arthur Erickson, the building's huge glass windows embrace the splendid views of cliffs, mountains, sea, and trees, giving context to one of the world's finest exhibits of Pacific Northwest Coast First Nations art. The MOA has a splendid collection of totem poles, some of which are displayed alongside other huge exhibits in the vast **Great Hall**. The museum does not limit itself to representing the Northwest Pacific area and there are works of art and artifacts from many other cultures. Some galleries are set aside for temporary exhibitions and some house the research collections where items are thoughtfully stored in glass filing drawers and clearly catalogued. On the museum grounds, totem poles and reconstructed Haida dwellings are set in the rain forest. The museum is open Tuesday from 11 AM to 9 PM; Wednesday to Sunday from 11 AM to 5 PM. An admission fee is charged, free all day on Tuesday.

Should you feel so inclined, from here you can follow the marked trails that lead down to **Wreck Beach**, a well-known and popular nudist beach. Or you can enjoy nature in a more cultivated form at the **Nitobe Memorial Garden** ((604) 822-6038, 6565 NW Marine Drive, a serene Japanese garden with a ceremonial teahouse. It's open in summer, daily from 10 AM to 6 PM; in winter, weekdays from 10 AM to 3 PM; an admission fee is charged. At the southwest end of the campus there's the **UBC Botanical Garden** ((604) 822-9666, at 16th Avenue and SW Marine Drive, where highlights include the **Asian Garden** and the **Physick Garden**, a sixteenth-century-style garden of medicinal plants. It's open daily 10 AM to 6 PM; an admission fee is charged.

In the eastern corner of False Creek, the silver geodesic dome that was built for the 1986 World's Fair is now home to **Science World** ((604) 268-6363, 1455 Québec Street at Terminal Avenue, where visitors come to grips with science and have fun through imaginative hands-on displays. The SkyTrain runs to the nearby Main Street Station. It's open daily; an admission fee is charged.

Keen gardeners and those who enjoy floral displays will love **Queen Elizabeth Park** ((604) 872-5513, at 33rd Avenue and Cambie Street. At a height of 150 m (492 ft) it's the city's highest point, where wonderful views and magnificent gardens

make a delightful place to stroll. Inside its dome-shaped **Bloedel Conservatory** exotic plants grow and brightly colored tropical birds fly free. It is open April to September, weekdays from 9 AM to 8 PM, weekends from 10 AM to 9 PM; the rest of the year, daily from 10 AM to 5 PM; an admission fee is charged. A few blocks away there's yet another manifestation of Vancouver's love affair with nature at the **Van Dusen Botanical Gardens** ((604) 261-0011, at 5251 Oak Street at 37th Avenue. In this 22-hectare (55-acre) garden there are geographical and botanical groupings of plants, a fragrance garden, a children's topiary garden where hedges are cut into animal shapes, and a maze. It's open July to August, daily from 10 AM

to 9 PM; October to April, daily from 10 AM to 4 PM; May, June and September, daily from 10 AM to 6 PM. An admission fee is charged, half price October to May.

The North Shore

On Vancouver's north shore the Coast Mountains rise steeply out of the sea, cut deeply by inlets and canyons. On the lower slopes are the smart residential suburbs of North and West Vancouver and beyond them, peaks and parks beckon hikers in the summer, skiers in the winter, and lovers of the great outdoors all the year round. To get there you can cross the spectacular **Lions Gate Bridge** that links the northern end of Stanley Park to Western Vancouver or the Second Narrows Bridge at

OPPOSITE: The seawall in Stanley Park, attracts cyclers, skaters, and a lone runner.
ABOVE: Downtown Vancouver.

Burnaby in East Vancouver. Alternatively, take the SeaBus. From there buses will take you to the viewing point of your choice.

Next to the SeaBus terminal is the **Lonsdale Quay Market** ((604) 985-6261, a lively waterfront development of shops and eateries centered around a busy public market selling produce. There are lovely views across Burrard Inlet of the city and it is a good spot to pause and orient oneself before exploring the spectacular sights the north shore has to offer. The market is open daily from 9:30 AM to 6:30 PM, Fridays until 9 PM.

At the north end of Capilano Road, the **Skyride** ((604) 984-0661, 6400 Nancy Green Way, awaits to lift you 1,100 m (3,700 ft) up **Grouse**

River as it rushes through a deep and narrow canyon surrounded by Douglas firs and Western Red cedars. It's a commercialized place and you are charged to cross the bridge; nevertheless it is a beautiful and awe-inspiring sight. It's at 3735 Capilano Road; if you're driving from downtown, pick up the Capilano Road from Lions Gate Bridge. The park is open daily year-round.

You can enjoy a similar but less commercialized experience at **Lynn Canyon Park and Ecology Centre** ((604) 981-3103. This thickly-forested parkland has nature trails through the rain forest, an ecology center, and a suspension bridge that crosses Lynn Creek. Like the bridge at Capilano

Mountain. The ride takes about eight minutes, and on a clear day it's a chance to enjoy panoramic views that take in Washington's Olympic Peninsula. In the winter this is one of the most popular ski resorts, being the closest to the city, but in the summer it's known as Cypress Beach because it's a great place to laze around soaking up the brilliant sunshine. There's a restaurant and bistro up here, as well as the new Feasthouse, which offers a sunset program combining traditional First Nations song and dance with a dinner of native foods. For information on the restaurants call ((604) 984-0661.

Near the foot of Grouse Mountain, the fantastically dramatic **Capilano Suspension Bridge** ((604) 985-7474 offers thrills for those with a head for heights. Set in a wild and wonderful parkland, this plank-and-cable bridge is 137 m (450 ft) long and sways 70 m (230 ft) above the Capilano

though only half as long, it crosses the creek at a height of 80 m (240 ft). There is no admission charge. If you're traveling by car, cross at Second Narrows Bridge, take Lynn Valley Road, and then head east along Peters Road.

A little further afield, the **Mount Seymour Provincial Park** overlooks the waters of Indian Arm, offering opportunities for hikers, horse riders, mountaineers, picnickers, view-seekers, and during the winter months skiers. Walking trails and a road climb eight kilometers (five miles) up the mountain to a lookout where there's a café, an information center, more walking paths, and views of eastern Vancouver. From here a chair lift takes visitors to the mountain top in July and August, while the more rugged follow the trail to the summit. To get there by car, take the Mount Seymour Parkway from Second Narrows Bridge, then turn off to the north on Mount Seymour Road.

A delightful way to see the impressive coastal scenery of **Howe Sound** is to take a trip aboard the refurbished *Royal Hudson*, a stately old Canadian Pacific Railway steam locomotive that pulled trains across Canada in the 1940s and 1950s. With a shrill whistle, a hiss, and the squealing of wheels, the train pulls away from North Vancouver Station at 10:30 AM and begins its 66-km (41-mile) journey northwest to the small logging community of Squamish along a route that runs through forests, up mountains, by waterfalls, all at a leisurely 20 mph. The train arrives at Squamish at approximately 12:30 PM and passengers have one and a half hours to explore — enough time to get to **Shannon Falls**

Southeast of Vancouver

To the east of Vancouver lies the fertile **Fraser Valley**, an area of parklands shadowed by mountains all around, a popular weekend escape for Vancouverites. The Trans-Canada Highway follows the Fraser River along its south shore, while Highway 7 runs along the north side. **Fort Langley National Historic Park** ((604) 513-4777, 56 km (35 miles) from Vancouver on the south side of the river makes an interesting stop. Once a trading post for the Hudson's Bay Company, the fort dates from 1827, and it was here in the Big House that British Columbia was officially proclaimed a crown colony. The fort with its wooden palisade has been restored and the buildings are open daily to the public.

for some lunch. There's an attractive option of returning to Vancouver by sea aboard the **MV Britannia**, a route that takes a little longer. The *Royal Hudson* runs Wednesdays through Sundays and holiday Mondays from early June to mid-September, and as it's a popular excursion you must book in advance. Contact BC Rail ((604) 631-3500 or (604) 984-5246 TOLL-FREE IN BRITISH COLUMBIA (800) 339-8752 TOLL-FREE ELSEWHERE IN NORTH AMERICA (800) 663-8238 FAX (604) 984-5505. Train buffs who've come this far will be delighted with Canada's second-largest collection of railway equipment at the new **West Coast Railway Heritage Park** TOLL-FREE (800) 722-1233 in Squamish, with vintage rail cars filled with artifacts, photos and information about the history of railroading in British Columbia. It's open daily from 10 AM to 5 PM, May to October; an admission fee is charged.

SPORTS AND OUTDOOR ACTIVITIES

With so many excellent opportunities within easy reach of the city center, outdoor pursuits are very much part of the Vancouver lifestyle.

From late November through Easter, it's a paradise for **skiing**. Just 15 minutes from downtown, Grouse Mountain ((604) 984-0661, 6400 Nancy Greene Way, offers runs that are suitable for those of all abilities. An aerial tramway takes skiers to the top; runs are lit at night. With your daily Skyride ticket (see WHAT TO SEE AND DO, above), you can also enjoy **snowshoeing, cross-country skiing, ice skating**, and **sleigh rides**. Neighboring Mount Seymour ((604) 986-2261,

---

OPPOSITE: B.C. Place Stadium in Vancouver. ABOVE: Sails charmingly interrupt Vancouver's shoreline and skyline.

1700 Mount Seymour Road, and Cypress Bowl ((604) 922-0825 (end of Cypress Bowl Ski Area Road, Exit 8 off Highway 1 westbound) also have good skiing and nighttime illumination. For ski information and conditions in the Vancouver area call the Snowphone ((604) 986-6262.

North of Squamish and 120 km (75 miles) northwest of Vancouver is the fashionable Whistler Resort. It is primarily famous for its skiing but also offers all manner of recreational activities that include **fishing, hiking, water sports, heli-hiking**, and simply sightseeing. The pseudo-European Whistler Village nestles between Blackcomb and Whistler Mountains, and caters to every need. For information contact Whistler Resort Association ((604) 932-3928 TOLL-FREE (800) 944-7853, 4010 Whistler Way, Whistler V0N 1B4. All lodgings in Whistler can be book through this agency. You can get there by train from North Vancouver, by hourly bus with Maverick Coach Lines ((604) 662-8051, Suite 210, 1150 Station Street, that operate from downtown Vancouver, or by car along Highway 99, the scenic Sea-to-Sky Highway.

Two more of Vancouver's popular pastimes are **cycling** and **in-line skating**, and there's no problem with rentals. The most convenient rental place is located next to the Westin Bayshore. It's open 9 AM to 6 PM. From the Bayshore you can roll your way along the seafront path which leads into Stanley Park and to the seawall promenade, where there are specially marked areas for skaters, bikers and joggers.

There are countless hiking trails of all kinds and lengths throughout the north shore parks. Close to the city center, Stanley Park has some scenic trails.

There's plenty of action to be had both in and on the water. If you fancy **sailing**, there are schools to teach you how to do it, and plenty of places where you can charter something, particularly around the Coal Harbour area and on Granville Island. **Windsurfing** tuition and equipment rentals are available at Kitsilano, Jericho, and English Bay beaches. Fraser Canyon is a good area for **canoeing** and **whitewater rafting**, while nearer downtown there's canoeing at False Creek. The Vancouver area has some excellent **scuba diving**, particularly in Howe Sound. Diver's World ((604) 732-1344, at 1817 Fourth Avenue West, and The Diving Locker ((604) 736-2681, 2745 Fourth Avenue West, rent out equipment, offer instruction, and organize scuba trips.

With 10 bathing beaches within the city limits **swimmers** are also spoiled for choice. The closest to downtown are the beaches in Stanley Park, all of which are good for swimming. Beaches are open from Victoria Day to Labor Day, guarded daily from 11:30 AM to 8:45 PM. Call the Vancouver Board of Parks and Recreation (swimming information)

((604) 738-8535 for more information. At Sunset Beach there's the Aquatic Centre ((604) 665-3424, 1050 Beach Avenue, which has indoor Olympic pools, a saltwater pool and a diving tank, and there's also the Kitsilano Pool ((604) 731-0011, an outdoor saltwater pool at Kitsilano Beach.

The Vancouver area has exceptionally good freshwater and saltwater **fishing**, with a good choice of lakes, rivers, streams, bays, and a variety of fish, being particularly well known for its salmon. You'll need a license and you should check the regulations carefully. Tackle shops sell licenses and can provide you with a list of current regulations: Bonnie Lee Fishing Charters ((604) 290-7447, 744 West King Edward Avenue; and Granville Island Boat Rentals ((604) 682-6287, 1696 Duranleau Street, on Granville Island, are two reputable outfitters.

NIGHTLIFE AND THE ARTS

True to its pleasure-seeking reputation, Vancouver is geared to entertainment. **Gastown** has a vibrant nightlife that draws visitors and residents alike. **Granville Island** has a concentration of theaters and art centers, as well as trendy microbreweries, while **Yaletown** is fashionable historic district of pool halls, art galleries and cafés. To check the listings you can pick up a free copy of the weekly arts and entertainment paper the *Georgia Straight*, or check the *Vancouver Sun* entertainment section, which appears each Thursday. There's also an **Arts Hotline** ((604) 684-2787 for the latest on performing and visual arts events in the city. Tickets for most cultural events are available, subject to handling charge, through **Ticketmaster** ((604) 280-3311, which has lots of outlets around the city. Bear in mind that reduced-price tickets are often available as the time of performance approaches.

The cultural heart of Vancouver beats downtown at the new Ford Centre for the Performing Arts, together with the Vancouver Playhouse and the Queen Elizabeth Theatre. The **Ford Centre** ((604) 280-2222, 777 Homer Street, presents world-class musicals, while the modern 3,000-seat "Queen E" ((604) 280-4444, Hamilton at Georgia, is the place to see ballet, opera, Broadway musicals and celebrity performers. The **Vancouver Playhouse** ((604) 872-6622, 160 First Street, is home to the city's main theatre company of the same name, presenting a mix of new drama and classic theater. Visiting dance companies also perform here.

The **Arts Club Theatre** ((604) 687-5315, 1585 Johnston Street, Granville Island, stages major theatrical productions, while smaller ones are performed in the adjoining Arts Club Revue. The **Vancouver East Cultural Centre** ((604) 254-9578, 1895 Venables Street, holds musical and theatrical events, and in Gastown the **Firehall Arts**

Centre, 280 East Cordova Street, the Touchstone theater company ((604) 687-8736 offers innovative theatre.

There are Theater-sports twice nightly on Fridays and Saturdays at the **Back Alley Theatre** ((604) 738-7013, 715 Thurlow Street, when two teams of actors compete for laughs by improvising plays on themes suggested by the audience. Front seats run the risk of audience participation.

Second only to Montréal as a major Canadian dance center, Vancouver's dance scene is as diverse as its cultural makeup, and ranges from traditional Japanese and Chinese dance to classical ballet. The **Vancouver East Cultural Centre** ((604) 254-9578 is home to the innovative Kokoro Dance

2120 Main Street, features the Big Band sound. Good places for mainstream jazz are the **Alma Street Café** ((604) 222-2244, 2505 Alma Street, and also at the **Glass Slipper** ((604) 877-0066, 185 East 11th Avenue. Blues fans should check out the **Purple Onion** ((604) 602-9442, at 15 Water Street, and the Arts Club Theatre (above) on Granville Island. The Coastal Jazz and Blues Society ((604) 687-0706 has a **hotline** with listings and directions to regular venues.

The spot for serious rhythm and blues is the **Yale Hotel** ((604) 681-YALE, at the north end of the Granville Bridge. **WISE Hall** ((604) 254-5858, 1882 Adanac Street, is the major venue for Celtic and other folk music, and big rock concerts are

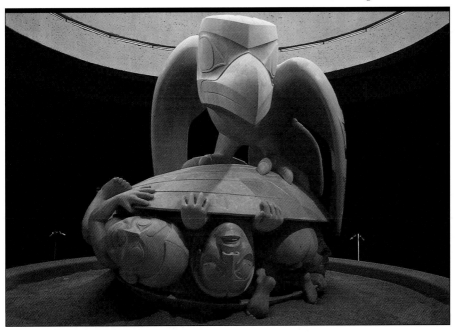

Company, and the **Firehall Arts Centre** ((604) 689-0926 (for dance company information) presents an annual series as well at the Dancing on the Edge Festival each July. The **Ballet British Columbia** ((604) 732-5003 can be seen at the Queen Elizabeth Theatre (see above) where world-class companies can also be seen. In **Robson Square Plaza**, free dance performances are held during the summer months.

Another cultural mainstay, the **Orpheum Theatre** ((604) 684-9100, at 601 Smithe Street, is a splendidly restored 1920s building that is home to the widely acclaimed **Vancouver Symphony Orchestra** ((604) 684-9100 and is the major venue for musical events. The **Vancouver Opera** ((604) 682-2871 presents four productions each season at the Queen Elizabeth Theatre.

Vancouver likes its jazz, and there's quite a mixture of venues. **Hot Jazz** ((604) 873-4131, at

often held at **GM Place** ((604) 280-4444, Pacific Boulevard North at Abbott Street. The **Commodore Ballroom** ((604) 681-7838, 870 Granville Street, is another major venue for rock and many other kinds of music.

On the dance club circuit, the classy-yet-cool **Richard's on Richards** ((604) 687-6794, 1036 Richards Street, one of the longest-running venues in the city, features live rock music and dancing nightly, while the very hip **Babalu's** ((604) 605-4343, 654 Nelson at Granville, has a versatile house band playing jazz, funk, soul, and rhythm and blues. Formerly called Graceland, **The Palladium Club** ((604) 688-2648, 1250 Richards Street, presents a diverse lineup of live dance music nightly. The dark and shiny **Luvafair**, at 1275 Seymour,

A stunning sculpture greets visitors to the University of British Columbia's Museum of Anthropology.

is one of Vancouver's see-and-be-seen spots, and the **Town Pump**, 66 Water Street, has live rock bands, a good location in one of the city's oldest neighborhoods, and a casual atmosphere.

WHERE TO STAY

Expensive

One of the city's top hotels is the **Four Seasons** ((604) 689-9333 TOLL-FREE (800) 286-6282 FAX (604) 689-3466, at 791 West Georgia Street, Vancouver V6C 2T4. Rising above the 200 fine shops of Pacific Centre Mall, this hotel embodies the excellent service, ultimate comfort and good taste which has become the trademark of this first-rate hotel

900 West Georgia Street, Vancouver V6C 2W6, one of the great railway hotels with over 500 accommodations. With a classical façade crowned with a steep green copper roof, this hotel is a Vancouver landmark, and within it the spacious public areas are furnished in grand style with chandeliers, antiques, an ocean of marble, and comfortable old-fashioned sofas and armchairs. The rooms are also spacious, but decorated in a much more low-key fashion, and business- and executive-class accommodation is offered. There's an indoor swimming pool, shops, cocktail lounges, a couple of good restaurants, and a popular nightspot. The service here is impeccable and the overall picture one of comfort and elegance.

chain. Rooms and suites are beautifully furnished, and there are indoor and outdoor swimming pools and tennis courts. There are several restaurants, including the first-rate Chartwell, and piano music plays in the delightful lounge.

The **Metropolitan Hotel Vancouver** ((604) 687-1122 TOLL-FREE (800) 667-2300 FAX (604) 689-7044, 645 Howe Street, Vancouver V6C 2Y9, is another leading hotel. The 197 well-furnished rooms and suites are individually designed and have marble bathrooms. The hotel has a business center, one of the city's best restaurants, an indoor swimming pool, a sun deck, racquetball courts, and even a library. Everywhere the needs and comforts of its guests are anticipated, and service is always close at hand.

For old-fashioned grandeur look to the **Canadian Pacific Hotel Vancouver** ((604) 684-3131 TOLL-FREE (800) 441-1414 FAX (604) 662-1929,

Rising above the Royal Centre mall is the city's largest hotel, the **Hyatt Regency Vancouver** ((604) 683-1234 TOLL-FREE (800) 233-1234 FAX (604) 689-3707, 655 Burrard Street, Vancouver V6C 2R7. There are 644 accommodations and several floors set aside for executive suites. Rooms are smartly decorated, some have balconies, and there are lots of nice touches. It has a good seafood restaurant, Fish & Co., pleasant lounges, a heated outdoor swimming pool, and access to racquetball and squash courts. The staff are knowledgeable and extremely helpful, and there's a bright and lively atmosphere.

Magnificently situated in the remarkable Canada Place waterfront complex is the **Pan Pacific Vancouver Hotel** ((604) 662-8111 TOLL-FREE IN CANADA (800) 663-1515 TOLL-FREE IN THE UNITED STATES (800) 937-1515, 300-999 Canada Place, Vancouver V6C 3B5. This hotel really does have everything. It's a member of the Leading Hotels of the World group, and all rooms and suites are luxurious, although there is an ultra-deluxe class available. With the Trade and Convention Centre also in the complex, it comes as no surprise to find that the excellent restaurants offer Japanese, Italian, and Pacific Rim cuisine along with spectacular harbor views. It has a business center, and a soaring, glass-topped lobby complete with waterfall.

Sutton Place ((604) 682-5511 TOLL-FREE (800) 961-7555 FAX (604) 682-5513, 845 Burrard Street, Vancouver V6Z 2K6, has a distinctly European accent. This is a relatively new hotel, furnished in classical French style with marble, antiques, and great elegance. The rooms, although on the small

dations. Rooms and suites are small but elegant with every amenity one could wish for. Some rooms have large balconies with views over Robson Square and fireplaces. Owner and general manager Eleni Skalbania's dedication to excellence is evident everywhere, and her personal touch makes this hotel a favorite of knowledgeable travelers. Executive facilities are available, and there's an excellent restaurant, The Bacchus, with its cozy fire-lit room romantically decorated in cherry wood and velvet. At high tea each afternoon guests choose from a street-side table by the French windows or a cozy fireside spot.

In the city's west end the **Westin Bayshore** ((604) 682-3377 TOLL-FREE (800) 228-3000 FAX (604)

side, match the public areas for style and grace, and the service is superb and personal. The hotel has 397 units and an adjoining block provides suites for long-stay guests. There's an attractive café, piano bars, an indoor pool, and tennis courts. Also European in style the **Georgian Court Hotel** ((604) 682-5555 TOLL-FREE (800) 663-1155 FAX (604) 682-8830, 773 Beatty Street, Vancouver V6B 2M4, is located opposite the BC Stadium and only a block away from the Queen Elizabeth Theatre. Antiques adorn the elegant lobby, the airy rooms are beautifully furnished, well-equipped, and many offer splendid views. There is an executive floor, and the first-rate William Tell restaurant.

Across from Robson Square the **Wedgewood Hotel** ((604) 689-7777 TOLL-FREE (800) 663-0666 FAX (604) 688-3074 E-MAIL wedgwood@portal.ca, 845 Hornby Street, Vancouver V6Z 1V1, is a smaller, privately owned hotel with 93 accommo-

687-3102, 1601 West Georgia Street, Vancouver V6G 2V4, is beautifully positioned near the edge of Stanley Park and set in grounds overlooking Coal Harbour. Rooms have large windows and lovely views, and the hotel offers a wide range of services including a children's activity program, restaurants, and an outdoor pool. The *pièce de résistance* is the private marina which brings float planes, fishing trips and cruises to the doorstep. This is the only hotel in Vancouver that is accessible from land, sea, and air.

Moving a few blocks away from Coal Harbour, the highrise **Shangri-La Pacific Palisades Hotel** ((604) 688-0461 TOLL-FREE (800) 663-1815 FAX (604) 688-4374, 1277 Robson Street, Vancouver V6E 1C4,

OPPOSITE: It's time for breakfast in bed in the penthouse suite at Vancouver's Wedgwood Hotel. ABOVE: The Pan Pacific Vancouver Hotel in the Canada Place waterfront complex.

is the pick of the hotels in the Robson Street area with its generous rooms with balconies overlooking Coal Harbour and Stanley Park. Its suites are particularly well-adapted for business travelers, but leisure travelers also enjoy the amenities, that include an indoor pool and bike rental.

In North Vancouver, the **Lonsdale Quay Hotel** ((604) 986-6111 TOLL-FREE (800) 836-6111 FAX (604) 986-8782, 123 Carrie Cates Court, North Vancouver V6M 3K7, is located next to the SeaBus Terminal on the top floors of the lively Lonsdale Quay Market. Its rooms and suites are attractively decorated, and there are some good views across Burrard Inlet. It has a restaurant, and a pub, and downtown is only 12 minutes away by SeaBus.

throughout in European style. It has a French restaurant and licensed lounge.

Just north of Lions Gate Bridge, you'll find the lovely **Park Royal Hotel** ((604) 926-5511 FAX (604) 926-6082, 540 Clyde Avenue, West Vancouver V7T 2J7, set in attractive grounds on the banks of the Capilano River, well-situated for beaches and mountains, and close to the Park Royal shopping center. The 30 accommodations are all attractive and airy, and there is a restaurant, an outdoor terrace for dining, and an English-style pub.

At the edge of Stanley Park on English Bay stands the much-loved **Sylvia Hotel** ((604) 681-9321, 1154 Gilford Street, Vancouver V6G 2P6. This delightful ivy-covered stone building has 115 rooms

South of downtown, the **Granville Island Hotel** ((604) 683-7373 TOLL-FREE (800) 663-1840 FAX (604) 683-3061 E-MAIL GIHotel@netminder .com, 1253 Johnston Street, Vancouver V6H 3R9, is a lively waterfront place that tends to attract a sporty crowd who take advantage of the tennis courts and the various charters that operate from the marina. The building has the warehouse-like appearance characteristic of Granville Island, and most rooms have waterfront views. The building incorporates a nightclub, restaurant, and a popular pub.

Mid-range

The **Barclay Hotel** ((604) 688-8850 FAX (604) 688-2534, at 1348 Robson Street, Vancouver V6E 1C5, is within walking distance of Stanley Park and offers some of the best value around. It has 90 accommodations and is attractively decorated

and suites (including housekeeping suites) some of which are located in a modern extension. The decor throughout is attractive, each room is different, and there's a restaurant and bar which both have beautiful views of the bay. Its popularity means that it is necessary to book well in advance.

For accommodation in the Gastown area, try the **Dominion Hotel** ((604) 681-6666 FAX (604) 681-5855, 210 Abbott Street, Vancouver V6B 2K8. This charming hotel is a late nineteenth-century brick building with antiques and relics of old Vancouver scattered throughout, and rooms that have been renovated. There is a restaurant, and breakfast is included in the room rate.

Inexpensive

The **Kingston Hotel Bed & Breakfast** ((604) 684-9024 TOLL-FREE (888) 713-3304 FAX (604) 684-9917, 757 Richards Street, Vancouver V6B 3A6, is a

European-style place where continental breakfast is included in the price. The rooms are small but clean; some have private bathrooms while others have hand basins. The hotel has a sauna and laundry facilities. Room rates range from inexpensive to moderate, and it is excellent value for money. East of downtown, the **Budget Inn-Patricia Hotel** ((604) 255-4301 FAX (604) 254-7154, 403 East Hastings Street, Vancouver V6A 1P6, has 24 simply furnished rooms with private bathrooms.

There's a wide range of **bed and breakfast** accommodation in metropolitan Vancouver. Among the agencies are: the Old English Bed and Breakfast Registry ((604) 986-5069 FAX (604) 986-8810, 1226 Silverwood Crescent, North Vancouver

Simon Fraser University, Room 212 McTaggart-Cowan Mall, Burnaby, Vancouver V5A 1S6. The University of British Columbia at Point Grey 16 km (10 miles) southwest of the center also offers year-round accommodation; information is available from the UBC Conference Centre ((604) 822-1010 FAX (604) 822-1069 E-MAIL reservations@brock .housing.ubc.ca, 5961 Student Union Boulevard, Vancouver V6T 2C9.

WHERE TO EAT

Vancouver's large number of restaurants reflect the city's rich ethnic mix in the wide variety of food they offer. You'll also find Pacific Northwest-

V7P 1J3; and Canada-West Accommodation B&B Registry ((604) 929-1424 FAX (604) 929-6692 TOLL-FREE (800) 561-3223, PO Box 86607, North Vancouver V4L 4L2.

Vancouver has two large Hostelling International **hostels**: Vancouver Downtown ((604) 684-4565 FAX (604) 684-4540 E-MAIL van-downtown@hihostels.bc.ca, at 1114 Burnaby Street, Vancouver V6E 1P1, with 240 beds; and Vancouver Jericho Beach ((604) 224-3208 FAX (604) 224-4852 E-MAIL van-jericho@hihostels.bc.ca, 1515 Discovery Street, Vancouver V6R 4K5, where there are over 300 beds and good self-catering facilities.

University accommodation is available from May to August at the Simon Fraser University, 20 km (12 miles) east of downtown. For details contact SFU Accommodations ((604) 291-4503 E-MAIL conference-accommodations@sfu.ca,

ern cuisine here, the region's own brand based on plentiful supplies of salmon and other seafood, game, herbs, and flowers. *City Food* is a free publication that comes out monthly and can be picked up at restaurants and bookstores. It's a good source of up-to-date information on the Vancouver area dining scene.

Expensive
Named Top Table by *Gourmet* magazine, **Diva at the Met** ((604) 602-7788, Metropolitan Hotel, 645 Howe Street, is known for its open kitchen from whence emanates the restaurant's unique international cuisine. Seasonal ingredients are emphasized and flavors are bold. The terraced room offers atmospheres ranging from lively to

---

OPPOSITE: Salmon on ice at Granville Market.
ABOVE: Produce for sale in Chinatown.

intimate. **Chartwell** ((604) 844-6715, at the Four Seasons Hotel, 791 West Georgia Street, is named after the English country home of Winston Churchill, and the restaurant imitates that ambiance with its warm wooden paneling and a glowing fireplace. Amid these gracious and tasteful surroundings, diners enjoy a wide-ranging progressive menu with strong Pacific Rim influences. Those who count the calories will find the menu especially pleasing.

William Tell ((604) 688-3504, at the Georgian Court Hotel, 765 Beatty Street, is another top Vancouver restaurant where a traditional interior and tables set with the finest china and crystal provide the setting for its haute cuisine. Swiss-French specialties appear alongside the classics, and local produce is mostly used. The wine list here is particularly good and the service superb.

Vancouver has some excellent French restaurants, and **Lumière** ((604) 739-8185, 2551 West Broadway, is among the best. French cuisine with influences from the East and West are served amidst furnishings of polished chrome and wood. The wine list is global. **Étoile** ((604) 681-4444, 1355 Hornby Street, also serves classical French cuisine adding its own contemporary spin. The *prix-fixe* menu changes every two weeks. A long-running favorite, **Le Gavroche** ((604) 685-3924, at 1616 Alberni Street, is set in a lovely old house in the city's west end. This restaurant has a mouth-watering menu, a democratic wine list, and excellent service. It is an ideal choice for a special occasion.

For a Chinese experience, try **Floata** ((604) 602-0368, 400-180 Keefer Street, located near the Dr. Sun Yat-Sen Park, in the third floor of a bright-red shopping plaza. It is the western flagship of a renowned Hong Kong restaurant, and despite its cavernous size, it's usually packed with diners enjoying dim sum served from steaming carts and lavish dinners of delicacies cooked up by its award-winning chef.

Moderate

South of the downtown peninsula, **Tojo's** ((604) 872-8050, at 202-777 West Broadway, offers Japanese food in sleek, sophisticated surroundings with an outdoor terrace and mountain views. You can choose to dine in a traditional tatami room, at a conventional dining table, or at the small sushi bar. The menu features all kinds of Japanese specialties as well as the chef's own innovative dishes, and freshness is the hallmark. Prices here range from expensive to moderate.

The best place in Vancouver specializing in Pacific Northwest cuisine is the highly acclaimed **Raintree at the Landing** ((604) 688-5570, 375 Water Street. The imaginative use of local seafood and organically grown produce results in some wonderful dishes, and an exceptionally

good wine list together with stunning views over the water of Grouse Mountain make a memorable meal. Over in West Vancouver, **Salmon House on the Hill** ((604) 926-3212, 2229 Folkstone Way, is another good place to sample Pacific Northwestern cuisine. Perched high above Vancouver, the restaurant commands wonderful views of Stanley Park and the city across the inlet. Seafood dominates the menu here, and it really is delicious.

At a beautiful location on Granville Island's waterfront, **Bridges** ((604) 687-4400, 1696 Duranleau Street, has a good seafood restaurant, a bistro, and a large terrace where you can enjoy beautiful mountain views. Across the creek, **A Kettle of Fish** ((604) 682-6661, 900 Pacific Street, serves deliciously fresh fish in a conservatory-style setting, and east of downtown, **The Cannery** ((604) 254-9606, 2205 Commissioner Street, has an extensive seafood menu and great harbor views.

For excellent and moderately priced French food, few places better the bistroesque **Le Crocodile** ((604) 669-4298, 100-909 Burrard Street, and in Stanley Park at Ferguson Point, the **Teahouse Restaurant** ((604) 669-3281, serves fine continental fare in a delightful Victorian house overlooking the bay.

Over in Kitsilano, at **Bishop's** ((604) 738-2025, 2183 West Fourth Avenue, exciting continental cuisine is presented with great style and served with enthusiasm. The restaurant is small and chic, and the atmosphere relaxed. Celebrated Italian chef Umberto Menghi has several restaurants in Vancouver, the most popular being **Il Giardino** ((604) 669-2422, 1382 Hornby Street. Here Italian classics reign, with game featuring prominently on the menu. It's extremely popular and reservations are required for both lunch and dinner. For imaginative Italian country cooking, go to **Piccolo Mondo** ((604) 688-1633, 850 Thurlow Street, where you'll find a seemingly endless menu and some very interesting dishes.

Some of the best Cantonese food can be found at the **Pink Pearl** ((604) 253-4316, 1132 East Hastings Street, a large restaurant where the emphasis is on seafood. A favorite for Northern Chinese cuisine is **Kirin Mandarin Restaurant** ((604) 682-8833, 102-1166 Alberni Street, where the menu is diverse, the surroundings sophisticated, and lobster and crab come fresh from the tanks. For a taste of Japan, try the **Kamei Sushi** ((604) 732-0112, 1414 West Broadway.

Inexpensive

We never miss a chance to drop by **La Bodega Tapas Bar** ((604) 684-8815, 1277 Howe Street, with its Spanish decor and intriguing specials

Coal Harbour divides Stanley Park from downtown's forest of highrise apartment buildings.

emphasizing creatively prepared meat dishes. If it's seafood you want, drop in on the **Only Other Fish and Oyster Café** ((604) 682-3474, 1517 Anderson Street, or rather, join the queue, because although this well-known and well-loved café has absolutely no finesse and no alcohol, it does have the freshest seafood you'll find anywhere.

Chinatown has a wealth of restaurants. The cheerful and unpretentious **Gain Wah** ((604) 684-1740, 218 Keefer Street, has authentic Cantonese fare including good *congee*, and you can enjoy Korean barbecue and sizzling hot pots in a casual atmosphere at **Arirang House** ((604) 879-0990, 221 Cambie Street. Our favorite lunch spot is **Ezugiku Noodle Café** ((604) 685-8606,

HOW TO GET THERE

Vancouver International Airport — Canada's second largest — is 15 km (nine miles) from downtown and about a 25- to 40-minute drive from town. The **Vancouver Airporter Service** ((604) 946-8866 TOLL-FREE (800) 668-3141, runs shuttles from the airport at 15-minute intervals, which stop at major downtown hotels and the Greyhound Bus Terminal, and operate from 6 AM to midnight. Ask the ticket agent to advise you of the hotel stop closest to your destination. Taxi stands can be found in front of the terminals.

1329 Robson Street, where steaming noodles are served at the stainless steel counter. In addition to Japanese fare, Robson Street is noted for its European restaurants, and one of its old favorites is **Heidelberg House** ((604) 682-1661, at 1256 Robson Street, a pleasant place in which to sample German specialties.

Pezzo ((604) 669-9300, at the corner of Robson and Thurlow, has cheap and good pizza and pastas, local beer and a stereo featuring the mellow voice of Mario Lanza. If Californian-Mexican food appeals, go to **Topanaga** ((604) 733-3713, 2904 West Fourth Avenue, a small café that serves hearty portions. For East Indian food, try the **Heaven and Earth India Curry House** ((604) 732-5313, 1754 West Fourth Avenue, in the Kitsilano area.

The First Narrows leads out from Vancouver into the Strait of Georgia.

When leaving Vancouver by air there is a $10 to $20 "Airport Improvement Fee."

VIA Rail ((604) 669-3050 TOLL-FREE IN CANADA (888) 842-7733 TOLL-FREE IN THE UNITED STATES (800) 561-3949 FAX (604) 640-3757 operates the *Canadian* three times a week from Toronto to Vancouver. Other points in the province connected to Vancouver by VIA Rail service include Kamloops, Prince Rupert, and Prince George. (Vancouver Island is accessed via bus ferry to Victoria or Nanaimo where there is train service up to Courtenay.) Trains depart from Pacific Central Station ((604) 669-3050 TOLL-FREE (800) 665-8630, at 1150 Station Street. **Amtrak** TOLL-FREE (800) 872-7245 TOLL-FREE IN THE UNITED STATES (800) 835-8725 operates one train daily from Seattle to Vancouver's Pacific Central Station. **BC Rail** ((604) 631-3500 TOLL-FREE (800) 663-8238 has daily service into North Vancouver from Squamish,

Whistler, Lillooet, and points in between, as well as regular service to 100 Mile House, Williams Lake, Quesnel, and Prince George. Its station is at 1311 West First Street, North Vancouver. **Rocky Mountain Railtours** ((604) 606-7200 TOLL-FREE (800) 665-7245 FAX (604) 606-7201, 1150 Station Street, Vancouver V6A 2X7 operates between Calgary, Banff and Jasper to Vancouver between May and October (see RIDE THE LEGENDARY RAILS, page 20, in TOP SPOTS).

BC Ferries ((604) 669-1211 TOLL-FREE IN BRITISH COLUMBIA (800) 223-3779 FAX (250) 381-2583 run from the Tsawwassen Ferry Terminal, 30 km (19 miles) south of downtown Vancouver, to Victoria (Swartz Bay), Nanaimo on Vancouver Island,

VANCOUVER ISLAND

Moored alongside the west coast of the British Columbia mainland and separated from it by the Georgia Strait, Vancouver Island stretches 450 km (280 miles) and covers an area of 32,000 sq km (12,000 sq miles). It is thus the largest island off North America's Pacific coast, and violates the 49th parallel, much to the annoyance of some. A chain of snow-tipped mountains runs north-south through the center of the island, splitting its personality between a rugged and sparsely populated west, with an exposed Pacific coastline cut by deep inlets, and a sheltered eastern shore of a much more

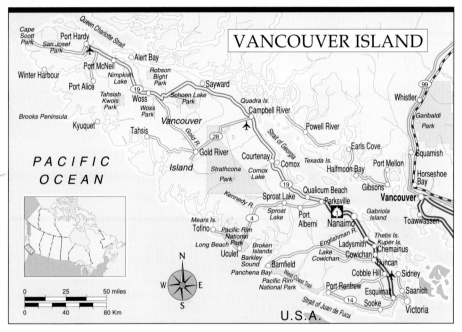

VANCOUVER ISLAND

and to the Southern Gulf Islands. They also operate a ferry from Horseshoe Bay, west of Vancouver, to Nanaimo, Bowen Island, and the mainland's Sunshine Coast. Twenty-four-hour recorded schedule information ((250) 386-3431 is also available.

Long-distance buses arrive at Pacific Central Station, Main Street at Terminal Avenue, including **Pacific Coach Lines** ((604) 662-8074 (from Victoria), **Maverick Lines** ((604) 662-8051 (from Squamish, Whistler, Pemberton, and Nanaimo), and **Greyhound** ((604) 482-8747 (from most mainland cities).

Motorists coming from the east will want to take the Trans-Canada Highway, while those coming from Seattle, Washington will take Highway 5, which becomes Highway 99 at the British Columbia border. The drive from Seattle to Vancouver takes about three hours.

tame character with white sandy beaches, gentle slopes, farmlands, and seaside towns.

The island is blessed with a gentle climate throughout the year, although the rainfall varies dramatically from place to place. The lowest rainfall and mildest temperatures are found at the southern end of the island, which is sheltered by the Olympic Mountains across the Juan de Fuca Strait. It is not surprising therefore that most of the island's population of 500,000 live in Victoria and the cozy seaside towns of the southeast, leaving the west side uninhabited for the most part, with a few small fishing communities dotted around.

The rain forests with their soaring red cedars and the lonely west coast shores seem a far cry from the neat lawns of Victoria and the snug towns of the southeast. It is this combination of ruggedly beautiful scenery, the sedate charm of Victoria, and people as gentle as the climate itself that makes

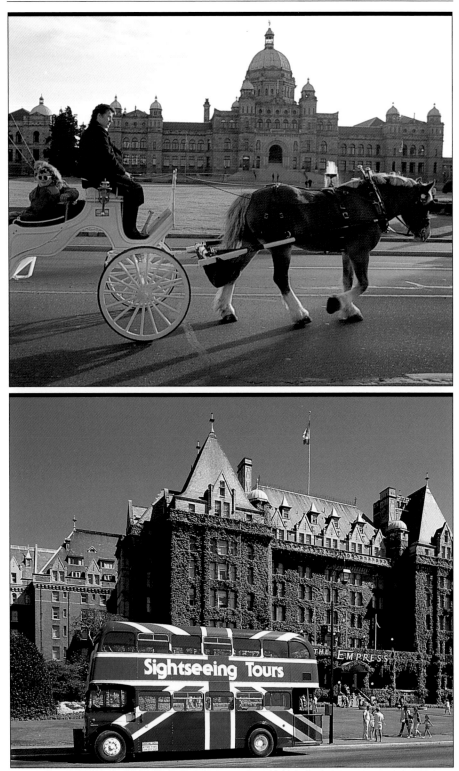

Vancouver Island so appealing to vacationers. The culture is equally diverse, for the British Empire was not the only society to leave its mark. The Haida, Kwagiutl, Cowichan, and Sooke natives who lived in fishing villages here long before the arrival of the white man have scattered the island with their totem poles, their crafts and legends, while their fishing skills seem to have found their way into the blood of the inhabitants.

Together with fishing, mining and logging are the island's main industries, and they are mostly found to the east of the mountain range. Stubbled mountainsides stand testimony to the latter and an impassioned battle rages over the island's particularly active logging program.

BACKGROUND

In 1774 Juan Perez of Spain visited Vancouver Island, and when Captain Cook landed at Nootka Island on the west coast in 1778 he did a little trade with the natives. In 1792 Captain George Vancouver put the island on the map when he charted the waters of Johnstone Strait. These visits had little effect on the lives of the island's native tribes and it wasn't until 1843, when the Hudson's Bay Company took control and founded a trading post on the island's southeastern tip, that things started slowly to change.

In 1849 Vancouver Island was declared a crown colony, with the Hudson's Bay Company administering it from Fort Victoria. Apart from some company farms established by the subsidiary Puget Sound Agricultural Company, little happened by way of colonization and the main concern remained fur trading.

The discovery of gold in the Fraser River during the 1850s and 1860s brought prospectors to Victoria, British Columbia's only port and source of provisions. As a result, the area developed into a typical boomtown, but when the gold fields were exhausted Victoria continued as an administrative center. The island united with British Columbia in 1866, and in 1871 Victoria was declared the provincial capital. It was intended to be the western terminus of the Canadian Pacific Railway, but this did not come to pass and the railroad stopped at Vancouver. This meant that industrialization also stopped at Vancouver and Victoria was left free to build itself a reputation as a center of genteel society. The other gift that the Canadian Pacific Railway gave Victoria was the building of the beautiful Empress Hotel in 1908, boosting a tourist industry that has flourished ever since.

GENERAL INFORMATION

Victoria's **Visitor Information Centre** ((250) 953-2033 FAX (250) 382-6539, 812 Wharf Street, Victoria V8W 1T3, is located on the waterfront across

from the Empress Hotel. The office is open daily. For **hotel reservations** in Victoria call TOLL-FREE (800) 663-3883. For information on the rest of Vancouver Island, contact the **Tourism Association of Vancouver Island** ((250) 382-3551 FAX (250) 382-3523, 302-45 Bastion Square, Victoria V8W 1J1. There are also information centers in towns throughout the island, including a major branch, the **Nanaimo Travel Infocentre** ((250) 756-0106, at 2290 Bowen Road, Nanaimo.

VICTORIA

Victoria has overcome its rough and ready beginnings, and has developed into a graceful city

that is both conservative and relaxed. Baskets of flowers adorn the lampposts, nineteenth-century buildings have been carefully renovated, tidy lawns and flowerbeds are all around. Victoria has been transformed from a raucous gold rush town into a colonial fantasy of a British seaside resort.

Victoria is British Columbia's capital, and with a population of 313,000 it is the province's second largest city. It is situated around a beautiful natural harbor at the southeastern tip of the island, sheltered by the mountains of Washington State, which lies only 32 km (20 miles) away across the Juan de Fuca Strait to the south. It boasts Canada's mildest climate with only 68 cm (27 inches) of

OPPOSITE TOP: Dignified survivors from the last century: a horse and carriage and the Parliament Buildings in Victoria. BOTTOM: The Empress Hotel. ABOVE: A Morris dancer.

rainfall a year and plenty of sunshine. While the rest of Canada is struggling through snow, Victoria is busy taking its official bloom count.

The love of beautiful gardens is not the only feature that Victoria has inherited from its British connections. It is a place that revels in and capitalizes upon its image as a last bastion of the British Empire. Old British traditions are fiercely preserved. Wander through one of the city's parks and the chances are that you'll see some croquet, cricket, or English bowls being played. You can ride around the city on a double-decker bus, stock up on Wedgwood china, Waterford crystal and tweeds in the shops, or take refreshment in one of the many pubs or tearooms. Just to make sure you

of the city is the **Inner Harbour** area, where Victoria's most majestic buildings overlook the lively little harbor which is constantly busy with the comings and goings of ferries, fishing boats, and yachts.

A large portion of the Inner Harbour is filled with the ivied grandeur of the **Empress Hotel** ℂ (250) 384-8111, a resplendent castle-like building that is the heart and very much the soul of Victoria. Designed by Francis Rattenbury and built by the Canadian Pacific Railway in 1908, the Empress became the place where Victorian polite society came to take tea. Today visitors flock here to experience an afternoon tea of cucumber sandwiches and scones with jam and clotted cream,

get the picture, somewhere around the Parliament Buildings you'll hear the whine of bagpipes.

Part of the reason for this "forever England" image is that the population is largely of British extraction, and the mild weather and low rainfall continues to make Victoria an attractive retirement home for the British. The main employers here are the government and tourism, and to keep the latter industry thriving the Britishness is carefully preserved and reinforced wherever possible, sometimes in ways that are rather garish, but it still keeps the visitors coming.

WHAT TO SEE AND DO

Downtown

Downtown Victoria is compactly laid-out within a small area, so walking is the easiest and most pleasant way of exploring it. The hub

served among silver teapots and cake stands in the desperately British ambiance of the Empress lobby. Tea at the Empress is very popular and should you wish to partake you should telephone to make a reservation. Behind the hotel stands the **Crystal Garden** ℂ (250) 381-1213, 731 Douglas Street, a large glass structure that was designed by Rattenbury and built in 1925. It once held an enormous saltwater pool, and its elegant ballroom was the scene of many social events. It is now an exotic conservatory with colorful tropical birds and monkeys among the greenery, overlooked by the ever-popular tearooms. It's open daily, year-round, and an admission fee is charged. You'll also find some of the best outlets for **native arts and crafts** along Douglas Street.

Across from the Empress, neatly clipped lawns and carefully arranged flowerbeds surround the stately **Parliament Buildings** ℂ (250) 387-3046, a

Gothic extravaganza of towers and domes that also overlooks the lovely harbor. Completed in 1897 and designed by the irrepressible Francis Rattenbury, these buildings remain the home of the provincial legislature. A statue of Queen Victoria dignifies the lawn to the front, statues of eminent Victorians stand on either side of the elaborate arched entrance, and the central copper-covered dome is crowned with a gilt statue of Captain George Vancouver. Free guided tours of the interior in a choice of languages operate daily during the summer months and on weekdays only during the winter. The buildings are also a remarkable sight at night, when they are outlined by thousands of little lights.

runs old movies, a pioneer village, a sawmill, and a reconstructed section of Captain George Vancouver's ship, *The Discovery*. In the section that deals with First Nations history, realistic displays allow the visitor to glimpse life in a Pacific Coast native village, and the museum's extensive collection of First Nations art and artifacts includes a collection of totem poles. The museum is open daily September to June from 10 AM to 5:30 PM, July and August from 9:30 AM to 7 PM; an admission fee is charged.

To the rear of the museum is a small grassy plot known as **Thunderbird Park** which is forested with modern totem poles carved with the image of the legendary thunderbird. At the south-

On the corner between the Empress and the Parliament Buildings stands the excellent **Royal British Columbia Museum** ((250) 387-3014. This is one of Canada's very best museums and the skill and imagination of its displays have made it one of Victoria's top attractions. It is devoted to all aspects of British Columbia's natural and cultural history from prehistoric times through to the present day. The second floor covers the province's natural history, while beautifully constructed dioramas depict aspects of the region's natural environment such as the rain forest, seashore, mountains, and ocean. The section dealing with the province's cultural history has some of the most popular and fascinating displays where sight, sound, and smell combine to give vivid and memorable impressions of life in the past. There is, for example, a detailed recreation of an early twentieth-century street, complete with a cinema that

ern edge of this park stands **Helmcken House** ((250) 361-0021, a heritage building dating from the 1850s that was originally the home of Fort Victoria's surgeon. Inside you can see period furnishings and a display of the doctor's medical equipment. It's open daily May to September with reduced winter hours; an admission fee is charged.

Victoria has its share of commercialized attractions, especially in the area around the Parliament Buildings. One of the better ones is the **Pacific Undersea Gardens** ((250) 382-5717, 490 Belleville Street, where you descend to the bottom of the harbor to look, through glass, at the marine life and some frolicsome scuba divers. Next to it the **Royal London Wax Museum** ((250) 388-4461 is

Victoria — OPPOSITE: Highland dancers step out. ABOVE: Rugby is another Old World activity that thrives here.

worth a look. The building was designed by Rattenbury and originally built in 1924 as the CPR Steamship Terminal. Inside you'll find 300 wax figures, including, of course, Queen Victoria. Both attractions are open daily, year-round; both charge an admission fee.

For a pleasant waterfront stroll continue westwards along Belleville Street past the ferry terminals and follow the coast to **Fisherman's Wharf**, a lively spot where fishing boats come and go and houseboats are moored. If you'd like to see Victoria from the water, boat trips leave from the Inner Harbour, in front of the Empress. Also along the waterfront, the brightly painted houses of **Waddington Alley** contain some interesting boutiques and art galleries.

The **Old Town** section of Victoria lies to the north of the Empress, along Wharf Street and the nearby streets and alleys. This is an area of narrow streets, squares, gaslights, cobbles, and buildings that date from the 1860s. The area has undergone extensive renovation and, as is so often the case, many of the old buildings now house chic cafés, restaurants, and shops. At **Centennial Square** you can see Victoria's original City Hall, and at nearby **Bastion Square**, site of the original Fort Victoria in 1843, the old criminal courthouse now houses the **Maritime Museum of British Columbia** ((250) 385-4222. On display here are model ships, nautical paraphernalia, and a Native American dugout canoe that voyaged from Victoria to England a hundred years ago.

Government Street, particularly where it runs through the Old Town, has some of the city's most interesting stores. Here are shops that have remained unchanged for the last 70 or so years and they wouldn't seem out of place in London's Jermyn Street. You can buy plaids, tartans, Waterford crystal, Wedgwood china, have yourself measured for a suit that will be made for you in England, buy your cigars at an old-fashioned tobacconist, or treat someone to delicious handmade chocolates. Also along the street are outlets for Canadian arts and crafts, and you'll see hardwearing Cowichan sweaters on sale that are made of naturally waterproof undyed wool and decorated with traditional First Nations designs.

Just north of Centennial Square, on the corner of Fisgard Street and Government Street, an ornate red gateway known as the **Gate of Harmonious Interest** marks the entrance to Victoria's old and colorful **Chinatown**. Once a flourishing community, it came into being in the 1850s when many Chinese arrived to work on constructing the Canadian Pacific Railway. Over the years Chinatown has dwindled in size and now scarcely covers two blocks, but it is still the site of the narrowest street in Canada and has a few interesting buildings, along with shops selling souvenirs, crafts, and exotic groceries.

At the southeastern edge of downtown, behind the British Columbia Provincial Museum, **Beacon Hill Park** offers a delightful retreat and a lovely spot to picnic. This hilly parkland of gardens, trees, ponds, and views stretches southwards to the Juan de Fuca Strait. At its southwestern corner a plaque marks the terminus of the Trans-Canada Highway.

Outside Downtown

About one and a half kilometers (a third of a mile) east of downtown in the Rockland area, a nineteenth-century mansion houses the **Art Gallery of Greater Victoria** ((250) 384-4101, 1040 Moss Street. It exhibits art from a variety of countries and periods, and has a particularly fine collection of Asian art that includes a Shinto shrine. The gallery is open daily; an admission fee is charged, free on Monday. Nearby stands the imposing **Craigdarroch Castle** ((250) 592-5323, 1050 Joan Crescent, a turreted baronial-style mansion of palatial proportions. It was built in 1890 by Robert Dunsmuir, a wealthy Scottish coal tycoon, in order to persuade his wife to leave her home in Scotland. The interior is richly decorated with wood paneling, stained glass, and period furniture. It is open daily, and an admission fee is charged.

Moving west of downtown, **Craigflower Manor** ((250) 387-4697, at Admirals and Craigflower roads, is one of Victoria's earliest buildings, dating from 1856. It was built on a farm for the Hudson's Bay Company subsidiary, Puget Sound Agricultural Company, in an early attempt to develop a settlement around the trading post. With original furnishings and household appliances, it makes for an interesting visit. Nearby stands the **Craigflower Schoolhouse**, which was built in 1855 and ended its days as a schoolhouse in 1911 to serve as a museum. It's open daily.

To the west of Victoria Harbour, the **English Village** ((250) 388-4353, at 429 Lampson Street, is a collection of replicated old English buildings. The highlight is the accurately reconstructed **Anne Hathaway's Cottage** furnished with sixteenth- and seventeenth-century antiques. The **Olde England Inn** offers accommodation and a restaurant serving English-style meals. The village is open daily, and an admission fee is charged.

Excursions from Victoria

The outstanding **Butchart Gardens** ((250) 652-5256, are located 21 km (13 miles) north of downtown Victoria on Brentwood Bay at 800 Bennevuto Avenue. Their history makes a classic ugly-duckling-to-swan story. Jenny Butchart was the wife of a wealthy cement manufacturer who, in the process of beautifying their large estate, decided to do something about the unsightly hole left by her husband's abandoned limestone quarry.

In 1904 she began the task of landscaping this eyesore by setting lawns, planting trees, creating beautiful arrangements of flowers, and by covering the sides of the pit with ivy. The success of this sunken garden inspired the Butcharts to continue their horticultural activities, and now their gardens cover an area of some 20 hectares (50 acres). There's a magnificent rose garden, which is best seen in July; a Japanese garden with lacquered bridges, summerhouses, and a waterfall; and a formal Italian garden with topiary hedges, a lily pond, and statuary. In the summer you can enjoy music in these delightful surroundings on the Concert Lawn and take a nighttime tour of the illuminated gardens.

Arm and then climbs Malahat Ridge where you have views across Saanich Inlet of the Gulf Islands, the mainland, and the distant peak of Mount Baker in Washington State.

If you'd like to explore some of the beaches and forests of the southwest corner of Vancouver Island, then pack your picnic hamper, maybe your tent as well, and head out of Victoria picking up Highway 14 bound for **Sooke**, some 42 km (26 miles) west of Victoria. In this logging town you'll find the Sooke Regional Museum and Travel Infocentre ((250) 642-6351, at 2070 Phillips Road, with its displays of local native craft (open daily in summer, closed Mondays in winter; admission is free). You can also pick up supplies

These are pleasure gardens so you won't find botanical labels among the flowerbeds, but the Horticultural Centre can answer any questions you may have.

Even in their winter greenery the gardens are worth the trip, and flowers will still be blooming in the greenhouses. You can have lunch or dinner in the Blue Poppy or the Dining Room restaurants making the leisurely visit that the gardens deserve. To get there from downtown Victoria, either take Highway 17 to the Keating Cross Road turnoff, from where you continue your journey in a westerly direction, or take the 17A direct. It's open daily at 9 AM; an admission fee is charged with discounts in the winter months.

To take a look at the coastal scenery northwest of Victoria, travel north out of the city on the Trans-Canada Highway, and after 16 km (10 miles) you'll hit **Malahat Drive**. The road skirts along Finlayson

for the rest of your journey in town. North of Sooke along Highway 14 you'll probably stop and follow a forest trail to one of the lovely beaches that line the coast here. The highway ends at the one-horse settlement of Port Renfrew, where you can observe some marine life in the tidal pools at **Botanical Beach** when the tide is low. The rugged West Coast Trail — a serious hiking undertaking — runs from here to Bamfield and forms a section of the famous Pacific Rim National Park. From here you can either retrace your steps along Highway 14 back to Victoria or you can take the logging road to Lake Cowichan where you have a choice of two roads, both of which connect with the Trans-Canada Highway at Duncan.

The beautiful Butchart Gardens on Tod Inlet outside Victoria.

Northeast of Victoria in the Strait of Georgia lie the lovely and temperate **Southern Gulf Islands**. Artists, retirees, and others drawn by the peace or the prospect of an alternative lifestyle inhabit some of the islands, which offer the visitor quiet beaches, beautiful vistas, accommodation, fishing, diving, and a host of other outdoor opportunities. From Swartz Bay, BC Ferries ((250) 386-3431 or (604) 669-1211, runs at regular intervals to Salt Spring Island, and operates another service to Pender, Mayne, Galiano, and Saturna Islands. Reserve ahead, and in the summer arrive well in advance of the departure time. For **bed and breakfast** accommodation, contact the Accommodations Group

Victoria are renowned for salmon and offer some excellent **deep-sea fishing**, and many companies in town offer charter trips. Fishing licenses are required, and regulations are complicated and constantly in flux; call ((604) 666-5835 for fish licensing information. Licenses are available province-wide from marinas, sporting goods stores, charter boat operators, and department stores.

The waters, particularly in the Georgia Strait, are excellent for **diving**, and are inhabited by a wide variety of marine life. Thetis Lake Park is a very pleasant spot for **swimming**. It is only a short drive northwest of downtown, and has a popular beach as well as more secluded spots. You'll also

of Salt Spring Island ((250) 537-5252 FAX (250) 537-4276 E-MAIL chamber@saltspring.com, Chamber of Commerce, Tourist Information Centre, 121 Lower Ganges Road, Salt Spring Island V8K 2T1.

SPORTS AND OUTDOOR ACTIVITIES

There are plenty of places offering **boating** or **sailing** charters, with or without crew. If you'd like to learn how to do it, there are a few schools around the Oak Bay Marina ((250) 598-3369. There are plenty of opportunities for **canoeing** in the area and sports outfitters can often supply information on package trips. There's **freshwater fishing** at Elk and Beaver lakes, which are only about a 15-minute drive north of Victoria, and there are several other lakes and streams a little further out. The waters that surround

find some beautiful beaches on the southwest coast along the stretch of Highway 14 between Sooke and Port Renfrew. There are several recreation centers in the Victoria area with pools. One of the best is the Crystal Pool Recreation Centre ((250) 380-7946, at 2275 Quadra Street.

Windsurfing is quite a popular pursuit in these parts, and there are plenty of places that give lessons. Some popular spots are Cadboro Bay, east of downtown near the university, and Elk Lake, which is about a 15-minute drive north of Victoria.

There are good **hiking** trails around some of the parklands northwest of Victoria, and lots more along the southwest coast between Sooke and Port Renfrew. At Port Renfrew, about 107 km (66 miles) from Victoria, there's the very challenging West Coast Trail to Bamfield (see PACIFIC RIM NATIONAL PARK, page 368).

NIGHTLIFE AND THE ARTS

Several free magazines are available that carry entertainment listings for the area. The Arts Council of Greater Victoria publishes *Arts Victoria*, and there's the *Monday Magazine* that, despite its title, comes out on Thursday.

The **Royal Theatre**, 805 Broughton Street, and the **McPherson Playhouse**, 3 Centennial Square, are both renovated older theaters that stage plays and concerts. Information on both can be obtained at ((250) 386-6121. The **University Centre Auditorium** ((250) 721-8480 at Finnerty Road also stages plays and dance events, and the intimate **Belfry**

Priding itself on its Englishness, Victoria has several pubs that serve British-style beer. **Spinnaker's Brew Pub** ((250) 386-2739, at 308 Catherine Street overlooks the harbor to the west of downtown, and is a pleasant place where you can sample some good ale brewed on the premises, take a brewery tour or just relax with a dart game. There is live music some nights.

WHERE TO STAY

Expensive

The château-like **Empress Hotel** ((250) 384-8111 FAX (250) 381-4334 TOLL-FREE (800) 441-1414, 721 Government Street, Victoria V8W 1W5, under-

Theatre ((250) 385-6815, 1291 Gladstone Street, tends towards contemporary drama.

The **Pacific Victoria Opera** stages three productions a year at the McPherson Playhouse, while the **Victoria Symphony** performs year-round, mainly at the Royal Theatre but can also can be heard at the University Centre Auditorium.

Victoria holds its own annual **Jazz Festival International** in late June. You can obtain information from the **Victorian Jazz Society** ((250) 388-4423. There's also the **Jazz Hotline** ((250) 658-5255 to contact for club and restaurant shows throughout the year. Downtown, **Hermann's Dixieland Inn** ((250) 388-9166, 753 View Street, has lots of atmosphere, hearty food, and the kind of jazz you'd expect from its name.

For jazz as well as live rock and blues, there's **Harpo's** ((250) 385-5333, at 15 Bastion Square, where top names often play.

went major renovation in 1989 and has emerged triumphantly with upgraded facilities and sympathetic redecoration. It is the island's largest hotel with 475 rooms and suites, all beautifully decorated with traditional prints and fresh flowers. Formal dining is in the lovely Empress Room. There is a modern bistro, and the famous afternoon tea is served in the 1920s elegance of the Palm Court or the Tea Lobby. There is an indoor pool, and shops complete the amenities.

Close to Beacon Hill Park, the **Beaconsfield Inn** ((250) 384-4044, 998 Humboldt Street, Victoria V8V 2Z8, is a restored early twentieth-century mansion beautifully decorated with wood paneling, stained glass, and furnished with antiques. This Old World elegance extends to the

OPPOSITE: The Victoria Eaton Centre. ABOVE: Afternoon tea in the Empress Hotel.

10 unique and lovely rooms, some of which have special features such as canopied beds or wood-burning fireplaces, and there are also a few "celebration suites" for honeymooners and lovers of luxury. The old-fashioned atmosphere is preserved by the absence of telephones or televisions in the rooms. The hotel has a lovely library where guests can attend a hospitality hour each afternoon, and breakfast — included in the room rate — is served in the attractive conservatory. Its sister hotel is the nearby **Abigail's Hotel** ((250) 388-5363, 906 McClure Street, Victoria V8V 3E7, which is a heritage Tudor-style mansion in much the same mold. It has 16 accommodations with similar features to the Beaconsfield, and again the library serves as a delightful social center. A gourmet breakfast is included in the room rates, which vary between expensive and mid-range.

In complete contrast is the modern highrise **Executive House Hotel** ((250) 388-5111 TOLL-FREE (800) 663-7001 FAX (250) 385-1323, 777 Douglas Street, Victoria V8W 2B5. It is one block away from the Inner Harbour and has 179 large accommodations, including suites with self-catering facilities. There's a restaurant, a popular pub, and an oyster bar. Rates range from expensive to mid-range. The **Clarion Hotel Grand Pacific** ((250) 386-0450 TOLL-FREE (800) 458-6262 FAX (250) 386-8779, at 450 Québec Street, Victoria V8V 1W5, is another modern hotel that overlooks the Inner Harbour. Rooms and suites are attractive, well-equipped, and each has a balcony and bathroom. The hotel has a pleasant dining room.

The **Laurel Point Inn** ((250) 386-8721 TOLL-FREE (800) 663-7667 FAX (250) 386-9547, at 680 Montréal Street, Victoria V8V 1Z8, stands on a headland overlooking the Inner Harbour and is surrounded by gardens. The coolly elegant rooms all have balconies with harbor views, and there is an indoor swimming pool, a tennis court, and a bistro.

The **Victoria Regent Hotel** ((250) 386-2211 TOLL-FREE (800) 663-7472 FAX (250) 386-2622, 1234 Wharf Street, Victoria V8W 3H9, stands at the water's edge and has excellent harbor views. There are 40 well-appointed accommodations, mostly one- and two-bedroom suites, some with fireplaces and all with kitchens. There's a waterside restaurant and marina facilities.

Close to the Parliament Buildings, the **Château Victoria Hotel** ((250) 382-4221 TOLL-FREE (800) 663-5891 FAX (250) 380-1950, 740 Burdett Avenue, Victoria V8W 1B2, is a highrise building with 178 accommodations each with a balcony. The hotel offers a good range of services; rooms and suites are available, some with a kitchen.

If you're considering a trip to the South Gulf island of Saltspring, you should make sure to stay at **Hastings House** ((250) 537-2362 E-MAIL hasthouse @saltspring.com, PO Box 1110, Ganges V0S 1E0.

If you weren't considering it, it's worth the trip just for the delight of staying at this inn. It belongs to the prestigious Relais & Châteaux chain and has 12 lovely rooms and suites well stocked with life's little luxuries. The half-timbered house resembles an old English country manor set in lovely grounds with views of Ganges Harbour, and first-class gourmet food is served in the graceful dining room. Guests can enjoy fishing, sailing and hiking nearby. The price includes full English breakfast. Book well in advance.

Some five kilometers (three miles) east of downtown there's the delightful Tudor-style **Oak Bay Beach Hotel** ((250) 598-4556, at 1175 Beach Drive, Victoria V8S 2N2. This seaside hotel has antiques in the lovely lobby and rooms which all differ in size and design. The hotel operates dinner cruises, whale watching tours, and fishing charters from the nearby marina, and it has an English-style pub and a seaside dining room.

Just outside Victoria (about 40 km or 24 miles from Victoria International Airport), **The Aerie** ((250) 743-7115 FAX (250) 743-4766 PO Box 108, Malahat V0R 2L0, is a lovely Relais & Château property, with a superb location offering breathtaking views across the fjords and Olympic Mountains. Sumptuous Mediterranean-style villas, including 10 rooms and 10 suites, are surrounded by acres of parkland. Activities abound with tennis courts, fishing, sailing, and hiking on site. When the day is done the spa, sauna, and whirlpool soothe the body from the day's exertions.

If you're planning an excursion to the southwest coast of the island, you might consider staying at the **Sooke Harbour House** ((250) 642-3421 FAX (250) 642-6988, 1528 Whiffen Spit Road, Rural Route 4, Sooke V0S 1N0, about 37 km (23 miles) from Victoria. Primarily an internationally famous gourmet restaurant, this large white house perched high above a bay also has 23 wonderful guestrooms. Rooms are lovingly decorated with original artworks and antiques, each with a name that underlines the theme reflected in the decor. All rooms have fireplaces, and some have four-poster beds, double Jacuzzis, balconies, or sun decks. Rates include breakfast and lunch, and special honeymoon packages are available.

Mid-range

Close to Parliament Buildings you can enjoy some old-fashioned comfort in an intimate atmosphere at the **Holland House Inn** ((250) 384-6644, 595 Michigan Street, Victoria V8V 1S7. This is a 1930s house, casually elegant with contemporary art adorning its public areas. There are 10 cheerful, antique-furnished rooms with balconies, some of which have four-poster beds and fireplaces. It's worth staying here for the gourmet breakfast alone. Rates include breakfast and vary from expensive to mid-range. Also close to Parliament, the **James Bay Inn** ((250) 384-7151 TOLL-FREE (800) 836-2649 FAX (250) 385-2311, 270 Government Street, Victoria V8V 2L2, is a large old house with character that offers good value and is thus very popular. The 48 rooms vary in amenities and size — some have private baths and some have kitchenettes.

For some fantasy accommodation try the **Olde England Inn** ((250) 388-4353 FAX (250) 382-8311, 429 Lampson Street, Victoria V9A 5Y9. It is part of a group of reconstructed sixteenth-century English buildings that include replicas of Shakespeare's birthplace and Anne Hathaway's

cottage and the like, and are just a short drive west of downtown in the Esquimalt district. Genuine antiques, including some canopy beds, furnish the rooms. The bathrooms are not, thankfully, sixteenth-century replicas. Prices vary widely from low mid-range to expensive.

The **Strathcona Hotel** ((250) 383-7137 TOLL-FREE (800) 663-7476 FAX (250) 383-6893, at 919 Douglas Street, Victoria V8W 2C2, is an old building that also houses a pub, a restaurant, and several nightspots. The rooms are modern with private bathrooms and lots of features that make it very good value. The **Hotel Douglas** ((250) 383-4157 TOLL-FREE (800) 332-9981 FAX (250) 383-2279, at 1450 Douglas Street, Victoria V8W 2G1, is also an older building with nice, modern rooms, some of which have private baths. There's a 24-hour café, a bar and laundry facilities. Room rates vary from the top of the inexpensive range to mid-range.

Inexpensive

Conveniently situated, the **Cherry Bank Hotel** ((250) 385-5380 TOLL-FREE (800) 998-6688, 825 Burdett Avenue, Victoria V8W 1B3, is a late nineteenth-century building with new extensions. The rooms are simply furnished and have no phones or television, but they are clean and adequate. There's a restaurant and bar, and you can join other guests in the Trivial Pursuit lounge. A full English breakfast is included in the price.

Victoria has an abundance of **bed and breakfast** accommodations ranging from the basic to the luxurious (see WHERE TO STAY, page 349, under VANCOUVER).

Hostelling International-Victoria (HI) ((250) 385-4511 FAX (250) 385-3232 E-MAIL victoria@ hihostels.bc.ca, downtown at 516 Yates Street, Victoria V8W 1K8, is a large, modern place with single-sex dormitories and good kitchen facilities.

The University of Victoria six kilometers (four miles) east of downtown offers **campus accommodation**. For details contact the University of Victoria Housing and Conference Services ((250) 721-8395, PO Box 1700, Victoria V8W 2Y2.

WHERE TO EAT

Expensive

Sooke Harbour House ((250) 642-3421, 42 km (26 miles) west of Victoria at 1528 Whiffen Spit Road, Rural Route 4, is one of Canada's best restaurants and offers some truly memorable dining. This is a large white house perched on a bluff overlooking a bay, with a spectacular view of the Juan de Fuca Strait and the Olympic Mountains beyond. The menu changes according to what is available that day, but you can expect to find flowers liberally used in delightful salads and as garnish, the freshest of fish, and free-range chicken. The presentation is pure artistry, the service knowledgeable, and the atmosphere informal.

Dinner is a far more formal affair at the distinguished **Empress Room** ((250) 384-8111, in the Empress Hotel, 721 Government Street. Wooden ceilings, pillars, and chandeliers create a setting that is splendidly traditional while the menu features Pacific Northwest cuisine and holds some pleasant surprises. Gentle piano or harp music enhances one's enjoyment of the excellent food.

Moderate to Inexpensive

Pagliacci's ((250) 386-1662, at 1011 Broad Street, serves dependable Italian food. There's usually a line outside and it is cramped inside, but everyone is fortunately very friendly, and putting your elbow in somebody else's pasta can prove to be a great icebreaker. There's a slightly Bohemian air about the **Herald Street Caffe** ((250) 381-1441,

An outdoor café in Victoria.

546 Herald Street, where you can inspect the work of local artists on display and enjoy some extremely good Italian and Californian food.

For Indian food try the **Taj Mahal** ((250) 383-4662, 679 Herald Street, where vegetarians will find themselves well-catered for. Along Fisgard Street in Chinatown, a goodly number of restaurants serve Sichuan, Hunan, and Cantonese food; for authentic Japanese food try the **Japanese Village Steak & Seafood House** ((250) 385-1615, at 734 Broughton Street. For an altogether English experience go to **Old Vic Fish 'n' Chips** ((250) 388-4536, at 1316 Broad Street, or on a rather more dignified note, take afternoon tea at the **James Bay Tearoom** ((250) 382-8282, 332 Menzies Street.

HOW TO GET THERE

Victoria International Airport is about 26 km (16 miles) north of downtown. There is an **airport bus service**, operated by PBM Transport ((250) 475-2010, that runs frequently. The trip to downtown takes around half an hour. Victoria is served by 50 flights each day that make the short trip from Vancouver International Airport and Seattle-Tacoma Airport, in addition to numerous direct flights from other major cities. Regular float plane and helicopter service to downtown Victoria is available from Vancouver and Seattle.

The *Princess Marguerite III* (which also carries cars) cruises daily between Seattle and Victoria's

ABOVE: The fearsome image of the thunderbird sits atop a totem pole in Victoria's Thunderbird Park. OPPOSITE: The handsome caboose of a vintage Canadian Pacific Railroad train.

Inner Harbour from mid-May to mid-September. The journey takes approximately four and a half hours. Contact **Clipper Navigation** ((250) 480-5555 TOLL-FREE IN THE UNITED STATES (800) 888-2535, for details and reservations. The *Victoria Clipper* is a jet-propelled catamaran, also operated by Clipper Navigation, that crosses between Victoria and Seattle in a mere two and a half hours, year-round. **BC Ferries** ((604) 277-0277 (24-hour recorded information) or (604) 669-1211 (reservations) TOLL-FREE IN BRITISH COLUMBIA (800) 663-7600 operate between Vancouver and Vancouver Island. From Tsawwassen, which is south of Vancouver on the mainland, ferries sail to Victoria and Nanaimo on Vancouver Island and to the Southern Gulf Islands. BC Ferries also operate between Horseshoe Bay (30 minutes north of Vancouver) and Nanaimo.

Black Ball Transport ((250) 386-2202 or ((206) 457-4491 in Port Angeles runs a ferry between Victoria's Inner Harbour and Port Angeles on Washington's Olympic Peninsula; it takes an hour and 35 minutes. **Washington State Ferries** ((250) 381-1551 or (IN THE US (206) 464-6400, operate daily, year-round between Sidney, just north of Victoria, and Anacortes, Washington with ports of call in the San Juan Islands. The approximate crossing time is three hours.

The **Pacific Coach Line** ((250) 385-4411 operates frequent service from Vancouver to Victoria via the Tsawwassen-Swartz Bay ferry crossing, with a journey time of three and a half hours. **Island Coach Lines** ((250) 385-4411 connects with other Vancouver Island towns. **Maverick Coach Lines** ((250) 662-8051 operates between Nanaimo and Vancouver also via the BC Ferries.

The **Esquimalt & Nanaimo Rail Liner** (VIA Rail) ((250) 383-4324 TOLL-FREE (888) 842-7733 runs to Duncan, Nanaimo, Qualicum Beach, Courtenay and points in between. The station is near downtown Victoria at 450 Pandora Avenue.

ELSEWHERE ON THE ISLAND

DUNCAN AND VICINITY

The rural town of Duncan, 60 km (38 miles) north of Victoria on the Trans-Canada Highway, is the gateway and supply center to the **Cowichan Valley**. The valley is still home to many Cowichan, and native craftsmen have collaborated with the town to produce the 80 or so totem poles clustered along the roadside. This is a good place to buy one of the famous Cowichan sweaters, as well as other native arts and crafts. Duncan's premiere attraction is the **Cowichan Native Village** ((250) 746-8119, 200 Cowichan Way, situated on a five-hectare (13-acre), tree-lined stretch of the Cowichan River. At the Longhouse Story Centre, a film explains the history and legends of the Cowichan people. At the carving house, visitors can see

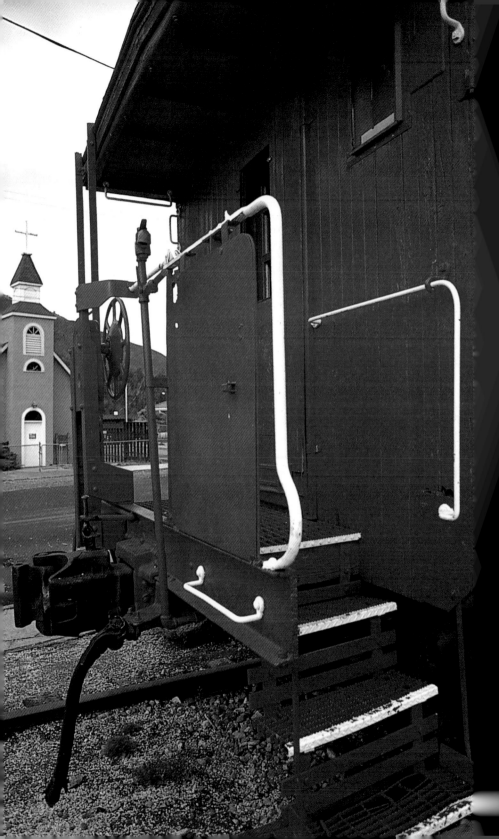

artisans at work, and at noon there's a salmon barbecue and dance presentation. The village is open daily from 9 AM to 5 PM; an admission is charged for the village and for the barbecue/show.

Highway 18 takes you 31 km (19 miles) westwards to **Lake Cowichan**, the largest freshwater lake on the island. It is known mainly for its good fishing but it is also good for swimming, camping, or canoeing, and the surrounding forest is laced with hiking trails. The valley is a lumbering area and one of the better logging roads will take you westwards from the lake to Port Renfrew on the island's west coast, the beginning of the Pacific Rim National Park's famous West Coast Trail.

About three kilometers (one and a half miles) north of Duncan the **British Columbia Forest Museum** ((250) 715-1113 offers a fascinating look at the history of the forestry industry in the province through both indoor and outdoor exhibits. Here you can take a ride on a narrow-gauge steam railway, visit a reconstructed logging camp, see old equipment, and walk through the surrounding forest. It's open daily May to September and an admission fee is charged.

Twenty kilometers (12 miles) north along the highway from Duncan lies the curious town of **Chemainus**. To avert the disaster that threatened when the town's sawmill closed down in 1983, the community set out to find itself a new source of revenue by commissioning murals to grace the town's buildings. The idea worked: visitors came to look, shops and restaurants opened, and murals depicting the town's history have spread like wildfire, covering not only walls but also litter bins and anything else that stands still long enough. BC Ferries operates from here to nearby **Thetis** and **Kuper islands**, part of the Southern Gulf Islands.

A little further north the attractive waterfront town of **Ladysmith** sits right on the 49th parallel which divides the mainland between Canada and the United States (aside from Victoria Island). The old buildings here have been nicely renovated and it makes a pleasant stopping place.

For lodging in Duncan there is the **Best Western Cowichan Valley Inn** ((250) 748-2722 TOLL-FREE (800) 528-1234 FAX (250) 748-2207, 6474 Trans-Canada Highway, Rural Route 4, Duncan V9L 3W8, located opposite the British Columbia Forest Museum. It offers 42 comfortable rooms and suites, a dining room, and a coffee shop. Prices are solidly mid-range.

At Ladysmith the **Yellowpoint Lodge** ((250) 245-7422 FAX (250) 245-7411, 3700 Yellow Point Road, Rural Route 3, Ladysmith V0R 2E0, is set in delightful parkland overlooking the sea, and inexpensive accommodation — with three full meals included in the rate — is available either in the main lodge or in rustic cottages. There is a saltwater pool, a hot tub, a sauna, sports facilities, and a restaurant.

NANAIMO

Nanaimo, 110 km (68 miles) north of Victoria, is the second largest city on Vancouver Island and a major deep-sea fishing center. Several First Nations tribes lived in peaceful coexistence here until the Hudson's Bay Company discovered coal in the 1850s. Nanaimo remained a thriving coal mining area until demand dwindled with the coming of the oil-burning ships, at which point it turned to logging and fishing. Now an important BC Ferries terminus with a direct link to the mainland, the town has adapted itself to the tourist industry. Increased facilities, renovated buildings, smart boutiques, jolly festivals, and inhabitants renowned for their friendliness draw many visitors.

In 1853 the Hudson's Bay Company built the fortified **Bastion** as defense against possible native attack. Now the symbol of Nanaimo, this stout fort serves as a museum, and during the summer months its three cannons are ceremonially fired each day at noon. To find out a little more about Nanaimo's history, visit the **Nanaimo Centennial Museum** ((250) 753-1821 at 100 Cameron Street, which is open daily during the summer and from Tuesday to Saturday in the winter.

The wealth of parks and lakes in and around Nanaimo gives anglers, boaters, canoeists, windsurfers, and hikers plentiful opportunities to pursue their sports. Departure Bay at the north end of town is a popular windsurfing spot and whatever equipment you need can be rented from an outlet actually on the beach. If island-hopping appeals to you, there's a regular BC Ferry service to nearby **Newcastle** and **Gabriola islands**. Newcastle Island is a provincial park inhabited only by wildlife, park keepers, and campers, while Gabriola Island, although home to a small artistic community, is also unspoiled, peaceful, and has some lovely beaches.

Just south of Nanaimo look for **Petroglyph Provincial Park** ((250) 387-5002 where you can see prehistoric carvings on the sandstone rock that were made by native people some 10,000 years ago.

The best place to stay around Nanaimo is the **Coast Bastion Inn** ((250) 753-6601 TOLL-FREE (800) 663-1144 FAX (250) 753-4155, 11 Bastion Street, Nanaimo V9R 2Z9, a large hotel on the waterfront with pleasant views from all of its rooms. The hotel has a café and a pub. The **Best Western Dorchester Hotel** ((250) 754-6835 TOLL-FREE (800) 661-2449 FAX (250) 754-6835, 70 Church Street, Nanaimo V9R 5H4, has rooms and suites with harbor views, a restaurant, a rooftop garden, and a library. Prices at both the Best Western Dorchester and the Coast Bastion fall into the expensive category. Conveniently situated for the Nanaimo Ferry Terminal is the **Colonial Motel** ((250) 754-4415 FAX (250) 753-1611, 950 Terminal Avenue North, Nanaimo V9S 4K4. Rooms have private bathrooms, cable television, telephones, and kitchenettes. Kayaks can be rented on site, and restaurants and shopping are close by. Rates are inexpensive.

PARKSVILLE TO PORT ALBERNI

About 38 km (24 miles) north of Nanaimo, **Parksville** is well situated for a variety of outdoor activities. It lies along a coastal stretch popular for its lovely, sandy beaches and waters said to be the warmest in Canada. To the west of Parksville lie wooded slopes threaded with nature trails, and

meters (five and a half miles) along the road in **MacMillan Provincial Park** stands the magnificent **Cathedral Grove**, an awesome sight that is not to be missed. Some of the Douglas firs in this grove are 800 years old and reach heights of 76 m (250 ft).

Halfway across the island, **Port Alberni** sits at the head of the deep-cutting Alberni Inlet that widens into the West Coast's Barkley Sound. It is a large town with a thriving lumber industry; a fact unfortunately borne out by the pungent smell that emanates from the mills. Its other main revenue comes from fishing, as anglers come here for the excellent salmon. From the harbor the stately **MV *Lady Rose*** ((250) 723-8313 takes passengers

in the winter months nearby Mount Arrowsmith attracts skiers. This is also where the scenic Highway 4 cuts westwards, crossing the island's central mountain range and leading to its star attraction — the magnificent Pacific Rim National Park, 154 km (96 miles) away.

After a steep five kilometers (three miles) along Highway 4, a deviation of about eight kilometers (five miles) to the left will bring you to **Englishman Falls Provincial Park** where the Englishman River rushes over waterfalls down into lush, ferny forest, and brims with rainbow trout and steelhead. With beautiful clear pools for swimming, it is a delightful spot to pitch a tent. Back along Highway 4, a further 20 km (12 miles) will bring you to **Little Qualicum Falls Provincial Park**. A delightful forest trail leads to this series of waterfalls and ice-cold pools, while nearby tree-fringed **Cameron Lake** teems with trout. About nine kilo-

down the inlet to Bamfield and Ucluelet via the Broken Islands. This cruise is a pleasant way to observe some of the wildlife of the sky and sea, and those intending to canoe or kayak around the Broken Islands are allowed to take their vessel aboard. You can rent whatever equipment you need for canoeing, kayaking, or diving from outlets in Port Alberni. The *Lady Rose* operates from April to September. Departures are daily at 8 AM.

From Port Alberni, Highway 4 continues towards the West Coast by **Sproat Lake**, which attracts many watersports enthusiasts and anglers. It proceeds through some beautiful mountain scenery, marred only by evidence of the extensive logging that has taken place in the area. The road follows the Kennedy River to Kennedy Lake, and

On Vancouver Island's Barkeley Sound eagles are so numerous that locals joke, "They're like crows to us."

then reaches the junction with the Ucluelet road where it bends sharply to the right and continues to Tofino.

There's a wide choice of motels and resorts in Parksville and several motels in Port Alberni. Back on the east coast there's some interesting accommodation at **Qualicum College Inn (** (250) 752-9262 TOLL-FREE (800) 663-7306 FAX (250) 752-5144 E-MAIL qcihotel@nanaimo.ark.com, 427 College Road, PO Box 99, Qualicum Beach V9K 2G4. This historic landmark building, once a boys' school, overlooks the sea and has 70 accommodations, including a few honeymoon suites. Fishing and golfing packages are available, and the prices are mid-range.

ing the spring when they return from their breeding grounds in the south. **Radar Hill** with its telescope offers a good viewing point, but for closer views there are whale-spotting boat trips that operate from Tofino. Humbler marine life can be seen in the tidal pools along the beach — you can look, but you are not allowed to remove any of the little creatures. Another interesting trip from Tofino runs to **Meares Island** where you can follow trails through unspoiled rain forest that has some ancient trees of majestic proportions.

The middle section of the park consists of the **Broken Islands**, 100 or so islands in Barkley Sound that can be reached by the MV *Lady Rose* passenger ship (see PARKSVILLE TO PORT ALBERNI, above),

PACIFIC RIM NATIONAL PARK

The ruggedly beautiful coastal strip that constitutes Pacific Rim National Park **(** (250) 762-7721, PO Box 280, Ucluelet V0R 3A0, stretches for a dramatic 72 km (45 miles) between Tofino and Port Renfrew and is made up of three sections, all very different in character and equally rich in wildlife. The most northerly section, known as **Long Beach**, lies between the villages of Tofino and Ucluelet and is a driftwood-strewn stretch of white sand and rock pounded by Pacific breakers. The weather is generally cold and wet here, but undeterred sportsmen and women don wetsuits to enjoy some superb surfing, swimming, canoeing, and kayaking. Hikers wrap up warmly and explore the magnificent trails through the rain forest. Porpoises, sea lions, and seals inhabit the waters. Gray whales can be spotted here, most frequently dur-

by charter from Port Alberni, or by boat from Ucluelet. The islands are popular with canoeists and kayakers, and the area also offers some wonderful scuba diving with plenty of shipwrecks to be seen, not to mention the world's largest octopi.

Many of the visitors come to Pacific Rim for the third section of the park, the **West Coast Trail**, a tough hiking trail stretching 75 km (47 miles) between Bamfield and Port Renfrew. The trail follows an historic lifesaving route for shipwrecked mariners and requires stamina and endurance, and hikers must carry all food and supplies for the six- to eight-day hike. This trail has become so popular that a quota system has been instituted limiting the number of hikers to 52 per

ABOVE: A kayaker's view of Barkeley Sound near Pacific Rim National Park — the roots of an ancient tree are claimed by the salt water. OPPOSITE: Sea anemone in a Pacific Rim tidal pool.

day. Trailheads are at Port Renfrew and Pachena Bay. Advance reservations are strongly recommended and can be made by calling TOLL-FREE (800) 663-6000. There is a nonrefundable reservation fee. For more information on the West Coast Trail, call the Bamfield Infocentre ((250) 728-3234 or the Port Renfrew Infocentre ((250) 647-5434.

At the entrance to Barkley Sound sits the little town of **Bamfield**, rather unusual in that its main highway is the inlet that divides it into two. A boardwalk two kilometers (one mile) long links East and West Bamfield.

In the Pacific Rim National Park area most of the accommodation is to be found at Tofino and Ucluelet. Bamfield also has a few lodges, resorts, and bed and breakfast places. In recent years fishing charters, lodges, resorts, and other kinds of accommodation have appeared in Bamfield in response to the growing demands of tourism, but during the high season the town still groans under the influx of tourists, mainly fishermen, so everything fills up quickly. You can explore Pacific Rim and the Broken Islands in high style from **Eagle Nook Ocean Wilderness Resort** ((250) 723-1000 TOLL-FREE (800) 760-2777 FAX (250) 723-9842 E-MAIL eaglenk@cedar.alberni.net, PO Box 575, Port Alberni, British Columbia V9Y 7M9. The resort is accessible by water taxi or ferry from Port Alberni (see PADDLE THE PACIFIC RIM, page 25, in TOP SPOTS).

QUALICUM BEACH TO CAMPBELL RIVER

Ten kilometers (six miles) north of Parksville, **Qualicum Beach** is a popular spot for anglers, sunbathers, and swimmers, with plenty of accommodation and facilities geared to visitors' needs. Alternatively, there are the quiet beaches of **Denman** and **Hornby Islands**, home to small communities and accessible by ferry.

A little further north, the towns of **Comox** and **Courtenay** sit in the lovely **Comox Valley**. Both are commercial centers that also serve as bases for the surrounding recreational areas. Golf courses, fishing lodges, mountain trails, and campsites abound, and during the winter skiers flock to the nearby slopes of **Mount Washington** and Strathcona Park's **Forbidden Plateau**.

Campbell River, the gateway to Strathcona Park, is another town that is dedicated to outdoor sports, with skiing, hiking, mountaineering, and canoeing all catered for. The scuba diving here is very highly rated, but above all it is famous for its salmon fishing, which is probably the best anywhere, while its first-class fishing lodges attract enthusiasts from all around the world. It is hardly surprising, therefore, that the town's central attraction seems to be the **Discovery Pier**, a boardwalk that has shelter and facilities for anglers. From here it is well worth a trip on the ferry to historic

Quadra Island to see the **Kwagiulth Museum and Cultural Centre** ((250) 285-3733 where there are displays of some fascinating carvings and ceremonial objects, many of which were seized by the authorities during the banning of potlatches — elaborate ceremonies involving ritual and feasting that were deemed heathen by the church. Potlatches were outlawed by the Canadian government in 1922 as part of a forced-assimilation program. The ban was lifted in 1951. The museum is open daily from 10 AM to 4:30 PM; closed Sunday and Monday off-season. An admission fee is charged.

From Campbell River, Highway 28 runs west to **Strathcona Park**, the largest on Vancouver

Island. It is a magnificent preserve of wilderness and wildlife that contains the **Golden Hinde**, the island's highest peak, as well as the magnificent **Della Falls**. Highway 28 cuts westwards across Strathcona Park to the small town of **Gold River**, where the *Uchuck III*, a converted mine sweeper, will take you along Nootka Sound to **Friendly Cove**, the place where Captain Cook first landed and met with the natives in 1778.

Comox and Courtenay both have a large number of inexpensive motels, and at Campbell River there are also a lot of fishing lodges. One of the most distinguished lodges in town is the **Painter's Lodge and Fishing Resort** ((250) 286-1102 TOLL-FREE (800) 663-7090 FAX (250) 598-1361, 1625 MacDonald Road, PO Box 560, Department 2, Campbell River V9W 5C1, open April to October. It overlooks the ocean and guests stay either in the main lodge or in cottages, where the rooms are very well-equipped. There's a heated outdoor pool, a pub, and seaside dining, and the lodge organizes just about any kind of package you could want. Prices here range from mid-range to expensive. At the **Strathcona Park Lodge (** (250) 286-8206, Highway 28, PO Box 2000, Station A, Campbell River V9W 5C9, there are many kinds of accommodation to be had: campsites, hostel accommodation, apartments, cottages, and chalets. The lodge organizes packages for every kind of outdoor sport, including rock climbing, canoeing, and sailing. **Tsa-Kwa-Luten Lodge (** (250) 285-2042 TOLL-FREE (800) 665-7746 FAX (250) 285-2532 E-MAIL gbryson@online.bc.ca, Lighthouse Road, Quadra Island, PO Box 460,

ceremonies; excellent films on aspects of Northwest Coast native culture are shown. The island is also a good place for **whale watching**. Seasmoke Tours **(** (250) 974-5225 TOLL-FREE (800) 668-6722 has been leading killer-whale watching educational tours for 20 years. You can choose a six-hour tour aboard their sailing yacht or the three-hour Zodiac tour.

Further north the highway ends at **Port Hardy**, where BC Ferries ply the scenic Inside Passage to and from Prince Rupert on the mainland, a 441-km (274-mile) journey (see CRUISE THE INSIDE PASSAGE, page 26, in TOP SPOTS). For the intrepid, trails run from Port Hardy to the splendidly isolated **Cape Scott** and **San Josef Provincial Parks**.

Quathiaski Cove V0P 1N0, at Cape Mudge, is owned and operated by the Cape Mudge First Nations band. Here guests can relax in an environment steeped in native history, culture, and architecture, and dine in the Big House where traditional West Coast fare is served. Accommodation is in the comfortable main lodge or waterfront cottages. All the typical island activities can be pursued here, including hiking, mountain biking, paddling, scuba diving, fishing, and beach combing.

NORTH ISLAND

The best reason for a stop at **Port McNeill** is to take the ferry to the island of **Alert Bay**, home of the **U'Mista Cultural Centre (** (250) 974-5403. On display here are more of the confiscated ceremonial objects that were used for the native potlatch

The Inside Passage ferry leaves from **Port Hardy** early in the morning, so most passengers spend the night somewhere in the vicinity. Always book ahead on nights before ferry departures. Comfortable rooms with shared bath and a hardy breakfast are the trademark of **This Old House (** (250) 949-8372 FAX (250) 949-8390 E-MAIL oldhouse@trinet.ca, 8735 Hastings Street, PO Box 2301, Port Hardy V0N 2P0. Built in 1925 and originally used as a boarding house, it's the oldest residence in Port Hardy. Jean, a former pilot and now part-time mail carrier, knows everything there is to know about the town. Hostel-type accommodation is also sometimes available here. For additional bed and breakfast listings,

Now you see them, now you don't: trees ABOVE of British Columbia's great forests are reduced to timber OPPOSITE to feed the printing presses of several nations.

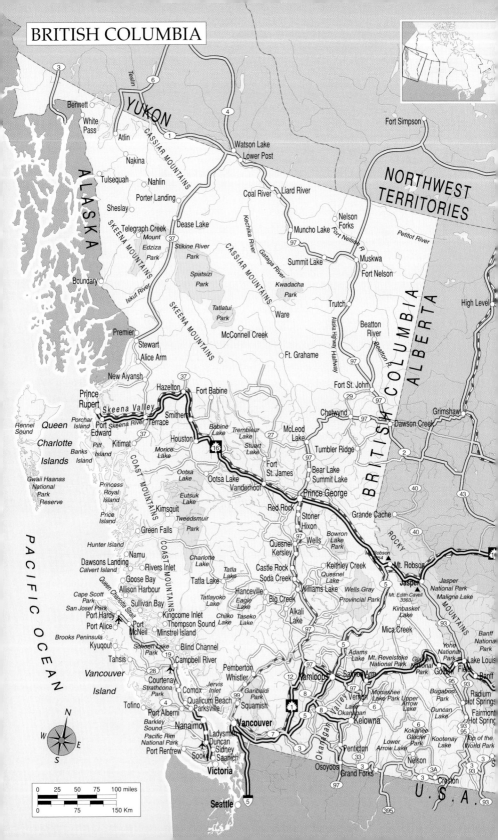

contact the **Port Hardy Visitor Information Centre** ((250) 949-7622, 7250 Market Street, PO Box 249, Port Hardy V0N 2P0; it's open from June 1 to Labor Day. If a hotel is more your style, the locally owned and operated **Airporter Inn** ((250) 949-9434, 4030 Byng Road, Port Hardy, is a reliable choice.

HOW TO GET THERE

A few airlines serve Vancouver Island cities and link with Vancouver, while there are also regular float-plane flights between Nanaimo and the mainland.

BC Ferries ((250) 381-1401 TOLL-FREE (888) 223-3779 run between Port Hardy in the northern part of the island and Prince Rupert on the mainland. This scenic trip along the Inside Passage takes 15 hours, with ferries operating every second day in the summer and once a week in winter. Reservations are required. BC Ferries also connects Horseshoe Bay in Vancouver with Nanaimo.

Island Coach Lines ((250) 724-1266 runs between Nanaimo and Port Alberni, and **Orient Stage Lines Ltd.** ((250) 723-6924 covers the run from Port Alberni to Ucluelet, Pacific Rim National Park, and Tofino.

Esquimalt & Nanaimo Rail Liner (VIA Rail) ((250) 383-4324 TOLL-FREE (888) 842-7733, 450 Pandora Avenue, Victoria, runs from Victoria to Courtenay, stopping at Courtenay, Nanaimo, Duncan, Qualicum Beach, and points along the way. You need to make reservations for trips during the summer.

If you're traveling by car, the road that connects Victoria to the North Island is the Trans-Canada Highway. To reach Ucluelet and Tofino on the West Coast you need to take Highway 4 from Parksville.

THE OKANAGAN VALLEY

This beautiful ribbon of valleys, lakes, and beaches lies in south central British Columbia and stretches from Osoyoos near the United States border to Vernon in the north — a distance of roughly 180 km (112 miles). It is centered around the Okanagan River and a long string of lakes, the largest being the magnificent 144-km (90-mile) Lake Okanagan, which according to First Nations legend is the home of the serpent-monster N'ha-A-Itk, or "Lake Demon," called Ogopogo in English after the popular nineteenth-century music hall tune, "The Ogopogo Song." The lakes are surrounded by arid, rolling hills, lakeside provincial parks, beautiful smooth beaches, and, inevitably, vacation resorts. Highway 97 runs the length of the valley and those who travel it can appreciate the fascinating Okanagan landscape that changes from a "pocket desert" around

Osoyoos, where cactus thrives and rainfall is lightest, to the green farmlands in the north. Throughout the valley orchards flourish, and many believe the Okanagan is at its most seductive during April and May when blossoms cover the trees and their scent fills the air.

The valley averages some 2,000 hours of sunshine a year, summers are hot, winters are mild, and the rainfall is low. This congenial climate, together with the vast tract of water that makes irrigation possible, has turned the area into a major fruit-producing region with crops of apples, peaches, grapes, apricots, cherries, plums, and pears. From late June to October the roadside is lined with stands selling these fruits. Vine-

yards cover the hillsides and eleven of the province's thirteen wineries are here, extending warm welcomes to the visitors who come to be shown around, to taste the wines, and to enjoy the hilltop views. The various fruit harvests are celebrated with events and festivals, and in early fall the whole valley joins in the biggest and jolliest one of all — the Okanagan Wine Festival ((250) 861-6654. The valley has the largest concentration of population in the interior; its main towns are Penticton, and Vernon. The valley has become a popular vacation spot and attracts Canadians from colder regions who come to soak up some of the abundant sunshine. In and around the main towns vacation resorts line the lakes and spread over the hillsides. There are noisy waterslide parks and theme parks. In the summer,

A steamer on Lake Okanagan calls at Kelowna.

water sports enthusiasts flock to the lakes, while the winter brings skiers to the nearby mountainsides. If you are in search of quieter beauty spots then by far the best way to visit the valley is by car. In this way you can appreciate the variation in the scenery and have the freedom to stop your car where you please.

GENERAL INFORMATION

Apart from the information available from the provincial tourist information offices, you can get more specific information on the region from the **Okanagan-Similkameen Tourism Association** ((250) 860-5999 FAX (250) 861-7493, 1332 Water

OSOYOOS

At the southern end of the Okanagan Valley, just north of the United States border, the little town of Osoyoos sits on the shore of Osoyoos Lake. The town has cultivated a Spanish look to suit its dry, sunny climate, and as is characteristic of the Okanagan Valley, it is a fruit-growing area that celebrates its harvests with colorful festivals. Sandy lakeside beaches and warm trout-filled waters make this a popular spot for sunbathing, swimming, angling, windsurfing, boating, and the site for a variety of water sports events. Although fruit-laden orchards cluster around the lake, cacti

Street, Kelowna V1Y 9P4. In addition, there is the **Penticton Wine and Information Centre** ((250) 493-4055, 888 Westminster Avenue West, and a smaller Information Centre along Highway 97, seven kilometers (four miles) south of downtown. At **Kelowna** you can drop in on the Travel Infocentre ((250) 861-1515, at 544 Harvey Avenue. **Vernon** has a year-round Travel Infocentre ((250) 542-1415, at 3700 33rd Street, and a couple of other seasonal centers stationed on the main highway at the northern and southern edges of town.

The Okanagan Valley is a popular resort area and there are masses of motels, resorts, and campgrounds that usually fall within the inexpensive and mid-range price brackets. For lists of **bed and breakfast** accommodation in the area contact the Okanagan Bed and Breakfast ((250) 764-2124, PO Box 5135, Station A, Kelowna V1Y 8T9.

and sagebrush grow on the arid hills that surround the town. This sandy area, which extends northwards to Skaha Lake, is often referred to as Canada's "pocket desert." It is a region that supports horned lizards, rattlesnakes, burrowing owls, and other life forms associated with the desert. Take Highway 3 slightly east of Osoyoos to **Anarchist Mountain** for views that allow you to appreciate fully the varied landscape.

West of the town Highway 3 leads into the neighboring Similkameen Valley. Highway 97 continues northwards following the Okanagan River through its valley past Vaseux and Skaha lakes, a route that is lined with orchards and, in the summertime, with stands selling succulent fruit. Eleven kilometers (seven miles) south of Penticton the **Okanagan Game Farm** ((250) 497-5405, occupies a large area of scrubland above Lake Skaha. A five-kilometer (three-mile) drive through the zoo allows visitors to see over 130 species of animals from all around the world and also has some good views of the lakes.

There are some 20 hotels and motels around the lakeside in Osoyoos, several with their own private beach and shaded lawns. Assistance with other options is available at the local **Visitor Info-centre** ((250) 495-7142 TOLL-FREE (888) 676-9667 FAX (250) 495-6161, at the junction of Highways 3 and 97, PO Box 227, Osoyoos V0H 1V0.

PENTICTON

The town of Penticton lies along Highway 97, 395 km (245 miles) east of Vancouver, between

the grape harvest in September but you don't have to wait until then to enjoy a taste of the local wine (see SPECIAL INTERESTS, PAGE 61, in YOUR CHOICE).

Along the Okanagan lakefront the pleasant **Art Gallery of the South Okanagan** ((250) 493-2928, at 199 Front Street, exhibits local and Canadian works, and can be visited Tuesday to Friday from 10 AM to 5 PM, Saturday and Sunday from 1 PM to 5 PM; an admission fee is charged, free on Tuesday.

About a 30-minute drive west of Penticton along Green Mountain Road lies the **Apex Resort** ((250) 492-2880, where there is a well-equipped ski center. From here, Highway 97 continues its scenic route along the west side of Lake Okanagan,

Skaha Lake and the southern shore of the larger Okanagan Lake. Its name is derived from Salish words meaning "place to stay forever," and the combination of a warm, dry climate and the lovely beaches of two lakes make it as appealing today as it obviously was to the natives who named it. The town is very popular with vacationers and has become tourist-oriented with water slide parks, motels, and other facilities lining Highway 97 as it cuts through the center of the town. The waters of the lakes are ideal for all kinds of water sports and during the high season the beaches get very busy.

The first orchards were planted here in 1874 and the town is now famous for peach-growing. In late July and August the **Penticton Peach Festival** celebrates the harvesting of the crop with sports events, music, dancing, and the extensive drinking of peach brandy. Penticton also celebrates

through orchards, vineyards, provincial parklands, and some smaller towns.

At Penticton there are a few places that stand out above the rest, such as the **Clarion Lakeside Resort and Conference Centre** ((250) 493-8221 TOLL-FREE (800) 663-9400, 21 Lakeshore Drive West, Penticton V2A 7M5. It stands on the shores of Lake Okanagan and offers top-line accommodation with all kinds of recreational facilities and services. The rooms are attractively furnished, all have balconies, and there's a restaurant, cocktail lounge, indoor pool, and a fitness center. Golf courses and tennis courts are nearby, and the beach and lake are at your disposal. Prices here range from expensive to mid-range. The **Best Western Inn** ((250) 493-0311 TOLL-FREE (800) 668-6746

Profiles in the Okanagan Game Farm: a mountain goat OPPOSITE and a bighorn sheep ABOVE.

is at 3180 Skaha Lake Road, Penticton V2A 6G4, and has 67 accommodations, including family and honeymoon suites, plus housekeeping units. There are indoor and outdoor pools, a sun deck and a restaurant, and the beach is nearby. Prices here are mid-range. Just across the road from Okanagan Lake Beach, the **Tiki Shores Condominium Beach Resort** ((250) 492-8769 FAX (250) 492-8160, 914 Lakeshore Drive, Penticton V2A 1C1, has one-, two-, and three-bedroom housekeeping units, some with rooftop patios. There's an outdoor pool, an indoor hot tub, and a (seasonal) restaurant. Prices fall into the mid-range category.

In the inexpensive bracket there's the **Three Gables Hotel** ((250) 492-3933, at 353 Main Street, Penticton V2A 1K9, which is in the city center but only a short walk away from the beach. Rooms have private bathrooms, and there's a restaurant and a pub.

Granny Bogner's ((250) 493-2711, 302 Eckhardt Avenue West, is widely held to be the best restaurant in the Okanagan. The theme is homey; the fare is European. It's open for dinner only, and reservations are essential. You can sample Greek specialties in pleasant surroundings at **Angelinis** on Skaha Lake Road, or some hearty good-value food at the **Elite Restaurant** ((250) 492-3051, 340 Main Street, where they do burgers, soups, and puddings. For Mexican food you should try **Taco Grande** at 452 Main Street.

KELOWNA

About halfway along Lake Okanagan, Highway 97 crosses a floating bridge to Kelowna, the largest city in the Okanagan Valley, with a population in the region of 70,000, and the center of this fruit-growing and wine-producing region. This attractive lakeside city with its many vineyards,

ture of life in those pioneering days. The site is open daily, and admission is free.

The province's largest and oldest winery is Kelowna's **Calona Wines** ((250) 762-9144 at 1125 Richter Street, where visitors are welcome to look around and taste the wine.

During the winter there's plenty of skiing on the slopes around Kelowna. Near the town on the other side of the lake is **Last Mountain**, which has chair lifts, a school, and something for skiers of all abilities, while about 57 km (35 miles) east of Kelowna is the **Big White Ski Area**, which is a ski resort with full facilities.

Continuing northwards along Highway 97 the scenery gradually becomes greener and cattle farming begins to take over from fruit growing.

Seventeen kilometers (11 miles) outside Kelowna lies the **Lake Okanagan Resort** ((250) 769-3511 TOLL-FREE (800) 663-3273 FAX (250) 769-6665, 2751 Westside Road, Kelowna V1Y7V8. This is an attractive lakeside resort set in landscaped gardens with luxurious condominiums, chalets, rooms and suites, and two dining rooms. It is an ideal haven for sports enthusiasts as it has tennis courts (some of which are floodlit for night games), a par-3 golf course, horse riding, heated outdoor pools, and a marina where guests go to water-ski, windsurf, and sail. Prices here run from mid-range to expensive.

In Kelowna the **Coast Capri Hotel** ((250) 860-6060 TOLL-FREE IN CANADA (800) 663-1144 FAX (250) 762-3430, 1171 Harvey Avenue, Kelowna V1Y 6E8, offers all the creature comforts you could want, with a heated pool, poolside café, restaurant, pub, and a cold beer and wine store. There are comfortable units and suites, all with television and telephone. Prices here are in the mid-range category.

The **Ponderosa Motel** ((250) 860-3982, at 1864 Harvey Avenue, Kelowna V1Y 6G2, has a warm, friendly atmosphere and low prices. It has 16 one- and two-bedroom housekeeping units, all with television. Tea and coffee is on the house and shops and restaurants are nearby. Not far from the lake and park, the **Willow Inn Hotel** ((250) 762-2122, 235 Queensway Avenue, Kelowna V1Y 6S4, has 40 rooms with telephones and televisions, and has a coffee garden. Prices are inexpensive and include full breakfast.

For dining, Kelowna has the popular **Earl's Hollywood on Top** ((250) 763-2777, 211 Bernard Avenue, a smart modern-looking place with a rooftop garden. It serves just about everything — tapas, pasta, ribs, steak, seafood and salads — and also has a busy cappuccino bar. It is open for lunch and dinner daily. There are all kinds of interesting snack items on the menu at **Jonathan L. Seagulls**

parks, gardens, and orchards is an island of greenery set among rolling semiarid hills. It has pleasant, sandy beaches and the lake provides plenty of scope for just about every water sport. The largest of Kelowna's parks is the lovely **City Park**, which has busy beaches, shady retreats, lawns, and tennis courts. In the summer it is sometimes the site of free outdoor concerts.

For a cruise of the lake and maybe a meal, get aboard the **MV *Fintry Queen*** ((250) 763-2780, a paddle wheel that moors in the City Park at the foot of Bernard Avenue. There are also evening cruises, which offer dining and dancing.

At the **Father Pandosy Settlement** ((250) 860-8369 south of downtown you can see some of the mission buildings that the oblate founded in 1859 and which formed the first white settlement in the valley. The original church and school still stand and some other buildings of similar age have been brought to the site to give the visitor a fuller pic-

Eventide along the South Thompson River at Kamloop's riverfront park.

((250) 860-8449, 262 Bernard Avenue, where you can enjoy lake views and, on weekends, late opening hours. At the attractive **Carmellie's Crêperie** ((250) 762-6350, 1862 Benvoulin Road, a wide choice of sweet and savory crêpes awaits, and the eclectic **Kitchen Cowboy** ((250) 868-8288, 353 Bernard Avenue, has a western decor and fare from basic hamburgers to sundried-tomato pizza that ropes in a trendy clientele.

VERNON

At the northern end of the Okanagan Valley, Vernon is surrounded by Kalamalka, Okanagan, and Swan Lakes, and has more of those pleasant Okanagan beaches that draw the vacationers. At the point where 25th Avenue crosses Highway 97 at the southern approach to the town stands **Polson Park**, where delightful oriental gardens offer a haven of shade and tranquillity. There's also a floral clock in the park. To acquaint yourself with the history of the town you should visit the **Vernon Museum and Archives** ((250) 542-3142, at 3009 32nd Avenue, where you can see old photographs of the town, costumes, carriages, displays on the pioneering days, and a collection of native artifacts. It is open Monday to Saturday and admission is free.

For a fascinating peek at the past take Highway 97 for 12 km (seven and a half miles) north of Vernon to the **O'Keefe Historic Ranch** ((250) 542-7868, one of the first ranches to appear in the area and one of the biggest in the entire province at the turn of the century. You can see O'Keefe's original log house, a general store, a blacksmith's shop, an early Roman Catholic church, and a fully furnished mansion house. Cornelius O'Keefe was one of the first cattle ranchers to come to the area, after which he seems to have made a valiant effort to populate the region. With his first wife he raised nine children, and after her death he remarried and had several more by his second wife. The O'Keefes lived at the ranch from 1867 until 1977, and many of their furnishings and possessions remain here. The site is open daily from mid-May to mid-October; an admission fee is charged.

Summer and winter, the **Silver Star Mountain Resort** ((250) 542-0224 TOLL-FREE IN THE UNITED STATES (800) 663-4431 FAX (250) 542-1236, PO Box 2, Silver Star Mountain V1B 3M1, 22 km (14 miles) east of town, has much to tempt outdoor lovers. From May to September it has some very pleasant hiking or cycling trails with views of the Coast Mountains. The resort, which has been built to look as though it's straight out of a Western, has accommodation, restaurants, and entertainment. In winter the bikes and boots are replaced by skis and snowmobiles, as the resort is awash with cross-country and downhill skiers. To get there, take 48th Avenue off Highway 97. En route you'll come

across a turnoff (Tillicum Road) that leads to **Cedar Hot Springs**, where you can relax in warm mineral spring water in a delightful forest setting.

In Vernon there are plenty of motels to choose from, but for something a little different try the **Vance Creek Hotel** ((250) 549-5191 FAX (250) 549-5177, PO Box 3002, Silver Star Mountain V0E 1G0. Like a set out of a spaghetti Western, the Vance Creek has a choice location in the center of the resort. Rooms on the first floor have kitchenettes, bunk beds, and private entrances. Fireplaces and Willow furniture add a touch of additional comfort to suites in the newer annex. Prices fall within the mid-range category.

The Silver Star Mountain Resort has good eating: The **Craigellachie Dining Room** ((250) 542-2459, at the Putnam Station Hotel, serves hearty meals including soups and sandwiches for lunch and traditional favorites such as barbecued spared ribs, lasagna, steaks, and pastas in the evening. The **Silver Lode Restaurant** ((250) 549-5105, at the Swiss Hotel Silver Lode Inn, serves authentic raclettes and fondues in a cheerful atmosphere.

HOW TO GET THERE

Greyhound TOLL-FREE (800) 661-8747 links Vancouver with Penticton, Kelowna, and Vernon. In Penticton the bus station ((250) 493-4101 is off Main Street between Robinson and Ellis streets. In Kelowna there is a station ((604) 860-3835 at 2366 Leckie Road, from which a regular service runs to Banff and Calgary; another links with Vernon, Kamloops and Prince George. In Vernon the Greyhound station ((604) 542-1415 is at 3700 33rd Street.

If you're driving north from Washington State, you'll probably want to take Highway 97. It runs northwards from the United States border through the Okanagan Valley. At the north end of the valley the Trans-Canada Highway links with Highway 97 and 97A, and motorists coming from Vancouver can take Highway 3 then 3A to Penticton.

GLACIER AND MOUNT REVELSTOKE NATIONAL PARKS

Just before it reaches the Rockies, the Trans-Canada Highway runs through Glacier National Park ((250) 837-7500 E-MAIL revglacier_reception @pch.gc.ca, PO Box 350, Revelstoke V0E 2S0, a rugged area high in the Columbia Mountains containing hundreds of glaciers, waterfalls, and rain forests. This is the birthplace of North American mountaineering and mountain climbing challenges abound. There are over 20 hiking trails — some short, some aimed at the more

The *Rocky Mountaineer* passes through Glacier National Park on its way from Alberta to the Pacific coast.

adventurous hiker. A number of backpacking trails are easily accessed. The more difficult trails often provide the best scenic rewards. The ski season begins in November and lasts almost to June. The spectacular terrain and heavy snowfalls of the Selkirk Mountains combine to produce some of the best ski touring opportunities in North America. Snow shoeing and winter camping. Avalanches are a danger here. At the center of the park, **Roger's Pass** has some magnificent views and the **Roger's Pass Centre** ((250) 837-6274, has maps of the park and pamphlets on the various trails. It's open daily year-round, and admission is free with your park pass.

Just west of Glacier, the smaller Mount Revelstoke National Park ((250) 837-7500 E-MAIL revglacier_reception@pch.gc.ca, PO Box 350, Revelstoke V0E 2S0 is a favorite destination for mountain bikers and hikers. Ten trails with differing levels of difficulty and great Rocky Mountain scenery make it a popular park. Two of the most accessible hikes consist of boardwalks that lead off into the countryside from Highway 1. The **Skunk Cabbage Trail** runs 1.2 km (three quarters of a mile) through towering skunk cabbage patches, and the **Giant Cedars Trail** is a 500-m (one-third-of-a-mile) jaunt through a majestic cedar forest where some of the trees are more than 1,000 years old. You can also drive the 24 km (14 miles) up the **Meadows in the Sky Parkway** (Summit Road) and from the top hike the one-kilometer (half-mile) trail to beautiful alpine meadows. Nearby, the **Revelstoke Dam** ((250) 837-6515 on Highway 23, has a visitor center and a free tour. It's open daily in summer 8 AM to 8 PM, with reduced hours in spring and fall.

At Roger's Pass, you'll find the moderately priced **Best Western Glacier Park Lodge** ((250) 837-2126, Glacier National Park, Roger's Pass V0E 2S0, with heated outdoor pool and 140 km (87 miles) of groomed hiking trails.

PRINCE RUPERT

Situated near the southern tip of Alaska's southeastern panhandle, Prince Rupert is a popular point of departure for trips into northern British Columbia, the Yukon and Alaska, and a pleasant place to spend a day or two.

Until the last decade, Rupert earned its living from the sea. Now that the fish stocks are depleted, the city is casting about for other ways to sustain its economy. Tourism perhaps. If it weren't for the fact that this is the rainiest city in Canada (more than 236 cm or 93 inches fall each year), Rupert would be awash with visitors. It has an excellent regional museum where you can learn about the area's first residents — the Tsimshian and Haida natives, some good seafood restaurants, and it is the gateway to one of the most beautiful valleys

in Canada, the Skeena. As it is, there's a steady flow of international visitors since this port town is a major transportation center. Both the ferries and the railroad begin and end here, and a few kilometers west of Rupert is the start of the scenic Stewart-Cassiar Highway, which runs to Watson Lake in the Yukon Territory.

GENERAL INFORMATION

The **Visitor Infocentre** ((250) 624-5637 TOLL-FREE (800) 667-1994 FAX (250) 627-8009 is located inside the Museum of Northern British Columbia, 101 First Avenue East. For advance information, write them at PO Box 669-SATC, Prince Rupert V8J 3S1. There is **Internet access** at the public library, 101 Sixth Avenue West. The major **rental car agencies** are located in the Rupert Square Shopping Centre on Second Avenue. Free transfers from these outlets to and from the airport and ferry docks can sometimes be arranged.

WHAT TO SEE AND DO

The **Museum of Northern British Columbia** ((250) 624-3207, 101 First Avenue West, is housed in an impressive building constructed to resemble a native longhouse. Inside is a small but excellent collection of Tsimshian and Haida artifacts including carved masks in wood and argillite (a rare black stone found only on the Queen Charlotte Islands which by law can only be carved by the Haida), reed baskets, and ceremonial dress. The gift shop is an excellent place to pick up regional souvenirs. Summer hours are Monday to Saturday from 9 AM to 8 PM and Sunday from 9 AM to 5 PM; winter hours are Monday to Saturday from 9 AM to 5 PM. An admission fee is charged.

The museum has a number of special programs. In June and July the **archeological harbor tour** offers a chance to learn about the Tsimshian culture with visits to archeological digs and historic villages and settlements. The Tsimshian have inhabited the area since before the time of the pyramids in Egypt. Across the street from the museum is the **carving shed** — where First Nations carvers can be seen at work in their studio. Hours vary but admission is free. Consult the museum for additional information on special programs.

A short walk from the museum will take you to the harbor front and, more specifically, to Cow Bay, the most delightful part of the town. The **Cow Bay Historic District** has souvenir and craft shops, good restaurants and a fishing village atmosphere that the rest of Rupert lacks, being cut off from the waterfront by the railway. The best souvenir **shopping** is here where native artwork can be found for sale in shops and workshops. This part of town is quite pleasant for strolling and browsing. But bring an umbrella.

The **North Pacific Cannery Village Museum**
((250) 628-3538 is British Columbia's oldest surviving salmon cannery and is a national historic
site and well worth the short drive along Highway
16 to Port Edward. Tours are give throughout the
day, along with a live one-woman performance
that relates personal stories from an important
chapter in the region's history. Visitors can see how
the cannery operated and learn about the hundreds
of First Nations people, Japanese, Chinese, and
Europeans who worked and lived there. The cannery is situated on the scenic Inverness Passage,
about 20 km (12 miles) south of Prince Rupert.
It's open daily, May 1 to September 30 from 9 AM
to 6 PM. An admission fee is charged.

WHERE TO STAY AND EAT

The inexpensively priced **Parry Place Bed &
Breakfast** ((250) 624-5887 TOLL-FREE (800) 565-3500
FAX (250) 624-8176 E-MAIL norwood@itytel.net,
133 Parry Place, Prince Rupert V8J 4B1, offers
comfortable rooms, some with private bath. Breakfast is a cornucopia of fresh fruits, pastries, and
bagels with cheese, smoked salmon. The hosts are
longtime residents — very knowledgeable, good
conversationalists, and most welcoming. They're
full of ideas for itineraries since they've boated
and camped all over the area, including the Queen
Charlotte Islands and Southeast Alaska. Parry
Place is close to the ferry docks, and pickup and
drop off can be arranged. French is spoken.

Downtown, the **Crest Motor Hotel** ((250) 624-
6771 FAX (250) 627-7666, 222 First Avenue West,
Prince Rupert V8J 3P6, offers run-of-the-mill mid-
range accommodation, with a lounge, coffee shop,
and restaurant at your service.

For an entirely unique experience stay at the
Inverness Bed & Breakfast ((250) 628-3375
E-MAIL duggle@well.com, 1889 Skeena Drive, Port
Edward V0V 1G0. It's located within the North
Pacific Cannery Village Museum (see WHAT TO SEE
AND DO, above). Rates are inexpensive and break-
fast is served at the historic Cannery Café. It's open
April 15 to October 30.

For no-frills lodging, the drab but tidy **Pioneer
Rooms** ((250) 624-2334, 167 Third Avenue, one
block east of MacBridge Avenue, has the cheap-
est sleeps in town. Laundry facilities are available.

If you ask locals where to find the best seafood, they'll undoubtedly recommend **Smile's
Seafood Café** (250) 624-3072, 1 Cow Bay Road,
which has been in business since 1934. **Cow Bay
Café** ((250) 627-1212, 205 Cow Bay Road, is good
too and has a nice view of the harbor. The chef at
the **Cannery Café** ((250) 628-3375 in nearby Port
Edward lived and worked at the historic North
Pacific Cannery before it's closure in the late 1960s.
The quaint building is the former mess house for
the cannery. Salmon, naturally, is the specialty.

Next to the Museum of Northern British Columbia, the moderately price **Pegleg's Seaside Grill**
((250) 624-5667, 3-101 First Avenue East, has a vast
menu including everything from seafood to Tex-
Mex and daily specials such as a halibut curry.
There's a very pleasant deck that looks out over
the Pacific Mariner's Memorial Park, with its
beslickered sailor pointing wistfully out to sea

HOW TO GET THERE

The **Alaska Marine Highway** ((907) 627-1744
or (907) 627-1745 TOLL-FREE (800) 642-0066,
PO Box 25535, Juneau, Alaska 99802 USA, links
Rupert with the Alaska panhandle, including

Skagway where there are bus, train and road connections to the Yukon. **BC Ferries** ((250) 624-9627
serve the Queen Charlotte Islands and Port Hardy
on Vancouver Island. The ferry docks are at the
west end of town on Fairview Road.

Greyhound ((250) 624-5090 has daily service
to Vancouver and Prince George. The station is at
822 Third Avenue West. The **VIA Rail** station ((250)
627-7589 is located toward the waterfront on Bill
Murray Way. Trains run to Prince George where
BC Rail continues to Vancouver (but an overnight
stay is required). The airport is on Digby Island,
and the ferry/bus connection to downtown takes
about 45 minutes. **Air BC** ((250) 624-4554, 112 Sixth
Street, and **Canadian Airlines** (250) 624-9181,
ground floor of Rupert Square Mall, Second Avenue, connect Rupert with Vancouver. Ask about
standby flights as they can sometimes be
cheaper than the bus or train.

Motorists will have no trouble getting into and
out of Rupert since there's only one road: Highway
16, the Yellowhead Highway from Prince George.

ABOVE: "North to Alaska!" The intersection of British
Columbia's Skeena and Cassiar highways beckons
the adventurer to northern British Columbia and
beyond. OVERLEAF: On the Queen Charlotte
Islands, sea kayaks bear classic Haida designs
representing the fauna of the region.

THE SKEENA VALLEY

From Prince Rupert, the Yellowhead Highway runs through a major cleft in British Columbia's Coast Mountains forming the **Skeena Valley**. It was once a vital trade and travel link for Tsimshian and interior native bands who's name for the valley, K'Shian, means "river of mists." One of the most beautiful drives in Canada, the Skeena's fog-shrouded karst mountain scenery is reminiscent of a Chinese silk painting. The drive is also an excellent opportunity to spot wildlife such as black bears, and bald eagles. Recreational possibilities abound along the valley.

The **'Ksan Historical Village (** (250) 842-5544, PO Box 326, Hazelton V0J 1Y0, is a replica of an ancient village along the Skeena River where for thousands of years the Gitksan people lived. Guided tours take visitors through longhouses where artifacts and multimedia exhibits tell the story of how the clan lived before and after European contact. On display are marvelously complex Chilkat blankets, "button" blankets, wood carvings including painted spirit masks, totem poles, and ceremonial costumes. There are dance performances periodically throughout the summer months. The village is open daily from mid-April through September. Admission is by donation, and guided tours of the three longhouses housing exhibits are offered several times daily.

THE QUEEN CHARLOTTE ISLANDS

Sometimes referred to as "the Canadian Galapagos" for their ecological uniqueness, the Queen Charlotte Islands, 130 km (78 miles) west of Prince Rupert, form an archipelago made up of two principle islands, Graham and Moresby, and 180 surrounding islets. Most of the islands' 5,000 inhabitants live on Graham Island, in six communities, and about a third of the islands' residents are Haida.

The **Visitor Information Centre (** (250) 559-8316 or (250) 559-8594 FAX (250) 559-8952 is in Queen Charlotte City on Wharf Street at the east end of town. They have information on Gwaii Haanas and the islands as a whole as well as natural history presentations. They sell the useful *Guide to the Queen Charlotte Islands* and detailed maps of the towns. For information specifically on Gwaii Haanas, contact the Superintendent, Gwaii Haanas (South Moresby National Park Marine Reserve) (** (250) 559-8818 FAX (250) 559-8366, PO Box 37, Queen Charlotte V0T 1S0.

WHAT TO SEE AND DO

Visitors are drawn to the Charlottes for a chance to see the ancient remnants of the Haida culture and for the archipelago's gorgeous wilderness

scenery. With its rugged west coast and sandy eastern beaches, the islands are a delight for view-seekers, and kayakers come from all over the world to paddle the waterways and coastline. Scuba divers find a watery paradise on Graham Island's west coast at Rennell Sound, where shore dives are possible from many points along the coastal logging road.

The Charlottes have about 120 km (75 miles) of paved roads, mostly along the shoreline on the east coast of Graham Island. In the northeast corner of Graham Island, **Naikoon Provincial Park (** (250) 557-4390 protects a wilderness of rain forest, sandy beaches, dunes, and bogs. In Old Masset (also called Haida) just to the west of Naikoon, there are many Haida sculptors creating works of art in silver, gold, argillite, and wood, as well as prints and woven baskets. You can see the artisans at work here and purchase crafts. On the southern end of Graham Island, in Skidegate, there is the **Queen Charlotte Islands Museum (** (250) 559-4643 with exhibits of Haida totem poles, masks, and carvings of silver and argillite, as well as a natural history exhibit on the wildlife of the islands.

From Graham Island there is hourly BC Ferry service to Moresby Island, a 20-minute crossing. Canada's newest national park, **Sgan Gwaii** — a UNESCO World Heritage Site — is located here, part of **Gwaii Haanas** (also known as South Moresby National Park Marine Reserve). Permission to enter the area is given by the Haida Gwaii Watchmen (** (250) 259-8225, PO Box 609, Skidegate, Haida Gwaii, V0T 1S0. The office is located at Second Beach, which is just north of Skidegate Landing along Highway 16. A journey to these sites begins with registration at the Parks Canada office (at the airport or in Queen Charlotte City) and an orientation session. The park, which covers the southern two thirds of the Queen Charlottes, is only accessible by boat or plane. There are some 500 archeological and historical sites here, maintained by the Haida Nation. The best way to experience the park is to go along with an experienced guide, such as **Moresby Explorers (** (250) 637-2215 TOLL-FREE (800) 806-7633, Beach Road, Sandspit, or **Queen Charlotte Adventures (** (250) 559-8990 FAX (250) 559-8983 TOLL-FREE (800) 668-4288, outside Queen Charlotte City on the road to Skidegate.

WHERE TO STAY

Most visitors stay and eat in Queen Charlotte, the largest town in the islands, but all of the islands' communities have a least some tourist facilities,

Queen Charlotte Islands — ABOVE: Haida in ceremonial dress. The drum at right bears the image of the killer whale. BELOW: An ancient Haida totem pole greets the dawn on Ninstits Island.

including many small bed and breakfast places; contact the **Queen Charlotte Travel Infocentre** ((250) 559-4742 FAX (250) 559-8188, 3922 Highway 33, PO Box 819, Queen Charlotte V0T 1S0, for a list of establishments. Reservations are recommended for Queen Charlotte City lodging.

HOW TO GET THERE

Year-round air service is available with Canadian Airlines International from Vancouver to Sandspit. For transportation from the airport to Queen Charlotte City, contact **Rikka Travel** ((250) 559-4400, 119 Third Avenue in Queen Charlotte City. **Rental cars** are available at Masset, Queen Charlotte, and Sandspit. From Prince Rupert, **BC Ferries** ((250) 559-4485 makes the six-hour crossing six times a week in summer, docking on Graham Island's south side. (Note that this is an open-sea crossing. Landlubbers may want to bring along their favorite seasickness remedy.) Reservations are strongly recommended. There is also daily floatplane service from Rupert to Sandspit, Queen Charlotte City, and Masset.

NORTHERN BRITISH COLUMBIA

A remote and sparsely inhabited area, Northern British Columbia has much in common with the neighboring Yukon Territory. Despite the logging and mining activities that have dominated the region's economy for 100 years, it remains virtually unspoiled—a land of great beauty and seemingly endless bounty. Intrepid travelers come for fishing, hiking through untouched mountain terrain, soaking in hot spring, and for the incomparable solitude.

Starting off from the Trans-Canada Highway (Highway 1) at Cache Creek, the **Cariboo Highway** (Highway 97) runs north, passing through the Fraser Valley to the interior ranch lands. Williams Lake is a major cattle-country pit stop. Further north along the Cariboo, you run into former mining country, then into the lumber and paper mill hub of Prince George. From Prince George the route divides: the northern section crosses the Rockies then joins the **Alaska Highway** at Dawson Creek; the west fork traverses the Hudson Bay Range, through the Skeena Valley with its First Nations villages to the port of Prince Rupert.

A flock of plovers takes to the air.

The North

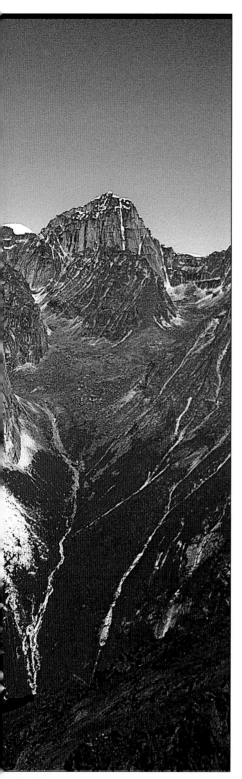

ONE COULD ARGUE THAT ALL OF CANADA IS THE NORTH. But for Canadians, "true north" is that vast stretch of country that extends from the 60th parallel beyond the magnetic North Pole. This North occupies a special place in the national mythology, forming a significant part of the identity of all Canadians — despite the fact that most of them have never been there. Northerners, for their part, call the rest of Canada "the outside." The Yukoners' history is as closely linked to that of Alaskans as to their fellow Canadians, and the Inuit majority of the northeast shares a common culture with the native peoples of Greenland.

Two-thirds of this surprisingly varied landscape constitute the Northwest Territories and Nunavut — a land of giant lakes, treeless tundra, and the hardy Dene, Inuit and other native groups who have thrived in this rugged environment for thousands of years. This is the least densely populated area in the world, with Canada's highest concentration of Aboriginal peoples (60%). Following decades of land-rights negotiations, on April 1, 1999, the former Northwest Territories was divided. The new border extends north from the Manitoba-Saskatchewan frontier for 500 km (310 miles), veers northwest for 1050 km (650 miles), hooks back east 500 km (310 miles) to 110' latitude, then cuts dead north to the Arctic Ocean. The territory east of this border has been named Nunavut (which means "our land" in Inuktitut), and includes the islands in Hudson Bay, James Bay, and Ungava Bay that are not within Manitoba, Ontario, or Quebec. The lands west of the new border will remain the Northwest Territories until a new name is chosen.

To the west of the Northwest Territories is the Yukon, distinguished from the rest of the North by its indigenous populations, its climate, its geography, and its history. Aside from its cultural and geographical differences, the Yukon is also more accessible than Nunavut and the western Northwest Territories primarily because of its transportation infrastructure. On the whole, the Yukon tends to attract more hikers and paddlers, while Nunavut and the Northwest Territories attract hunters and fishermen, though all three territories offer excellent opportunities for hiking, boating, fishing and hunting.

For the traveler who wishes to explore the North, several aspects of northern travel should be borne in mind. The first is that this is a vast, vast land. "The Canadian north," writes Pierre Berton, "is so big that you could drop the state of Texas or the British Isles in here and never notice either of them." Thus, you will want to choose a specific area to explore, depending on your interests, rather than trying to "do" the North. Second, a trip to Canada's North will probably require more

The Northwest Territories — A hiker surveys the Mackenzie Mountains.

than the usual amount of advance preparation and will certainly demand a significantly greater outlay of money.

Be aware that mosquitoes and changeable weather are major issues in the northern summer. A bug jacket over your T-shirt during the day will be as important as a sweater in the evening.

If you intend to do any wilderness hiking or paddling, you should obtain accurate and timely information about conditions to be expected and advise a friend or relative, and the nearest Royal Canadian Mounted Police detachment, where you are going and when you will be back.

Many of the Yukon's roads are now widened, straightened and paved, but major gravel roads

still exist. In the Northwest Territories highways are mainly all-weather gravel roads. Keep your headlights on at all times.

With the exception of Whitehorse in the Yukon Territory, northern communities are not under the 911 emergency system. See TRAVELERS' TIPS, page 425, for a list of police (RCMP) and medical emergency numbers for the North.

THE YUKON TERRITORY

In the far northwest corner of Canada, a rough triangular boundary defines the Yukon Territory's 483,450 sq km (174,000 sq miles). Bordered by

Skookum Jim ("skookum" means handsome), one of the discovers of Bonanza Creek, where the gold was "thick between the flaky slabs, like cheese sandwiches." The discovery touched off the 1896 gold rush.

British Columbia to the south and the Northwest Territories to the east, the northern tip of the triangle is cut through by the Arctic Circle and ends at the Beaufort Sea, home to musk oxen, polar bears, and beluga whales. Frozen wilderness defines the Yukon's southern boundary as well, where the largest nonpolar ice caps in the world are suspended over the saw-toothed mountains of Kluane National Park. In between all of this frozen water is a semiarid land that, were it not so far north, would be a desert.

The climate of the Yukon comes as a surprise to many visitors. Dawson City's temperature may drop below -50°C (-58°F) in January, but easily rise to 35°C (100°F) in July. The dry climate and long hours of sunshine contribute to this phenomenon.

The Yukon's aridity gives rise to another characteristic of the region: forest fires. Each year thousands of hectares burn. Fires are closely monitored, but generally allowed to take their own course. The prevailing notion is that burning and regrowth is a natural cycle of the habitat.

Some 1,300 species of flowering plants have adapted to ice, wind, and fire to thrive in the territory. Fireweed — so named because it is the first plant to revegetate land cleared by fire — is the Yukon's official flower, seen all summer long blazing along the roadways. The territory is home to 214 bird and 61 mammal species, as well as 28 species of fish. Only a few hardy tree varieties, such as spruce and lodgepole pine, poplar, birch, and willow, are able to tolerate the growing conditions in the Yukon. These trees tend to be smaller and spindlier than their southern relatives.

The Yukon's 33,000 human inhabitants are a ruggedly adaptable bunch as well. Situated 2,720 km (1,700 miles) from Vancouver, 1,440 km (900 miles) from Edmonton, hemmed in by lofty mountains to the south, they are extraordinarily isolated from the rest of Canada. In fact, Yukoners feel stronger ties with their Alaskan neighbors — with whom the Yukon shares its western border and many geographical and cultural characteristics — than they do with Canadians. Yukoners live in one of the earth's last frontier lands — and like all frontiers, it is full of hardship and opportunity. Yukoners, as you might expect, love and revere the outdoors: Though two thirds of them live in the capital city of Whitehorse, much of the residential area of this city rolls out into the countryside, with immediate access to mountain trails and river routes.

The Yukon has much to offer visitors: the ancient cultures of the regions' First Nations peoples, still alive in communities from Whitehorse to Old Crow; historic sites linked to the era of one of the world's greatest gold rushes; wilderness areas where barely a trace of human existence can be found; and some of the most splendid mountainscapes in Canada.

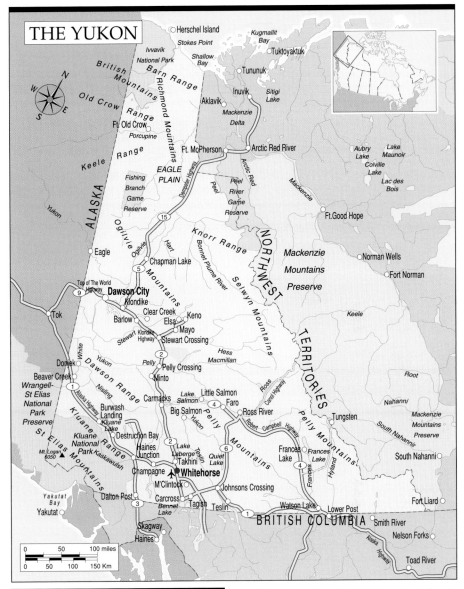

THE YUKON

Up until around 1800s the region now known as the Yukon was occupied exclusively by bands of Gwitch'in, Kaska, Tagish, Tutchone, and Teslin Hän natives — hunters and nomads who gathered in springtime into larger groups for fishing.

Beginning in the eighteenth century, Russian explorers began trading with the area's natives. Then in 1825 the explorer Sir John Franklin anchored off the Yukon's Arctic coastline. The Hudson's Bay Company moved into the interior in the 1840s, and United States traders arrived after Russia sold Alaska to the America in 1867.

Prospectors began to trickle into the Yukon in the 1870s, following a trail of gold strikes along the Rockies that had begun in California in 1849 and had continued into the interior of British Columbia. By 1882 there were 50 miners in the Yukon Valley searching for and finding small but promising amounts of gold. By the early 1890s the number had grown to nearly 1,000, centered mostly around the community of Forty Mile, near present-day Dawson City.

In 1896 a white prospector, George Washington Carmack, and his native brothers-in-law, Skookum Jim and "Dawson" Charlie, found gold, lots of it, in Rabbit Creek. Carmack brought word back that the rocks of Rabbit Creek had gold "thick between the flaky slabs, like cheese sandwiches." The three men staked their claims and Carmack renamed the creek, Bonanza. The gold rush was on.

Thousands of people poured into this remote corner of Canada, most arriving by way of Skagway, Alaska, and the upper Yukon River. These stampeders had to haul enough provisions to last out the year over the White or Chilkoot pass, then build a boat at the foot of Lake Bennett to carry them the remaining stretch to the Klondike gold fields near Dawson City. In the spring of 1898, Mounties counted 28,000 men and women leaving the shores of Lake Bennett in 7,000 make-

have put most mining operations in mothballs. In recent years, mining has been supplanted by tourism as the Yukon's leading industry.

WHITEHORSE

A hundred years ago, Whitehorse was not Whitehorse at all, but a stop on the Southern Tutchone and Tagish peoples' seasonal round of hunting and fishing. When the Klondike gold rush peaked from 1898 to 1900, Whitehorse became yet another stopping point, this time for the stampeders clawing their way to Dawson City, far to the north. Here on the banks of the Yukon, prospectors stopped to wring out their socks after traversing

shift boats bound for the Klondike. Amidst this hullabaloo, the town of Dawson was born.

Within a few years Dawson was left in the sawdust as gold seekers moved on to Nome, Alaska, where yet another big strike had been found. Gold mining in the Yukon continued (and continues today), but beginning in 1913 the Yukon's economy shifted from gold to other minerals, such as silver and lead at Keno Hill in the central Yukon. The construction of the Alaska Highway and the Canol pipeline and road brought new mineral exploration activity as well as bringing people, services, industries, and tourists to the Yukon. With the highway came permanent nonnative settlers, who finally outnumbered Yukon's native peoples.

Though the Yukon contains some 30% of Canada's natural resources, current low prices for precious metals, along with the cost of extraction,

the treacherous rapids upstream. Then in 1900 the White Pass & Yukon Railway was completed with its terminus in Whitehorse, and the settlement began to take shape. The building of the Alaska Highway through its backyard gave the town a further boost: In 1941, the population jumped from 300 to over 3,000. Today, Whitehorse, the territorial capital since 1953, has a population of around 22,000.

If someday there are cities built on planet Mars, they'll certainly look like parched and pragmatic Whitehorse. It's about as homely as cities come, but it grows on you — and quickly. Many are the stories of people who "came for a few days and stayed 20 years." But no matter the length of your stay, you'll discover that Whitehorse is a friendly town with fine, hot, and dry summers with daylight lasting long into the evenings. Everything you need for moving on into the remoter stretches of the territory is available here. There are quite a few historic buildings in the downtown area, and there are some worthwhile museums to explore.

General Information

Once in Whitehorse, your first stop should be the **Visitor Information Centre** ((867) 667-2915 FAX (867) 667-3546 E-MAIL yktour@yknet.ca, at the corner of Hanson Street and Second Avenue. They have stacks of information about the city and the territory, as well as interactive kiosks, video presentations, and helpful staff. Next door, the Whitehorse Public Library ((867) 667-5239, 2701 Second Avenue, has **Internet access** and is open daily. While there are **automated teller machines**

on the Interac and Plus systems in Whitehorse, Dawson City, and Watson Lake, Whitehorse has the territory's only ATM operating on the Cirrus system, located at the **Bank of Montréal** ((867) 668-4200, 111 Main Street.

What to See and Do

Though Whitehorse extends over an area of 259 sq km (162 sq miles), the downtown is small and a convenient place to get around. The center, laid out around Main Street, has four blocks of stores and an almost-bustling pace. Several interesting sights, however, are located outside of the downtown area. **Whitehorse Transit** ((867) 668-2831 makes the rounds. We recommend renting a car.

You may want to begin your downtown explorations with the Yukon Historical & Museums Association's 45-minute **historical walking tour**

((867) 667-4704, departing Monday to Saturday from the Donneworth House, at 3126 Third Avenue; a fee is charged.

Even if you're spending a very short time in Whitehorse, make a point to visit the **SS *Klondike* National Historic Site** ((867) 667-3970, near the downtown core at the Robert Campbell Bridge. In the territory's heyday, over 200 sternwheelers steamed up and down the Yukon River and its tributaries. Now only a few of these majestic ships are left, and the SS *Klondike* is the only one to have been restored to its earlier splendor. The park service interpretive tour and video are excellent. It's open daily 9 AM to 5:30 PM, with tours on the half hour. An admission fee is charged which includes a guided tour.

"Oh, for some of that gold," writes a wistful British Columbian in the **MacBride Museum** ((867) 667-2709 guest register. This log structure with a sod roof houses several fascinating exhibits, including an array of gold nuggets—each with its distinctive form — taken from a spectrum of Klondike creeks. Hands on exhibits allow visitors to get a sense of the weight of gold (it's 19 times more dense than water) and see a prospector's sluicebox in action. Archeology, culture, history, natural history, and transportation are other themes. Located on First Avenue between Steele and Wood streets, the museum is open June to August daily from 10 AM to 6 PM. An admission fee is charged.

Below the White Horse Rapids Dam you can see Chinook salmon completing the word's longest salmon migration at the **Whitehorse Fishway** ((867) 667-4263 or (867) 633-5965 (summers). This man-made fish ladder, located at the end of Nisultin Drive in suburban Riverdale, was built to allow the spawning salmon to fight their way upstream during their annual migration, bypassing the dam. There are interpretive displays and tanks that give you a fish's-eye view of the proceedings. The migration takes place in late July and August; the facility is open daily during the summer from 8 AM to 10 PM. Admission is free.

Whitehorse has its share of boutiques and corner pocket malls to browse in. The **Indian Craft Shop** ((867) 667-7216, 504 Main Street, across from the Gold Rush Inn, is a family-run operation selling First Nations arts and crafts. Parkas are available in stock or made to order, and beaded mukluks and moccasins, hides, furs, and souvenirs large and small are on offer. Nancy Huston, owner of **Midnight Sun** ((867) 668-4350, 205C Main Street, has made it her mission to find and market Yukon art and crafts. You'll find Yukon herbal teas, local jams and jelly, pottery, and prints as well as seventeenth-century First Nations trading beads

The Kluane Range, west of Whitehorse — You don't have to go far outside of town to find wide open spaces.

made into works of art and jewelry. The Jetsons-style sign of **Murdoch's Gem Shop** (867) 667-7716, 207 Main Street, is a downtown landmark. On display are "Klondike Kate's diamond belt" and the Yukon's largest selection of gold nugget jewelry.

Outside of the downtown area, there are several worthwhile sights. The **Yukon Art Centre** ((867) 667-8485, Yukon Place at Yukon College, off of Range Road N, is the best place in the territory to see art. Exhibits in this beautiful gallery showcase Yukon artists, both native and non-native, as well as internationally recognized visual artists. While you're on campus, you can find out if there is a prospector in your past at the **Yukon**

there are two more very good museums. The **Beringia Interpretive Centre** ((867) 667-8855, Alaska Highway Milepost 915, weaves First Nations creation myth and hard scientific evidence to tell the story of Beringia, the land bridge, created during the last Ice Age along which the first inhabitants of North America migrated from Asia. On this continent-sized land bridge, woolly mammoths and giant beavers as big as black bears roamed during the Pleistocene Age. The exhibits present the paleontological and archeological evidence of the age alongside Tlingit native stories about a great flood and how the clever Crow created the world. Fossilized remains include the tooth of a woolly mammoth weighing around five

Archives ((867) 667-5321 TOLL-FREE (800) 661-0408 E-MAIL yukon.archives@gov.yk.ca. Besides genealogical research, staff at the archives are prepared to help you find out more about any aspect of Yukon history. The archive has a file of ready-made historical photos, which get our vote for the best-value souvenir in the territory. Choose from portraits of handsome, Skookum Jim or that Yukon iconic image — toilers on the Chilkoot Trail — and many others. Hours are Tuesday and Wednesday from 9 AM to 5 PM, Thursday and Friday 1 PM to 9 PM and 10 AM to 1 PM and 2 PM to 6 PM on Saturday. On the drive up Two Mile Road, on the corner of Fourth Avenue, look for the **spirit houses**, a cluster of small, brightly colored shelters. This is a First Nations burial ground (and thus not to be disturbed).

Continuing onto the Alaska Highway from the Yukon College area, head for the airport where

kilograms (11 lb), dioramas showing the flora and fauna of the age and skeleton models of giant beavers and sloths. Interestingly, it was the gold rush that led to the discovery of this mother lode of ice age fossils and remains. As prospectors dug down into the permafrost to release the gold from the gravel, they also discovered (and continue to discover) these remains.

Next to the Beringia Centre is the **Yukon Transportation Museum** ((867) 668-4792, Alaska Highway Milepost 917. In a remote area like the Yukon, the history of European settlement is in many ways the history of transportation. The museum takes you on a fascinating historical journey from snowshoes to moose-skin boats to dogsleds, stage coaches, pioneer aircraft, railroad, riverboat and finally to the military vehicles that helped build the Alaska Highway. There's a very good film about the building of the White Pass & Yukon

Railway. It's open May 19 to September 14 daily from 9 AM to 6 PM; an admission fee is charged.

A hot soak at **Takhini Hot Springs** ((867) 633-2706, 17 miles north of Whitehorse, off the Klondike Loop Road, is surprisingly refreshing on a scorching Yukon summer's day. The hot pool has a grassy area surrounding it; bring a book and you can alternately soak and sun your afternoon away. It's open weekends starting in mid-May, daily from June 1 to mid-October; an admission fee is charged. Suit rental and lockers are available. There is horseback riding here as well.

During the gold rush hundreds of stampeders smashed their crude boats attempting to run the Whitehorse Rapids that once raced through **Miles**

have turned up remnants of stampeder encampments, as well as remains of early native use. Trips depart daily at 10 AM and 2 PM from the office of **Go Wild Tours!** ((867) 668-2411 E-MAIL arctic@yknet.yk.ca, on First Avenue (look for the moose head).

Excursions from Whitehorse

Not far from Whitehorse there are a couple of First Nations camps where visitors can see how Yukon native people lived prior to the arrival of European influences (for other camps see LISTEN TO ANCIENT VOICES, page 26, in TOP SPOTS). First Nations tourism is a rapidly changing and growing scene, so you may want to call or drop by the **Yukon**

Canyon, five kilometers (three miles) south of the city. The canyon's frothing water reminded the prospectors of horses' manes, which is where the capital city's name is believed to have originated. Now that the Whitehorse Dam has tamed the water, the canyon offers a pleasant float. You can take a two-hour Yukon River cruise on the **MV Schwatka** ((867) 668-4716, Miles Canyon Road off the Alaska Highway South, accompanied by narration that tells the story of those wilder times. Trips run daily from June 1 to September 7 at 2 PM; additional 7 PM cruises run every day from June 15 to August 15 inclusive. Advance reservations are recommended. The **Scenic Gold Rush Raft Float Tour** ((867) 633-4836, takes passengers through Miles Canyon on a two-and-a-half-hour narrated trip on a quaint (but seaworthy) craft that is a replica of the stampeders rafts. The boat makes a stop at Canyon City, where recent excavations

First Nations Tourism Association ((867) 667-7698 or (867) 667-7699 FAX (867) 667-7527, 1109 First Avenue, to find out about the latest offerings.

Atsua Ku (Grandma's Camp) Riverboat Adventures ((867) 668-6854 E-MAIL dsam@atsuaku.yk.ca, PO Box 5494, Whitehorse Y1A 5H4, takes travelers eight kilometers (five miles) down the Yukon River to visit historic First Nations cabins and an old steamboat wood camp. The trips can be done as lunch, supper or overnight trips with barbecue dinner. Included is wildlife watching, exhibitions of First Nations crafts, storytelling, and nature walks. About a 45-minute drive from Whitehorse is **Kwaday Dan Kenji (Long-**

OPPOSITE: Indigenous mountain goats graze at a Whitehorse wildlife preserve. ABOVE: At Silver City near Kluane National Park you can ramble among the decaying shanties and mining equipment of this boom-and-bust silver mining encampment.

Ago Peoples) ((867) 667-6375, located on the Alaska Highway two kilometers (just over a mile) south of Champagne (contact: Indian Way Ventures, PO Box 33031, Whitehorse Y1A 5Y5). Here you can come and enjoy hot tea and fresh *bannock*, fried biscuits. The family that runs this enterprise is researching and building a traditional First Nations camp showing how their ancestors lived before the introduction of European influences. It is open May to October 9 AM to 7:30 PM.

To see some of the countryside surrounding Whitehorse, drive the **Carcross Loop**, where unique and lovely scenery as well as gold rush and native history are found. Head out of Whitehorse south along the Alaska Highway, then take the Klondike Highway south. You'll shortly reach one of the most photographed scenes in the territory, **Emerald Lake**. Its turquoise hue is caused by the decomposed shells that are suspended in the water. Further along, the **Carcross Desert** is not a true desert at all but a former sandy lakebed, where winds have formed dozens of dunes. At Carcross, you'll want to stop and poke around. Tourism Yukon's **Visitor Reception Centre** ((867) 821-4431 is at the Old Train Depot. The friendly staff will help orient you to the tiny native town where log cabins line the unpaved streets.

Before the gold rush, Carcross (originally Caribou Crossing) at the foot of Lake Bennett was a seasonal hunting and fishing camp for the Tagish natives. During the stampede, Tlingit natives displaced them. The Tlingit who now live here are descendants of the tribe that once traveled and traded across the Chilkoot Trail and became renowned as porters when the gold rush was on. Sites in the tiny town include the **New Caribou Hotel**, built in 1900, the oldest in the Yukon, and the historic **Old North West Mounted Police Barracks**, which is now a curio shop.

You can retrace your route from Carcross back to Whitehorse or head east along Tagish Road through the village of Tagish and reconnect with the Alaska Highway to complete the loop. The distance from Whitehorse to Carcross is 74 km (47 miles).

Sports and Outdoor Activities

Many people come to the Yukon for its world-class **river running**. Resources are legion, but you might start your research by contacting the Yukon Canoe and Kayak Club ((867) 633-5625 FAX (867) 633-5630 E-MAIL bear@yknet.yk.ca, PO Box 5546, Whitehorse Y1A 5H4. In Whitehorse, canoes and kayaks can be rented from Kanoe People ((867) 668-4899 FAX (867) 668-4891 E-MAIL kanoe@yknet .yk.ca, PO Box 5152, Whitehorse Y1A 4S3. They also offers guided or unguided tours, fishing trips, and rent mountain bikes and camping gear. Also renting canoes is Up North ((867) 667-7905 FAX (867) 667-6334 E-MAIL upnorth@yknet.yk.ca,

PO Box 5418, Whitehorse Y1A 5H4, located across the Yukon River from the MacBride Museum.

Nahanni River Adventures (guided trips) ((867) 668-3180 TOLL-FREE (800) 297-6927 FAX (867) 668-3056 E-MAIL nahanni@yknet.yk.ca, PO Box 4869, Whitehorse Y1A 4N6, has guided trips for beginners and experts on the Tatshenshini, Yukon, Nahanni and other northern wilderness rivers. Tatshenshini Expediting ((867) 633-2742 FAX (867) 633-6184 E-MAIL tatexp@polar.com, 1602 Alder Street, Whitehorse Y1A 3W8, has guided **whitewater rafting** trips on the Tatshenshini, from day trips to 11-day excursions, and four- to six-day trips on the Alsek. They also rent rafts and canoes.

The area around Whitehorse affords great opportunities for **fishing**. A sport-fishing license is required, even to catch to the odd grayling by the side of the road. Licenses are available at sporting-goods stores. There are strict regulations governing seasons, sizes, and weights. Guided fly-fishing trips for two or three people are offered by Fly-Fishing Adventures ((867) 667-2359, PO Box 5971, Whitehorse Y1A 5L7, which also rents boats and equipment.

If you are in the Yukon in the spring or winter, take a **dog sledding trip** with Walden Guiding and Outfitting ((867) 667-7040; Blue Kennels ((867) 667-1342, PO Box 5484, Whitehorse, Y1A 5H4, or Sunshine Valley Guest Ranch ((867) 667-RIDE, PO Box 4211, Whitehorse, Y1A 3T3. Sunshine Valley also runs **packhorse trips** in the Yukon wilderness and offers French-speaking guides.

Several operations offer a full menu of activities from guided outdoor adventures to cultural trips: Arctic Vision ((867) 668-2411 FAX (867) 668-2642 E-MAIL arctic@yknet.yk.ca, PO Box 31210(v), Whitehorse Y1A 5P7, offers nature, birding, and cultural tours in the Yukon and Western Arctic. Big Bear ((867) 633-5642 FAX (867) 633-5630 E-MAIL bear@yknet.yk.ca, PO Box 5210, Whitehorse Y1A 4Z1, has canoeing, kayaking, hiking, rafting, and bicycle tours and rentals. Dutch and German are spoken.

Nightlife

Nightlife in Whitehorse centers around cold glasses of excellent Chilkoot Brewery ale, sipped late into the sunlit night on "The Deck" at the Yukon Mining Co., High Country Inn (see WHERE TO EAT, below). Another favorite gathering spot is the small terrace at Sam 'n' Andy's (see WHERE TO EAT, below). But before you've earned the right to kick back with the rest of Whitehorse's night creatures, you must see *Frantic Follies* ((867) 668-3225, at the Westmark Whitehorse Hotel. From Dawson City to Beaver Creek, every town in the Yukon will implore, if not order, you to see its "variety" show. Most of them are to be avoided, but the Whitehorse show is a happy exception. The follies pack in plenty of physical comedy, pulled off, in general, with flair, and the Robert Service recitations are truly funny. Even locals go at least once a year to see the new talent and get their fix of high-kicking showgirls. There are nightly performances. Reserve in advance as seats are often filled with coach tour groups.

Where to Stay

Easily the most luxurious accommodation north of 60th parallel, **Hawkins House** ((867) 668-7638 FAX (867) 668-7632 E-MAIL umbrich@internorth .com, 303 Hawkins Street, Whitehorse Y1A 1X5, is an unmissable painted-lady-style Victorian mansion in downtown Whitehorse. Fortunately, the interior is much more soothingly decorated. Rooms are small but beautifully and lovingly decked out in warm wood tones and packed with all the comforts you could ask for, including queen-sized beds, en-suite baths, sinks and refrigerators, and balconies. Two of the rooms have Jacuzzi tubs. A gourmet breakfast is served in the dining room each morning for an additional fee. Prices are at the high end of the mid-range category.

In the heart of downtown, there is the **Westmark Inn** ((867) 668-4700 FAX (867) 668-2789, at Second and Wood streets, Whitehorse Y1A 3T3, part of a northern chain. With 180 rooms this is the largest hotel in the Yukon. Rooms are spacious, nicely furnished, and well-decorated. There are lots of amenities close at hand, including a restaurant and bar, a travel agency, a gift shop, and a barber and a hair salon. Rates are at the top of the mid-range category.

At the end of Main Street, overlooking the Yukon River, the **Edgewater Hotel** ((867) 667-2572 FAX (867) 668-3014, 101 Main Street, Whitehorse Y1A 2A7, is a small, vintage hotel with 20 rooms and the excellent Cellar Dining Room (see WHERE TO EAT, below). Rooms are cozy and come equipped with extra-long beds and air conditioning. There is room service and some rooms are equipped with kitchenettes.

The slightly lower-priced **Best Western Gold Rush Inn** ((867) 668-4500 FAX (867) 668-7432, 411 Main Street, Whitehorse Y1A 2B6, is owned by one of Whitehorse's local characters who refers to himself as Gold Nuggie Dougie. Rooms are clean and comfortable, if lacking in the character one expects from the hunting-lodge-style lobby. There is a predictable restaurant and lounge.

A casual atmosphere, spacious rooms, full breakfast, evening snacks, and a host who will always go out of her way to make her guests' stay as carefree as possible are all trademarks of the **Four Seasons Bed & Breakfast** ((867) 667-2161 FAX (867) 667-2171 E-MAIL jeano@polarcom.com, 18 Tagish Road, Whitehorse Y1A 3P5. The house is located in a quiet residential area, a 15-minute walk from downtown and hillside hikes. Your host

can arrange guided tours, access to laundry facilities, and transportation. Prices are at the low end of the mid-range.

Haeckel Hill Bed & Breakfast ((867) 633-5625 FAX (867) 633-5630 E--MAIL bear@yknet.ca, 1501 Birch Street Whitehorse, Yukon, Canada Y1A 3X1, is located at the foot of Haeckel Hill in the rural suburb of Porter Creek, a five-minute drive from downtown. It makes an excellent base for day hiking and exploring the hilly countryside and forest trails; the proprietors are also tour operators who can arrange hiking, bicycling, and river trips. Rooms are sunny and comfortably furnished in white pine with a clean, uncluttered northern European touch. There's a sitting room with views

of the mountains and a fireplace. A breakfast of homemade breads and muffins is served each morning. Rates fall in the low end of the mid-range. German and Dutch are spoken.

There is no hostel in Whitehorse, nor is there a YMCA residence or university dormitory housing. In addition, camping is at a premium as hundreds of Canadian college students come north to supply labor for the Yukon summer tourist season. Bargain hunters traveling in groups of three or four can sometimes make arrangements with bed-and-breakfast establishments. For example, Four Seasons Bed & Breakfast (see above) regularly books their spacious double rooms, supplied with an extra cot, to three people for a very reasonable price.

A roadside marker denotes the international boundary between the United States and Canada.

For long-term stays, including winter vacations, **Wild Treats Vacation Property Rentals** ℂ/FAX (867) 633-3322 E-MAIL jwebster@yknet.yk.ca, 29 Wann Road, PO Box 9150, Whitehorse Y1A 4A2, rents cozy wilderness cabins.

Where to Eat

Hearty fare is served in Yukon restaurants; steak and seafood are featured on many menus. Arctic char, Alaska king crab, and Yukon or Taku River salmon are some of the local delicacies. You'll also find a variety of ethnic eateries with good, if not authentic, cuisine.

Locals and savvy tourists alike all seem to agree that the **Cellar Dining Room** (Edgewater Hotel)

Avenue at Main Street, has the best tabouli in town. It's open daily for breakfast lunch and dinner.

We love the **Pasta Palace** ℂ (867) 667-6888, 209 Main Street, for its inexpensive and delicious fare. The proprietors don't bother with atmosphere, but concentrate on serving some of the tastiest and best-value meals in the city. In addition to pastas there is an extensive selection of tapas and appetizers. Service is prompt and friendly.

Known locally as "The Deck," the **Yukon Mining Co.** (High Country Inn) ℂ (867) 667-4471, 4051 Fourth Avenue, is the place to go for an excellent cold one from the local Chilkoot Brewery and one of Heinz's juicy barbecued burgers. The best deal is the Deck burger. Also on the menu is

ℂ (867) 667-2572, 101 Main Street, is the best restaurant in Whitehorse. You'll pay top dollar for the excellent prime rib, Alaska king crab, or lobster and prawns served in the plush lower-level dining room The same great food is served in a more casual atmosphere — and for less money — in the Gallery upstairs from the Cellar.

Considering how far "north of the border" they are, **Sam 'n' Andy's** ℂ (867) 668-6994, 506 Main Street, serves fairly good Mexican food. The admittedly overpriced pitchers of margaritas draw the locals to the small, friendly terrace each evening. The post-modern **No Pop Sandwich Shop** ℂ (867) 668-3227, 312 Steele Street, is a trendy bistro-style place serving sandwiches and a number of daily specials, usually featuring fresh fish. On Sunday there is a popular brunch. Reservations are recommended. Also very popular locally, the **Talisman Restaurant** ℂ (867) 667-2736, 2112 Second

a range of seafood, pastas, and salads. There is surprisingly good sushi at the Yukon Mining Co. on certain nights; call to inquire about availability. To find The Deck, just look for the adjoining hotel, an aluminum tower in the neighborhood of the Robert Campbell Bridge.

There are several roasters in Whitehorse where a good cup coffee can be enjoyed. Our favorite is **Midnight Sun Coffee Roaster** ℂ (867) 633-4JOE, 4168C Fourth Avenue, where the organic brew is especially aromatic and the atmosphere is homey. They have great muffins and cookies, too. Another "must" on the Whitehorse scene is the **Alpine Bakery** ℂ (867) 668-6871, 411 Alexander Street, where you can purchase long-lasting expedition bread for your hiking or boating trip. All of the baked goods are terrific, all organic. They also offer homemade yogurt, European cheeses, and organic preserves made with Yukon berries. The Alpine has a reputation for being not only the best bakery in the Yukon, but one of the best in the country. It's open Tuesday to Saturday from 10 AM to 5:30 PM.

How to Get There
The **Whitehorse International Airport** is seven kilometers (five miles) from the downtown core, on a hill above the city. Until recently, there were no international direct flights to the Yukon. That changed with the introduction of a weekly Lufthansa flight from Frankfurt; additional international connections may be added as the Yukon becomes a more popular destination for Europeans.

Most people still fly into Whitehorse via a Canadian city. Daily service is available through Vancouver and Edmonton via **Canadian Airlines International (** (867) 668-7378, or from Juneau and Fairbanks, Alaska via **Air North (** (867) 668-2228. Flying to the Yukon is appallingly expensive. At certain seasons it is possible to arrange one-way charter flights to Vancouver or other Canadian cities for much less than the regular airline fare. The best place to make onward travel arrangements from Whitehorse is **Atlas Travel (** (867) 667-7823, in the Westmark Whitehorse Hotel.

Coming from British Columbia, motorists enter the Yukon via the Alaska Highway (Highway 1) or the **Stewart-Cassiar Highway**, which connects with Highway 1 near the Yukon-British Columbia border. From Alaska, Highway 1 leads from Fairbanks into the southwest corner of the territory. Those heading to Dawson City from Alaska

can pick up the **Taylor Highway** (Highway 5) at Tok, Alaska, and from there connect with the Top of the World Highway (Highway 9) which leads to Dawson City.

Greyhound ((867) 667-2223 TOLL-FREE (800) 661-8747 offers daily service from Edmonton. The trip takes 36 hours. The best place to break the journey is Liard Hot Springs. **Alaskon Express** TOLL-FREE (800) 544-2206 has regularly scheduled service from Alaska to the Yukon communities of Carcross, Whitehorse, Haines Junction, and Beaver Creek. Tickets may be booked at any Gray Line Office. In Whitehorse **Gray Line Yukon (** (867) 668-3130 is at 2288 Second Avenue. Cheaper fares are to be had on the **Alaska Direct Bus Lines (** (867) 668-4833 or (907) 277-6652, 125 Oklahoma Street, Anchorage, Alaska 99504-1210 USA, also runs through the Yukon, serving Whitehorse, Haines Junction, Burwash Landing, and Beaver Creek.

The most scenic way to get to the Yukon is via the Alaska State Ferries along the Inside Passage (see CRUISE THE INSIDE PASSAGE, page 26, in TOP SPOTS). Passengers can debark at Haines, Alaska, and follow Haines Road (Highway 3) up to Haines Junction where it connects with the Alaska Highway; or they can get off at Skagway, Alaska, where they can journey over the White Pass by railway (see RIDE THE LEGENDARY RAILS, page 20, in TOP SPOTS). From Skagway, travelers can also follow in the footsteps of the gold-rush stampeders by trekking the Chilkoot Trail (see SKAGWAY, ALASKA, below); or they can reach the Yukon by car via the Klondike Highway (Highway 2).

SKAGWAY, ALASKA

Described in 1898 as nothing more than "a spot of wet, mossy earth at the foot of a high mountain on the seashore," Skagway, Alaska, is one of the primary routes to the Yukon. A popular destination in itself, Skagway is swamped throughout the summer with short-term visitors: some 450,000 cruiseship passengers pass through each season. Most of the 2,500 people who work in Skagway are not residents, but come up only for the summer tourist season. Only around 300 live here year-round. A day is certainly enough time to rest up from your ferry trip, get a feel for the place and make your onward connections to the Yukon. The name, incidentally means, "place of the north wind."

General Information
The overburdened **Convention and Visitor Bureau (** (907) 983-2854 FAX (907) 983-1898, has town

The 1898 Klondike gold rush— "Tenderfeet" labor over the Chilkoot Pass from Dyea, Alaska, to Lake Bennett, British Columbia. ABOVE: A seasoned prospector, or "sourdough."

and trail maps and offers information and advice on all your travel and accommodation needs. **Internet access** is available at Soapy Station ((907) 983-2085, 745 Broadway, where there are also phone and fax facilities and laptop ports.

What to See and Do

The United States park service has done an admirable job of preserving the historical district of this boom-and-bust town, but behind the boardwalks and authentic false-fronted buildings, attractions, eateries, and hostelries of quality number only a few. Skagway's historical district is essentially a show for the passengers of the giant luxury cruise ships that dock by the threes and fours in its small

harbor. Much of downtown Skagway constitutes the **Klondike Gold Rush National Historic Park** which also encompasses the White Pass and Chilkoot Trail (as well as Pioneer Square in Seattle, Washington). The park Visitor Centre, Second Avenue and Broadway, is open daily 8 AM to 6 PM from May to September, 8 AM to 8 PM from June to August. The center offers films, ranger talks, and a worthwhile **walking tour of the historic district**; all activities are free of charge.

Dozens of operators — with mottoes such as "Why pay more?" — offer **sightseeing tours** around and about town. Take your pick. The one stand-out in the crowd is the Skagway Street Car Company ((907) 983-2908, whose costumed

ABOVE and OPPOSITE BOTTOM: Alaska State Ferries' MV *Matanuska* plies the Inside Passage. TOP: A Dawson cabin sports the traditional moose antler and knotty pine admorments.

interpreters take you around in a shiny yellow 1920s-vintage limousine.

For those who did not arrive in Skagway via boat, a taste of the Inside Passage can be had by booking on the **boat tours** to Haines or Juneau. Chilkat Cruises ((907) 766-2100 TOLL-FREE (888) 766-2103 operates a daily scheduled ferry shuttle service; Auk Nu Tours ((907) 586-8687 TOLL-FREE (800) 820-BOAT, runs the catamaran *Alaskan Dream* on day-long round-trip cruises to Juneau; and the Water Taxi ((907) 983-2083 offers a similar service to Haines.

And, don't worry — Skagway is not under attack; it's only helicopters and planes giving **flightseeing tours** to Mendenhall Glacier. You can hardly miss Temsco Helicopters ((907) 983-2900, near the harbor or Skagway Air Service ((907) 983-2218 E-MAIL skagair@ptialaska.net. They also have flightseeing tours of the spectacular Glacier Bay.

Skagway has two locally owned art and craft shops: **Inside Passage Arts** (907) 983-2585, and **Inhofe's Carvers Gallery** ((907) 983-2434, both located on Broadway. Inhofe's sells his own work and the works of his protégés, chiefly mastodon ivory carvings. At Inside Passage Arts the work ranges wider with Southeast Alaska native arts alongside the hand-carved silver jewelry of the owners. The rest of Skagway's shops are not noteworthy, running the gamut from expensive jewelry stores to trinket shops brimming with big-eyed seal T-shirts.

Excursions from Skagway

For many travelers, the sole reason for passing through Skagway is to access the famed 53-km (33-mile)-long **Chilkoot Trail**. A difficult hike that takes three to five days, it follows the route of the stampeders. The trail begins near the Dyea townsite northwest of Skagway. You must obtain a backcountry permit from the National Park Service before you begin your hike. Only 50 hikers per day are allowed to cross into Canada via the trail. Because of this quota, it may be necessary to obtain your permit as early as six months in advance if you wish to hike the trail at the peak season of mid-July to mid-August. Contact the **Klondike Gold Rush National Historic Park** ((907) 983-2921, PO Box 517, Skagway, Alaska 99840.

Where to Stay and Eat

If you decide to overnight in Skagway, we recommend **Whitehouse Bed and Breakfast** ((907) 983-9000 FAX (907) 983-3210 E-MAIL whitehse@ ptialaska.net, Eighth and Main, PO Box 41, Skagway, Alaska 99840. This historic house is located in a quiet street far enough away from Broadway to escape the constant hubbub but close enough for convenience. The spacious rooms have high ceilings and en-suite bathrooms. Full breakfast is served each morning in the dining

room. Prices are in the mid-range category. The **Skagway Inn** ((907) 983-2289 FAX (907) 983-2713 E-MAIL sgyinn@ptialaska.net, Seventh and Broadway, PO Box 500, Skagway, Alaska 99840, is a good choice, if you want to be in the center of the historic district. It's a European-style inn with cozy rooms decorated to commemorate "the girls" of Skagway's gold-rush days. Bathrooms are shared. Rates run from inexpensive to midrange. For budget travelers, the **Skagway Home Hostel** ((907) 983-2131 FAX (907) 983-2713, Third Street and Main, Skagway, Alaska 99840, has dormitory accommodation as well as inexpensive private double rooms.

It's difficult to make recommendations for restaurants in Skagway, whose dining establishments have begun to suffer from their success. On the ground floor of the Skagway Inn is **Olivia's** ((907) 983-2289, where Caesar salad is prepared at your table. Its reputation as the best restaurant in town is probably deserved, but standards are lamentably low here; nevertheless, reservations are recommended. The **Golden North Hotel** ((907) 983-2451, on Third Street and Broadway, has a restaurant with a delightful terrace, but service is slow. Also on Broadway, the very popular **Sweet Tooth Gertie's** ((907) 983-2450, 315 Broadway, is your best bet for a hearty breakfast. You can count on good solid food here, but be sure to arrive before the morning ferry passengers alight. They'll be hungry.

How to Get There

Skagway can be reached year-round via the **Alaska Marine Highway** ((907) 627-1744 or (907) 627-1745 TOLL-FREE (800) 642-0066, PO Box 25535, Juneau, Alaska 99802-5535, from Bellingham (Washington), Prince Rupert (British Columbia); and Wrangell, Petersburg, Sitka, Juneau and Haines (Alaska); and by air from Juneau, Haines and Whitehorse, Yukon. Road routes to Skagway are the Alaska and Klondike highways from the Yukon.

Once in Skagway, your options are the three Rs: road, rail, or ramble. The Klondike Highway takes you over the White Pass to the Yukon's capital city of Whitehorse. For bus service, there is **Rival Highway Tours** ((867) 667-7896, connecting Whitehorse to Skagway via Carcross and Fraser, British Columbia. Before the highway there was the **White Pass & Yukon Railway** ((907) 983-2217 TOLL-FREE (800) 343-7373 FAX (907) 983-2734, PO Box 435, Skagway, Alaska 99840. Ramblers backpack the steep Chilkoot Trail out of Dyea (see EXCURSIONS FROM SKAGWAY, page 402).

KLUANE NATIONAL PARK

Tucked in the southwest corner of the territory, a two-hour drive from Whitehorse, Kluane

(pronounced kloo-*ahn*-ee) National Park is the jewel of the Yukon, a designated UNESCO World Heritage Site. These 22,015 sq km (8,500 sq miles) of glaciers, marshes, lakes, and mountains are unsettled and virtually untouched. There are no ski lifts in Kluane waiting to whisk you to the top of a mountain, no teahouses at the end of the trail. "Kluane," said a transplanted Swiss couple we met there, "is the Swiss Alps without all the people." The Matterhorn of this alpine land is **Mount Logan** (6,050 m or 19,849 ft), Canada's highest peak and the second highest mountain in North America. It is part of the St. Elias Mountains, which contains six other peaks over 5,000 m (16,000 ft).

Much of the reserve's wilderness has been the homeland of the Southern Tutchone people for thousands of years. Many of the trails follow traditional paths of these First Nations people who still use them. The Champagne and Aishihik First Nations have a constitutional right to hunt and fish in the park and are co-managers of Kluane.

Because the park is undeveloped, the interior is only accessible to experienced alpinists (or those with the money to take a flightseeing tour, see WHAT TO SEE AND DO, below). Despite this, parts of Kluane are surprisingly accessible. Rafting, fishing in crystal clear waters, and wildlife watching are the chief activities.

General Information

Kluane has two visitor reception centers, staffed throughout the summer, where expert advice is available on what to see and do in the park. The **Kluane Park Visitor Centre** ((867) 634-2251 provides literature, information, and maps. It's open daily 8:30 AM to 9 PM. Within the same facility is the territorial **Visitor Information Centre** ((867) 634-2345. The **Sheep Mountain Visitor Centre** (867) 841-5161, Km 1707 Alaska Highway, is open daily 9 AM to 7 PM. An interpretive program runs

OPPOSITE and ABOVE: Kluane National Park — The St. Elias Lake Trail, "bear country."

through the summer months with guided hikes and presentations. Haines Junction is the place to stock up on provisions. **Madley's** has everything you need for camping, hiking as well as groceries, fresh produce, and smoked wild salmon which they will ship. Next door, the public library has the only public **Internet access** for miles around.

What to See and Do

You don't have to be a mountaineer to enjoy the many kilometers of trails throughout the park's front ranges. The best time of year for **hiking** is between June 15 and September 15, when temperatures range between a high of 28°C (82°F) and a low of 0°C (32°F). All overnight trips into Kluane

require registration at one of the visitor reception centers where you can also find out about how to avoid sneaking up on a bear (to begin with, always make noise as you are walking). The trailhead for the short hike to **St. Elias Lake Trail** (3.8 km or 2.4 miles) is 60 km (38 miles) south of Haines Junction on Haines Road. The trail leads through wood and meadow to backcountry camping along a lake visited by loons. The **Auriol Trail** (15 km or nine miles) is a popular overnight loop. The trailhead is seven kilometers south of Haines Junction on Haines Road.

Kluane is also a wonderful place for **paddling**. You can rent a canoe, kayak or raft and strike out on your own, or you can hook up with an outfitter (see OUTFITTERS, below).

Just east of the Sheep Mountain Visitor Centre, look for the scenic viewpoint marker for the turnoff (to your left) for **Silver City**, a ghost town

located five kilometers (three miles) down a gravel road. It's a worthwhile side trip where you can ramble among the decaying shanties and mining equipment.

The only way to get a glimpse at the St. Elias Mountains, short of mounting a major expedition, is to take a **flightseeing** tour with one of the local operators such as Trans North Helicopters ((867) 668-2177, located along the Alaska Highway east of the Sheep Mountain Visitor Centre. The helicopters will take you to the spectacular **Kaskawulsh Glacier**, part of the world's largest nonpolar ice field. Or you can arrange a **heli-hiking** trip. You'll be dropped off in an alpine meadow with panoramic views of Sheep Mountain, Kluane Lake and the St. Elias Mountains; from there you trek back to Trans North's Kluane base.

Haines Road is a gorgeous drive leading into an uninhabited corner of British Columbia before arriving at Haines, Alaska. At its highest point, the road cuts across a grand plateau guarded by glaciated mountains. Numerous creeks pass through the region, and this area has some of the continent's best river trips (see below).

Outfitters

Paddlewheel Adventures ((867) 634-2683, PO Box 2079, Haines Junction Y0B 1L0, across from the Kluane Park Visitor Centre, has canoe and mountain bike rentals, guided tours, and does bookings for a variety of other tours, including whitewater rafting, flightseeing, horseback riding, and llama hikes. The Tatshenshini Wilderness Area provides some of the best river running in the world. **Tatshenshini Expediting** ((867) 633-2742 FAX (867) 633-6184 E-MAIL tatexp@polar.com, 1602 Alder Street, Whitehorse Y1A 3W8, is one of the Yukon's longest established rafting and kayaking companies. They offer a range of adventures from one-day paddling trips along the Tat to the full 11-day Tatshenshini and Alsek riverrafting experience — this is the one that draws people from all over the world not only for its challenging rapids but for its unparalleled scenery. They also rent boats and all necessary equipment.

Where to Stay and Eat

In Haines Junction, the **Raven Motel** ((867) 634-2500 FAX (867) 634-2517, 181 Haines Road, PO Box 5470, Haines Junction Y0B 1L0, has comfortable rooms ranging in price from inexpensive to moderate. Rooms have direct dial telephones, en-suite bathrooms, and television. The restaurant (expensive) is among the best in the Yukon.

Rooms at the **Gateway Motel** ((867) 634-2371 FAX (867) 634-2833, PO Box 5460, Haines Junction

Yukon flora and fauna — ABOVE: Lichens flourish in an alpine meadow. OPPOSITE: A felled tree offers evidence of beavers.

Y0B 1L0, are of surprisingly high quality given the appearance of the building and office. Standing as it does at the junction of the Alaska Highway and Haines Road, few motels can compete with its stunning views of the snowcapped Kluane Mountain Range. Amenities include satellite television, complimentary coffee, and kitchenettes. The Gateway had a "For Sale" sign attached to it at the time of research, but the cigar-chomping owner (after offering to sell it to us) assured us that it was to remain in operation.

The **Cozy Corner** ((867) 634-2511 FAX (867) 634-2119, PO Box 5406, Haines Junction Y0B 1L0, is another good motel choice. The attached restaurant serves a generous breakfast.

One of the best ways to explore the region is to stay at **Dalton Trail Lodge** (/FAX (867) 667-1099, PO Box 5331, Haines Junction Y0B 1L0, nestled at the base of the St. Elias Mountains on Dezadeash Lake. Activities run from horseback riding to dog mushing, canoeing, hiking, fishing for king salmon and Arctic grayling, flightseeing, and snowmobiling all from the comfort of the casual lodge, log cabins, or private outposts. Visitors can opt for full-fledged, guided excursions or relaxed day-long forays into Kluane. The lodge has canoes stationed at many of the lakes, so day hikers can combine a canoe trip with a hike. Finally, the lodge has its own gold claim on Kimberly Creek where visitors can pan for nuggets and learn about placer mining. Full breakfast, a picnic lunch, and a hardy Swiss dinner are included in the prices, which are in the moderate category. German and French are spoken.

DAWSON CITY

At a latitude of 64° 4' north, Dawson City is a place of strange contradictions. Once the largest metropolis north of San Francisco, it now has a year-round population of less than 2,000. One of the most northerly of Canadian towns, it is also one of the hottest. In June, you can watch the sun sink below the horizon at one o'clock in the morning and stick around to see it come back up three hours later. The town's beer halls are loaded with frontier character, but it also lovingly preserves the cabins of two famous literary men, Robert Service and Jack London.

Dawson's gold rush atmosphere is what draws most visitors. Large portions of the town are part of a registered historical area administered by Parks Canada and the Klondike Visitors Association. Many of the buildings are authentic gold-rush era structures and the rest are good reproductions. The streets remain as they were in 1898, unpaved and lined by boardwalks. Museums, tours, panning for gold, gambling, old-time music, riverboat rides, and can-can girls are all part of the fun. Yet there is much more to Dawson City than turn-of-the-century revelry. Visitors who take a moment to look beyond the gold-rush glitter will also find a welcoming native community composed of descendants of the region's original inhabitants. Outdoor enthusiasts will find abundant opportunities for hiking, fishing, paddling and more, while motorists can enjoy some wonderfully scenic drives.

Background

The first wave of stampeders to arrive in Dawson City were totally unprepared for what lay ahead. The winter of 1897 was a season of shortages: There was not enough food to go around and fearful prospectors began to panic and hoard; candle and lamp oil was in short supply, leaving 3,000 of 6,000 inhabitants without with light for the winter in a land where daylight lasts only from 10 AM to 2 PM; 2,000 people were unsheltered or living in tents.

Despite its rough start, Dawson City was born and prospered. At the height of the gold rush, Dawson had a population of around 30,000, making it one of the biggest cities west of Winnipeg. Between 1897 and 1904, it is estimated that over

for the next 50 years. These days the little town of 2,000 year-round residents thrives on tourism.

General Information

Stop by the excellent **Visitor Reception Centre** ((867) 993-5566 on the corner of Front and King streets, for an orientation before you begin your explorations. It's open daily from May 16 to September 21, 8 AM to 8 PM. The building is a replica of the Alaska Trading Company building. **Parks Canada** ((867) 993-7200, maintains a counter here as well, where you can purchase a Parks Pass — worth the price if you're planning to visit more than three of their sites. For trip planning, you can contact the park service by writing: Superintendent,

$100 million in gold was recovered from the Klondike and its tributaries which covered an area of around 64 sq km (40 sq miles). It was a small pocket of land that glittered with gold, yet only a handful of prospectors went home millionaires. Tens of thousands were disappointed, for by the time they reached the gold fields, all of the best claims had been staked.

After the stampede, the population of Dawson City began to decline almost immediately. Many prospectors were soon discouraged and were lured by reports of other gold discoveries (e.g., Nome, Alaska in 1899). By 1906 the most easily worked placer mines (containing gold that is found lose in sand and gravel as opposed to "lode" gold that occurs in hard rock) were finished, leaving claims to be mined by large companies using huge and expensive dredges. The employment offered by these dredging companies kept Dawson City alive

Klondike National Historic Sites, PO Box 390, Dawson Y0B 1G0. The public library, in the Post Office Building, Fifth Avenue, has free **Internet access**; however, there is usually a long waiting list (we're talking days). It's better to shell out a few dollars to check your e-mail at **Harper Street Publishing** ((867) 993-6671. Call to get their current office location. While you are there, pick up a free copy of their *Guide to the Goldfields*, an annual publication with news, opinions, and essays about the North.

What to See and Do

Begin your visit to Dawson City with a **walking tour** through the historic downtown area. Tours are given by costumed interpreters and depart

Dawson City — OPPOSITE: The Palace Grande Theatre LEFT and a sunny seciton of the city's wooden sidewalks RIGHT. ABOVE: The "Pit" at the Windsor Hotel is a popular night spot.

from the Visitor Information Centre three times daily. The interpreters have an interesting rap, and this is also the only opportunity to see the interior of some of the restored historical buildings. You can, alternatively, rent an audio tape in English, French or German, for a self-guided walking tour.

On the riverbank near Queen Street, you can see an old, grounded sternwheeler, the **SS Keno**. Built in 1922 to ply the Stewart River around the mining hamlets of Mayo and Keno, it was the smallest in the Yukon fleet. Because of its diminutive size, the Keno would have been the first to break through the winter ice to Dawson — a welcome sight after long months without fresh vegetables. Tours of the newly restored boat are offered by the SS Keno National Historic Site ((867) 993-5462 FAX (867) 993-5683, C.P. 390 390 Dawson City Yukon, YIA 285.

A few blocks away from the river, the **Dawson City Museum** ((867) 993-5291, Fifth Avenue at Minto Park, features exhibits on the history of the gold rush. There are some 25,000 artifacts on display, though most of it will only be of interest to gold-rush buffs. Exhibits on the native Hän who populated the area before the gold rush and who still live here are lackluster. Silent films of the period, unearthed during a 1978 restoration project, are the best part of the museum's offerings. There's a coffee and gift shop. The museum is open from early June to Labor Day daily from 10 AM to 6 PM; an admission fee is charged.

The **Robert Service Cabin** is a two-room log structure in which the poet lived between 1909 and 1912. Actor Tom Byrne performs a daily recitation of the life and works of the "Bard of the Yukon" — who wrote such classics as "The Shooting of Dan McGrew" and "The Call of the Yukon." It's open daily from 9 AM to noon and 1 PM to 5 PM with recitals at 10 AM and 3 PM; an admission fee is charged. Farther south, on Eighth Avenue at the corner of Fifth, is the **Jack London Cabin**, where the writer lived briefly. Though his time in the Yukon was short, he collected the materials here for such classics as White Fang, "The Snow Wolf," and The Call of the Wild. There's a talk each day at 1 PM about London's adventures in the Klondike. It's open 11 AM to 3 PM and admission is free.

Souvenir shoppers should not miss the **Dawson Trading Post** ((867) 993-5316, on Fifth Avenue, a gold mine for those on the lookout for the unusual. Besides being a sports-and-adventure outfitter, the store sells local antiques, caribou antlers, and raw mastodon ivory. The **Klondike Nugget and Ivory Shop** ((867) 993-5432, has the Yukon's signature souvenir gold-nugget and mastodon ivory jewelry.

Dawson nightlife retains some of the frontier, whoop-it-up flavor of its heyday. The diminutive and beautifully restored **Palace Grande Theatre**

((867) 993-6217, King Street, was built in 1899 from materials that once made up two steamboats. Parks Canada restored the theater 1962, and now offers guided tours. The theater is also home to the much-vaunted Gaslight Follies. Best to tour the theater by day, but if you feel you must see the show, tickets are available at the Historic Post Office; shows run May 17 to September 14 nightly except Tuesday at 8 PM. It's safe to say that your evening might more wisely be spent elsewhere, say at **Diamond Tooth Gertie's Gambling Hall** ((867) 993-5575, at Fourth Avenue and Queen Street. At least here you'll have fun wasting your money. It's open from 7 PM to 2 AM with three floor shows each night, complete with can-can line. Minors are not admitted. It's open from mid-May to mid-September; an admission fee is charged.

The gaudy pink **Westminster Hotel** ((867) 993-5463, 975 Third Avenue, is the home of the "Pit" beer parlor and is stocked with local character and characters. Nightly entertainment is provided by same.

Excursions from Dawson City

A hike or drive up to **Midnight Dome** is another requisite of the Dawson City experience. Dawson sits at the foot of this mountain, and the summit affords views of the gold fields, Yukon River valley, Dawson, and the Ogilvie Mountains. Go up for the late-night sunset for the best vistas.

If you'd like to go with a group, **Gold City Tours** ((867) 993-5175, PO Box 960, Dawson Y0B 1G0, on Front Street across from the SS Keno riverboat, takes up to Midnight Dome. They also take sightseers out to the Bonanza Creek gold fields, and on a 12-hour trip via coach along the Dempster Highway to the Arctic Circle and back.

The twin-deck Yukon Queen takes passengers from Dawson City to Eagle, Alaska, a distance of 174 km (108 miles). The day-long cruise includes two meals and a stopover in Eagle. Trips run from mid-May to mid-September and passengers can choose one-way or round-trips. Book well in advance at Gray Line Yukon ((867) 993-5599 on Front Street near the visitor center.

Dawson City has some wonderful river excursions where you can meet and learn about the regional native cultures. **Ancient Voices Wilderness Camp** ((867) 993-5605 FAX (867) 993-6532 E-MAIL avwcamp@yukon.net, PO Box 679, Dawson Y0B 1G0 (see LISTEN TO ANCIENT VOICES, page 26, in TOP SPOTS) has an evening barbecue, drumming, and storytelling program as well as accommodation and adventure packages and programs including wilderness survival, arts and crafts, and

TOP: A motorboat ride up the Yukon River is a chance to spot wildlife such as moose and black bear. BOTTOM: Permafrost plays havoc with house foundations. These days, pilings that can be raised and lowered stablize the city's buildings.

women's workshops. **Fishwheel Charter Service** ((867) 993-6857, PO Box 891, Dawson Y0B 1G0, runs two-hour historical-cultural tours, where you can see a traditional native method of fishing. *Bannock* and tea are included in the trip.

The gold fields lie just south of Dawson City in the hills and creeks along the Klondike Highway. Though the rush is long over, you can pan for gold — success guaranteed — at **Claim 33** ((867) 993-5303, Mile 7 Bonanza Creek Road. But what's the fun in noodling around in a trough laced with gold flakes? Far better to roll up your sleeves and take your chances in a creek. **Goldbottom Mining Tours** ((867) 993-5023 FAX (867) 993-6715, PO Box 912, Dawson Y0B 1G0, runs escorted trips to an authentic placer mining operation where you'll see a gold processing demonstration and get an hour of gold panning in the creek (daily 11 AM to 7 PM) — rubber boots, pan, and shovel provided. They are located at Goldbottom and Hunker creeks, 30 km (19 miles) south of Dawson City and 15 km (just over nine miles) up Hunker Creek Road from the Klondike Highway.

After the first wave of individual prospecting, companies moved into the Yukon and began large-scale mining with dredges. Until it sank in the 1960s, **Dredge No. 4** ripped 22,000 grams of gold out of the ground each day. The largest wooden-hulled dredge ever built, it is now an historical monument. This dredge and others like it are responsible for the eerie, apocalyptic look of the landscape in the Klondike area. Floating in man-made ponds, the dredges scooped, sifted and spewed out creek gravel, creating huge, caterpillar-shaped mounds of tailings. It's open daily 9 AM to 5 PM, and is located 13 km (eight miles) south of Dawson City on Bonanza Creek Road (off the Klondike Highway).

The best way to get an idea of the extent of the gold fields is to take an **aerial tour** with Trans North Helicopters ((867) 993-5494. They also offer **heli-hiking** in the nearby Tombstone and Ogilvie mountains. The helipad is on the Klondike Highway, half a kilometer (about one quarter mile) south of Dawson City.

One hill over from Dredge No. 4, **Bear Creek** was for 60 years the home of the Yukon Consolidated Gold Corporation. This dredge support camp was where the gold ore was milled and melted down into bullion. This Parks Canada site has 65 buildings to tour illustrating the history of large-scale mining. The turnoff for Bear Creek is 16 km (10 miles) south of Dawson City, off the Klondike Highway.

Where to Stay

A welcome new addition to the mid-range to expensive accommodation available in Dawson City is the **Aurora Inn** (/FAX (867) 993-6860 E-MAIL rjansen@yknet.yk.ca, PO Box 1748, Daw-

son Y0B 1G0. Located on Fifth Avenue, the inn has spacious, sunny rooms with a contemporary Scandinavian look and locally made white pine furnishings. All rooms have en-suite baths. A European breakfast is served at an additional moderate cost. Some rooms come equipped with computers and the proprietors are happy to arrange a variety of supplementary services with its higher-priced rooms.

At the corner of Second and Queen streets, the **Downtown Hotel** ((867) 993-5346 TOLL-FREE (800) 661-0514 or (800) 764-GOLD FAX (867) 993-5076, PO Box 780, Dawson Y0B 1G0, is one of Dawson's two year-round accommodations. The rooms are comfortable and modern. The main building features a restaurant and the plush Sourdough Saloon. The annex (across the street) has a whirlpool. Rates are at the top end of the mid-range category.

The **Westmark Inn** ((867) 993-5542 TOLL-FREE (800) 544-0970 or (800) 999-2570, Fifth Avenue and Harper Street, Dawson Y0B 1G0, is part of the northern chain. It focuses most of its energies on the many coach tours that its parent company brings to Dawson City, but rooms for independent travelers are sometimes available. Though small, rooms are modern and richly furnished. There is room service, a dining room, lounge, and gift shop. Rates are solidly mid-range.

Nondescript but reliable, the **Triple J Hotel** ((867) 993-5323 TOLL-FREE (800) 764-3555 or (800) 661-0405, PO Box 359, Dawson Y0B 1G0, on Fifth Avenue, has a hotel, a motel, and small cabins. All units have private bath. The main hotel building includes a restaurant and lounge with a terrace. It's right next to Diamond Tooth Gertie's Casino, and it is open year-round. Rates are mid-range.

The First Nations-owned-and-operated **Bear Creek Bed & Bannock** ((867) 993-5605 FAX (867) 993-6532 E-MAIL kormendy@hypertech.yk.ca, PO Box 679, Dawson Y0B 1G0, offers inexpensive to mid-range bed and breakfast accommodation in Bear Creek, a quiet subdivision 10 minutes from Dawson. Guests stay in a four-room facility separate from the main house, and a continental breakfast including fresh *bannock* is served daily. Traditional First Nations arts and crafts are on display. Guests have use of a kitchen, living room, dining area, laundry facilities, and a large deck.

The **Dawson City Bunkhouse** ((867) 993-6164 FAX (867) 993-6051, on the corner of Front and Princess streets, PO Box 4040, Dawson Y0B 1G0 has clean, rustic accommodation including rooms with shared bath, or suites with private baths. Rates range from inexpensive to moderate.

Dawson has the Yukon's only Hostelling-International-affiliate, the **Dawson City River Hostel** ((867) 993-6823, PO Box 32, Dawson Y0B 1G0, directly opposite Dawson across the Yukon

At Ancient Voices Wilderness Camp, a moosehide is stretched on a rack for tanning.

River. It's open mid-May through September, has a kitchen and bike and canoe rental, and offers free pickup from the bus depot at designated times. To get there take the free 24-hour ferry from Front Street to West Dawson; the hostel is located 100 m (just over 100 yards) from the landing site.

Where to Eat

Good dining can be found in the local hotels, most notably the Downtown Hotel's atmospheric **Jack London Grill and Sourdough Saloon** ((867) 993-5346. The best restaurant in Dawson City, however, is **Marina's** ((867) 993-6800, Fifth Avenue between Princess and Harper streets. The pasta is heavenly. Located across from the Westmark, it can fill up quickly with hungry coach tour groups, so you may want to arrive a bit early for dinner.

Klondike Kate's ((867) 993-6527, corner King Street and Third Avenue, is housed in an authentic gold-rush-era building. The extensive menu features ethnic dishes such as gyros, falafel, "wraps" (like burritos), seafood, sandwiches, and domestic and imported beers. The breakfast special is one of Dawson's best buys. There's a covered patio in the rear. It's open daily 7 AM to 11 PM.

Along the riverfront, **River West Food & Health** ((867) 993-6339, Front and York streets, is a café where you can get sandwiches, salads, and soups at the counter. The coffee is good and you can order food to take out or to eat in.

How to Get There

You can fly from Whitehorse to Dawson City on **Air North** ((867) 668-2228. If you're driving from Alaska, you'll take the **Taylor** and **Top of the World highways** from Chicken to Dawson City. The **Klondike Highway** runs from Skagway, Alaska, through Carcross, Whitehorse, and on to Dawson. The section of the highway from Whitehorse to Dawson City is 537 km (333 miles) and the road is excellent. Bus service between Whitehorse and Dawson is provided by **Norline Coaches** ((867) 993-6010 (in Dawson City) or (867) 668-3355, 2191 Second Avenue (in Whitehorse).

YUKON HIGHWAYS

The Top of the World Highway

The Top of the World Highway (Highway 9) is a scenic drive that begins just across the Yukon River and leads 105 km (64 miles) to the border where it connects with the historic Taylor Highway (Highway 5). The trip begins with the free automobile and passenger ferry ((867) 993-5441, which operates 24 hours a day (apart from Wednesday mornings when it is closed for servicing from 5 AM to 7 AM.) Expect long lines in peak months. Heaviest traffic is from 7 AM to 11 AM and 4 PM to 7 PM.

This road began as a pack trail connecting Dawson City with Sixtymile and other neighboring mining communities. After crossing the Yukon River, the 175-km (110-mile) highway climbs rapidly above the tree line and meanders along mountain ridges with good views of the surrounding countryside. Moving on into Alaska, the Taylor Highway leads north to Eagle or south to Tetlin Junction and the Alaska Highway. The border area is a good place to spot rough-legged hawks, red-tailed hawks, merlins, and kestrels during spring and fall migrations.

The Alaska Highway

Hastily constructed as a military route during World War II, the Alaska Highway (Alcan) is now a tourist route to the northern frontier. As much a pilgrimage route as a road, the it attracts thousands every year, many of them retirees behind the wheel of their brand new recreational vehicles.

The Alaska Highway (Highway 1) starts at Dawson Creek, British Columbia, and travels northwest for 2,452 km (1,520 miles), ending in Fairbanks, Alaska. Along the way it cuts through the southwest corner of the Yukon. Even up until 10 years ago, sections of the road were unpaved. It is now entirely paved, though you will likely find some rough spots, as construction crews only have the precious summer months to upgrade and maintain the road.

First stop along the Canadian portion of the Alaska Highway is the "Gateway to the Yukon," **Watson Lake** (population: 1,795). Tourism Yukon operates the Visitor Reception and the Alaska Highway Interpretive Centre ((867) 536-7469, at the junction of the Robert Campbell and Alaska highways.

The next long stretch of road travels through **Teslin** and then skims past **Whitehorse**, after which the highway skirts **Kluane National Park**.

Spreading south from Alcan, the snow-covered **Icefield Ranges** can be seen behind the rugged Kluane Ranges. This is the most scenic part of the route. Plan to take your time.

As the Kluane Ranges taper off, you'll come to **Burwash Landing,** a tiny native village (population less than 100) which overlooks Kluane Lake. Here you'll find the very worthwhile **Kluane Museum of Natural History** ((867) 841-5561, Mile 1093 Alaska Highway. It has the Yukon's best natural history display along with fine exhibits of Southern Tutchone garments, tools, and weapons, as well as fossils. The museum has a stock of videos, which they will play on demand. It's open daily from mid-May to mid-September from 9 AM to 9 PM; an admission fee is charged. Oddity aficionados may be interested

---

The Dempster Highway runs from just east of Dawson City to Inuvik in the Northwest Territories.

to know that Burwash Landing is also the home of the "biggest gold pan in the world."

The last Canadian stop on the Alcan is **Beaver Creek** (population 140), the westernmost community in Canada. Like many other small Yukon and Alaskan towns, it began as a settlement during the construction of the Alaska Highway. It is situated 30 km (18 miles) south of the Alaskan border. There's a **Visitor Reception Centre (** (867) 862-7321, on the Alaska Highway, and directly across the street you'll find the **Westmark Inn Beaver Creek (** (867) 862-7501 TOLL-FREE (800) 544-0970 FAX (867) 862-7902, Mile 1202 Alaska Highway, Beaver Creek Y0B 1A0. The hotel has 174 rooms, a dining room, dinner theatre, recreation room,

the hamlet, going on to Faro, Ross River and various mining operations, and provides an alternative to the Alcan between Whitehorse and Watson Lake, through remote spectacular wilderness. If you need to break the drive from Whitehorse to Dawson City, you can bed down at the **Hotel Carmacks (** (867) 863-5221 FAX (867) 863-5605 E-MAIL hotelcar @yknet.yk.ca, PO Box 160, Carmacks Y0B 1C0.

The Dempster Highway

The start of the Dempster Highway (Highway 5) lies 40 km (25 miles) south of Dawson City. From here, this famed trek runs north 735 km (456 miles) to Inuvik, Northwest Territories, near the Arctic Ocean. The most northerly public road in Canada,

mini-golf, a recreational vehicle park, a laundry, a convenience store and a gas station. Unfortunately the only superlatives we can bestow on this Westmark are that it has the tiniest bathtubs we've ever encountered as well as the thinnest walls. Don't hesitate to ask to be moved if you get stuck next to noisy neighbors.

The Klondike Highway

The Klondike Highway (Highway 2) is a scenic, paved road leading from Skagway, Alaska, north through Whitehorse and on to Dawson City. About 180 km (112 miles) north of Whitehorse and 360 km (224 miles) south of Dawson, the village of **Carmacks** is located on a traditional First Nations trading site. In 1892, George Carmacks (later part of the group that precipitated the gold rush) established a small trading post here. The gravel-paved **Robert Campbell Highway** (Highway 4) intersects

the Dempster offers beautiful scenery, especially in early fall when the tundra plants take on autumn colors and migrating caribou are more easily seen.

Driving the Dempster Highway is no more difficult than traveling any other gravel road. Some precautions must be taken, however: The **Northwest Territories Visitor Centre (** (867) 993-6167 on Front Street in Dawson, across the street from the visitor center, is the place get information on traveling the Dempster and on visiting the Northwest Territories. For information on road conditions, call TOLL-FREE (800) 661-0750.

The **Klondike River Lodge (** (867) 993-6892, Klondike and Dempster Highways, Dawson Y0B 1G0, is the place from which to launch your trip up the Dempster Highway. Operated by the Gwitch'in Tribal Council, the lodge includes parking for recreational vehicles, a restaurant, a car wash, and a grocery store.

THE NORTHWEST TERRITORIES AND NUNAVUT

A vast frontier covering an area nearly half the size of the United States, the Northwest Territories and Nunavut are the North American continent's last true wilderness. The 67,500 Dene, Athapaskan, Inuit, and Anglo-Europeans who call these territories home are far outnumbered by the approximately 1,367,000 caribou which roam the land — these two territories have the world's lowest population density per square mile.

In the eastern areas the Inuit form a majority of the population. Although their traditional cul-

You should plan your trip to the Northwest Territories in advance, confirming accommodations and guide services prior to your departure. In many parts of the Northwest Territories transportation is limited to airplanes, snowmobiles, and all-terrain vehicles (ATVs) since there are no roads linking most communities. Dog teams are still used in winter and boats travel during warmer months when the ice comes off the water.

GENERAL INFORMATION

If you hear the call of the North, you're first response should be to get in touch with the government tourism agencies. The **Nunavut Tourism As-**

ture has suffered from contact with Anglo-European settlers, they remain a cultural force. In recent decades they have won significant victories in the fight to preserve a way of life that is so intimately tied to the land. These land-rights negotiations finally led to the partitioning, on April 1, 1999, of the old Northwest Territories into today's eastern Nunavut and western Northwest Territories.

For the adventurer, the Northwest Territories and Nunavut offer incomparable scenic wonders, along with abundant wildlife, world-class fishing, and opportunities to visit and learn from the native inhabitants. Recommended (if not indispensable) publications, should you decide to visit Nunavut or the Northwest Territories, include *The Nunavut Handbook* (Marion Soubliere, ed.) and *The Milepost* (see RECOMMENDED READING, page 435).

sociation ((867) 979-6551 TOLL-FREE IN CANADA (800) 491-7910, PO Box 1450, Iqaluit X0A 0H0, is the place to contact for planning your trip to Nunavut. Write or call **Northwest Territories Tourism** ((867) 873-7200 TOLL-FREE (800) 661-0788 WEB SITE www.nwttravel.nt.ca/, PO Box 610, Yellowknife X1A 2N5, for information on the Northwest Territories, including Yellowknife and the Western Arctic.

Many northern communities have **regional and local visitor centers** offering information and assistance as well as interpretive displays on the local culture and history. In communities that don't have visitor centers, you can usually get assistance at the community center and from hotel staff.

Inuvik, the town that stays up all summer — OPPOSITE: Our Lady of Victory Church is often called the Igloo Church. ABOVE: A downtown street is backlit by the midnight sun.

Travelers' Tips

THE BEST TIP WE CAN OFFER ANY TRAVELER is to get a good travel agent. There is no substitute — not even this sparkling chapter — for the information and helpful advice that a travel agent has at his or her command. In a world where fares, schedules, even routes are changing hourly, only someone with access to the latest information can give you the sort of guidance necessary to ensure a hassle-free vacation.

GETTING THERE

Almost all of the **major international airlines** fly to Canada, but Air Canada has more flights to more Canadian cities than any other airline. Also,

as you would expect, Air Canada has an extensive network of domestic airlines linking cities within Canada (see GETTING AROUND, below). Contact numbers for **Air Canada** are as follows: TOLL-FREE IN CANADA (888) AIR-CANADA; TOLL-FREE IN THE UNITED STATES (800) 776-3000 (for reservations) or (800) 488-1800 (for flight arrival and departure information); in Australia ((02) 9232 5222; in France (01 44 50 20 20; in New Zealand ((09) 379-3371 and in the United Kingdom ((0990) 247 226.

Other major airlines offering flights to Canada include: **American Airlines** TOLL-FREE (800) 433-7300; **Canadian Airlines** TOLL-FREE (800) 426-7000; **Delta** TOLL-FREE (800) 221-1212; **United** TOLL-FREE (800) 241-6522; **Northwest** TOLL-FREE (800) 447-4747; and **US Airways** TOLL-FREE (800) 428-4322.

One general tip regarding air travel to Canada — or anywhere else for that matter — is to get to the airport early. This is a contentious issue among frequent flyers, some of whom like to arrive at the airport just as the pilot is starting up the engines. But for us there are three compelling arguments in favor of heading for the airport ahead of time. One is that it gives you a safety margin in case you encounter a problem — a traffic jam, a flat tire, a detour — on the way. You would be surprised how many people miss planes because they didn't leave themselves time to absorb unexpected delays.

Secondly, by getting to the airport early you have a much better seat selection for your flight — and the longer the flight, the more important it is to have the seat you want. (If you are flying on a British Airways jumbo jet, for example, you can often get a seat upstairs, where it is more comfortable and the service is more attentive.) Thirdly, early arrivals at the airport avoid the long lines at the check-in counter, which means that the time that would otherwise be spent standing around shepherding one's luggage slowly forward can be spent reading, shopping, having drinks, having a meal — in a word, relaxing.

There are several **car-ferries** operating to Canada from points in the northeastern and northwestern United States. In the northwest, three ferry services operate between Victoria, British Columbia and Washington state: **Black Ball Transport** ((250) 386-2202 (in Victoria) or (360) 457-4491 (in Port Angeles) operates from Port Angeles; **Clipper Navigation** ((250) 382-8100 TOLL-FREE (800) 288-2535 from Seattle; and **Victoria San Juan Cruises** ((360) 738-8099 TOLL-FREE (800) 443-4552 from Bellingham with a stop in the San Juan Islands.

In the northeast, seasonal ferries connect Portland and Bar Harbor, Maine, to Yarmouth, Nova Scotia: **Prince of Fundy Cruises** ((207) 775-5616 TOLL-FREE (888) 341-7540, 468 Commercial Street, Portland, Maine 04101-4637 USA, operates from Portland; and **Bay Ferries** ((207) 288-3395 TOLL-FREE (888) 249-7245, 121 Eden Street, Bar Harbor, Maine 04609 USA, from Bar Harbor. Introduced in 1998, the superfast "Cat" takes 900 passengers and 240 vehicles across the Bay of Fundy and cuts the traveling time from six to two and a half hours. In Yarmouth, contact Bay Ferries ((902) 742-6800, 58 Water Street, Yarmouth, Nova Scotia B5A 1K9.

There are 13 principal border crossing points where the American highway system connects directly with the Canadian. Crossing into Canada by **car** is usually a quick, simple matter, although in peak season you might want to avoid the busier crossing points such as Detroit-Windsor and Niagara Falls. Once in Canada, no matter where you've crossed, you are only a short drive from the Trans-Canada Highway.

Greyhound TOLL-FREE (800) 661-8747 is the only company operating a cross-border service, but it has such a huge route system that you should have no difficulty in getting to most points in Canada from virtually anywhere in the United States. It also has a hugely complicated system of fares, discount fares, seasonal rates, unlimited-travel passes, and so on. Travel agents can usually help with such things. Major routes include New York–Montréal/Ottawa, Detroit–Toronto/Hamilton, Minneapolis–Winnipeg, and Seattle Vancouver/Edmonton/Calgary.

Although there is no regular passenger ship service between Europe and Canada, some **cargo lines** leaving from European ports accept passengers. Accommodations on board are usually comfortable and food plentiful if plain. Costs are less per day than they are on luxury cruise liners, but the trip is longer, so this option is not for those in a hurry. (The trip from Le Havre, France to Montréal, for example, takes 18 to 20 days.) For information on freighter travel, contact your travel agent or **Freighter World Cruises (** (818) 449-9200 FAX (818) 449-9573, 180 South Lake Avenue, Suite 335 Pasadena, California 91101.

Amtrak TOLL-FREE (800) 872-7245, the United States passenger railway system, has several routes serving Canada's East Coast and one route serving the West Coast. Major eastern routes are: New York–Montréal, New York–Buffalo–Niagara–Toronto, Chicago–Sarnia–Toronto, Cleveland–Buffalo–Niagara–Toronto, and Detroit–Windsor–Toronto. In the west, Amtrak connects Seattle, Washington with Vancouver, British Columbia.

TOURIST INFORMATION

Rather than having a central source of information for all of Canada, each of the provinces maintains a bureau that dispenses information on subjects of interest to tourists. In the GENERAL INFORMATION sections of the preceding chapters we have listed the local agencies; here, then, are the provincial tourism offices:

Travel Alberta ((403) 427-4321 TOLL-FREE (800) 661-8888 WEB SITE www.discoveralberta.com/html/Canada/Alberta/, PO Box 2500, Edmonton, Alberta T5J 2Z4.

British Columbia Tourism ((604) 685-0032 TOLL-FREE (800) 663-6000 WEB SITE www.tbc.gov.bc.ca/tourism/, Parliament Buildings, Victoria, British Columbia V8V 1X4.

Travel Manitoba ((204) 945-3777 TOLL-FREE (800) 665-0040 WEB SITE www.gov.mb.ca/itt/travel/explore/index.html, Seventh Floor, 155 Carlton Street, Winnipeg, Manitoba R3C 3H8.

Tourism New Brunswick ((506) 453-2444 TOLL-FREE (800) 561-0123 WEB SITE www.cybersmith.net/nbtour/, PO Box 6000, Fredericton, New Brunswick E3B 5C3.

Newfoundland and Labrador Department of Tourism, Culture and Recreation ((709) 729-2830 TOLL-FREE (800) 563-6353 WEB SITE www.gov.nf.ca/tourism/, PO Box 8700, St. John's, Newfoundland A1B 4K2.

Nova Scotia Tourism ((902) 425-5781 TOLL-FREE (800) 565-0000 WEB SITE explore.gov.ns.ca/, PO Box 456, Halifax, Nova Scotia B3J 2M7.

Northwest Territories Tourism ((867) 873-7200 TOLL-FREE (800) 661-0788 WEB SITE www.nwttravel.nt.ca/, PO Box 610, Yellowknife, Northwest Territories X1A 2N5.

Nunavut Tourism ((867) 979-6551 TOLL-FREE IN CANADA (800) 491-7910 WEB SITE www.nunatour.nt.ca/, PO Box 1450, Iqaluit, Nunavut X0A 0H0.

Ontario Travel ((416) 314-0944 TOLL-FREE (800) ONTARIO (416-668-2746) WEB SITE www.travelinx.com/, Queen's Park, Toronto, Ontario M7A 2R9.

Prince Edward Island Travel Information ((902) 368-4444 TOLL-FREE (800) 463-4734 WEB SITE www.gov.pe.ca/, PO Box 940, Charlottetown, Prince Edward Island C1A 7M5.

Tourisme Québec ((514) 873-2015 TOLL-FREE (800) 363-7777 WEB SITE www.tourisme.gouv.qc.ca/, PO Box 979, Montréal, Québec H3C 2W3.

Tourism Saskatchewan ((306) 787-2300 TOLL-FREE (800) 667-7191 WEB SITE www.sasktourism.com/index.html, Suite 500, 1900 Albert Street, Regina, Saskatchewan S4P 4L9.

Tourism Yukon ((867) 667-5340 WEB SITE www.touryukon.com/, PO Box 2703, Whitehorse, Yukon Y1A 2C9.

EMBASSIES AND CONSULATES

American Embassy ((613) 238-4470 100 Wellington Street, Ottawa, Ontario K1P 5T1.

American Consulates: Toronto ((416) 595-1700, 360 University Avenue, Toronto, Ontario M5G 1S4; **Montréal (** (514) 398-9695, Suite 1122,

OPPOSITE: All aboard! A railway station, though it may be small, is never far away. ABOVE: High over the Atlantic, an Air Canada jet engine glows in the first light of dawn.

South Tower, Complexe Desjardins, Montréal, Québec H5B 1E5; **Québec City** ((418) 692-2095, 2 place Terrasse-Dufferin (PO Box 939), Québec City, Québec G1R 4T9; **Halifax** ((902) 429-2480, Suite 910, Scotia Square, Halifax, Nova Scotia B3J 3K1; **Calgary** ((403) 266-8962, Room 1050, 615 Macleod Trail SE, Calgary, Alberta T2G 4T8; **Vancouver** ((604) 685-4311, Columbia Centre IV, 1095 West Pender Street, Vancouver, British Columbia V6E 2Y4.

Australian consulate general ((416) 323-1155, 175 Bloor Street E, Toronto, Ontario M5L 1B9.

British consulate general ((416) 593-1267, Suite 1910, 777 Bay Street, Toronto, Ontario M5G 2G2.

French Embassy ((613) 789-1795, 42 Sussex Drive, Ottawa, Ontario.

Netherlands Embassy ((613) 237-6471, 2020-350 Albert Street, Ottawa, Ontario.

Spanish Embassy ((613) 747-2252, 74 Stanley Avenue, Ottawa, Ontario.

TRAVEL DOCUMENTS

United States citizens, permanent residents of the United States, as well as British, Australian, New Zealand and Irish nationals, or citizens of most European Commonwealth countries, require only proof of citizenship to enter Canada (passport, birth certificate, voter registration card, or naturalization certificate). If the identification does not have a photograph on it, some form of additional photo identification may be needed. United States residents who are not citizens must show their Alien Registration Receipt Card. Travelers crossing the border with children should carry identification for them (passport or birth certificate), since Canadian and United States Customs and Immigration are taking measures to reduce parental and other kinds of child abduction. Children traveling with one parent or adult should bring a letter of permission from the other parent, parents, or legal guardian. Divorced parents with shared custody rights should carry legal documents establishing their status.

CUSTOMS

Customs regulations are similar to those in most countries, including the usual restrictions on bringing in meats, plants, and animals. Items intended for personal or professional use do not have to be declared, and you are allowed up to 200 cigarettes or 50 cigars, and 1.1 liters (40 oz) of wine or spirits duty-free. You can bring in gifts up to $60 in value. There are no currency restrictions.

Hunting and fishing equipment may be brought in duty-free as well, but all firearms and ammunition must be declared and a written description of each item, including serial numbers of guns, must be provided. Certain non-firearm weapons are also prohibited. Details of Customs regulations are available from Information Services, Revenue Canada, Customs and Excise, Connaught Building, Sussex Drive, Ottawa, Ontario K1A 0L5, or call Customs Canada TOLL-FREE (800) 461-9999.

If you are planning on purchasing furs or other animal products (e.g., antlers) check with your country's customs regulations to find out which animals are considered endangered and cannot be imported. The same consideration applies to Inuit art, which may be made of whalebone or mastodon ivory, neither of which can be brought into the United States.

TAXES

As a visitor to Canada you can claim a **tax refund** for some of the tax you pay on accommodation, as long as you stay less than one month in that accommodation. In addition, you may claim a tax refund for certain goods you take home. Look for the "Tax Refund for Visitors" brochure at Visitor Information Centres, ask for it at your hotel front desk, or write the Visitor Rebate Program, Revenue Canada, Summerside Tax Centre, Summerside, Prince Edward Island C1N 6C6.

WHEN TO GO

The decision of when to go will depend on what you are going *for*, and by now you should have a pretty good idea of what each region has to offer at what time of the year.

Generally speaking, the seasons in Canada's more temperate climes divide up as follows: winter occupies most of the long stretch from November to the end of March, summer occurs in June, July, and August, while the "shoulder" seasons of spring and autumn are largely confined to April through May and September through October.

The most temperate climate in all of Canada belongs to British Columbia, where mild summers fade gently into mild winters. In Vancouver, for example, the temperature seldom rises above 21°C (71°F) in summer, and seldom dips below freezing in winter. You will, however, need to take an umbrella: In December and January alone, meteorologists count on seeing 42 days of rainfall, an average that drops to about seven days in July and August.

Once you are east of the Rockies, the climate abruptly changes. The Prairie Provinces of Alberta, Saskatchewan, and Manitoba are known for their climatic extremes. In all three provinces you will find summers that are hot and sunny, though

punctuated by the occasional thunderstorm, followed almost immediately by winters that are very cold and generally dry. To give you some idea of the extremes of weather to be encountered in the Canadian prairies, in Saskatchewan temperatures of 45°C (113°F) have been recorded in summer and temperatures of -57°C (-70°F) in winter.

In Newfoundland and the Maritimes, winter temperatures seldom rise above freezing and can often fall far below, especially in the inland areas. Spring is brief — just time for the countryside to change from its winter to its summer wardrobe. The summer is comfortably mild, with temperatures in the high teens and 20s Centigrade (60s and 70s Fahrenheit). The autumn is gloriously colorful, particularly in New Brunswick, as trees erupt in a blaze of reds and golds.

In Ontario and Québec the winters are just as cold — often, in places, colder — and tend to be gray and damp in southern Ontario and snowy, bright and chilly elsewhere in the region. Spring is very pleasant and autumn is lovely, as in the Maritimes, but summer is considerably warmer and more humid, particularly in Toronto.

Not surprisingly, weather conditions in the Far North are more extreme than those in the southern provinces. But, some visitors are surprised to find out that northern summers can be hot. With the sun out as much as 24 hours a day (above the Arctic Circle), the temperature can reach a balmy 88°F/31°C. But even in July, you should be prepared for cool weather and take sweaters and a fall jacket.

Average monthly temperatures for nine Canadian cities are as follows:

Calgary
January	-10°C/14°F
April	4°C/39°F
July	16°C/62°F
October	6°C/51°F

Halifax
January	-5°C/24°F
April	4°C/39°F
July	18°C/66°F
October	9°C/49°F

Inuvik
January	-29°C/-20°F
April	-14°C/14°F
July	14°C/57°F
October	-8°C/17°F

Montréal
January	-8°C/15°F
April	6°C/42°F
July	21°C/70°F
October	9°C/49°F

St. John's
January	-5°C/24°F
April	1°C/35°F
July	15°C/59°F
October	7°C/45°F

Toronto
January	-5°C/23°F
April	6°C/43°F
July	21°C/70°F
October	10°C/50°F

Vancouver
January	3°C/37°F
April	9°C/48°F
July	17°C/63°F
October	10°C/50°F

OPPOSITE: Autumn leaves in New Brunswick. ABOVE: Winter in Canada is a time for bundling.

Whitehorse

January	-18°C/17°F
April	0°C/32°F
July	14°C/57°F
October	1°C/33°F

Yellowknife

January	-28°C/-18°F
April	-7°C/20°F
July	16°C/61°F
October	1°C/30°F

In the North, daylight hours are an important seasonal factor. Average daylight hours for seven northern Canadian cities are as follows:

	DEC	JUNE
Cambridge Bay	0.0	24.0
Dawson City	4.2	21.1
Inuvik	0.0	24.0
Iqaluit	4.5	20.8
Rankin Inlet	4.5	20.8
Whitehorse	5.4	19.1
Yellowknife	6.5	20.0

WHAT TO BRING

The criterion for what to pack should not be the desirability of having a particular article with you at any given time, but the undesirability of *not* having a particular article with you when you really need it. On that principle, here is our list of things you should never leave home without.

At the top of the list, by a wide margin, is a Swiss Army knife (or, to put it another way, two knives, two screwdrivers, a bottle opener, a can opener, a corkscrew, a toothpick, tweezers, nail file, and scissors). We would also throw in a miniature flashlight and a small travel alarm clock. You will need an adapter and/or transformer if you plan to bring electrical appliances that don't run on 110 volts or don't have an American-style plug.

Because even the most minor physical irritations or afflictions can ruin a trip if they strike at the wrong time (which is the only time they strike), we would be sure to include a small first-aid kit with such items as lip balm for chapped lips, aspirin, anti-diarrhea tablets, antiseptic ointment, a few bandages, and a few packets of tissues (which can also serve as toilet paper in an emergency). Resealable ziplock plastic bags come in handy when traveling — not least when you have items that you want to keep apart, or you want to segregate items that are damp or dirty or might be inclined to leak. By the way, everything we have mentioned so far will fit easily into a medium-sized plastic freezer bag.

If you are planning to travel by air and you want to take a Swiss Army knife, or anything else that might conceivably be considered a "weapon," be sure to pack it in the luggage you intend to check. You don't want to be mistaken for an armed passenger. On the other hand, if you are taking any battery-powered gadgets — shavers, cassette players, etc. — carry them with you on the airplane or take the batteries out before packing them, airline security personnel get understandably jumpy when unidentified objects with batteries in them show up on their X-ray screen.

Be sure to take with you lists of the numbers of all travel documents, cards, and checks you will be carrying, along with any telephone numbers included on them. This will greatly facilitate their quick replacement if lost. Also, take photocopies of your passport and any travel tickets: duplicates are issued more speedily if people can see a copy of the original — much more speedily in the case

of tickets or refunds. It is a good idea to get an international driver's license, obtainable from your automobile club, so that you can keep your home driver's license tucked away in a safe place. Always leave your inessential credit cards behind when you go on a trip, and of those you take with you carry only a couple in your wallet: any others should be tucked away in the same safe place as your passport, driver's license, extra travelers' checks, etc. It's just another way of ensuring that any loss causes only a temporary inconvenience.

When it comes to clothing, toiletries, jewelry, and gadgetry, it's up to you to decide what and how much you want to take. Canadians are very casual in their dress, so there is no need to take formal or semiformal wear beyond what your taste and your expected engagements require. There is, however, a need to take some warm clothing — a sweater or two perhaps, the odd woolen or corduroy garment, and a windbreaker—because even in summer, even in the hottest spots, it can turn quite cool in the evenings, especially if you happen to be on or near the water.

BASICS

TIME

Canada is divided into six time zones, including Newfoundland's own, typically quirky, time zone, which is only a half-hour ahead of Atlantic Standard Time in the Maritime Provinces. The other four time zones correspond to, and are continuations of, the four United States time zones: Eastern Standard Time, Central Standard Time, Mountain Standard Time, and Pacific Standard Time.

Atlantic Standard Time is four hours behind Greenwich Mean Time, so when it is 8 PM in London, it is 4 PM in the Maritimes (4:30 PM in Newfoundland). Québec and all of Ontario to the east of Thunder Bay are on Eastern Standard Time, five hours behind GMT. Manitoba and the eastern half of Saskatchewan are on **Central Standard Time;** the rest of Saskatchewan, Alberta and northeast British Columbia are on **Mountain Standard Time**. All of British Columbia west of the Rockies is on Pacific Standard Time, eight hours behind GMT.

All of Canada — with the mysterious exception of eastern Saskatchewan — observes Daylight Savings Time from the first Sunday in April, when the clocks are put forward one hour, until the last Sunday in October.

ELECTRICITY

The electric current is 110–120 volts AC, the same as in the United States, and the sockets only take American-type plugs with two flat prongs.

WEIGHTS AND MEASURES

Canadians, like just about everybody else in the world except their American neighbors, rely almost exclusively on the metric system. Thus, while Canadians are spared the old question, "How much is that in dollars?" they now have to face the new question, "How far is that in miles?" or "What is that in pounds and ounces?"

To make life easier for those not yet numerate in metrics, we have devised our own rough-and-ready (and of course approximate) system for making instant conversions on the spot. It is not only simple, but easy to memorize, so long as you remember that the colloquial term "a bit" here represents one-tenth of whatever it is next to. Thus: a meter equals a yard and a bit; a kilometer equals a half-mile and a bit; a kilogram equals two pounds and a bit (500 grams equals 1 lb and a bit); a liter equals an American quart and a bit.

For converting to degrees Fahrenheit, simply double the figure you are given in Celsius and add 30, topping it up by a couple of degrees when you get above 20°C. The temperature you come up with won't be precisely accurate, but it will be close enough. Note that when temperatures descend into the negative numbers the two scales begin to converge, thus: -40°C equals -40°F. (This may seem like an arcane bit of knowledge, but remember, this is Canada.)

SHOPPING HOURS

Shopping hours are generally from 9 AM to 6 PM, Monday through Friday, with late-night shopping in some stores until 9 PM on Thursday and Friday. Most shops and stores are also open Saturday and some local stores, especially during the summer, are open on Sunday from noon until 5 PM. Stores may have longer hours in summer months.

HEALTH AND SAFETY

You really haven't much to worry about in Canada, because health hazards are few and the health care is excellent. It can be expensive, though, so American visitors should check to make sure that their health insurance provides coverage in Canada, and overseas visitors should arrange short-term medical coverage for the period they expect to be there. An excellent medical emergency policy, which also includes personal travel insurance, is available from the **Europ Assistance Group** through its affiliates in a dozen or so countries, including: United Kingdom ((1444) 411999 FAX (1444) 458173, Sussex House, Perrymount Road, Haywards Heath, West Sussex RH1 IDN, England; and France ((01) 41858585 FAX (01) 41858305, 1 promenade de la Bonnette, 92230 Gennevilliers, France. A similar policy, similarly priced, is offered by **Wexas International** ((071) 5893315 E-MAIL mship@wexas.com, 45–49 Brompton Road, Knightsbridge, London SW3 1DE, England.

Another wise precaution is to carry a card in your wallet giving your blood type and listing any allergies or chronic conditions (including the wearing of contact lenses) that might affect treatment in an emergency.

Beyond that, it's always a good idea to have insect repellent with you, because in summer Canada has plenty of insects to repel, especially black flies and mosquitoes. A sunscreen lotion is also advisable, as the Canadian sun has a burning power out of all proportion to its heating power.

Emergency fire, ambulance, and police services are usually reached by dialing 911. For other emergencies or for areas not serviced by 911 (e.g., the

The world's first steam-powered clock keeps Pacific Standard Time in Vancouver's colorful Gastown district.

Northwest Territories and Nunavut), you should contact the operator by dialing "0." In the Yukon Territory, only Whitehorse operates a 911 emergency call system. For the rest of the territory, dial Royal Canadian Mounted Police ℂ (867) 667-5555; Medical ℂ (867) 667-3333. Yukon communities also have local police and medical emergency numbers, which you can get a list of from a visitor information center when you begin your trip.

CRIME

Crime? What crime? Canada may well be the most law-abiding of the world's industrialized nations. Violent crime isn't exactly unheard of, but it's not

heard of very often. The streets of Canada's cities are as safe at night as they are in the daytime.

All this law-and-orderliness notwithstanding, one should still take the same basic precautions here that a sensible person would take anywhere: leaving valuables in the hotel safe, locking your hotel room and car, not leaving valuable items visible in your car when unattended, not carrying all your cash and cards with you when you go out, not going for late-night strolls through questionable areas. There are no signs. In short, exercise your common sense, secure in the knowledge that Canadians can be counted on to exercise their common decency.

CURRENCY

Canadian currency resembles American currency in every important respect except value: The coins are in the same denominations and go by the same names (penny, nickel, dime, etc.), the paper notes are of uniform size (but in different colors according to value). There are no longer $1 and $2 bills. Instead there are $1 "loonie" coins, nicknamed the after the bird that appears on it, and the $2 "toonie."

At press time the **exchange rate** was: US$1 to C$1.50; and for the euro: €1 to C$1.65. Should you wish to be precisely *au courant*, visit the Universal Currency Converter WEB SITE www.xe.net/

currency/, or check your local newspaper. American dollars are widely accepted, but using them introduces an unnecessary complication into a transaction, as well as an unnecessary discourtesy.

As in all countries with hard currencies, the banks offer the best exchange rates—much better than hotels, for example. Banking hours are Monday to Thursday from 10 AM to 4 PM, 10 AM to 6 PM on Friday. Trust companies and credit unions tend to have longer hours and may also be open on Saturday morning. Most major credit cards are accepted anywhere you are likely to go—including American Express, MasterCard, Visa, Diners Club, Enroute, and Carte Blanche; consequently you are advised to carry a minimum of cash. If you prefer using non-plastic money, take it in the form of travelers' checks. They can be cashed everywhere, with proper identification (e.g. passport, driver's license), although the larger denominations will not always be welcome in places like restaurants that don't like being used as banks.

In general, however, we recommend floating through Canada on a raft of plastic: your bank debit card. All Canadian financial institutions have automatic teller machines (ATMs), and you'll find ATMs located in large and small shopping centers, airports, train stations, and even many gas stations and corner stores. Before you leave home check with your bank to be certain your ATM card is on the Plus or Cirrus network; they can also provide you with a booklet listing networks worldwide on which your card with operate.

GETTING AROUND

BY AIR

The country's two major carriers, **Air Canada** TOLL-FREE (800) 776-3000 and **Canadian Airlines International** TOLL-FREE (800) 426-7000, along with their regional partners, handle the bulk of the middle- and long-distance air traffic. Dozens of local independent carriers connect the remaining dots on the map. Thus there are very few places in Canada, even including remote islands, that are not accessible by air. The principal regional carriers include: **Air Alliance** ℂ (514) 393-3333, and **Inter-Canadien** ℂ (514) 847-2211 serving Québec; **Air Atlantic** ℂ (902) 427-5500 serving the Atlantic provinces; **Air BC** ℂ (604) 688-5515, and **Canadian Regional** ℂ (604) 279-6611 serving British Columbia and Alberta; **Air Ontario** ℂ (204) 632-1250 serving Ontario; and **NWT Air** ℂ (867) 423-1222 serving the Northwest Territories and the Yukon.

Anyone purchasing a round-trip trans-Atlantic flight from Europe to Canada on Air France, Continental, Air Canada, or United is eligible to purchase Air Canada's **Ameripass**. (Other transatlantic carriers also participate, but pass prices are higher.) The pass is bought in series of three to eight coupons—each coupon allowing one flight within North America to selected cities. At the time of research, three flights cost around $325, and eight flights around $930. There are restrictions, but it is a wonderful deal for those who want to cover a lot of ground in a short period of time. European travel agents should be able to provide information and make the bookings, or you can go directly to Air Canada.

BY RAIL

Canada's passenger rail carrier is the government-owned **VIA Rail** TOLL-FREE (888) 842-7733 WEB SITE www.viarail.ca. The VIA Rail network is

to arrival in Canada. Your travel agent will have all the particulars. Alternatively, contact VIA Rail's web site (see above), which lists their representatives throughout the world. Local and regional contact numbers for VIA Rail are found throughout the text.

BY BUS

Where there's a way, there's a willing bus to take you just about anywhere you want to go in Canada. Greyhound Canada has a nationwide route system, and there are five or six large regional companies that reach into the nooks and crannies that Greyhound misses. Bus service is frequent, quick

rapidly shrinking due to cuts in government funding, but there is still regular service between the major cities, and it is still possible to make the transcontinental journey by train in the comfort of your own rolling bedroom or roomette. This transcontinental service runs between Toronto and Vancouver, operating three times weekly, east and west, transiting Winnipeg, Saskatoon, Edmonton and Jasper, and passing through three spectacular mountain ranges en route: the Canadian Rockies, the Selkirks, and the Coast Mountains. It takes three days.

VIA Rail issues the **Canrailpass**, which makes possible substantial savings by allowing 12 days of coach-class travel over a 30-day period. Prices are $370 (low season) and $570 (high season). Sleeping cars are also available, but must be reserved at least a month in advance during the May to October high season. The pass must be purchased prior

and inexpensive, whether intercity or cross-country. The 5,000-km (3,000-mile) from Montréal to Vancouver, for example, takes 69 hours.

With Greyhound's **Domestic Canada Coach Pass** you can travel throughout five of the provinces as well as the Northwest Territories, Nunavut and the Yukon for periods of a week to two months. The pass is available for sale in Canada only, and costs between $209 and $495. You can buy it at any Greyhound Canada terminal, or ask a travel agent. There is also the **International Canada Coach Pass**, which is good on routes in all provinces excluding parts of Québec and the Maritimes; to include these areas you'll have to spring for the **Canada Coach Pass Plus**, available in 15-, 30-, and

OPPOSITE: A farm off Highway 1 in British Columbia. ABOVE: Goldie greets guests arriving by float plane at Eagle Nook Ocean Wilderness Lodge bordering the Pacific Rim National park.

60-day limits at a cost of $335, $440, and $545 respectively.

For detailed information contact **Greyhound Canada** TOLL-FREE (800) 661-8747 WEB SITE www.greyhound.ca, 877 Greyhound Way SW, Calgary, Alberta T3C 3V8.

By Car and Motor home

Canada, only slightly less than the United States, is a motorist's dream. The highway system may not be as sprawling as in the United States, but it doesn't have to be, since most of the places visited by tourists and natives alike are within easy driving distance of the Trans-Canada Highway.

In order to rent a vehicle in Canada, you must be at least 25 years old and you must have a credit card.

But, perhaps you had in mind something a bit larger: Each year hundreds of travelers hit the back roads of Canada in rented motor homes (recreational vehicles) and truck campers. This is the American equivalent of a "caravan," especially attractive for those who want to explore Canada as a family or group of friends. In order to rent a recreational vehicle, you must have a driver's license (that you've held for more than one year) and be at least 25 years old. It is strongly recommended that you reserve your recreational vehicle several weeks prior to departure. Contact your travel agent for information and reservations.

The gasoline may not be as cheap as in the United States, but it's far cheaper than in Europe.

The major car-rental firms are represented across the country, including: **Hertz** TOLL-FREE (800) 654-3001 TOLL-FREE IN CANADA (800) 263-0600 TOLL-FREE IN THE UNITED KINGDOM (0345) 555888; **Alamo** TOLL-FREE IN CANADA (800) 879-2847; **Budget** TOLL-FREE (800) 527-0700 TOLL-FREE IN THE UNITED KINGDOM (0800) 181181; **Dollar/Eurodollar** TOLL-FREE (800) 800-4000 TOLL-FREE IN THE UNITED KINGDOM (0990) 565656; and **Rent-a-Wreck** TOLL-FREE IN THE UNITED STATES (800) 535-1391 TOLL-FREE IN QUÉBEC (514) 521-5771 TOLL-FREE IN THE UNITED KINGDOM 011-44-21-772-8599 TOLL-FREE IN CANADA (800) 327-0116 Also represented is the largest Canadian rental car company, **National Tilden** TOLL-FREE (800) 387-4747, which has over 370 offices all over Canada.

If you are planning to rent a car in the summer, it's a good idea to reserve before you leave home.

By Ferry

There are both car and passenger ferry services available on most of Canada's major lakes and rivers, as well as between the mainland and the offshore islands. Ferries across the St. Lawrence and to Vancouver Island don't require reservations, but other ferries should be booked in advance — well in advance if you are taking a car with you.

Information on ferry transportation within various regions is listed under HOW TO GET THERE in the relevant chapters. The major lines include:

Alaska Marine Highway System ((907) 627-1744 or (907) 627-1745 TOLL-FREE (800) 642-0066, PO Box 25535, Juneau, Alaska 99802-5535 USA, operates between Bellingham, Washington, Prince Rupert, British Columbia, and Skagway, Alaska with stops in Juneau and Haines, and other Southeast Alaska ports.

Bay Ferries ((207) 288-3395 TOLL-FREE (888) 249-7245, 121 Eden Street, Bar Harbor, Maine 04609 USA operates a year-round ferry service across the Bay of Fundy between Digby, Nova Scotia and Saint John.

BC Ferries ((250) 386-3431 TOLL-FREE IN BRITISH COLUMBIA (888) 223-3779 FAX (250) 381-5452, 1112 Fort Street, Victoria, BC V8V 4V2 Canada, links Vancouver with Vancouver Island, Port Hardy, Prince Rupert, the Queen Charlotte Islands, the Gulf Islands and various southern British Columbia ports.

Marine Atlantic TOLL-FREE (800) 341-7981 FAX (902) 564-7480, 355 Purves Street, North Sydney, NS B2A 3V2; or P.O. Box 520, Port aux Basques, NF A0M 1C0, links the following cities: Saint John, New Brunswick–Digby, Nova Scotia; New Brunswick–Prince Edward Island; and Cape Breton Island, North Sydney, Nova Scotia–Port aux Basques, Newfoundland. During the summer, Marine Atlantic operates between Lewisporte (near Gander), Newfoundland and Happy Valley-Goose Bay, Labrador, with a stop at Cartwright, Labrador. Also during the summer, a coastal boat operates between St. Anthony, Newfoundland and ports north to Nain, Labrador. There is also a seasonal ferry between St. Barbe, on Newfoundland's Northern Peninsula, and Blanc Sablon, Québec.

Northumberland Ferries ((902) 566-3838 TOLL-FREE (888) 249-7245 FAX (902) 566-1550, 94 Water Street, PO Box 634, Charlottetown, Prince Edward Island C1A 7L3, links Caribou, Nova Scotia to Wood Islands, Prince Edward Island.

BY LOCAL TRANSPORTATION

Taxis can always be found at airports, railway stations, and major hotels. They can also be hailed in the street fairly easily in the larger cities; elsewhere they can be ordered by telephone. Rates are quite reasonable by American or European standards, and a tip of 15% or so is normal. In some provinces not all the taxis have meters, making it advisable to agree on the fare before beginning a journey.

In Toronto and Montréal the subway system provides a handy way of getting around. Subway tickets, which can be bought singly or in books, are on sale at newsagents as well as at the subway stations. If you choose to travel by bus, be sure to have the exact fare with you, as bus drivers do not carry change.

DRIVING

You will be required to carry a valid driver's license and it is recommended that you get an international driving permit as well (see WHAT TO TAKE, above). Any standard United States car insurance

policy is valid in Canada. If you have time, get a Canadian Non-Resident Inter-Provincial Motor Vehicle Liability Insurance Card from your insurance company. If the car you're driving is not registered under the name of one of the drivers or one of the passengers, bring written proof that you have permission from the owner to take the car into Canada.

The driving regulations will be familiar to anyone used to driving in the United States or in continental Europe: You drive on the right and pass on the left, vehicles approaching from the right have the right-of-way at intersections, the use of seat belts is compulsory, and driving under the influence of alcohol will incur stiff penalties.

In Newfoundland, Prince Edward Island, Québec, Ontario, Manitoba, and in the Yukon, Northwest Territories and Nunavut radar detectors are illegal even if not in use.

The speed limit on highways is usually 100 kph (60 mph), on smaller roads 80 kph (50 mph), and in towns 80 kph down to 50 kph (30 mph). You must stop if you come upon a school bus with its red lights flashing. You may turn right at a red light (except in Québec) if you stop first and make sure the road is clear. Some provinces require drivers to keep headlights on for periods after dawn and before sunset. In the Yukon, the law requires drivers to keep headlights on at all times when using territory highways.

Note: Fines for traffic offenses in Québec are much harsher there than elsewhere in Canada.

There are plenty of 24-hour service stations flanking the major highways, while those in town tend to close around 9 PM (7 PM in small towns, and all day on Sundays). Gasoline (or petrol) is sold by the liter (one liter equals about one quart; there are 3.8 liters to the gallon). Gas is a good deal more expensive than it is in the United States,

OPPOSITE: Made in America — a '57 Chevy sports Québec plates by the banks of the St. Lawrence. ABOVE: The ferry across the St. Lawrence to Rivière-du-Loup, at the base of the Gaspé Peninsula.

but cheaper than in Europe. Most stations take credit cards, and most are now self-service.

In the event of an accident, you should get to a telephone and dial the operator ("0") who can connect you with the police and emergency services. Members of automobile clubs affiliated with the Canadian Automobile Association (the American Automobile Association and most European automobile clubs are) should bring their membership cards along with them, as they are entitled to membership benefits. For more information contact the **Canadian Automobile Association** ((613) 226-7631, 1775 Courtwood Crescent, Ottawa, Ontario K2C 3J2; the **American Automobile Association** TOLL-FREE (800) 564-6222; the **United**

Kingdom Automobile Association ((0990) 500600; or the **Royal Automobile Club** ((0990) 722722 or (0345) 121345.

ACCOMMODATION

When it comes to accommodation in Canada, one is spoiled for choice. Wherever you go in Canada, you will find that there are types of accommodation to appeal to every taste and to suit every budget. If luxury and comfort are your priorities, there are deluxe hotels to rank with any in the world. If convenient locations while motoring are important, you will be pleased to know that there are motels in every price range sprinkled along the nation's main roads and highways. If economy is the paramount consideration, you will be able to get rooms at a YMCA, YWCA, university, or hostel in all but the most remote spots — and sometimes even there (see BACKPACKING, page 39, in YOUR CHOICE). If conversation and "character" count alongside economy, there is bound to be a bed-and-breakfast house to fit the bill.

If you will be staying in one place for a longish period, particularly with children or in a group, you will get both privacy and savings (on food) in an efficiency apartment in one of Canada's many apartment hotels. If rustic charm is what you're

looking for, there are delightful country inns spread across the country. If you want to get into serious rusticity, there is no better way than to stay on one of the hundreds of working farms and ranches that offer accommodation as well as hearty meals and healthy activities (see SPECIAL INTERESTS, page 58, in YOUR CHOICE). If you just want to get away from it all and hunt or fish or think about the human condition, there are some wonderful lodges in remote wilderness areas where Nature starts at your front door.

NATIONAL PARKS

National parks are federally administered, but locally supervised by park information centers. These centers are excellent sources of information, and are the place to pickup permits for fishing or backcountry camping. Exhibits on flora and fauna, interpretive talks and nature walks with park naturalists, and reports on weather and road conditions are often also part of the package.

Motorists must purchase permits when entering national parks, usually from a roadside booth at the park boundary. Each park has its own fee structure, and many offer pass programs. For additional information, contact **Parks Canada** ((819) 997-0055 E-MAIL parks_webmaster@pch.gc.ca, 25 Eddy Street, Hull, Québec K1A 0M5. The Parks Canada WEB SITE parkscanada.pch.gc.ca/ has a list of all park fees and pass programs as well as access to an on-line campground reservation system for a limited (but growing) number of parks.

CAMPING

There are thousands upon thousands of campgrounds throughout Canada, of every size and description. Many are in the national and provincial parks, some are municipally owned, others are privately run. Most are open from May until late September, with campsites costing from $10 to $15. Facilities usually include toilets, showers, a laundry, picnic tables, campfire sites, and power hookups for recreational vehicles. The fancier ones will also have a shop and a restaurant. Generally speaking, the privately run campgrounds will have more amenities and will be more expensive, while the public ones in the national and provincial parks will be more scenically situated.

As most campgrounds are run on a first-come, first-served basis, during the high season — July and August — it's a good idea to start looking for a site no later than mid-afternoon.

There are three **nocturnal nuisances** that can thoroughly spoil a camping vacation if you come unprepared. The first is that familiar bane, the mosquito. So bring plenty of insect repellent, as well as a tent fitted with a mosquito net. The second nuisance is scavenging animals — often, in

Canada, bears. These creatures can be discouraged by never keeping food in or near the tent (unless it's in the car), and by always disposing of un- eaten food and washing up the dishes immedi- ately after meals. No leftovers, no problems. Thirdly, even in midsummer, the temperature at night can suddenly drop, leaving you shivering unless you have brought enough warm clothing.

For lists of campgrounds write to the provin- cial tourism office in the area you plan to visit or contact Parks Canada (see above).

PRICES

With a few exceptions, we have deliberately avoided giving exact restaurant and accommoda- tion prices. This is because we have learned that the only thing you can absolutely depend on in this business is that the prices will have changed before the ink is dry (sometimes, surprisingly, for the better — as special offers and new types of discounts are introduced). We have therefore con- fined ourselves to price categories where hotels and restaurants are concerned. Hotels in the **expensive** category, for example, will charge over $150 a night for a double room; **mid-range** hotels will charge between $75 and $149; **inexpensive** hotels will charge less, sometimes much less. At restaurants listed as **expensive** you can expect to pay more than $50 per person for a meal, excluding wine; **moderate** restaurants will charge between $25 and $50; **inexpensive** ones will cost you less — some- times, again, much less. When hotels or restaurants fall at either of the two extremes — very expensive or very inexpensive — we have so indicated.

Another word about prices. All the prices given in this book, and the categories outlined above, are in Canadian dollars. Most travel guides tell you to remember that the Canadian dollar is worth about 20% to 30% less than the American dollar. My advice is precisely the opposite: forget that the Canadian dollar is worth less. Don't translate; think in United States dollars. This is because all the prices quoted in Canada are exclusive of the layers of taxes that are added later — sales taxes, goods and services taxes, even "taxes on taxes," as one hotel owner wanly pointed out to me. So by the time your bill is added in Canadian dollars, it will come to almost exactly the original, untaxed figure in American dollars. If you keep in mind this one simple trick, you will know a real bargain when you see one.

TIPPING

In general, you should tip more or less 15% — more if the service is outstanding, less if it is not so good. Tip porters $1 a bag, chambermaids $1 a day — rounding off the total upwards in deserv- ing cases, downwards in undeserving ones.

PUBLIC HOLIDAYS

National holidays include: New Year's Day, Good Friday, Easter Monday, Victoria Day (Monday nearest May 24), Canada Day (July 1), Labor Day (first Monday in September), Thanksgiving (second Monday in October), Remembrance Day (November 11), Christmas Day, Boxing Day (December 26).

In addition to the national holidays, each ter- ritory and province has its own local holidays.

LANGUAGE

Canada's two official languages are English and French, although the province of New Brunswick is the only officially bilingual area in the country. There are also 53 native languages spoken. Though French is the official language of the province of Québec, English is the mother tongue of 18% of the population of Québec, and is widely spoken, particularly around Greater Montréal.

French-speakers who wish to know more about the nuances and vocabulary specific to French as it is spoken in Québec can refer to the *Dictionnaire de la Langue Québécoise* by Léandre Bergeron (Éditions VLB), where they'll be fascinated to learn that a *dépanneur* is a convenience store (corner grocery store), *magasiner* is "to shop," and so on.

Even though English is widely spoken in Québec it helps to know a few phrases of French, especially if you are venturing outside of the province's urban areas.

Driving
arrêt   stop
autoroute   expressway
centre-ville   downtown
est   east
ouest   west
nord   north
sud   south
droite   right
gauche   left
pont   bridge
sens unique   one way
stationnement interdit   no parking
virage   turn
vitesse   speed

Conversations
au revoir   goodbye
bienvenue   welcome
bonjour   hello
bonsoir   goodnight, good evening
merci   thank you
s'il-vous-plaît   please

OPPOSITE: Ottawa's renowned Château Laurier.

Comment ça va?   How are you?
Pouvez-vous m'aidez?   Can you help me?
Où puis-je trouver…?   Where can I find…?
Quel est le prix?   How much does it cost?
Quelle heure est-il?   What time is it?

Shopping

ascenseur   elevator
chaussures   shoes
comptant   cash
cuir   leather
étage   floor, story
escalier roulant   escalator
prix réduit/rabais   discount or reduced price
rez-de-chaussée   main floor

sortie   exit
sous-sol   basement
vente   sale
vêtement   clothing

General

billets   tickets
calèche   horse-drawn carriage
gratuit   free
métro   subway
renseignements   information
reçu   receipt
salle de bain   washroom
souterrain   underground

MAIL

Although main post offices in Canada may open as early as 8 AM and close as late as 6 PM on weekdays, and some are open on Saturday mornings, you can avoid disappointment by going between 9 AM and 5 PM, Monday to Friday. In fact, you can avoid post offices altogether for most purposes, as stamps can be bought at hotels and from vending machines in airports, railway stations, shopping centers, and drugstores. Letters and postcards can be mailed at most hotels' front desks or at any red mailbox. At press time rates were $.46 for a first-class letter or postcard within Canada, $.55 to the United States, and $.95 to other countries.

If sending mail to a Canadian address, be sure to include the postal code. Also, we are told by the postal authorities that every year there are some Americans who think it is just as good to use American stamps as Canadian ones. It's not. Following are **postal abbreviations** for the provinces and territories: Alberta AB, British Columbia BC, Saskatchewan SK, Manitoba MB, New Brunswick NB, Newfoundland and Labrador NF, Northwest Territories and Nunavut NT, Nova Scotia NS, Ontario ON, Prince Edward Island PE, Québec QP, Yukon Territory YT.

If you want to **receive mail** in Canada, you can have mail sent to you ^{c}/$_o$ General Delivery at the main post office in the town or city where you wish to pick it up. But remember that it must be picked up within 15 days or it will be returned to sender. If you have an American Express card, or traveler's checks from American Express or Thomas Cook, you can have mail sent to you at any office of either company. It should be marked "Client Mail," and it will be held for you for as long as a month.

Telegrams are handled by CN/CP Telecommunications, while most good hotels now have telex and/or fax facilities available for guests' use.

TELEPHONES

The Canadian telephone system is completely integrated with that of the United States, which means that it is splendidly efficient and economical, and that no international codes are necessary for calls between the United States and Canada. As in the United States, for information on local telephone numbers dial 411; for information on long-distance numbers dial 1-555-1212. For calls requiring operator assistance — such as long-distance personal or collect calls, or for emergency calls — dial "0."

To place a long-distance call within the same area code, dial 1 + the number you are calling. To place a call outside your area code, dial 1 + area code + telephone number. For direct dialing of overseas calls, dial 011 + country code + city code + telephone number.

Calls placed in the evening or on the weekend are less expensive, although any call from a hotel will incur a (usually steep) surcharge. There are public telephones just about everywhere; they only accept Canadian quarters, and/or prepaid phone cards.

We have made an effort to provide the specific geographic limitations of the toll-free numbers listed in this book when this information was available. Generally speaking, TOLL-FREE refers to numbers available throughout North America, whereas limitations to Canada, the United States, or a specific province are indicated. TOLL-FREE IN

WESTERN CANADA means just that: you can use this number in British Columbia, Alberta, Saskatchewan, Yukon and Manitoba, but will not get through if you dial from elsewhere.

THE INTERNET

Canada is wired. Just about everywhere you go, you will find a bookstore, café, or public library offering access to the Internet for a nominal fee (and sometimes for free). If you've signed up for one of the global e-mail accounts before leaving home (Microsoft's HotMail is one of the most popular free e-mail services) then you are wired, too.

Where available, we have listed local Internet access points in the various destination sections under GENERAL INFORMATION. We found that most libraries offered access, but that actual availability varied greatly because of lack of equipment and high demand. In most cities, you can ask around and find the latest cybercafé where you can settle down with a coffee and get warming news from home.

The Internet is also becoming a powerful tool for researching and planning trips. Many, if not most, organizations, hotels, and tour operators listed in this book have home pages on the **World Wide Web**. Finding one of these home pages is usually a simple matter of logging onto your web browser (e.g., Netscape Navigator™ or Microsoft Internet Explorer™), locating the search function and typing in the name of the organization for which you are looking. You can also do keyword searches if you don't have a specific organization name in mind. Essentially, once on the web, your access to information is limited only by your ability to ask the right question.

Web sites are of varying quality. Some are quite useful, allowing you to retrieve information quickly, make contact via e-mail direct from the site, or even make a reservation at the touch of a button. Others will have you pulling your cyber hair out.

The following sites are ones that we found particularly useful in our research on this book. They offer essential information and pertinent services, as well as "links" to other home pages that will set you well on your way into cyberspace. (It is the nature of the web to be somewhat ephemeral, and you may find that some of these sites are no longer active.)

SITES

Reference
Canadian Yellowpages www.cdnyellowpages .com. This is a fairly well organized tool for address and telephone searches. It also offers classified ads, pictures of Canada, and links to other sites.
Ghosts of the Gold Rush www.gold-rush.org/. Find out if Great Aunt Lou climbed the Chilkoot Trail.
Lost Moose, the Yukon Publishers www .yukonweb.com/business/lost_moose/. These publishers specialize in northern literature, including the legendary *Lost Whole Moose Catalog*.
National Archives www.archives.ca. In English and French, this site contains written records, artwork, photographs, and maps that document the history of Canada and the workings of its government.
Sympatico www1.sympatico.ca:80/. This is a comprehensive site, operated by Bell Canada, with all things Canadian and more. It's very well organized, easy on the eye, and an excellent place to start research on the country in any category. The travel sections are especially good.
Universal Currency Converter www.xe.net/ currency/. A nifty way to find out what your dollar or euro is worth against any other currency, in real time.

Travel
Airline Network www.airnet.co.uk. Cheap flights departing from the United Kingdom. Unique in that it lists free stopovers.
Atevo www.atevo.com/. A comprehensive travel web site with all kinds of nooks and crannies to explore. It offers online reservations, but we found

OPPOSITE: At Montréal's busy Dorval Airport, workers keep up their nonstop pace. ABOVE: A phone booth in Vancouver's Chinatown.

the engine lacking. It's best used as an online magazine and travel-idea generator.

Rec.Travel Library — Canada www.travel-library .com/north_america/canada/index.html. A homespun site that has plenty of information, including personal advice and a list of answers to frequently asked questions about traveling in Canada. Strong on links to many other Canadian sites.

Travelocity www.travelocity.com. The best choice for straightforward air travel fare search and booking. Sign-up for automatic updates on air routes of your choosing. When the rate drops by $50 or more, you'll be notified via e-mail

Where Magazine www.wheremags.com. These are locally edited, ad-oriented destination magazines. The web site is useful and attractive. You can order magazines from the site, or browse the information on line for a number of Canadian cities, including Toronto, Winnipeg, and Vancouver.

Airlines

Air Canada www.aircanada.ca. Flight and departure information, reservations and the WebSaver program, a free service with last minute travel bargains to selected destinations. Sign up for automatic e-mail updates at this web site.

Canada Airlines International www.cdnair.ca. A slow site, but it has some interesting features. For example, you can ask its destination locator to list ticketing offices and hotels in your city of destination.

In addition, all of the following airline web sites allow you to get on e-mailing lists and book flights on-line:

American Airlines www.americanair.com
Continental www.flycontinental.com
Delta www.delta-air.com
Northwest Airlines www.nwa.com
United www.ual.com
US Airways www.usairways.com

Travel Guides

Alaska Highway www.peace.bc.ca
Mile marker by mile marker along this epic roadway.

Ferries

Alaska Marine Highway Ferry System www .dot.state.ak.us. Not a particularly glamorous or well-organized site, but key information is not difficult to find.

BC Ferries www.bcferries.bc.ca. Slick and useful. Access information about routes, schedules, fares, and online reservations.

Ground Transportation

Greyhound Canada www.greyhound.ca. An excellent site where you can download your choice of Adobe Acrobat .PDF (Portable Document Format) files of schedules.

VIA Rail www.viarail.ca. Attractive and very useful wit schedules, fares, and on-line reservations.

Visitor Information

Calgary Convention and Visitors Bureau www.visitor.calgary.ab.ca
Discover Banff www.discoverbanff.com/
Nunavut Handbook www.arctic-travel.com/ NUNATOUR/nt.html
Tourism Montréal www.tourism-Montreal.org
Tourism Toronto www.tourism-toronto.com
Tourism Winnipeg www.tourism-winnipeg .mb.ca
Tourism Vancouver www.tourism-vancouver.org
YukonWeb www.yukonweb.com/
Yukon Wild www.yukonwild.com/

RADIO AND TELEVISION

We are tempted to say that if you are in Canada you shouldn't be indoors, and leave it at that. We are further tempted to say that if you do find yourself indoors in North America, you certainly shouldn't be watching television. You know the reasons; you've probably seen a number of them already, wherever you live. Even so, it's difficult to convey the feeling of dull despair that comes over you when you contemplate a galaxy of up to 40 television channels — not one of which is shining brightly enough to engage your attention for more than a few minutes.

If it's any consolation, though, you are better off watching television in Canada then in the United States, simply because you have a choice of programs aside from the American ones (which nonetheless predominate even in areas beyond the reach of American stations). Its precarious finances notwithstanding, the CBC (Canadian Broadcasting Corporation) manages to produce some worthy programming of its own, while the French-language channels serve up the occasional treat. But don't be surprised when you switch channels to escape Teenage Mutant Ninja Turtles only to be confronted with Popeye *et son fils*.

The Canadian radio dial, like the American, features end-to-end music — classical, pop, rock, country, jazz — interspersed with talk shows, phone-ins, and news.

NEWSPAPERS AND MAGAZINES

Canadian journalism, too, closely resembles its American counterpart. With the exception of the *Globe and Mail*, which is published in Toronto, the newspapers are all local papers. Certainly, some big-city papers such as the *Toronto Star* are national, even international, in stature; but their main emphasis remains on coverage of their own communities. This enlightened parochialism benefits the visitor not only by providing a useful introduction to topics of local interest, but also by providing, through its listings and advertisements, a comprehensive guide to local events and entertainment. As a matter of fact, many of the places to go and things to do that we have recommended in this book were originally suggested to us by articles or reviews we came upon in the local press. So don't neglect this valuable resource whenever you arrive in a new place.

All of the larger newsagents in Canada have shelves that are identical to the ones you would expect to find in comparable shops in the United States — except that in addition to all the American newspapers and magazines you get the Canadian ones as well.

Recommended Reading

BACKHOUSE, FRANCES. *Women of the Klondike*. Whitecap Books, 1995.

BERTON, PIERRE. *The Mysterious North*. Toronto: McClelland and Stewart, 1956. *The Klondike Fever*. New York: Carroll and Graf, 1958.

BERTON, LAURA BEATRICE and PIERRE BERTON. *I Married the Klondike*. Toronto: McClelland and Stewart, 1996.

BROOK, STEPHEN. *Maple Leaf Rag*. London: Pan Books, 1989.

DRISCOLL, CYNTHIA BRACKETT. *One Woman's Gold Rush: Snapshots from Mollie Brackett's Lost Photo Album 1898–1899*. Kalamazoo: Oak Woods Media, 1996.

HARDY, ANNE. *Where to Eat in Canada*. Harvard Common Press, 1997.

MACKAY, CLAIRE. *The Toronto Story*. Toronto: Annick Press, 1990.

MACKAY, DONALD. *Flight from Famine: The Coming of the Irish to Canada*. Toronto: McClelland & Stewart, 1990.

MACLENNAN, HUGH. *Papers*. Calgary: University of Calgary Press, 1986.

MALCOLM, ANDREW H. *The Canadians*. New York: Times Books, 1985.

MCNAUGHT, KENNETH. *The Penguin History of Canada*. London: Penguin Books, 1988.

MILEPOST (THE), 50TH EDITION. Bellevue, Washington: Vernon Publications, 1998

MORGAN, BERNICE. *Random Passage*. Breakwater Books, Ltd., 1992.

MORTON, DESMOND. *A Peculiar Kind of Politics*. Toronto: University of Toronto Press, 1982.

MORTON, WILLIAM L. *The Canadian Identity*. Madison: University of Wisconsin Press, 1973.

MUISE, D.A., ed. *Reader's Guide to Canadian History, Vol. I.* GRANATSTEIN, A.L and P. STEVENS, eds. *Reader's Guide to Canadian History, Vol. II.* Toronto: University of Toronto Press, 1982.

PATTERSON, FREEMAN. *The Last Wilderness: Images of the Canadian Wild*. Vanier, Ontario: Canadian Geographic Society, 1991.

PROULX, E. ANNIE. *The Shipping News*. New York: Simon & Schuster, 1994.

RICHLER, MORDECAI. *The Apprenticeship of Duddy Kravitz*. London: Penguin Books, 1991. Broadsides. London: Vintage Books, 1991. Papers. Calgary: University of Calgary Press, 1987.

SOUBLIERE, MARION, ed. *The Nunavut Handbook: Traveling in Canada's Arctic.* Iqaluit, NWT: Nortext Press, 1998.

WALLACE, DONALD C. and FREDERICK A. FLETCHER. *Canadian Politics through Press Reports*. Toronto: Oxford University Press, 1985.

WELLS, E. HAZARD. Randall M. Dodd, editor. *Magnificence and Misery: A Firsthand Account of the 1897 Klondike Gold Rush*. Garden City, New York: Doubleday & Company, 1984.

For Children

CRAVEN, MARGARET. *I Heard the Owl Call My Name* and *Again Calls the Owl*. Laureleaf, 1993.

GALE, DONALD. *Shooshewan, Child of the Beothuk*. Breakwater Books, 1988.

SKOGAN, JOAN. *The Princess and the Sea-Bear and Other Tsimshian Stories*. Polestar Press, 1990.

Tucking in to an adult-size portion of *moules frites* (steamed mussels and French fries) in Montreal.

Quick Reference A–Z Guide
to Places and Topics of Interest with Listed Accommodation, Restaurants and Useful Telephone Numbers

Photography Credits

All photographs taken by Nik Wheeler and Robert Holmes, with the exception of those below:

David Henry: pages 12, 14, *left and right,* 15 *top and bottom,* 16, 18, 21, 22, 24, 25, 30, 31, 34, 35, 37, 38 *top,* 40, 41, 42, 43, 44, 47, 48 *top,* 49, 55, 56 *top and bottom,* 57, 58, 60, 61, 63, 64, *top and bottom,* 65, 83, 112, 119, 125, 127, 147 *left,* 148 *left,* 149, 150, 151, 152, 154, 160 *left and right,* 162, 165, 167, 171, 226, 227, 233, 234, 240 *left and right,* 241, 242, 244, 247, 278, 293, 294 *left,* 295, 297, 300, 302, 303, 304, 305 *top,* 307, 308, 309, 314 *right,* 319, 322, 323, 324, 325, 326, 327, *left and right,* 329, 332, 335, 339, 351, 368, 369, 376, 421, 427, 428, 432.

Laura Purdom: pages 27 *top and bottom,* 29 *top and bottom,* 45, 59 *bottom,* 62, 84, 381, 389, 394, 396, 397, 399, 402, 403 *top and bottom,* 404, 405, 406, 407, 408 *left and right,* 409, 411 *top and bottom,* 413.

Banff/Lake Louise Tourism Bureau: 305 *bottom.*

Dewitt Jones: 33, 46, 330, 333, 367, 383, 385 *top and bottom.*

Yukon Archives: Claude Lidd Collection: 75, Skookum Jim Oral History Collection: 392, McBride Museum Collection: 400, Vancouver Public Library Collection: 401.